STUDIES IN THE HISTORY OF CHRISTIAN MISSIONS

R. E. Frykenberg
Brian Stanley
General Editors

STUDIES IN THE HISTORY
OF CHRISTIAN MISSIONS

Susan Billington Harper

*In the Shadow of the Mahatma: Bishop V. S. Azariah
and the Travails of Christianity in British India*

Kevin Ward and Brian Stanley, *Editors*

The Church Mission Society and World Christianity, 1799-1999

IN THE SHADOW
OF THE MAHATMA

*Bishop V. S. Azariah and the Travails
of Christianity in British India*

Susan Billington Harper

WILLIAM B. EERDMANS PUBLISHING COMPANY
GRAND RAPIDS, MICHIGAN / CAMBRIDGE, U.K.

CURZON PRESS LTD
RICHMOND, SURREY, U.K.

Published jointly 2000 by
Wm. B. Eerdmans Publishing Co.
255 Jefferson Ave. S.E., Grand Rapids, Michigan 49503/
P.O. Box 163, Cambridge CB3 9PU U.K.
and by
Curzon Press Ltd
15 The Quadrant, Richmond, Surrey TW9 1BP UK

Printed in the United States of America

05 04 03 02 01 00   7 6 5 4 3 2 1

Library of Congress Cataloging-in-Publication Data

Harper, Susan Billington.
In the shadow of the Mahatma: Bishop V. S. Azariah
and the travails of Christianity in British India /
Susan Billington Harper.
p.   cm.   — (Studies in the history of Christian missions)
Includes bibliographical references and index.
ISBN 0-8028-3874-X (cloth: alk. paper)
1. Azariah, Vedanayagam Samuel, Bishop, 1874-1945.
2. Church of South India. Dornakal Diocese — Biography.
3. Church of South India — Bishops — Biography.
4. India, South — Church history — 20th century.
I. Title. II. Series.
BX7066.5.Z8 A934 2000
283′.092 — dc21
[B]   99-049030

British Library Cataloguing-in-Publication Data

A catalogue record for this book is available from the British Library.
Curzon Press ISBN 0-7007-1232-1

To my parents
James and Marjorie Billington

Contents

Maps and Illustrations

Maps

Illustrations

Illustrations are found between pages 220 and 221.

Abbreviations

ABCFM	American Board of Commissioners for Foreign Missions
ACPS	Andhra Christo Purushula Samajam
AH	Agatha Harrison
BHA	Bishop's House Archives, Calcutta
CENs	*Church of England Newspaper*
CIM	China Inland Mission
CISRS	Christian Institute for the Study of Religion and Society, Bangalore
CLS	Christian Literature Society for India
CM	M. K. Gandhi, *Christian Missions: Their Place in India,* ed. Bharatan Kumarappa (Ahmedabad, 2nd ed., 1957)
CMG	*Church Missionary Gleaner* (later, *CMO*)
CMO	*Church Missionary Outlook*
CMR	*Church Missionary Review* (later, *CO*)
CMS	Church Missionary Society
CMSA	Church Missionary Society Archives, University of Birmingham
CO	*Church Overseas* (later, *EWR*)
CP	*Christian Patriot*
CSAS	Centre of South Asian Studies, University of Cambridge
CUNV	*Church Union News and Views*
CWM	Council for World Mission
CWMG	*The Collected Works of Mahatma Gandhi* (New Delhi)
DDA	Dornakal Diocesan Archives
DDM	*Dornakal Diocesan Magazine*
ED, GOM	Madras Ecclesiastical Proceedings, Ecclesiastical Department, Government of Madras (IOL)

EWR	*East and West Review*
GCAH, UMC	General Commission on Archives and History, United Methodist Church, Drew University, Madison, New Jersey
GOI, HDP	Government of India, Home Department Proceedings (IOL)
GOI, PODOE	Government of India, Proceedings of the Department of Education (IOL)
Guardian	*Guardian* newspaper (Madras)
HF	*Harvest Field*
ICG	India Conciliation Group
ICG, FH	Agatha Harrison Papers, India Conciliation Group, Friends House, London
ICHR	*Indian Church History Review*
ICQR	*Indian Church Quarterly Review*
IESHR	*Indian Economic and Social History Review*
IJT	*Indian Journal of Theology*
IMC/CBMS, SOAS	Joint Archives of the International Missionary Council and Conference of British Missionary Societies, School of Oriental and African Studies, London
IMS	Indian Missionary Society of Tinnevelly (Tirunelveli)
IMSA	Indian Missionary Society of Tirunelveli Archives, Palayamkottai
IOL	India Office Library and Records, London
IRM	*International Review of Missions*
ISPCK	Society for Promoting Christian Knowledge for India
J&P	Judicial and Public Department (IOL)
J&PDR	Judicial and Public Department Register and Indexes (IOL)
JAS	*Journal of Asian Studies*
JSAS	*Journal of South Asian Studies*
LMS	London Missionary Society (later incorporated in CWM)
LP	Lambeth Palace Library, London
MACIPBC	Metropolitan Archives of the Church of India, Pakistan, Burma, and Ceylon; Bishop's College, Calcutta
MAS	*Modern Asian Studies*
MCCM	*Madras Christian College Magazine*
MDA	Madras Diocesan Archives
MDM	*Madras Diocesan Magazine*
MDR	*Madras Diocesan Record*
MII	*Man in India*
MMS	Methodist Missionary Society
MRW	*Missionary Review of the World*
MTDM	*Madras and Tinnevelly Diocesan Magazine*

NCC	National Christian Council of India, Burma, and Ceylon
NCCC	National Christian Council Correspondence (IMC/CBMS, SOAS)
NCCR	*National Christian Council Review*
NMI	*National Missionary Intelligencer*
NMS	National Missionary Society
NMSA	National Missionary Society Archives, Madras
PIMS	*Proceedings of the Indian Missionary Society of Tirunelveli (IMSA)*
R&S	*Religion and Society*
SAR	*South Asian Review*
SCM	Student Christian Movement
SIUC	South India United Church
SJT	*Scottish Journal of Theology*
SOCA	Selly Oak Colleges Archives and Library, Birmingham
SPCK	Society for Promoting Christian Knowledge
SPG	Society for the Propagation of the Gospel
SVM	Student Volunteer Movement
TE&TW	*The East and the West*
TMI-IMS	*The Missionary Intelligencer (Suvisesha Pirabalya Varthamani),* in IMSA
USCL·	United Society for Christian Literature
USPG	Archives of the United Society for the Propagation of the Gospel; USPG House, London; and Rhodes House, Oxford
UTCA	United Theological College Archives, Bangalore
VSA	Vedanayagam Samuel Azariah
WSCF	World Student Christian Federation
YDS	Yale Divinity School, Manuscripts and Archives, New Haven, CT
YMCA	Young Men's Christian Association
YMI	*Young Men of India*
YMI, B&C	*Young Men of India, Burma, and Ceylon*

A Note on Transliteration

With regard to transliteration and translation into English, I have aimed at maximizing consistency with primary sources and easing comprehension for the reader. Spellings of Indian place names are those used most frequently in the sources and during the period under investigation: Tinnevelly rather than Tirunelveli, Pallamcottah rather than Palayamkottai, Bezwada rather than Vijayawada, and so forth. Archaic spellings are abandoned only when required for consistency. Azariah's father's name was commonly transliterated from the Tamil as 'Vedanayagam' and from the Telugu as 'Vedanayakam.' Although Azariah used the Telugu spelling in Dornakal, for the sake of consistency I have chosen to use the Tamil transliteration throughout. Spellings of caste names are also those in ordinary usage at the time and, where there is little agreement in the primary source material, variant spellings are given in brackets: hence Yerukala (Erukala), etc. All works are in English unless indicated otherwise by transliteration or in brackets. Non-English titles or texts that were translated or transliterated during Azariah's lifetime are presented unchanged in order to avoid the confusion of newer, albeit more exact, systems. Where original transliterations of Tamil and Telugu are required, I use the Library of Congress systems.

Acknowledgments

The scholar who opened my eyes to Bishop Azariah's importance was the late bishop and historian, Stephen Charles Neill. Neill challenged me shortly before he died in 1984 to fulfill his own dream of producing a critical scholarly biography of Bishop Azariah. It has been a privilege to carry out his request.

Executing this commission would have been impossible without the support of many people from around the world. Thanks and appreciation are due, first of all, to the late Bishop Lesslie Newbigin and Dr. Tapan Raychaudhuri, who co-directed my doctoral studies in history at Oxford University. Special thanks are due as well to my good friend Rukmini Banerji, who first introduced me to the rich history and culture of India during our early years together as Rhodes Scholars in Oxford.

My bibliography reflects the host of other people who cooperated with me by granting interviews and engaging in personal correspondence. The Azariah family kindly granted me access to the bishop's correspondence with his wife and to other rare documents and photographs. Ambrose Azariah and Grace Aaron, Azariah's last surviving children, each provided several fascinating days of conversation and warm hospitality in their homes in Madras and Ottawa. Generous assistance was also provided for me in India by Rev. Peter and Dorothy Millar, the Bishops of Tirunelveli (Rt. Rev. Jason S. Dharmaraj) and Dornakal (Rt. Rev. D. Noah Samuel), Rev. and Mrs. Manickam, Rev. and Mrs. Muthuraj, Dr. and Mrs. John, the Sisters of Vishranthi Nilayam in Bangalore, Alison Weaver, Rev. and Mrs. Victor Manuel Raj, and the Rt. Rev. P. Solomon.

Rev. Vinay Samuel, his wife Colleen, and Miss Jothi Parker are among the many friends who helped to make my research in India especially interesting and pleasant. I am particularly grateful to Rev. Samuel for his intellectual inspiration and for directing me to Vern Middleton's attack on Azariah. I am also indebted to Eleanor Jackson for her advice in India and her comments on an earlier draft. Immanuel David, Rosalind O'Hanlon, and archivists in Calcutta (Joyce Austin and Mr. Mandal) and Bangalore (Fr. M. K. Kuriakose and Dr. Joseph Patmury) also offered many helpful suggestions during my research. Dr. and Mrs. Rajmohan Gandhi, Professor K. Swaminathan, V. T. Rajshekar of the Dalit Sahitya Akademy, and Rev. Jeyasingh of the National Missionary Society all contributed important insights to this study. Then too, I am grateful to those who assisted me with Tamil and Telugu translations: Professors E. Diwakar Abraham, R. S. Arulanandham, and Reginald of St. John's College, Tirunelveli, Mr. Edwin Joel of the Indian Missionary Society, Joy Tangayya, Mrs. B. S. Sharifa, Mrs. Geetha John, Vimala, and Danny Moses.

In England, the late Sister Carol Graham gave unstintingly of her time and provided me with a wealth of information about Dornakal and Bishop Azariah. I am grateful to librarians and archivists at the University of Birmingham (Dr. B. S. Benedikz), Rhodes House (Allen Bell), Yale Divinity School (Martha Lund Smalley and Sharon Laist), London's School of Oriental and African Studies (Rosemary Seton), the Library of Congress (Allen W. Thrasher), and Asbury Theological Seminary (Sylvia U. Brown) for their assistance. Rev. Charles Neill kindly permitted me to study Stephen Neill's private papers after his death; and the late Professor Bengt Sundkler generously lent me his entire collection of research notes, records of interviews, and personal correspondence for his 1954 study of the Church of South India. Several people with personal and family connections in India shared knowledge and resources with me, particularly Barbara Holmes, Sir John Lawrence, Peter Gwynn, and the Rt. Rev. James Matthews. I owe a special debt to Professor Robert Frykenberg and his wife Carol.

I am grateful to Judith Brown, the Beit Professor of Commonwealth History at Oxford University, for directing me to a book by almost the same title: *In the Shadow of the Mahatma: A Personal Memoir,* by Ghana'syandasa Birala (Bombay: Orient Longman, 1953). It is perhaps not an exaggeration to say that Birala's book and mine have nothing in common other than the first part of their titles.

Generous financial assistance for this study was provided by the Rhodes Trust, the Oxford University Bryce Studentship, Balliol College, the Arnold, Bryce, and Read Funds, Oxford's Committee for Graduate

Studies, the Beit Fund, and Mrs. James Clement. A Bernadotte Schmitt Research Award from the American Historical Association and a project for Research on Christianity within the Hindu-Muslim Context funded by The Pew Charitable Trusts also provided support for this work. Modified versions of several chapters have appeared in the *International Bulletin of Missionary Research, The Indo-British Review,* and *Pilgrim: The Magazine of the Friends of the Church in India.*

Finally, it remains to thank my family — both immediate and extended — for their support and encouragement during the production of this book. Anne and Duncan Fischer, Jim and Julie Billington, Tom and Susan Billington, Mr. and Mrs. Charles Harper, John and Margie McCarthy and all the Harper sisters, Jane Brown, and my late grandmother Marjorie Brennan all stood by me faithfully. Caron Cadle assisted heroically with the final manuscript. My husband Charles and my four young children welcomed Azariah as a member of our family. I am profoundly grateful to them. And I especially appreciate the assistance and inspiration of my parents, James and Marjorie Billington, to whom I have dedicated this book.

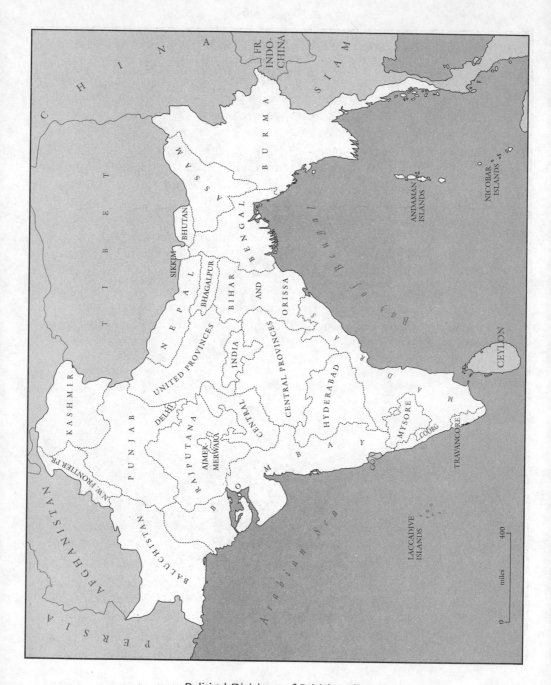

Political Divisions of British India

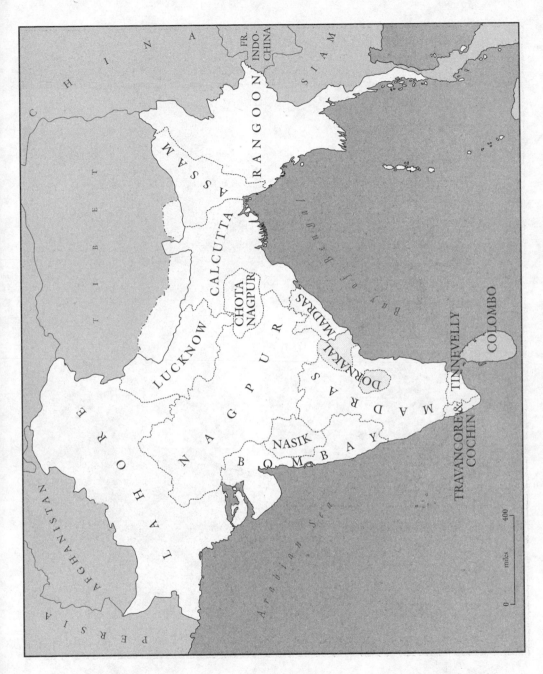

Ecclesiastical Divisions of British India: Anglican Dioceses in India, Burma, and Ceylon

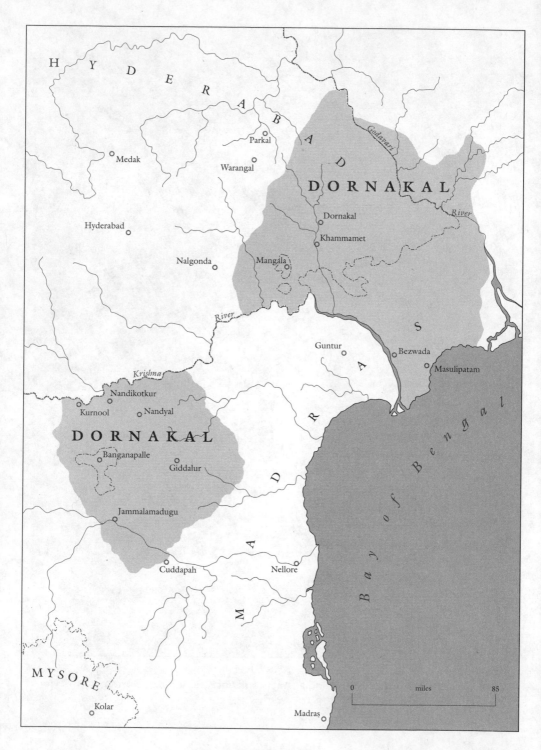

Dornakal Diocese

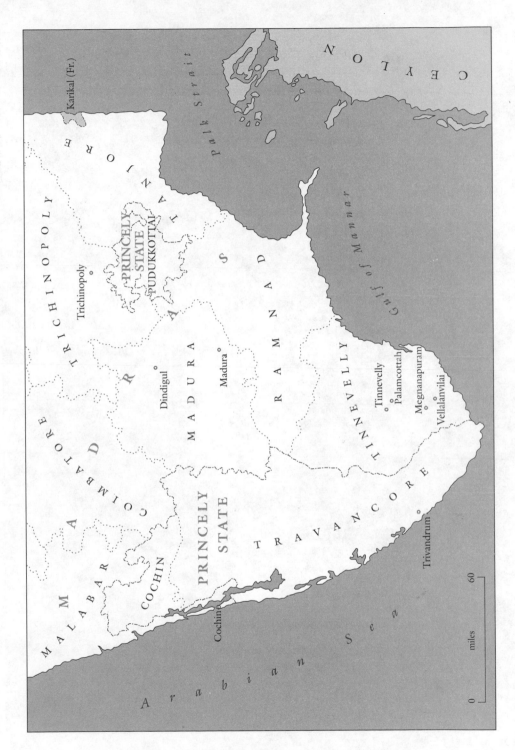

South India

Introduction

Vedanayagam Samuel Azariah (1874-1945) was the most successful leader of grassroots movements of conversion to Christianity in South Asia during the early twentieth century. He was the first and only native Indian bishop of an Anglican diocese from 1912 until his death in 1945. As both an effective evangelist to Indian villagers and a respected bishop in the British church hierarchy, Azariah provided a unique bridge between ordinary Indians and British elites during the late phase of their imperial association. He was equally at home with the 'untouchables' of rural India and the unreachables of the British Empire.[1] Azariah was a popular leader in rural Andhra, an esteemed builder of Protestant unification within India, and a pioneer in the Christian ecumenical movement globally. He was always in the middle — between different languages, different castes, different religious denominations, and different cultures.

1. 'Untouchable' is one of many names used historically to describe those groups belonging to the Panchama (or fifth) varna outside the Indian caste system. Some names, such as Depressed Class, Scheduled Class, or Harijan, were invented by government or political leaders on behalf of untouchable groups; others, such as Adivasi, Adi-Dravida, and Adi-Andhra, were invented by untouchable groups themselves. Different names were usually devised to reduce the stigma associated with older designations, or to unify several oppressed groups into one identifiable category for government benefits. Each, therefore, carries potent political and historical connotations. See S. Saraswathi, *Minorities in Madras State: Group Interests in Modern Politics,* (Delhi, 1974). The untouchable label is particularly unpopular among untouchables today, who prefer self-designations such as "Dalit." See 'What is "Dalit" and Dalitism?' *Dalit Voice,* II, 16 (1-15 June 1983), pp. 1-2, 11. However, for this book, I will favor historically apposite or descriptive terminology over currently acceptable terminology.

1

Through it all, he was a successful architect of peaceful progress in the violent first half of the twentieth century.

Why, then, is so little known today about such a remarkable and influential Third World figure? The reason, in part, is that most modern historians neglect Indian history and are innately hostile to religion in general and to Christian missionary activity in particular. But in larger measure, the neglect of Azariah is a by-product of the enormous attention devoted to the rise of secular nationalism and to the charismatic figure of Azariah's contemporary and sometimes opponent, Mohandas K. Gandhi.

Since Azariah was neither a defender of the old nor an apostle of the new political order, his extraordinarily consistent leadership of locally based religious transformations is simply off the radar screen of the modern university-media complex. If one must talk about either India or spirituality, it seems that Gandhi will cover the subject. Indeed, I have found that the only way to legitimize the study, let alone any public discussion, of Azariah in the university context is by stressing his relationship with Gandhi. Perhaps now that political ideologies seem to be losing some of their luster and religious movements appear to be showing unexpected strength, it may be possible to rediscover and to appreciate the importance, originality, and skill of a leader like Azariah. This book is an attempt to tell the life story of a humble yet effective leader who was one of the invisible builders of the world's largest democracy. It is also an attempt to rescue leaders who are rooted in religion and not focused on national politics from the arrogantly secular and narrowly political preoccupations of those who form public opinion.

I was introduced to this remarkable human being through several long conversations with the great missionary bishop and historian of Christianity, the late Stephen Neill. I felt the power and richness of religious and caste minorities in India while doing community fieldwork and study in India in 1984 and 1986. In the course of completing my doctoral dissertation in Commonwealth History at Oxford University under the magnificent co-supervision of Dr. Tapan Raychaudhuri and the late Rt. Rev. Lesslie Newbigin, I came to appreciate how this great evangelist combined extraordinary inner consistency with remarkable tactical flexibility.

In my study I found almost every cliché about Christian missionary activity to be incorrect. It was mainly westerners, not Indians, who pressed for the unprecedented elevation of a native Indian bishop; yet Azariah succeeded as a bishop far more with the Indian masses than with the missionaries or high officials of the Raj. He never fully embraced either of the secular ideologies then fashionable in India — nationalism or socialism. Nor did he use his unique position within the official religion of the British empire to become either an appendage of, or a rebel against, imperialism. He neither adopted all the amenities of western civilization nor theatrically flaunted his connection to the Indian villages in which he worked. He never identified himself irrevocably with any caste, social class, or ethnic group. In short, he had none of the 'identity crises' that historians routinely expect to find when modernity clashes with tradition.

He was, quite simply, a committed Christian totally preoccupied with winning and saving souls. In an age electrified by secular ideologies, Azariah remained devoted to a traditional religion. He sought to create an indigenous Indian form of Christianity, not a Christianized form of nationalism. Yet he was not the simple quietist that all this might suggest. He was also a dynamic leader and organizer. He lived and died working largely at the local level, and with the poor — those ordinary people in whose name contemporary historians like to speak but whose actual beliefs they often choose to discount.

Unlike Thomas Carlyle's heroic figures who changed history by the force of their titanic personalities, Azariah displayed his greatest strength in personal integrity and spiritual consistency. He was thrust into an extraordinary number of prominent positions precisely because he maintained inner stability during an age of rapid external change. He did not suffer from deep psychological neuroses and obsessions, nor indulge in secret immoralities, the favorite subjects of modern biographers (sometimes more aptly called pathographers). He was a complex man living in an even more complex age who coped successfully with paradox, conflict, and persecution thanks mainly to a solid inner core of religious faith.

It is hard for the critical-modern analytical mind to accept that such people really exist. Since Lytton Strachey's publication of *Eminent Victorians* in 1918, we have stopped trusting religious conviction as a positive motivating force in human history. Most modern biographies take religion seriously only when debunking its many pretensions, hypocritical postures, and false illusions. Religious rhetoric is rarely believed, if it is considered at all. Yet the Christian faith played such an outstanding and central role at every stage of Azariah's career that it is impossible to imagine his life or to explain his effectiveness without it.

Azariah's personal life was relatively serene. He was a happily married father of six children[2] who accepted wholeheartedly the basic doctrines of

---

2. A typical letter to his wife, Anbu, concludes: 'There's no wife like you! I thank my God upon every remembrance of you. When I think of you, my heart leaps in joy and thankfulness; and my eyes are wet with love. Kisses dear, kisses all over.' VSA to Anbu, 13 April 1910, Azariah Collection, Madras.

Christianity as defined by the Thirty-Nine Articles of the Church of England. He was the son of one of South India's first Indian Anglican priests and the uncomplicated product of the remarkably secure culture of South Indian Christianity. He shared with many British colleagues and Indian converts a general belief that British rule in India could fulfill a divine purpose by promoting the subcontinent's material improvement and, ultimately, spiritual redemption.[3] Azariah's belief in the transcendent purpose of empire and his successful leadership of an Indian branch of Britain's established church won him such trust and respect from British colleagues that shortly after Azariah's death in 1945, a fellow bishop recalled that:

> . . . in a discussion as to the possibility of an Indian being appointed Viceroy, one of those present remarked, "The only Indian who could possibly carry the job of Viceroy is the Bishop of Dornakal, but the Government would never have the sense to appoint him," an opinion from which none of those present dissented.[4]

Those who knew him would have trusted Azariah as the first Indian Viceroy and, although clearly not granting other Indians the trust they deserved, they also distrusted a government too conservative to appreciate Azariah's qualifications and to appoint him. One can only speculate as to how different the course of modern South Asian history might have been had an Indian like Azariah been appointed Viceroy. He became, in any case, his British associates' most trusted Indian advisor during the final tumultuous decades of the Raj, and a leader of efforts to 'indigenize' the church in India and to promote the welfare of the emerging new nation's disadvantaged populations.

Despite his prestige during his lifetime, Azariah has been virtually forgotten today outside of a narrow circle of Indian Christians, and his life and legacy have never been subjected to serious scholarly assessment. The existing corpus of writings on the bishop is substantial but limited in

3. On the 'theology of Christian imperialism' and its promotion by British Christians as diverse politically as the nationalist C. F. Andrews (during his early career at St. Stephen's College) and the conservative Brigadier General Sir Henry Page Croft, see Gerald Studdert-Kennedy, *British Christians, Indian Nationalists and the Raj* (Delhi, 1991).

4. Stephen Tinnevelly (Neill), 'Bishop Azariah of Dornakal,' *The Student Movement*, XLVII, 4, (March 1945), p. 84. This incident was also recorded in the first edition of the most widely circulated biography of Azariah in English: Carol Graham, *Azariah of Dornakal* (London, 1946), p. 9. However, the incident was deleted from her second edition (Madras, 1972). Such changes reflected the author's desire to be more sympathetic to nationalism and reduced the value of Graham's biography as a source on British views of Azariah before national independence.

both scope and objectivity. Several personal (and sometimes hagio-graphical) biographies have been written in English, Danish, Telugu, and Tamil, along with numerous shorter booklets, articles, and theses.[5] Taken together, these provide a valuable cumulative picture of Azariah's character and accomplishments which this book seeks to summarize rather than to duplicate. However, none of these studies plumbed the depths of the primary sources available throughout many continents, including Azariah's private correspondence with his wife, his letters and reports to missionary societies and church organizations, government ecclesiastical records, or other varied materials scattered throughout Great Britain, India, and North America. Nor has the 'oral history' (in story and song) of relatives, missionaries, church workers, and ordinary villagers in Tinnevelly (Tirunelveli), Dornakal, and throughout England and North America been systematically integrated into available studies. Nowhere has a complete bibliography of Azariah's writings been compiled. And nowhere has Azariah's life been interpreted in terms of the broader drama of South Asian history during the heyday and subsequent decline of the British Raj. This book attempts to fill in these gaps by providing the first comprehensive, critical scholarly study of Azariah's public life and legacy.

To understand the life of this neglected figure is to understand a new dimension of the complex period of transition between imperial and national rule in South Asia. The steadiness of Azariah's behavior and the constancy of his views are remarkable in light of the rapidly changing history of the institutions which he led, the regions in which he worked, and the nations between which he served as a trusted mediator. Azariah stands as a relatively fixed point of reference in the midst of stunning developments among upwardly mobile and mutually antagonistic untouchables and non-Brahmin castes,[6] increasingly expressive and competitive Tamils

5. Biographies of Bishop V. S. Azariah (hereafter VSA) by Carol Graham and J. Z. Hodge (English), Knud Heiberg (Danish), N. Premachendrudu (Telugu), and G. V. Job and D. A. Christadoss (Tamil), along with dozens of shorter biographical booklets, articles, and theses, are listed in the 'Bibliography of Works about Azariah,' pp. 408-11.

6. The term used for most non-Brahmin castes in missionary literature of this period was the Brahmin invective 'Sudra,' which demonstrates the extent to which Brahmin culture influenced the British and their dependents after the British East India Company's rise to power. 'Sudra' refers to the fourth varna in the Brahmanical social order *(varnaschramadharma)* and was applied even to high-ranking Telugu castes *(jatis)* such as Kammas and Velamas. This book attempts to employ specific *jati* names, or the terms 'non-Brahmin' and 'caste,' for those groups commonly called 'Sudras' in the primary literature. However, use of the derogatory label is occasionally necessary due to lack of specification in the source materials and to avoid inconsistency. 'Borderline' *jatis* such

and Telugus, hopeful but frustrated Indian nationalists, and idealistic but guilt-ridden western liberals. Subtle complexities in the process of read-justing caste, regional, communal, and national self-definitions at the end of the nationalist period are somehow made clearer when measured against the standard set by the bishop's personal stability and profes-sional stature.

Azariah's life seems to embody, contain, and sum up many of the dif-ficult tensions of his age between conflicting religious, cultural, and poli-tical ideals. It provides, in the words of Clifford Geertz, a metaphorical 'human recapitulation' of the many social transformations which accom-panied the transition from empire to independence.[7] This book is there-fore less a conventional narrative biography of Azariah's personal life than an analysis of his public life as it reflected the changes and controversies of Indian Christianity in the late Raj.[8]

Despite his many public successes, Azariah was on the losing side of the great movement of twentieth-century South Asia: secular nationalism.

as the Yerukalas (Erukalas) which were considered neither 'caste' ('varna') people nor outcaste people (like Andhra's Malas and Madigas) but were classified by the govern-ment as 'criminal castes and tribes' (along with Chenchus, Yenadis, 'Hill Reddis,' and Lombadies) will also be referred to wherever possible by their *jati* names. As in other cases, the 'Sudra' label will be employed only where absolutely necessary for consistency and where finer distinctions are not required for comprehension.

7. Anthropologist Clifford Geertz coined the phrase 'human recapitulation of a social transformation.' He, along with historian Charles Ryerson and sociologist Rob-ert Bellah, have creatively used the biographies of certain historical figures, such as E. V. Ramaswamy Naicker and C. N. Annadurai, as 'metaphors' for the history of the Tamil Renaissance. Charles Ryerson, *Regionalism and Religion: The Tamil Renaissance and Popular Hinduism* (Madras, 1988), pp. 1-24; Geertz's quotation is taken from p. 20. See also C. Geertz, *The Interpretation of Cultures* (New York, 1973).

8. The security and constancy of his family life and faith have enabled me to omit many biographical and personal details that did not seem particularly relevant to a study of his public life. Fulfilling the basic obligation to explore and document avail-able sources for the reconstruction of his public contribution has also left little room in the present study to pursue other potentially fruitful analytical approaches: com-parisons with the parallel experiences in India of Muslims and of both nonconformist and Roman Catholic Christians; and the critical perspectives that could be applied to his entire record by sociological, Marxist, subaltern, and perhaps even psychoanalytic historiography. Because this book is focused mainly on India and Britain, it has also not pursued the interesting subject of Azariah's broader international influence dur-ing his episcopacy. Particularly promising questions for further detailed study would be the extent of his influence on Western public opinion through frequent speaking tours and the nature of his broader international impact through ecumenical confer-ences.

He and his church were eventually overcome by the great onrush of Indian nationalist freedom fighters clad in *khadi* (or hand-spun cloth) who seemed to sweep more conciliatory sub-movements away in their wake. There is no trace of Azariah and his accomplishments in the voluminous literature on Indian nationalism, and he has been relegated to a mere footnote in the history of the modern Indian state.

His great contemporary, Mahatma Gandhi, was of course the inspiration for, and the beneficiary of, this massive popular movement against British rule. His fame seems inversely proportional to Azariah's obscurity (at least outside Indian Christian circles). Azariah admired the towering figure of Gandhi and paid him all due respects. He even joined the Mahatma in a notable political battle against separate electorates. But their fundamental religious and political disagreements prevented them from joining forces in their common missions to India's poor and, eventually, brought them into serious conflict over religious freedom.

Thus, as the sun set on the British Raj during its twilight years, Azariah lived in an ever lengthening shadow cast by the Mahatma across the subcontinental landscape. It was a shadow that seemed to darken the brilliance of all of Azariah's life and work, and it was a shadow that seemed to grow with every British retreat. Gandhi and Azariah met only a few times, but Gandhi privately considered Azariah to be his 'Enemy Number One,'[9] and Azariah was never able to escape his powerful critic's negative campaigns against both his life's work of Christian evangelism and British rule. These criticisms saddened his last years in Dornakal and obscured his historical legacy. Azariah lives in the shadow of the Mahatma as much today as he did during his lifetime.

8. Interview with Professor K. Swaminathan, Editor of *The Collected Works of Mahatma Gandhi*, 20 March 1986, Madras.

PART I

THE RISE

Late nineteenth-century India was the crown jewel within the global empire of Queen Victoria. However, the British Raj was more a continent than a country. It included today's Pakistan, Bangladesh, Myanmar, and Sri Lanka, along with the many regions and languages of present-day India. India was itself an empire dominated by two of the world's major non-western religions: Hinduism and Islam. And what seemed to be a dominant Hindu majority contained within itself yet another bewildering array of minority castes and ethnicities.[1]

Nowhere were these social and religious groupings more varied and complex than in South India, where caste divisions were complicated and reinforced by racial distinctions between darker-skinned, indigenous Dravidian peoples of the lower castes and lighter-skinned, Aryan peoples of the invading higher castes. Here, in a small Tamil village composed mainly of Dravidian groups, Vedanayagam Samuel Azariah was born — the man destined to become the leading Christian statesman of India and the most successful Christian evangelist among the untouchables.

1. Hinduism has assumed a denominationalist or world-religion character through a complex process of cultural, social, political, and religious construction over the last two hundred years. For guidance on conceptual problems inherent in the contemporary use of the term 'Hinduism,' and in the use and abuse of the concept of a 'Hindu majority,' see R. E. Frykenberg, 'Constructions of Hinduism at the Nexus of History and Religion,' *Journal of Interdisciplinary History,* XXIII, 3 (Winter 1993), pp. 523-50; 'The Emergence of Modern "Hinduism" as a Concept and as an Institution: A Reappraisal with Special Reference to South India,' in *Hinduism Reconsidered,* ed. Günther D. Sontheimer and Hermann Kulke, South Asian Studies No. XXIV (New Delhi, 1989), pp. 29-49; 'The Concept of "Majority" as a Devilish Force in the Politics of Modern India,' *Journal of Commonwealth and Comparative Politics,* XXV, 3 (Nov. 1987), pp. 267-74; and Romila Thapar, 'Syndicated Moksha?' *Seminar,* CCCXIII (1985), pp. 14-22.

The secret of his success lay in his spiritual purity and personal humility, and his stunning achievements were all the more remarkable for having occurred in a time of terrible tensions and unprecedented change. At every stage, he was a man with a mission. But he was at the same time a mediator in the middle. He was unique among successful Indians of his time in being able to communicate effectively with both the agrarian untouchables of India and the Oxbridge-educated elite of the British Raj.

To understand this unjustly neglected figure, we must re-create the remarkable community of Tinnevelly (Tirunelveli)[2] amid the arid plains of Tamil country and the life of his distinctive caste in the multi-ethnic patchwork of southern India.

2. As I explained in the opening note, I have chosen the archaic usage over the contemporary usage to maintain consistency with the historical sources. I recognize, regret, and apologize for the jarring anachronisms: for those of us accustomed to contemporary terminology it is difficult to revert to the older terms, with their highly British connotations. However, maintaining consistency with historical usage seemed a higher priority for this book than satisfying contemporary preference.

CHAPTER 1

Local Background: Secure Roots and a Spiritual Core

A spectacular breed of palm trees, the palmyras, dominate this otherwise dry land south of the Tambiravarni River ('copper-colored' river) on the southeastern tip of the Indian subcontinent. The people who scaled the palmyras, known as 'toddy-tappers' from the intoxicating alcohol made from the trees, came from the Shanar (now, Nadar) caste who spoke the poetic, ancient Tamil language of the region. On these red, sandy plains, one British missionary quipped, 'We have not the alternatives of being roasted one part of the year and frozen the other, but gently simmer over a slow fire the whole year round.'[1]

In this hot and sparse natural environment Protestant, or non-Catholic, Evangelical Christianity planted some of its deepest Indian roots. Christian missionaries arrived in Tinnevelly District before the British established direct political control over the area in 1801. Christianity was introduced in the eighteenth century by German Lutheran missionaries of the North European pietist tradition (in collaboration with the Society for Promoting Christian Knowledge, or SPCK), and was further strengthened in the nineteenth century under the Anglican auspices of the Church Missionary Society (CMS) and the Society for the Propagation of the Gospel in Foreign Parts (SPG).[2] Both were voluntary societies for

---

1. Robert Caldwell, *Lectures on the Tinnevelly Missions* (London, 1857), p. 28.
2. On early incursions into Tinnevelly by German missionaries sponsored by the King of Denmark with support from the SPCK, beginning with Christian Frederick

mission to non-Christians: the CMS expressed the 'low-church' Evangelical side of Anglican spirituality and the SPG expressed the 'high-church' Anglo-Catholic side. They worked side by side in Tinnevelly, where, despite their common evangelistic goals, they often fell prey to disagreements and rivalries. (Thus, their growing congregations tended to identify themselves as 'CMS Christians' or 'SPG Christians.')

Those most receptive to the Christian message in Tinnevelly were the semi-untouchable Shanars (now called Nadars, or 'lords'), an energetic one-fifth of the district's population whose hereditary occupation was bringing down the sap of the lofty palmyras.[3] By 1851, the Nadars of Tinnevelly and neighboring Travancore comprised more than half of the nearly 100,000 Christian converts registered with Protestant missions in India.[4] Conversion to Christianity was part of a rising aspiration in India to change status in the caste-dominated South Indian social hierarchy. The Nadar caste community and its strong Christian core were to be key agents of this change.

Azariah's paternal grandfather, a Nadar merchant known as Gnaniyar (or 'man of wisdom'), traveled through the countryside in a wagon, or

---

Schwartz in 1778, see Julius Richter, *A History of Missions in India,* trans. S. H. Moore (Edinburgh, 1908), pp. 96-127, particularly pp. 119, 127, 161-73; W. O. B. Allen and Edmund McClure, *Two Hundred Years: A History of the Society for Promoting Christian Knowledge, 1698-1898* (New York, 1898; reprinted, 1970), pp. 258-88. R. E. Frykenberg has correctly emphasized the important precedents set by the often-overlooked conversion movements which took place under Lutheran supervision in Tinnevelly as early as 1797, and the important role of conversions from the area's most important agricultural caste (the Vellalars) during this early period as well. See 'The Emergence of "Free" Religion under the Company's Raj in South India,' typescript from author, University of Wisconsin-Madison, 1984, p. 22; 'On the Study of Conversion Movements: A Review Article and a Theoretical Note,' *IESHR,* XVII, 1 (1980), pp. 125-26; and 'The Impact of Conversion and Social Reform upon Society in South India during the Late Company Period: Questions concerning Hindu-Christian Encounters with Special Reference to Tinnevelly,' *Indian Society and the Beginnings of Modernization, c. 1830-1850,* ed. C. H. Philips and M. D. Wainwright (London, 1976), pp. 193-95. Recognition of eighteenth-century Lutheran influence is also given in Hans Cnattingius, *Bishops and Societies: A Study of Anglican Colonial and Missionary Expansion, 1698-1850* (London, 1952) and S. C. Neill, *A History of Christianity in India: 1707-1858* (Cambridge, 1985), pp. 28-58, 212-22, 227-35.

3. *The Church Missionary Atlas* (London, 1896), pp. 145-46.

4. Of a total of 91,092 Christians, 51,355 belonged to Tinnevelly's CMS and SPG missions and to South Travancore's London Missionary Society (LMS). J. Richter, *op. cit.,* p. 201. On LMS work in Travancore, see Dick Kooiman, *Conversion and Social Equality in India* (New Delhi: South Asia Publications, n.d.).

bandi, drawn by bullocks or donkeys trading the coarse brown jaggery sugar from the local palmyra trees for grain and cotton.[5] Although relatively poor,[6] he was a link between the rustic villages of Tinnevelly and the newly installed English cotton companies in the larger city of Tuticorin and the more distant metropolis of Madras.[7]

Gnaniyar and his fellow Nadars occupied a middle position of 'semi-untouchability' in the caste system: between 'outcastes' and 'Sudras' (pronounced 'Shudras') in the caste hierarchy. Like the untouchables (here called Pallans and Paraiyans), they were barred from entering temples or courts of justice, and required to follow dress regulations forbidding women to cover the upper parts of their bodies. They were also forbidden the use of public wells and were subject to various prohibitions regarding spatial distance. Nadars were required to stay thirty-six paces away from high-caste Brahmins; their houses were limited to one story; they were forbidden to carry umbrellas and to wear shoes and gold ornaments. They could not milk cows, and Nadar women were not allowed to carry pots on their hips. Unlike the outcastes, however, many Nadars abstained from liquor and beef and disapproved of the remarriage of widows.[8]

As a merchant, Gnaniyar was not directly involved in the traditional, ritually polluting occupation of climbing and cultivating palmyra trees, and it is likely that his family held a relatively elevated position in the ranking of subgroups within his community.[9] Nevertheless, in the eyes of

---

5. Mercy Azariah, *Bishop Azariah of Dornakal: A Play* (Madras, 1948), p. 10; C. Graham, *Azariah of Dornakal* (London: SCM Press, 1st ed., 1946), p. 20; J. Z. Hodge, *Bishop Azariah of Dornakal* (Madras: CLS, 1946), p. 11; Group interview with K. Thasiah, C. Christian Devaraj, and other villagers in Vellalanvilai, 10 March 1986. Hereafter, Vellalanvilai interview.

6. C. Graham, *op. cit.,* p. 20; 'Bishop Azariah's Family and Early Life,' *DDM,* XXII, 5 (May 1945), p. 4.

7. In particular, Harvey Mills Company, Tuticorin (Vellalanvilai interview). Stephen Neill recounted in an unpublished draft of his autobiography that Azariah's grandfather used donkey teams to carry jaggery as far as Madras (Neill Collection, Oxford).

8. On the ranking of Shanars 'in-between' untouchables and Sudras, see Robert Caldwell, *Lectures on the Tinnevelly Missions, op. cit.,* pp. 44-45. Caldwell is amplified and discussed in Robert Hardgrave, *The Nadars of Tamilnad: The Political Culture of a Community in Change* (Berkeley, 1969), pp. 21-24.

9. Azariah's surviving children and grandchildren do not know to which subcaste their family belonged before conversion (A. J. Azariah to author, 26 Feb. 1988, Madras). Nadar subcaste distinctions were breaking down in the nineteenth century; hence it is often difficult to arrive at a consensus on questions of name, rank, or occupation of subcastes even among non-Christians. Hardgrave, *op. cit.,* p. 32.

other communities, he would have shared with all members of his caste the stigmas associated with their traditional occupation.

During succeeding generations, the Nadars became one of South India's most rapidly changing communities. By the year of Azariah's death in 1945, this formerly impoverished, semi-untouchable community had been transformed into one of the most economically and politically successful communities in the South.

The distinctive work of Protestant Christian missionary societies (the above-mentioned CMS, SPG, and the London Missionary Society, or LMS) spurred much of this change. Already by 1857, 43,000 converts had been received by the CMS and SPG missions in Tinnevelly alone.[10] As one missionary observed of these predominantly Nadar converts:

> Christianity and the palmyra have appeared to flourish together. Where the palmyra abounds, there Christian congregations and schools abound also; and where the palmyra disappears, there the signs of Christian progress are rarely seen.[11]

By the end of the nineteenth century, Tinnevelly had more Christians than any district in the Madras Presidency; and, among the Protestants, 95 percent were from the Nadar caste. Historian Robert Hardgrave has shown that the missions inspired spiritual and organizational unity in the previously fractionated community. Non-Christians joined Christian pacesetters in bringing political consciousness to the caste and uplifting it to take advantage of economic and educational opportunities in British India.[12]

The Nadar converts in Tinnevelly came primarily neither from the lowest sections of the caste (Kalla Shanars) nor from the highest (Nadans), but rather from the middle subgroups and particularly the climbers.[13] Conversion provided a pathway to caste advancement for middle-ranking Nadars, who, after receiving Christian education, were able to leave their former, polluting occupation in great numbers.[14] Christian missions helped Nadar women gain the right to cover their upper bodies during the violent breast-cloth controversy of the early- to mid-nineteenth century. Nadar women were frequently attacked, stripped, and beaten — and chapels and schools were

---

10. R. Caldwell, *Lectures, op. cit.,* p. 14.

11. *Ibid.,* p. 31.

12. R. Hardgrave, *op. cit.,* 43-70; and his article, 'The Breast-Cloth Controversy,' *IESHR,* V (June 1968), pp. 171-81.

13. *Ibid.,* p. 48.

14. *Ibid.,* pp. 48, 53.

burned — for the offense of wearing the breast cloths previously worn only by higher-caste Nair women. The position and influence of the missionaries helped Nadars to challenge their indigenous superiors, and Nadar Christian converts became leaders in the movement for social change.[15]

Economic and political conditions in the wake of British victory in the Mysore and Poligar *(Palaiyakkaram)* Wars (1755-1801), which subdued the power of feudal chiefs, were also favorable to Nadar advancement. Nadar merchants (like Azariah's grandfather) and moneylenders were better able to take advantage of improved transportation and communication created by the Pax Indika than were the relatively disadvantaged and locally bound palmyra tree climbers.[16] Trading cotton and tobacco, Nadar merchants established prosperous communities farther north and generally sought to disassociate themselves from members of the same caste in southern Tinnevelly. From about the 1860s, they frequently tried to lift their social status simply by adopting higher-caste manners and attributes, a process known as Sanskritization.[17] Although they were a family of merchants, Azariah's relatives did not seek advancement through Sanskritization but instead chose the different route of Christianization.

Like most of the palmyra-climbing Nadars, Azariah's ancestors were Saiva: a poor family of 'toddy-drawers' belonging to 'a very orthodox Hindu sect devoted to the exclusive worship of the god Siva, the destroyer.'[18] Azariah's grandfather was remembered as a particularly religious man who, while traveling through the countryside by *bandi,* 'always left the end of his bag of sweetstuff unfastened so that he could make an offering at any little shrine which he passed, or make a gift to anyone who asked him.'[19] Although the Nadars worshipped some of the familiar gods of the Hindu pantheon, particularly a son of Siva named Subramanya (or

15. D. Forrester, 'The Depressed Classes and Conversion to Christianity, 1860-1960', in *Religion in South Asia: Religious Conversion and Revival Movements in South Asia in Medieval and Modern Times,* ed. G. A. Oddie (New Delhi, 1977), p. 53; Bernard S. Cohn, *Colonialism and Its Forms of Knowledge: The British in India* (Delhi: Oxford University Press, 1997), pp. 139-143; R. Hardgrave, *op. cit.,* pp. 69-70, 265-66.

16. R. Hardgrave, *op. cit.,* pp. 96-97.

17. *Ibid.,* pp. 97-109. The success of this method of uplift has been disputed. D. Forrester has questioned Hardgrave's conclusion that Sanskritization failed (Forrester, *op. cit.,* p. 53, referring to Hardgrave, p. 129).

18. C. Graham, 'Bishop Azariah's Family and Early Life', in *op. cit.,* p. 4. This description was published in Dornakal to commemorate the bishop's death and is therefore likely to include the memories of Azariah's wife and children. In fact, most Nadars are Saiva, there being only one Vaishnava Nadar *kuttam.* See Hardgrave, *op. cit.,* p. 37.

19. C. Graham, 'Bishop Azariah's Family and Early Life,' in *op. cit.,* p. 4.

Murugan), missionaries tended to describe the most prevalent religious practices as 'demon-worship.' Many missionaries believed that Christianity was popular among Nadars precisely because it provided an attractive alternative to their former religion's 'bloody sacrifices' and 'devil dances.'[20] Missionary Robert Caldwell noted that deities favored by the highest Brahmin social groups received little notice from most Nadars.[21] Exclusion from Hindu temples contributed to the Nadar religion's decidedly anti-Brahmanical character. Indeed, some early Protestant missionaries to Tinnevelly denied that Nadars were "Hindu" at all because of the unorthodox nature of their religious practices.[22]

Azariah's father was born in 1821, probably in the village of Chettivillai.[23] He was given the name Velayudham, one of the many names of the popular deity Subramanya.[24] As a boy, he traveled with his father to exchange and to sell goods.[25] During these trips, they observed different aspects of the quickening group conversion movements taking place among Nadars between 1820 and 1835 in response to the pietistic brand of Christianity that was being preached by the missionaries.[26] In 1837, a

20. R. Caldwell, *Lectures, op. cit.,* pp. 47-49.

21. Although there were exceptions among the wealthier class or the more devout, among whom Gnaniyar may have been counted. R. Caldwell, *Tinnevelly Shanars,* 1st ed., pp. 8-29, quoted in R. Hardgrave, *op. cit.,* pp. 37-38.

22. R. Hardgrave, *op. cit.,* pp. 37-38. Similar observations have been made by modern missionaries regarding the unorthodoxy of much village 'Hinduism.' Ellis O. Shaw suggests that standard textbook descriptions of Hinduism are gravely deficient for not including the non-Brahmanical but widespread practices of much village religion. *Rural Hinduism: Some Observations and Experiences,* ed. S. P. Appasamy (Madras, 1986).

23. Chettivillai is also known by its Christian name, Chithambarapuram. Villagers of Chettivillai claim that it is the native place of Azariah's father, although other people believe that Megnanapuram (Bishop Jason Dharmaraj) and Vellalanvilai (Ambrose Azariah) were his native villages.

24. C. Graham, 'Bishop Azariah's Family and Early Life,' in *op. cit.,* p. 4. The year of his birth is given in A. J. Azariah, *A Biographical Sketch of Samuel Vedanayagam Thomas (1855-1890)* (Madras, 1970), p. 1. Murugan's popularity is reflected in some of the earliest Tamil heroic poetry: Hardgrave, *op. cit.,* p. 37; Nilakanta Sastri, *A History of South India: From Prehistoric Times to the Fall of Vijayanagar* (London, 1966), pp. 57-58, 143; K. Kailasapathy, *Tamil Heroic Poetry* (Oxford, 1968), pp. 35-36. The name Velayudham also refers to the three-pronged spear of Siva: Mercy Azariah, *op. cit.,* p. 15.

25. Vellalanvilai interview.

26. R. E. Frykenberg, 'The Impact of Conversion and Social Reform upon Society in South India during the Late Company Period,' in *op. cit.,* p. 201. In the nearby village of Nedu Vilai, a CMS mission was established in 1836, and 140 out of a total population of 338 villagers were baptized. S. C. Neill, *A History of Christianity in India: 1707-1858, op. cit.,* p. 466.

young Welsh missionary arrived who would transform this part of the Tinnevelly District into one of South India's most self-sufficient Christian areas and the training ground for the future Bishop of Dornakal. John Thomas (1807-70) began his life's work in the village of Megnanapuram (village of 'true wisdom'),[27] one of Tinnevelly's many Christian 'villages of refuge.' During Thomas's thirty-four-year tenure, a large mission compound was built, a school was opened, and, perhaps most notably, a semi-Gothic church with a spire 175 feet high was constructed on the site of a former Hindu shrine. Streets were straightened, houses were rebuilt in rows, trees were planted, and wells were improved.

The spoken tradition still preserved in Megnanapuram and surrounding villages describes his preaching against 'demons' and 'idols,' and his healing powers. 'John Thomas told us not to be afraid of devils; Christianity was the answer,' remembered one great-grandchild of early Tinnevelly Christians.[28] One story of Thomas's arrival in Megnanapuram recounts how he entered the village on horseback during an annual festival, fulfilling an oracle received by a *pujari*, or local Hindu priest, the year before, 'that the evil spirits would leave the place and go to the hills, because a white man would come here on a black horse, and the people would embrace the white man's religion.'[29] Upon arrival, villagers claim that Thomas overpowered a viper which was biting a worshipper at the village shrine and applied some healing medicine. The story continues:

> The news of the arrival of the white man on a black horse and of the miracle done by him brought all the villagers to the shrine. The white man was not such a fool as to let that opportunity slip away. He asked all the people to sit down, and . . . told them that the god they worshipped was not the true God, as it was made of stone, and had eyes that cannot see, legs that cannot walk, ears that cannot hear, a mouth that cannot talk, and so on, whereas his God was an immortal God who cannot be known in the image of an idol but can be seen only with spiritual eyes.[30]

27. Indian Christians remember that the village was called Saba Nilam (the 'Land of Curse') before their conversion to Christianity. M. Azariah, *op. cit.*, p. 14. In the reorganization of the CMS after the death of Rhenius in 1838, this village became one of six CMS mission centers in Tinnevelly. M. E. Gibbs, *The Anglican Church in India: 1600-1970* (New Delhi, 1972), p. 142.

28. Mr. K. Thasiah, aged 78 in 1986, whose great-grandfather was one of the first Nadars baptized by John Thomas in Megnanapuram. Vellalanvilai interview.

29. See M. E. Gibbs, *op. cit.*, pp. 142-43, for the full account from Emily Joseph of Megnanapuram, dated 29 August 1956.

30. *Ibid.*, p. 143.

Before the village would abandon the practice of making supplications to the goddess Bhadrakali for protection against epidemics, it appears to have been crucial that Thomas demonstrated the superior healing and protecting powers of the new God. The CMS missionaries to Tinnevelly presented Christianity as a replacement for, not a complement to, the worship of village idols and the associated fears of demons and diseases in very much the same way that Azariah and his colleagues would do in Dornakal seventy years later.

Thomas's missionary predecessor, Charles Rhenius, has also been credited with a miraculous healing. Christians in Megnanapuram like to tell the story of how Rhenius rescued the son of a Hindu priest from the deadly effects of a snake bite incurred while the boy's father was performing *puja* (worship ceremonies) beneath a Yelandai tree. The priest became a Christian, and Rhenius built a chapel on the site before the Yelandai tree, under which Azariah is also said to have prayed during his childhood.[31]

The repetition of certain themes in these oral accounts such as the healing of snakebites, the white missionary arriving on a black horse, and the practices of holy men beneath the Yelandai tree, suggests that general formulae guided these villagers in the construction of their historical stories.[32] There is no reason to believe that these stories are not based on some historical fact, but it is important to realize that they may also have been constructed according to certain forms that are structurally relevant in themselves and suggest unstated meanings to the community of transmission. Just as Christian missionaries have adapted stylized formulae from traditional Indian folk-song patterns to make new Indian Christian folk songs more highly evocative to listeners, so these stories reflect certain patterns and themes which deepen their resonance within today's living Indian Christian community.[33] A direct link is established between Rhenius, the missionary forebear, and Azariah, the successful native son, by their shared experience in the sacred space under the Yelandai tree where Rhenius conquered the devil and the false religion (symbolized by

31. Group interviews in Megnanapuram, 9 March 1986.

32. For a discussion of techniques of Tamil oral composition, see K. Kailasapathy, *Tamil Heroic Poetry, op. cit.,* pp. 135-228. The viper tradition also plays an important symbolic role in many legends of Christian heroes and 'holy men,' from St. Paul on Cyprus to St. Thomas in Mylapore.

33. As, e.g., in M. Thiel-Horstmann, 'Indian Christian and Traditional Folksong Patterns,' in *Asie du Sud, Traditions et Changements,* Colloques Internationaux du C.N.R.S. (Paris, 1979), pp. 87-91.

the snake and the neglectful Hindu priest-father) and built a chapel, and where India's rising indigenous Christian leader sought early spiritual communion with God.

In nearby Vellalanvilai, the village where Azariah's father was to become pastor, villagers still recount how John Thomas rode dramatically on his horse into their village, stopping to rest and to pray beneath their great banyan tree which sheltered a shrine dedicated to the goddess Essakiamman. Despite initial opposition to Thomas's preaching, the village *munsif,* or headman, decided to become a Christian and visited Megnanapuram continuously for three months to receive instruction for baptism. Under his leadership, four other families were baptized and formed the nucleus of a village congregation in 1841. Before long, all the Nadars of the village had embraced the new faith, dismantled the shrine to Essakiamman, and used the idol stones as the foundation stones for a new church.[34]

Azariah's father's conversion to Christianity seems to have been linked to his entrance into the British missionary school system. In 1839, at the age of eighteen, Azariah's father left his village to become a student at the recently opened CMS school in Megnanapuram. Shortly thereafter, he was baptized and given the new name 'Thomas Vedanayagam,' which combined the surname of the Welsh missionary with the nearest 'Christian equivalent' of his Hindu name (*Veda,* meaning 'Bible,' and *nayagam,* meaning 'master' or' leader').[35] Some versions of this story contend that in 1839 he came under the influence of Christianity and 'ran away' to the village of Megnanapuram, where he begged admission into the new religion. John Thomas then admitted him as a student in the mission school, the story goes, and accepted him as a candidate for baptism after a waiting period during which Azariah's father was tested for his 'sincerity.'[36] Other accounts suggest that the boy was more interested in education than in baptism. One local oral tradition maintains that he went to the CMS

34. This history was recounted to me by the great-grandson of Swamiadiyan Sudalaialumperumal, the headman who was first converted in response to Thomas's preaching (Vellalanvilai interview). The date of the first baptism was confirmed by the current Pastorate Chairman in Vellalanvilai, C. Christian Devaraj (Devaraj to author, 7 April 1987).

35. Translated as 'the Gem of the Christian Veda,' in M. Azariah, *op. cit.,* p. 15; C. Graham, *op. cit.,* p. 20; C. Graham, 'Bishop Azariah's Family and Early Life,' in *op. cit.,* p. 4.

36. C. Graham, *op. cit.,* p. 20; J. Z. Hodge, *op. cit.,* p. 11; and C. Graham, 'Bishop Azariah's Family and Early Life,' in *op. cit.,* p. 4.

school in Megnanapuram with his father's blessing and no apparent interest in Christianity.[37]

Whatever the real motives for Azariah's father's entrance into Christianity and the mission school, stories about this event also stressed the authoritarian role of the British missionary. Azariah's son Ambrose described how John Thomas selected children for admission to the boarding school in Megnanapuram:

> We are told that [John Thomas] would line [the children] up and reject most on the ground that one had a narrow forehead, another a head too small, that there was no grace in his face, that he looked sickly, that he came from a family too poor, that his family was too backward socially, that he did not look intelligent, and so on! As Thomas Vedanayagam was selected by John Thomas for admission in the boarding school, we can presume he had a broad-enough forehead, a well-formed head, that he had a pleasant face, that he was healthy, looked intelligent, and was from a family not too poor or backward![38]

To Azariah's family, the western missionary first appeared as a larger-than-life judge, and the missionary educational system as an exclusivist society dependent upon the mysterious whims of the all-powerful western missionary.

As far as we know, Azariah's grandfather (and presumably grandmother) never converted to Christianity; and, in this sense, Velayudham's baptism was unusual since most accessions to the church during this period in Tinnevelly involved whole families or even villages. This practice of group conversion tended to minimize social dislocation and provide protection from frequent persecutions.

Disincentives to conversion were strong in Nadar society during this period, particularly because of opposition to the growing influence of missions from upper-class Nadars, or Nadans.[39] Missionaries provided protection for Christian converts from the oppressions of these wealthy and powerful Nadan landlords in addition to offering education, medical aid, and other forms of assistance. With their traditional dominance thus

37. Vellalanvilai interview.
38. A. Azariah to author, 10 Aug. 1985.
39. R. Hardgrave, *op. cit.,* pp. 50-51; C. Graham, 'Bishop Azariah's Family and Early Life,' in *op. cit.,* pp. 4-5; and A. H. Grey-Edwards, *Memoir of the Rev. John Thomas: CMS Missionary at Megnanapuram Tinnevelly, South India, 1836-1870* (London, 1904), pp. 79-83.

threatened, the Nadans became the missionaries' greatest adversaries. Many Nadans supported anti-Christian societies: the Vibuthi Sangam (the Sacred Ashes Society), established in 1841 and allied with the Sadur Veda Siddhanta Sabha (Salay Street Society) of Madras after it was established in 1845; and the Society for Diffusing the Philosophy of the Four Vedas, organized to stop the mass conversions of the 1840s.[40] Confronted with such opposition, some converts sought the safety of Christian settlements; but most Christian families and villages were able to maintain their former community life largely intact after baptism.

After completing his education, Azariah's father chose not to follow his father's occupation but rather to enter the employ of the CMS, working for thirty years in most areas of Christian ministry from missionary preaching to pastoral care. At this time, Tamil catechists such as Azariah's father were employed by a European missionary 'to go before him — when he purposes visiting a village — in order to invite the people to come and listen, and to follow up his address by instructing more fully, and in greater detail, those who are willing to learn.'[41] Since Indian Christians were rarely ordained and promoted to positions of authority, the rapidly growing church faced a growing shortage of leadership. By 1842, John Thomas was responsible for visiting 500 communicants per month with the help of only one ordained Indian priest.[42] Few Indians were considered qualified to complete the western-style theological training necessary for ordination to the priesthood (an English-medium theology course which involved the study of Greek and Hebrew).

To solve this dilemma, John Thomas proposed a scheme to promote Indian church leadership, of which Azariah's father was a direct beneficiary.[43] In the face of considerable opposition from other missionaries, Thomas designed a new curriculum to meet the needs of local Indian Christian congregations. Experience in village ministry (at least fifteen

40. R. Hardgrave, *op. cit.,* pp. 50-51; S. C. Neill, *A History of Christianity in India: 1707-1858, op. cit.,* pp. 229-230. On the history of communal conflict provoked by conversions in Tinnevelly and Madras, and the persecutions of converts, see R. Frykenberg, 'Impact of Conversion and Social Reform,' in *op. cit.,* pp. 200, 207-8.

41. R. Caldwell, *Lectures on the Tinnevelly Missions, op. cit.,* p. 70.

42. S. C. Neill, *A History of Christianity in India: 1707-1858, op. cit.,* p. 399.

43. *Ibid.,* p. 400. This scheme was the product of a tradition — begun by the pietist Professor A. H. Francke (1663-1727) of the University of Halle, and imported to India by missionaries Ziegenbalg, Schwartz, and Rhenius — which challenged the exclusivist clericalism and tight ecclesiastical controls of much of the Anglican tradition. Thus, to many Anglican missionaries, it appeared to be "revolutionary."

years), loyalty to the church, and personal reputation, rather than academic accomplishments, became the criteria for acceptance in the training program, which included 'intensive study of the Bible in Tamil, an outline of church history, Christian doctrine based on the Thirty-Nine Articles of the Church of England, preaching (of which they already had considerable experience), and pastoral care and village problems.'[44] This innovation was similar to that instituted later by Azariah for training Telugu priests in Dornakal.

The fruits of Thomas's ideas were quickly evident. Five Indian deacons were ordained by 1851; ordinations took place again in 1856 and 1859; and Azariah's father was ordained deacon by the Bishop of Madras, Frederick Gell, on 31 January 1869, along with twenty-one other Indian deacons and twelve Indian priests.[45] This ordination in Pallamcottah (Palayamkottai) was the largest ever for India and represented the culmination of John Thomas's career as a missionary. The success of this Anglican scheme to train an Indian ministry contrasted sharply with a failed effort by French Roman Catholics to do roughly the same thing at the same time. Their inability to control the age of ordination (which they wanted to lower to help priests keep their celibacy vows), the lack of resources for a proposed seminary, and, above all, the seeming inability of French missionaries to adjust their conception of the priesthood to the simpler conditions of the Indian village — all contributed to the failure. In contrast, John Thomas was given the resources and support needed for training his priests, who, because they were usually older and married, were unencumbered by the problem of celibacy.[46]

Thomas Vedanayagam was subsequently ordained priest on 24 December 1871. He spent the years remaining before his death on 23 June 1889[47] as pastor of the congregation in Vellalanvilai. The village

44. *Ibid.,* p. 400. Although Hebrew and Greek ceased to be required of candidates, there is evidence that Thomas Vedanayagam acquired some knowledge of the languages anyway. See H. Whitehead, 'Vedanayakam Samuel Azariah,' *IRM,* XXXIV, 134 (April 1945), p. 184.

45. C. Graham, 'Bishop Azariah's Family and Early Life,' in *op. cit.,* p. 5; M. E. Gibbs, *op. cit.,* p. 251; S. C. Neill, *A History of Christianity in India: 1707-1858, op. cit.,* pp. 400-401.

46. These different experiences contributed to the relatively quick advance of the Anglicans and comparatively slow advance of the Roman Catholics in the ordination of Indians to the priesthood and the episcopacy. S. C. Neill, *A History of Christianity in India: 1707-1858, op. cit.,* pp. 298-99, 397-401; *The Story of the Christian Church in India and Pakistan* (Madras, 1972), pp. 96-98.

47. The date recorded on his tombstone in the churchyard of Holy Trinity Church, Vellalanvilai.

was composed mainly of Nadars employed by Vellalar landlords (hence the derivation of the name 'Vellalanvilai') who lived in the nearby village of Manad. During the second half of the nineteenth century, the Nadars purchased most of the land from the Manadu Vellalars, thus contributing to an overall increase of Nadar-owned land titles in the Tinnevelly District.[48] The first Vellalanvilai Nadars became Christians in the early 1840s, and by 1987 the village consisted of 516 Christian families engaged mainly in the cultivation of coconuts, rice, and bananas.[49]

Remembered for his piety and dedication, Thomas Vedanayagam adopted Anglicized models of religious practice (in liturgy, music, etc.) imported by the CMS. He built the semi-Gothic Holy Trinity Church upon the foundation stones taken from the preexisting shrine to the village goddess, Essakiamman. Apart from its location next to the village's giant banyan tree, there was little to distinguish his church and much of the liturgy within it from Anglican churches in England.

Azariah's father was married first to a Nadar wife about whom little is known[50] and, after her death, to a Christian from Kuppapuram (near the SPG center at Nazareth in Tinnevelly) named Ellen, who became Azariah's mother. His two sons by his first wife were men of considerable achievement. The first son, Ambrose V. Thomas (1850-1911), became the headmaster of the CMS High School in Megnanapuram which today bears his name. He taught himself both Greek and Sanskrit and placed great emphasis in the school on memorization of the Bible. This high school is believed to have produced more ordained Christian ministers than any school in the East.[51]

The second son, Samuel Vedanayagam Thomas (1855-90), was ap-

48. R. Hardgrave, *op. cit.,* p. 53. The current Vellalanvilai Pastorate Chairman, who lives in the rectory in which Azariah was born, described the process thus: 'This Nadar community worked hard and little by little they purchased the lands from the Manadu Vellalars and built houses. Because of the ownership of whole properties of the Vellalars, this name (Vellalanvilai) was published. Nowadays there are no Vellalars in Manad. They sold all the land and went away to places like Trichi and Thanjore towns' (C. Christian Devaraj to author, 7 April 1987).

49. C. Christian Devaraj to author, 7 April 1987. There is also a small village called Nainarpuram attached to the southeast of the village where Hindu 'Harijans,' who work the fields for daily wages, live today.

50. D. A. Christadoss, *Acariyā Attiyatcar* (Tirunelveli, 1974), pp. 2-3.

51. S. C. Neill, 'Vedanayagam Samuel Azariah,' in VSA, *Christian Giving* (London, 1954), p. 11. Ambrose Thomas was also headmaster of a CMS school in Colombo (D. A. Christadoss, *op. cit.,* p. 4).

pointed to a series of academic posts (teacher at the SPG College, Tiruchirapalli, in 1876 and, subsequently, headmaster of three schools: Wesleyan High School in Mannargudi, American High School in Madura, and Wesley College High School in Royapettah, Madras),[52] and became a noted Sanskrit scholar despite his early death at the age of thirty-five. After receiving BA and MA degrees in mathematics and English respectively, he undertook Sanskrit studies in response to the following experience, recounted by his grandson:

> It is said that one day while traveling with some Brahmin Pundits who were reading some slokas from the Vedas in Sanskrit, S. V. Thomas questioned them about the meaning of the slokas, and was told that they were too difficult to be understood by Non-Brahmins. He took this as a challenge and immediately started studying Sanskrit, and soon took the MS degree in Sanskrit coming first in Madras University and winning the University Gold Medal for Sanskrit that year.[53]

In the year of S. V. Thomas's death, it is believed that he was being considered for appointment as Professor of Sanskrit at Cambridge University.[54] That both of Azariah's elder half-brothers would have learned the sacred language of the Hindus and succeeded in following prestigious academic careers hardly one generation after their family's removal from semi-untouchable status indicates the degree to which their Christian education had provided a means for rapid social mobility.

Their eagerness to learn about Brahmin traditions was matched by a great reverence for British culture, with which their faith was intimately linked. S. V. Thomas was an avid reader and stylistic imitator of Thomas Babington Macaulay. He contributed articles to Christian periodicals such as *The Madras Christian College Magazine* and *The Harvest Field* on subjects ranging from South Indian missionary work to the Indian National Congress, of which he was harshly critical.[55] It was said that 'his writings were often mistaken by the press for those of an English gentleman, and were quoted as such.'[56] Thomas even produced a colloquial Tamil translation of Milton's *Paradise Lost* whose continuing popularity is reflected by

52. A. J. Azariah, *A Biographical Sketch of Samuel Vedanayagam Thomas, op. cit.,* p. 1.

53. *Ibid.,* p. 1.

54. *Ibid.,* p. 1.

55. *Essays by Samuel V. Thomas, MA (Medalist in Sanskrit, University of Madras),* bound volume of essays with no information on date or place of publication. Volume in the possession of Dr. D. Packiamuthu, Palayamkottai.

56. 'Introduction,' in *Essays by Samuel V. Thomas, op. cit.,* p. i.

its recent republication in Madras.[57] Azariah was to follow in his half-brother's steps by translating various Christian works into Tamil, notably Charles G. Finney's *Lectures on Revivalism* (1902), Andrew Murray's *Humility: The Beauty of Holiness* (c. 1902), St. Augustine's *Confessions* (n.d.), and selections from Bishop Andrewes' *Devotions* (1933).[58]

Thus, conversion to Christianity stimulated a process of advancement in Azariah's family, largely through educational achievements. Whereas Azariah's grandfather was a trader with, at most, a minimal elementary education, Azariah's father completed high school and ministerial training, and Azariah's elder half-brothers gained higher degrees and important positions in the missionary educational system. Azariah did not pursue any advanced degrees, but he was awarded an honorary degree from Cambridge University in 1920 and brought with him to Dornakal a deep appreciation for literacy and education.

Vedanayagam Samuel Azariah, the subject of our study, was born to Ellen and Thomas Vedanayagam on 17 August 1874 in the church rectory at Vellalanvilai and was baptized on 4 October. He was Ellen's first and only son, arriving thirteen years after the birth of their only other child, a daughter.[59] They chose the name Samuel after the Old Testament prophet whose parents, Hannah and Elkanah, had also waited many years for the birth of their first son.[60] It is less clear why he was given his other biblical name, Azariah.[61] He did not use the name until entering Madras Christian College in 1893, when he had an exchange (as related by his son) with its renowned Scottish principal, Wil-

57. Milton, *Poongavana Piralayam or Paradise Lost, Books I and II*, trans., S. V. Thomas (Madras, 1978). First edition: Trichinopoly: Southern Star Press, 1887. This work was mistakenly attributed to Ambrose V. Thomas in C. Graham, *op. cit.*, p. 23. From Graham, however, we learn that S. V. Thomas owned a printing press in Megnanapuram. Here Azariah learned techniques that were to be helpful later when establishing the Dornakal Diocesan Press.

58. Not all of these translations are available today, but they are known to exist (or to have existed). Letter from Grace Aaron to author, 9 Jan. 1987; *Extracts from Letters of Bishop Azariah*, with an Introduction by the Bishop of Madras (Madras, 1945), pp. 17-18. Azariah wrote in 1937 of Murray's book that 'next to the Bible that book has helped me most in my Christian life.' *Ibid.*, p. 18.

59. A 'married sister of Azariah' named Yovanna is a character in Scene 3 of M. Azariah, *op. cit.*, p. 23. Yovanna is also mentioned in D. A. Christadoss, *op. cit.*, p. 3.

60. 1 Samuel 1:4-20. This was a common practice among south Indian Christians wanting sons. Compare to: W. D. Clarke, 'In Memoriam: Samuel Satthianadhan,' *MDM*, I, 5 (May 1906), p. 245.

61. There was apparently 'no special reason.' C. Graham, 'Bishop Azariah's Family and Early Life,' in *op. cit.*, p. 6.

liam Miller, that was somewhat reminiscent of his father's humiliating introduction to missionary education:

> *Dr. Miller:* What is your name, boy?
> *Father:* Samuel, Sir.
> *Dr. Miller:* It is too common a name. Have you any other name?
> *Father:* Vedanayagam is my father's name.
> *Dr. Miller:* The name is too long and it is too much of a tongue-twister. What other name do you have?
> *Father:* Azariah, Sir.
> *Dr. Miller:* That is a good name. We will call you Azariah, Vedanayagam Samuel Azariah.[62]

Thus, the power of the western missionary educator extended even to the Adam-like renaming of his students.

Azariah passed his earliest childhood years in Vellalanvilai, where he attended the village church school and first learned to write by tracing letters in the dirt.[63] Years later as a bishop, Azariah credited his mother with instilling in him a deep appreciation of the Bible and of Christian prayer:

> My own earliest recollection of my mother is that she used to disappear suddenly on occasions: I used to cry and search for her and find her on her knees in an inner room in prayer. My mother had sanctified herself for the sake of her child. She taught me that my relationship to God was of far more importance than anything else, and she repeatedly impressed on me that I was born in answer to prayer and dedicated to the service of God.[64]

---

62. Ambrose Azariah to author, 10 August 1985, Madras. This account is corroborated almost exactly by Graham, who likely heard it from Azariah as well. C. Graham, *op. cit.,* p. 24. Once made Bishop of Dornakal, Azariah signed his letters 'V. S. Dornakal.'

63. Here 'the boys learnt to read from palmyra leaf books and traced their alphabet with their fingers on sand.' C. Graham, *op. cit.,* p. 21. Today Vellalanvilai offers a more modern, comprehensive education to an enlarged number of local youths at the 'Bishop Azariah Memorial School,' founded in 1963.

64. Speech at a Mother's Union Meeting in New Zealand in 1923, quoted in *The Church of South India, the Indian Missionary Society, Madras, and the National Missionary Society of India Jointly Celebrate the Birth Centenary of Bishop Azariah, 1974* (Madras: Diocesan Press, 1974), p. 23 (Henceforth *Birth Centenary of Bishop Azariah — 1974*).

By the age of ten, Azariah had committed to memory substantial portions of the Bible. 'All my love for the Bible and my knowledge of it came to me from my mother,' he claimed later.[65]

In 1885, Azariah became a student at the CMS High School in Megnanapuram where his half-brother Ambrose was both teacher and headmaster, exerting enormous influence over his young charge.[66] Azariah recalled later that:

> Many of us are what we are because of his influence, his prayers, his example. Yet there were many days when the time-table was forgotten; inspiration would make him devote one whole afternoon to Euclid, another to Algebra, again a whole morning to Scripture. These days are gone for ever . . . and with them is passing away the old Guru-Shisya (Master-Disciple) relationship between the teacher and the taught.[67]

The influence of Ambrose became even more important after the death of their father in 1889 when Azariah was only fifteen years old. As a surrogate father, Azariah's older half-brother inspired the future Bishop to place particular emphasis in later years on his role as a teacher in the Dornakal Divinity School and as an author of Telugu textbooks for seminarians.[68] In the year of his father's death, Azariah's mother moved to Megnanapuram to become matron of the CMS girls' school,[69] and Azariah matriculated at Church Missionary College, Tinnevelly (today: St. John's College, Palayamkottai). Here he took his F.A. (First in Arts) degree in 1892 and then served for a further year as a 'pupil teacher' to raise funds needed to complete his education.

During his tenure as a student in Tinnevelly, he is remembered primarily for establishing the Christian Brotherhood Association, which was dedicated to fighting rising caste spirit in the student hostels and to inspiring spiritual renewal. In addition to organizing prayer meetings, the organization published a Tamil journal, *Jeeva Thannair (Living Water)*, whose purpose was

65. C. Graham, *op. cit.,* p. 21.

66. The Eliot Tuxford School for Girls is now located on the site of the former CMS mission schools for boys and girls inside the mission compound built by John Thomas. Interview with R. Jeyakumar Devadason, Megnanapuram, 9 March 1986. The boys' school has been moved to another site outside the mission compound.

67. Quoted in C. Graham, *op. cit.,* pp. 22-23.

68. To be discussed below. See 'Bibliography of Azariah's Publications,' pp. 379-91.

69. D. A. Christadoss, *op. cit.,* p. 16.

mainly devotional and evangelistic.[70] Late nineteenth-century Tinnevelly had witnessed an increased awareness among Nadars of their caste rights and privileges and a corresponding growth of competition with other caste groups. Although Christian churches were officially opposed to caste, caste divisions still existed within most congregations. The social and economic mobility made possible through Christian education led, ironically, to heightened caste self-awareness and ambition. By 1894, Christians had widely adopted the title of their most virulent aristocratic Nadar opponents, the Nadans. Some literate Christians claimed that they were really Kshatriyas, or members of the warrior or ruler caste described by the ancient Hindu sage Manu. Azariah was not impressed by Indian Christians who helped to create and disseminate a new mythology of Nadar greatness, antagonizing other castes such as the Nadars' historical adversaries, the Maravars, and heightening caste consciousness within the Christian community itself.[71]

Azariah, therefore, began his student activist career by taking aim at the sins of his own people rather than at the sins of his British rulers. The Christian Brotherhood Association opposed caste in order to advance Christianity; but this was not an easy position to take in late nineteenth-century Tinnevelly. In 1893, an SPG missionary, J. A. Sharrock, established the Voluntary Society for the Suppression of Caste, but it attracted only three members in its first five years.[72] In choosing to take a stand against caste rights and privileges in his school, Azariah was beginning a long career of resisting dominant practices and opinions of his day on the basis of his confessional beliefs and western influences.

From February 1892 to January 1893, Azariah served as a monitor at the CMS High School in Palamcottah. His records reveal, not an extraordinary intellect, but a diligent student whose

> zeal, goodness, ability and industry . . . have been of great service to this Institution. To the students he has been kind and firm and has settled their differences without bringing them to other teachers. He has also been an example in study.[73]

---

70. The journal is still published by the Christian Brotherhood Association (Tirunelveli Diocesan Press, Palayamkottai).

71. R. Hardgrave, *op. cit.,* pp. 93-94.

72. Sharrock's refusal in 1892 to publish banns of marriage with the title Nadar provoked his congregation in Tuticorin to petition the Bishop of Madras in protest. They did not receive much sympathy from the bishop. *Ibid.,* pp. 93-94.

73. Note from the CMS High School Manager and Principal, Edwin Keyworth, 20 January 1893, Azariah Collection, Madras.

By the age of eighteen, Azariah had risen to the top of the missionary educational system in Tinnevelly and formed the ambition of becoming a Sunday School teacher.[74] His upbringing had exposed him to a conservative evangelical theology propagated by the CMS, and his faith found comfortable expression within the boundaries of the traditional Church of England and its associated institutions.

The following year, Azariah left the relatively parochial environment of Tinnevelly and ventured northwards to urban Madras. From February 1893 to March 1896, he was a student of mathematics at Madras Christian College, one of the colleges founded by the Church of Scotland's educational missions to privileged groups in India's cities. Here Azariah was exposed to a whole new type of liberal theology and a different, more elitist mission theory.[75]

Established in 1837 as St. Andrew's School by Church of Scotland missionary John Anderson, the college affiliated with the University of Madras by 1867 and was renamed Madras Christian College ten years later.[76] Anderson was inspired by the success of his fellow Free Church of Scotland missionary in Calcutta, Alexander Duff, to establish an English-medium school for the 'influential classes.'[77] Duff and his followers believed that Christian education of the urban elites was the first step in the conversion of India. They accepted a 'downward filtration theory' whereby education and, it was hoped, conversion of the top groups would have a leavening effect on the masses.[78]

74. *Ibid.*

75. Other notable Church of Scotland colleges were founded in Calcutta by Alexander Duff, in Bombay by John Wilson, and in Nagpur by Stephen Hislop.

76. The system of affiliating colleges was modeled after the University of London system: E. Jackson to author, 21 Jan. 1991, Birmingham; E. J. Bingle, 'A Hundred Years — 1837-1937: History of the Christian College,' *MCCM*, Centenary Issue (March 1937), p. 133.

77. Frykenberg, 'Modern Education in South India, 1784-1854: Its Roots and Its Role as a Vehicle of Integration under Company Raj,' *The American Historical Review*, 91, 1 (Feb. 1986), pp. 53-54. Anderson visited Calcutta to observe Duff's work before founding his own institution (see E. J. Bingle, *op. cit.*, p. 130). For a reassessment of Duff's achievement, see M. A. Laird, *Missionaries and Education in Bengal, 1793-1837* (Oxford, 1972), pp. 256-59.

78. M. A. Laird, *op. cit.*, pp. 207-8. This did not prevent Anderson from accepting admission of three pariah boys in 1838 at the cost of temporarily lowered enrollments when caste pupils withdrew from the school. John Braidwood, *True Yoke-fellows in the Mission Field: The Life and Labours of the Rev. John Anderson and the Rev. Robert Johnston, Traced in the Rise and Development of the Madras Free Church Mission* (London, 1862), pp. 74-97; S. C. Neill, *A History of Christianity in India: 1707-1858, op. cit.*, p. 320.

This mission strategy was not successful in producing conversions, although the Scottish colleges became wildly popular among India's most educated classes. By the time Azariah arrived at Madras Christian College, most educational missionaries had rationalized their failure to convert students by reconstructing the meaning and purpose of their Indian experience altogether. No longer was their mission to produce high-caste converts who would exit Hinduism and serve as inspirational leadership for a larger, multi-caste Indian Christian community; rather, it was to prepare Indian society as a whole for the reception of Christianity in the future by penetrating the mind of Hinduism and changing the thoughts and values of the entire culture. To achieve its goal of preparing India for the gospel through education, the so-called *praeparatio evangelica,* Madras Christian College sought to expose students to Christianity indirectly through the fruits of western culture and civilization, rather than directly through evangelism.

Azariah attended the college during the tenure of Principal William Miller (1862-1907), perhaps the most influential missionary in South India during the late nineteenth century.[79] Miller was educated in the Universities of Aberdeen and Edinburgh before being ordained in the Free Church of Scotland and taking up his position as Principal in Madras. He became a prominent figure in the Madras Presidency and was appointed to the Madras Legislative Council in 1893, the year Azariah entered the college. Miller became the leading spokesman in India of the *praeparatio evangelica* strategy, seeking to influence the whole non-Christian world with the message of the gospel without concern for immediate conversions.[80] By removing evangelization from the mandate of his college,[81] Miller began a movement among Christian colleges from about 1870 to turn their attention away from the problem of the salvation of non-Christian students

79. John McKenzie, 'Higher Education,' in *The Christian Task in India,* ed. J. McKenzie (London, 1929), p. 91. On Miller, see Kaj Baago, *Pioneers of Indigenous Christianity* (Madras, 1969), pp. 186-99.

80. S. C. Neill, *The Story of the Christian Church in India and Pakistan, op. cit.,* p. 127. Also J. McKenzie, *op. cit.,* pp. 91-93.

81. On Miller's defense at the Allahabad Conference in 1872-73 of the idea that, despite declining numbers of conversions in Christian schools, Christian education was one of the best methods of preparing India for Christianity, see G. A. Oddie, *Social Protest in India: British Protestant Missionaries and Social Reforms, 1850-1900* (Columbia, Mo., 1978), pp. 22-23. However, this type of argument was not completely absent even from the justifications made by the Baptist trio Carey, Marshman, and Ward for the establishment of Serampore College in 1818. E. Jackson to author, 21 Jan. 1991, Birmingham.

to focus more fully on the task of training a highly educated Christian elite — of which Azariah was a part — and of 'enlightening' wider Indian society more indirectly.[82]

The aims of Madras Christian College as described in its prospectus were:

> . . . simply to convey through the channel of a good education as great an amount of truth as possible to the native mind, especially of Bible truth. Every branch of knowledge communicated is to be made subservient to this desirable end.

However, the college curriculum included a broad range of subjects which extended beyond the narrower confines of more insular Christian educational programs:

> English, including reading, grammar and composition, writing and accounts, history, geography, arithmetic, mathematics, and algebra; the elements of astronomy and political economy; logic, moral philosophy, and natural theology; the evidences and doctrines of Christianity, etc.[83]

Under Miller, the school increased its enrollment, sharpened its academic standards, and further broadened the scope of its curriculum to include new subjects. Azariah arrived less than a decade after the introduction of a new course of studies for B.A. degree examinations which featured increased specialization and more advanced instruction in the physical and natural sciences.[84] Increased enrollment of students from the provinces — the relatively rural areas known in British India as the *mufassal* — necessitated the building of student hostels, which, interestingly, offered separate accommodation for students of different communities: Brahmin, Non-Brahmin, and Christian.[85] Coming from the rela-

82. S. C. Neill, *The Story of the Christian Church in India and Pakistan, op. cit.,* pp. 126-27.

83. E. J. Bingle, *op. cit.,* p. 130.

84. P. Cherian, 'Some Recollections of an Eventful Decade, 1880-1890,' *MCCM,* Centenary Number (March 1937), p. 170.

85. The first college hostel, opened in 1882, accommodated solely Brahmin or Vaishnava students. P. Cherian, *op. cit.,* p. 170; R. S. Macnicol, 'Landmarks in College History', *MCCM,* Centenary Number (March 1937), p. 145. In 1888, a hostel was opened for the accommodation of Christian students (presumably of all castes) and named after the late CMS Secretary in Madras, David Fenn. (*Ibid.,* p. 146.) In 1903, a hostel for Non-Brahmin students was opened as well. Known as Caithness Hall, this was the first hostel to accept students of different communities, although others were

tively conservative missionary schools of Tinnevelly, Azariah was thrust into a more cosmopolitan liberal environment, and into a student body which represented a wider range of socioeconomic and religious backgrounds.

This attempt by the Scottish missions to influence the cultural, moral, and spiritual beliefs of India through education was generally welcomed by Indians as a net benefit. Many non-Christian Indian students were willing to accept the teachings of Jesus without becoming members of an organized church via public confession and baptism.[86] However, a widespread revival and reinterpretation of Hinduism also took place in India during the nineteenth century, largely in response to the Christian missionary challenge. Isolated instances of conversion and a general suspicion of Christian intentions led to a period of heightened tension between Christians and Hindus immediately before Azariah's arrival in Madras.

The so-called 'Christian College Disturbance' of 1888 reflected the full intensity of the disagreements.[87] The college disturbance, which was provoked by a Brahmin conversion and, according to missionaries, by outside anti-Christian agitators, led to student strikes and wholesale chaos. The disturbance both reflected and worsened fears on the part of conservative Hindus in Madras that their customs and traditions were being undermined by the new religion. Reformist movements in Madras such as those that attempted to legislate against infant marriage owed much to the effects of western education upon Hindu social practices. However, the disagreement among the western-educated classes during the Age of Consent Bill controversy of 1890-91 dispelled the popular myth that these classes were necessarily in favor of reforms.[88]

The Hindu revival increased hostility to Christianity during Azariah's student days in Madras, but it did not seem to dampen his en-

---

to follow suit later. William Miller conducted an experiment in attempting to persuade students of different communities to share housing during retreats at the Mountain Home in Yercaud. However, the depth of resistance to these measures is reflected in the fact that when an inter-caste hostel was opened in 1919, the College Park Hostel, it maintained separate messes for Brahmin, Christian, and Non-Brahmin students. (*Ibid.*, pp. 151-3.) Separate messes may have been provided to cope with the different diets for vegetarians and non-vegetarians, but the issues of purity and pollution were almost certainly at stake as well. E. Jackson to author, 21 Jan. 1991, Birmingham.

86. S. C. Neill, *The Story of the Christian Church in India and Pakistan, op. cit.,* p. 126.

87. R. Suntharalingam, *Politics and Nationalist Awakening in South India, 1852-1891* (Tucson, Arizona, 1974), pp. 306-7.

88. *Ibid.,* p. 326.

thusiasm for Christian evangelism. Nor did the ecumenical atmosphere at Madras Christian College, where professors and students held many different and opposing opinions on religious, social, and political issues. The college did not encourage or enforce conformity to any single orthodoxy, as the varied debates and opinions expressed in the *Madras Christian College Magazine* demonstrated.[89]

In Madras, Azariah was able to make personal contact with many people of diverse views. In addition to meeting Hindu reformers, Azariah met Christians who were to be greatly influenced by nationalism, such as his classmate and future colleague in the National Missionary Society and the YMCA, K. T. Paul (1876-1931).[90] Among Azariah's other classmates were A. P. Patro, future leader of the non-Brahmin Justice Party and Minister of Education in the Madras Government from 1922 to 1927, and K. Venkata Reddi Naidu, Development Minister from 1922 to 1925 and then agent in South Africa and Law Member of the Madras Government.[91]

Significantly, young Azariah does not appear to have been involved in or influenced by the National Church of Madras, which was established during Azariah's student years by S. Pulney Andy and which, under the influence of growing nationalism and western liberal theology, attracted over one hundred members.[92] In Madras, Azariah was exposed for the first time to growing nationalism and protonationalism: his apparent general indifference to these developments is already striking at this young age.

Little is known about the details of Azariah's college career or why he chose to study mathematics.[93] He was probably influenced by his brother,

---

89. See, e.g., an article published in 1884 repudiating the claims of theosophy which did not succeed in convincing all of the students. The controversy is discussed in R. Suntharalingam, *op. cit.*, pp. 307-8. After its first fifty years of publication, the magazine reduced its scope to issues of more narrow college interest (see E. J. Bingle, *op. cit.*, p. 134).

90. After receiving a law degree, K. T. Paul began his career as headmaster of a mission school and then entered government employment. He served as General Secretary of the NMS from 1909 to 1914 and National General Secretary of the YMCA from 1916. See H. A. Popley, *K. T. Paul: Christian Leader* (Calcutta, 1938).

91. *Ibid.*, pp. 28-29.

92. K. Baago, 'The First Independence Movement among Indian Christians,' *ICHR*, I, 1 (June 1967), pp. 65-78; G. Thomas, *Christian Indians and Indian Nationalism, 1885-1950: An Interpretation in Historical and Theological Perspectives* (Frankfurt am Main, 1979), pp. 78-85.

93. No records of grades or activities are available in the Madras Christian College Archive, Tambaram.

S. V. Thomas, who completed a B.A. in mathematics in 1880,[94] and by CMS missionary to Tinnevelly in the 1890s, Thomas Walker, who received a mathematics degree at Cambridge in 1882 and argued that there was 'nothing like Mathematics for mental training and discipline.'[95] In the end, Azariah never completed his B.A. degree. He passed final examinations in English (ranking twelfth in his class) and in Tamil, but he was struck by a sudden illness, probably an attack of influenza, on the day of his final mathematics examinations.[96] He had the opportunity to take the mathematics exams after his recovery six months later, but Azariah chose not to — perhaps simply because of a 'lack of funds'[97] or because he had already committed himself (by March 1895) to a job as a YMCA secretary.[98]

Azariah's decision not to finish his B.A. may prefigure his later educational policy in the Dornakal Diocese, where he deemphasized the importance of higher learning as a form of skills relevant to village ministry. This policy was sharply criticized by many Telugus, who felt that Azariah had blocked their aspirations, in part because of his own alleged insecurity at not having attained a B.A. degree. His defenders countered that Azariah's policy rightly placed a holistic concern for village uplift (both spiritual and material) above the more individualistic ambitions for advanced degrees for a minority that would probably leave the villages. Azariah's son remembers that the bishop criticized people for flaunting their B.A.'s when they were not themselves 'B.A.,' that is, 'Born Again.'[99]

Azariah spent much of his time as a student engaged in Christian evangelistic activities sponsored by the YMCA: prayer meetings, Bible studies, and street preaching. By 1895, he was leading YMCA spiritual meetings and preaching bands in Madras, had attended the Third Indian National Convention of the YMCA as a delegate from Megnanapuram, and directed the opening of a new YMCA branch in Madras. When Azariah received an honorary degree from Cambridge University in 1920, an admirer wrote:

94. A. J. Azariah, *A Biographical Sketch of Samuel Vedanayagam Thomas, op. cit.,* p. 1.

95. Amy Wilson-Carmichael, *Walker of Tinnevelly* (London, 1916), p. 9.

96. Interview with A. Azariah, 3 June 1986, Madras; J. Z. Hodge, *op. cit.,* p. 11; C. Graham, *op. cit.,* p. 24. There are no records of the examinations in Madras Christian College Archives, Tambaram.

97. J. Z. Hodge, *op. cit.,* p. 11.

98. His son explained that he chose to take up the YMCA position rather than to delay for his exams. Interview with A. Azariah, 3 June 1986, Madras.

99. Interview with A. Azariah, 3 June 1986, Madras.

I remember how you willingly sacrificed your BA degree for the sake of the Master as a student of the Madras Christian College, and the Good Lord has rewarded you with a distinction that has not, to my mind, fallen to the lot of any other Indian Christian.[100]

Although we have no record today of Azariah's achievement (or lack of achievement) in his college classes, we do know that he was influenced by the 'high Christian ideals' of the faculty, whom he regarded with 'reverence and inspiration.'[101] Azariah always remembered William Miller's parting address to students in March 1896, when he 'committed us to God and with intense earnestness charged us to be faithful to the ideals of character and conduct that, through many years, the College had endeavored to place before us.'[102] Madras Christian College seems to have reinforced Azariah's admiration for the many values associated in his mind with both Christianity and the West. It also provided him with his first sustained exposure to people and ideas of widely differing traditions within India. Perhaps most importantly, it provided him with an introduction to the nondenominational Christian organization which was to broaden his horizons and serve as his vocational home for the next fourteen years: the YMCA.

100. James Devadasan to VSA, 17 July 1920, Azariah Collection, Madras.

101. For the college's centenary celebrations in 1937, Azariah wrote: 'The College may well be proud of the great men that have been at the helm during this past century since Anderson, Miller, Cooper, Skinner, Henderson, Macphail, Michie Smith, Russell, Kellett, Morren, Meston — are the few with whom I was personally acquainted, the very recital of whose names evokes wholesome memories of reverence and inspiration' (*MCCM,* Centenary Number [March 1937], pp. 122-23).

102. VSA, 'Commemoration Service Address,' *MCCM,* Centenary Number (March 1937), p. 111.

CHAPTER 2

Pan-Asian Ecumenism:
A Vision Beyond Nations

For the first two decades of Azariah's life, he was the parochial child of a subculture within a subculture of the Indian world. Secure in his native Anglican Tinnevelly, Azariah was suddenly thrust into contact, not so much with the rest of India or other Christian communities, as with the entirely new emerging reality of pan-Asian and worldwide Christian youth organizations seeking to break through all preexisting denominational boundaries to create a new Christianized world. Through these movements, Azariah developed a personal vision and sense of mission which transcended both the Anglicanism of Tinnevelly and the nationalism so popular with his student contemporaries.

The cosmopolitan city of Madras brought him into the ecumenical, student-generated attempt to break through all traditional denominations, religions, and caste boundaries. The Young Men's Christian Association provided the institutional base from which Azariah emerged as one of Asia's foremost ecumenical mission leaders. During his career with the YMCA from 1895 to 1909, Azariah's instinctive sense of the importance of missionary work acquired in the evangelical environment of Tinnevelly crystallized into a more fully developed ecumenical commitment to evangelism. Compared to the relatively insular atmosphere of Tinnevelly Anglicanism, the YMCA's multi-national scope and broad religious and social objectives expanded Azariah's intellectual and spiritual horizons beyond the confines of both his denomination and his nation. A brief look at the origins of the international YMCA movement during its high

36

tide of missionary optimism will help to explain how the organization often known today as a domesticated social and gymnastic club became an important vehicle for transmitting the faith in distant India.

The YMCA in India

The Young Men's Christian Association was created in the nineteenth century from an amalgam of different interdenominational organizations founded by young European and American men in response to changing work and living conditions in the Victorian period. In England, the YMCA was one of several socioreligious movements that arose to counteract the disruptive effects of industrial society on young men. The London Association was created on 6 June 1844 to provide for the spiritual welfare of young unmarried men of the commercial classes who had moved from farms to industrial centers to find employment and were confronted with difficult industrial living and working conditions.[1] Inspired by the pan-evangelical spirit characteristic of mid-nineteenth century British Protestantism, the YMCA was ecumenical from its inception. As YMCA founder George Williams discussed plans for founding the association with three other men in the drapery business, he said: 'Here we are, an Episcopalian, a Methodist, a Baptist, and a Congregationalist — four believers but a single faith in Christ. Forward together!'[2]

The same combination of rapid industrialization and spiritual revivalism helped to turn the YMCA almost unintentionally into an international movement. Early associations were established in Boston and New York to 'throw a kind of protecting influence around young men coming from the country to the city.'[3] Associations were formed in smaller New England towns, often without knowledge of each other. In Europe, associations often grew out of men's organizations originally formed to meet the needs of wandering journeymen apprentices.[4]

1. The name Young Men's Christian Association was adopted at the fifth meeting of the group in July 1844: C. P. Shedd, *History of the World's Alliance of Young Men's Christian Associations* (London, 1955), p. 23. See also Clyde Binfield, *George Williams and the Y.M.C.A.: A Study in Victorian Social Attitudes* (London, 1973).

2. R. Rouse, 'Voluntary Movements and the Changing Ecumenical Climate,' in *A History of the Ecumenical Movement, 1517-1948,* ed. R. Rouse and S. C. Neill (London, 1954), p. 327.

3. C. P. Shedd, *op. cit.,* p. 70. See also pp. 68-82.

4. *Ibid.,* p. 201.

Although these dispersed groups had no common origin, they united into a worldwide YMCA movement through the leadership, first, of the original London YMCA inspired by the international gathering at the Great Exhibition of 1851 and, later, of the World Alliance of YMCAs formed in Paris in 1855.[5] The number of associations grew quickly from 338 in 1855 to 2043 in 1876 and expanded beyond the original western boundaries.[6]

This was a new creation of the modern age: an international ecumenical movement of young men representing neither a single Christian denomination nor a single nationality.[7] In South Asia, branches were established, at first largely by and for Europeans, in Calcutta (1854),[8] Colombo (1859), Kandy (1861), Trivandrum (1873), and Lahore and Bombay (1875).[9] The early organizations were established voluntarily and were generally unaware of each other's existence; and so this early period of YMCA activity in India to 1889 has been aptly described as the 'Epoch of Introduction and of Isolation.'[10] The South Asian associations were established by Europeans and Americans who had come to India and Ceylon as teachers, missionaries, or businessmen.[11] Gradually, the associations came to include Indians and Sinhalas as full members, although the Calcutta branch long remained restricted to Europeans and Eurasians.

Later in the century, a powerful, largely forgotten upsurge of student missionary activity from America sparked an intense era of YMCA missionary activity in India. In 1886, a hundred young American men committed themselves to foreign missionary service at the first student sum-

5. *Ibid.,* pp. 15-40, 102.

6. *Ibid.,* p. 199.

7. *Ibid.,* pp. 41-101.

8. Nish, *Young Men's Christian Association of Calcutta, 1857-1957,* claims it was founded three years later than does Shedd. See E. Sharpe, *Not to Destroy but to Fulfil: The Contribution of J. N. Farquhar to Protestant Missionary Thought in India before 1914* (Uppsala, 1965), p. 152.

9. C. P. Shedd, *op. cit.,* p. 199. See also E. C. Worman, 'Early History of the YMCA,' published serially in *YMI,* Oct. 1922-Jan. 1923. Bound volume in YMCA Headquarters, UTC, Bangalore.

10. *YMI,* XIII, 1 (Jan. 1902), p. 19. E. C. Worman, *op. cit.,* pp. 1-3. Even the important future YMCA leader, David McConaughy, thought in 1893 that the first YMCA in India was established at Trivandrum in 1873. D. McConaughy, 'Second Paper,' *Report of the Third Decennial Missionary Conference, Bombay, 1892-1893,* I (Bombay, 1893), p. 191.

11. For example, early associations were formed due to the efforts of LMS representatives in Trivandrum (1870), the evangelistic tour of Rev. A. N. Summerville of Glasgow (1875), and the influence of Prof. Frank Sanders of Yale University and Jaffna College. *YMI,* XIII, 1 (Jan 1902), p. 19.

mer conference of the YMCA at Mt. Hermon School in Northfield, Massachusetts, sparking a nationwide wave of missionary volunteers which exceeded 2,000 within one year.[12] At the helm of this movement was a charismatic Princeton University graduate, Luther D. Wishard (1854-1925), who dreamed of building a world student movement through the missionary extension of the YMCA.[13] During a four-year world tour beginning in 1888, he laid the foundations for an aggressive global outreach program by the YMCA and its missionary wing, the Student Volunteer Movement (SVM), which was organized in 1888 by another dynamic YMCA secretary from Cornell University, John R. Mott (1865-1955).

John Mott became a Nobel Laureate and is remembered today as American Protestantism's foremost ambassador of missionary ecumenism. His parish was nothing less than 'the student community of the whole world.'[14] He served as National College Secretary of the YMCA from 1890 to 1915 and traveled more than two million miles during a lifetime that included frequent visits to India.[15] His tireless efforts to promote student missionary enthusiasm had a profound impact on students around the world at the turn of the century. Motivated by its 'watchword' slogan, 'the evangelization of the world in this generation,' his Student Volunteer Movement aimed to proclaim the gospel to the entire world, calculating that if each of the world's Christians witnessed to a hundred non-Christians, the whole earth would hear the Christian message by the year 1900 and be prepared for the millennium.[16] This was the vision that

12. C. P. Shedd, *op. cit.,* pp. 302-3. Evangelist Dwight L. Moody supported this movement, and the 'Cambridge Seven,' who had been inspired by Moody's campaign at Cambridge University in 1884, became the model for the American effort in 1886 to extend the influence of the Northfield missionary uprising. 'Historical Sketch of the Student Volunteer Movement for Foreign Missions,' Register of Ms. Group No. 42, pp. 7-8, SVM Archives, YDS.

13. C. P. Shedd, *op. cit.,* p. 354.

14. S. E. Ahlstrom, *A Religious History of the American People* (New Haven, 1972), p. 865.

15. He visited India during his 1895-97, 1901-2, 1912-13, 1928-29, 1936-37, and 1938-39 world tours. See III: 117/1930-32, 1936, 118/1950, 1953-54, Mott Papers, YDS. Also: *Experiences and Impressions during a Tour in Asia in 1912-1913, Being Extracts from Personal Letters of John R. Mott* (privately printed), Mott Papers, YDS.

16. The founders did not intend to convert the whole world, but rather to proclaim the gospel and thereby give each living person an opportunity to respond. Dana L. Robert, 'The Origin of the Student Volunteer Watchword: "The Evangelization of the World in This Generation,"' *The International Bulletin of Missionary Research,* X, 4 (Oct. 1986), pp. 146-49.

gripped Azariah during his student days in Madras and during his years as a YMCA secretary from 1895 to 1909.

Azariah first heard John Mott in December 1896 while attending a YMCA conference in Calcutta. Mott was promoting the Student Volunteer Movement on a 60,000-mile world tour during a 20-month period from 1895 to 1897 which took him to 22 countries and 144 educational institutions.[17] Azariah was impressed by Mott's intensity which contrasted so sharply with the more relaxed approach of his mentors at Madras Christian College. As Mott wrote about Miller's *praeparatio evangelica* strategy in later years:

> I was pained, in India, to hear the president of a Christian college rise to say that he did not expect conversions in this generation among their students, and I could hardly trust my ears when he added that the governing board at home agreed with him that they were not to expect conversions in this generation.

This strategy, Mott believed, was doomed to failure in both the short and long term:

> I said to myself: That is not the spirit that will win conversions in the next generation. It reminded me of the young preacher who went to Spurgeon [the popular nineteenth-century English Baptist preacher] to ask why he did not make converts in his ministry. "You do not expect to make converts after every sermon, do you?" Spurgeon asked. The young preacher replied, "Oh, no, of course I do not expect them after every sermon." "That is just the reason why you do not get them after any sermon," was Spurgeon's answer.[18]

Azariah agreed with Mott, and began to work actively for conversion through the efforts of the YMCA in Madras. 'What the SVM has done for the Western lands, the YMCA will increasingly do for India,' Azariah wrote to Mott in 1906, 'namely the calling out from the ranks of the young men volunteers who will pledge to devote their lives to carry the Gospel to the unevangelised regions of their country.'[19]

17. Records of World Tour, 1895-97, III: 117/1930-32, Mott Papers, YDS.
18. John Mott, 'An Unprecedented World-Situation,' c. 1913, I: 4/61, Mott Papers, YDS.
19. VSA to John Mott, 12 April 1906, I: 4/61, Mott Papers, YDS.

Beyond Nationalism:
Azariah's Pan-Asian Global Vision

While India's attention focused increasingly on the unfolding drama of rising nationalism, Azariah's attention turned to an even broader subject: the increasingly international character of Christianity and its varied cultural expressions in Asia. The climax of this phase of Azariah's career came in 1907 when he attended both the World Student Christian Federation (WSCF) Conference in Tokyo, the first of its kind ever to be held in an Asian nation; and the Fifth National Convention of the YMCAs of China, Korea, and Hong Kong, which met in Shanghai, China (and included delegates from eighteen Chinese provinces).

Azariah relished exposure to different Asian cultures and frequently compared them to Indian culture. 'The Native city! Ah! What a contrast to our Indian cities!' he wrote from Shanghai in March. 'The city is within walls, the whole city laid out in winding circular streets, very narrow, paved with stones. They are exactly as the narrow streets of Benares.'[20] He was both fascinated and disgusted by a thirty-two-course Chinese dinner given by one of the Shanghai YMCA Directors which included ducks' brains, birds' nests and sharks' fins.

> The last two courses were sent round but none of the guests is expected to partake of them. They leave it to show that they have had enough. . . . I tried the chop sticks, and I ate with them. . . . Of course the Chinese could do it a thousand times better than we can do. These dishes carried the Chinese flavour with them. They were quite repulsive to us.[21]

That evening, he spoke to the Convention on 'What Christianity Has Done in India,' and reflected afterwards on how China was giving him a fresh perspective on his experience as an Indian Christian. 'We never even reckon up what Christianity has done. It is quite a new experience when we come to tell it to people who know nothing whatever about India.'[22]

Azariah was struck by the beauty of Japan and the cleverness of its people: 'In printing, building, making nice articles they excel India,' he wrote home. 'The Japanese are certainly very tasteful in decoration. They have such a refined idea of colours. Their homes are clean, nice, well arranged,

20. VSA to Anbu, 20 March 1907, Shanghai, Azariah Collection, Madras.
21. *Ibid.*
22. *Ibid.*

and decked with pretty pictures of beautiful scenery.' But, while visiting the port city of Nagasaki, he was appalled to learn about the history of Japan's encounter with the West and its resistance to Christianity:

> Nagasaki is . . . the place where there was the greatest persecution of Christians. Christians were asked to trample upon the image of Christ and the Cross. Hundreds refused and were crucified. In the Roman Catholic Church there is an oil painting to show the crucifixion of these Christians. When one of the Buddhist Temples were [sic] built, the Christian carpenters of the city refused to build it, until compelled by Government. . . . I saw the hill from which the Christians are said to have [been] thrown down.[23]

Azariah was amazed by the forwardness ('freedom') of the Japanese women who managed restaurants: 'the ladies in charge come out and say: "Good morning, Gentlemen, How do you do? Please come in and have some tea."' But he was quite appalled by the subservience of wives who served YMCA delegates meals in their homes:

> As we entered we cast off our shoes and then I saw three ladies falling down to the ground before us. . . . We went and sat down on the floor of one of the rooms. Then we were introduced. We don't shake hands. As she is introduced the lady makes a deep bow, touches the ground with her forehead and that once, twice, and three times even. At the same time we have to do the same thing. Oh, it was curious. I succeeded in making the bows all right. As we left the house we again went through the rounds of bows.[24]

Despite the many cultural differences and his occasional feelings of alienation, Azariah maintained a clear sense of unity with Christians from other Asian cultures throughout this trip. This unity reached its fullest expression at the WSCF Conference in Tokyo, where Azariah met with 627 delegates, over 500 of whom came from Asia and included fifteen from India. 'The Conference opened with a season of prayer,' he wrote to his wife in April. 'When we began to sing "Holy, Holy, Holy" in English, German, French, Japanese, Korean, Chinese, I tell you, my whole frame thrilled with emotion. People from all nations, tribes and tongues praising God is indeed a memorable experience.'[25] All of Azariah's sense of alienation from other

---

23. VSA to Anbu, 27 March 1907, Kobe, Japan, Azariah Collection, Madras.
24. VSA to Anbu, 10 April 1907, Nagoya, Japan, Azariah Collection, Madras.
25. VSA to Anbu, 2 April 1907, Nikko, Japan, Azariah Collection, Madras.

Asian cultures — or from European cultures, for that matter — seemed to have dissolved in the commonality of Christian belief and worship.

The Tokyo conference elected Azariah as their vice-president and discussed strategies for evangelization in Japan, China, and India in the face of rising Asian nationalisms and concurrent efforts to revivify the national religions of Buddhism, Confucianism, and 'Higher Hinduism.' The conference report took the optimistic view that Asia's national movements were positive developments attributable to the beneficent influence of modern western civilization and to the gradual Christianization of these lands.[26] But the meeting also demonstrated the effects on Asian Christian students of the broader pan-Asian awakening that had been encouraged by the Japanese military defeat of Russia in 1905.

Azariah had a natural sympathy for the Asian awakening. The year before, he had helped to spread the growing spirit of Pan-Asian self-reliance when he escorted two Japanese YMCA secretaries, S. Motoda and T. Harada, on an evangelistic tour of India and reported that 'their messages are sure to do the Indians a lot of good. Great crowds flock to hear them everywhere.'[27] Azariah's enthusiastic address at the next year's Japanese WSCF Conference also appealed directly to this new sense of Asian confidence:

> No country can be fully evangelized except by its own sons. The fifty millions of Japan, the four hundred millions of China, and the three hundred millions of India can only be fully evangelized by the sons of Japan, China and India. . . . The nineteenth century can well be called the missionary century of the Occident. Fellow-students of Asia, shall we make the twentieth century the missionary century of the Orient? . . . Drawing our inspiration from the cross, let us go forth to make Jesus King of Asia![28]

26. G. S. Eddy, 'The Japan Conference,' *YMI*, XVIII, 7 (July 1907), pp. 87-91; G. Soundararaj, 'V. S. Azariah as YMCA Secretary', in *Birth Centenary of Bishop Azariah — 1974, op. cit.,* pp. 35-37; D. Lotz, '"The Evangelization of the World in this Generation": The Resurgence of a Missionary Idea among the Conservative Evangelicals' (Ph.D. thesis, Hamburg, 1970), p. 38.

27. VSA to John Mott, 12 April 1906, I: 4/61, Mott Papers, YDS. George Thomas, *Christian Indians and Indian Nationalism, op. cit.,* pp. 94-95.

28. VSA, 'Enlisting Students in the Extension of Christ's Kingdom,' in *Report of the Conference of the World Student Christian Federation: Held at Tokyo, Japan, April 3-7, 1907* (New York: WSCF), pp. 124-26. On the significance of the conference and Azariah's role, see Hans-Ruedi Weber, *Asia and the Ecumenical Movement, 1895-1961* (London, 1966), pp. 69-77.

Azariah's clarion call to convert Asia was, of course, different from a contemporary Asian nationalist's clarion call to free Asia from western domination. The rhetoric and enthusiasm of the Pan-Asian movement for Christian spiritual liberation paralleled those of early twentieth-century Asia's wider socio-political 'awakening,' but were fundamentally different in their goals. Perhaps because Azariah's own childhood experience gave him a secure sense of Christianity's legitimacy as an Indian religion, he never took the negative view that Asian conversion to Christianity represented a new form of Asian subordination to the West. Azariah never viewed Christianity as a 'western religion,' nor did he want it to become known as an 'eastern religion.' It was, to him, a universal religion that was truest to itself when transcending all national or regional boundaries.

The WSCF conference increased Azariah's appreciation for Christianity's supranational and extra-European identity. This early exposure to Christianity's pan-Asian and international character provided him with a broad perspective with which to counter the rising hostility of national leaders who opposed his commitment to evangelism and charged that his 'western' religion was incompatible with his Indian nationality. Gripped by an idealistic vision of regenerating India through missionary activism during his YMCA years, Azariah never accepted the charge that his efforts were not intrinsically patriotic.

Near the close of Christianity's 'great century' of expansion in Asia,[29] Azariah therefore joined the energetic, multinational YMCA membership in advocating India's acceptance not only of the Christian God, but also of the 'civilizing' effects of western culture and British rule. But he did so at the opening of a period in which many Indian nationalists were developing increasingly xenophobic attitudes towards western and, particularly, Christian missionary influences. He seemed quite unselfconscious about how his generally favorable views of British rule and of western Christian influence in India were beginning to sound more and more out of tune with the rising tenor of his age. His personal letters en route from Ceylon to China in 1907 almost guilelessly linked British power with divine power:

> There was a British Man of War or War Vessel standing in the harbour. And from that ship electric flash light was thrown on the waters and it lighted up every ship on the waters. The light was thrown on the entire horizon, powerful, bright, white light. It strongly reminded me of the

29. K. S. Latourette, *A History of the Expansion of Christianity: The Great Century, 1800-1914, in Northern Africa and Asia* (London, 1947).

search light of God falling upon human life. Nothing can hide in his light.[30]

What might have symbolized the menacing presence of foreign domination to a more self-conscious Indian nationalist, symbolized to Azariah the welcome searchlight of a beneficent God.

Thus, the awakening of Azariah's identity as an international Christian eventually alienated him from mainstream Indian nationalism in ways not too dissimilar from the alienation experienced by other Indian minorities such as the Muslims, particularly after the partition of Bengal in 1905 and the rise of the *swadeshi* movement for economic self-reliance.[31]

A 1907 editorial in the YMCA's journal *The Young Men of India* proclaimed:

> Every true citizen of India rejoices at the growing national spirit. . . . The Associations of India may play a great part in promoting the national spirit. . . . No organization is so closely in touch with great numbers of young men in all provinces . . . let the Association members realize that the Association is a national movement.[32]

The YMCA distinguished itself in India for its success in promoting Indian leadership within its ranks and for its general identification with the goals of Indian nationalism. However, these sensibilities did not extend to institutional participation in or support for secular political mobilization. When the British government issued the famous Morley-Minto constitutional reforms designed to win the allegiance of Indian liberals on the one hand, but also resorted to significant acts of repression such as the deportation of the extremist Lajpat Rai on the other, *The Young Men of India* did not advocate unconstitutional tactics in response. The achievement of political concessions from the British was not the purpose of the YMCA's existence nor the focus of its attention.

The YMCA expressed its broad nationalist sympathies by promoting Indians such as Azariah to positions of leadership and by establishing an atmosphere of equality and friendship between its Indian and western members. Azariah spent much of his YMCA career managing South Indian district headquarters in Madura and in his native Palamcottah, traveling frequently to YMCAs throughout India and to regional, national,

---

30. VSA to Anbu, 8 March 1907, Azariah Collection, Madras.

31. John R. McLane, *Indian Nationalism and the Early Congress* (Princeton, 1977), pp. 359-69; J. Brown, *Modern India: The Origins of an Asian Democracy* (Delhi, 1985), pp. 175-85.

32. *YMI*, XVIII, 8 (Aug. 1907), p. 99.

and international conferences. The future bishop had far greater opportunity to exercise responsibility in the YMCA than would have been possible in his native church of Tinnevelly with its more traditional and limited channels of advancement.[33] He was influenced predominantly by young American YMCA colleagues who were generally more sympathetic to Indian national self-determination than the British. However, British YMCA leaders, such as Scotsman J. N. Farquhar (with whom Azariah later edited The Heritage of India book series), were also relatively supportive of the national movement since they were somewhat removed from the British missionary establishment by virtue of their association with a suspicious ecumenical organization.[34]

Azariah embraced the ideal of missionary activism at the threshold of an era which became increasingly hostile towards his vision of national regeneration via conversion to Christianity. His belief that the solutions to what he regarded as India's spiritual as well as social, political, economic, and cultural problems were ultimately to be found in the Christian religion had only a small base of support in India. The growth of Hindu revivalism, particularly in the North, and of the perception that the Indian National Congress represented mainly Hindu interests, antagonized not only Azariah and much of the Christian constituency, but also the much larger Islamic minority which created the Muslim League in 1906. When nationalist leaders organized a mass meeting at the temple of Kali, *Kalighat,* in 1905 at which the *swadeshi* vow was taken before the mother-goddess, Christians as well as Muslims were disturbed by the symbolic association of Hinduism with the nationalist cause.[35]

Azariah's struggle during his pre-episcopal career to reconcile his Indian and Christian identities amid the overlapping and often conflicting imperatives of communal, national, and transnational loyalties took place entirely within the Indian branch of the International YMCA, to which we now turn our attention.

---

33. Stephen Neill argued that Azariah owed more to the YMCA than to the church itself when he was elevated to the episcopate. S. C. Neill, *A History of Christian Missions* (Harmondsworth, Middlesex, 1964), p. 366. Critics of Azariah's consecration charged at the time that his 'unorthodox' (i.e., non-Anglican) preparation for the bishopric would prove to be a disability in office because he would be essentially unfamiliar with the administrative, liturgical and pastoral demands of Anglican offices.

34. Eric J. Sharpe, *Not to Destroy but to Fulfil, op. cit.,* pp. 159-63, 193, 221-23. These suspicions only grew in upcoming decades. See G. Studdert-Kennedy, *British Christians, Indian Nationalists and the Raj, op. cit.,* pp. 129, 256-57.

35. E. Sharpe, *Not to Destroy but to Fulfil, op. cit.,* p. 221.

The Indian YMCA: The American Wave

Azariah was lifted from his provincial parish past into a new international vision by two American evangelists from the surging Student Volunteer Movement: David McConaughy (1860-1946) and George Sherwood Eddy (1871-1963).

The arrival of Gettysburg College graduate David McConaughy from the second Northfield Conference marked the beginning of the YMCA as an organized force on the Indian subcontinent. By January 1890, he had established a YMCA headquarters in Madras; and, as Secretary of the YMCA in India, he began systematic correspondence with more than 25 other Indian associations and established the national periodical, *The Young Men of India*. At the First Indian National Convention of the YMCAs in Madras in February 1891, 35 delegates from 17 associations joined the International Alliance of YMCAs, agreed to limit active memberships to young male Protestants (as was done in Europe and America), and offered associate memberships to men of any faith.[36]

The Indian YMCA promoted itself as an interdenominational Protestant organization which sought to develop harmonious relations with all churches rather than to become itself a new church. McConaughy described it as:

> not denominational, nor yet undenominational, but interdenominational, not apart from, but a part of the Church of Christ, the Young Men's Christian Association is, in short, the Church at work for young men by young men.[37]

Azariah's later involvement in the church unity movement was, in many respects, an attempt to recapture the ecumenical spirit that he, like other participants in the unity movement, had encountered for the first time in the YMCA.[38]

The goal of the YMCA in Madras, as elsewhere, was to meet the so-

---

36. C. P. Shedd, *op. cit.*, pp. 309-10. 'The members are of two classes: any young man of good character, introduced by two members, may become an Associate Member; any young man who is a Communicant Member of a Christian Protestant Church, may become an Active Member. Every Active Member is expected to take some definite part in the work of the various committees of the Association.' D. McConaughy, 'Second Paper,' *op. cit.*, p. 193. Membership fees were equal for both classes.

37. D. McConaughy, 'Second Paper,' in *op. cit.*, p. 189.

38. Bengt Sundkler, *Church of South India: The Movement towards Union, 1900-1947* (London, 1954), pp. 33-35.

called fourfold needs of young men: physical, intellectual, social, and spiritual. In the words of McConaughy, 'The finished product of the Young Men's Christian Association is a man – the coming man – with the muscle of an athlete, the brain of a scholar, the manners of a gentleman, and the heart of a Christian.'[39] The YMCA played an important role in the widespread development of what has been called 'muscular' Christianity in India during the late Victorian period.

The contrast between the 'manly' nature of Christianity and the 'effeminate' nature of Hinduism was a common theme in some popular missionary polemics and in other literature of the late British Raj. Sports and, specifically, the British public school games ethic helped diffuse throughout the British empire a moralistic ideology closely associated with Christianity and generally supportive of the British imperial enterprise.[40] Stories of the forcible introduction of boxing, rowing, football, cricket, ice-sliding, and swimming (and western trousers) to reluctant Indian students in Christian schools were not uncommon,[41] the stated purpose being to teach an ethic of fair play and decency necessary to good character and, specifically, to Christian conduct.

The ideal of the manly citizen was one whose body was as fully trained as his mind and spirit. In the words of George Barne, Bishop of Lahore, they would be 'men of character and courage, serving their fellow-men, fighting for truth and justice, constantly engaged in killing dragons, valiant men in thought and action.'[42] Under the guidance of McConaughy and his successors, the YMCA influenced a new generation of Indian leaders to admire 'manly' principles and practices derived from a vigorous, robust type of Christian culture popular in late Victorian Britain and North America.

39. D. McConaughy, 'Second Paper,' in *op. cit.,* p. 189.

40. J. A. Mangan, *The Games Ethic and Imperialism: Aspects of the Diffusion of an Ideal* (New York, 1986). The important role of the YMCA is overlooked in this study.

41. Cecil Earle Tyndale-Biscoe (1863-1949), head of the CMS School in Shrinagar from 1890 to 1947, provides an excellent description of the forcible introduction of sports in *Tyndale-Biscoe of Kashmir: An Autobiography* (London, 1951). The enormous popularity of cricket and football in India today suggests, however, that resistance to these sports was short-lived.

42. Rt. Rev. George Barne, former Bishop of Lahore, 'Foreword,' in *Tyndale-Biscoe of Kashmir, op. cit.,* pp. 9-10. (Barne was Bishop of Lahore from 1932 to 1949.) According to Mangan, Tyndale-Biscoe was the best example of a 'muscular' missionary at work in India, 'the preux chevalier of imperial Christian knights.' Mangan, *op. cit.,* pp. 177-91. See also G. Studdert-Kennedy, *British Christians, Indian Nationalists and the Raj, op. cit.,* pp. 226-36. Other important examples were T. L. Pennell (1867-1912) and A. G. Fraser (1873-1962).

In the early stage of the YMCA's history, spiritual work was regarded as the association's first and foremost duty. Nowhere was this emphasis more clearly illustrated than in the Madras branch where Azariah was first drawn into YMCA activities. The main focus was a Bible study class, street preaching in Tamil, and hospital visitations, which were all considered part of the 'spiritual side' of the work.[43] Sponsorship of Bible classes became a key criterion for admission of associations to the Second Indian National Convention.[44]

The Madras YMCA actively evangelized its own members, both Christian and non-Christian. Urban associations in India were composed mainly of students and young professionals from the English-educated elites. In order to attract high caliber native members and to win the respect of missionaries in the field who were often skeptical of the YMCA, the association tended to send unusually well-qualified secretaries to foreign countries such as India. McConaughy, Wishard, and their contemporary John Trumbull Swift (1861-1928), who was posted to Japan, all had university educations and, in this respect, were not representative of the majority of YMCA officers in the West during the period.[45] By 1903, 15 out of the 20 YMCA secretaries in India were university graduates.[46] The membership in urban areas reflected similarly high attainments. In March 1896, the occupational distribution of YMCA membership in Madras was: 'Students 171, Clerks 109, Teachers 35, Lawyers 6, Physicians 5, Mechanics 18, Soldiers 2, Merchants 29, Missionaries 27, Signallers 5, Miscellaneous 30.' As *The Young Men of India* noted with a tone of self-congratulation, 'this distribution clearly shows that the YMCA is appealing to the right class of young men.'[47]

All active members were in full communion with a Protestant Christian church, though many were considered to be merely 'nominal' Christians by the evangelical YMCA leaders, who persistently tried to deepen their membership's faith through Bible studies, observing a daily time of prayer (the SVM's so-called 'Morning Watch') and inspirational addresses.

43. D. McConaughy, 'Second Paper,' in *op. cit.,* pp. 192-93.
44. E. C. Worman, *op. cit.,* p. 10
45. C. P. Shedd, *op. cit.,* p. 310.
46. *YMI,* XIV, 3 (March 1903), p. 46.
47. *YMI,* VII, 3 (March 1896), p. 28. Although the occupational distribution did not include nationality, the total membership of 437 included '152 Native Christians, 142 Hindus, 8 Mahomedans, 86 Eurasians, 46 Europeans, 1 Parsi and 2 Coorgs.' *Ibid.* (Coorgs, whose religion stands firmly within the Hindu tradition, were still classified separately, both here and below.)

But McConaughy was particularly anxious to keep the Madras association doors open 'to all young men without distinction of race, rank or religion'[48] through associate memberships for non-Christians. By 1894, 302 of the 430 YMCA members in Madras were 'native Indian young men,' of whom 202 were Hindu, 12 were Muslim, 3 were Parsis, and 85 were 'native Christians.' Thus, non-Christians outnumbered Christians 217 to 213, a development which McConaughy welcomed. The people most thoroughly excluded from associations in Madras and elsewhere were the Roman Catholics, who first gained admission to a YMCA in Mexico City in 1907.[49]

The YMCA made a concerted effort to convince non-Christian associate members and visitors of the superiority of Christianity over its alternatives.[50] The Second National Convention of YMCAs in India, which met in Bombay in April 1892, passed the resolution: 'That Associations be exhorted to do everything in their power towards extending the privileges of their work to the non-Christian communities around them.'[51] It was hoped that, by providing an inviting meeting place for men of different faiths, Christian members would be able to influence non-Christians towards accepting the Christian gospel. As David McConaughy wrote: 'the influence of the Active Members is brought to bear upon the Associate Members constantly, in all departments, not merely in religious meetings; the Secretary is always accessible, and finds frequent opportunities for conversation with the members.'[52]

Hindus began striking back at the YMCA during Azariah's years as a student in Madras. The conversion of Mr. Ramanujam Chetty (a high-caste Komati) in 1894 caused a great uproar and provoked the Hindu community in Madras to establish a Young Men's Hindu Association (YMHA).[53] The YMHA adopted a policy of admitting only Hindus 'so as not to hurt the caste feelings of orthodox members,' and sought to provide a defense against what it perceived as a YMCA assault on Hindu

---

48. E. C. Worman, *op. cit.,* p. 5.

49. C. P. Shedd, *op. cit.,* p. 342.

50. D. McConaughy, 'Second Paper,' in *op. cit.,* p. 194.

51. C. P. Shedd, *op. cit.,* p. 362. Efforts to involve non-Christians in YMCA activities were pursued more energetically and persistently than efforts to include non-Protestant Christians, particularly Roman Catholics.

52. D. McConaughy, 'Second Paper,' in *op. cit.,* p. 193.

53. This was, in fact, the second Hindu organization of this kind to be established during the YMCA's first five years in Madras. The first one had only a brief life. See *YMI,* V, 7 (Sept. 1894), p. 49; *YMI,* V, 8 (Oct. 1894), p. 57.

traditions. In return, the YMCA criticized the Hindu association for intolerance and defended the liberty of all people to change their faith. By December, *The Young Men of India* reported that Mr. Ramanujam had relapsed after being virtually imprisoned in his home, besieged by tearful relatives, and required to undergo the 'humiliation of *maha-prayaschittam,* the necessary expiatory ceremonies.'[54] Despite the establishment of the YMHA, the YMCA managed to retain a sizable number of Hindu associate members. In 1896 the balance of Christian to Hindus in the YMCA was 152 to 142 (in addition to 8 Muslims, 1 Parsi, and 2 Coorgs).[55]

By 1889 other religious groups established organizations similar to the Christian association to provide alternatives for their own young men. The progressive theistic Hindu reform movement in Bombay, the Prarthana Samaj, established the Students' Brotherhood. The more defensively communalistic Hindu social reform movement, the Arya Samaj, established the Arya Kumar Sabha, or Young Men's Arya Association. The occult Theosophical Society established the Young Men's Indian Association; the non-violent Jains established the Jain Young Men's Association; and the more militaristic Sikhs established the Young Men's Sikh Association in Lahore and the Khalsa Young Men's Association in Amritsar.[56] Each of these non-Christian associations replicated the YMCA's organization and methods by providing social clubs and centers of instruction for their respective religions.[57] The purpose of some, such as the Theosophists' Young Men's Indian Association in Madras, was explicitly to save young men from Christian influence.[58]

Azariah became a secretary in the Indian YMCA at a time when the association was seeking to expand both its Christian and non-Christian Indian membership.[59] Azariah was attracted to McConaughy's belief that the YMCA in India was not a 'foreign mission' and, indeed, that there were no distinctions between foreign and home fields:

---

54. What was regarded as 'disgusting humiliation' by the association was regarded as a sign of reform by *The Hindu,* which complimented the community for receiving Mr. Ramanujam back. *YMI, V,* 10 (Dec. 1894), pp. 73-74.

55. *YMI,* VII, 3 (March 1896), p. 28.

56. J. N. Farquhar, *Modern Religious Movements in India* (London, 1929), pp. 25, 80-81, 125, 278, 329, 343, 444.

57. *Ibid.,* p. 25. See also p. 444.

58. *Ibid.,* p. 278.

59. C. P. Shedd, *op. cit.,* p. 362.

Come with me to Calvary, and . . . take your stand there with me upon that only point on all the earth high enough to see that there is no such thing as a foreign field and a home field.[60]

This early YMCA generation sought to establish in each country self-sustaining indigenous leadership,[61] and by 1896 the expenses of the YMCA in Madras were largely met by local membership fees.[62] In comparison with more traditional western missionary societies, the YMCA was relatively quick to promote Indians to positions of leadership and to establish an association controlled by indigenous constituencies.[63] At the Madras association's establishment in 1890, an educated Indian was appointed Assistant Secretary;[64] and at the First Indian National Convention of YMCAs the following year there were 26 Indian delegates, 2 Anglo-Indian, and 7 European. At this convention, plans were discussed for the appointment of an Indian evangelist, and the plans were realized with Azariah's appointment in 1895 as the first Tamil Agent of the Indian National Union of YMCAs.[65]

The YMCA had some difficulty convincing young Indian Christians that its plans for Indianization were sincere. Many Indians, including K. T. Paul, one of the YMCA's greatest future leaders, were initially skeptical. Paul was Azariah's contemporary at Madras Christian College, and he refused to sign a volunteer card in response to John Mott's 1895-96 appeal for Indian student evangelists because 'serving God is not serving a foreign mission.'[66] By the time Paul reversed his decision seventeen years later and became one of the association's leading secretaries, the YMCA had itself become an effective mouthpiece for the grievances of men like Paul. *The Young Men of India* often expressed the frustration of young In-

60. Quoted in *ibid.,* p. 342.
61. E. C. Worman, *op. cit.,* p. 5.
62. *YMI,* VII, 3 (March 1896), p. 28.
63. C. P. Shedd, *op. cit.,* p. 310.
64. *Ibid.,* p. 309.
65. As we shall see below, he was also appointed as the General Secretary of the YMCA in Madura. Azariah began training for both positions in 1895 while serving as an Assistant Secretary in Madras (E. C. Worman, *op. cit.,* pp. 6, 13). Indeed, one of Azariah's closest American YMCA colleagues claimed later that his main purpose in going to India was to develop national leaders for India's evangelization. Donald F. Ebright, 'The National Missionary Society of India, 1905-1942: An Expression of the Movement toward Indigenization within the Christian Church' (Ph.D. thesis, University of Chicago, 1944), p. 71.
66. K. T. Paul, 'The Call to Missionary Service,' *YMI,* XXIV, 2 (Feb. 1913), p. 103.

dian Christians at the 'patronizing, condescending spirit' of missionary societies.[67]

Azariah shared some of these feelings after he left Madras Christian College to become a full-time association secretary. But he and contemporary S. K. Datta saw the YMCA less as a foreign body than as a vehicle for giving greater responsibilities and freedoms to Indian Christians than conventional missionary societies did. The association provided Indian Christians with an unusually large scope for developing independently their own ideas and abilities.[68] The YMCA's progressive indigenization program prepared some of the most talented Indian Christians of Azariah's generation, including Paul and Datta, for leadership in the decades ahead.[69] At the end of his YMCA career in 1909, Azariah wrote to John Mott:

> The YMCA and its Secretaries have done me great help in every way. I enjoyed their confidence as perhaps no Indian worker enjoys under the Missionary Societies. The liberty, the confidence, and the fraternal feeling — are treasures I enjoyed during these 13 years. There is at present in India no service in connection with foreign missionary Societies that is calculated to develop the Indian's powers so much as the Young Men's Christian Association.[70]

Although attempting to indigenize the leadership, the YMCA in Madras still conducted its affairs along essentially western lines. Its facilities and activities resembled those in western countries. When Azariah joined the Madras YMCA, it offered the use of reading rooms and a library to its membership;[71] it sponsored lectures (on subjects like temperance), commercial classes (e.g., typewriting, phonography, first aid), the monthly

---

67. G. Thomas, *Christian Indians and Indian Nationalism, op. cit.,* p. 144.

68. D. F. Ebright, *op. cit.,* p. 81.

69. E. M. Jackson, *Red Tape and the Gospel: A Study of the Significance of the Ecumenical Missionary Struggle of William Paton (1886-1943)* (Birmingham, 1980), p. 73; R. Rouse, 'Voluntary Movements and the Changing Ecumenical Climate,' in *op cit.,* p. 328; M. E. Gibbs, *op. cit.,* p. 341; S. C. Neill, *The Story of the Christian Church in India and Pakistan, op. cit.,* p. 154; C. Graham, *op. cit.,* pp. 24-26. See also: *YMI,* XIII, 1 (Jan. 1902), pp. 19-20 which notes that, in 1899, there were 10 Indian and 15 foreign Secretaries represented at the First General Secretary's Conference.

70. VSA to John Mott, 25 May 1909, I: 4/61, Mott Papers, YDS.

71. The YMCA did not, however, accept western literary influences uncritically. It rejected all 'skeptical books' along with 'corrupt ones . . . coarse novels and publications of worthless character (that) hurt men by bringing impure images into their minds.' *CP,* VI, 48 (28 Nov. 1895), p. 3.

publication *The Young Men of India,* music, games, and frequent social gatherings. The government set aside athletic grounds for the YMCA's exclusive use in playing tennis, badminton, cricket, baseball, and football (soccer). Furthermore, the association required egalitarian social standards and disallowed any observance of caste regulations in its buildings or functions. McConaughy reported in 1896:

> In the restaurant of the Young Men's Christian Association in Madras the man of highest caste now sits with men of other castes and of no caste and eats food prepared by a cook who is an outcaste.[72]

The YMCA leadership often condemned Western sectarian prejudices along with Indian caste prejudices, thereby planting the seeds for future ecumenical advances in South India:

> Within the walls of the Association all are equal without distinction of caste or creed. Be he a Brahman, be he a Sudra, or be he a Churchman, be he a Dissenter — all stand on one platform and thus a feeling of fellowship and equality is fostered between all the members.[73]

In its early stages in India, the YMCA adopted what one Indian church historian has called a path of 'structural indigenization.' Indians assumed leadership of organizations whose intrinsic structures retained their original western forms and showed little concern for 'the environment, the style of life and the traditions of the people.'[74] Azariah was apparently content with the western patterns of conduct and organization he encountered in the Madras YMCA. Only later, when attempting to establish associations in the smaller towns and villages of Madura and Tinnevelly Districts, did Azariah find it necessary to give YMCA structures and priorities a more distinctively Indian form.

72. *CP,* VII, 7 (13 Feb. 1896), p. 6.
73. *CP,* VI, 48 (28 Nov. 1895), p. 3.
74. I. David, 'The Development of the Concept of Indigenisation among Protestant Christians in India from the Time of Henry Venn' (M.Th. thesis, United Theological College, Bangalore, 1975), pp. 7-37. Quotation on p. 107.

Azariah as a YMCA Secretary:
The Impact of Eddy

Azariah became an active member of the YMCA and its missionary wing, the Student Volunteer Movement, in 1894 while he was a student at Madras Christian College.[75] It was the year of Chetty's disputed conversion, and Azariah led YMCA Bible studies, prayer meetings, and organized open-air Preaching Bands in the streets of Madras.[76] There is no evidence that he compromised his Christian evangelism in the face of increased resistance to YMCA activities by Hindu and other religious groups. Seeking conversions of non-Christians remained Azariah's central and unfaltering goal. By 1895, he was deeply involved in the association's evangelistic activities. He represented the village of Megnanapuram at the Indian National Convention of YMCAs in Madras in December 1894, and, shortly thereafter, he delivered an evangelistic address entitled 'Why Am I a Christian?' to a 'Reason Meeting' at the Blacktown (then Georgetown) branch of the YMCA.[77]

Azariah was chosen to manage the opening of the Madras association's third branch in Royapetta in 1895. In March, he became an Assistant Secretary in the Madras YMCA and embarked on a year's part-time training to become the first Tamil Agent of the Indian National Council of YMCAs and General Secretary of the association in Madurai.[78] At the

75. 'V. S. Azariah — An Appreciation', *YMI*, XX, 9 (Sept. 1909), p. 144; VSA, 'Smaller Associations,' in *Proceedings of the Fourth Indian National Convention of the YMCAs held at Calcutta, 26-30 Dec. 1896*, p. 44. The primary sources for Azariah's YMCA career are *The Young Men of India (YMI)*; private correspondence in the Azariah collection, Madras; Mott and Eddy Papers at YDS; and interviews with Indian Christians in Madras and Tinnevelly.

76. His activities were first reported in a 1894 issue of *YMI*, V, 7 (Sept 1894), p. 55.

77. Unfortunately, *YMI* contains no record of the contents of this address. *YMI*, V, 2 (Feb. 1895), p. 19.

78. There is a great deal of confusion in both primary and secondary sources over Azariah's exact titles during his employment with the YMCA. He has been described as 'South India Traveling Secretary' (Hodge, *op. cit.*, p. 15), 'Traveling Secretary' (H. Whitehead, 'Vedanayakam Samuel Azariah,' in *op. cit.*, p. 184), 'branch secretary' (G. Soundararaj, 'V. S. Azariah as YMCA Secretary,' in *Birth Centenary of Bishop Azariah — 1974* [Madras: Diocesan Press, 1974], p. 36), and 'Area Secretary for Tamil Nadu' ('Important Events in Bishop Azariah's Life,' in *Birth Centenary of Bishop Azariah — 1974*, *op. cit.*, p. 85). There is equal confusion over his new title after a significant promotion in 1902: 'Associate General Secretary' (H. Whitehead, *op. cit.*, p. 184), 'Joint General Secretary of the National Council' ('Important Events in Bishop Azariah's Life,' in *op. cit.*,

age of twenty-one, he was placed in charge of the YMCA headquarters in Madurai, from which he began a decade's work of developing the YMCA's smaller, more indigenous associations in the towns and villages of Madurai and Tinnevelly Districts. Thus Azariah began full-time employment as a YMCA secretary, not among western-educated elites in Madras, but among the much poorer Christian converts of rural South India.

In Madurai, Azariah is remembered even to this day for his missionary work and inspirational spiritual leadership. He held worship services in both Tamil and English, taught Sunday school, and delivered papers on topics such as biblical archaeology (one was entitled '"Stones Crying Out" or the Testimony of the Bible from Ancient Monuments,' delivered on 14 August 1896). Azariah was not content merely to advertise YMCA meetings; he relentlessly visited all members to ensure their attendance. After one meeting in 1896 on 'Personal Bible Study for Spiritual Growth,' twenty-one signed a declaration that they would devote the first half hour each day to Bible study (the so-called 'Morning Watch').[79] He traveled extensively to visit YMCA branches, to establish new ones, to organize devotional and educational meetings on a wide range of topics, and to attend various conventions. In 1897, he covered 3,465 miles and delivered 126 addresses to both Christians and non-Christians.

His extensive travels led to disappointment at the spiritual apathy of association members.[80] Apart from occasional references to India's great diversity, size, and difficult journeys by bullock cart over 'the worst specimens of public road,' his writings are dominated by penetrating criticisms

---

p. 85), 'All-India Traveling Secretary' (G. Soundararaj, *op. cit.*, p. 36), and 'Associate General Secretary of the All-India YMCA' (D. A. Christadoss, 'Azariah the Christian Leader,' in *Birth Centenary of Bishop Azariah — 1974, op. cit.*, p. 44). Even more confusion is introduced if titles are translated from Tamil sources such as D. A. Christadoss, *Acariyā Attiyaṭcar.* I have used the most authoritative source available, the *YMI,* for Azariah's titles. Thus, in March 1895 he began training to become the first 'Tamil Agent of the Indian National Council of YMCAs.' He was also sometimes called the 'Tamil Agent of the Indian National Union,' or simply the 'Tamil Secretary.' After his promotion, Azariah was listed as the 'Associate National Secretary of the Indian National Council' or 'Tamil Secretary for the National Council.' Throughout his tenure with the YMCA, he also held positions as the General Secretary of the Madura and, then, the Palamcottah and Tinnevelly YMCA headquarters. The National Council of YMCAs of India in New Delhi was unable to provide any further information about Azariah's career (D. S. Chinnadorai to author, 29 March 1986; A. K. Chowdhury to author, 16 May and 2 Sept. 1986.)

79. *YMI,* VII, 2 (Dec. 1896), p. 139.

80. VSA, 'What I Saw,' *YMI,* VII, 9 (Sept. 1896), p. 98.

of the Indian Christian community's lack of spirituality and missionary enthusiasm:

> How sad to find Christians eaten up with pride of caste and wealth, sunk in worldliness and superstition, given in various instances to fashionable forms of vices, and lacking in zeal for the Master's cause.[81]

Focusing mainly on spiritual edification, his activities in 1897 included organizing a convention in Palamcottah during which 408 people pledged to observe the 'Morning Watch.' He taught Sunday school to Hindu boys in Tinnevelly, gave lectures on astronomy, and in 1899 shifted his headquarters formally to the southern city of Palamcottah.

One reason for this shift was his marriage on 29 June of the previous year to Anbu Mariammal Samuel (1876-1950), one of the most highly educated Christian women in the Tinnevelly District.[82] In their lifetime together, she would raise six children and become an active participant in women's education in the Dornakal Diocese. In 1898, Anbu and Azariah disregarded and reinterpreted various Indian marriage traditions — corresponding with each other during their engagement, not following customary dowry procedures, and marrying on a Wednesday. It happened to be an 'auspicious' day for weddings according to Hindu tradition; but Azariah chose the date primarily because it was St. Peter's Day in the Christian calendar, and he desired his wife to be as helpful as Peter's.[83] This provides a good example of the manner in which Azariah, as a young man, drew from differing Indian and western social and religious traditions. He rejected some commonly followed patterns of behavior, while often quietly attempting where possible to reconcile Christian and Hindu practices. As we shall see, the Christian marriage ceremony became the focus of Azariah's boldest liturgical experiments in synthesizing Christian and local Hindu traditions.

Despite the shift of headquarters to their native Palamcottah, Azariah and his wife saw relatively little of each other during their first years of mar-

---

81. VSA, 'The Needs of India,' *YMI*, IX, 3 (March 1898), p. 31.

82. She completed one of the first First in Arts courses administered by Sarah Tucker College in Palamcottah. 'Sarah Tucker Institute' affiliated with Madras University in 1896, becoming the first women's college in South India. *CP*, VI, 48 (28 Nov. 1895), p. 2; *CP*, VI, 49 (5 Dec. 1895), p. 5.

83. That Azariah's wedding budget was a mere 40 rupees has become an important part of the oral tradition about Azariah in Tinnevelly today, and has also been enshrined in the drama about Azariah's life by D. Packiamuthu, *Valikāṭṭi* (Tirunelveli: IMS, 1963; Madras: CLS, 1974). See also D. A. Christadoss, *Acariyā Attiyaṭcar, op. cit.*, p. 40.

riage. Azariah spent 151 days traveling a total of 1,973 miles in 1899, and he traveled more than 7,200 miles and attended eight conventions in 1900 and 1901. The demand for his participation in various conferences, summer camps, and further conventions increased. During the next eight years he delivered speeches and sermons, conducted Bible studies and prayer meetings, and arranged literary meetings, debates, lectures, concerts, social gatherings, and sporting events in YMCA branches throughout South India. In some locations he established YMCA reading rooms and libraries for which he also purchased books on a wide range of religious and secular subjects.

Azariah's principal partner — and friend — during these itinerant years was the American Congregationalist George Sherwood Eddy, who eventually became the YMCA's chief evangelist in Asia. A graduate of Yale University and Princeton Theological Seminary, Eddy arrived in Calcutta in 1896 to take up a position as Traveling Secretary for the Student Volunteer Movement under the auspices of the YMCA and the American Board of Commissioners for Foreign Missions. In 1911, he was appointed YMCA Secretary for Asia, but he returned to Europe during the First World War to work as YMCA Secretary with British and American armies in France, an experience that contributed to his becoming a pacifist.[84]

Eddy began his work in India with English-speaking Hindu and Muslim students. Failing to witness any lasting conversions, he decided in 1899 to switch his emphasis to the South Indian 'masses': the outcaste and lower-caste groups which were converting to Christianity in rural areas — Azariah's native people. He learned Tamil and accompanied Azariah on frequent visits to YMCA branches, churches, and colleges throughout South India — to preach the gospel, to persuade young men to join the missionary cause, and to encourage them to abandon loyalty to all traditional social practices associated with Hinduism and caste.[85] As Eddy wrote about their common purpose as they traveled:

84. Later in his life, from 1921 to 1957, Eddy led the Fellowship for a Christian Social Order, an influential liberal Christian organization that hosted traveling seminars for a total of 1500 American leaders to England, continental Europe, and the Soviet Union in an attempt to develop a Christian approach to reforming industrial capitalism. Eddy also became involved in improving race relations in America, helping in 1936 to organize the Christian Socialist Delta Cooperative Farms in Mississippi, which provided land for both black and white Protestant families of evicted sharecroppers. See G. S. Eddy, *Eighty Adventurous Years: An Autobiography* (New York, 1955). A study that portrays Eddy's widespread influence during the interwar period is Richard W. Fox, *Reinhold Niebuhr: A Biography* (New York, 1985).

85. 'Corres: Report Letters from India,' I: 3/52, Eddy Papers, YDS. See also, G. S. Eddy, *Pathfinders of the World Missionary Crusade* (New York, 1945), pp. 140-41.

Our objective was both individual and social. Seeking to work with all Christian forces as one team, we hoped to raise up Indian leaders for the Christianization of their own land, and ultimately to change the whole social order, building a new India as part of a new world.[86]

Azariah became one of India's most fervent promoters of the SVM watchword, writing in 1904 that '"Evangelization of India in this generation" ought to be written large on the walls of our YMCAs as well as on the hearts of our active members.'[87] His commitment to seek conversions to Christianity inspired Eddy, who described Azariah in 1902 as 'full of the Holy Ghost and of wisdom, and a man of much prayer . . . I never met an American student at Northfield or in the colleges who has so deep a Christian life.'[88]

In time, Azariah and Eddy grew apart because of differing views on Christianity's social mission. Azariah did not share Eddy's later pacifism and his view that the Christian social vision was best expressed by the British Labour Party under Ramsay MacDonald (a 'successful application of Christianity to politics: all the idealism of Liberal Christianity without the sentimentality; all the realism of Marxism without the cynicism').[89] Azariah steadfastly resisted association with any secular social ideologies. But in their early YMCA years, they shared the common dream that India's social regeneration would be brought about by Christian evangelization.

Employing the preaching techniques of American revivalism, Azariah and Eddy sought to bring about radical conversions to an evangelical faith similar to those seen in Northfield. During a month's visit to Jaffna,[90] Eddy and Azariah held about a hundred meetings for Christians and Hindus. As many as 1,200 attended one of them, in which over a hundred Hindus and 'many more' nominal Christians 'publicly confessed Christ.'

They did not achieve such results in Jaffna immediately. An initial attempt to expose 'Hinduism' for its 'Pantheism, Polytheism, Idolatry, Caste and its incongruous Incarnations' in contrast to Christ provoked such opposition from the Hindu press and Hindu students that Azariah

86. G. S. Eddy, *Pathfinders of the World Missionary Crusade, op. cit.,* p. 141.

87. VSA, 'Missionary Work and the Spirit of the Association,' *YMI,* XV, 3 (March 1904), p. 45.

88. Report Letter No. 28, I: 3/55, Eddy Papers, YDS.

89. R. W. Fox, *op. cit.,* p. 78.

90. This was part of a three-month tour of South India; see Report Letters Nos. 28-31, I: 3/55, Eddy Papers, YDS.

and Eddy moved from apologetics to more purely personal appeals for salvation. Their subsequent sermons focused on the themes of sin, conversion, consecration, service for others, and the evils of the caste system, and often provoked emotional responses from their audiences. At one college meeting, Eddy reported, 'one prominent teacher rose and confessed his sin with tears, saying that he had never been converted, but that now, thank God, he was saved.'[91]

Azariah and Eddy claimed that a thousand conversions took place during their 1904 tour of 21 associations in South India, which involved 32 meetings in various schools, colleges, villages, and churches. A Harvard graduate who attended both the Northfield Conference and a 1903 South Indian YMCA Student Camp remarked on the striking similarity between the two meetings: 'the same general program (including Bible studies and evangelistic missionary appeals) . . . the same mingled spirit of hard work and real fun . . . the same ever deepening purpose as the conference drew to a close.'[92] The spirit of revivalism seemed to be transcending international boundaries. This Christian revivalism was also mixed with a deepening sense of loyalty to India, as Azariah recalled after traveling to the Bombay area for a 1906 meeting:

> Today we had a good meeting. They were having special meetings for the workers and they were all tender and broken-hearted. So God's word took hold of their hearts. Many wept. The meeting lasted from 8:00 to 12:35 a.m. Several wept and one rolled on the floor. Several women broke down as they confessed their indifference to the needs of India. There has been great rejoicing on account of God's work in this morning meeting.[93]

Azariah helped to 'indigenize' the YMCA by adjusting its activities to the needs of smaller towns and villages where western influence was less pronounced. Several of Azariah's articles in *The Young Men of India* and speeches at YMCA conferences stressed the ways in which smaller associations of the YMCA differed from those in Madras and other urban centers.[94] Associations in Presidency cities were housed in expensive build-

---

91. Report Letter No. 31, *ibid.*

92. E. C. Carter, *Among Indian Young Men* (Cambridge, MA, March 1904), pp. 26-27.

93. VSA to Anbu, 11 Sept. 1906, Mehamadabad, Azariah Collection, Madras.

94. VSA: 'The Mutual Relations of the Associations,' *YMI*, XII, 2 (Feb. 1901), pp. 23-25; 'Associations in Small Towns,' *YMI*, XVI, 2 (Feb. 1905), pp. 39-41; 'Smaller Associations,' *op. cit.*, pp. 40-44.

ings and offered a full range of activities for a varied membership (European and Indian, Christian and non-Christian). Associations in the villages were led by local Christian catechists and tended to offer only prayer meetings and Bible studies to small groups composed almost exclusively of Indian Christians.

Azariah believed this spiritual work was central to the needs of the villages. His early village tours impressed on him an 'appalling' indifference to spiritual matters and inordinate interest in temporal concerns among non-Christians.[95] He was also disillusioned with the condition of many village YMCAs in Madurai and Tinnevelly Districts under those he considered to be mainly 'nominal' Christians.[96] Thus, Azariah tightened the rules governing active membership (requiring daily prayer and Bible study) and the foundation of village associations (requiring weekly meetings of the Bible and Prayer Union for at least a year before establishment).[97]

Azariah also worked to expand the activities of smaller associations to include all four areas of the YMCA ideal (spiritual, physical, intellectual, social). In district centers, he sought to widen the association's membership to include educated Hindus and Christians employed in schools and government. Hindu communities were not always pleased with the Christian emphasis in these smaller associations, and Azariah encountered resistance in trying to establish new YMCA rooms in the town of Tinnevelly during the period from 1898 to 1901. The District of Tinnevelly was wracked by communal violence during this period, much of which centered upon resistance to Shanar (Nadar) upward mobility.[98] Despite Azariah's efforts to underplay his own Nadar background and to broaden the YMCA's membership to non-Nadars, his association may also have been perceived with some suspicion and resentment as yet another organizing forum for Nadar assertion.

Impressed by the work of an association in Travancore, Azariah added new activities to the smaller associations: the writing of vernacular essays and the use of popular lyrical forms of music to balance the dominance of English in urban associations and national conventions.[99] He

95. VSA, 'Tamil Secretary's Report,' *YMI*, X, 7 (July 1899), p. 113.

96. VSA, 'What I Saw,' *op. cit.,* pp. 98-99.

97. 'Letter from an Indian Pastor of Tinnevelly,' *YMI*, X, 10 (Oct. 1899), p. 162.

98. Arun Bandopadhyay, 'The Communal Riots in Tinnevelli in 1899: Some Reconsiderations,' in *Caste and Communal Politics in South Asia*, ed. Sekhar Bandopadhyay and Suranjan Das (Calcutta, 1993), pp. 29-45.

99. VSA, 'A Visit to South Travancore,' *YMI*, VII, 11 (Nov. 1896), pp. 121-22. See also VSA, 'What I Saw,' *op. cit.,* pp. 98-99; 'Smaller Associations,' *op. cit.,* pp. 42-43. He

used the YMCA as a base for teaching temperance (requiring members to sign cards pledging not to drink). He criticized Christians for 'pride of caste and wealth,' for 'worldliness and superstition,' for engaging in 'fashionable forms of vices,' and for being 'slaves of heathen practices and superstitious fears.' Although Azariah was occasionally critical of India's non-Christians, he reserved his harshest criticisms for Christians themselves — exhorting them to a higher standard of spiritual and moral life. Above all, Azariah attempted to inculcate in his membership the virtues of regular daily prayer (the 'Morning Watch') and evangelistic witness to non-Christians.[100]

The smaller and larger YMCAs differed most in the area of 'manly' sports, Azariah observed. In the smaller associations 'most of the people will be workmen who will have had enough of physical exercise in their daily work.' Although 'native games will be very attractive if they are arranged on moonlight nights when only these men could be brought together,' he concluded that 'on physical lines we may not have to do much.'[101] The vast majority of Indian Christians in the villages came from outcaste or low-caste backgrounds. They were already engaged in manual labor; and unlike their more educated urban counterparts, they regarded the YMCA's emphasis on physical fitness as onerous. Azariah helped the YMCA to 'indigenize' its practices. But since Indian society contained many levels of indigenous reality, Azariah argued that the YMCA needed to differentiate its mission according to the needs of the specific people being served.

The YMCA as a Locus for International and Interracial Relations

As one of the few institutions in India that cut across international as well as national and subnational boundaries, the YMCA became an arena for expressing international and interracial disagreements and occasionally

---

noticed that the work in Travancore was more highly developed than that in his districts ('A Visit to South Travancore,' *op. cit.*, pp. 121-22).

100. VSA, 'The Life of Faith,' *YMI*, IX, 6 (June 1898), pp. 83-84; 'The Needs of India,' *op. cit.*, pp. 30-31; 'Lessons in Prayer,' *YMI*, XI, 11 and 12 (Nov. and Dec. 1900), pp. 192-93, 210-11; 'The Tamil District Conference,' *YMI*, VIII, 7 (Aug. 1897), p. 98; 'The Morning Watch,' *YMI*, VIII, 8 (Sept. 1897), pp. 124-26; 'Oh To Be Nothing,' *YMI*, X, 1 (Jan. 1899), pp. 7-8.

101. VSA, 'Smaller Associations,' *op. cit.*, p. 43.

for effecting rapprochements. Many British YMCA leaders in India did not like the new methods and 'enthusiastic, evangelistic, missionary-minded type of leader' exemplified by Americans like Eddy. Concerned to protect their relations with missionary societies in colonial possessions, many more reserved Britons preferred to hold their American counterparts at arm's length.[102] The British hoped to reduce the freedom of the North American International Committee and its influence over the YMCA's worldwide activities by placing the American committee under the control of the relatively weak Central International Committee.

Although the British were ultimately unable to achieve this reorganization, this question of central oversight remained a source of tension in the YMCA for half a century.[103] The YMCA in India was perhaps less aware of this conflict than the YMCAs in England and America. McConaughy, for instance, received a warm welcome and support from British missionaries and pastors in Madras, and worked amicably throughout his career with British YMCA secretaries.[104] What had been a difficult conflict between Christians in the West was mollified greatly when transplanted into the Indian context. A similar relaxation of persistent western interdenominational tensions in the Indian setting was to become an important factor in the successful unification of episcopal and nonepiscopal Protestant churches in South India several decades later. Azariah does not appear to have felt the effects of the American-British YMCA conflict, except perhaps at the end of his YMCA career when the American leadership protested his entrance into Anglican orders.

The experience of working with young western laymen in the YMCA offered Azariah the opportunity for friendships that, by his own admission in his 1910 speech to the Edinburgh World Missionary Conference, were sadly lacking between Indians and foreigners in the more established churches and missionary societies.[105] The YMCA's policy of promoting In-

---

102. C. P. Shedd, *op. cit.*, p. 292. The British YMCA leadership opposed Luther D. Wishard's early missionary campaign, and McConaughy was aware of the delicacy of his position while touring England in 1899. *Ibid.*, pp. 292, 305-6.

103. *Ibid.*, pp. 292, 306-7, 327, 662-63. It has been claimed that the British failure to subordinate the energetic missionary endeavors of the North American International Committee to the control of the Central International Committee enabled the YMCA to conceive of its mission in global rather than European-American terms. *Ibid.*, pp. 292, 306-8.

104. *Ibid.*, p. 309, and *YMI*, XIV, 3 (March 1903), p. 46.

105. VSA, 'The Problem of Co-Operation between Foreign and Native Workers,' *op. cit.*

dians to leadership positions on terms of equality with Westerners created an atmosphere of goodwill between Indians and Westerners — particularly Americans — which was highly unusual for the period.[106]

Eddy's friendship with Azariah also taught him much about the challenges and rewards of deep interracial friendships. Eddy met Azariah in Calcutta in 1896 and recounted later, 'for fifteen years he was my best friend, Indian or foreign.'[107] Indeed, Eddy wrote in 1949 that Azariah was 'the best friend I ever had,' and in 1955 that Azariah was 'the greatest man whose life I was ever privileged to share.'[108] Eddy's recollections of his friendship with Azariah indicate the extent to which it was exceptional for the time:

> I remember an early conversation between us that was crucial. When I questioned Azariah about our friendship, he replied that he supposed we were as close friends as an Indian and a foreigner could ever be. This seemed to me to imply that he felt some subtle racial barrier between us and that I would be kept at arm's length in a sort of second-class friendship. When I showed that his attitude struck me like a blow, he was amazed that any foreigner would want a complete and equal friendship with an Indian. . . . From that frank moment Azariah and I became close and equal friends.[109]

Extant reports of their preaching tours evoke a remarkably compatible and peaceful sense of common purpose that developed between the two young men of vastly different cultures. Eddy wrote during their 1898 tour of 'dark Cochin':

> At midnight our boat was waiting for the turn of the tide. It was a long rakish craft, fitted with a rude lateen-sail, made of thatch. In the stern was a little cabin, just big enough for three of us [Eddy, Azariah, and McConaughy] to sleep abreast. . . . Soon we were out on the backwater;

106. Edward C. Carter, a graduate of Harvard University who served as traveling secretary for northern India, was another close companion of Azariah during his YMCA years. See E. C. Carter, *Among Indian Young Men, op. cit.;* 'Indian Christian Leadership and the Indian Church,' *YMI,* XXIV, 3 (March 1913), pp. 154-57. Bad relations are a more common theme in *The Christian Patriot.* See, e.g., *CP,* VII, 8 (20 Feb. 1896), p. 4; *CP,* VII, 15 (9 April 1896), p. 4.

107. G. S. Eddy, *Pathfinders of the World Missionary Crusade, op. cit.,* pp. 139-40.

108. G. S. Eddy, *Religion and Politics in India, op. cit.; Eighty Adventurous Years, op. cit.,* p. 53. These estimations included friends such as Reinhold Niebuhr. R. W. Fox, *op. cit.*

109. G. S. Eddy, *Pathfinders of the World Missionary Crusade, op. cit.,* pp. 139-40.

the moon was rising over the palms on the shore. . . . We were slipping down with the tide towards Travancore, and the Equator. The low monotony of the boatmen's song was the last thing we heard as we fell asleep:

> Anywhere with Jesus we can go to sleep,
> While the shadows lengthen and about us creep.
> Anywhere without Him, dearest joys would fade,
> Anywhere with Jesus, we are not afraid.[110]

Azariah was genuinely touched by Eddy's gestures of friendship, writing to his wife Anbu in 1899: 'Mr. Eddy subscribes (his) letter thus: "Your affectionate brother in Christ G. S. Eddy." How loving in tone is the letter . . . we have fresh cause for thanksgiving this year!'[111] In a 1909 letter to John Mott, Azariah wrote:

> I cannot put down in words what under God I owe to men like Eddy, Carter, McConaughy and Larsen. I count among them my *friends:* which is so rare in India as far as the different nationalities are concerned.[112]

Azariah was involved in many YMCA activities characterized by an atmosphere of relative equality between Indians and Europeans. *The Young Men of India* reported that, at a 1908 conference (or 'camp') in Palamcottah for Tamil YMCAs, 'the unusual sight (for Tinnevelly) of Europeans sitting on the floor to share the plain curry and rice with Indian students made a great impression on the delegates.' Here Azariah led a session on 'the Model Student Association' which was described as 'one of the most helpful sessions in the whole Camp.'[113]

Azariah's experience of equality and close friendships across racial barriers in the YMCA prepared the way for his later comfortable relationships not only with western missionaries and clerics but also with outcaste Malas and Madigas of Telugu country. From an early age, Azariah equated racist attitudes with caste prejudice and regarded Christian love

---

110. G. S. Eddy, *Report Letter No. 14 — Sept. 1898, In Dark Cochin,* I: 3/51, Eddy Papers, YDS.

111. VSA to Anbu, 13 Feb. 1899, Azariah Collection, Madras. David Packiamuthu captures the spirit of this close friendship in the first act of his play, *Valikāṭṭi, op. cit.*

112. VSA to J. Mott, 25 May 1909, I: 4/61, Mott Papers, YDS. L. P. Larsen was a YMCA secretary from Denmark. See Knud Heiberg, *V. S. Azariah: Biskop af Dornakal* (Copenhagen: Det Danske Missionsselskab, 1950), pp. 15-16.

113. 'The Fourth Tamil Camp,' *YMI,* XIX, 6 (June 1908), pp. 98-99.

as the best solution to both evils. In 1896 he enjoined colleagues in the YMCA to practice this law of love with greater seriousness:

> The chief qualification needed to successfully work among the people of India in general is unqualified sympathy and love. . . . This may seem trivial to many, but I know from experience that this is the great secret of success among our people. When the Indian sees that we are afraid to touch him for fear of soiling our fingers, that we will not condescend to visit him at his poor and perhaps dirty dwelling, that we will not sit on the meagre seat he may offer us at his house — when he sees this, I say, he sets us down at once for men of words and not of action. The Indian is quick in observation. He sees how far the law of love and kindness, which our Master so elaborately expounded and we perhaps so ardently preach, has taken hold of our lives. This spirit of love . . . has no counterpart in India. People here are already oppressed and trodden down by the cursed caste system. They do not want any more of that in another shape.[114]

Azariah's vision for healing interracial and intercaste tensions — both to him different forms of the same fundamental hatred — was essentially evangelistic: to spread the 'law of love and kindness' preached by Jesus but having 'no counterpart in India.' Racial sin did not emanate only from the West; India was also prone to it and, worse, lacked the Christian resources for healing it. It is telling that, although Azariah clearly understood the hurt feelings of the Indians he describes, he never described himself as a victim but rather as one equally capable of racial hatred. Nor did he idealize Indian practices, but rather he likened caste prejudices to the very western racialist prejudices he abhorred.

The solution to both interracial and intercaste conflicts was not, he suggested, to worsen them through self-righteous condemnation, but rather to solve them through self-examination, confession, and, ultimately, conversion. To this end, he began to turn his attention increasingly to the spiritual state of India and to the missionary responsibility of his fellow Indian Christians.

114. VSA, 'Smaller Associations,' *op. cit.,* p. 41.

CHAPTER 3

Indigenous National Base:
A Nonpolitical Missionary

What was the proper Christian approach to spreading the faith when it was seen by growing ranks of Indian nationalists as subordinate to western political and economic interests? One approach was to discard Christianity or subordinate it to nationalism; another was to accept Christianity as a subordinate category of imperial control. Azariah had an altogether different perspective which involved both indigenizing Christianity within the vast Indian subcontinent, and transcending both in India and the world the divisions that blunted the central Christian message and confused those still in need of receiving it.

Far from rejecting the faith associated with his western rulers, Azariah actively recruited Indians to serve as Christian missionaries in India. He grew increasingly distressed by the lack of missionary zeal among Indian Christians during his YMCA years, and began to challenge his countrymen ever more insistently to evangelize their own land. Using census materials from 1891 and 1901 to demonstrate how many areas of India remained unevangelized, Azariah published articles[1] and a book imploring Indian Christians to take missions more seriously.[2] He wrote in 1904:

1. For example, VSA, 'The Needs of India,' *op. cit.,* pp. 30-31; 'Unoccupied Fields,' *YMI,* XVI, 2 (Feb. 1905), pp. 25-27; 'Missionary Work and the Spirit of the Association,' *op. cit.,* pp. 43-46; 'The Unoccupied Fields of India,' *YMI,* XVII, 1 (Jan. 1906), pp. 12-16.

2. *Introductory Lessons on India and Missions for Mission Study Classes,* 1st ed. (Calcutta: Student Volunteer Movement of India and Ceylon, 1908). See the Bibliography for later editions in English, Tamil, Telugu and Malayalam.

Should foreign missionary work be the peculiar privilege of Europeans residing in their homeland? No. Those living in the midst of heathen darkness also must be made to feel their duty to their Saviour and their fellowmen. . . . "Evangelization of India in this generation" ought to be written large on the walls of our YMCAs as well as on the hearts of our active members. . . . Let us inspire the young men with the ambition to sacrifice their all for India and for Christ. Let us appeal to their patriotic spirit. Let us exalt the noble calling of a missionary over and above that of a Vakil, a businessman or a High Court judge.[3]

In his calls for Indian self-evangelization, Azariah was clearly influenced by the national consciousness that was growing in the country as a whole. He used the language of patriotism, nobility, and sacrifice familiar to young Indian nationalists of the period, mixed in with traditional missionary rhetoric about 'heathen darkness.'

The nationalist critique of western missions has been so successful that many Indian Christians still seek to legitimize their experience as a subcontinental minority by exaggerating the nationalist credentials of their forebears. Yet, Azariah's campaign to replace European with indigenous missionaries was inspired more by evangelical than by nationalist zeal. This approach may have come as an unpleasant surprise to some Indian Christian nationalists. But it was the missionary enthusiasm of the Student Volunteer Movement and of evangelical missionaries such as Thomas Walker of Tinnevelly that inspired Azariah and most other Indian Christians of his generation to believe that they were themselves capable of, and responsible for, building a new India through Christian evangelism rather than through nationalist politics.

To be sure, the indigenous missionary movement was influenced by growing nationalism, and the Christian missionary enterprise itself helped fuel growing self-awareness of caste, ethnic, regional, and even national identities among Indian converts. Christian teaching contributed to the development of ethnic self-assertion among Tamil Christians; and this, in turn, contributed indirectly to the rise of other forms of regional and national consciousness in the rural South.

Links between Christianity and rising indigenous self-awareness among other groups have been observed in Africa where, primarily through the impact of vernacular translations of Scripture, Christian missionaries have 'uncapped the springs of indigenization.' By stimulating cultural self-

3. VSA, 'Missionary Work and the Spirit of the Association,' *op. cit.,* pp. 44-46.

understanding, the missionaries acted as agents of indigenous reconstruction rather than arms of imperial combat.[4] In India Christian missionaries helped to stimulate the Bengali and Tamil renaissances via their historical, ethnographic, and linguistic work. The renaissance of Tamil language and literature probably began with the publication in 1856 of Irish-born missionary Robert Caldwell's *A Comparative Grammar of the Dravidian or South Indian Family of Languages,* and the first Tamil novel was written by Indian Christian convert Samuel Vedanayagam Pillai (1826-89).

Significantly, Robert Caldwell stands among the eight bronze statues honoring the makers of Tamil culture erected on the Madras Marina by the (post-independence) Dravida Munetra Kazhagam (DMK) government in 1968. With him stand two other Christian missionaries: George Uglow Pope and Joseph Constantius Beschi. Caldwell and Pope both came to India in the late 1830s under the auspices of non-Anglican missionary societies (the LMS and the Wesleyan Methodist Missionary Society, respectively) before beginning their service to Tamil language and culture under the Anglican SPG: Beschi served as a Jesuit missionary to Tamil country a century earlier. G. U. Pope is remembered for his valuable editions of the Tamil classics and for his instruction of Tamil at the University of Oxford; J. C. Beschi is remembered as one of the founders of literary prose in Tamil whose mastery of the Tamil language also enabled him to produce both grammars and notable Tamil poetry. That Caldwell, Pope, and Beschi should rank today as three of the most important figures in the history of the Tamil language and culture is, in the words of a more recent Bishop of Madras, 'a nice commentary on the popular view that the only work of missionaries has been to destroy native cultures.'[5]

In both the African and Indian cases, the stated aim of the Protestant missionaries (to convert the natives) was in the short run less historically important than the inescapable cultural consequences of their work, and particularly their translations of the Bible and recording of other vernacular literature.[6] Foreigners such as Caldwell, Pope, Mott, and

---

4. Lamin Sanneh, 'Christian Mission in the Pluralist Milieu: The African Experience,' *IRM,* LXXIV, 294 (April 1985), pp. 199-211. See also *Translating the Message: The Missionary Impact on Culture* (Maryknoll, NY, 1989).

5. Lesslie Newbigin, *Unfinished Agenda* (London, 1985), pp. 218-19. M. A. Laird, *Missionaries and Education in Bengal: 1793-1837* (Oxford, 1972), pp. 55-8, 265; Charles Ryerson, *Regionalism and Religion: The Tamil Renaissance and Popular Hinduism* (Madras, 1988), pp. 60-81.

6. I am grateful to Professor Sanneh for his suggestions on this subject in an interview on 17 Sept. 1987, Cambridge, MA.

Eddy stirred up awareness of ethnic and national identity among Indian Christians and other Indians who did not necessarily adopt their faith. The marginalization of Christian influence in much of India during the last decades of the Raj occurred at least in part because of the resourcefulness with which Indian society responded to the Christian challenge by revitalizing its own rival traditions and identity.

The young Azariah got his first real sense of what was meant by the Indian nation as a whole from his participation in YMCA and SVM conferences. As Mott wrote after his 1901-2 tour of India, 'The Indian Empire reminded me vividly of a continent rather than a nation. . . . In a field so vast . . . the only way I could hope to touch the entire movement among the young men was through conventions.'[7] As a result of Mott's initiative, attendance at major national conferences was a regular feature of Azariah's YMCA career. He participated in four such gatherings in December 1901 alone.[8]

Such meetings helped Azariah and his young Indian Christian colleagues to achieve a sense of identity and unity as a pan-Indian, interdenominational and multi-caste community. John Mott's exhortations to assume responsibility for the evangelization of their nation helped to galvanize them into a national movement. As Mott wrote about the purpose of his 1901-2 tour: 'The problem in India and Ceylon to which I devoted more attention than to any other one thing was that of getting more of the strong Christian students to dedicate their lives to the evangelization of their own countrymen.'[9] Mott, the foreigner, seems to have been at least partly responsible for persuading Azariah and his contemporaries that missionary work was itself an inviting field for national self-expression.

Azariah's inspiration for Indian missions also came directly from his daily studies of Scripture and from western Christian literature. He collaborated with Eddy in 1899 on a biography of the great evangelical preacher, Charles G. Finney (1792-1875), who emphasized dramatic personal confessions of belief and is often described as the 'father of modern revivalism.' Azariah also translated portions of Finney's *Lectures on Revivals*

7. Mott to Hofmeyr, 21 Jan. 1902, World Trip 1901-2: Records, III: 117/1936, Mott Papers, YDS.

8. The South India Conference of the SVM in Madras, Dec. 14-17; and three in Allahabad: (1) the YMCA Conference of the Association Secretaries of India, Burma, and Ceylon, Dec. 22-24, (2) the National Convention of the YMCA of India and Burma, Dec. 26-29, and, (3) the Conference of the Secretaries of the International Committee in India and Ceylon, Dec. 30–Jan. 1.

9. Mott to Hofmeyr, 21 Jan. 1902, *op. cit.*

(1835) into Tamil, and produced with Eddy several Tamil pamphlets on prayer, studies of Paul's Letters to the Galatians and Ephesians, and a brochure entitled 'Divisions and Unity of the Body of Christ.' Azariah's early literary activity was almost entirely designed to make inspirational western Christian literature more accessible to Tamil Christians in order to excite the Indian church with missionary vision. As Azariah wrote to John Mott in 1906:

> We are greatly in need of the sort of literature that you have used to rouse up the missionary interest of the Church. We have to study your methods and adapt them to India.[10]

Azariah requested permission to translate portions of Mott's book *The Pastor and Modern Missions* into the Indian vernaculars, and remained throughout his life committed to including western Christian literature in the vernacular corpus of literature he was building for the Indian church.

Azariah envisaged the YMCA playing an evangelistic role in India similar to that of the Student Volunteer Movement in the West whose watchword he repeated frequently, seeking 'to put before the Christian students the duty of the evangelization of India . . . the calling out from the ranks of the young men volunteers who will pledge to devote their lives to carry the Gospel to the unevangelized regions of their country.'[11] This vision eventually prompted Azariah to leave the YMCA and to become a missionary with an indigenous missionary society he helped to establish.

Throughout, Azariah saw his faith as a form of patriotism, conceiving of India's evangelization as an activity of surpassing value for his homeland. Contrary to Hindu nationalist charges that Christian missionary work in India was unpatriotic, Azariah argued that conversion to Christianity promised national as well as individual salvation. Although close associations with western missionaries often led outsiders to believe that Indian Christians were denationalized dependents of imperialism, the missionary enterprise was itself becoming an increasingly internal, Indian matter.

10. VSA to J. Mott, 12 April, 1906, I: 4/61, Mott Papers, YDS.
11. *Ibid.*

From Foreign to Indigenous Mission

The stated objective of most foreign missionaries from at least the mid-nineteenth century had been to establish self-governing, self-supporting, and self-propagating churches in mission lands.[12] However, in practice, many western missionary societies had been reluctant to hand responsibility over to native Christians. Most missions were slow to execute the devolutionary ideal of establishing independent national churches in the field.[13] The missionaries' unwillingness to share duties with capable Indian Christians was at least partly attributable to paternalistic if not racist-imperialist sympathies.[14] Some Indian Christians — particularly the poor and less educated ones — also desired to be dependent on foreign societies. One of nineteenth-century India's most preeminent native pastors, W. T. Sathianadhan, predicted in 1873 that, unless the Indian church was weaned from its dependence on foreign societies, 'the native churches will entwine themselves like parasites about Missionary Societies, and their increasing number will entail such an amount of expenditure as the Home Churches and Societies, with ever-increasing calls upon their liberality, will not be able to meet.'[15]

12. Although British and American sources commonly claim that the pioneering advocates of indigenization were Rufus Anderson of the American Board of Commissioners for Foreign Mission (Secretary from 1832) and Henry Venn of the Church Missionary Society (Secretary from 1841), pietist Lutherans (not to mention Jesuits) provide earlier precedents in South India. See R. Frykenberg, 'The Impact of Conversion and Social Reform upon Society in South India during the late Company Period,' in *op. cit.*, pp. 187-204. Indeed, native Tamil priests Sathianadhan and John Devashayam played important roles within the remarkably indigenous ethos of the Tinnevelly church of the late eighteenth and early nineteenth centuries. Credit for church indigenization must therefore go to C. F. Schwartz and C. T. Rhenius as much as to Anderson and Venn. On Anderson, see William R. Hutchison, *Errand to the World: American Protestant Thought and Foreign Missions* (Chicago, 1987), pp. 77-90. On Venn, see C. Peter Williams, *The Ideal of the Self-Governing Church: A Study of Victorian Missionary Strategy* (Leiden, 1990); and T. E. Yates, *Venn and Victorian Bishops Abroad: The Missionary Policies of Henry Venn and Their Repercussions upon the Anglican Episcopate of the Colonial Period, 1841-1872* (Uppsala, 1978).

13. D. J. Fleming, *Devolution in Mission Administration: As Exemplified by the Legislative History of Five American Missionary Societies in India* (London, 1916).

14. Michael Hollis, *Paternalism and the Church* (Oxford, 1962). Interview, 7 Sept. 1984, Manormead, Hindhead. Hollis was Anglican Bishop of Madras from 1942 to 1947 and the Church of South India's Bishop of Madras from 1947 to 1954.

15. W. T. Sathianadhan, 'The Native Church in South India,' *Report of the General Missionary Conference held at Allahabad 1872-73* (London, 1873), pp. 251-52. Not surprisingly, W. T. Sathianadhan's son Samuel became a founding Vice-President of the NMS.

Sathianadhan's warning proved remarkably prescient.[16] When S. Pulney Andy established the National Church of India in Madras in 1886 as a self-supporting, self-governing church unburdened by western sectarian differences, he received only limited support from both missionaries and Indian Christian colleagues.[17] The missionaries objected that a new church would weaken already existing native churches, few of which were self-supporting, and would contribute to a multiplication of sects. Indian pastors also resisted recruitment into the new church because, Andy claimed, they preferred to be maintained by foreign missions and viewed dependence on Indian congregations as beneath their dignity. By 1898, interest in the new national church was waning universally.

Azariah's Tinnevelly Indo-Anglican church was more independent of its parent western domination than many other churches in India. Local CMS missionaries such as John Thomas had actually put mission theory into practice by trying to establish self-governing, self-supporting, and self-propagating churches. As the boy Azariah watched his father serve as one of the church's more prominent leaders, he developed confidence in the Indian church's ability and right to self-governance. Azariah was also encouraged by the YMCA's promotion of Indian leadership. Ecclesiastical models, rather than political models, gave Azariah a secure belief in the Indian church's ability to manage her own affairs and prompted him to launch India's first two major indigenous missionary societies: The Indian Missionary Society of Tinnevelly in 1903 and the National Missionary Society in 1905.

Indian Christians had undertaken internal evangelism before. Indeed, the initial successes of western missionaries were probably much more dependent on forgotten Indian pioneers than the missionaries cared to admit; and Azariah was conscious of several precedents within the Tinnevelly Diocese.[18] A study of conversion in India has noted that, 'even during the nineteenth century when Christian white missionaries were involved in evangelism in [India], the actual gospel work was largely done by

16. G. W. Houghton, 'The Development of the Protestant Missionary Church in Madras 1870-1920: The Impoverishment of Dependency' (Ph.D. thesis, University of California, Los Angeles, 1981).

17. *Ibid.,* pp. 281-94.

18. VSA, 'The Indian Missionary Society of Tinnevelly and Fields for Work,' *HF* (new series), XVI, 1 (Jan. 1905), pp. 19-20. Both Rhenius and Caldwell established native missionary societies. See R. Frykenberg, 'The Impact of Conversion and Social Reform upon Society in South India,' in *op. cit.,* p. 203; and H. W. Tucker, *Under His Banner: Papers on the Missionary Work of Modern Times* (London, 1886), pp. 52-53.

Indians.'[19] By 1858, there were four Indian workers for every foreign Protestant missionary and probably a similar proportion among Roman Catholics.[20] Missionary reports aimed at European readers often referred to these merely as 'native workers,' if at all.[21] As one historian has observed, Azariah was described in CMS reports only as 'a "native worker" in 1902, and was named "Azariah" for the first time in 1903.'[22]

Despite their obscurity in the West, Indian Christians employed by foreign missions always performed many critical functions, such as translating inaccessible languages, gathering cultural, geographical, economic and political information, and acting as virtually autonomous teachers and evangelists in rural areas where living conditions were more primitive and where Europeans did not believe they could survive. The Scottish Presbyterian mission ordained Narayan Seshadri to the full status of missionary in 1854 and placed him in charge of work at Indapur and Jalna (about 200 miles northeast of Bombay) from 1862 until his death in 1891. In the latter half of the nineteenth century, many foreign missions in South India established small native evangelistic bands to work locally among non-Christians. W. T. Sathianadhan organized a 'Preachers' Association' in 1887 whose forty-two members were drawn from over six castes and were financially self-supporting.[23] By 1904, G. S. Eddy was able to assert that 'almost all the older and stronger missions of South India have organized missionary societies in the native churches.'[24]

Although most of these societies worked only within their own local culture areas, several Indian societies were formed with a wider missionary vision for work throughout India and abroad. The Home Missionary Society established in 1898 by the American Baptist churches in Telugu country sent Indian missionaries to unevangelized jungle tribes within their own districts, to hill tribes of the Kurnool District and the Nilgiris, and to the Telugu and Tamil people in Natal, South Africa. Eddy publicized the

19. Sunder Raj, *The Confusion Called Conversion* (New Delhi, 1986), p. 13.

20. S. C. Neill, *A History of Christianity in India, 1707-1858, op. cit.,* p. 361.

21. Schwartz called these Indian workers his 'Helpers,' while Rhenius used the terms 'Pastor' or 'Catechist.' The Tamil term was *upadesiar,* meaning territorial or 'parish' leaders, caregivers or 'pastors.'

22. D. F. Ebright, 'The National Missionary Society of India, 1905-1942,' in *op. cit.,* p. 73.

23. G. Houghton, *op. cit.,* pp. 117-20. For an impressive list of other small, localized indigenous missions, see D. F. Ebright, *op. cit.,* pp. 60-63.

24. G. S. Eddy, 'Signs of Promise in India: The Missionary Spirit in the Native Church,' *MRW* (June 1904), pp. 430-31. Copy in II: 6/101, Eddy Papers, YDS.

development of Indian missionary initiatives, arguing in several articles that, in the face of such efforts, greater responsibility should be given the Indian church to determine its own destiny.[25]

Most of these earlier indigenous groups were established by western missions and thus lacked organizational or financial identities apart from their parent societies.[26] Azariah's Indian Christian missionary movement at the turn of the century took a new step by establishing autonomous missionary societies with self-supporting and self-governing organizational structures for sending Indian missionaries throughout India and abroad to evangelize 'foreigners.' The IMS and NMS were by far the largest and most ambitious Indian missionary endeavors of their kind. Founded by Indian Christians, they remained organizationally distinct from western societies and forged their links instead with other native Indian churches.

Azariah played a foundational role in each of these pioneering associations. The IMS was the missionary wing of Tinnevelly's congregations (supported first by CMS congregations and eventually also by SPG congregations) to unevangelized areas, both in India and abroad. The NMS was an interdenominational society aiming to spread Christianity in India and surrounding territories such as Afghanistan, Tibet, and Nepal. Freedom from official control by foreigners gave both the IMS and the NMS greater independence in recruitment, financing, and evangelistic strategy than the earlier European- and American-based movements. However, both societies sought foreign advice and counsel, particularly in choosing fields of work that avoided competition with other missionary forces in India. Azariah's leadership helped produce in the IMS and NMS a remarkable example of a movement that achieved independence from and equality with western missionary societies without developing any major hostility in working relationships.

Indigenous Mission to the Telugus

Accounts of the origins of the IMS by its founders and their successors suggest that it was inspired, first and foremost, by a series of spiritual revivals within the diocese during the last decade of the nineteenth century.

25. *Ibid.*, p. 433. Also G. S. Eddy, 'The Missionary Spirit,' *YMI*, XIV, 10 (Oct. 1903), pp. 169-71.
26. D. F. Ebright, *op. cit.*, pp. 60-63.

The evangelistic itinerancies of CMS missionary Thomas G. Ragland (1815-58) through relatively untouched areas of northern Tinnevelly District after 1853 were undertaken with the help of both western and Indian colleagues, and provided one important model for the IMS.[27] Other spiritual revivals in Tinnevelly during the 1890s created new prayer and preaching groups: the Christian Brotherhood Association organized by Azariah and fellow students at Church Missionary College, the 'Band of Faith' in 1891, and the 'Tinnevelly Band of Hope' in 1892, which later became the Diocesan Children's Mission under the leadership of Samuel Pakianathan, the first IMS missionary. These revivals increased the Tinnevelly church's missionary fervor and attracted important financial support from the enthusiastic faithful.

Two inspirational western works, *Foreign Missions and Home Calls* by A. H. Arden and *The Key to Missionary Service* by Andrew Murray (one of Azariah's favorite Christian writers), encouraged Tinnevelly Christians to increase evangelistic outreach and to pray for India's salvation.[28] On 3 December 1899, a special day of intercession for the regeneration of India was held, and some participants vowed to spend at least one hour each day thereafter praying for their country and diocese. Another evangelistic revival associated with CMS missionary Thomas Walker and the village of Tuckerammalpuram in 1899 attempted to introduce the methods of the English evangelical Keswick Convention. 'Tinnevelly Keswick' evolved into the Tinnevelly Church Prayer Union, an important ministry for spiritual renewal.[29]

Azariah credited A. H. Arden for having given him the idea of founding an indigenous missionary society. Arden argued that even the poorest church had no right to evade its responsibility to support foreign missionary work. The contention that church resources must be reserved for home needs was specious, Arden claimed, in light of the many historically proven benefits that foreign work gives to a home church. In addition to increasing the home church's spiritual fervor, 'the money and labour spent upon Foreign Missions

27. VSA, 'The Indian Missionary Society of Tinnevelly and Fields for Work,' *op. cit.*, pp. 19-20. Azariah also noted that Tinnevelly had sent evangelists to both the Kois (Godavary District) and the Todas (Nilgiris Hills).

28. A. H. Arden authored his works anonymously thus: *Foreign Missions and Home Calls,* 'By the Author of "Are Foreign Missions doing any Good?"' (London, 1893) and *Are Foreign Missions Doing Any Good?,* 'By the Author of "Foreign Missions and Home Calls"' (London, 1894). Bibliography listings are under Arden.

29. Joseph Abraham, *Fifty Years' History of the Indian Missionary Society of Tirunelveli (1903-1953)* (Palayamkottai, 1955), pp. 1-4.

have made an abundant return in increase of trade and in colonial extension.'[30] The best way for a poor church (or nation) to remain poor, Arden concluded, was to hoard its resources rather than to give them away.

Arden's argument that poverty at home was no excuse for avoiding missionary responsibilities abroad struck Azariah with great force. British missionaries had expressed grave doubts about the Tinnevelly church's ability to support its own missionaries, persuading Azariah and his colleagues to drop the idea of a Tinnevelly missionary society in 1897. But as the spiritual fervor and financial security of the Tinnevelly church increased, the proposal for a missionary society was revived in 1902[31] and led directly to the formation of the IMS the following year.

Azariah argued that the IMS was founded by 'a nucleus of true believers in every part of the district longing and praying for the awakening of India.'[32] Other accounts credit Azariah with almost sole personal responsibility for its creation.[33] Azariah was certainly the preeminent leader within the society from its inception. He was inspired during a month-long evangelistic visit to Jaffna in 1902, conducted in partnership with Eddy, by the fervor of the Student Foreign Missionary Society of Jaffna which had been established in 1899, 'to send the Gospel to Tamil-speaking peoples in neglected districts of other lands.'[34] This small, courageous group caused Azariah to reevaluate the relative inactivity of his larger, more prosperous native church in Tinnevelly, though Eddy may also have prodded him to action.[35]

30. A. H. Arden, *Foreign Missions and Home Calls, op. cit.,* p. 59. He quotes one calculation that the United States was making a return of 13 percent per annum on the money invested in its early missionary work in the Sandwich Islands (Hawaii). Arden did not write his book with Indian Christian audiences in mind. Foreign missions, as he conceived them, were always sent out by western churches to 'heathen lands.'

31. VSA, 'The Indian Missionary Society of Tinnevelly and Fields for Work,' *op. cit.,* pp. 17-29; 'The Missionary Effort of the Tinnevelly Church,' *CMR,* LIX (1908), pp. 554-60; *Introductory Lessons on India and Missions, op. cit.,* pp. 93-96.

32. VSA, 'The Indian Missionary Society of Tinnevelly and Fields for Work,' *op. cit.,* p. 18.

33. See, e.g., G. S. Eddy, 'Religion and Politics in India,' II: 6/125, Eddy Papers, YDS.

34. Its first missionary, J. K. Shinnatamby, was sent to India in 1899. For fifty years the Anglican church in Jaffna had already supported a mission to neighboring islands, 'The Native Evangelical Society,' and an energetic 'Women's Foreign Missionary Society' had also been established. Letter No. 22, 'Corres: Report Letters from India,' I: 3/53, Eddy Papers, YDS; D. F. Ebright, *op. cit.,* pp. 63-67. For journals of their tour, see Letter Nos. 28-31, 'Corres: Report Letters from India,' I: 3/55, Eddy Papers, YDS.

35. Eddy's original account credits Azariah with recognizing the need to recruit

Azariah led the 'immediate and creative activity' in Tinnevelly which brought the new missionary society into being. He initiated a systematic study of the latest census reports to determine which areas of India were still unreached by Christian missionaries. He held meetings with local pastors and laymen to discuss forming an indigenous missionary society, privately circulated a draft constitution, and published an appeal to Tinnevelly Christians to undertake foreign missionary work. On 12 February 1903, Azariah presided as Honorary Secretary at the founding meeting of the Indian Missionary Society of Tinnevelly, for which he served as General Secretary from 1903 to 1908.[36]

The constitution of the IMS specified that its 'chief aim is to foster missionary spirit in the Indian Church by indigenous efforts and propagate the Gospel in India or other countries.' It limited membership to 'all communicant Christians of Tinnevelly,' later altered to 'Christian Indians.' Westerners could not be members but were welcomed to participate in the society's affairs as visitors and to promote its interests through private as well as public means.[37] The founders sought advice from both the Bishop of Tinnevelly and Madura, Samuel Morley, and from the CMS's superintending missionary, E. S. Carr. These Europeans were given the honorary positions of Patron and Vice-Patron respectively.[38] On 23 October 1903, the IMS defined its own relationship to the diocese as fully autonomous but insisted that the society remain on good terms with the mother church.[39]

Azariah was proud that the IMS belonged solely to Indian congregations and maintained complete independence from foreign control, even in financial matters.[40] To the challenge, 'Should not the Native Church become entirely free from foreign support before it commences such a work as this?' Azariah answered, 'Foreign missionary work will give great stimulus to the cause of self-support. It has been found in Tinnevelly that those Churches which are keen on rising to what is technically called self-

more Indians as missionaries; but, in a later interview, Eddy suggested that he issued a 'personal challenge' to Azariah imploring him to found a similar society in Tinnevelly. G. S. Eddy, *Pathfinders of the World Missionary Crusade, op. cit.,* p. 143; *Eighty Adventurous Years, op. cit.,* pp. 53-54. For an interview account, see D. F. Ebright, *op. cit.,* pp. 66-67.

36. D. F. Ebright, *op. cit.,* pp. 66-69; VSA, 'The Indian Missionary Society of Tinnevelly and Fields for Work,' *op. cit.,* pp. 18-19.

37. For example, Rev. E. A. Douglas shared the speaker's platform with V. Gnanamuthu at a public meeting for the IMS in 1903, 7 July 1903, PIMS, IMSA.

38. *Ibid.*

39. 23 October 1903, PIMS, IMSA.

40. VSA, 'The Indian Missionary Society of Tinnevelly and Fields for Work,' *op. cit.,* pp. 19-20.

support are also the Churches that evince a deep interest in the foreign mission.' Furthermore, he added, quoting Arden, 'It is a general rule . . . that earnest support to Foreign Mission is usually accompanied by increased gifts to home work.'[41]

Despite its separate identity, the IMS remained in close fellowship with the Indo-Anglican church and soon established links with other churches in Europe and America as well. When, in 1928, the Conference of British Missionary Societies called for a 'mission of help' from India, Azariah was pleased that India could 'share with our parent Churches any spiritual gift that the Spirit of God may have bestowed upon ourselves.' This request suggested to him that Britons at last believed that 'there are Indians who have so learnt at the feet of Christ and have so assimilated the truth as it is in Jesus to our own racial and religious part that . . . the truth can be presented with an appealing power to some, at least, in the old country to whom it has not hitherto appealed with the same force.'[42]

From 1903 until 1909, Azariah promoted the IMS while concurrently serving as YMCA Secretary. He stimulated the missionary zeal of Tinnevelly congregations by sending written appeals, speaking at public and private meetings, editing a new journal called *Suvisesha Pirabalya Varthamani (The Missionary Intelligencer)*, arranging and participating in evangelistic tours by lay volunteers, and seeking previously unevangelized territories to which the society could send its missionaries.

Initial resistance to the IMS came from Protestant missionaries of older western societies in Tamil country who feared the IMS would introduce Indo-Anglicanism as a new denomination in their mission areas. The older societies were clearly possessive toward territories ('mission fields') they had long occupied. So the IMS decided to send its first charge, Samuel Pakianathan, to a virgin mission field in 'malarial' Telugu-speaking regions of eastern Hyderabad, then a Muslim-controlled princely state and now a part of Andhra Pradesh.[43] After being repelled by some form of public or government resistance at their first mission site, Pakianathan and his colleague P. Devasahayam purchased a building previously used for the sale of alcohol with six acres of land in the railway village of Dornakal as the site for their new mission.

This was an ironic place to begin, in view of the Nadar Christians'

41. *Ibid.,* pp. 23-25.

42. VSA, 'Mission of Help to the Older Churches,' *NCCR*, L, 2 (Feb. 1930), pp. 59-61.

43. VSA, 'The Indian Missionary Society of Tinnevelly and Fields for Work,' *op. cit.,* pp. 22-23.

strong adherence to temperance principles, which they hoped would liberate them from the social stigma (and ritual pollution) associated with the
manufacture of intoxicating toddy from Tinnevelly's palmyra trees. Yet,
for the arriving missionaries, establishing their mission in an unused
toddy shop was not unlike building a Christian chapel on the site of a former Hindu shrine. In both cases, Christians saw themselves overthrowing
idols and stigmas of the past in favor of the new faith.[44] This spot in
Dornakal became the center of the mission where Azariah volunteered his
services in 1908 and where a new diocese was formed after he was elevated
to the episcopate in 1912.

At the very time that nationalism was finding political expression in
the establishment of the Indian National Congress and was gaining appeal under the *swadeshi* (or 'economic self-reliance') banner, Azariah
moved in the opposite direction: away from politics and toward the
evangelization of an isolated and impoverished rural area. To be sure,
Azariah was aware of developments in the broader national arena through
contacts with western-educated professionals in the Madras, Bombay, and
Calcutta YMCAs, and he gave a patriotic flavor to his repeated calls for
missionary volunteers to work for India's sake. In 1908 he wrote:

> Garibaldi, the Italian patriot, calling for volunteers to save his country,
> said: 'young men, I have nothing to offer you but cold, hunger and rags,
> let him who loves his country follow me.' Thousands of the youth of It-
> aly — the flower of the nation — followed him and laid down their lives
> for the freedom of their motherland. Shall we do less for our land and
> our Master?[45]

Azariah invoked the memory of nationalist heroes to motivate young recruits to similar sacrifice in the mission field; only now the goal was spiritual rather than political liberation.

But it is inaccurate to suggest that nationalism was the prime motivating factor for indigenous mission, or that 'Patriotism entered the religious sphere . . . , and there arose the popular urge to nationalize religion
just as much as nationalize politics.'[46] Azariah was drawing on nationalist

44. For examples of Tinnevelly's destruction of idols and reuse of Hindu shrines
and temples, see *Mission of Sawyerpooram, Part Second, Journal of the Rev. G. U. Pope,* 5th
ed. (London, 1846), pp. 17-18; *Mission of Sawyerpooram, Part Third, Report of the Rev. G. U.
Pope, January 1845,* 4th ed. (London, 1847), p. 5.

45. Quoted in *Birth Centenary of Bishop Azariah, 1974, op. cit.,* p. 25.

46. Joseph Abraham, *Fifty Years History of the Indian Missionary Society of Tirunelveli
(1903-1953), op. cit.,* p. 4.

sentiment to bolster the missionary cause rather than drawing primary in-spiration from that sentiment.

At the turn of the century, most Nadar Christians were more inter-ested in local issues of social, economic, and ritual preferment than in the political activities of the seemingly remote, mainly urban, higher-caste na-tionalists.[47] The intensifying regional and caste preoccupations of the so-called 'backward' groups in the Madras Presidency led to the flowering of non-Brahminism in the twentieth century and precluded any sustained sympathy for Brahmin-led nationalist calls for *swaraj* or Home Rule.[48] This was not an unwelcome development to some Britons whose antipa-thy toward upper-caste interests resulted in ICS support for the Justice Party by 1918 and 1919. Although Azariah distanced himself from narrow Nadar aspirations during his YMCA years and even more so during his ca-reer in Dornakal, he responded more to the clarion calls of localized reli-gious and cultural movements than to the more distant calls of national political ones.

There is almost no textual evidence, even of an indirect kind, to sup-port the theory that the founders of the IMS were motivated by anything other than the biblical commission to preach the gospel to nonbelievers, so forcefully advocated in the western missionary tracts of the 1890s. The study of Scripture and prayer, in the context of spiritual revival, led the founders of the IMS to conclude that missionary service was a duty in-cumbent on all Christians. This responsibility involved sacrificial giving of money and lives to foreign, and in Dornakal's case, mainly outcaste people. Recognizing themselves not as dependent converts (what critics were to call 'rice Christians') but rather as spiritually mature Christian witnesses, the Indian founders aimed to work as equal partners with west-ern missionaries and with Indo Anglican church officials.

Nationalist propaganda which castigated Indian Christians as inher-ently 'unpatriotic' did, however, begin to affect Azariah's evangelism at about this time. Already in 1903, Azariah and Eddy found that Hindu au-diences were increasingly defending 'all that was theirs' and resisting 'all that does not praise or tolerate the national religion.'[49] Rising Hindu op-position prompted them to stop attacking Hinduism and to focus instead on the revivalist theme of overcoming sin and attaining personal salva-

47. R. Hardgrave, *The Nadars of Tamilnad, op. cit.*, pp. 43-94; Arun Bandopadhyay, 'The Communal Riots in Tinnevelli in 1899,' *op. cit.*

48. E. F. Irschick, *Politics and Social Conflict in South India: The Non-Brahman Move-ment and Tamil Separatism, 1916-1929* (Bombay, 1969).

49. Letter No. 32, 'Corres: Report Letters from India,' I: 3/55, Eddy Papers, YDS.

tion.[50] While this shift was partly tactical, their written testimony suggests a consistent internal dependence on the type of spiritual awakenings that had stirred the Tinnevelly church in the 1890s. Azariah and his colleagues invoked the names of westerners — Ragland, Arden, and Murray — to legitimize their revival-based IMS, more than the names of Indian leaders, let alone politicized nationalists.

Even their models for indigenization were taken from western-based Christian agencies rather than from Indian-based or Hindu ones. In solving the issue of how the missionaries would be supported financially, the IMS founders looked to the model established by the evangelical China Inland Mission (CIM) forty years earlier. They were impressed that CIM missionaries were offered no salary but were asked to depend on God to provide for their needs via contributions from the faithful.[51] Perhaps more importantly, CIM missionaries adopted Chinese habits of life and therefore provided a model for indigenization. Azariah and his colleagues drew upon this foreign missionary organization rather than a culturally similar and indigenous Indian model — such as that of the *sannyasin* who also lives by alms. The IMS considered itself to be part of a trans-national Christian movement and did not choose to legitimate an indigenous non-Christian model. Even the small, relatively short-lived IMS Brotherhood that was established in 1907 when two Brahmin converts joined the Dornakal mission to work as bachelors without salary or other emolument was shaped more by the brotherhoods established by Oxford and Cambridge Universities than by any Indian ascetic traditions.[52]

Once again, the transnational character of Azariah's Christian perspective prompted him to resist 'false' man-made barriers of nation (caste, denomination, etc.). Participation in international, interdenominational student movements such as the YMCA and the SVM gave Azariah an early distaste for parochialism in all its manifestations and a preference for subordinating nationalist or sectarian appeals to the universal and unifying claims of his religion. Azariah later wrote that 'the religion of Christ is one of the most dynamic factors in the world. It always bursts its boundaries . . . [and] . . . refuses to be confined to any one race, class or caste.'[53] None of Azariah's writings indicates a negative desire to send western mission-

50. Letter No. 31, 'Corres: Report Letters from India,' I: 3/55, Eddy Papers, YDS.

51. 5 March 1907, PIMS, IMSA.

52. 'V. S. Azariah,' *NMI*, III, 10 (June 1909), p. 80. On the brotherhoods, see M. E. Gibbs, *op. cit.*, pp. 303-16.

53. VSA, 'The Communal Award,' *Guardian*, X, 31 (8 Sept. 1932), p. 368.

aries home. On the contrary, although he criticized missionaries for being too slow to entrust responsibilities to Indian Christians, he contended to the end of his life that India still needed missionary help (both men and money) from other countries. At the same time, the IMS reflected Azariah's recognition that Indian Christians shared responsibility for the 'evangelization of the world' with churches everywhere. Indeed, in Azariah we find one of the earliest non-western statements of the 'partners in mission' theory which has come to animate the CMS and other modern missionary agencies.

The founding of the IMS was a bold initiative on the part of Tinnevelly's Christians in a domain where the leaders (although not the foot soldiers) had hitherto been mainly westerners. Ethnic self-assertion was beginning to displace the inertia of dependency. But precedents for the IMS had been established in complete isolation from Indian nationalism. The itinerant CMS missionary to Tinnevelly, Thomas G. Ragland (1815-58), claimed to have laid the foundation for 'a genuine native missionary society' before his death; but his work was inspired by missionary fervor and by his society's commitment to founding self-propagating churches, not by protonationalism. Protestant Christian missionaries, European and Indian, focused on a broader 'unlocking' of caste, regional, and ethnic aspirations which, as we shall see, were expressed in a multitude of different ways, in nearly total isolation from political nationalist movements.

Indigenous Mission as National Expression

Azariah's second indigenous missionary enterprise owed more to national political developments, and particularly to the *swadeshi* movement, than had the IMS. The National Missionary Society (NMS) was born near the center of the political crisis that followed the partition of Bengal in 1905 and the rise of anti-foreign activities. It was established on 25 December 1905 in Serampore College near Calcutta by 16 Indian delegates from seven political divisions in India and Ceylon, representing five denominations and speaking eight Indian languages.[54] Once again, it was the brain-

54. Detailed studies include D. F. Ebright, 'The National Missionary Society of India, 1905-1942,' in *op. cit.;* J. M. Jayasingh, 'The History of the National Missionary Society of India: A Critical Study' (M.Th. thesis, Asian Centre for Theological Studies and Mission, Seoul, Korea, July 1983); Eric Sharpe, *Not to Destroy but to Fulfil, op. cit.,* pp. 223-37; *The National Missionary Society of India, 1905* (Calcutta: Baptist Mission Press,

child of Azariah and Eddy, who was the only non-Indian delegate at Serampore.

Azariah and Eddy enlisted three of the Indian Christian community's most distinguished elders, Raja Sir Harnam Singh, Kali Charan Banerji, and S. Sathianadhan, to help provide for all of India's churches what the IMS had provided for Tinnevelly: a self-supporting, self-governing mission. Among its founding delegates were some of the most highly educated nationalists in the Indian Christian community: Bepin Chandra Sircar, Nirmal Chandra Mukerji, Sumant Vishnu Karmarkar, the Muslim convert R. Siraj-ud-din, Jashwant Rao Chitamber, and the Burmese brothers L. T. Ah Son and Ah Pon.[55]

Azariah was elected the society's first General Secretary, and served in this capacity until 1908, with K. T. Paul as its first Treasurer. The Constitution adopted by the founders stated:

---

n.d.); *The First Ten Years of the National Missionary Society, 1905-1916* (Salem: T.A.C. Press, n.d.); *In His Footsteps: Report of the National Missionary Society of India, 1936* (Madras: NMS Press, 1936), copy in NMSA, Madras; G. Thomas, *Christian Indians and Indian Nationalism, 1885-1950, op. cit.,* pp. 146-54.

55. Raja Sir Harnam Singh (1851-1930) was a convert from the royal house of Kapurthala and manager of the Kapurthala Estates in Oudh, and was knighted in 1899. Kali Charan Banerji (1847-1907) was a Brahmin convert, lawyer, newspaper editor, professor at Free Church College, translator of the New Testament into Bengali, and founder of the Calcutta Christo Samaj in 1887. Samuel Sathianadhan (1861-1906), son of W. T. Sathianadhan, was educated at Corpus Christi College, Cambridge, and became Professor of Mental and Moral Philosophy at Presidency College, Madras, Fellow of both the Royal Statistical Society in London and University of Madras, Assistant to the ICS Director of Public Instruction and author of numerous books and articles. B. P. Sircar was a Hindu convert who received an M.A. degree in Canada, was ordained in 1904, and became a YMCA activist. N. C. Mukerji was a brilliant Brahmin convert who suffered from leprosy and became Principal of Ewing Christian College, Allahabad. S. V. Karmarkar was the son of a Brahmin convert from Poona, who received a B.D. degree at Yale, was ordained and worked with the American Marathi Mission, the YMCA, the British and Foreign Bible Society, and other Christian organizations. R. Siraj-ud-din was Professor of History and Logic at Forman Christian College and a founder of St. Andrew's Brotherhood, Lahore, which was dedicated to evangelizing the educated classes. J. R. Chitamber was the son of a Maratha Brahmin convert and Principal of Methodist College, Lucknow. In 1930, he became the first Indian bishop of the Methodist Episcopal Church of South East Asia. L. T. Ah Son was a musician and teacher at Baptist College, Rangoon, and his brother, Ah Pon, was a doctor and an ordained medical missionary. They were the sons of Adoniram Judson's first converts. See C. E. Abraham, *The Founders of the National Missionary Society of India* (Madras, 1947); D. F. Ebright, *op. cit.,* Appendix II, pp. 251-54; W. D. Clarke, 'In Memoriam: Samuel Satahianadan,' in *op. cit.*

The object of the Society shall be to evangelize unoccupied fields in India and adjacent countries, and to lay on Indian Christians the burden of responsibility for the evangelization of their own country and neighbouring lands.[56]

The NMS restricted membership to Indian Christians (others would be honorary members or members of a European Advisory Board) and forbade solicitation of funds outside India. The elderly Vice-President, Kali Charan Banerji, persuaded the society to remain institutionally linked with established churches rather than to create a new sectarian organization. In 1887, he had tried to build a more authentically Indian Christianity by establishing a transdenominational church, the Calcutta Christo Samaj; but he recognized that the Samaj had merely become another sect within Christianity, and he urged NMS delegates not to commit the same error. The society aimed to facilitate inter-church cooperation and to draw divided churches closer together.

Azariah played an interestingly mixed role in the discussions that founded the society. He sided with the older conservatives (President Raja Sir Harnam Singh and Vice-Presidents K. C. Banerji and S. Sathianadhan) on the issue of organization, but with the younger radicals on the issue of finances. He advocated adopting a western-style organization like the IMS with elected committees in opposition to those favoring a less formal structure and a more 'spiritual expression.'[57] At the same time, he challenged his colleagues to resist soliciting financial support from non-resident westerners and, instead, to raise funds from less wealthy indigenous churches and individuals on the subcontinent.

Azariah's decision to reject less centralized, more Hindu-type models of organization later led to the criticism that the NMS was 'too well organized, too respectable, too much in harmony with western institutions that are controlled by some machine in some centre.'[58] A western member of the Advisory Board answered this criticism by demonstrating that many indigenous Hindu models were themselves highly organized. Azariah's own consistent preference for western organizational models prevailed not only in his structuring of the IMS and NMS but also in the administrative apparatus he was to establish later in the Dornakal Diocese.

56. *Proceedings of the National Missionary Society: Minute Book* (Dec. 1905-Dec. 1923), NMSA, Madras. Copy in D. F. Ebright, *op. cit.,* pp. 92-93. See also *The Meeting at Serampore* (Madras, 1947).

57. D. F. Ebright, *op. cit.,* pp. 89-90.

58. 'National Missionary Society,' *NMI*, II, 5 (Jan. 1908), pp. 40-41.

The NMS received enthusiastic support from Christian journals, churches, and missionary societies throughout India and abroad. Azariah spent much of the three and a half years after its foundation traveling the length and breadth of India promoting the NMS cause, establishing a hundred society branches in 1906 alone. Largely because of his efforts, 'by the close of the first five years, scarcely a local church in all India had not listened to the message of the NMS.'[59] The *National Missionary Intelligencer (NMI)* and five vernacular papers helped to publicize the society's work. Azariah recruited the society's first missionary, James Williams, from among the Indian delegates attending the 1907 World Student Christian Federation Conference in Tokyo to begin work in the predominantly Muslim village of Fazlabad in the Punjab in August of that year. The society's second and third missionaries were sent in 1909 to Okara in the Punjab and to Nukkar Tehsil in the United Provinces respectively. By 1910, missions had also been established in the Omalur Taluk, two hundred miles west of Madras, and in the Karjat-Karmala Taluks in the Bombay Presidency.

Azariah propelled this missionary activity forward by arguing that, because of India's great pluralism, 'work among the Panjabis of the North is as much foreign service to the Bengalee or the Madrasee, as it is to the Englishman or American.'[60] He pointed out that, although 'the missionary idea is novel to the Indian mind,'[61] it is a universal obligation rooted in Christ's parting commission, 'Go ye into all the world and make disciples of all nations.' He urged Indian Christians to familiarize themselves 'with the arguments uniformly used in stirring up the Western Churches to missionary duty,'[62] and was not hesitant to quote western authors John Mott and Andrew Murray and London's Lambeth Conference in support of indigenous missions. The society's formula of 'Indian money, Indian men and Indian management' was derived directly from nineteenth-century western missionary statesmen Henry Venn (of the British CMS) and Rufus Anderson (of the American Board of Commissioners for Foreign Missions, or ABCFM), and its constitution was adopted symbolically in the pagoda of Henry Martyn (1781-1812), the evangelical East India Company chaplain and missionary pioneer.[63]

59. D. F. Ebright, *op. cit.,* p. 104.
60. VSA, 'The National Missionary Society of India,' *HF* (new series), XVII, 7 (July 1906), p. 251.
61. *Ibid.,* p. 248.
62. *Ibid.,* p. 249.
63. See Sherwood Eddy's important Letter No. 36, 22 Jan. 1906, I: 3/57, Eddy Papers, YDS.

More than the IMS, the NMS used the rhetoric of national aspiration to appeal to politically aroused students and to young people of India. The *NMI* described its '*swadeshi* missions' and suggested that in certain areas of India, such as the east coast of the Northern Circars, the society benefited from 'the *swadeshi* aspect of the appeal.'[64] Editorials claimed that NMS work contributed to 'the common cause of our National Redemption,'[65] which alone was capable of unifying the selfish communal divisions which handicapped any patriotic effort 'to secure the advancement' of India.[66] Azariah's NMS colleague K. T. Paul noted that, in winning support for the NMS from three Ceylonese Christian communities, 'the *Swadeshi* responsibility is accepted on all hands and the *Swadeshi* privilege recognized.'[67] N. C. Mukerji of Allahabad called on the Indian church to relate its faith more directly to political events by formulating 'a body of teaching which would do for our nationalist movement what Christian Socialism has done for the Labour Movement in England.' Using the Christian notion of true brotherhood to condemn the British subjection of India, Mukerji urged the NMS to 'let our countrymen feel that instead of being a hindrance, Christianity is an ally and an incentive to their national aspirations.'[68] Clearly, the NMS generally wished to participate in the 'nation's' development, and began to appropriate nationalist language to advance the society's interests.

Though the NMS was broadly influenced by the spirit of nationalism, it distanced itself from the negative, anti-British strain of political nationalism that it detected behind the emergence of terrorism in Poona and Bengal. At the society's opening meeting, some delegates opposed the use of the word 'national' in the society's name because of its 'political significance.' The title was accepted reluctantly and only after 'all attempts to secure another satisfactory word which would be expressive of the essential indigenous character of the movement failed.' The report continued:

> It is hoped that the Society will soon reclaim the word, if it has undesirable associations in the minds of any, and will under this name rally all the Indian Christians under the common banner of Christ.[69]

64. 'Branches Old and New,' *NMI*, III, 6 (Feb. 1909), p. 51.

65. *NMI*, III, 8 (April 1909), pp. 61-62.

66. *NMI*, III, 9 (May 1909), pp. 69-70.

67. *NMI*, II, 11 (July 1908), p. 102.

68. 'The Indian Christian Attitude towards Indian National Aspirations,' *NMI*, II, 9 (May 1908), pp. 84-85.

69. *The Meeting at Serampore* (Madras, 1947), p. 2, copy in NMSA, Madras. See also VSA, 'The National Missionary Society of India,' *op. cit.*, p. 246.

In 1907, the *NMI* journal denied an 'imaginary' contention made in the *Central Christian Advocate* of Kansas City that the NMS was created by the national movement in order to reject European authority. An *NMI* editorial countered:

> We shall not pause to point out that not many prominent Native Christians have identified themselves with the Nationalist Political movement. Our main desire is to point out to the writer that it is *not* 'impatience towards European authority' that brought the National Missionary Society into existence, but it is a whole-hearted conviction on the part of the Indian Christians that 'the evangelization of the hitherto untouched parts of the country' should be undertaken by 'means of Indian men (and women too) supported by Indian money.' . . . The continent of India needs our work as well as the work of the Foreign Mission societies. Here is room and opportunity for all.[70]

Reports in the *NMI* and the *Christian Patriot* denied that the society favored *swadeshi* and *swaraj* in their 'degraded' aspects or that it was motivated by 'the same jealousy of the foreigner that marks the sinister side of *swadeshi*.'[71] The most detailed monograph on the subject also concludes that the NMS did not emerge from jealous or anti-foreign attitudes,[72] although it describes the society as 'Indian Christian nationalism in action,' with officers who were 'sincere nationalists.'[73] While many of its founders were generally sympathetic to the national movement, they were members of a relatively small and elite, western-educated group. (The Brahmin cast of NMS founders contrasts with the Nadar cast of the IMS founders.) The vast majority of Indian Christians came from rural depressed class backgrounds in South India whose close association with British missionaries and involvement in regional and lower-caste initiatives made them less interested in, and even hostile to, what many perceived as primarily a Brahmin political cause.

Westerners generally drew more links between indigenous missions and the national movement than did Indian Christians. The British missionary and Principal of the Church Missionary College in Tinnevelly, Rev. H. Schaffter, urged the IMS and, indirectly, the NMS to consider themselves as Christian expressions of *'swadeshism'* and to claim as their

---

70. *NMI,* II, 4 (Dec. 1907), p. 28.
71. 'Notes,' *NMI,* II, 12 (Aug. 1908), p. 122; D. F. Ebright, *op. cit.,* p. 99.
72. D. F. Ebright, *op. cit.,* p. 100.
73. *Ibid.,* pp. 103, 143.

inheritance the mottoes, '*Bande Mataram, Swadeshi* and *Swaraj.*'[74] The 1908 New Year's Message to the NMS membership, penned by C. F. Andrews in the *NMI,* even suggested that 'Christ loves India far, far more than the greatest Indian Patriot who has ever lived.'[75] Both a CMS Report for 1905-6 and other western observers attributed the society's inspiration and strength to the influence of the national movement.[76]

The nearly total preoccupation with secular nationalism by western-ers and western-educated Indians threatens to distort the historical reality that was experienced by the bulk of the NMS membership. The early is-sues of the *NMI* make frequent and repeated references not to Indian na-tionalists, but to the great western missionaries of Asia and Africa: Ziegenbalg, Carey, Livingstone, Hudson Taylor, and Adoniram Judson.[77] The Christianization of Korea was presented as an inspirational model for mission in Asia.[78] The story of Scottish missionary John Gibson Paton's civilizing crusade against cannibalism, infanticide, the strangling of wid-ows, constant war, witchcraft, polygamy, and other 'nameless immorali-ties' in the Hebrides Islands was recounted in the most imaginative orientalist style.[79] The NMS saw itself as part of a worldwide Christian movement more than an Indian national movement, and cited messages from the Archbishops of Canterbury and York to stress the point.[80] To be sure, its founding in the nationalist center of Calcutta in 1905 suggests that its leaders shared in the general desire of educated Indians to manage their country's own affairs, and its subsequent popularity benefited from the desire to shed the image of Indian Christianity as a 'foreign' faith. However, far from attempting to isolate itself from continued western in-fluences, the NMS sought to integrate itself into the corporate life of a universal church reinvigorated by a predominantly western missionary movement.

The later adoption by the NMS of a more radically 'indigenous'

74. 'Notes,' *NMI,* II, 12 (Aug. 1908), p. 122.

75. C. F. Andrews, 'A New Year's Message,' *NMI,* II, 5 (Jan. 1908), p. 35.

76. According to D. F. Ebright, *op. cit.,* pp. 99-100. The society's most 'indige-nous' later projects — the Christa Seva Sangha and the Christukula Ashram in Tirupattur — were initiated by westerners Jack C. Winslow and E. Forrester Paton (who co-founded the ashram with S. Jesudason).

77. *NMI,* II, 3 (Nov. 1907), pp. 19-21; II, 4 (Dec. 1907), p. 29; II, 5 (Jan. 1908), p. 36; III, 10 (June 1909), pp. 80-81.

78. 'Korea: The Marvellous Successes of the Gospel,' *NMI,* II, 10 (June 1908), pp. 95-97.

79. J.N.R. (author), 'John Gibson Paton,' *NMI,* II, 12 (Aug. 1908), pp. 116-21.

80. *NMI,* III, 9 (May 1909), pp. 72-73.

character apparently contributed to its decline rather than to any greater acceptance in India. The European Advisory Board was dismissed in 1920 and the society assumed the vernacular name 'Bharat Kristya Sevak Samaj' (or, Indian Christian Service Society). But many Indian churches were alienated by its call for radical indigenization, and few new converts were gained by making it a more nationalist movement.[81] Most of the original affiliated churches preferred to retain familiar western aspects of their worship rather than to accept the new and more 'indigenous' version of NMS, which seemed to borrow unduly from a Hindu culture that was even more alien to many former outcaste Christians. Azariah himself became alienated from the NMS even earlier in 1906-9, when he made the most momentous decision of his life: to go himself to Dornakal as a simple IMS missionary to the outcastes.

81. J. M. Jayasingh, *op. cit.*, pp. 144-45, 207-11.

PART II

THE REIGN

Azariah was elevated as the first Indian Anglican bishop in an atmosphere of surprising controversy; but his reign brought equally surprising growth and harmony. As he moved from the worlds of Tinnevelly Indo-Anglicanism and Pan-Asian student evangelism into British imperial and church politics, he necessarily became embroiled in historic church-state controversies and served as a lightning rod for racial and other prejudices. His secure grounding in a specific sacramental spirituality and traditional church activities enabled him to absorb hostile pressures without bitterness and to become late imperial India's most successful mass evangelist and church builder.

CHAPTER 4

Bishop in the British Empire: Church-State Conflict under the Raj

Azariah's unusual path to an unprecedented bishopric began with his decision actively to pursue rather than merely to promote missionary work. Increasingly frustrated with the broad but unfocused national scope of his work, he confided to his wife during one of his interminable itinerancies for the NMS in 1906 that 'I feel afraid that if I did this long I would simply grow *unreal*.' Azariah's dissatisfaction with the NMS seems to have been grounded primarily in a suspicion that the society's emerging liberal nationalistic profile would detract from its evangelistic mission. He admitted in his most private correspondence that he persevered in the NMS work 'simply because of Mr. Eddy and *not* because I feel that it is the Lord's will for me,' and concluded:

> The Missionary cause has my entire heart. But as far as the particular Society is concerned, I do not have strong convictions on certain aspects of it. And still I am called upon to defend it, to speak for it, to support the very thing I feel doubtful about in private. I feel miserable . . . in this business.[1]

Finding himself in the paradoxical situation of promoting an indigenous national project largely for the sake of a liberal-minded foreign friend, Azariah began to search for ways to fulfil his own missionary call-

---

1. VSA to Anbu, 17 Aug. 1906, Azariah Collection, Madras.

ing, rather than simply satisfy a westerner's enthusiasm for the Indianization of missions.

Azariah received what he interpreted as a divine 'call' to conduct evangelism in a specific locality sometime between 1906 and 1909.[2] In 1909,
he resigned from both the YMCA and the NMS to become Superintending
Missionary of the more locally activist IMS in Dornakal. The precipitating
event occurred just after Azariah had completed an address on the importance of missionary service at Memorial Hall, Madras, when a student in
the front row whispered loudly, 'Why doesn't *he* go as a missionary!'[3]
Azariah had been considering doing so and took this as God's message to
him. After a proposal to unify the IMS and the NMS failed in early 1909,
Azariah decided to offer himself as a full-time missionary to the IMS.[4]

In April, the IMS accepted Azariah's offer of missionary service and
appointed him Superintending Missionary for the Dornakal field at a salary of RS 60 per month.[5] This appointment involved considerable sacrifice for Azariah, who was poised to take on new international responsibilities for the YMCA. As a YMCA colleague recalled a few years later:

> It was [Azariah's] love for the Church that made him . . . refuse the
> higher salary offered by the YMCA, and decline their offer to send him
> to the YMCA convention at Oxford and to the Constantinople Student
> Conference, and . . . go to Dornakal to work among the poor people
> there.[6]

Although Azariah subsequently maintained close links with the NMS and
the YMCA, welcoming their workers in Dornakal, he now turned his back

2. Different dates for this event have been suggested. See, e.g., D. Packiamuthu,
'Azariah, the Apostle of India,' in *Birth Centenary of Bishop Azariah, 1974, op. cit.,* p. 82
(who sets the date as 1909); and J. Z. Hodge, *op. cit.,* p. 17 (who claims Azariah came to
the decision shortly after August 1906).

3. This story has been told by Azariah and by virtually all biographers, although
the Rev. Alfred Bunyan believed that a suggestion by Henry Whitehead precipitated
Azariah's resignation from the YMCA and his move to Dornakal. Interview, 29 March
1986, Dornakal.

4. The NMS had invited the Tinnevelly-based IMS to affiliate itself with the national organization in 1908 but then rejected the conditions under which the IMS desired to affiliate. *Original Minute Books: Proceedings of the Executive Committee,* I, 4 Aug.
1908; 11 March 1909; 13 May 1909; 14 July 1909, NMSA, Madras.

5. Resolution XIII, 'Offer of Secretary Mr. V. S. Azariah,' 13 April 1909, PIMS,
IMSA.

6. Mr. J. R. Isaac, Letter to *The Mail,* 11 Feb. 1912; quoted in *Birth Centenary of
Bishop Azariah, 1974, op. cit.,* p. 20.

on other international opportunities and gave himself fully to the local mission work of his home society.

To strengthen Azariah's position in the field, the IMS Executive Committee asked the Bishop of Madras, Henry Whitehead (1853-1947), if he would send Azariah to Dornakal as an ordained Anglican priest. (Previous IMS missionaries had all been laymen.)[7] Whitehead liked the idea and persuaded Azariah in March 1909 to take an accelerated course for ordination under the bishop's private tuition. Whitehead did not reveal to Azariah why he was abbreviating the normal ordination training, but it was almost certainly because he and his wife, Isabel, had already identified Azariah as their candidate to be the first Indian bishop.

After several months of intensive work at the Whiteheads' Ootacamund residence (May, June, September, October), Azariah was ordained deacon on 29 June, commissioned to begin his IMS work in Dornakal in July, and ordained priest on 5 December.[8] As he studied for ordination, Azariah also launched his work in Dornakal, the small railway depot in the Warangal District of southeastern Hyderabad State. Here, within the favorite hunting grounds of the Nizam of Hyderabad, he would develop his career as missionary to the depressed and non-Brahmin classes.

The year 1909 was therefore a crucial turning point for both Azariah's career and Indo-Anglicanism. Azariah was turning away from broad interdenominational organizations to more narrow denominational work in what was to him a foreign area of South India. At the same time, he was turning for guidance to Whitehead — an upper-class Englishman and member of the long line of liberal westerners who imagined themselves to be the true champions of Indianization. Azariah was moving away from the American Sherwood Eddy, who had previously succeeded in persuading Azariah not to pursue Anglican ordination in 1901-2. The cosmopolitan Eddy seems to have regarded Indians with a complicated mix of high-minded compassion and upper-class disdain, and he saw Azariah's return to a backward parish as the end, not the beginning, of a promising career. Eddy later wrote:

> [Azariah] chose for his field the most degraded, drunken, carrion-eating devil-worshipers in Hyderabad. The poverty of the people, struggling to live on four or five cents a day, was abysmal. In fact, the people were so

7. Resolution XIII, 13 April 1909, PIMS, IMSA.
8. 1909 Folder, Azariah Collection, Madras.

degraded that I did not expect to see any appreciable results in our life-time. I pleaded with Azariah not to throw away his life there, and I said good-bye fearing I should never see him again.[9]

Contrary to Eddy's predictions, Azariah rapidly made Dornakal the center of the fastest-growing mission field in India and the headquarters of an expanding Indo-Anglican diocese. But in early 1909, it still seemed risky to abandon two influential posts and his native Tinnevelly, in order to work as an ordinary priest and missionary among depressed class groups in an unfamiliar and seemingly unpromising rural area.

Azariah moved in 1909 to the isolated Dornakal railway station, which was surrounded on all sides by tiger-infested jungles and tracts of dry land without access to roads. Here he lived first in a tent, unprotected from dangerous wildlife, and began the strenuous work of evangelizing non-Christian Telugu villagers and supervising new Christian congregations.[10] Traveling by foot, bullock cart, and bicycle, with his food and Bible tracts hanging in a bag suspended from the handlebars, Azariah visited families in their simple houses, talked to small groups of men sitting in the shade of trees, preached to crowds gathered in the evenings to hear him, and, on Sundays, performed priestly duties for nascent congregations.[11] By January 1910, shortly after the death of an infant son, his wife and four young children joined him in Dornakal. 'He gave us this sweet boy *in order that* he might take him to Himself and through this that he may teach us many precious lessons,' Azariah tried to comfort Anbu before the move.[12] Together again, the Azariah family set up a home in two rooms of the old brewery and began their lifelong work of service to Andhra villagers.

This story of his humble beginnings as a missionary in Dornakal has been overshadowed by the publicity generated by his simultaneous rise to an Anglican bishopric in 1912. Soon after Azariah launched his village missionary work, he was concurrently thrust into an international whirl-

9. G. S. Eddy, *Eighty Adventurous Years, op. cit.,* p. 54. Elsewhere, Eddy described Azariah's decision as a 'heroic sacrifice': Eddy, *Pathfinders of the World Missionary Crusade, op. cit.,* p. 147.

10. Interview with Azariah's daughter, Grace Aaron, 24-25 Sept. 1985, Ottawa, Ontario, Canada.

11. D. A. Christadoss, 'V. S. Azariah — Missionary Priest,' in *Birth Centenary of Bishop Azariah, 1974, op. cit.* pp. 42-43

12. Their four living children were Mercy (b. 8 April 1899), Edwin (b. 11 June 1901), George (b. 24 Dec. 1903), and Grace (b. 10 May 1908). They would have two more sons in Dornakal: Henry (b. 5 June 1911) and Ambrose (b. 31 Jan. 1916). A total of three children died in infancy. VSA to Anbu, 31 March 1909, Azariah Collection, Madras.

wind of ecclesiastical and imperial politics. Bishop Henry Whitehead's three-year battle to appoint him as the first Indian Anglican bishop brought Azariah into a new world of Anglican politics and made him an international symbol of the purported success of the Empire's 'civilizing mission.' It also changed his life forever.

Azariah's 1912 consecration as the first Indian bishop of the Anglican church was the most significant event in his personal and professional life. It made him a leading representative of the Indian Empire's loyal subject populations; it was a milestone in the history of the overseas Anglican church; and it thrust the established church's bishops in India into newly public and progressive roles.

But the road to consecration was long and tortuous. The battle over his appointment opened up new and unexpected rifts between the imperial state and its established church, and between various Christian subgroups. When Henry Whitehead first proposed the idea in 1909, he had little notion of the obstacles that would stand in the way of Azariah and would ultimately prevent consecrations of other Indian bishops in the waning years of the Raj. However, he was aware of one dramatic fact which should have served as a warning sign: Anglican church and missionary expansion in India had generally occurred in spite of the British government rather than because of it. The church had never been free to appoint new bishops for India. Now Whitehead was proposing to do just that, and more: to appoint a new bishop not only for India but also from India. This was a doubly controversial move.

Church-State Conflict in Anglican India

Azariah was consecrated as the first Indian Anglican bishop on Sunday, 29 December 1912, in St. Paul's Cathedral, Calcutta. On that momentous day, in the presence of eleven British Anglican bishops, the Governor of Bengal, and a large crowd of western and Indian supporters, the Anglican church announced to the world that it was opening the floodgates to Indian leadership in the church. 'We . . . welcome to the high office of a ruler in the Church of God one whom we believe will render loyal and efficient service, . . . the forerunner of a long line of Indian Bishops in the years yet to come,' the Reverend Canon E. S. Sell enthused in his sermon.[13] Ten

---

13. Rev. Canon Sell, 'Strengthened with Might,' in *The Glorious Company of the Apostles and Other Sermons* (Madras, 1927), p. 15.

days later, Azariah was installed as bishop in the newly created diocese of Dornakal. He was thirty-eight years old.

With this consecration, the Anglican church made a complete break with precedent. Azariah became the first Indian bishop, not only of the Anglican church, but of any Christian church outside the small and ancient Syrian Christian churches of St. Thomas, most of whom had themselves been dependent on bishops from Mesopotamia until the sixteenth century.[14] All other churches in India lagged behind the Anglican church in consecrating indigenous bishops. The Roman Catholic church had appointed three Goan Brahmins as bishops in the seventeenth century,[15] but did not appoint native Indian bishops again until 1923.[16] Both the Roman Catholic and Syrian churches could be considered particularly 'foreign' because they used the liturgical languages of Latin and Syriac.

14. The so-called 'Thomas Christians' began appointing Indian bishops only from 1896, although there had been earlier precedents. The Synod of Diamper in 1599 marked the beginning of a deep schism in the Syrian church between those who pledged allegiance to the Roman Catholic Church (and hence came under the jurisdiction of foreign bishops sent either by the Pope or by the Portuguese, who were given the right to appoint bishops under claims of the *Padroado*) and those who retained allegiance to the eastern churches (sometimes known as the Malankara Church). After the Syrian break with the Roman Catholics (over the famous oath of the Koonen Cross), leaders of the Malankara Church consecrated one of their own members as bishop (Parambil Tumi, known as Thomas de Campo) in a ceremony performed by priests (without any episcopal involvement) in 1653. By 1665, the Eastern Church established communion with the Jacobite Patriarch of Antioch, from whom it then received many of its future bishops. See A. M. Mundadan, *Indian Christians: Search for Identity and Struggle for Autonomy* (Bangalore, 1984), pp. 8-14; S. C. Neill, *The Christian World,* unpublished lecture series, Neill Collection, Oxford, and *A History of Christianity in India: The Beginnings to 1707, op. cit.* See also Leslie W. Brown, *The Indian Christians of St. Thomas: An Account of the Ancient Syrian Church of Malabar* (Cambridge, 1956, 1982).

15. They were given the title of Vicars Apostolic, signifying their role as direct representatives of the Pope in episcopal orders but without territorial titles taken from the area in which they were to work. S. C. Neill, *The Christian Society* (London, 1952), pp. 241-42; *A History of Christianity in India: The Beginnings to 1707, op. cit.,* pp. 335-41; A. M. Mundadan, *op. cit.,* pp. 140-44.

16. In that year it conferred episcopacy on Tiburtius Roche of Tuticorin in Tamil Nadu. In the centralized Roman Catholic Church hierarchy, progress towards indigenization of the episcopate depended very much on the actions of the Pope. It was the strong initiative of Pope Pius XI which led to the relatively rapid progress of episcopal indigenization in India and elsewhere after the consecration in Rome of 12 bishops of different races in October 1926. The first non-European Cardinals (who stand above bishops in the church hierarchy) were appointed by Pope Pius XII. S. Neill, *The Christian Society, op. cit.,* pp. 241-42; and *A History of Christian Missions, op. cit.,* pp. 521-27.

The arrival of Evangelical (or Protestant) missions and the subsequent dissemination of Bibles translated into Indian vernacular languages, combined with the rising force of Indian nationalism, provoked older churches in India to seek a more genuinely Indian identity under native leadership. But even indigenous Protestant churches in India continued to rely on foreign bishops until well into the twentieth century. The Methodist Episcopal Church in southern Asia waited until 1931 to consecrate an Indian, and the Lutheran church lingered until 1955.[17] The Anglican church also acted in India before anywhere else except West Africa, where, as we shall see, it consecrated Samuel Adayi Crowther in 1864. The first indigenous Anglican bishops were consecrated in China in 1918,[18] Japan in 1923,[19] Uganda in 1947,[20] and Iran in 1961.[21] Thus, the appoint-

17. Brenton Thoburn Badley, *The Making of a Bishop: The Life-Story of Bishop Jashwant Rao Chitambar* (Lucknow, 1942), p. 5. There are a number of striking similarities between the careers of Azariah and J. R. Chitamber, the first Methodist bishop. Chitambar committed himself to Christian work under the influence of John Mott and Robert Wilder, who visited Lucknow in February 1896. (He signed the pledge to keep the 'Morning Watch' and committed himself to take up direct Christian work unless prevented by God.) He accompanied Azariah as fellow delegate to Tokyo in 1907 and to Edinburgh in 1910, and was a co-founder of the NMS. The first Indian Lutheran bishop was Raja Manickam of Tranquebar, 1955. S. Neill, *The Story of the Christian Church in India and Pakistan, op. cit.,* pp. 155-56.

18. Tsae-Seng Sing was consecrated assistant bishop in the Chekiang Diocese of the *Chung Hua Sheng Kung Hui* (the Anglican church in China) in October 1918. Ding Ing-ong was consecrated assistant bishop in Fukien Diocese in April 1927. (Interestingly, the diocesan bishop, John Hind, tried to persuade Ding to become diocesan bishop with himself as assistant, but testified that 'the climate of opinion in the Fukien church, alike among missionaries and Chinese church members, was not ready for this.') The Roman Catholic Church in China had a similar experience to that in India. The first Chinese Roman Catholic bishop was Lô Wen-Tsao (1617-91) whose brief tenure as Bishop of Basilinopolis (1685 to his death) was followed by a long period of 'regression.' Six Chinese bishops were among those consecrated by Pius XI in 1926. G. Hewitt, *The Problems of Success: A History of the Church Missionary Society 1910-1942,* II (London, 1977), pp. 246, 266, 286; G. K. A. Bell, *Randall Davidson: Archbishop of Canterbury,* II (London, 1935), pp. 1227-29.

19. J. S. Motoda and J. Y. Naide were consecrated as Bishops of Tokyo and Osaka respectively in the *Nippon Sei Ko Kwai* (The Holy Catholic Church of Japan), a united Anglican church. It is interesting to note that Archbishop Davidson began to encourage the NSKK to consecrate a bishop of Japanese birth in 1917. The Methodists preceded the Anglicans in Japan by consecrating Yoitsu Honda as bishop of the American Episcopal Methodist Church in 1907. The Roman Catholics waited until 1927 to consecrate a Japanese bishop, Mgr. Hayusake. G. Hewitt, *The Problems of Success, op. cit.,* pp. 310-11.

20. Assistant Bishop Abere Balya.

21. Bishop Hassan Barnabas Dehqani-Tafti.

ment of Azariah was a pathbreaking step, not only for the Anglican church globally but also for all Christian denominations in India.

Azariah's appointment was additionally important because it necessitated the creation of a new diocese. The growth of an Indo-Anglican ecclesiastical structure on the subcontinent, complete with chaplains, bishops, clergymen, and Gothic-styled churches, brought the Church of England continually and increasingly into conflict with the Government of India's official policy of noninterference in Indian religious affairs.[22] The proliferation of bishoprics in India, Burma, and Ceylon (designed to accommodate not only the growing number of Britons abroad but also the Anglican church's expanding Indian and Eurasian membership) provided a serious, if largely unrecognized point of tension between church and state at the turn of the century. The church in India confronted a variety of frustrating, state-imposed obstacles to its growth, and Anglican bishops and missionaries in India generally regarded their association with the government as a hindrance to their work. Strongly conflicting opinions arose regarding the extent to which the government should be involved with promoting Christianity on the subcontinent. The complex legal and political battle surrounding the creation of the Dornakal Diocese is only one of many illustrations of broadening civil-ecclesiastical discord which belies the widely accepted notion that church and state formed a close partnership in which both parties participated in a semi-official imperial system of mutual support and promotion.[23]

The relationship between Christianity and British rule in India was governed by a long-standing 'official' policy of tolerance, which was later

22. Henceforth the Government of India, or the Indian government, are terms used to designate the government of the Raj *in India* under British rule. (The British government, in contrast, was located *in Britain*.) The Government of India (Governor-General in Council), the Government of Bengal (Government of Fort William, or Governor-in-Council for Bengal), and the Government of Madras (Government of Fort St. George, or Governor-in-Council for Madras) are also distinct from the governments of individuals, such as Curzon's government.

23. This theory receives detailed documentation in L. F. Knoll, 'State and Religions in British India: 1814-1865' (Ph.D. thesis, Graduate Theological Union, Berkeley, California, 1971). Although Knoll's thorough study of Ecclesiastical Department records in Madras provides an interesting history of church-state interaction, his conclusions suffer from a lack of perspective that might have been achieved by consulting other primary source materials such as those available in church and missionary society archives. The partnership theory is also a common theme in general histories such as Kenneth and Helen Ballhatchet, 'Asia,' in *The Oxford Illustrated History of Christianity*, ed. John McManners (Oxford, 1990), pp. 488-518.

articulated for the East India Company in Lord Macaulay's 1835 Minute on Education: 'We abstain, and I trust shall always abstain, from giving any public encouragement to those who are in any way engaged in the work of converting natives to Christianity.' It was restated for the Indian government in the Queen's Proclamation of 1858:

> Firmly relying on the truth of Christianity . . . we disclaim alike the right and the desire to impose our convictions on any of our subjects . . . and we do strictly charge and enjoin all those who may be in authority under us that they abstain from all interference with the religious belief or worship of any of our subjects on pain of our highest displeasure.[24]

But this policy of nonintervention was difficult to enforce and provoked continuing controversy. Evangelicals such as Charles Grant (1746-1823) and William Wilberforce (1759-1833) successfully pressured the government to allow the Anglican church and missionary societies fuller access to India. The small handful of Europeans who exercised power over vast numbers of non-Christian peoples in India decided mainly for political and economic reasons to extend British patronage to Indian religious institutions. The East India Company administered revenues to Hindu temples, propitiated Hindu deities, and provided for the ceremonies, festivals, and rituals associated with the great temples. In 1817, these procedures were regularized, and the Company assumed direct legal responsibility for the support and maintenance of Hindu deities. The English East India Company's Raj has therefore been described with some justification as a 'Hindu Raj.'[25]

The Church of England planted its first roots in India shortly after the English East India Company received its original charter from Queen

---

24. Both quoted in D. A. Low, *Lion Rampant, op. cit.,* pp. 119-20.

25. R. E. Frykenberg, 'Conversion and Crises of Conscience under Company Raj in South India,' in *Asie du Sud, Traditions et Changements,* Colloques Internationaux du C.N.R.S., no. 582, p. 312; 'The Emergence of "Free" Religion under the Company's Raj in South India,' in *op. cit.,* pp. 14-16; 'The Impact of Conversion and Social Reform upon Society in South India during the Late Company Period,' in *op. cit.,* pp. 210-15. See also C. Y. Mudaliar, *The Secular State and Religious Institutions in India: A Study of the Administration of Hindu Public Religious Trusts in Madras* (Wiesbaden, 1974), pp. 1-53, particularly, pp. 16-23. Furthermore, it was Indian Christians who were left with fewer rights in British India than any other group after the passage of the East India Act of 1813. They were excluded from certain jobs and professions, and were liable both to be deprived of property, wives, and children upon conversion, and to be punished in public by caning for refusing to participate in certain Hindu ceremonies. S. C. Neill, *A History of Christianity in India 1707-1858, op. cit.,* p. 173, and R. E. Frykenberg, 'The Emergence of "Free" Religion,' in *op. cit.,* pp. 24-28.

Elizabeth in 1600 requiring that Anglican chaplains oversee the spiritual life on its ships and in its factories. As the British extended their commercial and military presence in India during the next three centuries, so also did the Anglican church gradually increase its influence. Company and military chaplains ministered to British residents, soldiers, and much of the growing Eurasian population. Before the first bishop was sent to India in 1814, chaplains worked under the remote supervision of the Bishop of London, and no Anglican could be confirmed or ordained in India. These early chaplains were paid from local Company revenues and apparently did not engage in serious evangelistic activity. In the seventeenth century, only one baptism of an Indian according to Anglican rites was recorded.[26]

The situation had changed by the late eighteenth and early nineteenth centuries when the so-called 'pious chaplains' undertook vigorous missionary work in India. Under the inspiration of the Cambridge evangelical leader Charles Simeon (1759-1836), they won Indian converts and translated the Bible into Indian vernaculars.[27] After the Crown assumed direct control of the Indian government in 1858, the government took responsibility for appointing chaplains and paid their salaries from tax revenues.[28]

Since the chaplains and priests ministered primarily to Europeans, extraecclesiastical societies arose to evangelize foreign populations; the Society for Promoting Christian Knowledge (SPCK) was founded in 1699, the SPG in 1701, and the CMS in 1799. Missionaries for India first received limited permission to work in British-controlled territories in the East India Company Charter Act of 1813, and were given unlimited freedom twenty years later in the Charter Act of 1833. This development was a victory for evangelicals against the powerful anti-missionary lobby in Parliament led by Company Director Sir Stephen Lushington, who believed that evangelistic activity in India threatened British material interests.

After rejecting a proposal for government patronage of Christian missions in 1793, Parliament approved the extension of the Anglican episcopate to India in 1813, responding again to the evangelicals and rebuffing the East India Company. The East India Act of 1813 provided for the appointment of a bishop for India with an episcopal seat in Calcutta that included all 'British territories in the East Indies and Parts aforesaid' (i.e., within the Company's Charter). In 1817, the island of Ceylon was added

26. M. E. Gibbs, *The Anglican Church in India, op. cit.*, pp. 8-11; S. C. Neill, *Anglicanism*, 4th ed. (New York, 1977), pp. 208-11.

27. S. C. Neill, *Anglicanism, op. cit.*, pp. 323-24; *A History of Christianity in India, 1707-1858, op. cit.*, pp. 255-61.

28. S. C. Neill, *Colonialism and Christian Missions* (London, 1966), pp. 99-100.

to the diocese, followed by Australia and New Zealand in 1823.[29] The new
Bishop of Calcutta was the first Anglican bishop 'east of Suez,' with three
new archdeacons assisting him in the Presidency capitals.

The bishop could not be appointed according to traditional English
methods without a preexisting diocesan electoral apparatus (the Dean
and Chapter of a cathedral or collegiate college). So the government revived a procedure used in the sixteenth century under Edward VI whereby
the Crown nominated bishops directly.[30] The royal letters patent issued
after the 1813 Act appointed Thomas Fanshawe Middleton (bishop 1814-
22) to the new episcopal see and classified him and his archdeacons as
civil servants to be paid from local Company revenues — 5,000 pounds
sterling per year for the bishop and 2,000 pounds per year for each archdeacon. Middleton, like bishops in England, was made subject to the
Archbishop of Canterbury and to English ecclesiastical laws governing
such matters as liturgy and use of the Book of Common Prayer;[31] but the
letters safeguarded the authority of the Governor-General and Governors
in India, gave the Crown the right to cancel the appointment, and with-
held from the bishop a seat in the House of Lords. These civil restrictions
on the bishop's authority prompted one church historian to call the letters patent 'a travesty of episcopacy.'[32]

Middleton's episcopate was launched in virtual secrecy for fear that
his appointment might provoke protests either from British officials opposed generally to 'missionary meddling' in India or from the Indian population.[33] The sermon preached at his consecration was not published, as
was the usual custom, and he received no public reception or even a formal residence when he arrived in Calcutta in 1814. The secretiveness may

29. M. E. Gibbs, *op. cit.,* pp. 51, 82.

30. Using letters patent rather than the normal procedure of the *congé d'élire,* or
'permission to elect' a bishop, which was granted by the Crown to the Dean and Chapter of a diocesan cathedral. The use of letters patent was permitted by an Act of 1547.
S. C. Neill, *A History of Christianity in India 1707-1858, op. cit.,* p. 261. For text of letters
patent, see C. J. Grimes, *Towards an Indian Church: The Growth of the Church of India in Constitution and Life* (London, 1946), pp. 229-38.

31. M. E. Gibbs, *op. cit.,* p. 266. Such laws were often grossly inappropriate within
the Indian context: *ibid.,* p. 56.

32. Grimes, *op. cit.,* p. 63. As the number of Anglican dioceses increased in the
nineteenth century, the Bishoprics Act of 1878 mandated that only 26 British bishops
were to have seats in the House of Lords.

33. S. C. Neill, *History of Christianity in India, 1707-1858, op. cit.,* p. 262; M. E. Gibbs,
op. cit., p. 57; J. McLeod Campbell, *Christian History in the Making* (London, 1946), pp. 88-
89.

have been unnecessary, because the initial response to the importation of the English ecclesiastical establishment was surprisingly subdued. Most non-Christian Indians seemed to accept the idea that the British regime would follow the practice of previous Hindu and Muslim rulers by giving its faith some official recognition.[34]

Bishop Middleton's greatest opposition came from within his own church and the Company's Court of Directors. It proved difficult to su-perimpose his new episcopal authority onto the already existing chap-laincy and upon a rapidly growing missionary population that looked to their independent home societies for authority. Middleton had been com-missioned to license all Anglican clergy in India. But India's civil and mili-tary chaplains were accustomed to receiving instructions and appoint-ments from civil authorities (the Governor-General-in-Council, the Governors of other Presidencies, or the Commander-in-Chief in the area). The Governor-General during Middleton's tenure, Lord Moira, argued that chaplains should be appointed by the new bishop, but the Company's Court of Directors overruled him and insisted, instead, that chaplains simply be appointed by seniority. Patronage in India was a perquisite which the Company Directors simply would not surrender to either the Church or the Crown.[35]

Middleton faced even greater problems in extending his authority over the growing number of missionaries who, in the words of a later bishop, 'seemed to wander at their own sweet will, rather than to be settled in one particular place.'[36] 'I must either license them or silence them . . . there is no alternative,' Middleton lamented; but 'how can I silence men who come to India under the authority of a clause in the charter?'[37] In the end, Middleton concluded that his letters patent from the Crown gave him jurisdiction over chaplains only, and he gave up trying to license An-glican missionaries or to ordain Indian clergy.

Parliament clarified the original letters patent at the request of Middleton's successor, Reginald Heber (bishop 1823-26). He was conse-crated at Lambeth Palace on 1 June 1823 without the secrecy of the pre-ceding decade.[38] The India Bishops and Courts Act of 1823 tightened the

34. S. C. Neill, *A History of Christianity in India: 1707-1858, op. cit.,* p. 262.
35. M. E. Gibbs, *op. cit.,* p. 58.
36. Quoted in S. C. Neill, *A History of Christianity in India: 1707-1858, op. cit.,* p. 263.
37. Quoted in *ibid.,* p. 263. On the problem of episcopal relations with mission-ary societies, see Hans Cnattingius, *Bishops and Societies, op. cit.*
38. Previously vociferous opponents of missions to the East, such as Canon Syd-ney Smith, chose to remain silent and the church was less fearful of causing damaging

bishop's control over missionaries, loosened the Anglican ministry's attachment to the Crown, and gave the Bishop of Calcutta the right to ordain Indians to the Anglican ministry.[39] During his short tenure, Heber ordained a Tamil convert, Christian David, and a Muslim convert, Abdul Masih, to Anglican orders, brought all Anglican clergymen working in the Calcutta Diocese under his authority, and promoted the church's evangelistic mission in India, calling himself 'the chief Missionary of the Society in the East.'[40]

Heber survived the Indian climate and his rigorous travel schedule for only four years, and his two successors, John Thomas James (bishop 1827-28) and John Matthias Turner (bishop 1829-31), both died less than two years after their arrivals. Therefore, when the Company's charter came up for renewal in 1833, Parliament lessened the bishop's burdens by establishing additional bishoprics in the Bombay and Madras Presidencies and by elevating the Bishop of Calcutta to the status of a Metropolitan. The church, like the state, now looked to Calcutta as its center of authority, and the bishops assumed prestigious roles in official ranking.[41] Once again, there was surprisingly little opposition from the non-Christian Indian population which bore the brunt of increased costs, and opposition to the Indian episcopacy from the liberal Lord William Bentinck was apparently based on his disapproval of Protestant establishment in Ireland more than any concerns about the Indian situation.[42]

Thus the Anglican church's destiny in India was inextricably linked with that of India's British rulers.[43] Whether this connection ultimately helped or hurt the Christian enterprise in India is a complex question. Al-

---

political effects in India. Derrick Hughes, *Bishop Sahib: A Life of Reginald Heber* (Worthing, 1986), pp. 87-88, 194-95.

39. Indian ordinands were exempted from making the oath of allegiance to the Crown required of candidates in England. S. C. Neill, *A History of Christianity 1707-1858, op. cit.,* p. 267. Derrick Hughes, *op. cit.,* p. 85.

40. Quoted from his farewell address to the SPCK in London before departure for India. S. C. Neill, *A History of Christianity in India: 1707-1858,* p. 267; J. M. Campbell, *op. cit.,* pp. 92-96.

41. In the Madras Presidency, the bishop was preceded only by the Governor and the Chief Justice. L. Newbigin, *Unfinished Agenda: An Autobiography* (London, 1985), p. 214.

42. John Rosselli, *Lord William Bentinck: The Making of a Liberal Imperialist, 1774-1839* (Berkeley, 1974), p. 212.

43. By the late nineteenth century, one-fourth of India's Anglican clerical body was supported by Indian taxation mandated by Acts of Parliament. H. W. Tucker, *Under His Banner, op. cit.,* pp. 45-46.

though Christianity may have benefited in early times from its close association in the popular imagination with the prestigious empire in India, the state connection became a serious liability with the advent of the national independence movement.[44] Azariah later described the educated Christian nationalist's embarrassment at the Indo-Anglican church's dependence on any British government:

> He feels that such a dependence compromises his position before his non-Christian compatriots. The Hindu knows that His Majesty has proclaimed strict neutrality in matters concerning the religion of the peoples of India: and yet his Indian Christian brother is a member of a Church in which the King's aid has to be sought to create a new diocese, to sub-divide an old one, for the consecration of a Bishop, and even for the consecration of an Indian Bishop. Why should his Majesty, he rightly asks . . . appoint the chief ministers and directors of one of the religious sects followed by nearly a million of the peoples of India?[45]

As Azariah's criticism suggested, the extension of Anglicanism outside the British Isles during the colonial era produced complex legal and constitutional problems for the Church of England.[46] Anglican bishops generally came to regret their church's state connection well before the advent of popular Indian nationalism in the early twentieth century. They saw the state connection as a legal and cultural hindrance to the church's growth and development. As the British had expanded territorial control in India and the number of Indo-Anglicans had increased during the nineteenth century, the Church of England in India was required to obey laws whose authority rested upon the consent of a distant Parliament (the church's chief law-making body since the Reformation), and whose stipulations were suited to ecclesiastical life in Britain rather than India.

Azariah lamented that the Anglican church in India was unable to create new dioceses, to subdivide old ones, or to consecrate new bishops without government approval. It had been especially awkward for his early British predecessors in India not to be allowed to change the *Book of Common Prayer* or even to change the requirement that Anglican ordinands be

44. D. A. Low, *Lion Rampant, op. cit.,* pp. 113-47.

45. VSA, 'Self Government for the Church of England in India,' *HF,* XLIII (I in new series), 12 (Dec. 1923), p. 449.

46. This subject is reviewed in G. W. O. Addleshaw, 'The Law and Constitution of the Church Overseas,' in *The Mission of the Anglican Communion,* ed. E. R. Morgan and R. Lloyd (London, 1948), pp. 74-98.

'learned in the Latin tongue.'[47] By denying the church liberty to control its institutional expansion, to adapt its work to Indian conditions via liturgical reforms, or to relax Greek, Latin, and English language proficiency requirements, the government had forced most bishops in India to conclude that their association with the state was a nuisance rather than a benefit.[48]

Some legal adjustments had been made over time to accommodate the growing variety of circumstances in which the Anglican church had to operate outside Britain. After the American War of Independence, a Parliamentary Act of 1786 had waived the required oath of obedience to the Crown as a prerequisite for consecration; but the need remained for a royal license and for consecrations to take place in London.[49] Bishops in India and elsewhere frequently challenged civil control over ecclesiastical affairs, but to no avail. Governor-General Bentinck limited the church's right to define the nature and degree of a chaplain's authority during the Calcutta bishopric of Daniel Wilson (bishop 1832-58), despite Wilson's protest against government interference in spiritual matters.[50]

The growth of Empire in non-Christian lands seriously challenged the statutory authority of Parliament over church law and structure. Church-state relations in religiously plural territories could never be established, as they had been in England, on a theory of society which conceived of the church and state as part of a unitary whole guided by God's supreme reason.[51] Government regulation of ecclesiastical affairs was generally expected in England, where the House of Commons was composed mainly of Anglicans and bishops sat in the House of Lords. But expectations were different in multi-religious foreign territories such as India, even before the development of parliamentary democracy. The British policy of non-interference in Indian religious affairs was the Raj's political answer to religious pluralism, but it did not apply to the Anglican church itself.

47. S. C. Neill, *Anglicanism, op. cit.,* p. 327.

48. S. C. Neill, *A History of Christianity in India: 1707-1858, op. cit.,* p. 266.

49. On the development of episcopacy in America, see F. V. Mills, *Bishops by Ballot: An Eighteenth Century Ecclesiastical Revolution* (New York, 1978).

50. T. E. Yates, *Venn and Victorian Bishops Abroad: The Missionary Policies of Henry Venn and Their Repercussions upon the Anglican Episcopate of the Colonial Period 1841-1872* (London: SPCK, 1978), pp. 28-29; M. E. Gibbs, *op. cit.,* p. 116.

51. The theory was expressed by Richard Hooker (c. 1554-1600) in his *Treatise on the Laws of Ecclesiastical Polity*. For a nineteenth-century defense of this theory, see W. H. Fremantle, *The World as the Subject of Redemption: Being an Attempt to Set Forth the Functions of the Church as Designed to Embrace the Whole Race of Mankind* (1883 Bampton Lectures) (London, 1885).

Future Anglican bishops would disagree with certain government policies, but most divines agreed with Azariah that Britain's expanding influence on the subcontinent was a providential historical development bringing India closer to her ultimate destiny of redemption in Christianity. Leaders of the Indian Anglican establishment played an important although still inadequately understood role in helping to define and to articulate the framework of religious assumptions which served to justify the imperialism of the Raj.[52] But most bishops still wished to free their church in India from Erastian shackles in order to execute better their own imperial Christian mission.

The tensions between church and state in British India came to a head over the issue of extending the episcopate itself. Pressure to establish more bishoprics in India grew steadily during the nineteenth century for three primary reasons. Firstly, ecclesiastical divisions in the British Empire were coterminous with civil divisions (as they had been in the Roman empire). Thus, steady territorial gains meant comparable increases in the size of each diocese and in the workload of each bishop. Secondly, the success of Anglican missionary societies in attracting Indian converts was steadily increasing the Church of England populations in most dioceses. By the end of the nineteenth century, Indian congregations outnumbered European and Eurasian congregations by a ratio of three to one.[53] And, thirdly, episcopal reforms initiated in England fundamentally altered the position of Anglican bishops both at home and abroad. This third, domestic English development had important implications for India that historians have generally overlooked.

By the 1840s, the Church of England had begun to take new interest in her rapidly proliferating 'daughters' overseas. Consecrations for overseas bishops were moved from the secluded Lambeth Palace Chapel to Westminster Abbey in 1847; a 'Colonial Bishoprics' Fund' was established in 1841 to endow thirty new dioceses in thirty years; and church facilities were markedly increased for training overseas recruits.[54]

Most important of all was a dramatic shift in the Church of England's understanding of the episcopate itself under the influence of the

---

52. See G. Studdert-Kennedy, *British Christians, Indian Nationalists and the Raj, op. cit.;* and 'Christian Imperialists of the Raj: Left, Right and Centre,' in *Making Imperial Mentalities: Socialisation and British Imperialism,* ed. J. A. Mangan (Manchester, 1990), pp. 127-43.

53. C. J. Grimes, *Towards an Indian Church, op. cit.,* p. 88.

54. W. F. France, *The Oversea Episcopate: Centenary History of the Colonial Bishoprics Fund, 1841-1941* (London, 1941); J. M. Campbell, *op. cit.,* pp. 113-15.

Tractarian movement. Many eighteenth-century bishops had been grossly negligent of their dioceses, spending most of each year in London at the House of Lords. Thanks largely to the influence and example of Bishop Samuel Wilberforce (1805-73), nineteenth-century bishops were increasingly preoccupied with performing spiritual duties within their dioceses. Wilberforce's diligent stewardship of his Oxford Diocese from 1845 virtually revolutionized the idea of episcopacy. By the end of the century, English bishops were less involved in London's political life and more involved in local affairs: synods of their clergy, diocesan conferences, and educational and missionary organizations. The newly responsible bishops also utilized episcopal visitations, rural deans, and their 'bishop's veto' (designed by the 1874 Public Worship Regulation Act to help keep 'popery' out of the Church of England) in order to strengthen their influence over diocesan affairs.

These changes led to an increased workload for every bishop, and to pressure for dividing larger dioceses into smaller units and creating suffragan bishops to assist with the bishop's work.[55] Assisted by the revival in 1870 of the Suffragan Bishops Act of 1534, the church formed ten new bishoprics in England between 1847 and 1910.[56]

Thus, diocesan growth in late nineteenth-century India paralleled similar growth in England, and bishops sent abroad carried with them a greater inner commitment to serve their diocesan clergy and laity. Confronted by overseas dioceses often as large as the United Kingdom itself, these more conscientious bishops felt added stress, which in turn increased the pressure to reduce the size of their jurisdictions by creating new bishoprics and by ordaining suffragan bishops, which was made possible for bishops in India by the Colonial Church Act of 1874.[57]

---

55. Owen Chadwick, *The Victorian Church: Part II* (London, 1970), p. 347.

56. Manchester, 1847; Truro, 1876; St. Alban's, 1877, Liverpool, 1880; Newcastle, 1882; Southwell, 1884; Wakefield, 1888; Bristol, 1897; Birmingham, 1905; Southwark, 1905. (Ripon was formed in 1836.) The movement for appointing suffragans began in 1870 when the dioceses of Canterbury and Lincoln appointed respectively the suffragan bishops of Dover and Nottingham. Today diocesan bishops are vastly outnumbered by suffragans in the two provinces of Canterbury and York.

57. Had the eighteenth-century conception of the episcopate survived into the nineteenth and twentieth centuries, it is likely that the pressure to multiply dioceses in India, as well as in England, would have been substantially reduced. Cecilia M. Ady, 'From the Restoration to the Present Day,' in *The Apostolic Ministry: Essays on the History and the Doctrine of Episcopacy*, ed. Kenneth E. Kirk (London, 1946), pp. 441-60; J. R. H. Moorman, 'The Anglican Bishop,' in *Bishops: But What Kind? Reflections on Episcopacy*, ed. Peter Moore (London, 1982), pp. 116-26; Owen Chadwick, *op. cit.*, pp. 342-47.

One aspect of the intensifying debate between Tractarians and evangelicals in mid-nineteenth-century England was the problematic question of the proper relation of overseas bishops to missionaries.[58] The high church view, articulated most forcefully by Bishop Wilberforce, held that the episcopate was such an essential foundation for the church that, without a bishop, a 'church' could not exist *(ubi episcopos, ibi ecclesia)*. From this position it followed that every mission should be led by a bishop. The contrary view, propagated by Henry Venn during his tenure as CMS General Secretary from 1841 to 1872, contended that the bishop was the 'crown' of the church, whose foundations had to be laid by a prior vanguard of missionaries and whose bishops should be chosen from among native converts.

In contrast to Wilberforce's position that bishops (inevitably, European) should lead missions to unevangelized lands, Venn believed that missionary evangelists should create self-governing, self-supporting, and self-propagating native churches which would, when sufficiently mature, appoint their own native bishops. Venn rejected the high church belief in 'missionary bishops' for unevangelized lands, claiming in an 1857 memorandum on the extension of the Indian episcopate that 'if a "missionary bishop" should be sent out . . . his *episcopal* functions must be for the most part laid aside.'[59] He argued that missionary bishops would become little more than European superintendents whose very presence further hindered 'euthanasia of mission,' the desirable process whereby missions voluntarily gave way to a native church under a native bishop. Both the evangelical CMS and the high church SPG favored the extension of the episcopate overseas, but their fundamental disagreement about the relation between evangelism and the ecclesiastical hierarchy underlay several key controversies in the late nineteenth century.

The missionary motive behind the proliferating episcopate in India posed the most serious challenge to the state's historic posture of religious neutrality; and the government's efforts to stymie episcopal growth dramatically reinforced a growing desire within the Indian episcopate for

58. The following discussion is based on an analysis by T. E. Yates, *op. cit.,* pp. 16-20, 99-109.

59. Quoted in *ibid.,* p. 105. On Venn, see also C. Peter Williams, *The Ideal of the Self-Governing Church: A Study of Victorian Missionary Strategy* (Leiden, 1990); Max Warren, ed., *To Apply the Gospel: Selections from the Writings of Henry Venn* (Grand Rapids, 1971); and Wilbert R. Shenk, *Henry Venn — Missionary Statesman* (Maryknoll, NY, 1983), and 'The Contribution of Henry Venn to Mission Thought,' *Anvil,* II, 1 (1985), pp. 25-42.

disestablishment.[60] The Indo-Anglican church was still legally bound to civil authorities, having no rights of self-government independent of those granted by the state and needing civil consent for most ecclesiastical acts. Bishop Wilberforce failed to obtain Parliament's approval for the creation of missionary bishops for native churches within existing dioceses in 1853. Parliament defeated a plan proposed in 1865 by Bishop Cotton of Calcutta (bishop 1858-66) for a new bishopric in northern India at Lahore, and rejected similar proposals again in 1871 and 1872. Nor would Parliament accept a scheme devised by Cotton's successor, Bishop Milman (bishop 1867-76), for enjoining the Crown, Parliament, and the Indian government to cooperate with bishops in England and India to create new dioceses.[61] As a result, all dioceses created in India after the 1833 Charter Act were brought into being by what Bishop Stephen Neill described as a series of 'subterfuges.'[62]

Between 1813 and 1929, the number of bishoprics in India, Burma, and Ceylon increased from one to fourteen.[63] The establishment of bish-

60. The Anglo-Catholic critique of state control over the church and its bishops helped to move Anglicanism beyond British territorial control in Africa. Wilberforce's conception of 'missionary bishops' as spiritually rather than legally ordained authorities inclined him to believe that the Anglican church should be free to create dioceses outside the dominions of the Crown. His advocacy of this position led to the first consecration in 1861 of a 'missionary bishop' to an area without a preexisting church or state support when C. F. Mackenzie was appointed 'Bishop of the Mission to the Tribes Dwelling in the Neighbourhood of the Lake Nyassa and the River Shire' in central Africa. The legal problems this presented the government were suggested by a letter from Bishop Gray, the Metropolitan of the Church of the Province of South Africa, who was responsible for Mackenzie's charge:

> The Foreign Office is at present in a flutter about the possibility of issuing a licence without defining the limits of the Central African Diocese. They have referred the question to the Law Officers!! Shall I name the Mountains of the Moon? (Quoted in S. C. Neill, *Anglicanism, op. cit.,* p. 304)

Mackenzie's consecration established an important precedent in the process of defining the legal position of Anglican dioceses outside British territories. The problem was settled during a protracted battle in the 1860s over the heresy trial and excommunication of the first Bishop of Natal, J. W. Colenso, during which the Church of England lost coercive jurisdiction over churches in self-governing colonies.

61. J. Richter, *A History of Missions in India, op. cit.,* p. 274; C. J. Grimes, *Towards an Indian Church, op. cit.,* pp. 83-84; M. E. Gibbs, *op. cit.,* p. 280; J. M. Campbell, *op. cit.,* p. 308.

62. S. C. Neill, *Anglicanism, op. cit.,* p. 327.

63. Detailed discussions of episcopal extension in India may be found in: W. F. France, *The Oversea Episcopate, op. cit.;* J. Richter, *A History of Missions in India, op. cit.,* pp. 273-80; C. J. Grimes, *Towards an Indian Church, op. cit.,* pp. 83-92; E. J. Palmer, 'The Angli-

oprics in Madras (1835) and Bombay (1837) by the 1833 Charter Renewal Act, and in Australia (1836) and Colombo (1845), reduced the original Calcutta Diocese to a more manageable size. But the annexation of the Punjab, the Central Provinces, Oudh, and Burma left the Bishop of Calcutta with an even larger diocese than Middleton had possessed originally in 1813. The church was in a double bind: the geographical scope of its jurisdiction grew with the expansion of empire, but imperial authorities were limiting its ability to exercise that jurisdiction.

To cope with increasing demands for episcopal oversight, the church devised new ways to appoint bishops without an Act of Parliament. It procured a legal decision permitting new, privately endowed dioceses to be established in territories lying outside East India Company rule at the time of the 1833 Act — leading to the creation in 1877 of new dioceses in Rangoon (for Burmese territories annexed after 1833) and Lahore (for Delhi, the Punjab, the North-West Frontier, Kashmir and Baluchistan, and Sindh, which was transferred from the Bombay Diocese).[64] A see was also created for Travancore and Cochin in 1879 on the basis of the Jerusalem Bishopric Act of 1841,[65] which provided legal precedent for the consecration of either British or foreign subjects as Anglican bishops outside the limits of British rule. Other legal maneuvers permitted the reorganization of two assistant bishoprics in Madras (formed in 1877) into the single Diocese of Tinnevelly/Madura in 1896, and the subdivision of the Calcutta Diocese into the Dioceses of Chota Nagpur (1890), Lucknow (1893), Nagpur (1902), and Assam (1915). Finally, the Dornakal and Nasik Dioceses were established in 1912 and 1929 to reduce the geographical areas under the Bishops of Madras and Bombay.

By raising private endowments to fund the new dioceses, discovering legal loopholes, and, occasionally, disregarding the law completely, the church managed to increase its episcopal presence to what it regarded as a more acceptable but still inadequate level. Because of this improvisational process, the status of bishops in India, Burma, and Ceylon became one of

can Communion: India,' in *op. cit.*, pp. 202-3; and H. Whitehead, *Indian Problems in Religion, Education, Politics, op. cit.*, pp. 100-102. Excellent documentation may also be found in the papers of M. E. Gibbs, IOR Neg 7667, I Gen. part a, IOL, London.

64. M. E. Gibbs, *op. cit.*, p. 280.

65. Formally, the Bishops in Foreign Countries Act, which provided for the establishment of a joint bishopric whose incumbent was appointed alternately by the Crowns of England and Prussia. Interestingly, an Arab was not appointed to the Jerusalem bishopric until the 1970s. 'The Jerusalem Bishopric,' seminar given by P. Urwin, Oxford, 5 May 1987.

the most 'irregular' of any church in the world. By 1924, seven bishops were appointed by royal letters patent and paid either entirely by the government or by the government from endowment funds raised in India and England; the Bishop of Travancore and Cochin was appointed by the Archbishop of Canterbury and paid by the CMS; the Bishop of Chota Nagpur was appointed by the Metropolitan and paid by the SPG; the Bishop of Tinnevelly and Madura was appointed by the Bishop of Madras with the approval of the Metropolitan and paid by the CMS, the SPG, and private endowments; the Bishop of Dornakal was appointed by the Bishop of Madras with the approval of the Metropolitan and paid entirely from endowments; the Bishop of Colombo was appointed by a Diocesan Synod and paid by endowments.[66] Bishop Henry Whitehead concluded in 1924 that, 'to the legal mind the whole position of the Church of England in India (is) utterly chaotic and impossible,'[67] and Azariah described the situation as 'hopeless confusion.'[68] Even a later church historian was driven to exclaim: 'For incredible muddle, complexity and anomaly has it ever had a parallel in any Church in Christendom?'[69]

The picture that emerges from this history is hardly the simplistic one of an established church marching triumphantly alongside a growing and confident empire. It is rather that of an established but overstretched church struggling to find a place in the expanding empire by ingenious and, often, illegal schemes designed to minimize opposition from the imperial government.

Of course, new bishoprics would not have been allowed to multiply in India, Burma, and Ceylon without some degree of tacit consent or, as Azariah expressed it, 'common sense, mutual goodwill and obligations of fellowship'[70] on the part of both civil and ecclesiastical sectors. As Whitehead observed later:

> The Church in India has been obliged to step over the legal fences by which it is theoretically restricted. [But] . . . the system has worked well

66. As summarized by Henry Whitehead, *Indian Problems in Religion, Education, Politics, op. cit.,* p. 90. Among other legal problems Whitehead noted that, according to letters patent, Commissioners Delegate were to be chosen from a body that no longer existed and the clergy were to be disciplined by officials who no longer existed.

67. *Ibid.,* p. 91.

68. VSA, 'Self Government for the Church of England in India,' in *op. cit.,* pp. 447-48.

69. Grimes, *Towards an Indian Church, op. cit.,* p. 103.

70. *Ibid.*

because all parties have been anxious to make it work. . . . It has been said that this disregard of the law 'debauches the consciences' of the bishops and clergy. Perhaps I am no fit judge on this point, as I worked the system as a bishop for twenty-three years without scruple. But as nobody wants the law to be strictly observed, neither the members of the Church, nor the Government of India, nor the Crown nor the Houses of Parliament. . . . I cannot think that anyone's conscience has been a bit the worse for treating it as a dead letter.[71]

The tacit consent between church and state to treat the law as a 'dead letter' did permit expansion of a kind of Indo-Anglicanism in South Asia, but not without continuing opposition from government officials that was powerful enough to persuade the church in India to break its ties with the state altogether in the first decades of the 1900s. Once respect for the existing law had become thoroughly eroded, there seemed little reason for continuing the semblance of a specious 'Establishment.'

The break began with the development of a system of synodical government which laid the groundwork for church independence in 1930. An informal meeting of bishops in Bombay in 1863 had led to more formal gatherings in 1873 and 1877 and to the first Episcopal Synod in 1883. The bishops passed their first resolution indicating their desire to establish a synodical system in 1877.[72] The Episcopal Synod then played an increasingly important role in the development of the Indo-Anglican church; by 1910, it initiated plans for the establishment of a Provincial Synod of bishops, priests, and laymen.

Once again, it was western clerics who accelerated the path to independence for the Indian church. New impetus came for disestablishment in 1902, when Bishop Reginald S. Copleston (c. 1845-1925) moved from Colombo to the Metropolitan see of Calcutta. During his tenure as Bishop of Colombo (1875-1902), Copleston had overseen the disestablishment of the Anglican church in Ceylon in 1886, and he was eager to direct the church in India towards the same goal.[73] His last Episcopal Synod as Metropolitan (and Azariah's first as bishop), in December 1912-January 1913, has been described as 'one of the most momentous meetings in its history.'[74] The

---

71. Henry Whitehead, *Indian Problems in Religion, Education, Politics, op. cit.,* pp. 100-101.

72. *Minutes of the Episcopal Synod of the Province of India and Ceylon, 1863-1908* (Calcutta, 1911), res. 7, p. 14.

73. M. E. Gibbs, *op. cit.,* pp. 262-77.

74. *Ibid.,* p. 339.

bishops specified that the Provincial Synod's members would henceforth be elected by diocesan councils, which already existed in larger and older dioceses but were now also to be established in newer and smaller dioceses. Synodical government was to provide the church with greater autonomy from the state, which the bishops chided for slowness in establishing new dioceses, appointing new bishops and adapting to Indian circumstances. 'We should go steadily forward with our plans for Synodical Government, and if Disestablishment comes, let it come,' wrote the Bishop of Madras on 2 January 1913.[75]

The plans were also welcomed by growing numbers of Indian Christians who sought a more unified and dignified identity than was afforded by their continued self-identification as 'SPG Christians' or 'CMS Christians.' Despite legal notification that an Act of Parliament would be needed, the Episcopal Synod resolved in March 1915 to move ahead to build on 'that measure of freedom in their administration which has characterized their work in the past' and to establish advisory diocesan and provincial councils until such time as they could achieve greater powers of self-government. The legal barriers were lowered in 1919 when Parliament passed an Enabling Act which gave the Church of England greater control over its own affairs, and opened the way for ecclesiastical structures in India to gain freedom from their burdensome dependence on the state.[76]

Azariah's appointment to the Dornakal Diocese provides an excellent example of how the church deliberately circumvented civil restrictions on its growth. The complex negotiations and calculated steps leading up to Azariah's consecration were led by the brilliant and fascinating figure of Bishop Henry Whitehead. He generated vociferous opposition, but was able to engineer a decisive turning point in the development of an independent and indigenous Indo-Anglican church.

Bishop Henry Whitehead as Bridge Builder

The success of the missionary enterprise among untouchable and low-caste groups created a massive demographic shift in the Indian church's membership during the nineteenth century. Indian Christian congrega-

---

75. Ms. 2966: 223, Palmer Papers, Lambeth Palace Library, London.
76. M. E. Gibbs, *op. cit.,* p. 351; *Proceedings of the Meeting of the Provincial Council of the Church of the Province of India, Burma and Ceylon,* Second Session held at Calcutta, Jan. 28-Feb. 3, 1926, Record of Decisions, pp. 41-43, BHA, Calcutta.

tions had always vastly outnumbered European and Eurasian congregations: this trend accelerated by the century's end. Anglican bishops could
not plausibly deny episcopal rank or supervision to Indian converts, and
the generally accepted (if never fully realized) division between an ecclesiastical establishment for Europeans and Eurasians on the one hand and
missionary societies for native converts on the other was no longer even
theoretically tenable. The creation of the Dornakal Diocese under the
leadership of Bishop Azariah bridged this gap even if it did not end all the
controversy.

The Dornakal Diocese was established to provide episcopal oversight
for some Telugu-speaking regions of the northern Madras Presidency and
the southeast corner of the Nizam's Dominions. Conversion movements
among untouchable groups in these areas had brought over a million people into Christian churches of various denominations during the last
three decades of the nineteenth century. This rapid growth continued in the
twentieth century, increasing the total Indo-Anglican population in Telugu
country tenfold — from 22,356 in 1894 to 225,080 in 1940.[77]

By the turn of the century, the new Bishop of Madras, Henry Whitehead (1853-1947), recognized his need for assistance in overseeing the expanding Telugu churches and identified Azariah as the man for the job.
Whitehead had been a fellow and tutor of Trinity College, Oxford, and
was the brother of the famed philosopher Alfred North Whitehead.[78] Hav-

---

77. *DDM,* V, 1 (Jan. 1928), p. 7; VSA, *A Charge Delivered at Bezwada on Wednesday,
October 29th, 1941* (Dornakal: Mission Press, 1941), p. 4; S. C. Neill, *The Story of the Christian Church in India and Pakistan, op. cit.,* pp. 117-18.

78. Henry Whitehead's papers and correspondence were destroyed after his
death, chiefly because of the Church Missionary Society's failure to recognize their importance (letter from his nearest living family relation, Barbara Holmes, 19 Oct. 1986).
Nor were his papers kept by the Oxford Mission in Calcutta (letters from the Mission's
General Secretary, Graham P. Newell, 31 Oct. 1985, and from the Rt. Rev. J. D. Blair, 15
Nov. 1985), by the Madras Diocese (apart from printed quarterly and monthly letters
contained in an incomplete set of the diocesan magazines in the diocesan headquarters), or by Trinity College. (Indeed, a signed copy of Whitehead's book *Indian Problems,*
which had been donated by Whitehead to his college library and which still contained
his personal letter to the Principal, was found for sale at an Oxford bookshop during
the course of this research.) Henry Whitehead's papers were important not only for
their descriptions of Christian activity in Bengal and Madras during the period from
1883 to 1922, but also for their valuable ethnographic observations such as those contained in his book *The Village Gods of South India.*

Victor Lowe, the biographer of Alfred North Whitehead, was also unable to lo-
cate the letters between Henry Whitehead and his brother and concluded that they
had been destroyed (letter from V. Lowe, 10 June 1985). Nor were later Bishops of Ma-

ing received top degrees in both classics and mathematics at Trinity, Henry Whitehead began his career as a lecturer at Oxford in the former subject from 1878 to 1883. He was ordained to the priesthood in 1879[79] through the influence of the Tractarian movement whose mentor, John Henry Newman, made annual visits to the college as an honorary fellow and met Whitehead on several occasions. The Oxford Mission to Calcutta was founded in 1879 and sent university men to work among Indian students and educated populations by providing boys' schools and hostels, along the lines of the Cambridge Mission to Delhi. The Oxford Mission began as a religious brotherhood of four university graduates who established a boarding school for Indian Christian boys in Calcutta and, by the century's end, a successful hostel for non-Christian students.[80]

Whitehead served as the mission's Honorary Secretary in Oxford[81] until 1883 when he offered himself to the Metropolitan, Edward R. Johnson, for the Calcutta mission. Johnson persuaded him to accept, instead, the 'extraordinarily important job' of Principal of Bishop's College in Calcutta. After a traumatic parting from his disapproving father, Whitehead voyaged to Calcutta, where he experienced the further trauma of discover-

dras, Michael Hollis and Lesslie Newbigin, aware of the existence of any collections of Henry Whitehead's papers (letter from Hollis to V. Lowe, 25 April 1969; interview with author, 7 Sept. 1984). One of the few scholars privileged to examine Whitehead's private papers and to interview his wife Isabel was Bengt Sundkler of Uppsala University, Sweden, to whom I am deeply indebted for allowing me to study his notes and for his valuable consultation. Sundkler compiled a sizable bibliography of Whitehead's writings in his book *Church of South India, op. cit.,* p. 439. The listing of Henry Whitehead's published writings and addresses in the bibliography of this book, taken in conjunction with the sixteen items in Sundkler's bibliography, may represent only part of Whitehead's total life's output but comprise together the largest such bibliography compiled to date.

Apart from autobiographical details provided in his own writings (especially his 'Pastoral Letter' and 'Diary,' published in the Madras diocesan magazines and his book *Indian Problems*), there is very little biographical information available on Henry Whitehead. Among the best sources are George Longridge, *A History of the Oxford Mission to Calcutta,* 2nd ed. (London, 1910); Arthur H. B. Brittain, ed., *The Secunderabad Magazine: A Record of Church Work in an Indian Parish,* III, June 1900-April 1901 (Madras, 1901), p. 30; *MDR,* XIV, 1 (Jan. 1900), p. 2; Bengt Sundkler, *Church of South India, op. cit.;* M. E. Gibbs, *op. cit.;* 'The Rt. Rev. Bishop Whitehead,' *HF,* XLII, 6 (June 1922), pp. 216-17.

79. According to all sources except *MDR,* XIV, 1 (Jan. 1900), p. 2, which puts his ordination in 1880.

80. J. Richter, *A History of Missions in India, op. cit.,* p. 325.

81. *The Oxford Mission to Calcutta,* First Annual Report: Michaelmas 1880, Oxford.

ing only one student enrolled for instruction. Whitehead raised the enrollment to forty during the next decade,[82] joined the Oxford Brotherhood in 1890, was appointed Superior of the Oxford Mission in 1891, and became Bishop of Madras in 1899, where he served until his retirement to England in 1922.

Whitehead had been frustrated by his lack of missionary success during sixteen years in Calcutta. The long-range strategy of the Oxford Mission was to convert the upper classes, not so much by direct evangelism as by exposure to the fruits of Christian civilization through western education. At the annual meeting of the Oxford Mission to Calcutta held at Trinity College in 1890, Whitehead explained that the mission's strategy was to allow modern western education slowly to undermine Hinduism among the educated classes in Bengal. The mission not only ran hostels; it initiated special lectures and published a student journal called the *Epiphany,* which attracted a readership of perhaps ten thousand by the end of the decade.[83] Whitehead explained that:

> I do not feel in the slightest degree anxious or nervous simply because we do not produce any immediate results in the way of conversion, or because the results are slow. . . . I feel perfectly sure that, if we only go to work faithfully and patiently, while education undermines Hindooism and leaves us a clear field, in the end Christian truth will win its way.[84]

But he eventually lost patience after his mission had failed to produce more than a handful of conversions to Christianity by the turn of the century. Western education seemed to be producing agnostics by destroying 'those religious feelings which would lead men to seek after any religious truth whatever,' and producing a state of 'religious paralysis and religious indifference.'[85] In the Oxford Mission's Annual Report for 1897, Whitehead wrote: 'it cannot be said that the general body of educated

82. Whitehead taught all of his students to play cricket, one of his proudest accomplishments. B. Sundkler's interview with Isabel Whitehead, Sept. 1947, Reading. Sundkler Collection, Uppsala.

83. This 1899 estimate was based on a circulation figure of five thousand, plus readership gained because, the mission claimed, 'the paper circulates to families, and to students' clubs, so that for every person who has a copy of the *Epiphany* sent him, probably some two or three at the very least will read it every week. A circulation, therefore, of about five thousand represents a body of something like ten thousand readers every week.' *The Oxford Mission to Calcutta: Annual Report,* 1899, pp. 19-20.

84. *The Oxford Mission to Calcutta: Annual Report,* 1890, pp. 29-30.

85. *The Oxford Mission to Calcutta: Annual Report,* 1896, p. 17.

Hindus are any nearer to Christianity now than they appear to have been thirty or forty years ago . . . [and] there are scarcely any signs as yet that the educated classes, as a whole, are moving in the direction of Christianity. In many respects they seem to be moving away from it.'[86]

Yet Whitehead could not help but note that Christianity had most successfully taken root, and was continuing to spread at an unexpectedly rapid rate, among untouchables and low-castes in rural India. He began to believe that Christian missionary societies should invest more of their resources where they would count — in the work among the very rural, economically disadvantaged populations where the harvest was being reaped. With his consecration as Bishop of Madras, Whitehead changed course completely and became a leading advocate of this 'mass movement' work.[87]

Whitehead argued that the lower classes were 'craving for life' denied them by 'the tyranny and oppression of a thousand years,' and that missionaries were the first people to treat India's outcastes 'as human beings.'[88] Western missionaries should abandon their elitist, top-down strategies and should adopt a new bottom-up strategy for converting India. The hostile educated classes might even be led to reconsider the claims of the Christian faith if this strategy proved successful. In a 1906 issue of his diocesan magazine, he wrote:

> For the last century, the Brahmans, the educated classes and the caste people among the Hindus, have had the gospel preached to them all over India in every form that the ingenuity of missionaries can devise, and, as a body, they have turned a deaf ear to it. No doubt, Christian teaching has greatly influenced their ideas and moral standards, but to Christianity itself they have been profoundly indifferent. But they will not and cannot remain indifferent to the conversion of four million pariahs to Christianity, and their elevation from a state of hopeless degradation to a position of power and influence.[89]

Rapid church growth in the Telugu districts of the Madras diocese particularly caught the bishop's attention. The successful IMS mission in Dornakal attracted Bishop Whitehead to Dornakal in 1906 to baptize 46

---

86. George Longridge, *op. cit.,* p. 146.

87. See especially H. Whitehead, *Our Mission Policy in India* (Madras, 1907).

88. H. Whitehead, *Work among Indian Outcastes* (London, 1912), p. 4.

89. H. Whitehead, 'The Future of Christianity in India,' *MDM,* I, 11 (Nov. 1906), p. 529.

new IMS converts. On arrival, he discovered 300 more catechumens, mainly of outcaste Mala background, also under instruction for baptism. Henceforth, Whitehead and his wife became active supporters of the IMS mission, offering financial help for training new converts and for supporting missionaries.[90]

When Azariah formally joined the mission in 1909, there were approximately 30,000 Indian Christians associated with the Indo-Anglican church in Telugu regions (which included Dornakal), with an increase of between 2,000 and 3,000 converts per year.[91] Whitehead's prediction of 1908, that the Telugu church could soon expect as many as 10,000 people per year seeking baptism,[92] was realized and exceeded in Azariah's lifetime. In 1925 alone there were 17,000 new converts to the church.[93]

New congregations spread over a very large area, and the duty of traveling for confirmations rapidly became burdensome for Whitehead:

> I was on tour from the end of September last year till the middle of March this year [he wrote in May 1909] and am still sadly behind hand with my confirmations in the Telugu country. If I can carry out my present programme I shall have been 11 months on tour by next Christmas . . . and still the work will be in arrears.[94]

At the Episcopal Synod of January 1908, Whitehead initiated procedures to appoint an assistant bishop specifically for missionary work in Telugu districts.[95] By the close of the year, the bishop made preliminary arrangements for a salary and asked Metropolitan Copleston (Metropolitan, 1902-13) to obtain government approval for appointing an assistant bishop, either European or Indian.[96]

90. Minutes for 9 July 1906, 27 Jan. 1908, 2 April 1908 (in which the IMS refused the suggestion of Mrs. Whitehead to establish a branch of the mission in Madras), 6 June 1908, 14 July 1909, in *PIMS,* IMSA.

91. Government of India, Department of Education, Ecclesiastical, No. 7 to the Secretary of State for India, 21 Sept. 1911; and A. G. Cardew, Government of Madras to the Home Department, Government of India, No. 69, 4 Oct. 1909, both in 5: 1/2, Dornakal, MACIPBC. Also, Nos. 66-67, Nov. 1909, GOI, HDP, IOL.

92. *MTDM*, III, 3 (March 1908), pp. 80-81.

93. *East Anglican Daily Times,* 3 May 1927, quoted in *Birth Centenary of Bishop Azariah, op. cit.,* p. 20.

94. Whitehead to Copleston, 20 May 1909, 5: 1/1, Dornakal, MACIPBC.

95. The Synod approved his intention to appoint an assistant, on the understanding that the assistant bishop would not be a voting member of the Synod. *Minutes of the Episcopal Synod of the Province of India and Ceylon, 1863-1908, op. cit.,* Res. 17, p. 79.

96. Whitehead to Copleston, 17 Nov. 1908, 5: 1/1, Dornakal, MACIPBC.

Copleston, another Oxford don with decidedly high church views, proved a willing collaborator with Whitehead. Both men had been criticized by the CMS for their 'ritualism': Copleston during his earlier tenure as Bishop of Colombo and Whitehead shortly after his arrival in Madras in 1899.[97] Both men's experiences in South Asia moderated their strict Anglo-Catholic opinions, and both developed extremely cordial relations with the CMS and the evangelical wing of the church. Whitehead's transformation from loyal Tractarian to ardent ecumenist and promoter of mass evangelism illustrates the general rule that 'the situation in the mission field tends to have a broadening effect upon the individual missionary.'[98]

Both Copleston and Whitehead became avid students of Indian culture: Copleston as the leading western authority of his generation on Buddhism who was able to preach in Tamil, Hindustani, and Bengali by the end of his tenure as Metropolitan; Whitehead as an expert in South Indian folk religion who was similarly well versed in the relevant vernaculars.[99] Both favored distancing the church from the state by instituting synodical government, and both shared a Tractarian-inspired enthusiasm for the appointment of a missionary bishop to the Telugu regions of the Madras Presidency and Hyderabad State.

Private correspondence reveals that Whitehead decided before April 1909 to appoint Azariah to the post,[100] and that Whitehead's energetic

97. T. Walker to Durant, 1 April 1901; *Minutes of the Tinnevelly CMS Missionary Conference*, 6 April 1901; H. Schaffter to Durant, 10 April 1901; T. Walker to Durant, 4 April 1901; all in Sundkler Collection, Uppsala, Sweden.

98. B. Sundkler, *Church of South India, op. cit.*, p. 52. See also pp. 50-60. Whitehead's metamorphosis would seem to illustrate G. A. Oddie's observation that circumstances and developments in India, rather than social and educational backgrounds in the West, were the most important factors contributing to British missionary involvement in Indian social reform. G. A. Oddie, *Social Protest in India, op. cit.*, pp. 9-17. See also Brian Stanley, 'The Reshaping of Christian Tradition: Western Denominational Identity in a Non-Western Context,' in *Unity and Diversity in the Church*, ed. R. N. Swanson (Oxford, 1996), pp. 399-426.

99. Copleston's most famous work, *Buddhism Primitive and Present in Magadha and in Ceylon* (London, 1st ed., 1892; 2nd ed., 1908), is still regarded as a competent textbook by scholars today, as is Whitehead's *Village Gods of South India* (1st ed., London and New York, 1916; 2nd ed., Calcutta, 1921; republished in Delhi, 1976, and New York, 1980).

100. Correspondence between Whitehead and the Metropolitan in 1909 indicates that Azariah had already been discussed and approved privately as the candidate for the office. Copleston assured Whitehead in May that he approved of 'the general plan, the person, and the ultimate hope' proposed by Whitehead. Whitehead to Copleston, 20 May 1909, 5: 1/1, Dornakal, MACIPBC.

wife Isabel was almost certainly originally responsible for identifying Azariah as a potential bishop and for persuading her husband to pursue the idea.[101] The bishop kept his decision a secret, particularly from Azariah, who had not yet begun his work in the IMS Dornakal mission. If Azariah were to learn of his imminent appointment before his arrival in Dornakal, Whitehead wrote to John Mott in April 1909, this would

> to a very great extent take the edge off the sacrifice he is making [and would] give envious people a handle for saying, what is entirely untrue, that he knew all along before he made his offer to the IMS that he was selected for the bishopric, and that he offered himself for the mission in order to qualify for the episcopate.[102]

When Azariah left the YMCA for Dornakal, neither he nor his colleagues, with the exception of Whitehead, Copleston, and John Mott, knew of Whitehead's secret plans. Bishop Whitehead did not reveal his cards until the night before Azariah's ordination as deacon on 29 June 1909, when he informed Azariah of his intention to make him a bishop. This revelation set off a three-year storm of controversy. It would take all of his vision and skills of leadership to negotiate the many issues that threatened to block Azariah's promotion.

The British Debate over Azariah's Consecration

Protests against Whitehead's plan came for different reasons from the church hierarchy led by the Metropolitan, from the Governments of Madras and India, from both Anglican and nonconformist missionaries, and from Indian Christians themselves. The bishop responded by modifying but not abandoning his plan.

101. B. Sundkler's interview with Isabel Whitehead, Sept. 1947, Reading. Sundkler Collection, Uppsala. *Mrs. Whitehead's Work — An Appreciation,* by an anonymous author, p. 4, in Whitehead Collection, County Donegal, Ireland. (I am grateful to Barbara Holmes for granting me access to what remains of the family's papers.) Little information is available on Mrs. Whitehead apart from secondary descriptions of her artistic and social service interests in biographies of Azariah. (She was a painter, an enthusiastic hostess, President of the YWCA, and founder of the Social Service League in Madras). Henry Whitehead gave credit to his wife for Azariah's appointment during a tour of the Dornakal Diocese after his 1922 retirement from Madras. See G. Abraham to Metropolitan, 24 June 1935, 422: 19A, D Series, USPG.
102. H. Whitehead to J. Mott, 26 April 1909, 1: 99/1740, Mott Papers, YDS.

The Metropolitan objected to Whitehead's 1908 proposal to appoint an Indian as an assistant without a seat in the Synod on the grounds that it was too timid and would not grant the first Indian bishop enough authority. The first Indian bishop should have independent jurisdiction over a diocese of his own, Copleston protested, rather than be appointed as subordinate to an Englishman in 'a half-hearted act of trust.'[103] Whitehead agreed that his plan was only 'a first step towards a higher ideal,' but reassured the Metropolitan that the new assistant would be given 'very large and independent functions of government and responsibility.' Whitehead claimed that he needed help in the Telugu districts immediately and feared a possible legal rejection if they attempted to establish a new diocesan bishopric in the Madras Presidency. The Metropolitan was disappointed that Whitehead was unwilling to pursue the 'fuller method' and reiterated that 'a tentative act of trust in our Indian brethren does not meet my views.'[104] Later Copleston wrote to the CMS:

> it is of the utmost importance that the first indigenous Bishop should stand on no lower level than his foreign colleagues. And so I have desired that he should have a Diocese of his own, and a seat in the Synod among the rest.[105]

Copleston also worried that Whitehead's proposal to establish an Indian Bishopric Fund to support future Indian bishops would create undesirable racial distinctions in the church:

> If you at all understand my aims — the aims of my life — for the Indian Church, you cannot expect that I should feel kindly towards any scheme for an 'Indian Bishopric Fund.' Such an institution would be a definite recognition of race distinction; not less so than one from which Indians should be excluded. The Christian principle, as I understand it, is not that of the fair balance of races, or — as the politicians have it, 'Communities,' but that of the indifference of race.[106]

Foreshadowing debates over minority preferences that have dominated Indian, not to mention American, politics for much of this century,

103. Whitehead to Copleston, 20 May 1909, 5: 1/1, Dornakal, MACIPBC.
104. Copleston to Whitehead, 26 May 1909, *ibid.*
105. Copleston to C. E. C. Bardsley, St. John Baptist's Day, 1912, 5: 1/2, Dornakal, MACIPBC.
106. Copleston to Whitehead, 26 May 1909, 5: 1/1, Dornakal, MACIPBC. See also Whitehead to Copleston, 20 May 1909, 5: 1/1, Dornakal, MACIPBC.

Copleston placed his church squarely on the side of those who believed that racially based preferences would worsen rather than heal racial divisions.

Nevertheless, Whitehead gained Copleston's consent to present to the Governments of Madras and India a plan containing the following provisions: (1) that an assistant bishop be appointed without independent jurisdiction under an oath of allegiance to the Bishop of Madras and to the Metropolitan, (2) that the new assistant bishop's salary be provided by a Diocesan Fund based on voluntary contributions with no state revenues, and (3) that an Indian priest could be appointed to the post basically to relieve the diocesan bishop of most missionary work.[107]

With this compromise in hand, the bishops then sought government authority to act. In January of 1910, the Governments of Madras and India agreed to all the provisions, but insisted upon two safeguards: (1) that the Archdeacon of Madras rather than the assistant bishop be in charge of the diocese in the bishop's absence, and (2) that the assistant bishop be commissioned under royal license by the Archbishop of Canterbury, even if consecrated in India.[108] In the first instance, the Governments of India and Madras wanted to prevent the possibility of an Indian national from assuming, even temporarily, the duties of a Presidency bishop or from having authority over chaplains during the bishop's absence. Government officials had apparently not forgotten the 'white mutiny' over the Ilbert Bill in 1883, and were still scared by the idea that an Indian should ever have authority over Englishmen.[109] In the second instance, the Governments of India and Madras wanted to restrict the freedom of the Metropolitan and the bishops in India to consecrate future bishops without obtaining necessary permission from the state.

This was not the first time that government officials had thwarted the Metropolitan's ambition to appoint bishops independently. Copleston had previously clashed with the Government of India over episcopal freedom in 1905, when he sought to fill vacancies to the sees of Chota Nagpur and Travancore/Cochin without the usual commission from the Archbishop of Canterbury under the royal license. The government insisted that Copleston and the Indian bishops delay their proceedings until the usual permission had been obtained. The civil authorities

107. Whitehead to Copleston, 5 July 1909, *ibid.*
108. Whitehead to Copleston, 11 Jan. 1910, with enclosure: Government of Madras, Ecclesiastical Department Memo No. 525-1, 3 Jan. 1910, *ibid.*
109. Edwin Hirschmann, *The 'White' Mutiny: The Ilbert Bill Crisis in India and the Genesis of the Indian National Congress* (New Delhi, 1980).

suspected, quite rightly, that the Metropolitan was trying to bypass certain aspects of state control in order to gain greater freedom from lay control for the church in India. A Minute from the Judicial and Public Department of 7 December 1905 expressed the fear that, if the Metropolitan and his bishops used such liberty to increase the number of bishoprics in India without government consent, this 'might give rise to serious misapprehensions in the minds of the people of India.'[110] Bearing this earlier conflict in mind, the Indian government insisted that Copleston and Whitehead obtain the formal commission to consecrate Azariah issued under royal license by the Archbishop of Canterbury,[111] and the bishops consented to the government's stipulations.

Whitehead had originally hoped to consecrate Azariah in early 1910, but now delays seemed inevitable. The Metropolitan received complaints from unnamed clergymen in Madras that Azariah, as a newly ordained priest, would be too inexperienced for the job of bishop. Copleston seemed to hesitate at this juncture and, when Azariah accepted his invitation to the 1910 World Missionary Conference in Edinburgh, the Metropolitan advised that the consecration be delayed until Azariah gained more practical experience as a priest in Dornakal.[112]

The bishops used the resulting hiatus, not to retreat, but rather to fortify and even to radicalize their position. The Episcopal Synod met at Allahabad in November 1910 and challenged the government by reversing its opinion of 1908 and resolving that a fully independent diocesan bishopric should be founded in Telugu country.[113] Knowing that he would never gain the necessary Parliamentary consent to establish this new diocese, Whitehead resorted to an arrangement, used also in Chota Nagpur and Tinnevelly, which he freely admitted was 'makeshift' and 'legally unsound.'[114] He obtained permission from the Crown to appoint an assistant bishop but, under the authority of the Synod, authorized Azariah to exercise autonomous episcopal oversight within an independent diocese. Azariah would therefore be an assistant bishop in

---

110. 'Consecration of Indian Bishops,' Minute, 7 Dec. 1905, 3860, J&P, IOL.

111. H. C. Woodman (Additional Deputy Secretary to the Government of India, Home Department) to the Chief Secretary to the Government of Madras, No. 510, 27 Nov. 1909, GOI, HDP, IOL.

112. Copleston to Whitehead, 31 Jan. 1910, 5: 1/2, Dornakal, MACIPBC.

113. Resolution 11, *Minutes of the Episcopal Synod held at Calcutta from 1910-1936*, p. 4, BHA, Calcutta; Copleston to Whitehead, 7 July 1911, 5: 1/2, Dornakal, MACIPBC; M. E. Gibbs, *op. cit.*, pp. 342-43.

114. Whitehead, *Indian Problems, op. cit.*, pp. 100-101.

the eyes of the government, but a diocesan bishop in the eyes of the church, with fully independent jurisdiction and voting membership in the Episcopal Synod. Only when the Church of England in India was disestablished in 1930 would Azariah gain legal status as a diocesan bishop. Until then, he was technically breaking the law by performing the full duties of his office.

Other new difficulties still stood in the way of final government permission to appoint an Indian bishop. A strong objection to Azariah was voiced in the London-based India Council by the conservative Sir James Thomson.[115] He claimed that Indian Christians were generally incompetent and that no native priest was capable of handling a bishop's responsibility:

> The Bishop of Madras seems to be taking example by our larger opening of the door to native talent in civil administration: [but] the material is different.[116]

Thomson warned that Whitehead was giving Azariah too much authority and that the government should reserve the right to appeal the assistant bishop's orders. The Council's subsequent consultation with a legal advisor concluded that such a safeguard would be unnecessary, but Thomson remained dissatisfied and reaffirmed the need 'to help Bishop Whitehead to safeguard himself and his people.'[117] Thomson also warned that Azariah would have difficulty maintaining his 'rank' with British missionaries in South India:

> I doubt if I should find one [missionary] who would support this proposal of the Bishop's to have a native priest entrusted with a Bishop's work.

115. Thomson was educated at Aberdeen University, was appointed to the ICS after the 1869 examination, and served in several posts in Madras, Godavari, and Travancore/Cochin until his retirement in 1906. He became a member of the Council of India in 1908, where he and Lee-Warner were considered the most conservative members. John Morley concluded that Thomson was 'no good at all.' See Stanley Wolpert, *Morley and India: 1906-1910* (Berkeley, 1967), pp. 152, 268.

116. 'Proposal to appoint an Assistant Bishop in Madras: Note of dissent by Sir James Thomson,' 8 May 1912, 2341, J&P, IOL.

117. Note from Sir James Thomson, 15 July 1912, 2341, J&P, IOL. See also in 2341, J&P, IOL: Minute 1912; Thomson to M. C. Seton, 20 May 1912; E. J. Turner to Thomson, n.d.; note from Thomson, 5 June 1912; Seton to Sir William Lee Warner, 8 June 1912; Seton to Sale, 8 July 1912; Sale to Seton, 9 July 1912.

Nor did Thomson believe that Azariah would be successful with 'the rest of the Ecclesiastical Establishment of the English Church':

> The man must either fulfil his office or permit derogation from it. And human nature is human nature even in a Christian priest: sometimes more so than less.[118]

Thomson was clearly motivated by stereotypically negative views of native priests and Indian Christians. Yet he also accused the government of discriminating against Indians by not offering, in the case of Dornakal, to support the missionary bishopric with tax revenues. 'It is not easy to understand why the revenues of India should provide church privileges for the white man, but not for the black.'[119] Thomson's disingenuous concern with racial equity was thus summoned to mask his belief that Indian Christians were incapable of leading their own ecclesiastical institutions.

Fortunately for Azariah, Thomson's dissent was outweighed by the support of several other key members of the India Council, and by the liberal Secretary of State, the Marquess of Crewe (Secretary, 1910-15). The strongest advocate of Whitehead's plan appears to have been Sir Steyning William Edgerley,[120] who objected to the Government of India's requirement that the Archdeacon of Madras have authority over the assistant bishop during the diocesan bishop's absences. This, Edgerley protested, 'looks like . . . racial discrimination in the very last place where we ought to find it.'[121] The government safeguard was defended by the powerful Sir Arthur Hirtzel,[122] who argued that, although objectionable in itself, the provision would protect British chaplains (some of whom were supposedly 'jealous' of Azariah's promotion) from being placed unwillingly under the native bishop's authority. Hirtzel advised retaining the provision, at least for the time being, in order to 'let the shy horse have a good look at

---

118. 'Proposal to appoint an Assistant Bishop in Madras: Note of dissent by Sir James Thomson,' in *op. cit.*

119. *Ibid.*

120. Edgerley was educated at Balliol and entered the ICS in 1877. He served in a variety of posts in Bombay (Private Secretary to the Governor, 1889-95; Secretary to the Government, 1897; Member of the Council, 1907), and became a member of the Council of India in 1909.

121. Arthur Hirtzel to Seton, 2 April 1912, 2341, J&P, IOL.

122. Hirtzel was Secretary to the Political Department at the India Office from 1909 to 1917, and Permanent Under-Secretary until 1930. John Morley considered Hirtzel his 'right hand man' during his tenure as Secretary of State.

the unaccustomed object first.'[123] Hirtzel joined Edgerley and Crewe in supporting Azariah's appointment, which the India Council approved on 14 May in time to permit the December 1912 consecration.[124] Prejudice toward Azariah, the 'unaccustomed object,' was thus wrestled to the ground through the imperfect but effective art of compromise.

Newspaper accounts of Azariah's appointment in early 1912 generated rumors which caused concern in both London and Madras. Controversy erupted in Parliament on 23 April 1912, and the Undersecretary of State for India, Edwin Montagu, had to assure the House of Commons, through his spokesman, that Azariah had not yet been appointed and that 'no part of the remuneration of the post, if it be sanctioned, will be provided from Government funds.'[125] The same questions were raised in the Madras Legislative Council, whose members were assured that 'the Assistant Bishop, if appointed, will not be a Government servant and his salary

123. Hirtzel to Seton, 19 April 1912, 2341, J&P, IOL.

124. 'Reference Paper,' 3926/11, J&P, 6 Nov. 1911 and 'Minute,' J&P 3926, 1911; both in 2341, J&P, IOL. Hirtzel indicated that certain letters concerning the Azariah debate were removed from the file at the Secretary of State's instruction. Although the reason for this is not given, it could possibly have been Crewe's desire to protect the contents of this debate from public exposure (Hirtzel to Seton, 2 April 1912, 2341, J&P, IOL; see also Whitehead to Copleston, 15 Aug. 1911, and other items in 5: 1/2, Dornakal, MACIPBC).

That Hirtzel favored Azariah's elevation to the episcopacy is further proof of Studdert-Kennedy's argument that, by overlooking the religious dimension of the Secretary's life and thought, Stanley Wolpert has misrepresented Hirtzel as a mere conservative opponent of liberal proposals (a 'potent deterrent to liberalizing change'), but with a contradictory and inexplicable commitment to the evolution of Indian nationalism (G. Studdert-Kennedy, *British Christians, Indian Nationalists and the Raj, op. cit.,* pp. 73-80). As Hirtzel's advocacy of Azariah (and of the later church unity movement spearheaded by Azariah) suggests, this contradiction finds its resolution in the christological domain. Hirtzel's liberalism was derived from his commitment to the Christian missionary endeavors which, if supported enthusiastically, would insure that 'when Indians come to govern themselves in accordance with Indian ideas, Indian ideas are to be Christian ideas' (quoted in *ibid.,* p. 79). Azariah's appointment was thus an important step in the Christian 'imperialist's' plan, for it marked the stage at which the British race (the superior race, Hirtzel argued, because it was Christian) passed a significant portion of its imperial trusteeship to an Indian who would assist the British in their historical mission of promoting the collective redemption of humankind in Christ. Azariah promised to be a willing partner in the Christian imperialist's mission and thus he was to be encouraged in his leadership.

125. Debates on Indian Affairs, House of Commons, Session 1912 (2 and 3 George V), 20 Feb. 1912 to 6 March 1913, Comprising Extracts from *The Parliamentary Debates* (London, 1912), col. 79.

will not be paid from public revenues.' The Government of Madras also admitted that it was 'not aware of the exact legal position [the Assistant Bishop] will occupy in relation to the Bishop of Madras, but his sphere of work will be determined from time to time by the latter.'[126]

In the midst of this palaver, Whitehead went to London to lobby for Azariah with the heads of missionary societies, the Archbishop of Canterbury and the former Viceroy, Lord Curzon. On 4 July 1912, while the Bishop of Madras was still in London, the King issued his Royal License to the Archbishop of Canterbury empowering him to commission the bishops in India to consecrate Azariah as Assistant Bishop in the Madras Diocese. The Metropolitan received the commission on 19 July 1912. Despite further complaints from Thomson and others, a date was set in December for the consecration with the approval of both the India Office in London and the Governments of India and Madras.

As different government branches in India and Britain bickered over Whitehead's plan, Azariah's appointment was also being debated in the wider Anglican arena. Some British Anglicans did not like his lower-caste background, but the majority were thankful that he did not represent the imitatively westernized Indian professional elite. As the editor of the Anglican *Church Times* wrote in 1913:

> [Azariah] will not present Christianity as an alien religion but as the embodiment of eternal truth. The new prelate is no Europeanized babu, decked in borrowed plumes from Piccadilly and affecting for good or for evil the fashions of the Sahib. The establishment of the Indian Church will be near at hand.[127]

The Anglican establishment in England welcomed Azariah's appointment precisely because he was not a high-caste, English-educated Indian. Azariah symbolized what many Britons regarded as the genuinely Indian peasant masses rather than the westernized upper classes whose rising national aspirations and European 'pretensions' were regarded, on one level, as ridiculous and, on another level, as threatening to the permanence of empire.

The consecration permitted the reassertion of a familiar imperial theme, articulated by Tories such as Salisbury, Lytton, and Curzon in

126. Proceedings of the Council of the Governor of Fort St. George, Jan. 1911 to June 1912, vol. XXXIX, pt. 1 (Madras, 1912), pp. 907-8, in Legislative Council Proceedings, Madras, 1911-12, V/9/2492, IOL.

127. Editorial, *Church Times,* 24 Jan. 1913, quoted in B. Sundkler, *Church of South India, op. cit.,* p. 372, n.18, and in Sundkler collection.

earlier years, that urban, western-educated Indians did not represent the 'real' India of 'voiceless millions who can neither read nor write . . . the ryots and the peasants whose life is not one of political aspiration but of mute penury and toil.'[128] As a Nadar from Tinnevelly, Azariah represented formerly low-caste and untouchable groups whose rejection of high-caste Hindu domination conveniently reinforced the British Empire's own rationale for resisting the increasingly troublesome Indian National Congress. For most interested Englishmen, Azariah's appointment did not pose a serious threat to the imperial ethos but rather provided a satisfying example of how Britain's presence in India served to protect and even to promote the weak and powerless. Although some of these same Britons might have shared Thomson's prejudice against low-caste Indians, their pleasure over the symbolism of Azariah's appointment generally outweighed any concern for the efficacy of church leadership in India.

Whitehead faced significant opposition, however, from Anglican missionary societies whose field workers did not believe that an Indian could run a diocese. He discovered by August 1911 that many CMS missionaries opposed his proposal on the grounds that mission districts in the Hyderabad State were not yet self-sufficient enough to support the first Indian bishopric. These missionaries accepted the assumption almost universally held, by imperialists and nationalists alike, that Indians needed training in self-government for successful independence. Even Gandhi maintained at this time that Indians needed to prepare themselves for self-government through various disciplines of self-control and self-purification. However, the freedom to manage the vast array of Christian schools, churches, hospitals, and other institutions imported to India by westerners was a limited form of freedom indeed, which amounted to little more than the obligation to run foreign institutions.

Whitehead shared the missionaries' concern that Dornakal Christians were not yet ready to take over a full-fledged Anglican diocese. Recalling an argument raised by the SPG in 1864 against an Indian bishop for Tinnevelly, Whitehead wrote to Copleston:

In their opinion the districts in the Hyderabad State are precisely those in which European control is at present most needed. There is much

128. Quoted in J. Brown, *Modern India: The Origins of an Asian Democracy, op. cit.,* p. 139.

force in this contention and I should not be willing at once to set it aside. The future growth of the Dornakal mission under Azariah's guidance may, and I think will, prove that European control is less needed than the missionaries imagine. But it would undoubtedly be better if the first independent Indian Bishop would be appointed to a see where the Indian congregations were riper for self-support and self-government. An independent diocese in the Telugu Country must after all be for many years a pauper diocese entirely dependent on a foreign missionary society for its support. An Indian bishop under these circumstances could not have the independence which he ought to have. For the present, therefore, I am myself in favour of consecrating an Assistant bishopric.[129]

Even Whitehead could not envisage Azariah as more than an assistant bishop in a 'pauper diocese,' and he continued to disagree with Copleston's more radical plan for Azariah's autonomous bishopric.

Azariah's appointment opened up new fissures between missionaries in the field and mission administrators in London, while also causing the low-church CMS and the high-church SPG to reverse their normal positions toward bishops: the evangelical CMS argued for giving Azariah greater episcopal responsibility, while the Anglo-Catholic SPG issued a rare challenge to episcopal authority by opposing Azariah's appointment altogether.

The Parent Committee of the CMS in London endorsed the more radical plan for a full diocesan bishopric in 1912, and agreed to include one of its Telugu mission districts (Khammamett) in the new diocese. This outraged some CMS missionaries in India, but the London Committee prevailed and, within a decade, the CMS relinquished the remainder of its Telugu missions in the Madras Presidency to Azariah's care.[130] Knowing that Azariah had stronger support from CMS administrators in distant London than from some CMS missionaries in India did not make Azariah's early years as a bishop any easier.

129. Whitehead to Copleston, 15 Aug. 1911, 5: 1/2, Dornakal, MACIPBC.
130. By 1917, the Metropolitan reported that seven CMS clergy in Ellore wished to be transferred from the Madras Diocese to the Dornakal Diocese and added, 'I believe I am right in saying that four years ago some of them had expressed very strongly their determination not to work under an Indian Bishop. Certainly many of the Madras missionaries took this position. The change is a most wonderful testimony to the depth and power of Bishop Azariah's work. A more splendid indication of the wisdom of making the experiment could hardly be imagined.' H. H. Montgomery, *The Life and Letters of George Alfred Lefroy* (London, 1920), p. 248.

The London-based India Sub-Committee of the SPG, by contrast, argued that Azariah was ill qualified and that Whitehead had overstepped his authority by appointing him without wider consultation. In a gesture completely uncharacteristic of an Anglo-Catholic society renowned for loyalty to bishops, the SPG Sub-Committee passed a resolution on 24 January 1912 opposing Whitehead's plan to consecrate the 'recently ordained priest, of no marked distinction.'[131] This objection was eventually overruled by both the Secretary of the SPG and the Archbishop of Canterbury, who argued against trying to micro-manage the affairs of bishops in India,[132] despite his own private worries about Azariah's relative lack of experience.[133] In the end, Azariah proved to be such a competent leader and administrator that, within a decade, the Synod extended his diocese to cover an area roughly the size of England.[134]

Whitehead was criticized even more strongly by nonconformist missionaries for attempting, through the consecration of Azariah, to further a larger scheme for Anglicanism as the state religion of India. A series of articles by the Congregationalist missionary to South India, Bernard Lucas (d. 1920), asked how the government intended to maintain its position of strict religious neutrality when it permitted the appointment of Anglican bishops to oversee the fieldwork of Anglican missionary societies. Claiming that the government had allowed Anglican bishops as 'State Officials' to be involved actively in evangelizing Indian populations, Lucas wrote:

> It is an anomalous position, because these Bishops are as much Government servants as Chaplains, and if the principle of a strict neutrality in religious matters were observed, they would be precluded altogether from taking any part in missionary work quite as much as Chaplains.[135]

131. 'Resolution of the India Sub-Committee,' 24 January 1912, 178: 357, Davidson Papers, Lambeth Palace.

132. Davidson to Stenning, 27 Jan. 1912, 178: 361-62, Davidson Papers, Lambeth Palace.

133. The Archbishop said to Azariah in a 1910 meeting: 'Well, you have been in orders only a year: That gives ground to the opposition.' VSA to Anbu, 8 July 1910, Azariah Collection, Madras.

134. Reaching just beyond Singareni in the North and Cuddapah in the South, to just beyond Kurnool in the West and Masulipatam in the East.

135. Bernard Lucas, *HF*, XXXII, 9 (Sept. 1912), p. 329. On Lucas, see G. Studdert-Kennedy, *British Christians, Indian Nationalists and the Raj, op. cit.*, pp. 135-37, in which he notes Hirtzel's attraction to Lucas's liberal theology. See also Kaj Baago, *Pioneers of Indigenous Christianity, op. cit.*, pp. 200-206; and Brian Stanley, 'The Reshaping of Christian Tradition," in *op. cit.*, pp. 411-12.

The fact that Azariah would not be paid by the government did not solve the fundamental problem that the Anglican Church interpreted the letters patent issued to its bishops in India as a license to encourage state-sanctioned evangelism of Indian populations. The appointment of an Indian bishop brought the Indo-Anglican church one step closer to a crisis which Lucas felt could be resolved only by disestablishment.

Whitehead denied that Anglican authorities were planning a state-sponsored episcopal church for India and expressed his own dissatisfaction that the letters patent required him to apply for a King's mandate before consecrating Azariah. Whitehead professed to dislike the state connection as much as Lucas, who summarized the situation as follows:

> At present the heads of the Episcopal Church in India are Government servants supported out of Government funds and responsible to Government for their work. We have, therefore, a Church in India actively engaged in the propagation of Christianity amongst the people of India whose responsible heads are Government officers, and it is simply impossible for the Government to maintain that pledge of religious neutrality to which they are committed. . . . Mr. Azariah's appointment is distinctly, if not exclusively, a missionary appointment, necessitated by the work, not of the Ecclesiastical Department, but of the Church of England Missionary Societies . . . it is this fact which makes it a political and not merely an ecclesiastical question. Under the present conditions the Government are being identified with the missionary work of the Indian Episcopal Church and unless these conditions are altered they will become increasingly identified with it.[136]

Lucas predicted that, in the event of large accessions from the Hindu community in Dornakal or elsewhere, aggrieved Hindus might accuse the government of interference in religious matters.

In fact, the mass movements of outcastes in Dornakal did not much interest caste Hindus until the franchise expanded along communal lines and Gandhi's anti-untouchability campaign brought the issue into focus more than two decades later. Lucas's argument articulated, however, the desire strongly felt by some Anglicans and most nonconformists for church disestablishment in India. As we have seen, in the year of Azariah's consecration, the Episcopal Synod took another important step towards making that desire a reality.

136. Bernard Lucas, *HF*, XXXII, 11 (Nov. 1912), pp. 407-8.

The Indian Perspective
on Azariah's Consecration

On the Indian side, the response to Azariah's consecration was equally complex and surprising: there was little concern from Hindus and Muslims but much concern from Indian Christians. In Calcutta, for example, the event passed unnoticed in the daily newspaper, *The Bengalee,* edited by the great nationalist champion of better representation for Indians in the Indian civil service, Surendranath Banerjea. The appointment of the first Indian bishop was overlooked in favor of political events such as the Twenty-Seventh Indian National Congress sessions held at Bankipur, and religious events such as the Theosophical Convention and the Inaugural meeting of the All-India Cow Preservation Society. *The Bengalee* reported on a sermon from the Bishop of Lahore — about the December 1912 attempt to murder the Viceroy in Delhi — but the consecration of the first Indian bishop passed unnoticed.

The Madras-based weekly newpaper *The Hindu* gave Azariah's consecration only slightly more notice. 'Yesterday at St. Paul's Cathedral, the first Indian clergyman belonging to the Church of England was made a Bishop,' the paper reported. 'There was a great gathering of clergymen, and Bishop Copleston, who leaves India very soon, presided.' Without mentioning Azariah's name, the short telegraphed article then went on to describe the differences between Bishop Copleston and his successor, Bishop Lefroy.[137] The faceless new Indian bishop was thus passed over in favor of his British colleagues, and the significance of his appointment was obfuscated entirely. It is doubtful that such newspapers would have ignored such an event if the new Indian bishop had hailed from a more elite background: the appointment of a Bengali Brahmin as the first Indian bishop, for example, most certainly would have created a considerable stir, if not controversy. However, non-Christian elites were basically uninterested in the appointment of a mere 'Indian clergyman' (read: former 'low caste' or 'untouchable') to a position of prominence in a church that was regarded primarily as the home of British rulers and Indian outcastes.[138] The marginalization of Azariah's ministry by Indian elites therefore began with the very date of his consecration.

---

137. *The Hindu — Madras,* XVIII, 2 (9 Jan. 1913), p. 5.
138. I am indebted to Mahatma Gandhi's grandson, Rajmohan Gandhi, for focusing my attention on this aspect of the Indian response to Azariah's appointment during two conversations in Madras in February 1986.

Locally in Dornakal, Muslim officials from the Nizam of Hyderabad's government consented to the establishment of the Dornakal Diocese more readily than their Christian official counterparts from the British Raj had done. Purchase deeds in today's Dornakal Diocese Compound
suggest that the church had no difficulty procuring permission from the
local Taluqdar and Bunjudar of Dornakal, or from higher authorities in
the Nizam's government, to buy land or to erect buildings for religious
purposes.[139] Dornakal was clearly a backwater area that few government
officials cared about; and IMS missionaries reported that the Nizam himself was more concerned for the lions in Dornakal than for the 'tribals.'
Yet villagers today also recall (and the historical record affirms) that the
Nizam's administration was so pleased to have the church working
among poor people in the remote Dornakal area that it donated three
hundred acres of land to the diocese free of charge as part of its benefac-
tions to charitable institutions.[140] The Nizam also gave Azariah free first-
class railway passage throughout the state, and he at least once asked
Azariah to talk with him while passing through Dornakal on a train.[141]

The more vociferous indigenous opposition to Azariah's consecration came from Indian Christians rather than from Indians of different religions who, at this stage, were not threatened by his proposed work with
outcastes. Different factions within the Indian Christian community fired
off strongly critical petitions to the Metropolitan and bishops in India,
the Archbishops of Canterbury and York, the Bishop of London, the relevant missionary societies, the Secretary of State for India, and the Governor of Madras. One such document, signed by 'members of the Church of
England' in Tinnevelly, castigated Azariah for allegedly lacking experience, sanctity, advanced university or theological education, high social
position, and repute among Hindus.[142] Another petition, which claimed
to represent over a thousand adult communicant members of the Church

139. See, e.g., V. S. Azariah to Maulvi Syed Ahmed Ulla Sahib, Esq., Dornakal,
July 31, 1911; Syed Ahmed Ulla, Taluqdar and Bunjudar of Dornakal, to V. S. Azariah,
31 July 1911; Director General, H. H. the Nizam's Government, Revenue Department
to V. S. Azariah, 27 July 1912 and 16 Oct. 1917; DDA.

140. 12 July 1911, Minutes of the Executive Committee, Minute Book, 1903-22,
PIMS; interviews with Alfred Bunyan, 29 March 1986, and with Rev. M. Daniel, 8 April
1986, Dornakal.

141. Interviews with Alfred Bunyan, 29 March 1986, and Rev. M. Daniel, 8 April
1986, Dornakal.

142. 'Members of the Church of England' to The Lord Bishops of the Province
of India and Ceylon, n.d. (Nurul Islam Press, Tinnevelly), 178: 369-70, Davidson Papers, Lambeth Palace. Copy with signatures in 5: 1/4, Dornakal, MACIPBC.

of England in the Telugu districts and Madras, attacked Azariah on similar grounds and added unfavorable references to his nonconformist associations in the YMCA.[143] Some Telugu Christians resented the appointment of a Tamil; others protested the exclusion of Indian Christians from the consultative process;[144] and the Episcopal Synod itself complained that Whitehead's secretiveness in planning Azariah's appointment had contributed to the opposition.[145]

Whitehead defended himself vigorously against these protests, writing to the Metropolitan:

> the opposition has been promoted by unworthy motives and even, I am sorry to say, by malicious falsehoods and slander. Four sick passions that are the curse of the Church in South India — race prejudice, caste feeling, party spirit and personal jealousy — have all been concentrated on this appointment.[146]

In a similar letter to the Archbishop of Canterbury, Whitehead argued that the protests from Indian Christians were inspired by 'unworthy motives, race prejudice, caste feeling, party spirit and jealousy.'[147]

143. 'Christians in communion with the Church of England and living in the Diocese of Madras' to Copleston (Vest & Co., Madras, n.d.), 178: 371-72, Davidson Papers, Lambeth Palace. Copy with signatures in 5: 1/4, Dornakal, MACIPBC.

144. '. . . we beg the Synod to consider very carefully the result of imposing an Assistant Bishop on an unwilling Diocese which has never been consulted as to his pay and position. We protest against the secrecy with which all arrangements have been made.' See 'Christians in communion with the Church of England and living in the Diocese of Madras' to Copleston (Vest & Co., Madras, n.d.), 178: 371-72, Davidson Papers, Lambeth Palace. Copy with signatures in 5: 1/4, Dornakal, MACIPBC.

145. C. H. Gill to Copleston, 10 Feb. 1912, 5: 1/5, Dornakal, MACIPBC. See also (i) 'The Indian Christian Community in Communion with the Church of England, and living in the Diocese of Madras to the Archbishop of Canterbury' (Vest & Co., Madras, n.d.); (ii) C. M. Soondram to Davidson, n.d., (iii) letter from VOX POPULI in the *Indian Patriot,* 23 April 1912; letter from CMS in the *Indian Patriot,* 30 April 1912; letter from C. G. Marshall to the *Madras Times,* 20 March 1912 (which claims mistakenly that Azariah would be paid from state revenues and questions the propriety of this in light of the declared neutrality of the Crown and government in matters of religion), all in 178: 386-88, Davidson Papers, Lambeth Palace.

146. Whitehead to Copleston, 8 Nov. 1911, 5: 1/2, Dornakal, MACIPBC.

147. Whitehead to Davidson, 6 June 1912, 178: 389-90, Davidson Papers, Lambeth Palace. See also Whitehead to Copleston, 14 Sept. 1911, 5: 1/2, Dornakal, MACIPBC. By race prejudice, Whitehead was referring to internal Indian prejudices against the darker-skinned Dravidian races.

Whitehead added that one of the main organizers of the protest in Madras,

The Episcopal Synod, the Archbishop, and others were persuaded by Whitehead's defense of Azariah and also by letters and counterpetitions received from Indian Christians in Azariah's support. One such petition from Tinnevelly Christians that was circulated in both the Tamil and Telugu areas implied that Azariah's opposition was organized by Tinnevelly Christians of different caste origins who were unable to accept 'another Tinnevelly Christian who is not a relation of theirs, attaining a position above their own.'[148] Azariah's consecration thus became an occasion for the open articulation of interregional and intercaste disputes, but their effect was limited by the closed nature of the episcopal selection process, which did not require clerical or congregational consent, and by the constancy of Henry Whitehead's patronage.

Whitehead's zeal for indigenization and sympathy for Indian nationalism led him to minimize the continuing power of subnational loyalties to undermine many of his plans for Dornakal and for church unity, and to make the appointments of bishops in Indian Protestant churches controversial up to the present day.

The controversy over Azariah's consecration was not a simple confrontation between a monolithic bloc of oppressed Indian Christians and an opposing monolithic bloc of conservative and racist British Christians trying to thwart Azariah's elevation. Azariah and his Indian Christian colleagues were not fighting a nationalist battle against the dark forces of imperialism. It was, rather, a controversy that accurately reflected the complexities and contradictions inherent within both British and Indian societies during the last decades of the Raj. Azariah was promoted by liberal westerners against the wishes of many less liberal westerners and Indians. His appointment opened up rifts within the established church, within the British, Indian, and Madras governments, within and between various missionary societies, and within factions of Indian Christianity itself. Azariah and his supporters weathered these and no doubt other controversies that lie outside the reach of this study. But there were invisible costs, and Azariah himself faced enormous new personal and professional challenges.

C. M. Soondram, bore a personal grudge against Azariah for refusing to speak at a meeting organized by Soondram in protest against another speaker's 'gross immorality.'

148. 'Petition for Rev. V. S. Azariah's appointment as Bishop of Dornakal,' 5: 1/6, Dornakal, MACIPBC. See also 5: 1/5 for further letters and petitions in Azariah's favor. This same argument had been used in 1878 by Nadar Christians to prevent the proposed appointment of a Vellalar to the bishopric in Tinnevelly.

CHAPTER 5

Bishop in the Indian Church: Race and Identity Formation

The Search for an Indian Episcopal Identity

Azariah was publicly silent about the controversy surrounding his appointment. But private letters reveal it was a time of great inner turmoil for the bishop and his wife. At first he felt overwhelmed at being singled out by the British establishment for promotion, writing to his wife in August 1909, 'All these great privileges and blessings come unsought for. I feel most unworthy of it all. Pray that we may be kept quite humble at all these things and that all glory may go to Him through whose Grace we are what we are.'[1]

He soon felt apprehension over the secrecy surrounding the plans and wondered how he and his wife would fulfill the many expectations being thrust upon them. He worried that the IMS would think he was ignoring his responsibilities in Dornakal by spending so much time with Bishop Whitehead. He also worried about the burden that would fall on his wife who was coping with four young children, 'a conservative, old, superstitious mother,'[2] the recent death of their baby boy, and an impending move to rural Dornakal. He wrote to her from the Whiteheads' hill station home:

1. VSA to Anbu, 2 Aug. 1909, Azariah Collection, Madras.
2. VSA to Anbu, 31 March 1909, Azariah Collection.

138

Mrs. W[hitehead] and I talk a lot about you. I feel all the time anxious how you are going to rise to the occasion. To dine with the Bishop, to lead in all big meetings, to be introduced to the Governor — things of this sort will be quite out of your way. Your instinct will be to take the last place. You can't behave in such a way that people will look up to you as a big person. And, yet, God can give you even the Grace. I am praying that He who led us so far, will even now lead us on.[3]

If Azariah had worries about his own abilities to be a bishop, he did not express them. However, his concerns for his wife's ability to perform the official duties of 'a big person' within the Raj probably reflected his own worries.

As a new, highly visible symbol of Indian Christianity, Azariah would set precedents for future Indian bishops in every aspect of his demeanor. Azariah got a first taste several months after his consecration when he participated in the consecration of the new Bishop of Lahore in Simla. Azariah was the center of attention at this event, as the Metropolitan wrote shortly thereafter:

> I believe his appearance in this way, in so important a function, at the centre of Empire, will do real good — bring home to many who had given the matter little or no thought what we have done in making him a Bishop. I think every one was favourably impressed by his appearance and manner. Almost the whole of official Simla was there, including the Viceroy and Lady Hardinge.[4]

As the first Indian bishop 'at the centre of Empire,' Azariah would become an important symbol of Christianity's growing presence in India, of the church's liberal views on Indian leadership, and of the Raj's success in winning loyal subjects. His every move would be carefully observed — sometimes even by the Raj's highest officials. In 1909, the meaning of this future was just beginning to dawn on Azariah as he trained for ordination with the Whiteheads in Ootacamund.

During the difficult period of uncertainty leading up to his consecration, Azariah was confronted with the challenge of defining, for himself and for India, a suitable identity for a first Indian bishop. One of the first steps in this process of identity construction was to decide what clothes he should wear. This challenge was made more complex and per-

---

3. VSA to Anbu, 9 Sept. 1909, Azariah Collection.
4. H. H. Montgomery, *The Life and Letters of George Alfred Lefroy, op. cit.,* pp. 238-39.

sonally embarrassing by the well-intentioned but domineering efforts of westerners. The Whiteheads were particularly anxious that Azariah, their symbol of the new age of church indigenization, should establish Indian norms distinguishing him from his English colleagues.

During Azariah's residence with the Bishop of Madras in preparation for his consecration, Isabel Whitehead decided to tackle the problem of identifying suitable vestments. She initially assumed that Azariah would wear the costly coat and breeches donned by other English bishops (like 'a Highlander going to a funeral').[5] Azariah found this awkward:

> My new suits and the black suit and long coat came today. Mrs. Whitehead wanted me to put on the long coat for dinner. She would not listen to all my pleadings to excuse. And so I had to dress myself up in it. It is rather too grand for a poor fellow like me![6]

Dinner that night seemed to Azariah something like a costume party for which he had reluctantly 'dressed up.' Isabel ignored his 'pleadings to excuse' and pressured him to don a 'grand' outfit that offended Azariah's every sensibility, not so much because of its western appearance as because of its expense and pretentiousness.

Worse than her initial directive to dress like Bishop Whitehead were her subsequent directives to wear Indian dress. Mrs. Whitehead pressured Azariah to add a turban, the classic symbol of oriental dignity in the West, to his episcopal attire. The West's sentimental attachment to the turban was well illustrated by an article of 1896 in which a European writer lamented its replacement by a modern round cap:

> The turban, which is honorable alike for its appearance, its venerable age, and the associations which it always seems to carry with it of oriental dignity and politeness, is rapidly being ousted by that loathsome and intensely vulgar little round cap, which obtrudes its hideousness upon our sight from one end of India to the other.[7]

Azariah and most of his peers wore exactly such 'loathsome and intensely vulgar' modern round caps during their student days at Madras Christian College. Although many South Indians still wore turbans for a wide vari-

---

5. Alec R. Vidler, *The Church in the Age of Revolution: 1789 to the Present Day* (Middlesex, 1961), p. 252.
6. VSA to Anbu, 26 May 1909, Azariah Collection, Madras.
7. 'How Should Indians Dress?' *CP*, VII, 17 (23 April 1896), p. 5.

ety of functions, many students chose alternative (or no) headgear, possibly because of the turban's association either with the rustic cloths wrapped around the head by coolie workers for protection from the sun, or with India's princely, martial, or elitist, Brahmin-dominated traditional culture.[8]

Azariah wished to avoid identification with any of these extremes, and had already adopted the western practice of removing headwear to show respect (the opposite of the Indian practice of covering the head to show respect). Azariah considered a turban to be as inappropriate and foreign as it was to most westerners. The future bishop, therefore, resisted Mrs. Whitehead's pressure to wear a turban even more vehemently than her pressure to wear an English bishop's garb, writing to his wife from the Whitehead's house in Ootacamund that 'Mrs. Whitehead is taking me to task for not buying a turban!'[9]

The ambitious Isabel persisted, however, in searching for other Indian models for episcopal dress. She studied the existing indigenous episcopal attire of bishops from the Syrian Orthodox churches (even though most of them came from the Middle East rather than India) — prompting Azariah to write from the Whitehead home in September 1909:

> We had quite an exciting time over the visit of the Patriarch of Antioch. His Holiness the Patriarch, His Grace Mar Dionysius of Malabar, and their Chaplains came up this afternoon for tea. I acted as chaplain receiving them at the doorstep. I was serving tea also. . . . Mrs.

8. The ongoing popularity of turbans during this period is suggested by the many photographs of prominent figures such as Radhakrishnan, C. Rajagopalachari, Sarvepalli Gopal, or members of the Legislative Assembly in Madras, in which they are wearing turbans. Azariah and his peers were likely using their headgear to make a statement about modernity and its separation from traditional caste domination. Later in Dornakal, Azariah's son recalls, Azariah regarded turbans as unnecessary because, unlike peasants, clergy did not need protection from the sun. (Interview with Ambrose Azariah, 2 March 1986, Madras.)

9. VSA to Anbu, 21 May 1909, Azariah Collection, Madras. Although Azariah desisted at this stage, some Indian Christians did wear turbans during this period. See, e.g., the 1905 photograph of NMS founders in which three delegates are wearing turbans: Siraj-ud-din of Lahore, Chitamber of Lucknow, and Karmarkar of Bombay. (Two of these were sons of Brahmin converts, and one was a Muslim convert whose family was said to be related to notable Muslim saints whose tombs were located in Srinigar, Kashmir.) See RG 32, IV; 23/239, Eddy Papers, YDS. One photograph of Azariah in a procession in Tinnevelly pictures him in a turban, but this was clearly a special ceremonial occasion and we do not know if Azariah was pressured against his will to don it.

Whitehead was all the time engaged in noting their dress to suggest what the dress of Indian Bishop [*sic*] should be. It seems when the Bishop was consecrated he spent £500 on dress alone. I am saying all along that the expensive English episcopal dress should not be imported to India.[10]

To fully appreciate Azariah's concern about importing expensive British episcopal clothing standards to India, the modern reader must recognize that, with five hundred pounds sterling — equivalent in those days to 7,500 rupees — Azariah and his wife could have bought a three-to-four bedroom house.

Impelled at least in part by such terrifying clothing costs, Azariah successfully resisted Mrs. Whitehead's attempts to dress him up as the Indian bishop of her own extravagant and highly orientalist imagination. The Syrian paradigm was dropped along with the turban; and after further haggling, Azariah substituted a simple cassock for the costly English coat and breeches donned by the other bishops.[11]

Azariah won this battle, but continued to construct his new identity under the Whiteheads' well-intentioned but intrusive gaze. In good colonial ethnographic fashion, the Whiteheads photographed every scene of this fashion show at their hill station residence. The Azariah family photo album today contains one photo of Azariah in English bishop's clothes topped with a turban (and standing next to Bishop Whitehead), another of Azariah alone in the simpler cassock he chose but still wearing the turban, and, finally, a noticeably more relaxed picture without any turban and in his preferred cassock (standing once again next to the traditionally attired Bishop Whitehead).[12] Paradoxically, westerners had urged an Indian to indigenize according to Indian paradigms that the Indian believed inappropriate; and the Indian adopted western dress opposed by orientalizing westerners.

The Whiteheads' campaign to orientalize their first Indian bishop forms a fascinating but hitherto unreported chapter in the British Raj's crusade at the time of the great Imperial Durbar of 1911 to enliven civic rituals through the introduction (or reintroduction) of orientalized cos-

10. VSA to Anbu, 5 Sept. 1909, Azariah Collection, Madras.
11. As one historian has written of the 'younger churches'' persistent use of western clothing styles: 'Native priests were dressed up like European clergymen, and even native bishops, when there came to be such, adorned themselves in the riding attire of eighteenth-century English prelates.' Alec R. Vidler, *op. cit.*, p. 252.
12. Family photo album, Azariah Collection, Madras.

tumes and regalia.[13] Indian compatriots at different levels of the civic polity were being pressured to adopt European ideas of proper Indian dress during this time, and they creatively negotiated solutions that defined a newly emerging and highly complex Indo-British code of manners and respect. Through Azariah, the Indo-Anglican church also contributed to this process of bolstering the dignity of the Raj through orientalization of its official religious institutions. That Azariah's particular solutions to the problems of whether to wear a turban or western dress did not satisfy his British mentors suggests that, at least in some cases, this process of orientalization was less successful than has generally been recognized.

The small but symbolic indignities Azariah experienced during this time of identity formation are illustrated by the Whiteheads' ultimately successful campaign to persuade him to shave off his fashionable mustache before entering the conservative Episcopal Synod in 1912. One wonders how Azariah must have felt when, after shaving for the consecration, he discovered that Bishops Lefroy, Palmer, and Foss Westcott sported mustaches with beards for the ceremony, and that impressive mutton-chop sideburns still colonized most of Metropolitan Copleston's face.[14]

Although Azariah had successfully rejected the turban for his episcopal uniform, the Whiteheads continued to pressure him to wear turbans for public functions, especially outside India. In April 1910, he embarked with Mrs. Whitehead on his first trip to Europe and Great Britain to speak at the Edinburgh World Missionary Conference. Mrs. Whitehead persuaded him to purchase two turbans (one brown and one white silk) for his trip, but he conceded in a letter to his wife from aboard the outgoing *R.M.S. Otranto* that he 'had not had the courage to show them out yet.'[15] As if to heighten his own embarrassment at donning what he regarded as an artificial Indian costume for the benefit of his English mentor, those in charge of the ship sponsored two fancy dress balls for which European passengers also dressed themselves up as Orientals. Azariah was not invited, but described this bizarre event:

13. Bernard S. Cohn, *Colonialism and Its Forms of Knowledge: The British in India* (Delhi: Oxford University Press: Delhi, 1997), pp. 106-62; David Cannadine, 'The Context, Performance and Meaning of Ritual: The British Monarchy and the "Invention of Tradition," c. 1820-1977,' in *The Invention of Tradition*, ed. Eric Hobsbawm and Terence Ranger (Cambridge, 1983), pp. 101-64.

14. Azariah to Mrs. Whitehead, 3 Oct. 1912, Sundkler Collection, Uppsala. See the frontispiece to Eyre Chatterton, *A History of the Church of England in India, op. cit.*

15. VSA to Anbu, 11 April 1910, Azariah Collection, Madras.

This evening there was a Fancy Dress Ball in the I class. Everybody dressed himself or herself in most fanciful costumes and went to dinner. We of the II class stood at the entrance and had a peep. Japanese costumes, Malay costumes, and even an Indian lady's dress were worn by ladies. The lady . . . painted her face also in dark brown. When I write this there is dancing going on in the upper deck.[16]

Eight days later, Azariah wrote again to his wife:

They have a fancy dress ball up on the deck. I dressed up a gentleman as an Indian Prince! I put on him my white *Veshti,* lace turban, and he got a long white sheet to use as melvessa. Miss Morgan dressed up a girl like an Indian girl. Prizes were given to the best dressed. The Indian girl got a II Prize. My man did not get any.[17]

As Azariah assisted fellow passengers in acting out their imaginary perceptions of the Orient, his anxiety about his own identity grew, and he became increasingly annoyed by Mrs. Whitehead's attempts to impose her ideas on him.

Mrs. Whitehead comes often to my chair in the deck and talks for a long time. She's full of plans for England and I am afraid rather tiresome in her plans. I am feeling more and more that while in England it is better for me to be independent. She rather wishes me to be directed by her

16. *Ibid.*
17. VSA to Anbu, 19 April 1910, Azariah Collection, Madras. The tension, embarrassment, and, sometimes, humor produced when Indians and Europeans imagined the experience of the 'other' through dramatic enactments are deeply revealing. Compare Azariah's descriptions of Westerners dressed as Indians with Henry Whitehead's description of Telugu schoolboys performing a musical drama of the life of Joseph:

The dresses looked as though they had been borrowed from some Hindu Dramatic Company in the town. They were an extraordinary assortment of garments, Indian and European. The actors whitened their faces with chalk, producing a most ghastly effect, and they walked up and down the stage flourishing sticks, swords, and pocket handkerchiefs. Jacob looked like an elderly Hindu of the olden school, Joseph like a spoilt child of a Hindu Raja, with a much bespangled coat and with his cheeks painted white, with bright patches of red. He walked up and down the stage flourishing his pocket handkerchief, till one gradually felt profound sympathy for his brothers. When he was finally sold for 30 pieces of silver, a Hindu merchant in the audience justly remarked, 'It is too much, he is not worthy of it.' 'A Diary of the Bishop's Tour,' *MTDM,* V, 8 (Aug. 1910), pp. 294-95.

ideas. I am afraid this will make it often unpleasant for her as well as unpleasant for me. I am praying much about this. Please pray also that God may guide me to behave tactfully.[18]

Azariah must have shown extraordinary tact, because Mrs. Whitehead wrote to Anbu from the ship that '[Azariah] has been so kind to me, and it is very nice to have a friend on board, though I don't see much of him.'[19] But Isabel Whitehead was clearly insensitive to her effect on Azariah. What seemed to her a scarcity of conversations seemed to Azariah a virtual bombardment.

Isabel Whitehead was a domineering woman, even by the already domineering standards of many British memsahibs. She had a penchant for annoying other Britons as well as Indian Christians. Edwin Montagu called her 'a beastly woman' after a 1913 meeting, and blamed her for blocking Bishop Whitehead's chances for promotion to the Metropolitan see. Her personality prompted Montagu to ruminate in his diary on the generic problem of the formidable memsahib:

> The fact is that however confidently it may be said that the Englishman has succeeded in India, the Englishwoman has been a conspicuous failure. She feels race prejudice far more than the man (so, bye-the-bye, do the Indian women), and she has so little to do. She cannot do the parson's daughter or squire's wife among people she does not understand, in districts where she is only allowed to remain a short time. So she degenerates, reads little, gets unhealthy and embittered by the many separations from her family. Her pluck, which is tremendous, is rather wasted. I am all for bachelors in India. In innumerable cases the women spoil their husbands' lives completely (e.g., Gubbay, Whitehead, etc.) by separation as well as by being there.[20]

Isabel Whitehead's self-appointed role as mentor to the new Indian bishop intensified her domineering tendencies. Subconscious racial prejudices and imperialist sympathies may have contributed to her patronizing relationship with Azariah,[21] but her well-intentioned orientalizing

18. VSA to Anbu, 11 April 1910, Azariah Collection, Madras.
19. Isabel Whitehead to Anbu, 16 April 1910, Azariah Collection, Madras.
20. *Edwin Samuel Montagu Diaries, 1912-1913*, pp. 79-80, 84-85, D. 523/38-40, IOL, London.
21. She seems to have had a warmer, although still patronizing, relation with Azariah's wife. In one letter to Anbu, she asked Anbu to pray for her reunion with her son Constantine, after eighteen months' separation (Isabel Whitehead to Anbu, 16 April

was an even more obvious cause. At times, Indian Christians like Azariah felt as oppressed by their visionary liberal benefactors as by die-hard reactionaries.

Azariah landed in Naples on 22 April 1910, where he got his first glimpse of the western world. From his small pension (ten minutes' walk from Mrs. Whitehead's more expensive hotel), Azariah could see Mount Vesuvius smoking. He visited local museums and the City of the Dead in Pompeii, but was more interested in living Italians. He described his 'first impression of Europe' to his wife after twenty-four hours on shore:

> We see white boatmen, white jutka wallahs, white sweetmeat sellers, white vegetable sellers, white porters, white cigarette selling boys. I have not met with *a single* dark man.[22]

To see white men performing all of the menial tasks they would never perform in India amused Azariah. The great and exalted white man of India seemed reduced, all of a sudden, to the level of ordinary people. After hearing missionaries complain for years about poor sanitation in India, he was also surprised to find in Naples that 'in the streets they have latrines in worse form than in Madras. Men make water without the least sense of shame; a woman even talking to him all the time he is doing it!'[23]

Azariah traveled through Rome and Pisa, where he was 'thrilled' to see sites visited by the apostles Peter and Paul, and fascinated by the historical interplay between ancient Rome and Christianity. The defeat of ancient Roman forms of worship reminded him of South Asian religions:

> There are whole lots of Museums containing ancient sculpture. Thousands of Jupiter, Venus, Saturn, Apollo, Mercury cut in marble or bronze have been dug out and are now placed in the Museum. As, I suppose, one day our Sivas, Vishnus, Nelliappan [?], Minakshis will be placed in the Museums.[24]

He saw Roman Catholicism as a new form of idolatry ('worship of Virgin Mary, making of images, altars, etc. etc. are probably all borrowed from the ancient heathen Rome') that confined religion to priests when the

---

1910, Azariah Collection, Madras). One expects that Anbu was more sympathetic than Edwin Montagu about the English memsahib's forced separations from children.

22. VSA to Anbu, 22 April, 1910, Azariah Collection, Madras.

23. *Ibid.*

24. VSA to Anbu, 27 April 1910.

streets of Rome abounded in irreligion ('Theatres, Plays etc. find full attendance. Churches are visited only by a corresponding few').

Traveling on to England in a third-class compartment (Mrs. Whitehead was in the second class), he was disappointed with the appearance of Westminster Abbey, amazed by the busy London night life, and impressed by the thousands of churches that 'rise everywhere' in the countryside. However, his annoyance with Mrs. Whitehead led him seriously to consider abandoning the Whiteheads and his training for the bishopric altogether by the time he reached the Edinburgh Conference in June. After talking with Sherwood Eddy, his good friend, Azariah wrote to Anbu:

> Mr. Eddy has heard from his friends in India that Mrs. Whitehead was trying her utmost to spoil me by taking me round and taking away my own individuality. It is sad to hear of all this. I wanted to write and tell the Bishop that he should leave me out of account in maturing his plans. But Mr. Eddy says I ought not to do so. So I remain quiet. 'Thy Will, O Lord, be done!'[25]

Although bowing to Sherwood Eddy's advice, Azariah continued to look for ways to maintain his independence. While in Edinburgh, he quietly arranged to return to England a fortnight later than he initially intended because, he wrote to Anbu, 'I want if possible to avoid arriving with Mrs. Whitehead — this is absolutely private.'[26]

His irritation with Mrs. Whitehead was one factor prompting him to deliver a radically critical speech on the subject of racial relations between missionaries and their foreign converts at the Edinburgh Conference. To the shock of the gathered crowds, Azariah argued that racial alienation infected the missionary enterprise with 'a certain aloofness, a lack of mutual understanding and openness, a great lack of frank intercourse and friendliness.' He pleaded with the assembled missionaries to give up their paternalistic attitudes for true cooperation based on spiritual friendships under the sovereignty of Christ, 'the great Unifier of mankind':

> I do not plead for returning calls, handshakes, chairs, dinners and teas, as such. I do, on the other hand, plead for all of them and more if they can be expressions of a friendly feeling, if these or anything else can be

25. VSA to Anbu, 16 June 1910, Azariah Collection, Madras. Mrs. Whitehead was not the only liberal westerner guilty of being overbearing. Azariah had experienced similar pressure from his confidant in this instance, Sherwood Eddy, during their NMS collaboration, as noted in the previous chapter.
26. *Ibid.*

the outward proofs of a real willingness on the part of the foreign missionary to show that he is in the midst of the people, to be to them, not a lord and master, but a brother and friend. . . .

Through all the ages to come the Indian Church will rise up in gratitude to attest the heroism and self-denying labours of the missionary body. You have given your goods to feed the poor. You have given your bodies to be burned. We ask also for *love*. Give us FRIENDS![27]

Azariah called for friendship that would be 'more than condescending love,' and it struck the missionary community 'like a bomb,' Isabel Whitehead reported to Anbu. 'Half the audience was delighted and the other half very angry.'[28] Of course Mrs. Whitehead was part of the 'delighted' faction, little realizing that she was part of the problem. She and the bishop were pleased that Azariah had been courageous enough to reprimand conservative missionaries for racialism, and to suggest that a universal (as opposed to purely indigenous) form of Christianity was the only solution. Azariah's speech included a rousing call for interracial cooperation in the cause of Christ:

The exceeding riches of the glory of Christ can be fully realised not by the Englishman, the American, and the Continental alone, nor by the Japanese, the Chinese, and the Indians by themselves — but by all working together, worshipping together, and learning together the Perfect Image of our Lord and Christ. . . . This will be possible only from spiritual friendships between the two races. We ought to be willing to learn from one another and to help one another.[29]

Azariah did not speak about politics. He described the rising aspirations of 'a new generation of Christians who do not wish to be treated like children' as evidence of 'the success of missionary work' rather than of nationalist fervor. But Azariah echoed political nationalism with his insistence that 'There can never be real progress unless the aspirations of the native Christians to self-government and independence are accepted, encouraged, and acted upon.'[30]

Azariah's speech drew, not just on his recent discomfort with Isabel

27. 'The Problem of Co-operation between Foreign and Native Workers,' in *World Missionary Conference, 1910: The History and Records of the Conference: Together with Addresses Delivered in the Evening Meetings* (Edinburgh, 1910), pp. 306, 311, 315.

28. Isabel Whitehead to Anbu, 2 July 1910, Azariah Collection, Madras.

29. *Ibid.,* p. 315.

30. *Ibid.,* p. 312.

Whitehead, but on a childhood of missionary schools and ten years of working for the YMCA. 'The problem of race relationships is one of the most serious problems confronting the Church to-day,' he concluded. 'The bridging of the gulf between the East and West, and the attainment of a greater unity and common ground in Christ . . . is one of the deepest needs of our time.'[31]

Azariah returned to Dornakal and to the controversy surrounding his candidacy for the bishopric with a new sense of purpose and a quiet determination not to accept an English interpretation of what it meant to be Indian. But he now faced daily the awkward realization that, in being groomed for the first Indian bishopric, he was also being sculpted into a living symbol of Indian Christianity for and by westerners.

Azariah was regarded, because of his race, as the Synod's natural pace-setter for Indianization, but he sometimes disappointed the non-Indians in their orientalizing expectations. His British episcopal colleagues eventually adopted Azariah's simpler cassock, and then went further to present themselves in a more 'Indian' manner than Azariah himself. Stephen Neill, Bishop of Tinnevelly from 1939 to 1945, wrote in later years: 'It has always amused me that, whereas I the foreigner always went to Church barefoot, Azariah, the Indian, always wore leather shoes.'[32]

Azariah took an independent approach to the dress issue, and was unafraid to adopt western forms of respect (such as wearing shoes) even as his British colleagues adopted Indian forms of respect (by shedding their shoes). He also tried to diffuse the subtle tension surrounding these decisions with humor. To westerners who advocated 'Indian' practices he considered inappropriate, he suggested introducing 'the real Indian ecclesiastical vestment. . . . Nothing at all!'[33]

Western pressure to Indianize increased during the last decades of the Independence movement as India also focused greater attention on the meaning of clothing. Changing clothing styles were important instruments of cultural and economic identity construction in South Asia at the individual, family, caste, and regional levels. Once *khadi*, or home-spun cloth, was adopted by Indian nationalists as a symbol of their resistance to British rule during the noncooperation movement, clothing styles became an important component of political identity formation as well. Gandhi shed first his western clothes and then his Indian clothes down to the

31. *Ibid.*, p. 306.
32. S. C. Neill, 'Bishop Azariah,' *op. cit.*, p. 38.
33. That is, nothing above the waist or below the knee. *Ibid.*

loincloth as an act of political defiance and identification with India's poor.

Ironically, however, when given the opportunity to choose, Gandhi's Harijans (his name for untouchables, meaning 'children of God') showed a persistent preference for more modern and western-style clothing which, they believed, separated them symbolically from the stigma of their past untouchability. Azariah's contemporary and ally, the untouchable leader B. R. Ambedkar, chose to represent his people in European clothes rather than the loincloth, and this trend persists in Dalit communities today.[34]

To the dismay of Gandhi's many western Anglican admirers, Indian Christian converts from the depressed classes also often adopted western rather than Indian norms, particularly when 'indigenous' models were derived from Hindu traditions to which they felt little attachment. Early Shanar (later Nadar) converts in Tinnevelly embraced western Gothic architecture, especially if church steeples were higher than any nearby Hindu temple gopuram. 'Pukka' (or substantial and permanent) stone churches were preferable to any indigenous alternatives. Indian converts wanted their churches to demonstrate an elevated, distinctively Christian (and therefore, from their point of view, British) status. Thus, a stone Gothic church was infinitely preferable to the more 'indigenous' thatched mud hut or simple altar that was often eulogized by westerners but represented to converts little but their former poverty and ritually polluting semi-untouchability.[35] Far from being a weak concession to domineering missionaries, westernization represented a symbolic challenge by long-suppressed lower classes to an oppressive indigenous social order. In this context, indigenization along the lines expected by western orientalizing indigenizers would have been viewed as just another form of oppression.

Westerners rather than Indians often championed twentieth-century efforts to use Hindu temple architecture for Christian churches, as in the case of the church at Christukula Ashram founded by E. Forrester-Paton and S. Jesudason. But most Indian Christian converts had little interest in the Indianizing efforts of westerners such as J. C. Wins-

---

34. Emma Tarlo, *Clothing Matters: Dress and Identity in India* (Chicago, 1996), pp. 251-83.

35. Nor was there much interest in imitating mosques, apparently because they excluded women in worship, although probably also because of the converts' desire for distinctiveness from other Indian religious traditions. S. C. Neill, *A History of Christianity in India, 1707-1858, op. cit.,* p. 411; *A History of Christian Missions, op. cit.,* pp. 536-39; *The Story of the Christian Church in India and Pakistan, op. cit.,* pp. 163-65; A. T. Fishman, *For This Purpose* (Madras, 1958), p. 79.

low, who modeled the Christa Seva Sangha community at Poona on Indian ashrams.[36] They were proud of their new Christian (and, by association, European) identities and wanted their places of worship to reflect this distinctiveness and separation from their former poverty and stigmatization.

In the opinion of one former South Indian bishop, most twentieth-century church Indianization had an artificial quality because it was initiated by westerners without strong guidance or support from the majority of Indian Christians.[37] It was perhaps as difficult for many liberal westerners, as it was for Indian nationalists to accept that, in many situations, Indian Christians desired closer identification with the West than with their own native traditions. Christianity, in its Anglican mission-mediated forms, appeared to provide for many the most clear and straightforward path out of the demeaning cultural matrix from which converts wished to escape.

Azariah developed an increasingly secure and unselfconscious sense of his Indian Christian identity during his years in Dornakal, but he could never entirely avoid western pressure to Indianize. During the Whiteheads' regular visits to Dornakal, Mrs. Whitehead berated the bishop and his family for eating English breakfasts rather than South Indian *iddli*.[38] When Azariah named a new Christian village in his diocese 'Whitehead Farm,' the Whiteheads insisted that he rename it 'Vedanayagapuram,' to give Azariah credit for its establishment and to make the settlement appear more Indian.[39] The village of Kiritipuram ('crown village') adjacent to the town of Dornakal was apparently named after both King George V and Azariah, whose 'crownings' were commemorated by a small stone

36. E. B. Havell, 'Christian Architecture in India,' *MTDM*, IX, 2 (Feb. 1914), pp. 49-51, advocates the use of Hindu architecture for Christian churches.

37. Interview with Bishop Michael Hollis, 7 Sept. 1984, Manormead, Hindhead. See also K. M. de Silva, 'From Elite Status to Beleaguered Minority: The Christians in Twentieth Century Sri Lanka,' in *Asie du Sud. Traditions et Changements,* Colloques Internationaux du CNRS, No. 582, p. 349.

38. Interview with Ambrose Azariah, 2 March 1986, Madras.

39. There is some disagreement about the original name of the village. One account claimed it was first called 'Whitehead Farm' (interviews with Rev. M. Daniel, 29 March and 8 April 1986, Dornakal), while another claimed it was first called 'Conconda' after Henry Whitehead's son, John Henry Constantine (nicknamed 'Concon'), who later became one of the world's great mathematicians (interview with Ambrose Azariah, 24 March 1986, Madras). Both accounts agreed, however, that the Whiteheads were responsible for persuading Azariah to change the name to Vedanayagapuram.

monument which still stands in the village today.[40] The association of Azariah's consecration with a royal coronation reflected the village's unmistakable pride at their bishop's prestigious position in the British Raj as well as basic sympathy for the monarchy and British rule in India. Azariah's own son George was named after the King, whose Proclamation Azariah witnessed personally during his 1910 trip to England.[41]

That westerners, rather than Indian congregations in Dornakal, exerted pressure on Azariah to develop an Indian persona shows how Indian nationalism had influenced the British but left Andhra's rural Christian communities (among others) relatively untouched. 'To be indigenous,' another Anglican divine has written, 'means simply to be free to respond to Christ and to the world without any of the self-consciousness which is imposed by the attitudes of others.'[42]

This kind of self-consciousness plagued India during the years of the British Raj. British imperial rule altered many aspects of India's self-perception to conform to western representations of India. Many Indians came to view themselves through the eyes of western philosophers, educationalists, economists, poets, and missionaries; and the self-questioning provoked by western critiques led to new Indian understandings of their national identity by the end of the nineteenth century.[43] It was as if India had collectively decided to don a metaphorical 'Indian' costume tailored by the West.

But a reverse process was also taking place: Indian nationalist critiques of western culture, politics, and values began to influence British self-perceptions. Critical Indian portraits of the West, and of British rule in particular, caused British Christians such as C. F. Andrews and Verrier Elwin to lose confidence in the Raj and to reject British for Indian values and customs, sometimes literally exchanging their western dress for Indian costumes. Indian nationalism influenced mainstream Anglicans to a degree that has perhaps been underappreciated.

---

40. Interview with Rev. M. Daniel, 8 April 1986, Dornakal. The stone pillar capped with a crown appears to have been placed there on the occasion of the King's silver jubilee in 1935.

41. VSA to Anbu, 11 May 1910, Azariah Collection, Madras.

42. John V. Taylor, 'Selfhood — Presence or Persona?' in *The Church Crossing Frontiers: Essays on the Nature of Mission in Honour of Bengt Sundkler*, ed. P. Beyerhaus and C. F. Hallencreutz (Uppsala, 1969), p. 176.

43. J. M. Brown, *Modern India: The Origins of an Asian Democracy, op. cit.*, pp. 147-49. Also B. T. McCully, *English Education and the Origins of Indian Nationalism* (New York, 1940); C. H. Heimsath, *Indian Nationalism and Hindu Social Reform* (Princeton, 1964).

The impact of Indian nationalism — often transmitted through western agencies — was therefore highly uneven across the Indian Christian community. To Azariah and many outcaste Indian converts, Indianization seemed more a British than an Indian idea. Azariah's western friends seemed unable to understand that Azariah was at least as uncomfortable wearing a turban as the European gentleman at the fancy dress ball on the *R.M.S. Otranto*. The bishop's discomfort was felt in differing degrees by most Indian Christians of his generation, who were increasingly either influenced or irritated by Indian nationalism.

Race and the Church

Why did so few Indian bishops emerge in a church whose bishops, Azariah's experience suggests, were so committed to developing Indian leadership? Why, when the Anglican church was willing in 1912 to place an Indian Christian in authority over a full-fledged multiracial Indo-Anglican diocese whose membership included British chaplains, missionaries, and congregations, did this not happen again for decades? Episcopal records, both before and after Azariah's consecration, suggest that the bishops wanted to appoint more Indians to the episcopate. What were the factors that stopped further progress in this direction?

The church had discussed the idea of appointing a native Indian bishop on several occasions during the nineteenth century, but each time largely jurisdictional obstacles stood in the way, along with some caste and racial prejudices.[44] British Anglicans seemed unable to put their theo-

---

44. The subject arose in a 1857 debate over the creation of a new diocese centered in Agra in the North-Western Province (later known as the United Province of Agra and Oudh, and then as Uttar Pradesh; but not the same as the North-West Frontier Province). The CMS resisted the appointment of a foreign missionary bishop in favor of 'a resident bishop who is familiar with the language and habits of the Native Christian Church, and who fully enjoys its confidence. But the question will then arise whether a *native* will not be the proper person' (quoted in S. C. Neill, *A History of Christianity in India, 1707-1858, op. cit.*, p. 274; M. E. Gibbs, *op. cit.*, p. 194; and T. E. Yates, *op. cit.*, pp. 104-6). In a memorandum on the extension of the Indian episcopate, the society reiterated its position that missionaries and evangelists should lead the way in establishing a native church rather than foreign missionary bishops who would, they argued, retard the emergence of indigenous bishops.

The proposal for a bishopric at Agra was dropped largely because of CMS missionaries' lingering belief that missionaries and chaplains ordained in England and supported largely by foreign agencies ought not to be subject to the jurisdiction of an

ries about Indian church leadership into practice at the highest level, and Indian bishops remained nothing but an empty dream. The Roman Catholic Church was even less successful in realizing its goal of indigenizing the church hierarchy in India. Although Rome stressed the importance of

---

Indian bishop consecrated in India. They protested that the Indian bishop's authority would be severely limited if it did not include control over the appointment and salaries of missionaries and chaplains serving within the diocese. Therefore, Neill contends that organizational and financial considerations more than racial prejudice hindered the early emergence of an Indian bishop (S. C. Neill, *Colonialism and Christian Missions, op. cit.*, p. 108).

The idea of appointing an Indian bishop was raised again in the following decade by Azariah's father's mentor, CMS missionary John Thomas. Unlike the church in the Punjab, the Tinnevelly church was relatively advanced in financial self-support. Only the Ugandan church in Africa had gone further in realizing Henry Venn's vision of self-governing, self-supporting, and self-propagating churches with indigenous church councils and speedy transfers of authority to the native clergy (the so-called 'euthanasia' of mission). By 1864, John Thomas wanted to place fifteen self-reliant congregations under the jurisdiction of an Indian bishop.

The Metropolitan at the time, Bishop Cotton, approved of appointing an Indian, but only as an assistant to the Bishop of Madras. This modified plan was then undercut by a report to Cotton from the SPG missionary in Tinnevelly, Robert Caldwell, questioning the Tinnevelly church's ability to maintain itself financially apart from the missionary societies. Caldwell doubted that an Indian bishop could operate effectively as a diocesan leader or that a suitable episcopal candidate could be found among the Tamil clergy. 'Things appear to me to be about as ripe at present for our having a native Governor as for our having a native Bishop' (M. E. Gibbs, *op. cit.*, pp. 252-53). By 1866, the plan for an Indian bishop was abandoned, although it was referred to repeatedly by the Bishop of Madras, Frederick Gell (bishop 1861-99), in subsequent charges to the diocesan clergy as part of his efforts to encourage the indigenous church to become more self-supporting, self-governing, and self-expanding. He considered the plan for a native bishop to be merely postponed and suggested that native chaplains be appointed instead (Frederick Gell, *A Charge Delivered on the 1st of November 1866 in St. George's Cathedral, Madras, at the Second Visitation of Frederick Gell, Bishop of Madras* [Madras, 1867], pp. 30-32; *A Charge Delivered on the 27th of October 1869 in St. George's Cathedral, Madras, at the Third Visitation of Frederick Gell, Bishop of Madras* [Madras, 1869], p. 11).

The CMS continued to explore the possibility of an Indian bishop for Tinnevelly in the 1870s without success. It chose a British missionary, Edward Sargent, as assistant bishop for the CMS mission areas in Tinnevelly in 1877. At least two Tamil clergymen were subsequently advanced as possible candidates for Tinnevelly bishoprics. But the first, William Sathianadhan, was rejected because of his caste affiliation as a Vellalar in contrast to Tinnevelly's Nadar majority. The other candidate, Vedanayagam Viravagu, was put forward in 1880 for a minuscule bishopric to be created in the north of the district but declined the offer, and the plan was therefore deemed 'premature' (M. E. Gibbs, *op. cit.*, p. 254; S. C. Neill, 'The Participation of In-an indigenous priesthood from 1845, mission historian Stephen Neill has noted that 'these injunctions met with singularly little response.'[45] An abiding belief in the white man's superiority combined with bad previous experiences with Goanese priests and a less venturesome phase of Jesuit activity in Asia help to explain the Roman church's delay.

It is commonly supposed that the Anglican church was slow to appoint Indian bishops because of stubborn racial prejudice. But nineteenth-century church records suggest that British bishops resisted the establishment of Indian bishoprics mainly in an effort to affirm the equality of races against widespread prejudice. To many nineteenth-century western church leaders, Indian bishops would lead to a racially divided church: a 'dual episcopate' in which English diocesan bishops would oversee European congregations and Indian assistant bishops, Indian congregations.[46]

---

dian Christians in Political Affairs,' in *The Church Crossing Frontiers: Essays on the Nature of Mission in Honour of Bengt Sundkler,* ed. P. Beyerhaus and C. F. Hallencreutz [Uppsala, 1969], pp. 78-79).

45. S. C. Neill, *A History of Christian Missions, op. cit.,* pp. 403-5.

46. See M. E. Gibbs, *op. cit.,* p. 254. Racist pressure to segregate the native and European churches under separate bishops began very early in India, and the bishops consistently took a firm stand against it. In 1838 a CMS missionary influenced by Tractarian ideals proposed unsuccessfully that the church in India subdivide its three dioceses and create suffragan bishops in each new area (T. E. Yates, *op. cit.,* pp. 78-83). Bishop Samuel Wilberforce's unsuccessful motion to Parliament in 1853, examined above, would have allowed the creation of missionary bishops (probably Europeans rather than Indians) for the Indian congregations within existing bishoprics (Julius Richter, *A History of Missions in India, op. cit.,* p. 274). The Bishops' Conference in 1873 decisively rejected a proposal for assistant bishops as opening the way for 'an inferior class of Bishops' without the freedom and independence necessary to execute the duties of their office (E. J. Palmer, 'The Anglican Communion: India,' *Episcopacy Ancient and Modern, op. cit.,* pp. 205-6; see also *Church Missionary Society: Resolutions passed by the General Committee, July 22, 1873, on the Appointment of Coadjutor Bishops in India,* 1: 1, Bishops, MACIPBC). This decision was crucial, argued a former Bishop of Bombay in 1930, for avoiding the 'considerable temptation to appoint Indian bishops as assistants . . . [which] would have become a cause of much ill-feeling today' (E. J. Palmer, 'The Anglican Communion: India,' *op. cit.,* p. 207).

The possibility that the episcopacy might be divided along racial lines was always imminent. Records of the Episcopal Conference in 1888 indicate that, although the bishops were steadfastly opposed to 'the idea of two churches, one for Europeans and one for Natives,' their views were not shared by people in England (*Report of the Episcopal Conference,* Calcutta [handwritten], 16 Jan. 1888, p. 3, BHA, Calcutta). In fact, Henry Venn and the CMS were by the late 1860's advocating racially defined episcopates because Venn feared that racially integrated churches would always be dominated by Europeans. See C. Peter Williams, *The Ideal of the Self-Governing Church,* pp. 43-47.

The threat of a racially divided church reemerged in the negotiations over Azariah's appointment. In his remarks at Azariah's consecration, Metropolitan Copleston warned the church against allowing this sort of racial division to emerge through the appointment of future Indian bishops.[47] That the next two Indians elevated to the episcopate were appointed only as assistants to European bishops (S. K. Tarafdar for Calcutta in 1935 and J. S. C. Banerjea for Lahore in 1937), and that this trend was also followed in China, Japan, and Africa,[48] suggests that the bishops may have bowed to the very pressures they had hitherto successfully resisted.

Another important factor influencing the church and missionary societies to delay appointing indigenous bishops was the perceived 'failure' in the 1880s and 1890s of the CMS's two most progressive experiments in indigenization: the first in Tinnevelly and the second in Africa. In 1863, the CMS initiated a system of church councils in Tinnevelly designed to give its elected members a greater measure of freedom despite the continued presence of missionary chairmen and of a missionary council. The reforms were drastically curtailed, however, after Bishop Sargent's death in 1889 when the society concluded that 'grave evils had entered into the life of the Church, and that in many areas order had been replaced by chaos.'[49]

The CMS believed in retrospect that it had transferred too much responsibility too quickly to Indian clergy who, it contended, were unequipped to cope with western-style administrative and financial responsibilities. Insufficient episcopal oversight after the deaths and retirements of the missionary chairmen of the church councils had apparently increased the troubles, and Tinnevelly's progress towards indigenization was delayed for another thirty years. Only in the twentieth century would missionaries wonder if their institutional structures and expectations had been inappropriate for the Indian village context. At the time, they tended to blame Indian Christians for their 'childlike' inadequacy. The Tinnevelly missionaries reimposed 'iron control' during Azariah's childhood and greatly influenced the future bishop's determination to end the paternalistic relationship between western missionaries and Indian Christians.[50]

47. C. Graham, *Azariah of Dornakal, op. cit.,* p. 40; M. E. Gibbs, *op. cit.,* p. 343.

48. S. C. Neill, *A History of Christian Missions, op. cit.,* pp. 525-26.

49. S. C. Neill, 'The Participation of Indian Christians in Political Affairs,' *op. cit.,* p. 68.

50. Whether the CMS objections were valid or not (most secondary sources have concluded they had some validity although further investigations may reveal otherwise), it is undeniable that the society's response worsened relations between the mis-

Many church leaders were also haunted by the perceived 'failure' of the Anglican church's first experience with a bishop of non-European race. Samuel Ajayi Crowther (c. 1807-99)[51] was consecrated in Canterbury Cathedral in 1864 as a missionary bishop[52] to West African countries beyond British jurisdiction (eastern Nigeria, principally along the Niger river). Freed from slavery as a boy and raised as a Christian, Crowther became a tireless missionary and translator of Christian texts into the Yoruba language. He accepted his episcopal post reluctantly, mainly in deference to his mentor Henry Venn and after receiving reassurances from the government that he would have no jurisdiction over European missionaries. Like Azariah, he was promoted by a visionary westerner.

By the year of Crowther's death, disciplinary scandals and European criticisms of Crowther and of Africans on the mission staff had severely undermined his reputation and credibility. The reasons for his supposed failure have been hotly disputed. Henry Venn has been accused of instituting his ideal of a native episcopate prematurely and in a doctrinaire fashion without either considering the practical difficulties or consistently supporting Crowther's mission. European missionaries of the CMS have been accused of using Crowther as a 'sacrificial victim' in a racially inspired vendetta against African church leadership. Crowther has also been faulted for lenience, weak judgment, and weak discipline.[53] Whatever the fundamental causes, the failure of Crowther's bishopric had an enormous impact on the future development of an indigenous Anglican episcopate in Africa. To many Anglican churchmen, Crowther became 'a symbol not

---

sionaries and many Tinnevelly Christians by the century's end. *Ibid.*, pp. 68-69; J. Richter, *A History of Missions in India, op. cit.*, p. 431; S. C. Neill, *Creative Tension: The Duff Lectures, 1958* (London, 1959), pp. 68-69.

51. On the history of Crowther's bishopric, see Lamin Sanneh, *West African Christianity: The Religious Impact* (London, 1983), pp. 75-76, 81-89, 168-78; T. E. Yates, *op. cit.*, pp. 110-17, 124-63; J. B. Webster, *The African Churches among the Yoruba, 1888-1922* (Oxford, 1964); S. C. Neill, *A History of Christian Missions, op. cit.*, pp. 306, 377-78, 396; Max Warren, *Social History and Christian Mission* (London, 1967), pp. 23-50.

52. Practical considerations rather than capitulation by Crowther's mentor, Henry Venn, to Tractarian ideals account for the appointment of Crowther as bishop to a mission field. See Yates, *op. cit.*, pp. 153, 162.

53. It was fellow Anglican Roland Allen who in 1927 first suggested that Crowther had been the victim of an impossible situation. Bengt Sundkler, *The Christian Ministry in Africa* (London, 1962); Roland Allen, *The Spontaneous Expansion of the Church* (Grand Rapids: Eerdmans, 1962), pp. 140-41; S. C. Neill, *A History of Christian Missions, op. cit.*, pp. 377-78, 396 (additional note); S. C. Neill, *Anglicanism, op. cit.*, p. 341; T. E. Yates, *op. cit.*, pp. 158-63; Lamin Sanneh, *West African Christianity, op. cit.*, pp. 169-73.

only of African leadership but also of the supposed failure of African leadership,' so that, 'for half a century and more, Africans were considered to be insufficiently "mature" for leadership in the Church.'[54]

The hesitancy of the Anglican church to appoint native bishops in India was almost certainly conditioned by this perceived fiasco in Africa. Church leaders in India were keenly aware of African precedents. CMS Secretary Rev. Canon E. S. Sell described in the sermon at Azariah's consecration a Ugandan experiment in church indigenization as a model for Azariah to follow in Dornakal.[55]

Socioeconomic factors also inhibited the elevation of an Indian to the episcopacy and to other positions of leadership in the church. Most British missionaries in the first half of the nineteenth century had belonged to the growing lower middle class of skilled mechanics, artisans, and tradesmen. The British carpenters, printers, bookbinders, weavers, mechanics, smiths, coopers, cabinetmakers and tinplate workers who comprised the bulk of the early nineteenth-century missionary population were not joined by a sizable number of British university graduates until later in the nineteenth century (in contrast to the earliest Evangelical [Protestant] missionaries trained at Halle University). Not all early nineteenth-century missionaries were from the 'mechanics class': Charles Simeon's 'pious chaplains' and missionaries came from Cambridge University, for example. But there was a sizable nineteenth-century petit bourgeois missionary class which seems to have had a psychological need to identify a lower class over which it could feel superior. This may have intensified the paternalistic attitude which many mis-

---

54. B. Sundkler, *The Christian Ministry in Africa, op. cit.,* p. 46. Crowther was succeeded by three European bishops and, although a number of Africans were appointed as assistant bishops in following years, no African diocesan bishop was appointed again until 1952. It is interesting to note that Africans generally opposed the appointment of British successors. As we shall see, this contrasts with the Dornakal experience where the indigenous church virtually insisted that a European successor to Azariah be appointed.

Crowther's humiliation and the choice of a European successor created a strong backlash among African Christians, whose growing separatist sentiments led subsequently to the prolific growth of Africa's independent churches. The appointment of African assistant bishops to serve under Europeans, beginning with James Johnson in the Niger Delta, created further animosity among African congregations and widened the separatists' rift with Anglicanism (L. Sanneh, *West African Christianity, op. cit.,* pp. 168-78).

55. Rev. Canon Sell, 'Strengthened with Might,' in *The Glorious Company of the Apostles and Other Sermons* (Madras, 1927), p. 17.

sionaries of this period developed toward the populations of their host countries.[56]

Then, as the educational qualifications of missionaries serving in India rose, opportunities for native leadership seemed to diminish.[57] By the turn of the century, the church in India recruited its bishops almost exclusively from highly qualified missionaries in India or Englishmen with previous Indian experience, and abandoned its earlier practice of recruiting less experienced bishops directly from England.[58] As the pool of talent in India 'improved,' competition for leadership positions stiffened, and most bishoprics remained in the hands of the same British educated class that controlled the appointments.

Two years before Azariah's consecration, an SPG missionary, J. A. Sharrock, argued that Indian Christians were comparatively unequipped to handle a bishop's responsibilities:

> So long as there are urgent appeals for Oxford and Cambridge men to do all the real work, which the Indian clergy at present cannot do; and so long as the Indian Church can neither support itself nor govern itself, the consecration of Indian bishops would only throw the Church back, as the Indians themselves well know. While English missionaries are a necessity, Indian bishops are an impossibility.[59]

Sharrock conceded that a self-supporting and self-governing church was 'an ideal at which we should aim,' but claimed that most clergy and laity, both English and Indian, believed that 'the Church is not yet sufficiently advanced, and that a suitable body of men does not yet exist.'[60]

This argument did not deter Whitehead and Copleston, who were suspicious of arguments that so closely resembled those of British government officials anxious to safeguard their political power. Even the more liberal-minded Britons who professed long-term desires for Indian self-

---

56. Although these missionaries condemned caste practices among Indian converts, they nevertheless made themselves into an exclusive caste in India. This contradiction between their Enlightenment-based opposition to caste or class and their own behavior was remarked upon by Bishop Heber and others. M. Warren, *Social History and Christian Missions, op. cit.,* pp. 36-56; Michael Hollis, *Paternalism and the Church, op. cit.*

57. M. Warren, *op. cit.,* p. 50.

58. M. E. Gibbs, *op. cit.,* pp. 338-39.

59. J. A. Sharrock, *South Indian Missions: Containing Glimpses into the Lives and Customs of the Tamil People* (London, 1910), p. 280.

60. *Ibid.,* p. 279.

government had increasingly during the late nineteenth century excused British inaction on the grounds of an immediate scarcity of native talent. Those few Indians who qualified for ICS positions were, like Azariah, often posted in remote and inaccessible areas where British officials preferred not to live and where Indian officials would pose less of a threat to British supremacy than in the centers of power.[61]

Unlike the Indian professional elites who filled scarce ICS positions, Indian Christians came mostly from outcaste or low-caste backgrounds, and this further prejudiced some Britons against them. The Indian Christian community in Tinnevelly preserves in its oral tradition a story that epitomizes the condescending manner with which some missionaries greeted the news that a Tinnevelly Christian of Nadar background was to be made a bishop. One Miss Ardill was said to have exclaimed that Azariah should be given at his consecration a *kurukkanthadi* (a T-shaped wooden pole used to climb palmyra trees and carried by climbers on their shoulders), instead of a bishop's staff.[62] Nadar Christians viewed the *kurukkanthadi* as a symbol of stigma rather than status. Far from a positive suggestion for indigenization, Tinnevelly Christians understood Miss Ardill's comment only as the insult it was meant to be.

That an Indian Christian without a college degree should be permitted to occupy a seat in the Episcopal Synod alongside distinguished Oxford and Cambridge graduates was an idea which many Britons also found difficult to accept.[63] Indeed, Azariah would probably not have been consecrated in 1912 had not a small group of liberal-minded church lead-

61. See Brajendra Nath De, 'Reminiscences of an Indian Member of the Indian Civil Service,' memoirs published serially in *Calcutta Review*, CXXXII-CXXXVI (April 1953-July 1956). I am grateful to Barun De for having drawn my attention to this interesting memoir. On British strategies for coping with new demands made by western-educated Indians, see J. M. Brown, *Modern India: The Origins of an Asian Democracy* (Delhi, 1985), pp. 138-43. See also Francis G. Hutchins, *The Illusion of Permanence, op. cit.;* John R. McLane, *Indian Nationalism and the Early Congress, op. cit.,* pp. 21-49; Anil Seal, *The Emergence of Indian Nationalism* (Cambridge, 1971), pp. 131-93.

62. Interview with David Packiamuthu, 13 March 1986, Perumalpuram, Tirunelveli. Miss Ardill was undoubtedly related to the conservative CMS missionary in Palamcottah, R. F. Ardill, who was also critical of Azariah's consecration, as we shall see in a following chapter.

63. At the time of Azariah's consecration, all other Indian bishops except two were Oxbridge graduates of considerable distinction, and the two others were graduates of Trinity College, Dublin: Reginald Stephen Copleston (fellow and tutor of St. John's College, Oxford), Henry Whitehead (fellow and lecturer of Trinity College, Oxford), Edwin James Palmer (first-class Lit. Hum., fellow and tutor of Balliol College, Oxford), Ernest Arthur Copleston (Reginald's younger brother, St. John's College, Ox-

ers taken advantage of a nondemocratic ecclesiastical system that did not require popular approval.

Azariah's backers, Whitehead and Copleston, were both sensitive to the rising national aspirations of the English-educated elites in India. Whitehead arrived in India just before the founding of the Indian National Congress in 1885, and he sympathized with reformist political leaders such as G. K. Gokhale (1866-1915) who called on the British to give Indians a greater share of the responsibility for their country's government. Whitehead allied himself with the liberal tradition of British government in India which looked forward to eventual Indian self-government and specially admired the Viceroy of India from 1880 to 1884, Lord Ripon.[64] Whitehead's decision to make Azariah a bishop was to some degree an attempt to provide an ecclesiastical answer to nationalist demands that he had already recognized as legitimate in the civil arena.

Azariah's appointment was also Henry Whitehead's answer to the moral problem of racism, which, he believed, was undermining the British position in India. He criticized his compatriots for encouraging divisions of caste, region, race, and nationality, and hindering both Indo-British relations and an effective united Indian nationalism. Whitehead had been shocked to see social and racial relations deteriorating between Indians and Englishmen in Calcutta, and he saw this social bitterness exacerbating India's political problems.[65] He and his wife organized frequent racially mixed social events, and exhorted his Madras diocese to do likewise. After holding a garden party for Europeans and Telugus, he wrote:

> I wish that garden parties of this kind, at which Europeans and Indians could meet together, were more common all over India. . . . I feel sure that the bitterness that now characterizes the political movement in India is largely due to social causes. The growing desire for political power is inevitable, but there is no need why it should be marked by such

---

ford), Rollestone Sterritt Fyffe (Emanuel College, Cambridge), George Alfred Lefroy (first-class Theological Tripos, Trinity College, Cambridge), Charles Hope Gill (Queen's College and Ridley Hall, Cambridge), George Herbert Westcott and Foss Westcott (fourth and fifth sons of Regius Professor of Divinity at Cambridge, Brooke Foss Westcott, a famous new Testament scholar; both sons at Peterhouse, Cambridge), Arthur Acheson Williams (Trinity College, Dublin; fellow of Madras University), Eyre Chatterton (honours in classics and literature, Senior Moderator, and Gold Medallist in Ethics and Logic, First Theological Exhibitioner, Trinity College, Dublin).

64. Whitehead, *Indian Problems in Religion, Education, and Politics, op. cit.,* pp. 199-224; R. J. Moore, *Liberalism and Indian Politics: 1872-1922* (London, 1966).

65. Whitehead, *Indian Problems,* pp. 270-301.

strong anti-English feeling. If Englishmen as a body in India would only be more courteous in their behaviour to their Indian subordinates and fellow-workers, and seek for opportunities of showing them a little sympathy, we should never have heard of the unrest, except as a perfectly natural and legitimate agitation on the part of educated Indians for an increased share in the government of their own country.[66]

Racial alienation and the simmering, silent hatred that undergirded many interactions between Britons and Englishmen provided a seemingly insurmountable barrier to forming the types of friendship Whitehead and Azariah desired. In contrast to Whitehead's optimistic view of interracial parties, British Parliamentary Under Secretary of State Edwin Samuel Montagu described a 'bridging-the-gulf' party in Lahore during his 1912-13 India tour as 'indescribably horrible.' All of the Indian guests (three Indian ladies and 'hundreds of prosperous looking Indian gentlemen . . . in costumes varying from frock coats to brocade') stood together and talked while being absolutely ignored by the Englishmen (who played tennis and badminton) and the Englishwomen (who 'gossiped' together). Montagu concluded that such parties did more harm than good.[67]

Azariah's consecration drew attention to the missionaries' success in bringing non-European races into the church but also heightened anxieties about the church's changing racial composition. At exactly this moment in 1910, the British author John Buchan published his popular schoolboy's adventure story, *Prester John*, which features an attack on the British Empire led by a rebel 'Kaffir King' disguised in the legitimizing cloak of a black African Christian minister. This story played to the primitive fear that beneath the veneer of even the most seemingly civilized black Christian minister lay some terrifying pagan essence. The protagonist, Laputa, delivers a sermon to the Free Kirk in Scotland but then disappears to a dark beach to perform a secret pagan ritual. Beneath the many onion-skin layers of his personality lay only 'something strange and great and moving and terrible.'

Buchan's story suggested that non-white Christians preaching equality between blacks and whites in God's sight might be secretly working to undermine the Empire. Laputa's idealistic sermon to the Scottish congregation forecastd a day when Negroes would have something to teach the British about civilization, but it was really only a euphemistic mask for his sinister plot against the white races. This popular story

---

66. *MTDM*, III, 9 (Sept. 1908), pp. 327-28.
67. *Edwin Samuel Montagu Diaries, 1912-13*, D. 523/38-40, IOL.

struck a resonant chord in the British public imagination at a time of heightened anxiety about the future of the empire. Some Britons may have subtly seen even the saintly Azariah as a mysterious Indian bishop whose real agenda could be threatening.

Whitehead hoped that Azariah's appointment would both mollify the Indian community and challenge those westerners who believed that white races should never be under the authority of non-white races. British missionaries were placed under Azariah's jurisdiction in the new Dornakal Diocese. Whitehead believed on practical grounds that an Indian would be better equipped than an Englishman to work in rural villages of the Telugu areas.

The subsequent history of Indian bishops suggests, however, that the bishops underestimated the many obstacles at different levels of Indian and British societies to realizing their interracial ideals. Whitehead chose a Tamil for the Dornakal post, thereby placing the first 'indigenous' bishop in a 'foreign' diocese. As Azariah's later career demonstrates, the Telugu congregations in Dornakal Diocese did not necessarily consider Azariah to be a fully sympathetic, let alone 'indigenous' representative of their interests. That the first Indian bishop should be regarded as something of an alien in his own diocese suggests that Whitehead — for all his vision and leadership — took insufficient account of the complex cultural, ethnic, linguistic, and caste differences that might impede the work of the Indian church on a national scale.

The Continuing Lack of Indian Bishops

Azariah's episcopal appointment was heralded in 1912 as the beginning of a new age for indigenous church leadership.[68] 'Rejoice in the appointment of Indian Bishops and ask for many more,' said Copleston;[69] and Bishop Whitehead predicted the appointment of more Indian bishops in the 'not far distant' future in a sermon delivered at Cambridge in the same year.[70]

However, the hopes of both the Metropolitan and his colleague in Madras were disappointed for the next three decades. No other Indians were made diocesan bishops during Azariah's lifetime. Of the thirty-four appointed to Anglican dioceses in India, Burma, and Ceylon from 1912 to

---

68. Rev. Canon Sell, 'Strengthened with Might,' in *op. cit.,* pp. 13-23.
69. Carol Graham, *Azariah of Dornakal, op. cit.,* p. 40; M. Gibbs, *op. cit.,* p. 343.
70. *MTDM,* VII, 9 (Sept. 1912), pp. 263-72.

1945, all were British except Azariah and C. K. Jacob, an Indian who was consecrated Bishop of Travancore and Cochin after Azariah's death in 1945.[71]

Azariah had no Indian diocesan colleagues during his career. Although two Indian assistant bishops were appointed to Calcutta (1935) and Lahore (1937),[72] Azariah remained what one historian has called a 'native curiosity'[73] in the Episcopal Synod to the end of his life.

The failure to follow up on the 1912 initiative is particularly startling in light of the almost unanimous agreement among European church leaders that Azariah's work in Dornakal was enormously successful. Already in 1917, the Metropolitan wrote confidentially to the Archbishop of Canterbury and the heads of London's major missionary societies praising Azariah for having won the esteem and affection of English missionaries in Dornakal, many of whom had previously 'expressed their entire unwillingness to work under him.' Azariah had developed such a degree of trust with his fellow Indian workers that the Metropolitan felt 'quite a new sense of what the life and power for the work of Evangelization of the indigenous Indian Church will be when under Indian leaders — provided they are, more or less, of the type of Bishop Azariah.'[74] The Archbishop of Canterbury responded, in turn, that Azariah's consecration marked 'a new departure in the Mission Field on the right lines.'[75] So pleased was the Anglican establishment with Azariah's work that his diocese was enlarged from an area roughly the size of Wales to one roughly the size of England within a decade of his conse-

---

71. Gibbs claims that Nirod Kumar Biswas was the second Indian diocesan bishop. He was consecrated Bishop of Assam in 1946, whereas C. K. Jacob was consecrated the year before, as Gibbs's own appendix demonstrates. Gibbs, *op. cit.,* pp. 380, 414, 416. Neill also claims that Azariah had one Indian diocesan colleague at the time of his death. S. C. Neill, *The Story of the Christian Church in India and Pakistan, op. cit.,* p. 155.

72. Unlike Azariah, who was given complete administrative control over a designated area while serving simultaneously as an assistant to the Bishop of Madras from 1913 to 1921, the assistant bishops of Calcutta and Lahore were given no independent jurisdiction over subdivisions of their dioceses and, hence, no diocesan seats in the Episcopal Synod such as that occupied by Azariah from the date of his consecration. Azariah suggested that they should be given such limited privileges in 'Circular Letter,' 16 Nov. 1942, 1: 4, Episcopal Synod, MACIPBC.

73. G. Thomas, *Christian Indians and Indian Nationalism, op. cit.,* pp. 232-33.

74. Metropolitan to the Rt. Revd. Bp. Montgomery, et al., 11 June 1917, 5: 2/7, Dornakal, MACIPBC.

75. Archbishop of Canterbury to the Metropolitan, 7 Aug. 1917, 5: 2/7, Dornakal, MACIPBC.

cration.[76] There is simply no indication that the church failed to appoint more Indian bishops because of displeasure with Azariah's performance, as had been the case with the pioneering bishopric of Samuel Crowther in Africa.

Yet there is also surprisingly little evidence in the preserved archival records of Indian Christian frustration or anger about the continuing lack of Indian bishops during these decades of growing nationalism. The problem was hardly referred to until the 1940s — and then only in the context of more general criticisms of the missionary establishment. In the highly charged anti-imperialist atmosphere of the Quit India movement with its promise of imminent independence, several Indian Christians compared the Anglican church's reluctance to transfer ecclesiastical control to Indian leaders with the British government's similar unwillingness to relinquish political control. The former principal of Serampore College, C. E. Abraham, argued that Azariah's long isolation as the only Indian bishop illustrated the church's insincerity in its stated goal of devolving authority from foreign missions to the native church. The Anglican church, like the British government, 'continually promised freedom for Indian people and in actuality always tried to delay it.'[77] An Anglican priest, M. C. Chakravarty, described the church in India as 'a side-show of British imperialism, an instrument subtly devised for the perpetuation of British domination in this country.'[78] Why, he asked, were there so few Indian church leaders and so little discontent with British dominance of the Episcopal Synod during the three decades leading up to independence?

The nationalist critique of the Indian church implied that non-Indian church leadership was responsible for excluding Indians from the episcopal ranks. It was true that Anglican churchmen often harbored aloof and condescending attitudes towards Indians. Before disestablishment of the church in 1930, the complex and undemocratic nature of the appointment system permitted the continued exclusion of Indians from the Synod.[79] Both the church and the government abandoned Copleston and Whitehead's enthusiasm for episcopal indigenization. But, after dis-

76. C. Graham, *Azariah of Dornakal, op. cit.,* pp. 42, 48.

77. G. Thomas, *Christian Indians and Indian Nationalism, op. cit.,* p. 233. Note also the similarities described by E. C. Bhatty between the foreign-based administrations of the government and the missionary societies. *Ibid.,* pp. 233-43.

78. *Ibid.,* p. 235.

79. Bishops were appointed by a variety of methods before disestablishment of the church in 1930. The Crown, with the advice of the Secretary of State for India, appointed bishops under letters patent for Calcutta, Madras, Bombay, Lahore, Rangoon,

establishment and the introduction of more democratic methods of episcopal selection, the pattern of exclusion did not change.[80] Many segments
of the Indian Christian population continued to prefer British bishops to

Lucknow, and Nagpur. Bishops under the commission of the statutory Bishops of Calcutta, Madras, and Bombay (Assam, Chota Nagpur, Nasik, Dornakal, Tinnevelly, and
Madura) were appointed by those bishops. If either the Bishop of Madras or the
Bishop of Bombay was the commissioner, they required the Metropolitan's assent as
well (E. J. Palmer, op. cit., pp. 206-7). The Bishop of Travancore was appointed by the
Archbishop of Canterbury, and the Bishop of Colombo first by the Crown and then by
the Diocesan Synod after disestablishment of the Church in Ceylon in 1886 (ibid., pp.
207-8). The church in India and Burma appointed seventeen more bishops according
to these diverse procedures between the date of Azariah's consecration and church disestablishment in 1930. Of these, seven appointments were transfers from other sees
and the remaining ten bishops chosen mainly from the missionary population. Although the Bishop of Madras offered Azariah the opportunity to become Bishop of
Tinnevelly, Azariah refused and the church failed to use any of its seventeen opportunities to elevate other Indians to the episcopate.

Indian bishops were also absent from the church in Ceylon where relatively early
disestablishment permitted diocesan clerical and lay participation in episcopal elections. When Reginald Copleston was transferred from the see of Colombo to Calcutta
in 1902, his brother, Ernest Arthur Copleston, was chosen as his successor by five senior bishops from the Church of England to whom the independent church entrusted
the appointment. The 'free' church in Ceylon continued to choose English bishops until 1964, when it elected Harold de Soysa as bishop. (E. A. Copleston served as bishop
until 1924, when he was succeeded by Mark Rodolph Carpenter-Garnier [1924-38],
Cecil Douglas Horsley [1938-48] and Archibald Rollo Graham-Campbell [1948-64].)
See Gibbs, op. cit., pp. 339, 413.

80. When the church achieved its independence from English civil control on
1 March 1930, the choice of episcopal nominees was turned over to diocesan governing bodies. At this time, individual bishops of the new Church of India, Burma, and
Ceylon lost all rights of coercive jurisdiction but, in exchange, obtained the 'right to be
free in all spiritual matters from the direction or interposition of any civil government'
(Gibbs, op. cit., p. 357). The new church's constitution contained several alternate
methods for the appointment of bishops. Bishops of so-called 'missionary dioceses'
(those whose finances were still temporarily controlled by missionary societies) were
appointed directly by the Metropolitan, but 'fully organized' dioceses were to elect
bishops through their own governing bodies.

Of the ten bishops appointed by the church in India and Burma in the period
between disestablishment and Azariah's death, none were native Indians — Madras:
Arthur Michael Hollis (1941-47); Rangoon: George A. West (1934-55); Lahore:
George D. Barne (1932-49); Travancore and Cochin: Bernard C. Corfield (1938-44);
Chota Nagpur: George N. L. Hall (1936-57); Lucknow: Sydney A. Bill (1939-47);
Tinnevelly: Stephen C. Neill (1939-45); Nagpur: Alexander O. Hardy (1937-48); Nasik:
Henry C. Read (1944-57); Bhagalpur (Patna): Thomas Lenman (1943-54).

This count excludes the three westerners appointed in 1945 after Azariah's

Indian ones. Given the opportunity to choose, a more indigenous and democratic church did not necessarily prefer Indian bishops. Democratization did not necessarily lead to indigenization; in fact, it may have hindered it.

Azariah declined comment on the absence of other Indian diocesan bishops for most of his career. He himself generally appointed Englishmen rather than Indians to important positions in the Dornakal Diocese: three European archdeacons and a European assistant bishop shouldered much of the responsibility for his diocesan administration. He may have sought to prove that white men could work successfully and harmoniously under Indian authority. But Azariah's lack of protest about his racial isolation in the Synod and his unwillingness to rely more on native Indian talent within his diocese indicated that, whatever his motives, the promotion of Indians was not his highest priority. Not until 1942 (and,

---

death: George C. Hubback (Calcutta, 1945-50), G. T. Selwyn (Tinnevelly, 1945-47 CSI), and A. B. Elliot (1945-47 CSI). Also excluded from the above calculations are the two western bishops appointed to Colombo between 1912 and 1945: Mark R. Carpenter-Garnier (1924-38) and Cecil D. Horsley (1938-48). These five bishops, together with Azariah, C. K. Jacob, and the 27 bishops appointed in India and Burma between 1912 and Azariah's death, bring the count up to 34, the above-mentioned number of bishops appointed in India, Burma, and Ceylon between 1912 and 1945.

In the Chota Nagpur, Travancore/Cochin, and Tinnevelly dioceses, large rural Indian Christian populations elected European bishops in 1936, 1938, and 1939 respectively. After 1945, more Indians were elected to episcopal posts; but only after political independence and the formation of the united Church of South India in 1947 was the Anglican church on the subcontinent placed under the control of a predominantly Indian episcopal body.

Even under the democratic post-independence election procedures, foreign bishops continued to be elected to serve in India. For example, Bishop Lesslie Newbigin served with great distinction as Bishop of Madura in the newly formed Church of South India from 1947 to 1959 and as Bishop of Madras from 1965 to 1974. It is clear that race was only one of a large number of factors affecting the outcome of episcopal elections in India and elsewhere during this period. Despite the striking difference between the African and Indian responses to the appointments of European successors to the first native bishops (anger in Africa and, as we shall see, relief in Dornakal), the African church continued to elect Europeans in later years. In a 1961 election of a new Archbishop for western Africa, the African candidate received some European support but not enough to win against the European candidate, Cecil Patterson, who was supported by many Africans. S. C. Neill, *A History of Christian Missions, op. cit.,* p. 526.

The 'indigenization' of church leadership in India was clearly not the result of democratic reforms accompanying disestablishment. On the contrary, democratization slowed down the indigenization of Anglican church leadership.

ironically, at the prompting of Tinnevelly's 'barefoot' bishop, Stephen Neill) did Azariah break his silence and formally protest the church's failure to appoint more Indian bishops in a circular letter to his episcopal colleagues.[81] Stephen Neill had urged the Synod and church to appoint more Indian bishops and moved the formation of a committee, led by Azariah, to devise proposals for removing obstacles in the way of such a development.

According to Azariah's committee report, the chief factor inhibiting the naming of more Indian diocesan bishops was the democratization brought about by church disestablishment. The chances of an Indian being elected bishop actually decreased after the church gained its independence from civil control in 1930, he contended, when the new Church of India, Burma, and Ceylon placed most episcopal elections into the hands of the dioceses. 'According to the present Constitution whereby Bishops are elected by the Dioceses themselves, there does not appear to be much chance for any of the Dioceses with large Indian Church populations to elect Indians as Diocesan Bishops.'[82] Regarding the dioceses of Tinnevelly, Travancore, and Chota Nagpur which had elected foreign bishops after disestablishment, Azariah explained that 'the large Rural Christians [sic] probably think they need a European Bishop to watch over their interests. Communal and personal jealousies also often come into play.'[83]

Azariah's conclusion was based on grassroots experience in his own diocese where intercaste and interregional rivalries led many to conclude that 'we would prefer to be ruled by a European to being ruled by an Indian as the former has generally a broad outlook and no vested interests in this country.'[84] The widespread preference for European over native church leaders did not end with the coming of national independence. Bishop Neill wrote as late as 1952 that:

> In the (Anglican) Church of India, the inclination still to elect European and not Indian bishops is so strong as to cause some dismay to those who believe firmly in the principle of indigenous leadership.[85]

---

81. 'Circular Letter,' 16 Nov. 1942, 1: 4, Episcopal Synod, MACIPBC.

82. *Ibid.*

83. *Ibid.*

84. *Manifesto of the Layman's Association of the CMS Churches of the Dornakal Diocese,* 5: 2/6, Dornakal, MACIPBC.

85. S. C. Neill, *The Christian Society, op. cit.,* p. 253. See also G. W. Houghton, 'The Development of the Protestant Missionary Church in Madras 1870-1920,' *op. cit.*

In order to elect more Indians to diocesan bishoprics, Azariah recommended that the church find ways to subvert its own constitution, just as the old Church of England in India had subverted the legal restrictions on its expansion. Azariah proposed that the problem be solved by appointing Indian assistant bishops who, after a few years of episcopal ministry under their diocesan bishops, would be given independent spheres of authority within the boundaries of the diocese:

> The procedure here proposed avoids the difficulty created by the electoral system which we have adopted in our Constitution for choosing Bishops. The Assistant Bishops will be appointed by nomination of the individual Diocesan Bishops — preferably by nomination of a panel, from which the Synod will appoint a Bishop. When once the Episcopal ministry of these Assistant Bishops is appreciated, the people will raise no difficulty to accept them as Diocesan Bishops — if necessary, over smaller areas than are now included in a Diocese. As Bishop Whitehead used to say when I was appointed: 'If he fails, only a small area will be threatened with disaster!' This procedure will satisfy the Constitution as it is at present. There is no provision for the appointment of the first Bishop of a fully organized Diocese. Approaching that stage through the back door of Assistant Bishops is the only possible method now, and it is as well that this is so.[86]

The problem Azariah confronted in 1942 was remarkably similar to that which his mentor Henry Whitehead had faced three decades earlier. In both cases, the Episcopal Synod was dominated by British bishops, and the most vocal opposition to Indianization came from Indian clergy and laity. Now as then, the most effective solution to the problem appeared to be the appointment of Indian assistants. The Synod made an exception to its policy against a 'dual episcopate' in 1922 when it decided that 'in some places it might be advisable to appoint Assistant Bishops as a temporary expedient or as a step intended to prepare the way for a division of the Diocese,'[87] and this permitted the appointment of two Indian suffragans. Azariah justified his 1942 recommendation that this method be employed again by claiming that Indian appointees would benefit from apprenticeships as assistants to more experienced diocesan (and European) bishops.

When Azariah procured consent from the Synod and the General

---

86. *Circular Letter,* 16 Nov. 1942, *op. cit.*

87. Quoted in 'Assistant Bishop,' *DDM*, XII, 1 (Jan. 1935), p. 12. In the same issue, see also pp. 11 and 13 and 'The Bishop's Letter,' pp. 8-10.

Council to appoint an Assistant Bishop for Dornakal in 1935, he chose an Irish CMS missionary and Archdeacon, A. B. Elliot, for the post. Azariah's principal reason for appointing the Irishman was that he doubted the abilities of Dornakal's Mala, Madiga, and caste converts to handle the responsibilities of episcopal office. In a 1934 letter, Azariah suggested that all Telugu clergymen in his diocese lacked the education, age, and experience needed for the job:

> If I look around in the Diocese for an *Indian* who is likely to be acceptable as Bishop, the field of choice is very limited. There are two or three men who are likely to be accepted as Bishop if the sole consideration was their own personal spiritual life: but their education is only up to the Matriculation standard. They will not command the respect of the European Missionaries and the Indians. There are a few younger men of both educational and spiritual qualification. . . . Some years hence they are sure to be considered as possibilities for this sacred office. Their age and experience is against them now. These considerations leave me no choice but to look around for an Assistant from among the European Missionaries. Perhaps this is not a disadvantage in a Diocese with an Indian Diocesan.[88]

Ironically, Azariah rejected Telugu candidates on the very same grounds upon which his own critics had sought to reject him before his 1912 consecration. He seemed more cautious than his mentors Whitehead and Copleston about 'taking a chance' on an Indian appointee. This decision and his controversial educational policy (examined below) left a legacy of bitterness in Dornakal in later years, particularly among the more educated Telugu converts. But there was little Telugu opposition to Elliot's appointment at the time, apart from a complaint by 'SPG Christians' that Azariah had chosen a CMS missionary.[89] Most Christians in the diocese appear to have preferred western missionaries to Indian clergymen. One SPG Christian later criticized Azariah for expelling 'the saintly and self-sacrificing European missionaries, who have spent their energy, money and blood for the SPG Telugu Church.' He also argued that SPG territories should have a separate bishop, presumably chosen from among the remaining Europeans.[90]

After Azariah's death in 1945, many Christians in the Dornakal Dio-

---

88. VSA to Metropolitan, 13 Nov. 1934, 5: 2/4, Dornakal, MACIPBC.
89. G. Abraham to Metropolitan, 24 June 1935, 422: 19A, D Series, USPG.
90. Memorial by P. Yesudas, 17 July 1939, 524: 1, D Series, USPG.

cese campaigned vigorously for a European bishop, rather than an Indian, to be elected as his successor. Numerous petitions to the Metropolitan complained that the aspirations of 'Andhra Christians' had been ignored under the 'Native Tamil Bishop.' One letter accused Azariah of imposing on Andhra's Christians 'a most dissatisfied life with strenuous struggle for their betterment,' and criticized Azariah for distancing the Dornakal church from 'the Mother Church of England, just as a child was forcibly removed from the hands of her mother: making us to lament the loss.' The authors decried 'the tyrannical yoke of this Indian Bishop,' citing particular dissatisfaction with his educational policies. Some congregations professed to be considering desertion to 'CATHOLISM' [*sic*], an occurrence which, they said, 'could never have taken place if we had an English Bishop.'[91] Another petition asserted that Telugus had been held back in their social, religious, political, and educational development 'under the leadership of a Native Tamil Bishop' and urged the election of 'ONLY an EUROPEAN BISHOP,' [*sic*] preferably the current assistant bishop, A. B. Elliot.[92] One missive claiming to represent 360 congregations criticized Azariah's administration, called on the Metropolitan to 'grant us a *fresh* English bishop who is not trained by the treacherous late Tamilian bishop,' and concluded with the chorus: 'We want English Bishop! We want English Bishop! We want English Bishop!'[93] Although one petitioner favored an Indian for the post, he dismissed all native clergymen as incompetent and recommended the election of a native layman, which the Metropolitan informed him was impossible under the church constitution.[94] Another letter called for the election of a Telugu bishop, but only one from 'a decent family and (with) a good College and Theological education', an apparent call for an educated caste candidate. The writer feared that an Indian bishop would be less able to obtain financial support from missionary societies and that, 'among Indians, the non-Andhras (Tamilians) will find a place.' Although he claimed that 'most of us in the

91. 'Your Most Obedient Children of Congregations in Andhra Diocese' to the Metropolitan, undated, 5: 2/7, Dornakal, MACIPBC.

92. T. Emmanuel Prianadhudu to the Metropolitan, 17 Jan. 1945, 5: 2/7, Dornakal, MACIPBC.

93. '360 Congregations of Dornakal Diocese' to the Metropolitan (undated), 5: 2/7, Dornakal, MACIPBC. See also in same file a telegram from CMS Church's Laymen's Association, Ellore, to the Metropolitan (undated), requesting a European bishop.

94. A. Andrews to the Metropolitan, 22 Feb. 1945, 5: 2/7, Dornakal, MACIPBC; Metropolitan to A. Andrews, 5 March 1945, 5: 2/7, Dornakal, MACIPBC.

Diocese feel that we ought to have an Indian again, as our next Bishop,'[95] all other preserved archival records suggest that the vast majority of Dornakal's congregations favored a European successor.

In the end, five Europeans, three Tamils, and three Andhras were nominated for the Dornakal post. After most withdrew their names from consideration, Elliot was elected by a vast majority as Bishop of Dornakal,[96] and the retiring Irishman reluctantly accepted in a letter to the Metropolitan:

> Though many have voted for me it is undoubtedly desirable that there should again be an Indian Bishop of Dornakal. In the hope that I can help to further this by accepting, preparing an assistant bishop or bishops and then making way for another election, I accept your call to be Bishop of Dornakal.[97]

The story of Azariah's consecration, bishopric, and succession suggests that intercaste and interregional competition for control of the church's considerable resources, combined with attitudes of dependency typical of colonial situations, created unexpectedly complex resistance to indigenization. Azariah's appointment had been essentially a European idea brought to fruition against considerable indigenous opposition. The European Synod's failure on numerous occasions to promote Indians to positions of leadership, particularly between 1912 and 1930, produced little indigenous protest. Diocesan clergy and laity in India, Burma, and Ceylon demonstrated little interest in appointing Indian bishops until political independence was imminent. Even then, this interest was confined mainly to educated Indian Christians with nationalist sentiments. Former outcastes, who filled the vast majority of Anglican churches in the Dornakal diocese, apparently considered British bishops preferable to most Indian alternatives, particularly Tamils. They regarded British missionaries and bishops as powerful patrons more likely to protect their interests than Indian bishops preoccupied with the interests of their particular caste or language group. Indian bishops were also regarded as less effective at garnering financial and other support from western sources.

95. Seelam Jacob to the Metropolitan, 27 March 1945, 5: 2/7, Dornakal, MACIPBC.

96. Elliot received 32 votes, another European received 16, and the only remaining Indian received 3 votes. See Metropolitan to the Bishops of Chota Nagpur and Madras, 12 April 1945, 5: 2/7, Dornakal, MACIPBC.

97. A. B. Elliot to the Metropolitan, 27 April 1945, 5: 2/7, Dornakal, MACIPBC.

Critics of Azariah's career focused much of their ire on his Tamil identity. The 1945 petitions reflected the influence of the broader cultural and political 'Andhra movement' which swept through the territory of the Dornakal Diocese during Azariah's lifetime and vented much of its frustration against Tamil neighbors to the south.[98] The Telugu-Tamil controversies that so weakened the effectiveness of the Justice Party in the 1920s had many cultural dimensions, as was demonstrated in the campaign that led to the creation of a separate Telugu-language university for Andhra in Vijayawada on 26 April 1926. The campus lay within the boundaries of the Dornakal Diocese, and Azariah was invited to deliver a convocation address there in 1929,[99] but the 1945 petitions against the appointment of further Tamil bishops for the Telugu church indicated how deeply anti-Tamil sentiments had penetrated rural Andhra society. The Dornakal church stressed the use of indigenous Telugu musical and dramatic idioms in worship and evangelism, and this may have made Telugu Christians more self-consciously aware of their Telugu heritage than most non-Christian Malas and Madigas. But rising Telugu objections to Tamil dominance over ecclesiastical affairs echoed similar objections expressed by secular counterparts against perceived Tamil political and cultural domination. Sir Charles Todhunter in a 1919 minute for the Government of Madras observed that 'the Telugu . . . has for officers one set of foreigners (Englishmen), and if and when they depart he does not want to exchange them for another set of foreigners (Tamils).'[100]

The formerly untouchable Telugu Christians were not generally prepared to accept Tamil authority during this period, and were almost equally hostile to competing Andhra ascendancies. Rivalry persisted within the church between Malas and Madigas, each of whom hoped to benefit from the objective arbitration of a western bishop in their recurrent disputes. Though continued British leadership was not desired by many educated Indian Christians, particularly those in urban areas, pro-British sentiment continued among less confident rural Indian Christians and appears to have had continuing influence on episcopal appointments after 1930. The church was in the unenviable position of discovering that the very instrument it had chosen to facilitate the process of indigeni-

98. P. Raghunadha Rao, *History of Modern Andhra* (New Delhi, 1978; revised ed., 1983), pp. 69-124.

99. 'Andhra University, Third Convocation, 1929. Addresses by V. S. Azariah and the Vice-Chancellor Mr. R. C. Reddy,' copy in Azariah Collection, Madras.

100. Quoted in Eugene F. Irschick, *Politics and Social Conflict in South India, op. cit.*, p. 246, n. 58. See also pp. 244-51.

zation in India, disestablishment, had virtually eliminated the short-term prospects for an indigenous episcopate.

The bishops' evident frustration at their inability to convince the Indian church of its rights and responsibilities regarding self-government belies the nonconformist charge that Anglican bishops constituted a fundamentally conservative force blocking the more progressive aspirations of the laity.[101] It seems equally doubtful that Azariah remained the only Indian bishop because of 'the extreme reluctance of Western churches and missions in India to relinquish the dominant hold they had in the affairs of the Christian movement in India.'[102] On the contrary, the greatest challenge to the appointment of Indian bishops came from Indian Christians who, in the case of Azariah's appointment, were unable to prevail. Synodical reforms and disestablishment, both of which placed greater decision-making powers in Indian hands, did not lead to Indianization of the Synod but rather to continued dependence on western leadership.

Of course, not all bishops in India favored rapid indigenization. The Bishop of Lahore from 1899 to 1913, G. A. Lefroy, vigorously opposed the appointment in 1907 of S. K. Rudra as principal of St. Stephen's College (Delhi) with the argument that no Indian would have 'the same power of vigorous and effective leadership or would be trusted and followed by the Indian Professors and students themselves at all in the same way as (would) a good Western (Principal).'[103] Lefroy did not greatly alter his opinions about Indian leadership during his ensuing tenure as Metropolitan from 1913 to 1919, and this probably contributed to the paucity of Indian episcopal appointments via undemocratic means during those years. But even Lefroy demonstrated a softening of his attitude towards Indian aspirations when, at the suggestion of C. F. Andrews, he publicly supported South African Indians in their *satyagraha* struggle of 1913.

Lefroy was supported in his position by five of his episcopal col-

---

101. During the ongoing negotiations for the united Church of South India, critics of the episcopacy like the non-Anglican J. J. Banninga of Madura noted that the laity 'have usually sought progress and the bishops have been the conservative element,' and argued that allocation of greater powers to bishops would be 'a conservative rather than a progressive force' that 'puts the power into the hands of the bishops to keep the church as it has been' rather than placing authority 'in the hands of the laity to make the Church be what they think it ought to be.' J. J. Banninga to Bartlett, 21 July 1928, Sundkler collection, Uppsala.

102. G. Thomas, *Christian Indians and Indian Nationalism, 1885-1950, op. cit.,* pp. 232-33.

103. Quoted in *ibid.,* p. 155.

leagues, while two opposed him. Significantly, Azariah gave only modified consent, in contrast to the Bishop of Madras' urging to take more radical action.[104] And by 1917, Lefroy favored transferring all remaining CMS Telugu missions to Azariah's diocese, remarking that 'it was delightful seeing Bishop Azariah among his people; the true leadership, together with the entire sympathy and mutual understanding.'[105] By the early 1940s, leading European bishops such as Stephen Neill, Michael Hollis, and Foss Westcott were at least as determined to end the 'foreignness' of the Anglican leadership in India as highly educated Indian Christian nationalists.

The church's decision to encourage the mass movements of depressed classes into Christianity propelled western missionaries and bishops into becoming the protectors and patrons of previously powerless people. Once the control of episcopal appointments was placed more firmly in diocesan hands, these converts were understandably reluctant to jettison their relatively disinterested new defenders in favor of Indians who seemed less powerful and more likely to favor 'foreign' or rival castes.

104. Hugh Tinker, *The Ordeal of Love, op. cit.,* pp. 77-78, 83.
105. H. H. Montgomery, *The Life and Letters of George Alfred Lefroy, op. cit.,* p. 248.

CHAPTER 6

Bishop in Andhra:
Local Transformation through Conversion

B ack in Dornakal, Azariah continued his work of church building. He
turned the small IMS mission outpost in Dornakal into the center of
India's fastest-growing Anglican diocese. In so doing, he forged an original, independent path — following neither the western norms preferred by
most villagers nor the Indian norms preferred by most westerners and Indian nationalists. His goal was nothing short of transforming both the
structure and the worldview of rural Telugu life. He presented Christianity as a new and sacramental framework for Andhra's depressed and non-
Brahmin classes. Traditional moral, socioeconomic, political, legal, and
spiritual priorities were all to be thoroughly reordered. Azariah's success
with the so-called 'mass movements' in Andhra eventually caught the eye
and earned the disapproval of the broader non-Christian Indian community, including Gandhi. But few if any of Azariah's critics have bothered to
study the actual history of Dornakal Diocese under Azariah's guidance.

Azariah's approach to mission in Dornakal was, first and foremost,
orthodox and church-centered. He believed it was impossible to be Christian outside the institutional 'Body of Christ.' Christian life found its
proper social and historical expression, Azariah asserted, only through the
one, holy, catholic, and apostolic church founded by Jesus Christ and
functioning as 'the one instrument of His spirit's special operation in the
world.' Azariah disagreed with Hindu reformers such as Manilal C. Parekh
and Keshub Chunder Sen, who argued that one could be a Christian while
having 'little to do with organized forms of Christianity of any kind.' The

176

bishop held this view to be nothing more than a 'parody' and a 'presumption' since 'the Church is not an association that individuals can or may organize for their own convenience,' but is rather 'a new creation' established in history by God himself on the first Easter day to continue the work of Jesus Christ on earth. This orthodox position did not win Azariah many friends in an age and culture dominated by triumphant heterodoxies, beginning with Gandhi's idiosyncratic interpretation of the *Bhagavad Gita* and extending to Christian reinterpretations of theology as well.[1] But it proved to be a steady guide to Azariah in Dornakal, where he worked from 1909 until his death in 1945.

The Dornakal diocese lay in the land of the Telugus, or Andhras,[2] which was divided politically between the British and the Nizam of Hyderabad, but united by a common language and ancient heritage. Comprising a triangular area extending along the seacoast from just north of Madras to the border of Orissa and westward to Bellary beyond the subcontinent's center, it encompassed 61,378 square miles in 13 districts of the Madras Presidency and 41,512 square miles in 9 districts of the Nizam's Dominions.[3] There were fertile coastal areas nourished by the Kistna (Krishna), Godavari, and Pennar Rivers, hilly inland regions of the Eastern Ghats and the great plains of the Deccan. Most of this territory had once been part of the kingdom of Telingana, and later belonged to a powerful Muslim Governor of the Deccan, known as the Nizam-ul-mulk. The territory north of the Coromandel Coast (the so-called 'Circars' or 'Northern Circars' of Ganjam, Vizagapatam, Godavari and Kistna), was given to the

1. On Gandhi, see Margaret Chatterjee, *Gandhi's Religious Thought* (Notre Dame, IN, 1983). On Christian reinterpretations, see G. V. Job, et al., *Rethinking Christianity in India Today,* ed. D. M. Devasahayam and A. N. Sudarisanam (Madras, 1938). See also M. M. Thomas, *The Acknowledged Christ of the Indian Renaissance* (London, 1969), p. 80; and VSA, *The Church and Evangelism, op. cit.* (1936), pp. 32-37.
2. The classical name Andhra is generally preferred by Telugu speakers. The name of today's state, Andhra Pradesh, translates as 'country of the Andhras.' 'Andhra' was commonly used alone to refer to Telugu-speaking regions as they existed before incorporation into the modern state.
3. The 13 districts of the Madras Presidency in which Andhras were concentrated at the time of the 1931 Census were Ganjam, Vizagapatam Plains, Godavari East Agency, Godavari East Plains, Godavari West, Kistna, Guntur, Nellore, Cuddapah, Kurnool, Anantapur, Madras City, and Chittoor. The 9 districts of the Nizam's Dominions were Hyderabad City, Atraf-i-Balda, Warangal, Karimnagar, Adilabad, Medak, Nizamabad, Mahabubnagar, and Nalgonda. 'Statistics of Telugu Christianity,' *DDM,* XI, 8 (Aug. 1934), p. 6; J. B. Williams, *Research Studies in the Economic and Social Environment of the Indian Church* (Guntur, 1938), Tables 1A and 1B.

French in 1757 and, after pressure from Robert Clive, to the British in 1765. The Nizam ceded the southern districts of Cuddapah, Kurnool, and Bellary (known as the 'Ceded Districts') to the British by 1800.

Economic and social conditions varied widely across the Telugu area. Under the British, coastal Andhra became one of India's great grain producers. An extensive irrigation system helped to control the Kistna and Godavari Rivers, boosted the production of rice and sugarcane, and ameliorated persistent problems of flood, famine, and epidemic.[4] Economic conditions were harsher in the less fertile inland districts where forests provided some timber (primarily teak and sal) and arable lands were farmed for millet, cotton, indigo, and some rice. Dornakal itself was situated in a forested area used by the Nizam for hunting and gaming.

The emerging Indian Christian community in Andhra was composed almost entirely of former untouchables who lived on meager daily wages from agricultural and leather work, and were the first to suffer during famines such as those of 1832-33, 1865-66, and 1876-77.[5] A gradual erosion of economic and social security caused by the dislocating effect of western rule upon the *jajmani* system during the nineteenth century left the depressed classes with fewer strong patrons and, in most cases, a lower standard of living than before. As the system of reciprocal duties and services which had hitherto regulated rural village society slowly weakened, the depressed classes were freed to some extent from social pressure enforced by higher castes to consider the claims of new western missionary patrons.[6]

In the Nizam's districts, the lack of effective legal safeguards against the power of the landlords *(maktedars* and *pattedars)* to subject tenants to serfdom and slavery *(baghela* and *vetti chakiri)* made the plight of the poorest agricultural laborers especially onerous. A lack of control over revenue collectors made the lowest groups in the social hierarchy desperate for the

4. On the difficulties of measuring the irrigation system's effectiveness, see E. Whitcombe, 'Irrigation and Railways,' in *The Cambridge Economic History of India,* ed. D. Kumar and T. Raychaudhuri, pp. 677-737.

5. On the role of Telugu Christians in building irrigation systems during the latter famine and the conversion movements that followed the crisis, see John E. Clough, *Social Christianity in the Orient* (New York, 1914).

6. D. B. Forrester, 'The Depressed Classes and Conversion to Christianity, 1860-1960,' *op. cit.,* pp. 41-43. Clough's record demonstrates, however, that persecutions continued despite such changes. See J. E. Clough, *op. cit.* See also A. T. Fishman, *Culture, Change and the Underprivileged: A Study of the Madigas in South India under Christian Guidance, op. cit.;* P. Hiebert, *Konduru: Structure and Integration in a South Indian Village, op. cit.*

kind of protection which outside missionaries — particularly Europeans — provided. In the earliest days of the IMS mission to Dornakal, Mala converts looked to IMS missionary Samuel Pakianathan for help in an ultimately successful court case over water resources against a local landlord (*dora*). Without missionary backing, the local Malas would probably not have had the courage to confront the powerful *dora,* who was reputed to steal sheep and cows without penalty.[7] Azariah's son Ambrose remembers that the advocacy of IMS missionaries such as the Rev. Gell Knight against oppressive upper castes was one of the primary reasons for untouchable, tribal, and low-caste receptivity to Christianity in Dornakal.[8]

The mass movements to Christianity occurred in Andhra during a time of dramatic regional awakening and self-assertion on many levels. A rediscovery of Telugu culture was already underway when Azariah arrived in Dornakal, partly rooted in the influence of earlier western Christian missionaries. Telugu journals proliferated from one to twenty during the period from 1858 to 1905,[9] and English education spread[10] and created a new type of Telugu elite instructed in western liberal principles and skeptical of many practices common to orthodox Hindu society.

By the second half of the nineteenth century, Telugu elites in the districts under direct British rule were relatively receptive to new stirrings of both regional and national political sentiment. But this was less true at

---

7. Interview with Rev. Daniel, 31 March 1986, Dornakal. Rev. Daniel's father was a Mala weaver named Butchayya who converted to Christianity under the influence of the IMS and took the new Christian name, Job. He took the case against the *dora,* Madavarazu Narasimha Rao, to the district court with the help of Samuel Packianathan.

8. Interview, 23 March 1986, Madras.

9. Beginning with the publication of the Bellary Christian Association's *Satya-doota.* P. Raghunadha Rao, *History of Modern Andhra, op. cit.,* pp. 73-76.

10. Noble College (known then as English School) was founded in Masulipatam by CMS missionary Robert Noble in 1843, with a mission particularly to Brahmin elites. See John Noble, *A Memoir of the Rev. Robert Turlington Noble: Missionary to the Telugu People of India* (London, 1867). Noble College's importance as a centerpiece in Andhra's emerging cultural self-identity helps to explain why Azariah's later closure of the college caused a particularly strong outburst of criticism from upwardly mobile Christian populations. Other milestones were the University of Madras (1857), a second grade college in Rajahmundry (1873), Hindu College in Visagapatam (1878), and Dhallikota College in Berhampur (1879). For a study of one of the patron saints of the Telugu revival, see Peter Schmitthenner, *Telugu Resurgence, 1800: C. P. Brown and Cultural Consolidation in South India* (New Delhi: Manohar, in press). This study is based on a revision of his University of Wisconsin Ph.D. thesis (1991) entitled 'Charles Philip Brown: The Legacy of an East India Company Servant and Scholar of South India.'

the outcaste or lowest caste levels of Telugu society, to which missionaries now increasingly turned their attention. And it was even less true in the districts under the Nizam's control, where Urdu was the required language for education and administration and English education had not yet penetrated.[11] This was the region to which Azariah brought a religious and social message that provided the society's poorest inhabitants with a new sense of purpose and confidence both as Christians and as Telugus.

Anglican Missions and 'Mass Movements' in Andhra

Government officials played an important role in bringing the first Anglican missions to Andhra. Both the CMS and the SPG sent their first missionaries to Telugu-speaking regions at the request of civil servants bent upon the evangelization of India.[12] Anglican missions proved as unsuccessful in Andhra as they had been in Bengal in converting the society's elites through educational institutions.[13] The English school established in Masulipatam, like the great Scottish colleges in the Presidency cities, provided high-quality education but few conversions. The school's academic success led to its elevation in 1893 to college rank, but its illustrious founder Robert Noble lived to see only eleven students baptized.[14]

11. P. R. Rao, *op. cit.,* pp. 67, 74.

12. The CMS established its first Telugu mission in 1841 after discovering that civil and military officials in the Telugu country had been praying for missionaries to come and had raised 2,000 to 3,000 pounds sterling toward their support. In response to an appeal from John Goldingham, the Collector of the Guntur District from 1836 to 1841, the society centered its operations in Masulipatam, the largest town on the eastern coast between Madras and Calcutta and the site of an East India Company factory since the seventeenth century. Likewise, the SPG founded its mission at Cuddapah in 1842 after receiving a petition from a former civil servant, William Howell, who had resigned in 1822 to engage in full-time evangelistic work for the London Missionary Society in Cuddapah and gained a hundred converts in twenty years. The SPG accepted Howell as a missionary when he was episcopally ordained in 1842 and sponsored his work in Cuddapah. W. D. Clarke, *The Centenary of the South Indian Mission of the Church Missionary Society* (Madras, 1914), pp. 21-24. Copy in 1913-14: 34, G2 I2/0, CMSA. Also M. E. Gibbs, *op. cit.,* pp. 151, 260; C. Graham, *Azariah of Dornakal, op. cit.,* pp. 63-70.

13. J. W. Pickett, *Christ's Way to India's Heart* (Lucknow, 1937), pp. 11-21.

14. Noble witnessed the conversions of nine Brahmins, one Velama, and one Muslim. Two baptisms of students in 1852 resulted in a temporary boycott of the school. Although the numbers were small, these converts were greatly influential: one

The rising and sizable non-Catholic, Evangelical communities in Andhra, as in other parts of India, depended on conversions from the lowest ranks of the social hierarchy.[15] These so-called 'mass movements'[16] of

---

became a judge, another a magistrate, one a minister and missionary, two were headmasters, seven were assistant-masters of English schools, and one edited a vernacular Christian magazine. *The Church Missionary Atlas* (London, 1896), pp. 143-44. See also John Noble, *op. cit.* In contrast to Noble, whose mission to elites followed the example of the Jesuit missionary, Robert de Nobili, CMS missionary G. T. Fox focused on Andhra's low-castes and outcastes. See Henry W. Fox, *Memoir of G. T. Fox: Missionary to the Teloogoo People* (London, 1861).

15. The Protestant church in the Punjab grew from 3,823 in 1881 to 483,081 in 1947 due to accessions of sweepers and landless laborers. Between 1870 and 1914, most of the Chuhras of Sialkot district converted to Christianity. The Nadar movements of Tinnevelly were examined in Chapter One. For discussions of mass movement activity, see D. B. Forrester, *Caste and Christianity: Attitudes and Policies on Caste of Anglo-Saxon Protestant Missionaries in India* (London, 1980), pp. 83-92; J. C. B. Webster, *A History of the Dalit Christians in India* (San Francisco, 1992); T. V. Philip, 'Protestant Christianity in India since 1858,' in *Christianity in India: A History in Ecumenical Perspective*, ed. H. C. Perumalil and E. R. Hambye, *op. cit.*, pp. 267-72. Of course, group conversion movements also occurred in the Roman Catholic Church, beginning with the sixteenth-century conversion *en masse* of the Paravas. On the Parava community, see S. B. Kaufmann, 'A Christian Caste in Hindu Society: Religious Leadership and Social Conflict among the Paravas of Southern Tamilnadu,' *MAS*, XV, 2 (April 1981), pp. 203-34; 'Popular Christianity, Caste and Hindu Society in South India 1800-1915: A Study of Travancore and Tirunelveli' (Ph.D. thesis, Cambridge University, 1980). However, later movements to the Catholic church were not as large as those to the Protestant community. See A. Meersman, 'The Catholic Church in India since the mid-19th Century,' in *Christianity in India: A History in Ecumenical Perspective, op. cit.*, p. 253. On South Indian Protestant mass movements, see D. B. Forrester, 'The Depressed Classes and Conversion to Christianity, 1860-1960,' and G. A. Oddie, 'Christian Conversion among Non-Brahmans in Andhra Pradesh, with Special Reference to Anglican Missions and the Dornakal Diocese, c. 1900-1936,' both in *Religion in South Asia: Religious Conversion and Revival Movements in South Asia in Medieval and Modern Times*, ed. G. A. Oddie (New Delhi, 1977), pp. 35-66 and 67-99 respectively. See also by G. A. Oddie, 'Christian Conversion in the Telugu Country, 1860-1900: A Case Study of One Protestant Movement in the Godavery-Krishna Delta,' *IESHR*, XII, 1 (Jan.-March 1975), pp. 61-79; and 'Christianity in the Hindu Crucible: Continuity and Change in the Kaveri Delta, 1850-1900,' *ICHR*, XV, 1 (June 1981), pp. 48-72. These authors trace the movements back to the late nineteenth century although there are earlier precedents, as R. E. Frykenberg argues in his articles referenced in the opening of Chapter 1. See also S. C. Neill, *A History of Christianity in India, 1707-1858, op. cit.*, pp. 215-35.

16. It was widely agreed, even by those who commonly used the term, that 'mass movements' was an inappropriate name for describing conversion movements, which rarely involved more than a small proportion (about 3 percent) of the total Indian population. They were 'mass' movements less in the sense that they attracted huge

depressed classes to Christianity across India swelled the total Indian Christian population from 1,862,634 in 1881 to 6,290,292 in 1931.[17] In both the eastern and western portions of Azariah's future diocese, group conversion movements of outcaste Malas and Madigas were sparked largely by newly converted Indian Christians and spread through local networks of family and *jati*.[18]

The movements in Azariah's future diocese took place within the broader context of similar group movements to Christianity which were sweeping through Telugu country under the auspices of both American Baptist and American Lutheran missions. By 1912, the American Baptist Telugu Mission reported 61,687 church members on its rolls, almost all of them former Madigas brought into the Christian fold through the initial leadership of leather worker and agricultural laborer Yerraguntla Periah of Ongole. This mission alone baptised between 1,500 and 3,500 Madigas annually.[19]

---

numbers of converts than in the sense that the converts entered the church *en masse*, i.e., in family or *jati* groups. 'Group,' 'communal,' or 'people' movements have all been suggested as alternatives better approximating the movements' group or caste-based character. J. W. Gladstone, *Protestant Christianity and People's Movements in Kerala, 1850-1936* (Kannamoola, Trivandrum, 1984), pp. 7-9; J. W. Pickett, 'Christian Mass Movements in India,' *MRW*, LIX, 4 (April 1936), p. 167; and *Christian Mass Movements in India, op. cit.*, pp. 21-22. The less than satisfactory term 'mass movement' has been adopted for the purposes of this study in deference to its contemporary usage during the period under investigation.

17. 'The India Census,' *DDM*, X, 11 (Nov. 1933), p. 9. These figures do not include accessions in the Indian states, Burma, or Ceylon. The total Christian population of India, Burma, and Ceylon in 1931 was 6,819,829, almost half of which were Protestant Christians. *Directory of Christian Missions and Churches in India, Burma and Ceylon, 1940-1941* (Nagpur, 1940), p. 37. Statistics based on census data were used frequently in mass movement literature and sometimes contradicted each other. Elsewhere, Azariah stated that the total Indian Christian community in India and Burma in 1931 numbered only 5,990,234, with a growth rate of 34 percent between 1921 and 1931. VSA, 'The Christian Church in India,' in *Moving Millions* (Boston: The Central Committee on the United Study of Foreign Missions, 1938), p. 172.

18. The most effective agents for the spread of Christianity were not the missionaries but rather Indian Christians who spread the news about their new faith informally among their own people. Isolation of new converts in mission compounds tended to hinder this process of transmission. T. V. Philip, 'Protestant Christianity in India since 1858,' in *op. cit.*, p. 272; Sunder Raj, *The Confusion Called Conversion* (New Delhi, 1986), pp. 13-14. The indigenous transmission system is described in J. Clough, *op. cit.*

19. John C. B. Webster, *A History of the Dalit Christians in India* (San Francisco, 1992), pp. 40-44.

The mass movement in the CMS territory of the Krishna-Godavari delta, which increased Christian membership from 260 in 1861 to 11,356 in 1894, began with the conversion of a Mala headman named Pogolu Venkayya, who was known for daring exploits of highway robbery before his baptism in 1859. His testimony regarding the claims of Christianity set into motion the conversion movements that eventually brought thousands of Malas and, later, Madigas into the church.[20]

Similarly, the mass movements in the western territories under SPG auspices were sparked by the conversion of another Mala 'outlaw' named Akutu Nancharu.[21] Rev. William Howell met and spoke with Nancharu while the latter was an inmate in the Cuddapah jail, and Nan-

20. Venkayya himself was said to have persuaded over 700 people from his family and *jati* to be baptized. See G. A. Oddie, 'Christian Conversion in the Telugu Country, 1860-1900,' in *op. cit.*, pp. 67-69; *The Church Missionary Atlas, op. cit.*, p. 144; C. Graham, *Azariah of Dornakal, op. cit.*, pp. 68-69; J. B. Williams, *Research Studies in the Economic and Social Environment of the Indian Church, op. cit.*, p. 9.

21. It is significant that both of these pioneer converts regarded the missionaries as potential champions of their causes with the police and in the law courts. Missionaries often provided converts with legal assistance and frequently defended them against persecutors. See A. T. Fishman, *Culture Change and the Underprivileged: A Study of the Madigas in South India under Christian Guidance* (Madras, 1941), pp. 16-17. Protection from what converts described as police harassment was one of the common motives for conversion. For example, Yerukalas (Erukalas), who were commonly identified as 'burglars' as well as basket weavers and soothsayers, complained that they were frequently blamed for burglaries they never committed. One Yerukala convert in Dornakal testified: 'In former times when a theft occurred, whoever might be the thief, the village authorities used to arrest us and put us in prison for some days. But since we have become Christians we are free from such troubles. No one is bold enough to touch us without the permission of our pastor.' *DDM*, IX, 8 (Aug. 1932), p. 11. In 1912, CMS missionaries observed a decrease in the numbers desiring Christian instruction after the Nizam's Inspector-General of Police rescinded an order that placed certain lower castes under police supervision but exempted Christian enquirers. When the Nizam extended this exemption to all lower classes, the missionaries recorded, 'one of the motives which has figured largely in the accessions of recent years no longer exists.' *Minutes of the 125th Telugu Missionary Conference held at Bezwada, Sept. 29–Oct. 2, 1912,* in 1912: 205, G2 12/0, CMSA. Yerukalas and Waddars were the groups most anxious for missionary protection from police intimidation and harassment, according to G. A. Oddie, 'Christian Conversion among Non-Brahmans in Andhra Pradesh, with Special Reference to the Anglican Missions and the Dornakal Diocese, c. 1900-1936,' in *op. cit.*, pp. 75-76. As we shall see below, Malas and Madigas were also frequently accused of crimes, and, whether they were guilty or not, the fact that missionaries offered them any support at all, moral or otherwise, was apparently significant enough to ignite an interest in conversion. See also J. W. Pickett, *Christ's Way to India's Heart, op. cit.*, p. 42.

charu persuaded Howell to send two Christian teachers to his village. The subsequent evangelistic work of two Telugu brothers, Alfred and Basil Wood, in the SPG areas between the Red and Black Hills led to the baptisms of some 1,700 Christians (with over 1,000 others receiving instruction in the faith) in the period from 1852 (the year of the first baptism) to 1870. The famine of 1876-77 devastated this community and led to persecution by Hindus, who blamed the newly converted Christians for the catastrophe. However, the Christian community benefited in the long run when recipients of church-sponsored famine relief asked for baptism in later years. There were 10,000 members on the SPG church rolls in the western part of Azariah's future diocese (near Cuddapah) by the end of the century, and nearly 20,000 by the year 1920.[22]

Conversions to Christianity occurred in Andhra at a faster rate than in almost any other South Asian region during Azariah's lifetime. During the first four decades of the twentieth century, the Indian Christian population grew at a faster rate than other major communal groups. Between 1921 and 1931, an average of 12,855 converts joined the church each month. The Indian Christian population of India and Burma increased at a rate of 32.5 percent during this decade, with Protestant Christians increasing at a rate of 41 percent.[23]

The rate of growth in Telugu-speaking areas was among the fastest on the subcontinent.[24] The total Anglican Christian population in the Dornakal Diocese increased from 56,681 in 1912 to 225,080 in 1941, a number which exceeded the total number of Anglican converts for all of

22. C. Graham, *op. cit.,* pp. 66-67. On the mass movements, mainly of Madigas, to the Baptist churches in Andhra, beginning with the above-mentioned dramatic conversion story of Yerraguntla Periah and his wife in 1866, see J. Clough, *op. cit.,* pp. 140-43 and A. T. Fishman, *Culture Change and the Underprivileged, op. cit.,* pp. 5, 10-15. Both Clough and Fishman stress that Periah and his many friends and relatives who converted to Christianity formerly participated in Vaishnavite or Saivite reform movements or were members of the Nasriah sect whose guru, Nasr Mohammed Mastan, had advocated high ethical standards and the abolition of caste.

23. This compared to rates of 13 percent for Muslims and 10.4 percent for Hindus. *Directory of Christian Missions and Churches in India, Burma and Ceylon, 1940-1941, op. cit.,* pp. 34, 36, 38.

24. The number of Protestant Christians increased at a rate of 183.8 percent in Hyderabad State and 54.8 percent in the Madras Presidency, the greater part of this increase taking place in the Telugu regions. *Ibid.,* p. 42; 'Statistics of Telugu Christianity,' *DDM,* XI, 8 (Aug. 1934), pp. 6-7. The increases in the Telugu districts for Protestant and Roman Catholic Christians were 52 percent for the Madras Presidency and 152 percent for the Hyderabad State. VSA, 'Evangelization and Its Challenge,' *NCCR,* LIV, 1 (Jan. 1934), p. 9.

Japan, Korea, and China combined.[25] In 1932, the Dornakal church baptized a record number of 11,532 converts and sustained this general level of accession throughout the decade.[26] In 1936, about 200 converts were baptized each week, for an annual total of 11,400.[27]

Protestant missionaries greeted the mass movements with mixed emotions. Although aiding the church quantitatively, the movements brought in hordes of uneducated, poor converts whom many missionaries felt ill equipped to serve. By 1933, roughly 80 percent of India's Protestant Christians were mass movement converts from depressed class backgrounds.[28] In Telugu regions, group conversions of outcaste Malas, Madigas, and, in later decades, low-caste non-Brahmins accounted for almost all of the Anglican church's growth.

The Malas were traditionally weavers, although competition from industrial mills had forced most of them to become agricultural workers by Azariah's time. The Madigas were traditionally leather workers engaged in the tanning of skins and the making of leather articles. Certain other social functions were exclusively performed — but never shared — by these two castes. They dug graves and monopolized two key roles in festivals for village goddesses: cutting the neck of the sacrificial animal and sprinkling blood-soaked grain in the fields. They provided village officers with manual assistance, beat drums, and provided trumpets and fanfare on festive occasions. Both castes also had the 'right' to eat the carrion of village cattle, and they performed other specialized communal tasks in certain villages such as *neerukattu* (watering the fields).

Since the Malas and the Madigas occupied the lowest status in society, they were prohibited from drawing water from common wells and from living in the main village. Their touch was considered to be pollut-

---

25. Excellent although occasionally inconsistent statistics of Anglican church growth in the Dornakal Diocese may be found in *DDM*: V, 1 (Jan. 1928), pp. 1-2; V, 4 (April 1928), p. 11; V, 11 (Nov. 1928), p. 6; V, 12 (Dec. 1928), p. 1; VI, 6 (June 1929), p. 3; VIII, 11 (Nov. 1931), p. 1; X, 1 (Jan. 1933), 'Statistics for the Year 1931'; X, 5 (May 1933), 'Statistics for the Year 1932', X, 11 (Nov. 1933), p. 4; XI, 6 (June 1934), p. 19; XI, 8 (Aug. 1934), pp. 6-9; XI, 11 (Nov. 1934), p. 6; XII, 4 (April 1935), p. 19; XIII, 5 (May 1936), p. 2; XIV, 3 (March 1937), p. 2; XV, 3 (March 1938), p. 1; XVIII, 4 (April 1941), p. 1. See also VSA, *A Charge Delivered at Bezwada on Wednesday, October 29th, 1941, op. cit.,* p. 4.

26. *DDM*, X, 11 (Nov. 1933), p. 4.

27. VSA, 'India: A Present Urgent Opportunity,' in *The Spirit of Missions* (U.S.A., autumn 1937), p. 543; *A Charge Delivered at Bezwada on Wednesday, October 29th, 1941, op. cit.,* p. 4.

28. J. W. Pickett, *Christian Mass Movements in India, op. cit.,* pp. 302-3.

ing, and washermen and barbers would not serve them. In addition, these two untouchable groups had a long-standing rivalry over which occupied the higher position in the social hierarchy, causing them to observe strict segregation even among themselves, living in separate hamlets and refusing to share the same food or the same wells.[29]

Among the non-Brahmin castes susceptible to Christian conversion in Andhra were the Telagas, Kammas, Kappus, and Reddis (landowners and farmers), and Yadowas (shepherds, or Gollas).[30] The Telugu missions were even more successful in converting substantial numbers of borderline and tribal groups such as Waddars (stonecutters and diggers, also known as Vadderas or Oddars), Yerukalas (pig traders, basketmakers, and soothsayers, also known as Erukalas and Erkalas), Lombadies (nomadic gypsies or 'carriers,' also known as Banjaras, found throughout western and southern India),[31] and Mandulas (another nomadic tribe of snake charmers and swine traders many of whom apparently converted to Christianity to obtain protection from their ruthless headman, Kunda Puchiah of Masulipatam).[32]

To appreciate fully the size of the rising mass movements, however, it is important to remember that collective accessions of Malas, Madigas,

29. For more on these groups and on the age-old animosity between them, see Sydney Nicholson, 'Social Organization of the Malas — An Outcaste Indian People,' *Journal of the Royal Anthropological Institute of Great Britain and Ireland,* LVI (Jan.-June, 1926), pp. 91-103; T. R. Singh, *The Madiga: A Study in Social Structure and Change* (Lucknow, 1969); and N. Subha Reddi, 'Community-Conflict among the Depressed Castes of Andhra,' *Man in India,* XXX, 4 (Oct.-Dec., 1950), pp. 1-12; Edgar Thurston, *Castes and Tribes of Southern India,* IV (Madras, 1909), pp. 292-325, 329-87; J. Abraham, *Fifty Years' History of the Indian Missionary Society of Tirunelveli, 1903-1953, op. cit.,* pp. 76-77; Knud Heiberg, *V. S. Azariah af Dornakal, op. cit.,* p. 79; C. Graham, *Azariah of Dornakal, op. cit.,* p. 53.

30. VSA, 'The Bishop's Letter,' *DDM,* IX, 6 (June 1932), pp. 1-4; G. A. Oddie, 'Christian Conversion among Non-Brahmans in Andhra Pradesh, with Special Reference to Anglican Missions and the Dornakal Diocese,' in *op. cit.,* pp. 67-99; James G. Manor, 'Testing the Barrier between Caste and Outcaste: The Andhra Evangelical Lutheran Church in Guntur District,' *ICHR,* V, 1 (1971), pp. 27-41; J. Abraham, *Fifty Years' History of the Indian Missionary Society of Tirunelveli, 1903-1953, op. cit.,* pp. 71-79; J. W. Pickett, *Christ's Way to India's Heart, op. cit.,* pp. 2, 40-45, 48-50, 100-117.

31. Edgar Thurston, *Castes and Tribes of Southern India, op. cit.,* IV, pp. 207-32; J. Abraham, *Fifty Years' History of the Indian Missionary Society of Tirunelveli, 1903-1953, op. cit.,* pp. 68-70; J. Manor, 'Testing the Barrier between Caste and Outcaste,' in *op. cit.,* pp. 29-30; J. W. Pickett, *Christ's Way to India's Heart, op. cit.,* pp. 106-7.

32. The IMS reported that 636 Mandulas had received baptism by 1955. J. Abraham, *op. cit.,* pp. 73-76.

Adivasi (tribals or aboriginals), and non-Brahmin castes to Christianity occurred not only in the Anglican church but also in each of the other prominent churches and missions in Andhra: the United Lutheran Church, the American Baptist (or "Lone Star") Telugu Mission, the Canadian Baptist Mission, the London Missionary Society, and the Wesleyan Methodist Church of Medak. Azariah estimated in 1935 that there were roughly 800,000 Christians in the Telugu country, as compared to roughly 200,000 in the Dornakal Diocese.[33] Regarding non-Brahmin caste conversions, he estimated in 1932 that a total of 26,000 'Sudras' — mainly Kammas — from 41 subcastes had joined the major Protestant churches in Andhra, almost half of them converting during the previous five years.[34] Reports made during an annual united evangelistic campaign by the Anglican, Methodist, and (London) Telugu Missions concluded in 1935 that 'the movement to Christ among the caste people in the villages is so strong, well established and growing that there can be no doubt about the issue.'[35] Shortly afterwards, Azariah wrote: 'I believe we have about 50,000 Christians of caste origin in all missions of the Telugu country.'[36]

Building a Church and Diocese for the Dornakal Mission

Shepherding the conversion of depressed classes, tribals, and non-Brahmin castes through direct evangelism, teaching, and grassroots humanitarian aid was the central occupation of Azariah's life. His efforts in this area earned him widespread acclaim as the Christian leader in India 'with the most successful experience in mass movement work.'[37] As we have seen, when Azariah moved with his family to Dornakal he assumed leadership of the small band of IMS missionaries from the mission's base in an unused brewery purchased from a local businessman. The mission purchased nine acres of land for buildings, cultivation, and gardening purposes, for

33. 'The Bishop's Letter,' *DDM*, XII, 12 (Dec. 1935), p. 4.

34. 'The Bishop's Letter,' *DDM*, IX, 6 (June 1932), p. 1. These figures do not include accessions to the Wesleyan Methodist Church of Medak, but see F. Colyer Sackett, *Posnett of Medak* (London, 1951), pp. 50-53, 81-87.

35. A. Rumpus, 'Report on the United Evangelistic Campaign 1934,' *DDM*, XII, 3 (March 1935), p. 12.

36. 'The Bishop's Letter,' *DDM*, XII, 12 (Dec. 1935), p. 4.

37. J. W. Pickett, *Christian Mass Movements in India, op. cit.,* p. 6.

which they paid a fixed yearly revenue of five rupees to the Nizam's government, and received permission to build a chapel on the site.[38]

The IMS mission area lay in the Warangal District's Manukota Taluq, a hilly, forested game-hunting region with a population of 60,000, only 1,005 of whom were Christians at the time. The early IMS missionaries were struck by its isolation ('this taluk is quite innocent of a post office'), its illiteracy (one state school and some purportedly ineffective *pial*, or raised platform, schools in larger villages), its drunkenness ('without any *abkari* [or excise] control as in the British provinces, liquors are as free and plenty [sic] as water' and 'one can scarcely see a sober person, local liquors being sold in the open streets'), and its 'superstition and witchery' ('people caught by small pox or cholera are left to their fate, lest Durga [goddess of slaughter] should be incensed').[39] The Indian missionaries' critique of rural Telugu life was no more positive than most earlier western missionary critiques: indigenization of mission did not alter the typically negative perspective on the degradation of local non-Christian society.

Seven Mala families from the village of Beerole, 24 miles southwest of Dornakal, were the first to respond to the IMS appeal for converts.[40] They learned about Christianity from IMS agents invited to Beerole by an interested Mala named Gopoji Venkayya. Upon making Venkayya's acquaintance in the town of Manukota (where Venkayya had come to pay taxes), the IMS missionary offered to come to Venkayya's village to provide education 'in the name of God.' This offer was accepted and led to the mission's first baptism of 33 adult Malas by Henry Whitehead in Dornakal on 6 August 1906, and of their 13 infant children on the following day. By 1909, the IMS was training Mala catechumens for baptism in 28 surrounding villages.[41]

38. Rev. K. Luke, *Dārnakal Tiranalvēli Indiyan Miṣanari Sanghamu: 1905-1956* (Vijayawada, 1956), pp. 6-7. VSA to Maulvi Syed Ahmed Ulla Sahib, 31 July 1911; Syed Ahmed Ulla to VSA, 31 July 1911; W. S. Butterfield to anonymous, 1912, DDA. It is worth noting that the IMS missionaries first attempted unsuccessfully to establish a mission headquarters in the village of Manukota. The conversion of a Yerukala thief from this village, named Rudrakshi Sunkadu, led to the creation of a congregation there several years later. K. Luke, *op. cit.*, pp. 16-18.

39. 'Diary of the Bishop's Tour,' *MDM*, II, 4 (April 1907), pp. 156-61; J. Abraham, *Fifty Years' History, op. cit.*, pp. 15-16.

40. A detailed account of the transmission of Christianity from village to village in the IMS mission area is available in K. Luke, *Dārnakal Tiranalvēli Indiyan Miṣanarī Sanghamu, op. cit.*

41. Three of these villages were Medidapalli, Thodelagudam, and Savattapalli. J. Abraham, *op. cit.*, pp. 27-28; K. Luke, *op. cit.*

When this small mission post became the center of the new diocese in 1912, Azariah began the long process of integrating the ever-increasing flow of converts into a fully organized church through baptisms, confirmations, ordinations, and the day-to-day activities of his own disciplined life as a bishop.

Throughout his career, Azariah's daily routine began and ended in solitude. He rose at five o'clock every morning and spent between two and two and a half hours in Bible study and prayer, a discipline he 'couldn't live without.' He also withdrew from conversation most evenings for theological study. His life of prayer, reading, and study provided essential spiritual, intellectual, and personal nourishment for his ministry, and his private letters were infused with the enthusiasm and inspiration he derived from reading the Bible and other books. In one nine-day period when returning from Palestine to Colombo on board the *R.M.S. Osterley,* Azariah read a classic of the British Empire, *Letters of General Gordon to His Sister* ('a splendid book'), *Tent Work in Palestine, Jews according to St. Mark,* three other unidentified 'big books,' and the biblical books of Judges, 1 and 2 Samuel, 1 and 2 Kings, Zechariah, Haggai, and parts of Isaiah, Jeremiah, and Ezekiel.[42]

A second hallmark of his bishopric was his devotion to a sacramental ministry. As his co-worker recalled later: 'Prayer was the very mainspring of his existence; the ordered worship of the Church was his delight; the sacraments and the Word of God were the very bread of life.'[43] Azariah traveled constantly through the villages of Dornakal Diocese to examine, baptize, and confirm new Christians, to celebrate holy communion, and to ordain the new Indian Christian leaders into the clergy. He was always most at home in the villages, where he paid careful attention to even the smallest details of rural life.

The typical larger Dornakal village was described by Azariah's co-worker, Carol Graham, as a deeply divided but interdependent network of subgroups, beginning with Brahmin homes clustered round the temple, then moving to the landlord's double-storied and sometimes richly carved and decorated buildings, and to the portions of the village owned by shepherds, potters, carpenters, goldsmiths, and the like. The outcaste homes were grouped together beyond a rigid dividing line, often in poor repair

42. He also enjoyed introducing Anbu to books, writing to her on 24 June 1920, 'I was very glad to get your letter . . . and especially that part where you criticise the book I sent you. I think it is a true criticism and I am very proud that you have learnt to read a book like that with a critical eye and that you can pick out the best in any book!' VSA to Anbu, Azariah Collection, Madras.

43. Carol Graham, *Azariah of Dornakal, op. cit.,* p. 17.

and filled with stagnant pools and refuse. 'The squalor of the outcaste hamlet has to be seen to be believed,' Graham reported.[44]

Into this setting Azariah brought his decorated episcopal robes and the gifts of the sacraments of baptism, holy communion, and confirmation. He paid special attention to the performance of the liturgy as a sacred drama, making full use of theatrical elements that would impress the villagers. One visitor from England remembered:

> [T]he splendour of his full convocation robes, snow-white rochet and scarlet chimere appear[ed] suddenly from a temporary vestry in a cattle-shed amid the drab dust-colour and general unbleached appearance of an Indian Village congregation. "Yes," he said, "I want them to know something of the glory of the church and how can they when most of them see nothing beyond the village chapel?"[45]

Azariah's regalia pointed the attention of villagers beyond their poverty to something more glorious. The typical Telugu village chapel-cum-school had walls of palmyra leaf or mud and stone, with thatched roofs constantly in need of repair. Only a few could afford to build roofs of timber and bamboo with salt earth on top. The chapels were dark inside with tiny windows and little room for people, who usually sat on floors painted with cow dung. The altar was either a table or a mud structure built against the east wall topped with a stone. Azariah stepped into this environment dressed in radiant robes symbolizing the glory of God. He appeared as the chief actor in a sacramental drama designed to bring Christian faith to rural Andhra, and to transform the villagers' very hopes and expectations.

Azariah is remembered as a bishop who loved the villages and gave his life for their uplift. But he is remembered especially for his kindness toward even the most humble converts, and his interest in the details of their lives. He learned to speak fluent Telugu in a way that villagers understood and appreciated. As one Indian woman co-worker recalled:

> Bishop Azariah had the admirable and extra-ordinary power of remembering names and faces. During his tours in the diocese there were many occasions of meeting village Christians individually and in groups. One can hear his beautiful voice calling out, 'Kantayya, how do you do,' 'Shanthamma, is the quarrel over your chicken ended?' When he conducted services he used to keep the whole congregation wakeful and at-

44. *Ibid.*, pp. 53-54.
45. *Ibid.*, pp. 86-87.

tentive by calling out names and giving out many questions on the scripture taught. Very often Marthamma, Jeevamma and Premamma were more prompt in answering than their husbands who were chided. There was no way of escape.[46]

Azariah was a bishop of the villages, not of Lambeth or Cambridge or the great cities of India.

The new church and community were literally created through the sacred ritual of baptism; 5,947 new Christians were baptized in Dornakal Diocese in 1920, and 10,319 in 1930.[47] Most were baptized by total immersion in nearby tanks or rivers in groups of between 10 and 150.

Reports sent in to Azariah from his clergy gave a picture of great religious turmoil in the villages, of groups defecting from one religion and joining another in a bid to improve their lives. Thus a pastor's report in 1932 stated simply:

> At A— 50 people were lately baptised. The chief Mala threw down the shrine of the village goddess in front of his house and in the same place put up a small shed, in which he asked for the baptisms to take place. At B— some six years ago six families apostatised (sic) and joined the Brahmasamaj. They have now all come back and brought back the remaining non-Christians who have also received baptism. Now there is a good congregation 77 in number, newly baptised 34. At C— 34 baptisms. They gave up drinking for the last year and a half. The whole village here do not drink now. At D— there are 48 baptised Christians. They also do not drink. On Christmas Day they had a love feast in token that they should not drink.[48]

The Dornakal diocesan records are chock-full of such suggestive testimonies. Baptism was the dividing line between the old and the new, and Azariah continually stressed its sacred and practical importance.

As Azariah traveled through the villages, he was usually greeted with great ceremony and processions featuring garlands, bands, toms-toms, and fireworks. On the road to the village of Atlapragadakondur for an immersion baptism of 103 people in January 1935, Azariah described 'enthusiastic demonstrations accompanied by band, fireworks, etc.' and being 'stopped constantly by eager villagers, anxious to garland us [with mari-

---

46. Mrs. C. William, 'The Evangelist Bishop — As I Knew Him,' in *Birth Centenary of Bishop Azariah, 1974, op. cit.,* p. 47.

47. *DDM*, VIII, 11 (Nov. 1931), p. 8.

48. *DDM*, IX, 5 (May 1932), p. 13.

golds] on the way. . . . One of the party counted that he had seventy-two garlands to his share that day!'[49]

Azariah began the ceremony by questioning the baptismal candidates, who had spent between six and eighteen months training with local clergy (the time period usually depended on the candidate's level of literacy; between 90 and 95 percent of the new converts were illiterate). At each village, Azariah questioned the candidates for baptism, not resting content with memorized answers but asking about many aspects of their spiritual experiences. At a minimum, each candidate was required to memorize and understand the baptismal vows and the essential articles of Christian belief.

Azariah frequently tried to turn people away from baptism who he believed were inadequately prepared, sometimes unsuccessfully. One baptism of 27 people from 6 castes included two 'zenana ladies . . . [who] had traveled twelve miles for the Baptism. Each and every one was dead keen on Baptism. My efforts to postpone the Baptism of one or two of them for various reasons were futile.'[50]

After questioning and singing, the baptismal party would usually move to the nearest river or body of water, each candidate carrying new white clothes under his or her arm. Bishop Azariah would stand in the water up to his waist, and begin to receive candidates. Carol Graham described a typical riverside baptism thus:

> There is a solemn hush while the Creed is recited and the promises are made. Then all are called in turn by their new names, family by family. Abraham, his wife Sarah, his children Peace, Hope and Joy. John, his wife Mary, his children Jewel-of-the-Lord, Servant-of-Jesus, and God's-beloved. Gone are the old, ugly outcaste names and gone is the old life of degradation and fear. As they step down into the clear running water under the blue eastern sky, and come up again with shining faces and joyful hearts, they know that they are indeed children of the Father of all Who has loved and saved us in Christ Jesus.
>
> As each family comes out of the river the new, clean white garments are put on and, when all is over, there follows the happy procession back to the village. . . .[51]

At the end of each baptism, Azariah required all new Christians to place their hands on their heads and repeat the slogan: 'Woe unto me if I

---

49. 'The Bishop's Letter,' *DDM*, XII, 2 (Feb. 1935), p. 1.
50. 'The Bishop's Letter,' *DDM*, VIII, 9 (Sept. 1931), pp. 1-2.
51. Carol Graham, *Dornakal: Every Christian a Witness* (London, 1945), p. 28.

preach not the Gospel,' thereby directing them to the responsibility of grassroots lay evangelism, the key to local church growth.

After further training and experience in the Christian faith, new Christians were encouraged to become full communicant members of the church through confirmation. Azariah typically went on confirmation tours throughout his diocese in the increasing heat from mid-February to the end of April. On these tours, he stressed the theme that the Church is the Body of Christ brought into being to manifest Christ to the world. Just as the Church was empowered through the coming of the Holy Spirit at Pentecost, so the confirmation candidates would be empowered through the laying on of hands at confirmation. He tested all candidates in their knowledge of their vows, the Lord's Prayer, the Creed, the Commandments, and certain other facts about confirmation before allowing them to participate in the ceremony. And he continually stressed the importance of adequate preparation so that confirmation would be 'a time of real consecration, self-surrender and infilling of the Holy Spirit.'[52]

Bishop Azariah described one confirmation service in a small forest village called Lankapalli in 1934 where he was greeted by ninety-six confirmation candidates and a few hundred Christians 'from the neighbourhood.' As the chapel could seat only thirty people, the local pastor erected a big *pandal* (or rough shed) which covered the whole width of the main village lane (thereby blocking travel of all people, animals, and carts for three hours). Azariah examined the candidates, gave an address, and invited eight people at a time into the chapel for the laying on of hands:

> The entire village lane was filled with a large concourse of Christians reverently on their knees invoking God's blessing. When the service was nearly over, came two candidates running breathless, hot with perspiration, but with eager faces anxious to rush into the chapel to receive the Bishop's blessing. They were however stopped and were told they must wait for the Confirmation at the next centre. No, they would not listen: had they not most anxiously and keenly looking [*sic*] forward to this day to receive the gift of Confirmation? One was a Lambadi convert, and the other a caste woman too. The Pastor came and whispered into my ears that they were very keen souls, and they would find it most difficult to

52. 'The Bishop's Letter,' *DDM,* XII, 6 (June 1935), p. 2, where he implored his pastors to institute a retreat for confirmation candidates on a model established in Scandinavia.

be at the next centre which was twenty-two miles away from that place. I agreed to go over the service for them once again. They came into the chapel, the questions were asked and answered, the prayer for the Holy Spirit was said over them and to their great joy they received the laying on of hands. We came away rejoicing too.[53]

The other rituals of communion, marriage, and funerals all helped the church to link the everyday events of village life with religion. Seeing the sanctification of all human life as the necessary outcome of an incarnational faith, he also encouraged smaller ceremonies to consecrate tools, sanctify a child's first day at school, the coming of age, the dedication of a house, or the blessing of a harvest. As Azariah said:

> The Worship of the Lord's Day anywhere in India should not ignore the natural desire of the villagers to have a good monsoon, to have a plenteous harvest, and to draw to God at times of epidemics. The Litany was evolved during a time of plague. Processional recital of litanies are a great comfort to Indian people.[54]

Azariah sought not to desacralize village life through the introduction of a westernized Christianity, but instead to resacralize village life through a Christianity that he believed to be universally relevant.

The bishop's new church in Dornakal became the institutional focus for a broad effort on the part of the depressed classes to improve their status in society. The new religion brought complex changes into their social and economic life and altered their roles within village ritual and culture. The Dornakal church became a principal provider of education, medical care, and a variety of other social services which, in the West, were devolving rapidly from churches to governments during the same period. Azariah became the leader of a new 'community,' rather than simply a new religious organization.

As the bishop developed into the powerful head of a challenging social movement in Andhra, he was sometimes criticized for being too autocratic and for discouraging the educational aspirations of Telugu Christians. But the vast majority of accounts indicate that, although he was a Tamil, he succeeded in becoming a much respected and beloved leader of Telugus, known affectionately as *Thandrigaru*, or 'Honored Father' of the diocese. Like many early western missionaries to India,

53. 'The Bishop's Letter,' *DDM*, XI, 4 (April 1934), pp. 5-6.
54. 'Worship in the Indian Church,' *DDM*, XII, 10 (Oct. 1935), p. 8.

Azariah committed the remainder of his life to his 'mission field.' He refused to abandon his rural ministry even when invited to become the bishop of his native Tinnevelly in October 1928.[55] He toured the villages of his diocese, eventually by car but still where necessary by bullock cart, until his death, and was buried next to the indigenous-style cathedral he built in Dornakal. Christians in rural Andhra today still describe Azariah as different from other church leaders (and particularly other Tamil missionaries). 'All others filled their bags and went away, but Bishop Azariah emptied his for the Lord,' villagers in Beerole recounted in 1986. 'He gave *all* his life to us.'[56]

The most notable aspect of the IMS mission strategy under Azariah's leadership was the encouragement of group conversions in order to minimize the social dislocation of converts after baptism and to provide the strength of group solidarity in the face of hostility from non-Christians. The IMS conservative theology also required an uncompromising condemnation of the beliefs of popular Hinduism such as idol worship and other 'superstitious' practices. Azariah had abandoned negative forms of evangelism after his early experiences with Sherwood Eddy: in Dornakal he promoted a positive vision of Christianity rather than a negative view of non-Christian faiths. However, negative rhetoric about Hinduism's faults was transmitted through the diocese more informally. For example, a song learned by some Indian and European missionaries during this period, 'The Vanity of Idol Worship,' used a vibrant tune from the Telugu tradition to ridicule various Hindu practices.

What's the use of worshipping idols?

Forgetting the Creator, you are worshipping the creation;
even though you know that no benefit comes from worshipping idols.

What's the use of worshipping idols?

Christ is there to wash away your sins but, because you do not care,
you still give more prominence to idols than to God,
    and you are storing up your sins.

55. D. Packiamuthu, *Valikāṭṭi*, Act III, Scene 2.
56. Group interview in Beerole, A. P., 4 April 1986. Just what the 'others' took in their 'bags' from Dornakal remained unspecified (perhaps money? perhaps enhanced prestige in the church?). The central point was that Azariah sacrificed everything for them.

What's the use of worshipping idols?

You have a stone to grind your medicines;
     You have a stone to wash your clothes;
You have a stone to wipe your feet;
     You have a stone to mark your grave.
The same stone, you worship as God.

What's the use of worshipping idols?

You bring a new pot into your house and worship it as a goddess.
But, this pot is made only by man with clay.
What's the use of worshipping idols?

You cut a tree down in the forest from which to make tools,
     beds, and other things.
The carpenter makes an idol from the same wood,
     paints it with permanent colors,
and then you prostrate yourselves before it.

You get metals and make utensils.
Then you take the same metal and fashion it into a God to worship.
You stupid people.

What's the use of worshipping idols?

You bring stones into Temples and call them
by the names of 'people' who have died
     (Rama, Krishna, Venkateshawa).
You worship them as if they were great Gods.

What's the use of worshipping idols?

To transport things you use an ox.
To plow and to harvest you use an ox.
Then you worship that same ox.

What's the use of worshipping idols?

A man will make something beautiful and you will worship it.
But, there's no use in worshipping man-made things.

What's the use of worshipping idols?[57]

57. Sung to author, in Telugu, during an interview with an elderly priest in
Dornakal, Rev. Daniel, 8 April 1986. Although Rev. Daniel was able to sing this lyric

Azariah and his IMS colleagues regarded evangelism as their first duty, relying heavily on indigenous networks of communication via inter-village family and *jati* ties to transmit their gospel message. Invitations came to visit villages, and the missionaries had little trouble in encouraging a rapid but fundamentally family and *jati*-based conversion movement. More aggressive means were needed to carry the Christian message beyond caste boundaries; in later years, Azariah instituted a hugely successful annual 'week of witness' in which all members of the Dornakal church, lay and clerical, joined Telugu workers from the SIUC and the Wesleyan Methodist Church in a march through the villages to spread the gospel. By 1933, 23,567 Dornakal Christians took part in the week-long campaign, during which 60,000 handbills were given away and 8,850 religious books and Scripture portions were sold. 341 new villages asked for Christian instruction, and Azariah estimated that, if the church had the financial resources to provide the teachers desired, 27,000 people could be brought into the church as a result of this campaign alone.[58]

Azariah's second priority was the training of teachers and pastors for the quickly proliferating village congregations. In Dornakal, as in other mass movement areas, the first request from Christian inquirers was to 'send us a teacher.' The teacher conducted training for baptism and confirmation, organized village worship, and, eventually, became the central figure in the many social improvement projects sponsored by the church: elementary education for children, literacy classes for adults, medicines and simple remedies for common diseases, temperance campaigns, and building and maintaining village chapels and schools. To train such village workers, Azariah established a Teacher's Training Institute in 1917 to prepare village elementary school instructors,[59] and by 1931 the mission supported 45 Telugu workers in 126 villages.[60] Once stationed in a village, the teacher cooperated with specialists such as the IMS doctor who toured the diocese to disseminate health services and information and to refer

---

from memory, he said it has not been used since the 1930s because of offense caused to Hindus. A version of this lyric may be found in *Andhra Christian Lyrics* (Baptist edition, Madras, 1939), no. 432, p. 300.

58. 'The Bishop's Letters,' *DDM*, IX, 12 (Dec. 1932), pp. 1-3; *DDM*, X, 9 (Sept. 1933), pp. 1-5; and *DDM*, XII, 9 (Sept. 1935), pp. 1-3.

59. *TMI-IMS*, XIV, 9 (Sept. 1917), p. 77.

60. VSA, 'The Training of the Village Worker in India,' *IRM*, XII (July 1923), pp. 360-67; *The Twenty-eighth Report of the IMS of Tinnevelly, 1930-31* (Palayamkottai, 1931), p. 5.

the seriously ill to a medical dispensary Azariah established in Dornakal in 1923.[61]

Azariah rejected the more radical mission strategy of rapid diffusion of the gospel message without building a strong local ministry through education.[62] The recruitment and training of a sizable corps of Telugu clergymen was central to the bishop's vision for establishing self-sufficient local congregations, and Azariah's work in this area resembled the system established in Tinnevelly by his father's mentor, John Thomas.[63]

The Dornakal Divinity School was founded in 1920 to train ordination candidates, and by 1934 its 115 graduates formed the nucleus of the diocesan clergy.[64] It was '. . . a simple family affair where the ordinands lived with their wives and families in small cottages built round a quadrangle. Every week-end they spent out in the villages, often with the local Pastor who had actually been sold as a boy by his father in payment of a bad debt and bought back by Bishop Azariah for ten rupees,' Azariah's co-worker remembers.[65] Azariah created the seminary's curriculum, wrote many of its textbooks, and taught many of its courses. Subjects included the Scripture, early church history, Anglican doctrine, Hinduism, Islam, and practical experience in the villages. His textbooks included vernacular expositions of biblical texts (*First and Second Corinthians* [1931, 1943], *Acts of the Apostles* [c. 1934], *Revelation* [1939], *Job* [1940], *Amos* [n.d.]); his inspirational meditations on various Christian topics and aids to worship

61. See, e.g., *DDM,* VI, 7 (July 1929), p. 16; M. Azariah, 'Thirty Years' Report of the Dornakal Mission,' in *op. cit.,* pp. 7-8. Medical work began in a hired house in the Dornakal bazaar, named St. Luke's Dispensary. In 1927, the dispensary was renamed 'The Bishop Whitehead Hospital' after Bishop and Mrs. Whitehead donated the money to buy a bigger building.

62. This strategy, adopted by The China Inland Mission, deemphasized education. This turned out to be one of that mission's greatest weaknesses. Ruth A. Tucker, *From Jerusalem to Irian Jaya: A Biographical History of Christian Missions* (Grand Rapids, 1983), p. 185.

63. S. C. Neill, 'Vedanayagam Samuel Azariah, 1874-1945,' in VSA, *Christian Giving, op. cit.,* pp. 9-10.

64. VSA, 'The Bishop's Letter,' *DDM,* XI, 9 (Sept. 1934), pp. 1-5. The IMS was criticized by Telugu Christians for its alleged failure to promote Telugus to positions of responsibility in the church, the common mistake of so many western missionary societies. See I. Victor Manuelraj, 'An Evaluation of the Work of the Indian Missionary Society of Tirunelveli in the Dornakal Field from 1954 to 1974,' (B.D. thesis, Serampore University, 1976), p. 52.

65. Carol Graham, *Between Two Worlds,* privately published in England, n.d., p. 29.

(*Collections of Prayer Meditation* [1934], *Worship in the Indian Church* [1935], *Missionary Litanies* [1936], *Lessons on Miracles* [1937], *Christian Giving* [1939], *Sabbath or Sunday* [1942], *Pentecost Spirit* [1975]), his historical investigations (*Introductory Lessons on India and Missions* [1908], *India and the Christian Movement* [1935], *The Church and Evangelism* [1936, 1956]), and his books on aspects of Anglican practice (*Holy Baptism* [1919], *The Pastor and the Pastorate* [1936], *Holy Matrimony* [1941], *Confirmation* [1942]).[66]

In his writings, Azariah attempted to bring the fruits of western biblical and historical scholarship to bear upon the specific needs and conditions of the rural South Indian church. He made use of works both ancient (Eusebius) and modern (Brooke Foss Westcott and Edwin Hatch),[67] and drew from diverse interpretive schools (from the liberal Adolf von Harnack to the more conservative E. C. Hoskyns and C. H. Turner).[68] Azariah utilized the works of F. J. A. Hort *(Christian Ecclesia)* and A. C. Headlam (Bampton Lectures) to demonstrate how the historical roots of Christian unity were relevant to South India's ecumenical aspirations.[69]

66. See 'Bibliography of Azariah's Publications.'

67. Eusebius (c. 260-c. 340) was bishop of Caesarea from about 315 and is known as the 'father of church history' principally for his *Ecclesiastical History,* which treats the period from the Apostolic Age till his own day. B. F. Westcott (1825-1901) was Regius Professor of Divinity at Cambridge and prepared, with F. J. A. Hort, an important critical edition of the Greek New Testament, in addition to biblical commentaries and a long series of theological works, before becoming Bishop of Durham in 1890. As noted elsewhere, he was also the father of Azariah's colleagues Foss and George Herbert Westcott. E. Hatch (1835-89) was Oxford's reader in ecclesiastical history. His 1880 Bampton Lectures, *The Organization of the Early Christian Churches,* traced the origins of the episcopate to financial administrators of Greek religious associations.

68. A. v. Harnack (1851-1930) was a patristic scholar whose seven-volume history of Christian doctrine demonstrated a liberal theology which stressed ethics at the expense of religious experience and metaphysics (which he considered an alien intrusion into Christian theology from Greek sources). E. C. Hoskyns (1884-1937) was dean of the chapel of Corpus Christi College, Cambridge, and argued in his famous 'The Christ of the Synoptic Gospels' that the 'historical Jesus' of liberal Protestantism was unhistorical. C. H. Turner (1860-1930) was a patristic and New Testament scholar of Magdalen College, Oxford, who produced the definitive edition of early Latin ecclesiastical canons.

69. F. J. A. Hort (1828-92) was a New Testament scholar of Trinity College, Cambridge. His *Christian Ecclesia* was published posthumously in 1897. A. C. Headlam (1862-1947) was Regius Professor of Divinity at Oxford when he delivered his Bampton Lectures in 1920 entitled *The Doctrine of the Church and Christian Reunion,* which aimed to provide an ecclesiological foundation for unity between the Anglican church and other denominations. On Azariah's use of them, see B. Sundkler, *Church of South India, op. cit.,* p. 181.

Azariah undertook a detailed study of Paul's epistles to the Corinthians to demonstrate why the church of Corinth provided a particularly good model for the church in India. The Corinthian church, like the Indian, was composed primarily of Gentiles from the lower classes whose failure to abandon pagan practices and bitter internal disputes seriously hurt the life of the church.[70] Azariah's writing sought not to break new ground in biblical or historical scholarship, but rather to utilize resources from the West to create a comprehensible Telugu Christian literature for a previously almost wholly illiterate population. To this end, he purchased and managed a printing press for the diocese, thereby following in the footsteps of his half-brother, Ambrose V. Thomas, who ran a press in Megnanapuram and taught the young Azariah valuable printing techniques.[71] The introduction of the printing press, along with increased literacy and the provision of teachers, had been the key elements in the dissemination of pietistic Christianity throughout the Tinnevelly region, and Azariah adopted a similar strategy in Dornakal.[72]

Few of Azariah's books had a serious impact outside Dornakal or India, with the notable exception of his work on *Christian Giving*, which was published first in India (in English and several Indian vernaculars) and then posthumously in London and New York.[73] In this book, the leader of what Whitehead had called a 'pauper diocese' described the importance and joy of charitable giving, despite the circumstances. The book emerged not so much from theoretical reflections as from practical experiences of poverty in the villages. As his co-worker recalled:

> He toured tirelessly from village to village conferring with the Elders. What exactly did tithing involve? 'How much does your family spend in a month? On what you eat, on the clothes you wear? On the tobacco you smoke or the bangles your women-folk buy? How does this compare with what you give to God?' In a society which still lived largely by barter such an unknown quantity as income was almost impossible to assess and intricate calculations went on far into the night, but the rate of giving did go up. God's hen with every egg it laid and God's patch of earth

---

70. J. Z. Hodge, *op. cit.,* pp. 99-100.
71. Interview with S. C. Neill, 12 May 1984, Oxford.
72. R. E. Frykenberg, 'The Impact of Conversion and Social Reform upon Society in South India during the Late Company Period,' in *op. cit.,* p. 197.
73. See 'Bibliography of Azariah's Publications.'

with all it produced became commonplace and family occasions were blessed with special offerings.[74]

Azariah wanted to teach his depressed class congregations to give — whether by saving portions of rice or dedicating extra eggs — at least in part to free his diocese from its dependence on the West. The result was a book that challenged the West itself to rediscover the deeper theological meaning and practical benefits of giving.

The provision of education was central to the IMS enterprise in Dornakal and helped attract many depressed class conversions.[75] However, Azariah deemphasized the importance of higher education for converts and promoted instead vocational education that fostered the dignity of manual labor and furthered overall village uplift. Azariah and the other Tamil missionaries mixed the mud, carried the wood, and otherwise fully participated in the construction of Dornakal's first chapel.[76] The IMS established an 'industrial' school whose primary purpose was to promote self-sufficiency of village congregations by providing training in useful trades. Beginning as a boarding school with two students in 1906, the Dornakal Training School grew within thirty years to accommodate 126 boys and 55 girls in trades such as weaving, carpentry, leatherwork, agriculture, farming, gardening, tape weaving, tailoring, and dressmaking.[77]

Azariah retained this vocational emphasis in later decades by establishing other trade schools and, to the distress of Telugu Christians, by closing high schools in Bezwada and Ellore and Noble College in Masulipatam.[78] The bishop argued that Christian education ought to promote the general socioeconomic improvement of the villages. The 'literary' education offered in most Christian mission schools tended to destroy traditional vocational aspirations and to lure rural converts to the cities in pursuit of more prestigious jobs as clerks, teachers, or preach-

74. Carol Graham, *Between Two Worlds, op. cit.,* p. 29.

75. P. M. Simon, 'Evangelistic Work at Alampur,' *DDM,* X, 10 (Oct. 1933), p. 9.

76. *The 11th Annual Report of the IMS of Tinnevelly, 1913-14,* pp. 20-21, IMSA.

77. M. Azariah, 'Thirty Years' Report of the Dornakal Mission of the Indian Missionary Society of Tinnevelly, 1903-1933,' *DDM,* XI, 12 (Dec. 1934), pp. 6-7; Joseph Abraham, *Fifty Years' History of the Indian Missionary Society of Tirunelveli, op. cit.,* pp. 89-91; Henry Whitehead, 'The Bishop's Diary,' *MDM,* XVI, 3 (March 1921), pp. 51-59; *DDM,* V, 10 (Oct. 1928), pp. 13-15.

78. The bishop closed Noble College reluctantly for financial reasons. The college fell into debt in the mid-1930s when it lost fee-paying students to the newly opened Hindu College and the SPG was unable to make up the difference. See VSA to Waddy, 1 Aug. 1935, 396: 2, D Series, USPG.

ers.[79] Azariah therefore directed diocesan resources away from higher education and towards schools that taught new trades and improved methods for the traditional occupations of weaving and leatherwork. In a 1930 letter, the bishop described his educational goals as follows:

> Our Christian community comes from the most poverty-stricken classes in the land. The ordinary man's income is at the most 6-d a day and a woman's 3-d a day. They live by daily wages, earned by doing unskilled field labour, for their Hindu caste neighbours. Any education given to such people must, we believe, include education to prepare them for life. Our aim then is to produce . . . a new generation of men — men who will not be ashamed of manual labour, men who will be willing to go back into the village with the knowledge of some handicraft, and settle down there to earn an honest livelihood and to become centres of light, in their turn, creating a sturdy, self-respecting, rural Christian manhood.[80]

Whatever the merits of Azariah's policy, it caused offense to many Telugu Christians, who regarded it as an effort to suppress their legitimate aspirations.[81]

In his defense of vocational training and manual work, the bishop joined Gandhi and other modern Hindu social reformers in strongly repudiating the predominant Indian system of values which stigmatized manual work and relegated its laborers to the lowest social ranks. Upon hear-

---

79. VSA, 'The Church in Rural India,' *DDM*, V, 10 (Oct. 1928), p. 8; 'The Bishop's Letter,' *DDM*, VII, 6 (June 1930), pp. 1-3.

80. VSA to W. F. France, 26 Nov. 1930, 331: 47, D Series, USPG. See also 8 Oct. 1919, *PIMS*, IMSA. In 1916, the average monthly earnings of a family of Mala fieldworkers were about six rupees (*MDM*, XI, 6 [June 1916], p. 185). It should be emphasized that the IMS strongly supported the goal of attaining literacy and, where possible, the opportunity of further education. Azariah and his IMS colleagues are remembered as having brought both 'God and literacy' to rural areas of Andhra Pradesh (interview with Dr. M. Santosham, President of the IMS, 28 Feb. 1986, Madras). However, Azariah recognized that education frequently undermined the goals of village development because the well educated left the villages for greater opportunities in towns or cities. He stressed the importance of vocational education, not out of disrespect for higher education per se, but in the interest of common village uplift.

81. This sentiment was well expressed in interviews with Alfred Bunyan (8 April 1986, Dornakal) and Bishop P. Solomon (1 April 1986, Dhyana Ashram, Paloncha). See also criticisms in *Manifesto of the Laymen's Association of the CMS Churches of the Dornakal Diocese*, 5: 2/6, Dornakal, MACIPBC. The general problem as experienced by Telugu Christians is discussed in A. T. Fishman, *Culture Change and the Underprivileged, op. cit.*, pp. 34-57.

ing of the Dornakal mission's village uplift work in 1910, 'two members of a well known Nationalist Society' told Azariah, '"you have been doing all these years what we are still only talking about!"'[82] When G. V. Varky, Parliamentary Secretary of Education Minister for the Madras Presidency, visited Dornakal in 1938, he described Azariah as a *karma yogi*, or man of action, whose commitment to village reconstruction resembled that of Gandhi's Wardha Scheme of education which emphasized traditional village industries (spinning, etc.) rather than Nehru's secular vision of socialist modernization.[83]

Azariah also shared Gandhi's interest in women's uplift and was responsible for training widows as Bible women to teach in villages, promoting women as village elders and deaconesses, encouraging women's education, and starting a home for unmarried mothers in Khammamett, where they received training and were prepared for reintegration into village society as 'valued marriage partners.' In this work, he was assisted by his quiet and well-educated wife, Anbu, who took on increasing responsibilities over the years.

Anbu served as President of the Mothers' Union in Dornakal, which maintained branches throughout the diocese. Each year she produced two pamphlets on subjects concerning Christian family and home life which could be read aloud to village members. Through the Mothers' Union, Anbu managed a wide network of women's social and evangelistic work, sick visiting, and an annual festival with preaching, processions, inter-village singing competitions, sports, and games. By 1931, the Mothers' Union had 688 branches with 5,480 members.[84]

Bishop Azariah also enlisted Anbu to educate the wives of seminarians at the Dornakal Divinity School. 'Whenever he was at home the

82. H. Whitehead, 'The New Movement in India and the Old Gospel,' *The East and the West,* IX, 1 (Jan. 1911), p. 5.

83. D. Packiamuthu, interview, 13 March 1986, Perumalapuram, Tirunelveli; and *Valikāṭṭi,* Act III, scene 6. On pioneering work of Christian missions in rural reconstruction, see A. T. Fishman, *Culture Change and the Underprivileged, op. cit.,* pp. 35-36. Also, interview with Ambrose Azariah, 23 Feb. 1986, Madras.

84. Interviews with Carol Graham, 19 Dec. 1984, Oxford; 22-23 April 1985, Farnham; 7 and 21-23 Oct., 4 Nov., 1986, Woking. See also C. Graham, 'Women in the Indian Church,' *IJT,* VII, 4 (Oct.-Dec. 1958), p. 149; 'History of the Mothers' Union in the Dornakal Diocese,' typescript, Graham Collection. Carol Graham's educational work in Dornakal, for which she authored a series of short books listed in the bibliography, was central to Azariah's campaign for village uplift. On St. Mary's Home for unwed mothers in Khammamett, see Elva Jackson, *Indian Saga* (Devonport, New Zealand, 1980), pp. 59-60.

Bishop never missed his daily lecture . . . and every day in the hottest hours Mrs. Azariah would proceed under a large umbrella to take her classes for the wives.'[85] Azariah recognized that educated wives greatly increased the effectiveness of his pastors, an insight he probably gained from his happy experience with Anbu herself. He used to enjoin his seminarians 'to get on their knees every day to thank the Lord for their wives.'

Azariah also instituted a pioneering program to foster women's leadership in the villages through their election as church elders. By 1944, there were almost 2,000 women elders in 800 Dornakal villages, perhaps only 20 of whom could read or write but each of whom were perceived to be the leaders of their communities:

> They are often responsible for keeping the Church clean, calling the women to services, taking up the offerings on the women's side and generally keeping order among the women and children. Often they go round on Saturday evening asking the women: 'Have you got your grain offering ready? Have you washed your clothes? Don't forget to get up early tomorrow,' and so on. They are also trying to raise the moral standards of the women, healing quarrels, and even taking part in the village courts when a case concerning a woman has to be tried.[86]

These responsibilities were significant in rural areas where women were allowed few rights of leadership, even on the most informal of village *panchayats*. But Azariah believed that village uplift began with the uplift of home and family life. He used to argue that 'no village could be better than its women,' and that village uplift therefore must begin with women.

When Azariah was installed as bishop of the new Dornakal Diocese on 8 January 1913, Bishop Whitehead commissioned him to exercise episcopal jurisdiction over three mission fields within the borders of the Nizam's Dominions: the IMS Dornakal mission, the CMS Khammamett mission, and the SPG Singareni mission. Between 1919 and 1922, his diocese was enlarged to include the CMS district of Dummagudem and all of the remaining Telugu mission districts of the CMS and SPG in the Madras Presidency.[87]

---

85. Carol Graham, *Between Two Worlds, op. cit.,* p. 29, Graham Collection.

86. Carol Graham, 'M.U. Overseas Meeting, Dec. 5th, 1944,' typescript, Graham Collection.

87. This new territory encompassed much of the districts of Kurnool, Cuddapah, Kistna, West Godavari, and the Bhadrachalem division of East Godavari. The western

Thus, within one decade, Dornakal was transformed from the headquarters of a small indigenous missionary society into the center of one of India's largest and fastest-growing Anglican dioceses.[88] Having begun as the supervisor of the six Indian clergy, 172 lay workers, and about 8,000 Indian Christians associated with the Dornakal (IMS), Khammamett (CMS), and Singareni (SPG) missions, Azariah became the episcopal director of a vast conglomeration of Christian congregations and institutions. Many were still dependent on the pastoral and financial ministrations of powerful western missionaries, and all were experiencing rapid growth of membership. Azariah was confronted with the challenge of unifying diverse western missions and quickly expanding rural congregations under one institutional umbrella. As the only Indian of his generation with substantial authority over western missionaries and as a 'foreign' Tamil in the midst of an increasingly assertive Telugu population, Azariah faced a formidable task.

The Influence of Western
Mission Theory on Indigenization

Azariah built his church in Dornakal not on virgin soil but in a field already populated by diverse and sometimes competing missionary societies. He had to coordinate their work with the local church, and draw Anglican mission agents into his diocesan structure. He was largely guided by mission theories imported from the West in creating his own strategies for evangelism, but in every case he devised new tactics appropriate to Indian villages.

One of Azariah's first administrative challenges was to integrate the IMS work of the small missionary band from Tinnevelly into diocesan life.

side of his diocese (composed of former SPG areas surrounding the towns of Kurnool, Nandyal, and Cuddapah) was separated from the eastern portion of his diocese (composed of former CMS areas between the Kistna and Godavari Rivers) by a large tract of territory occupied by the Lutheran Church. See map of the Dornakal Diocese. See also 'Statistics of Telugu Christianity,' in *op. cit.*, p. 6; C. J. Grimes, *Towards an Indian Church, op. cit.*, pp. 89-90.

88. Between 1921 and 1931, the number of Protestant Christians increased at a rate of 183.8 percent in Hyderabad State and at a rate of 57.8 percent in the Madras Province, both of which were substantially higher than the average of 41 percent for Protestant Christians throughout India and Burma. Much of the increase in Hyderabad and Madras was caused by the Telugu movements. *Directory of Christian Missions and Churches, op. cit.*, p. 42.

Although the IMS was a fully indigenous mission administered by Indian men with Indian money, its similarity to a home-based committee administering funds to missionaries in the field has led at least one scholar to describe its missionary efforts as nothing more than 'replicas of foreign missionary societies.'[89]

The IMS had indeed modeled itself after a foreign missionary society committed to indigenization: the China Inland Mission. Established by Yorkshireman Hudson Taylor in 1865, the China Inland Mission was a nondenominational 'faith' mission with a conservative evangelical gospel message and a strong emphasis on identifying with the foreign culture through language, dress, and manners. Taylor's society broke precedent with other British societies by accepting missionaries from working-class backgrounds with relatively little education, and by requiring mission affairs to be directed from the field rather than by remote 'home committees' in London. It considered its primary task to be evangelism, with education, medical assistance, and other social work as secondary goals.[90]

The IMS reproduced some but not all of the China Inland Mission's distinctive characteristics.[91] The Indian society had a similarly conservative evangelical focus, but its strong ties to the Anglican Church in Tinnevelly prevented it from attaining the China Inland Mission's broad nondenominational appeal. When the IMS headquarters at Dornakal became the new diocesan center in 1912, it became virtually impossible to distinguish IMS policy from that of the Anglican church, since both were subject to Azariah's authority and reflected his priorities.[92] The China Inland Mission's ideal of immersion in the foreign culture provided Azariah and the IMS with valuable guidelines for respecting local Telugu customs. All IMS missionaries learned the vernacular and stressed the importance of cultural continuity after conversion.

89. I. David, 'The Development of the Concept of Indigenisation,' in *op. cit.,* pp. 37, 107.

90. 5 and 6 March 1907, *PIMS,* IMSA; S. C. Neill, *A History of Christian Missions, op. cit.,* pp. 333-36.

91. Azariah, like most China Inland Mission agents, did not have a college degree, but the Indian society placed much more emphasis on recruiting educated missionaries than its Chinese counterpart.

92. Many accounts of Azariah's life underestimate the degree to which Azariah owed much of his later success as a missionary bishop to the unstinting support of IMS workers who continued to work in Dornakal until the late 1980s. The last IMS missionary to Dornakal, Victor Manuelraj, only departed from the diocese shortly after the field research for this book was completed.

Azariah continued this tradition in Dornakal by advocating both 'structural indigenization' (by which the control of western missions was transferred to Indians) and 'cultural indigenization' (by which western-style institutions and forms of religious expression were transformed into their Indian equivalents).[93] The bishop was committed to building a self-sufficient church under an Indian priesthood and to planting the roots of Christianity deeply in Telugu soil. However, Azariah was also committed to maintaining the Indian church's membership both in the multi-national Anglican communion (whose Lambeth Conferences he attended in 1920 and 1930) and in the 'universal' church (whose ecumenical character he enhanced as a participant in South Indian Protestant church unity negotiations). He was never comfortable with the more radical doctrines of the educated, urban-based 'cultural indigenizers' who rejected the traditional institutional church and orthodox theology in favor of allegedly more 'indigenous' alternatives derived from non-Christian models.[94] Azariah advocated ecclesiastical indigenization within fixed boundaries established by Christianity's historical experience.

Azariah inherited a vast conglomeration of Indian Christian congregations still dependent for money and personnel on British (and Tamil)[95] missionary societies. British Anglicans recognized that the creation of the Dornakal Diocese under an Indian bishop presented an excellent opportunity for the realization of Henry Venn's rarely implemented vision of a self-supporting, self-governing, and self-propagating church free from reliance on foreign support.[96] But Azariah's diocese was actually modeled

93. This useful distinction was drawn by I. David in 'The Development of the Concept of Indigenization among Protestant Christians in India from the Time of Henry Venn,' in *op. cit.,* pp. 7-41.

94. He was unhappy with the findings of the liberal 'Rethinking Christianity Group,' whose prominent members included P. Chenchiah, V. Chakkarai, Bishop Appasamy, S. Jesudason, P. Devasahayam, Eddy Asirvatham, and A. N. Sudarisanam. See *Rethinking Christianity in India Today* (Madras, 1938). Chenchiah (1886-1959) was a lawyer and Chief Justice of Pudukottai High Court. He and his associates were particularly influenced by Indian nationalism. On the participation of westerners in the development of liberal indigenous theology, see Kaj Baajo, *Pioneers of Indigenous Christianity, op. cit.,* pp. 71-84. See also R. H. S. Boyd, *India and the Latin Captivity of the Church: The Cultural Context of the Gospel* (Cambridge, 1974).

95. Although the struggle for autonomy from western missionary societies is the central focus of this investigation, it is important to note that Azariah also had to assert authority over IMS missionaries. The bitter resignation of Solomon Pakianathan in 1911 suggests that this was not always an easy process. See 12 July 1911, *PIMS*, IMSA.

96. I. David, *op. cit.,* pp. 3-30.

on the ideas of another Englishman, Henry Whitehead's radical friend Roland Allen (1868-1947), an Anglican parish priest and former missionary to China.[97] Paradoxically, but by now predictably, Azariah chose to follow a path to church indigenization that was more cautious and conservative than that advocated by either of these two westerners.

Azariah had been exposed to the ideas of Henry Venn from his earliest childhood in Tinnevelly, where they had deeply influenced his father's mentor, John Thomas. Henry Whitehead introduced his young protégé to the ideas of Roland Allen in 1912 just after Allen had published a startling new book criticizing modern western missions for having strayed in their missionary methods from apostolic precedent.[98]

The pattern for mission established by St. Paul, Allen contended, was to lay the foundations of new churches in a relatively short period of time (about six months) and then to move on to other mission fields so that the newly planted churches would grow not under the direction of the apostles, but by the power of the Holy Spirit. Similarly, modern missionaries should give young churches freedom as quickly as possible in order to encourage them to develop traditions in worship, liturgy, music, and administration suitable to their own culture. Allen generally approved of Venn's 'three-self' formula, but objected strongly to Venn's gradualism by arguing that self-government and self-propagation need not await self-support.[99] Allen's scheme for immediate church independence did not find much favor with missionaries, who found it difficult to resist the temptation to consider themselves indispensable religious authorities and financial benefactors. Nor, in this age of continuing imperial expansion, did his suggestion that the church abandon its confidence in the moral superiority of western culture find much favor.[100] Allen's books

97. For a good summary of Allen's life and contribution, as well as a bibliography, see Charles H. Long and Anne Rowthorn, 'The Legacy of Roland Allen,' *International Bulletin of Missionary Research,* XIII, 2 (April 1989), pp. 65-70.

98. Roland Allen, *Missionary Methods: St. Paul's or Ours::A Study of the Church in the Four Provinces* (1st ed., London, 1912; 2nd ed., London, 1927; 6th ed., Grand Rapids, 1962).

99. I. David, *op. cit.,* pp. 17-23. Azariah agreed with Allen on this although for different reasons, as will be explored below. See VSA, 'Self-Support: False or True,' *IRM,* XXVII, 107 (July 1938), pp. 361-71; 'Self-Support,' *NCCR,* LVIII, 10 (Oct. 1938), pp. 536-43.

100. Allen's works were virtually ignored for many years. He himself estimated that his theories would not be appreciated until about the year 1960. Only two of his works have been regularly reprinted. See Lesslie Newbigin's 'Foreword,' in Roland Allen, *Missionary Methods: St. Paul's or Ours?,* 6th ed., *op. cit.,* pp. i-iii. That there has recently

had the unwelcome effect of challenging missionaries to examine their relations, not only to the foreign cultures in which they worked, but also to their own western culture.

Bishop Whitehead was one of the first western churchmen to recognize and publicly endorse Allen's ideas. In an introduction to Allen's 1912 volume which reflected his own frustrating experience in Calcutta, Whitehead agreed that the failure of modern missions could be traced to a departure from apostolic precedent:

> We neglect the open doors and then spend time and money largely in preaching to people who show no willingness to accept the faith. We found Churches and keep them in leading strings for a hundred years, and even then are not within measurable distance of giving them independence. We transplant to the mission field the elaborate system of teaching and organization with which we are familiar at home. We impose discipline upon our converts as an external law and authority. . . . where St. Paul conspicuously succeeded, we have conspicuously failed. May it not be because we have worked upon widely different principles?[101]

Hoping that Azariah would avoid the mistakes made by his western predecessors, Whitehead provided him with a copy of Allen's book on missionary methods in early 1912 to serve as a guide in Dornakal.[102] In many respects, Allen and Azariah shared a deep affinity. Azariah's plea at the 1910 Edinburgh conference that western missions 'give us friends' resem-

---

been a rediscovery of Allen's prophetic writings is evidenced by works such as Vincent J. Donovan, *Christianity Rediscovered: An Epistle from the Masai* (London, 1985). Allen shared Whitehead's deep appreciation for the Anglo-Catholic tradition garnered at Oxford, and, although Whitehead was fifteen years older than Allen, they both died in 1947.

101. Henry Whitehead, 'Introduction,' in Roland Allen, *Missionary Methods: St. Paul's or Ours?*, 2nd ed., *op. cit.*, pp. viii-ix.

102. Whitehead was equally impressed with Allen's later works, such as *The Spontaneous Expansion of the Church and the Causes Which Hinder It, op. cit.* (the first British edition was published in 1927). Whitehead commended Allen on 21 August 1928 for producing an argument on the voluntary clergy overseas that was 'unanswerable,' but asked, 'Why is it printed privately and not given the widest possible circulation? It ought to be broadcasted and read by all the bishops, archdeacons, parish priests, parish councillors, communicants and earnest churchmen and churchwomen throughout the Anglican communions. . . . It convicts me of past sins.' Quoted in David Paton, 'Biographical and Theological Essay,' in *Reform of the Ministry: A Study in the Work of Roland Allen,* ed. David M. Paton (London, 1968), p. 95.

bled Allen's condemnation of missionary paternalism.[103] Azariah was particularly impressed with Allen's portrayal of the contrast between the Pauline church and modern missions. In a letter to Isabel Whitehead in April 1912, Azariah wrote:

> I have been enjoying Mr. Roland Allen's volume immensely. I like his fearless conclusions — I may say reckless — it thoroughly suits my militant spirit! . . . I wish someone would send a copy of this book to all South India's Church of England missionaries. . . . You know how practical the book is to me. It is a warning voice in time . . . that at least in Dornakal things need not be so. And may I say by the Grace of God they *shall not be so?*[104]

Allen showed Azariah how powerful western missionaries often inhibited the emergence of native Christian leaders. In a letter to Bishop Whitehead in May 1912 that was directly inspired by reading Allen, Azariah wrote, 'in Missions conducted by European Missionaries the need for more Bishops, or even for a Bishop, is not felt much, because the missionaries are themselves Bishops.'[105] The apostolic model explicated by Allen provided a biblical foundation for Azariah's policy of encouraging ecclesiastical self-sufficiency in his diocese and discouraging dependence on western missionaries and finances. It also added legitimacy to his struggle for authority over powerful European missionaries. The Bishop of Dornakal's subsequent tendency to see the ancient church as a model for Dornakal owed much to this early exposure to Roland Allen's so-called 'biblical primitivism.'

Azariah frequently compared the apostolic church's mission to pagan Gentiles in the Roman Empire with his own church's mission to Hindus in the British Empire.[106] His efforts to create Christian villages not dependent on missionary societies bore the unmistakable imprint of Allen. The bishop encouraged newly installed teachers to appoint voluntary lay readers from among the Christian village headmen to conduct services, and a *panchayat*

---

103. I. David., *op. cit.,* pp. 21-23.

104. VSA to Isabel Whitehead, 17 April 1912, Sundkler Collection.

105. VSA to Henry Whitehead, 2 May 1912, Sundkler Collection.

106. Azariah used evidence from the historical works of Harnack *(Mission and Expansion of Christianity)* and K. S. Latourette *(The History of the Expansion of Christianity)* in addition to St. Luke's *Acts of the Apostles.* See, e.g., VSA, 'The Place of the Church in Evangelism,' in *Evangelism: International Missionary Council Meeting at Tambaram, Madras, December 12th to 29th, 1938* (London, 1939), pp. 32-47; *The Church and Evangelism, op. cit.* (1936).

to take charge of discipline, within one year of their arrival at a new village. Although Azariah found this policy increasingly difficult to institute as the church grew, he continued to prod teachers to devolve responsibility rapidly to new converts and move on to other villages. Apart from receiving a priest once a month to administer sacraments, the newly established congregations would quickly become largely self-sufficient.[107]

Azariah continued to consult Allen during his tenure in Dornakal and invited him to address a conference of Dornakal's clergy in December 1927 concerning the barriers to church growth created by the existence of a stipendiary professional clergy and the advantages of ecclesiastical self-support. Apparently, Allen's lectures were enthusiastically received by Dornakal's clergymen,[108] as were his writings. When Allen arrived in Dornakal, he discovered that his books were completely sold out and that he was being quoted 'in season and out of season.'[109] Allen had long been a keen observer of Azariah's work in Dornakal,[110] and was particularly intrigued by the educational techniques Azariah developed for instructing villagers about topics such as prayer without making them dependent on foreign concepts. In a 1912 letter, Azariah described how he had abandoned the set form of the Telugu Lord's Prayer ending with the Aramaic 'Amen' and permitted converts to devise forms more tailored to their own needs, such as:

> Oh Father who art in Heaven, You are our Father, we are Your children. Keep us all well. Heal my rheumatism and my child's boil. Keep us from all wild animals, the bear and the tiger. Forgive us our sins, our quarrels, angry words, all that we have done since morning. Make us good. Bring all the castes to kneel down to You and call You Father.[111]

To Allen, this exemplified truly indigenous prayer because 'Mr. Azariah is not concerned to set forth his subject in any predetermined order. He is not concerned with any desire to create a Christian of any certain type. His sole object is to assist his hearers to learn the meaning of prayer.'[112] Azariah was one of the very few Anglican bishops with whom

---

107. *MDM*, XI, 2 (Feb. 1916), p. 37.

108. 'Diary of a Visit in South India,' in *Reform of the Ministry, op. cit.*, pp. 106-19.

109. *Ibid.*, pp. 107, 116.

110. From perhaps as early as 1910. See Letter from the Bishop of Assam (George Clay Hubback) to R. Allen, 20 Sept. 1928, *Reform of the Ministry, op. cit.*, pp. 163-64.

111. 'An Illustration from V. S. Azariah,' in *The Ministry of the Spirit: Selected Writings of Roland Allen*, ed. David M. Paton (London, 1960), p. 131.

112. *Ibid.*, p. 131.

Allen shared such an understanding. Most were exasperated by Allen's prophetic teachings, which they found difficult to integrate with their administrative duties and with the liturgical requirements of the *Book of Common Prayer*.[113]

Azariah's subsequent establishment of a self-governing diocesan organization with increased power for the laity and indigenous leaders bears the mark of Allen's early influence and suggests that Allen's writings may have had more impact on Anglican missionaries in this period than has previously been supposed.[114] Azariah was also indebted to John Mott, whose Continuation Committees organized after the 1910 Edinburgh conference helped advance the case of transferring responsibility from foreign missionary societies to native churches. Under Mott's presidency, the Calcutta Missionary Conference of 1912 resolved:

> that the work carried on by Foreign Missionary Societies should be gradually transferred, as opportunities offer, to the Indian Church, and that suitable plans and modifications of existing organizations should be adopted, wherever necessary, so that this principle may be carried out by missionary bodies.[115]

The establishment of the National Missionary Council in 1912 provided indigenous churches with more unified organizational support for their missionary efforts. The National Missionary Council's decision to change its title to the National Christian Council of India, Burma, and Ceylon (NCC) in 1923 further reflected the growing emphasis on indigenous church-based missionary work. The Jerusalem meeting of the International Missionary Council (1928) urged missionary societies from 'older churches' to establish relationships with 'younger churches' based on partnership rather than leadership. Following the direction provided at Edinburgh and Jerusalem, Azariah took the lead at the 1938 International Missionary Council meeting at Tambaram in stressing that the

113. David M. Paton, 'Biographical and Theological Essay,' in *Reform of the Ministry, op. cit.,* p. 23.

114. According to one view, 'Allen's ideas had little influence on Anglican missions during his lifetime. His Spirit-centered ecclesiology seemed idealistic and impractical to the leadership of a highly institutionalized church closely associated with the British empire.' Long and Rowthorn, *op. cit.,* p. 69.

115. Quoted in VSA, 'The Transfer of Responsibility from the Mission to the Church,' *MDM,* XIV, 11 (Nov. 1919), p. 256. Azariah frequently mentioned the importance of Mott's influence on this development. See, e.g., VSA, 'The Church's Ideal,' *CMR,* LXXI (1920), p. 153.

church should be the center of missionary activity as 'the divinely appointed instrument of evangelism to the world.'[116] The Bishop of Dornakal was involved intimately in all of these developments as President of the NCC from 1928 to 1945, and the widely discussed statements issued by these conferences provided guidance and support for Azariah's diocesan reforms.[117]

Clearly, indigenization strategies did not come to Azariah entirely from western sources. His work in Dornakal was also influenced by the growing Indian national movement and, particularly, by the liberal policies enshrined in the Montagu-Chelmsford Report of 1918 and in the Government of India Act the following year. In a speech to the Madras Missionary Conference in 1919, Azariah suggested that the Indian Christian's desire to achieve autonomy from foreign missionary societies (or, as he phrased it in the political terminology of the day, 'an immediate grant of Home Rule and Swaraj in the Church'), provided fresh impetus for devolving ecclesiastical control to the local church.

> The scheme for political reforms with its transferred and reserved subjects is whetting the appetite for independence and freedom for self-expression in Indian Christian young men. The church cannot surely lag behind the State.[118]

In a sermon delivered the following year for the 121st anniversary of the CMS in London, Azariah observed:

> 'Responsible government,' 'Home rule,' 'Transferred and reserved subjects' — these have become familiar phrases in modern India. Is it to be wondered at that the Indian Christian is attracted by the glamour of these ideas, and expects it in the sphere of church and mission administration? . . . The national spirit of India demands liberty for the Church.[119]

Indeed, the Bishop of Dornakal's approach to missionary devolution was almost identical to that espoused in the political arena by liberal nationalists who left the increasingly extremist Congress Party after the appearance of the Montagu-Chelmsford Report to form 'The National

116. VSA, 'The Place of the Church in Evangelism,' *op. cit.* (1939), p. 33.

117. *Ibid.,* pp. 40-41 and VSA, 'The Church's Ideal,' *op. cit.* (1920), p. 153.

118. VSA, 'The Transfer of Responsibility from the Mission to the Church,' *op. cit.* (1919), p. 257.

119. VSA, 'The Church's Ideal,' *op. cit.,* pp. 158-59.

Liberal Federation of India.' Like the liberal nationalist politicians, Azariah wanted gradual ecclesiastical reform, whereas the increasingly extremist 'young theologians want entire autonomy at one step.' The bishop remarked that 'sober minds will . . . be willing to wait and will gladly welcome the caution and sanity' implied in the otherwise 'irritating words' of the 1912 Calcutta Missionary Conference that mission work should be transferred to the Indian church 'gradually' and 'as opportunities offer.'[120] By 1935, Azariah's statements on the subject of devolution from mission to church reflect a new urgency dictated by increasing hostility to Christian missions (which will be explored in a later chapter):

> At a time when the spirit of nationalism sweeps over the land, and everything un-Indian is looked upon with suspicion, it is a moral and spiritual obligation upon all missionaries, and missionary societies from abroad and upon all Churches in India to seek to do everything they possibly can, to make it possible, both in appearance and in reality, to identify the Christian movement with the indigenous Church and indigenous leadership.[121]

Azariah faced many practical difficulties in trying to build an indigenous church in Dornakal. He first set out to build a single diocesan organization to replace the variety of missionary organizations within his diocese. He regarded the Anglican Telugu missions inherited by the Indian church as fundamentally flawed by the autocratic power they gave to district missionaries. But merely to transfer the power of the district missionary 'from one individual who is a European to another individual who is an Indian' would not be an effective method of devolution.

> If autocracy is condemned, it must be condemned irrespective of the nationality of the autocrat. . . . Without a strong Committee of the laity or common people of the community, individual leadership might degenerate into Indian Swadeshi Nawabism.[122]

Thus, in addition to placing Indians in leadership positions, Azariah tried to improve the representative character of the church by building an ecclesiastical organization that included advisory councils of local laity. As

120. VSA, 'The Transfer of Responsibility from the Mission to the Church,' *op. cit.,* p. 257.

121. VSA, *India and the Christian Movement, op. cit.* (1935), p. 89.

122. VSA, 'The Transfer of Responsibility from the Mission to the Church,' *op. cit.,* p. 259.

Azariah's diocese was enlarged to include all Telugu Anglican missions and other contiguous areas under the Diocese of Madras by 1922, the bishop established a synodical organization to increase lay participation and to unite all churches connected with missions in his diocese under the primary authority of Indian Christians without undue interference from European missionaries.[123] Each Christian village, or group of villages, in the diocese was placed under the care of the lay teacher who was responsible for congregational worship, for education, and for the informal disciplinary *panchayats* composed of village elders. Fifteen or twenty-five such villages or groups of villages were led by ten to fifteen teachers under the overall authority of an ordained pastor, who visited each village at least once a month to administer the sacraments. The pastor was authorized to call formal *panchayats* of village elders to consider serious disciplinary cases whose results, in turn, were reported to the Bishop's local council (composed of both clergy and laymen) and, occasionally, to the bishop himself, who alone possessed the power of excommunication and restoration.

The pastor was assisted in the administration of the finances, property, education, evangelism, pastoral work, and discipline by a Pastorate Committee (or quarterly meeting or church committee) that included both the pastor (or chairman) and lay members elected by communicants. Groups of three to four Pastorates constituted a Deanery, which was administered by a Deanery Committee led by an Indian Deanery Chairman and including lay representatives elected by the Pastorate Committees.

By 1931, Azariah had transferred all of the Telugu areas previously controlled by the powerful European District Missionaries of the CMS and SPG into the control of 25 Deanery Chairmen, each responsible for the affairs of as many as 10,000 Christians and 100 to 150 teachers and rural schools. At the next higher level appeared the eight Church Councils, whose lay members were elected by the Deanery Committee members. Above this stood the Episcopal Synod, which authorized Azariah to organize the whole Dornakal Diocese under one Diocesan Council with the bishop as its President. This body of some one hundred chosen lay and clerical leaders met for its first session in December 1921 (and biennially thereafter), and provided the central administrative authority for the diocese. Among its many responsibilities, the Diocesan Council elected both

123. For Azariah's own descriptions of his diocesan organization, see VSA, 'The Christian Church in India,' *op. cit.* (1938), pp. 174-78; *A Charge Delivered to the Clergy of the Diocese of Dornakal at Bezwada, October 7, 1931* (Madras: Diocesan Press, 1931), pp. 4-7. Also Archdeacon Emmet, 'Lay Work in Dornakal Diocese,' *DDM,* X, 4 (April 1933), pp. 7-10; B. Sundkler, *Church of South India, op. cit.,* pp. 58-59.

clerical and lay representatives to the General Council of the Church of India, Burma, and Ceylon (known as the Provincial Council before 1927).

Azariah's organizational reforms transferred the power of selecting and recommending candidates for ordination from the bishop to the laity, and also devolved a wide variety of responsibilities from European missionaries to the Indian clergy and laity. Church proceedings were made more accessible by conducting all Diocesan Council and Committee meetings in Telugu (though Diocesan Council meetings used both Telugu and English). The bishop hoped that such changes, when installed quickly as in Dornakal, would stop dependency on missionary societies and ensure that 'in all church organizations Indian laymen predominate.'[124]

Azariah's reforms were only partly successful. The Dornakal Diocese developed an unusually high percentage of Indian workers and low percentage of western missionaries. By 1940, 157 of 168 ordained workers were listed as 'indigenous' and only 11 as 'foreign.'[125] But Azariah was less successful in increasing the role of the laity in church affairs. Movements protesting an alleged lack of lay participation under Azariah's 'dictatorship' developed in both CMS and SPG districts during the 1940s. That these protests were motivated at least in part by personal grievances appears clear from counterpetitions denying the allegations and from the fact that some of the protest leaders had been disciplined by the church for marrying their deceased wives' sisters, an indigenous practice discouraged under Anglican marriage guidelines. However, the establishment by critics of rival Laymen's Associations caused the bishop no small trouble during the last years of his life; these Associations became forums for criticizing Azariah's educational policy as well.[126]

Several organizational changes that Azariah instituted in the 1930s

124. VSA, 'The Christian Church in India,' *op. cit.* (1938), pp. 174-75.

125. Although many dioceses did not classify their workers according to race, the Dornakal figures compared favorably to figures for ordained workers in the Bombay Diocese (29 Indian and 40 European) and for Chota Nagpur (34 Indians and 17 English). *Directory of Christian Missions and Churches, op. cit.,* pp. 308-9.

126. See, e.g., *Resolutions and Memorandum submitted by the Independent Lay Representatives of the CMS Churches of the Dornakal Diocese to the Most Reverend the Metropolitan of India,* 6 Dec. 1943; VSA to the Metropolitan, 11 Dec. 1943; Metropolitan to VSA, 14 Dec. 1943, all in 5: 2/1, Dornakal, MACIPBC. Also N. T. Gnanaprakasan to the Metropolitan, 14 Nov. 1943; *Memorandum Submitted by the Laymen's Association of the CMS Churches of the Dornakal Diocese to the Most Reverend the Metropolitan of India* (Masulipatam: Hindu Press, n.d.), Metropolitan to VSA, 22 Nov. 1943; N. T. Gnanaprakasan to the Metropolitan, n.d.; *Manifesto of the Laymen's Association of the CMS Churches of the Dornakal Diocese,* all in 5: 2/6, Dornakal, MACIPBC.

demonstrated his own continued willingness to rely upon missionary help from abroad. Although the bishop had hoped that the Indian Deanery Chairmen would take on most of the responsibilities of the European District Missionary, he soon discovered that the formation of Deaneries and removal of District Missionaries vastly increased his own correspondence and office work. At the same time, the rapid growth in confirmations[127] further increased Azariah's itinerant episcopal responsibilities. To handle all this work, he subdivided the diocese into three Archdeaconries encompassing the territories of the eight Church Councils previously under the bishop's direct authority.[128] He filled the posts of Archdeacon with three European missionaries who henceforth carried much of the diocese's burden of finances and administration. When Azariah procured permission to appoint an Assistant Bishop, he again appointed a European missionary to the post.

Azariah's thinking about the relation of the church in India to its mother church in England evolved from his impassioned pleas for rapid indigenization as a young YMCA secretary to a pragmatic decision in later years that the Indian church still needed the aid of foreign missionary societies and a share in both the spiritual and material riches of the Anglican communion. Azariah had never advocated the forced expulsion of European missionaries or finances from India, believing as much in 1910 as in 1931 that devolution should be voluntary and gradual.[129] However, he moderated his views on self-support. In 1905, Azariah had challenged the NMS to be self-supporting and not to accept funds if offered by non-resident westerners.[130] By 1938, after shepherding his im-

127. 21,515 people were confirmed between 1920 and 1930. Whereas in 1915 it was possible to hold confirmations in 20 centers, by 1931 it was necessary to travel to 55 centers, and even this did not satisfy the demand. VSA, *A Charge Delivered to the Clergy of the Diocese of Dornakal at Bezwada, October 7, 1931, op. cit.,* p. 6.

128. The first covered the area encompassed by the Nandyal Church Council, the second the Kistna Church Council, and the third the remaining work in the Deccan and in Dummagudem.

129. 'I think the Westerner will be for years to come a necessity.' VSA, 'The Problem of Co-operation between Foreign and Native Workers,' *op. cit.* (1910), p. 315. 'The rich heritage of Christian experience and culture that England possesses by reason of generations of its Christianity is something India has not got; and I believe English Christians owe it to God and to the Church of India to send us some of their best sons and daughters to pass this inheritance on to us. This is the service that we still expect of our mother Church of England.' VSA, *A Charge Delivered to the Clergy of the Diocese of Dornakal at Bezwada, October 7, 1931, op. cit.,* pp. 24-25.

130. D. F. Ebright, 'The National Missionary Society of India, 1905-42,' in *op. cit.,* p. 89.

poverished church in Dornakal for almost three decades, Azariah concluded that the pressure to become self-supporting had produced disastrous pastoral results (smothering the spirit of evangelism, neglecting the nurture of Christians, and refusing to teach new inquirers or to baptize catechumens)[131] and had become 'a source of irritation to the indigenous Church.'[132] Azariah now fully agreed with Allen that Venn's original missionary policy of withholding the right to both self-government and self-propagation until Indian congregations were financially independent was founded upon a fundamental ecclesiological error:

> The indigenous Church is the *fruit* of missionary labour, but not the *possession* of missions; and it is on the side of missions a serious and fatal misunderstanding of the nature of the Church to consider any indigenous Church in any stage of development to be in an inferior position because it receives financial support. The support given to one Church by another is not charity but fraternal help. The missionary agencies must act fully on the idea that Churches which are equal members of Christ's Body should receive fraternal help, which fact excludes the stipulation of rights, conditions or restrictions. Where rights are connected with support, the equal and fraternal members of Christ's Body easily take on the relation to each other of *controlling benefactors to irritated recipients of charity.*[133]

Azariah's sensitivity on this subject developed out of his experiences not just in Dornakal but at numerous international conferences, which continued to impress upon him the theological ideal of the worldwide church as the unified 'body of Christ' whose parts are all equally valuable. Azariah increasingly emphasized that the church, rather than extra-ecclesiastical societies, was the principal instrument of evangelization. Once an indigenous church possessed a diocesan organization and a native ministry, as in Dornakal, Azariah argued that missionary societies should step aside and become the church's helper rather than its leader. 'The work must henceforth be, not mission-centric, but church-centric,' he wrote in 1938.[134] For Azariah, whether or not European missionaries occupied prominent positions in his diocese or financial support came from the West was less important than whether or not those positions and that

---

131. VSA, 'Self-Support: False and True,' *op. cit.* (1938), pp. 365-66.
132. VSA, 'Self-Support,' *op. cit.* (1938), p. 537.
133. *Ibid.*, pp. 537-38. (Italics in original)
134. VSA, 'The Christian Church in India,' *op. cit.* (1938), p. 169.

money were placed under the clear authority of the native church. Azariah was motivated less by a nationalistic impulse to replace Europeans with Indians, or sterling with rupees, than by a yearning to give institutional authority to the Indian church that was equal to the authority of churches in other nations.

By building an ecclesiastical structure designed to survive his lifetime and that of his successors, Azariah differentiated himself from many other Indian religious leaders whose popularity was based mainly on a cult of personality and whose following largely disintegrated soon after they or their self-appointed successors died. The Hindu-Christian movements that developed around Chet Ram in the Punjab, around Kandiswammy Chetti in Madras, and around Subba Rao in Andhra called extreme attention to their leaders' personalities and rejected the church and its sacraments as necessary for salvation.[135] In contrast, Azariah subordinated his own personality to the institutional church, which he viewed as a living body not dependent upon him but necessary for salvation.

Azariah built a church, rather than a personality cult, because he focused his life on three central priorities: the study of the Bible, regular participation in holy communion, and ongoing service for others. As he wrote to a friend in 1937, the study of holy scripture 'turns you away from yourself, delivers you from introspection and places your heart and mind on God.' The sacrament of holy communion 'places your heart and soul on the finished work of Christ.' Furthermore,

> It saves you from any temptation to go far away from the Cross and Resurrection — objective acts which constitute the starting points of our Christian life. Whatever my feeling may be, or grasp of realities at any particular moment, whatever my failures may be, my being is immersed in the contemplation of something that happened apart from myself and yet which is the pivot around which my life must move. And this creates in us a dependence upon another and a humility that are the prerequisites of any growth in the spiritual life.

And, finally, the call to service for others 'comes out of the merciful heart of God and is meant to make us feel our nothingness and strive to find by prayer and quiet the strength and purification necessary for the

135. Kaj Baago, *The Movement around Subba Rao, op. cit.; Pioneers of Indigenous Christianity, op. cit.*, pp. 81-84, 207-14; J. N. Farquhar, *Modern Religious Movements in India, op. cit.*, pp. 150-56.

task.'[136] These spiritual disciplines of study, communion, and service gave Azariah the inner strength he sorely needed to weather the storms in church and society to which we shall now turn.

136. Quoted in *Birth Centenary of Bishop Azariah, 1974, op. cit.,* p. 24.

1. Shanars (renamed Nadars) practice their hereditary occupation of climbing palmyra trees in Tinnevelly District, c. 1910. Azariah's family hailed from this caste, and his grandfather was a merchant of palmyra tree products.
(Source: J. A. Sharrock, *South Indian Missions: Containing Glimpses into the Lives and Customs of the Tamil People.* Westminster: SPG, 1910, p. 76.)

2. St. Paul's Church, Megnanapuram, built by C.M.S. missionary John Thomas between 1844 and 1868. Its 175-foot spire is a landmark for many miles around.
(Source: Azariah Family Newsletter, 31 Jan. 1991, in author's possession.)

3. Holy Trinity Church, Vellalanvilai, Tinnevelly District, built by Azariah's father, Thomas Vedanayagam, between 1871 and 1889.
(Source: Azariah Family Newsletter, 31 Jan. 1991, in author's possession.)

4. The village school (now named Azariah Memorial School) in Vellalanvilai where Azariah learned to read from palmyra leaf books and to trace the alphabet with his fingers on the sand.
(Source: Azariah Family Newsletter, 31 Jan. 1991, in author's possession.)

5. B.A. Class, Madras Christian College, 1895. Azariah is seated at the extreme left on the floor.

(Source: *Birth Centenary of Bishop Azariah, 1974*. The Church of South India, the Indian Missionary Society, Madras, and the National Missionary Society of India: Madras, 1974.)

6. V. S. Azariah in 1868: a YMCA Secretary
for Madurai and Tinnevelly Districts.
(Source: Azariah Family Album, in the
possession of Ambrose Azariah, Madras.)

7. Founders of the National Missionary Society of India, Serampore, 25 Dec. 1905. Standing (left to right): S. N. Mukerji (Lahore), W. S. Ratnaval (Calcutta), R. Siraj-ud-din (Lahore), E. A. de Alwis (Kandy), J. W. N. Hensman (Calcutta), J. R. Chitambar (Lucknow), B. P. Sircar (Calcutta). Seated (left to right): J. M. Gulam Masih (Manipuri, U.P.), G. S. Eddy (Madras), S. V. Karmarkar (Chairman: Bombay), V. S. Azariah (Secretary: Palamcottah). Seated on floor (left to right): K. T. Paul (Madras), L. T. Ah Son (Rangoon), N. C. Mukerji (Allahabad). Missing from picture: Rajah Sir Harnam Singh, K. C. Banerji, S. Sathianadhan, and Ah Pon.

8. The former brewery which served as the Indian Missionary Society's headquarters in Dornakal, c. 1910. In the early days, the adjacent tent housed the future Bishop of Dornakal and his family.
(Source: Azariah Family Album, in the possession of Ambrose Azariah, Madras.)

9. Indian Missionary Society missionaries to Dornakal, with their families, c. 1909-1911.
Standing (left to right): Mr. K. Muthusamy, Rev. V. S. Azariah, Mr. J. Srinivasagam. Seated (left to right): Mrs. Muthusamy, Mrs. Samuel Pakianathan, Rev. Samuel Pakianathan, Mr. Solomon Pakianathan, Mrs. Solomon Pakianathan, Mrs. Anbu Azariah, and Mrs. Srinivasagam.
(Source: *Birth Centenary of Bishop Azariah, 1974*. The Church of South India, the Indian Missionary Society, Madras, and the National Missionary Society of India: Madras, 1974.)

10. The making of an Indian bishop, c. 1909:

10a. Azariah with his mentor,
Bishop Henry Whitehead of Madras,
c. 1909. Here the first Indian bishop-
designate dons the British long coat and
trousers, with the 'oriental' turban.
(Source: Azariah Family Album, in the
possession of Ambrose Azariah, Madras.)

10b. Azariah substitutes the coat and trousers
for a simpler cassock, but retains the turban.
(Source: Azariah Family Album, in the possession of
Ambrose Azariah, Madras.)

10c. By consecration day, Azariah abandons the turban as well. Here he is pictured with fellow bishops. Azariah is seated third from the left. Metropolitan Reginald Copleston is seated in the center and Bishop Henry Whitehead is seated third from right.

(Source: *Birth Centenary of Bishop Azariah, 1974.* The Church of South India, the Indian Missionary Society, Madras, and the National Missionary Society of India: Madras, 1974.)

10d. The new Indian bishop, fully robed with crosier, after his consecration in Calcutta on December 29, 1912.

(Source: *Birth Centenary of Bishop Azariah, 1974.* The Church of South India, the Indian Missionary Society, Madras, and the National Missionary Society of India: Madras, 1974.)

11a. Azariah chats with his mentor, Bishop Henry Whitehead, date unknown.
(Source: Azariah Family Album, in the possession of Ambrose Azariah, Madras.)

11b. Isabel Whitehead, 1916.
(Source: Azariah Family Album, in the possession of Ambrose Azariah, Madras.)

12. Azariah with his family in 1929. Standing (left to right): sons George, Henry, Edwin.
Seated (left to right): daughter Grace, wife Anbu, son Ambrose, V. S. Azariah, and daughter Mercy.
(Source: *Birth Centenary of Bishop Azariah, 1974*. The Church of South India, the Indian Missionary Society,
Madras, and the National Missionary Society of India: Madras, 1974.)

13. The face of Christianity in the Dornakal Diocese:

13a. A Telugu pastor with his wife in front of a village prayer house, c. 1938.
(Source: Carol Graham, *Christ Among the Telugus*, London: SPG, 1938.)

13b. Members of a village congregation in Dornakal Diocese.
(Source: Carol Graham, *Christ Among the Telugus*, London: SPG, 1938.)

13c. A Palm Sunday procession in
Dornakal Diocese, c. 1945.
(Source: Carol Graham, *Dornakal: Every
Christian a Witness*, London: SPG, 1945

13d. The altar in a village prayer house, c. 1945.
(Source: Carol Graham, *Dornakal: Every Christian a Witness*, London: SPG, 1945.)

13e. Baptism in Dornakal Diocese, date unknown.
(Source: Azariah Family Album, Madras.)

14. Dornakal Cathedral:

14a. West front.
(Source: *The Story of Dornakal Cathedral*,
Madras: Diocesan Press, n.d.)

14b. South verandah.
(Source: *DDM*, Special Cathedral Double Number, Feb.-March, 1939, vol. XVI, 2 & 3.)

14c. Cathedral interior.
(Source: *DDM*, Special Cathedral Double Number, Feb.-March, 1939, vol. XVI, 2 & 3.)

14d. Congregation at prayer in Dornakal Cathedral.
(Source: *The Story of Dornakal Cathedral*, Madras: Diocesan Press, n.d.)

15. The faces of Christian education in Dornakal Diocese:

15a. Vocational training at the Mission Weaving School, Giddalur, c. 1945.
(Source: Carol Graham, *Dornakal: Every Christian a Witness*, London: SPG, 1945.)

15b. Diocesan teachers-in-training stand outside their homes in Dornakal, date unknown.
(Source: Azariah Family Album, Madras.)

15c. Divinity School, Dornakal.
(Source: *Silver Jubilee: Diocese of Dornakal: 1912-1937,* Mysore: Wesley Press and Publishing House, n.d.)

15d. Women's class in a Dornakal village.
(Source: Carol Graham, *Christ Among the Telugus,* London: SPG, 1938.)

16. Stained glass window, formerly in the Chapel of the United Society for the Propagation of the Gospel (USPG) in London, depicts Azariah holding a model of Dornakal Cathedral. The maker of the stained glass was L. C. Evetts. The window is now located in the USPG archives in Partnership House.
(Source: The United Society for the Propagation of the Gospel, Partnership House, 157 Waterloo Road, London.)

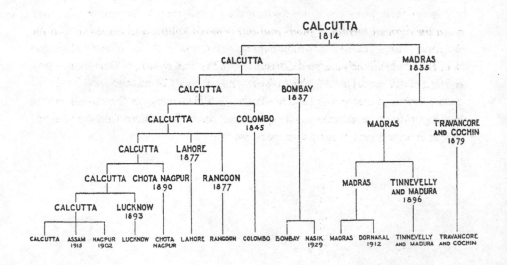

17. Increase of the Episcopate: 1814-1929.
(Source: Cecil John Grimes, *Towards an Indian Church: The Growth of the Church of India in Constitution and Life*, London: SPCK, 1946, p. 168.)

PART III

THE RESOLUTIONS

Azariah's triumphant elevation to a position of unprecedented authority for an Indian empowered him to begin resolving several broader ecclesiastical, social, and cultural quandaries of the late Raj. As a unique native Indian statesman in the Anglican church, he was well positioned to deal with the conflict between missionary societies and churches in India as well as with the broader denominational divisions within Christendom. As the bishop of one of the most dramatically growing Christian dioceses in all of Asia, he also faced the immense practical challenges of rooting the new faith in an ancient, sometimes intractable local Indian culture.

Azariah resolved these daunting problems by adopting a pragmatic approach that was neither purely western nor aggressively indigenous. He successfully navigated the difficult terrain of inter- and intra-church affairs, and helped to lead the Anglican church into its first union with non episcopal churches since the Reformation. He also brilliantly adapted Christianity to the local culture of Dornakal — providing a classic model for the Third World of how to mix Christian essentials with the particularities of indigenous culture. Azariah's achievements in these areas earned him a worldwide reputation as one of the most successful modern Christian leaders ever to emerge from the extra-European world.

CHAPTER 7

Overcoming Divisions in Christendom

The Resistance of Missionary Societies

As Azariah's friend, Sherwood Eddy, watched Azariah process down the aisle at his consecration next to the aging English Metropolitan, it suggested to him 'the passing of one regime and the beginning of a new and indigenous development in Indian missions.'[1] Sadly, however, 'regimes' rarely give up leadership easily, even within the church.

Henry Whitehead described Azariah's consecration to a CMS missionary as 'a great step forward';[2] but many missionaries did not agree, and they fought Azariah's efforts to obtain and exert his authority over their missions in Dornakal. Although, as we have seen, Azariah ultimately succeeded in maintaining a remarkably warm and cordial relationship with the missionary establishment during his episcopal career, this overall harmony was frequently disrupted by jurisdictional disagreements which soured other positive relations.

While most missionary societies were committed in theory to the early establishment of self-sufficient churches, they were often unable or unwilling to act upon this commitment, as Azariah had noted in 1910:

> The aim of the Missionary Societies, we know, is to develop self-governing Churches and to give freedom and scope to indigenous leadership,

---

1. S. Eddy to J. E. Tracy, 15 Jan. 1913, quoted in K. Baago, *A History of the National Christian Council of India, 1914-1964* (Nagpur, 1965), p. 15.
2. H. Whitehead to Bardsley, 17 Jan. 1913, Series G2 I2/0, 1913: 15, CMSA.

and to strive to make themselves unnecessary in the field. But the Societies have not convinced the natives that this is their aim.[3]

The battles that Azariah was obliged to fight with the CMS and the SPG, the two major Anglican societies sponsoring work in his diocese, illustrate how underlying fears and prejudices weakened the cross-cultural and interracial unity of the church.[4]

The area initially committed to Azariah's care in the Nizam's Dominions included the former CMS mission area of Khammamett, which ranged over 5,000 square miles and, in 1913, contained 350 village congregations with 5,689 baptized Christians and catechumens led by six ordained priests and 126 Christian agents.[5] This district provided the first test case for Azariah of the difficulties of asserting his episcopal authority over western missionaries in the field.

On Henry Whitehead's advice, the Khammamett mission was separated from the CMS Telugu Mission's administrative system in 1912 and placed under the joint authority of the new Indian bishop and the CMS Corresponding Committee in Madras, which retained the authority to administer the society's grants. Whitehead advised Azariah to appoint a sympathetic new CMS recruit as Superintending Missionary of the Khammamett district.[6]

The society insisted that the candidate chosen as 'the first European missionary privileged to work under an Indian Bishop' be both amenable to the idea and able to offer wise counsel,[7] since missionaries in the field and in Madras were opposing the transfer of the mission to the Dornakal Diocese. The CMS Corresponding Committee in Madras feared that pri-

3. VSA, 'The Problem of Co-operation between Foreign and Native Workers,' *op. cit.* (1910), p. 312.

4. The bishop's relationship with his home society, the IMS, does not appear to have been comparably difficult. Although the above-mentioned resignation of IMS missionary Solomon Pakianathan because of 'differences of opinion' with other workers suggests that internal relations may have been strained occasionally, archival evidence provides an overall impression of harmony and cooperation between Azariah and the IMS. T. Waller to Durrant, 17 Jan. 1912, Series G2 I2/0, 1912: 17, CMSA.

5. *Khammamett in 1913* (Madras, 1914); copy in Series G2 I2/0, 1913-14: 83, CMSA; *Proceedings of the Madras Corresponding Committee,* 3 Dec. 1912, Series G2 I2/0, 1912: 228, CMSA.

6. Henry Whitehead, *Memorandum on the Proposed Arrangements for the Bishopric of Dornakal,* 17 June 1912, Series G2 I2/0, 1912: 106, CMSA.

7. E. Sell to Durrant, 29 Jan. 1913, Series G2 I2/0, 1913-14: 17, CMSA; *Khammamett in 1913, op. cit.;* Memorandum on Khammamett and Dornakal from Canon Sell, and private comments on Memorandum, Series G2 I2/0, 1912: 132-33, CMSA.

vate donations to the Khammamett mission would stop under an Indian bishop, and they agreed to transfer Khammamett only if the CMS would retain control over financial administration and participate in appointing the Superintending Missionary.[8] Missionaries in the Telugu areas argued that it would simply be 'impossible' to hand authority over to the Dornakal diocese, and that the move would destroy 'unity of policy' in Telugu missions and give the IMS too much control.[9] But these objections by missionaries in the field were dismissed by the Corresponding Committee in Madras:

> It is quite clear that they look at the matter from a different and less progressive standpoint than we do. However, they make no definite proposals and the conclusion we draw is that after having grumbled a little they consider the matter as now closed.[10]

The Madras group decided to withdraw authority over the Khammamett district from missionaries in the field whose methods of administration were regarded as too traditional for the new diocese and to retain for themselves the 'ultimate control' of the district's affairs in order to 'safeguard the interests of the society.'[11] The society's secretary in Madras pleaded with the field missionaries to help make the Dornakal bishopric 'a success' by agreeing to the transfer and assisting in the training of Dornakal's workers to develop 'a system of Indian administration, side by side with our existing administration, which is governed by the Society and administered by Europeans.'[12] He added that, 'so long as the Society fur-

8. Series G2 I2/0, 1912: 132-33, CMSA; J. Cain to Durrant, 8 Aug. 1912, Series G2 I2/0, 1912: 148, CMSA; *Proceedings of the Madras Corresponding Committee*, 29 Aug. 1912, Series G2 I2/0, 1912: 162, CMSA; E. Sell to Durrant, 2 Sept. 1912, Series G2 I2/0, 1912: 163, CMSA; *Proceedings of the Madras Corresponding Committee, 29 Oct. 1912*, Series G2 I2/0, 1912: 191, CMSA.

9. They believed the Indian mission had made some serious mistakes, which they had observed with 'great regret.' The goals of Indian men, money, and methods had not been promoted, and, in their estimation, a reluctance to consult Indian lay and clerical members of the District Church Councils would lead to future problems. They also resented the implication that they had not made sufficient use of Indian men, money, and methods in Khammamett. *Minutes of the 125th Telugu Missionary Conference Held at Bezwada*, Sept. 29–Oct. 2, 1912, Series G2 I2/0, 1912: 205, CMSA. See also Canon Edward Sell to Durrant, 21 Aug. 1912, Series G2/I2/0, 1912: 153, CMSA.

10. E. Sell to Durrant, 31 Oct. 1912, Series G2 I2/0, 1912: 192, CMSA.

11. *Ibid.*

12. Circular letter from E. Sell to Penn, 3 Sept. 1912, Series G2 I2/0, 1912: 193, CMSA.

nishes funds it must exercise a certain amount of control, but it is desired that such control should not hinder the development of new methods.'

The 'progressive' CMS wanted, in a general way, to facilitate the development of an indigenous church within its mission territory, but fell short of submitting itself fully to the authority of the new native bishop. In part, they may have recognized the vast amount of detailed work such authority would entail for the new bishop and his fledgling church. But they also seem to have had an underlying distrust in the ability of Indians conscientiously to administer funds and to perform as truly equal partners in the missionary enterprise. Settlements generally favorable to Azariah were reached by January 1913 on the transfer issue and the appointment of a Superintending Missionary,[13] but ambiguities remained in the definition of jurisdictions which were to cause future problems for Azariah in his relations with the missionary societies.

Few British missionaries envisioned in 1912 that, within ten years, Azariah would be in charge of all Anglican missions in Andhra. When a rumor that such a proposal was being considered was circulated among CMS agents in 1912, it was vehemently denied.[14] Some missionaries were alarmed that Azariah's rise seemed to stimulate the aspirations of Indian Christians for greater responsibilities in church affairs. Conservative CMS missionaries like R. F. Ardill in Palamcottah believed that the consecration was fueling destructive Indian ambitions and signaled a dangerous

13. Henry Whitehead to Durrant, 18 July 1912, Series G2 I2/0, 1912: 129, CMSA; *Resolution and Recommendation of Parent Committee,* 11 Dec. 1912, Series G2 I2/ P5 1904-13, 1912: 191, CMSA; *Proceedings of the Madras Corresponding Committee,* 3 Dec. 1912, Series G2 I2/0, 1912: 228, CMSA; E. Sell to Durrant, 29 Jan. 1913, Series G2 I2/0, 1913: 17, CMSA. The settlements were not reached, however, without more objections from missionaries in the field being sent directly to London. See Penn to Durrant, 13 Nov. 1912, Series G2 I2/0, 1912: 221, CMSA.

Within a year of his enthronement as bishop, Azariah was called upon to serve as Superintending Missionary of the Khammamett district (and Mrs. Azariah as director of the boarding school) when the new appointee, Mr. Cranswick, was obliged by his wife's malaria to go to Australia. E. Sell to Waller, 29 Jan. 1914, Series G2 I2/0, 1914: 7, CMSA. Interestingly, Azariah refused to have anything to do with the society's financial arrangements during this time. *Minutes of the Madras Corresponding Committee,* 6 Feb. 1914, Series G2 I2/0, 1914: 10, CMSA. The reasons behind this decision remain a matter of speculation. The superintending missionary that Azariah replaced believed, however, that more responsibility for financial support should be given to the Indian church and that, regarding details, 'no one can speak more practically or usefully than Bishop Azariah — he has many thoughts on the subject.' G. H. Cranswick to Waller, 27 July 1914, Series G2 I2/0, 1914: 104, CMSA.

14. E. Sell to Durrant, 4 Nov. 1912, Series G2 I2/0, 1912: 215, CMSA.

change in status between Indian and European Christians. 'The general ferment now at work in "native" public opinion in India has begun to affect our Christian Community . . . and this has been moved to more powerful action by the consecration of Bishop Azariah,' Ardill wrote in June 1913.[15] Indian Christians now believed that they might achieve equality with Europeans, he complained, and even that 'the European can be done [away] with altogether':

> Indeed there is now some talk of the European being a 'usurper' living on the Funds that ought to come to the Indian Church and getting a salary much beyond his Indian brother.[16]

Although he denied that he personally objected to Azariah, his former student at Church Missionary College in Tinnevelly, Ardill had accused Azariah of promoting the dangerous idea 'that the missionaries should stand aside and no longer play the part of "fathers"' during a meeting in the Tinnevelly diocese the previous year. Ardill recalled, disapprovingly, Azariah's contention that Indians 'had been long enough under "tutelage" and now should be allowed to think for themselves.'[17]

When the inconceivable occurred and Azariah's diocese was extended to include other Anglican Telugu missions, there was relatively little resistance from the now experienced CMS, but stubborn resistance from the more conservative SPG. When Azariah distributed a draft constitution for his new diocesan council administrative system in early 1923, the CMS agreed to the plan despite another round of complaints from missionaries in the field.[18] The affairs of the CMS missions were thus placed under the jurisdiction of a locally appointed governing body, the Kistna Administrative Committee, that was directly answerable to the Diocesan Council (although three of the society's nine missionaries to Andhra continued to serve on the committee). Azariah continued to have

---

15. R. F. Ardill to Durrant, 20 June 1913, Series G2 I2/0, 1913: 68, CMSA.

16. *Ibid.*

17. *Ibid.*

18. The Telugu missionaries wanted the Madras Corresponding Committee to remain the mission's controlling body for an indefinite period of time, but they were overruled once again. Instead, the society's leadership in London concluded that 'there will be no necessity for a reference on any matters, except finance, to the Secretary at Madras,' whose job would be more like that of a treasurer than that of a secretary. E. F. E. Wigram to VSA, 9 Nov. 1922, Series G2 I2/L17, 1917-24: 322, CMSA; see also 1917-24: 287-88, 339; VSA to E. F. E. Wigram, 18 Jan. 1923, Series G2 I2/P6, 1913-24: 10-11, CMSA.

minor jurisdictional disagreements with CMS missionaries in his diocese over issues such as where to station the society's new recruits, but sympathetic leadership in London generally assured the bishop's right to control such decisions.[19]

This cooperation reflected a larger CMS initiative to support diocesan organizations in India in preparation for disestablishment. Having agreed upon the undesirability of the existing system that tied the church in India to the *Book of Common Prayer* and to British government control, in 1922 the CMS joined ranks with the Indian bishops to help lay the financial and constitutional foundations for an autonomous church. The respectful treatment afforded Azariah by the CMS headquarters in London, despite objections from missionaries in the field, reflects this broader change of policy: this contributed both to the eventual severance of the Church of India from the Church of England and to closer cooperation between the many Anglican missions in India. Under pressure to create unified dioceses and in response to a new generation of young field missionaries in the 1920s and 1930s who were more prepared to cede church leadership to Indians, the CMS, SPG, the 'Brotherhoods' from Oxford, Cambridge, and Dublin, and other religious communities joined ranks as never before.[20]

The SPG was the slowest to surrender control over its Telugu missions. When episcopal supervision of its mission areas passed from the Bishop of Madras to Azariah in 1920, administration of the society was transferred from a committee in Madras (only one of whose members had ever visited the missions) to a Bishop's Telugu Mission Committee composed of missionaries and elected representatives of the local church. Azariah wanted to give his diocese still greater responsibility over affairs in the SPG area and soon replaced the committee with a more representative supervisory body, similar to the Kistna Administrative Committee in the CMS area.[21]

19. See, e.g., correspondence between Azariah, E. F. E. Wigram (the India Group Secretary at CMS headquarters), and R. W. Peachey (former Chairman of the Bezwada and Ellore District Church Councils and then Secretary of South India Missions) over where to station Miss Langdale-Smith. Wigram asserted that it was up to Azariah, not Peachey, to decide the issue. Series G2 I2/L17, 1917-24: 277, 284, 287, CMSA; Series G2 I2/P6, 1913-24: 64, 80, CMSA. Peachey was one of the CMS Telugu missionaries to resist the transfer of Khammamett in 1912. E. Sell to Durrant, 21 Aug. 1912, Series G2 I2/0, 1912/106: 153, CMSA.

20. G. Hewitt, *The Problems of Success, op. cit.,* pp. 58-64.

21. For correspondence related to this controversy, see 25: 114, 124-25, 128, 130, 133-34, 137 (Dornakal), CLS Series, USPG; and 35: 24, 54, 57, 65, 75-76 (Dornakal), CLR Series, USPG.

The bishop's 1925 proposal for this Nandyal Administrative Committee provoked strong resistance from the home society, which wanted the number of missionaries on the committee to parallel the increase in local church members. Azariah objected that 'it is not right, as a principle, that on a Diocesan Committee, missionaries should have such a preponderating role,'[22] and he was supported by SPG missionaries in the field — a curious reversal from the earlier dispute with the CMS in which Azariah was opposed by missionaries in the field. The SPG's insistence upon safeguards to protect its grants, institutions, and missionaries infuriated Azariah, who noted that the CMS had demanded no such protection and concluded:

> If . . . we are in a state when representatives of English Missionary Societies should 'watch' the Diocese or Diocesan Council to see that the interests of their particular Society are safe-guarded — the Diocese is not ready to live its own life. 'Safeguards' and 'watching the interests' imply lack of confidence and as such I find it impossible to accept them.[23]

When Azariah threatened to withdraw his proposal completely, the SPG chose to apologize ('there was no intention of conveying a lack of confidence . . .') and to accept Azariah's plan.[24]

With the establishment of Nandyal's local governing body under diocesan jurisdiction, relations between Dornakal and the SPG warmed considerably. As with the CMS, institutional changes were strengthened by personnel changes, as an older generation of missionaries gradually gave way to a new generation more alert to growing Indian nationalism and more sympathetic to Indian Christian aspirations. Azariah pushed this process along by requesting the retirement of missionaries unable or unwilling to adapt. In a lengthy correspondence during 1920 and 1921,[25] the bishop requested that the SPG retire an ageing and largely deaf missionary who, Azariah believed, would have trouble fitting into the new order of things. Although he expressed gratitude for the Rev. A. Britten's forty-five years of service in Nandyal and Giddalur, Azariah criticized the

22. VSA to A. M. Murray, 6 Oct. 1926, 35: 75-76 (Dornakal), CLR Series, USPG.

23. *Ibid.*

24. A. M. Murray to VSA, 26 Oct. 1926, and A. M. Murray to VSA, 2 Dec. 1926, 25: 133, 137 (Dornakal), CLS Series, USPG.

25. VSA to Pascoe, 23 Oct. 1920, 62: 76; VSA to King, 25 April 1921, 62: 132; A. Britten to Dolphin, 13 July 1921, 62: 163a; Britten to Dolphin, 19 July 1921, 62: 169; also, 62: 173, 176, 183, 193, 195, 218, 224, 246, 254, all in (Madras, Tinnevelly, Dornakal) CLR Series, USPG.

missionary for a domineering, disciplinarian approach which he believed had discouraged Indian pastors from taking initiative and acting responsibly. The society was preparing to follow the bishop's recommendation against Britten's vehement protests when declining health, perhaps mercifully, forced Britten's retirement.

In the area of finances Azariah met with his most difficult and sensitive challenges. The extraordinary success of the mass movements in Dornakal drew attention, and extra funds, from the British societies. Although the 1920s were generally years of retrenchment for missionary societies,[26] special appeals launched in Britain during the 1920s and 1930s, often with Azariah's personal participation, led to a relative increase in money for the Telugu mass movements. Azariah regularly delivered sermons and published articles in England about the mass movements. At the well-attended 1920 CMS 'Annual Sermon' in London, he estimated that 50 million outcastes could be brought into the church with western help.[27] An Azariah family scrapbook contains dozens of reports from western newspapers and journals of Azariah's addresses and activities during trips to Great Britain, America, and Australia, and suggests that Azariah's influence was widely felt by churchgoing populations in the western world.[28]

These campaigns were promoted by the church institutions with the heroic supporting efforts of interested individuals such as the Whiteheads and Canon D. S. Johnson of Manchester. The only agency in England formally collecting money for Dornakal (apart from those collecting for the CMS and SPG) was the Dornakal Diocesan Association, chaired by Sir William Barton with Isabel Whitehead's help as secretary. But Henry Whitehead served as Azariah's commissary in England, frequently appealing for private support and lobbying for missionary society grants and salaries for Dornakal. Canon Johnson also launched two mass movement appeals with Azariah's help in 1918 and in 1927-28. Johnson persuaded churches throughout his Manchester Diocese to each provide 20 pounds sterling per year for the upkeep of village schools in the Dornakal Diocese,

26. The number of Protestant missionaries in India dropped from 5,201 in 1912 to 5,063 in 1938, despite the steady growth during the same period of the Protestant Christian community from about 1,000,000 in 1914 to about 2,500,000 in 1936. G. Hewitt, *The Problems of Success, op. cit.,* pp. 11, 49.

27. VSA, 'The Church's Ideal,' *op. cit.* (1920), pp. 148-63. See also his 1937 CMS 'Annual Sermon': 'The Unity Which Christ Wills,' *CMO,* LXIV (July 1937), pp. 150-52 (copy in CMSA, AR(MS), 1936-37, cited in G. Hewitt, *op. cit.,* p. 110).

28. Clippings Album, Azariah Collection, Madras.

which were then named after their English sponsors. Azariah delivered a sermon in Manchester Cathedral on 19 June 1930 about the mass movements in Dornakal that is still remembered by elderly parishioners today.[29]

In areas such as Dornakal where additional funds were provided from abroad for the education, training, and appointment of teachers and the provision of Christian literature, substantial increases in the numbers of annual baptisms usually occurred.[30] Other missionaries, particularly from north India, resented such a large proportion of dwindling missionary resources being allocated to mass movements in the South, and accusations of mismanagement were hurled without much evidence. In a series of bitter exchanges with the SPG in the late 1920s and early 1930s, Azariah was obliged to defend himself against several rumors related to his allocation of funds in the diocese.[31] The society's slowness and seeming reluctance to accept his denials of wrongdoing (presented with ample documentation from the diocese's extensive financial records) embittered Azariah. It made more difficult his continuing effort to assert authority over SPG missionaries who were still reluctant to look to the bishop rather than the home society for financial directives.[32] Yet Azariah suc-

29. Letter from Manchester parishioner Bert Shepherd to author, undated, Stockport. On Johnson's special fund-raising appeals for the mass movements, launched in cooperation with Azariah and the National Christian Council in India, see G. Hewitt, *The Problems of Success, op. cit.,* pp. 106-12.

30. The CMS Mass Movement Commission reported the following figures in 1928:

	Baptized adherents	Under instruction for baptism	Number of baptisms annually
The Punjab	37,669	4,000	1,909
United Provinces	8,726	2,858	275
Western India	5,000	900	284
Bengal (Santal area)	8,000	300	350
Telugu	68,807	45,733	7,104
Travancore	38,500	2,900	700
Tinnevelly	25,000	1,500	700

From G. Hewitt, *The Problems of Success, op. cit.,* p. 109, who argues that the large numbers for the Telugu missions were at least partly attributable to the funds raised by Canon Johnson.

31. See, e.g., VSA to S. Waddy, 19 April 1929, 324: 40; VSA to Waddy, 23 April, 363a: 18; VSA to Waddy, 23 May 1933, 363a: 18; VSA to Waddy, 5 July 1934, 369: 4, all in (Dornakal), D Series, USPG.

32. VSA to France, 5 Feb. 1941, 524: 3 (Dornakal), D Series, USPG.

ceeded in exerting his authority over all areas of diocesan financial life, and in avoiding entirely the types of scandals that so marred the earlier bishopric of Samuel Crowther in Africa.

In negotiating relations between his emerging indigenous church and its 'parent' missionary societies, Azariah had the additional difficulty of local pressure from Telugu converts to maintain ties to missionaries. In contemporary Dornakal, foreign missionaries — both western and Tamil — are still often remembered in idealized terms as nothing less than self-sacrificing saints. A lyric sung in some Dornakal villages today recalls:

> Listen to the good deeds the missionaries from England, Ireland and Tinnevelly have done in India,
> Although we did not know them (they were not our friends), still they have come and worked hard for God, despite the hot sun.
> They have constructed schools and churches. They dug wells for the oppressed people.
> Words are not sufficient to describe their good works.[33]

These works in schools and hospitals touched many people, and their provision of clothing and food for young schoolchildren is still described with special appreciation. Western missionaries were often singled out for particular praise. They were often remembered for treating people of different castes and economic levels (particularly those of the lowest groups) with respect and impartiality. One local pastor reflected that, 'when they were living like animals, the missionaries instructed them.'[34] British missionaries were remembered affectionately and with some amusement by the long form of their names ('Father Arthur Frederick Ryder Bird'), and are still prayed for by people in the villages.[35] Often the westerners were perceived as men and women of enormous spiritual depth who cooperated with and worked humbly under Indian authority. Sister Carol Graham of the Women's Union is remembered for praying two hours every morning, and the Dornakal community bade Sister Stanton of the Church Army farewell with an affectionate lyric that is still remembered and sung today:

---

33. Sung by Mrs. Peram Kantama, 4 April 1986, Beerole. Many of the songs praising Azariah also stress the missionary character of his work with the IMS.
34. Interview with Rev. Pasunori Ratnam, 5 April 1986, Madiripuram.
35. Interview with Mr. David, 9 April 1986, Dornakal.

> She taught English, Sunday School too,
> Come back, don't go away,
> Write letters to us at least once a week![36]

The work of an American Episcopal missionary to Yellendu in the Khammam District is so well remembered that contemporaries still say of him:

> Because of his love for the people, if you go in the forest, even the trees whisper 'Shriver, Shriver, Shriver.'[37]

In contrast to (but in conjunction with) these idealized memories, recollections of Azariah's difficulties with western missionaries also still persist, particularly in the minds of the Telugu Christian community's more educated and prominent members. Bishop Elliot's successor, Bishop P. Solomon, attested to the reality of Azariah's ongoing disagreements with missionaries who preferred not to serve under an Indian bishop.[38] A former pastorate chairman recalled how the older generation of missionaries frequently clashed with Azariah over their loss of authority in managing schools and churches.[39] Some missionaries were remembered for both good and bad relations with Azariah, as was the above-mentioned Father Arthur Frederick Ryder Bird, who tried to stop Azariah from taking control of mission schools and hospitals but still maintained excellent relations with him.[40]

This mixed picture of Azariah's relations with foreign missionaries reflects the complex range of factors influencing Azariah's creative solutions to these various jurisdictional and financial problems. The external pressure of rising political nationalism combined with internal pressure for greater ecclesiastical autonomy from newly assertive educated Indian Christian converts. This assertiveness was articulated mainly by elites

---

36. Sung by Rev. M. Daniel, 8 April 1986, Dornakal, who also recalled Sister Carol's devotion and a spirit of cooperation between Azariah and the missionaries. Interviews also on 29 and 31 March 1986.

37. Interview with Mr. David, 9 April 1986, Dornakal.

38. Interview with Bishop P. Solomon, 31 March 1986, Dhyana Ashram, Paloncha.

39. Interview with Rev. Alfred Bunyan, 29 March 1986, Dornakal.

40. Interview with Alfred Bunyan, 29 March 1986, Dornakal. Azariah is said to have addressed him as 'Father' (all other missionaries he addressed as 'Mr.') and to have visited him on his deathbed in England. (Interview with Mr. David, 9 April 1986, Dornakal.)

against local pressure for continued dependency on the West, and caused a slow and hardly perceptible deterioration in formerly stable relationships between western providers and Indian Christian recipients. Azariah led the movement to place the formerly unequal relationship upon a new foundation of equality between mission and church.

In Dornakal, the picture was complicated by the presence of a Tamil bishop whose efforts to place western missionaries more squarely under the Dornakal church's authority were sometimes resented by Telugus themselves. Strong bonds of affection had developed over one hundred years of interaction between highly literate if paternalistic British missionaries and Telugu Christians who gathered, as they liked to sing, 'like ants around the sweet jaggery *(cheruku belam)* of the gospel.'[41] These ties were challenged by Azariah's strategy for diocesan autonomy, and his struggles with missionary societies to assert the Indian church's independence were sometimes misinterpreted as efforts to replace European dominance with Tamil dominance, rather than as efforts to raise the Telugu church to its full place in Christendom.

Azariah resolved his controversies with western missionaries and their societies by avoiding the extremes of continued dependency or permanent separation. He chose to transcend the hurt, suspicion, and distrust engendered by these conflicts and, instead, to use the conflicts to build a new type of partnership with his western benefactors. Throughout his bishopric he maintained a remarkably cordial overall relationship with western missionary societies — who could not afford to lose his favor, just as he could not afford to lose theirs. This relationship resembled an aging marriage — with its complex mix of affection, disappointment, and frustration — more than a war between enemies.[42] The bishop insisted on change despite personal fondness for western colleagues, and he sometimes recommended limited and short-term separations (not divorce) between mission and church so that the relationship could be rebuilt on a

41. A popular dancing song composed by Canon Subbayya begins: 'Wherever there is jaggery, there are ants. In the same way, where people preach the Gospel, the people from surrounding areas gather. Victory! Hallelujah!' Sung by Mr. Kumari Joseph Samuel, 5 April 1986, Madiripuram.

42. This analogy was used for the broader relation between Britain and India by Sir John Lawrence, who has argued: 'to consider the relation of Britain and India purely, or even mainly, in terms of aggression worked out in a colonial situation ignores many of the positive features of a four hundred year relationship that was similar to that of an aging marriage.' Sir John Lawrence, *India and Britain: More than a Marriage of Convenience,* offprint from the author.

newly solid foundation. Despite protests of different kinds from the marriage's Telugu 'children,' Azariah managed to save and improve this troubled union.

The Resistance of Christian Denominationalism

The unity of the church was threatened not only by conflicts with Anglican missionary societies. The western missionary enterprise had imported multiple denominations to India, so that the Indian Christian church was itself divided into many sections. Some Indian Christians identified themselves with bizarrely inappropriate titles such as British Anglicans, Canadian Baptists, or German Lutherans. These divisions seriously weakened the witness of an already small minority church in a non-Christian land. As Azariah argued at the Lausanne Conference on Faith and Order in 1927,

> Unity may be theoretically a desirable ideal in Europe and America, but it is vital to the life of the Church in the mission field. The divisions of Christendom may be a source of weakness in Christian countries, but in non-Christian lands they are a sin and a scandal.[43]

Azariah tried to shock the western church out of its complacency. Denominationalism was taken for granted in the West, but Indian Christians could ill afford divisions, outnumbered as they already were by non-Christians on the subcontinent. Worse still, Indian converts exploited denominational divisions to preserve former caste divisions, with different caste groups being baptized into different denominations. Azariah identified Christian disunity as a serious problem early in his career, and spent over three decades battling for unity between the Anglican church and other Christian denominations.

Azariah helped to jump-start the twentieth-century ecumenical movement at a meeting between representatives of the Church of England in India and the South India United Church (a united Congregational-Presbyterian church) at Bishop Whitehead's Madras residence in 1910. This meeting sparked a process that led, after many years of painstaking labor and negotiation, to the first reunification of episcopal (Anglican)

---

43. VSA, 'The Necessity of Christian Unity for the Missionary Enterprise of the Church,' in *Faith and Order: Proceedings of the World Conference, Lausanne, August 3-21, 1927,* ed. H. N. Bate (London: Student Christian Movement, 1927), p. 495.

and non-episcopal (Congregational, Presbyterian, Methodist) Churches since the Reformation, in 1947. Although the new Church of South India came into being two years after Azariah's death, he participated in virtually all of the major interdenominational meetings leading up to its formation.

These negotiations were a different kind of struggle for Azariah, forcing him to defend church teachings on issues such as historic succession against nonconformist challenges to Anglican faith and order. A brief survey[44] of Azariah's contribution to the formation of the Church of South India is helpful for understanding not only another dimension of his prolific activity, but also the distinctive contribution which he made to the historic 1947 settlement as the preeminent spokesman for Indian Christians during a quarter century of negotiations.

Azariah was intimately involved with all of the major personalities and organizations who pioneered South Indian ecumenism: the Tinnevelly (mainly Nadar but also Vellalar) church, Madras Christian College, the YMCA, the IMS, the NMS, Sherwood Eddy, John Mott, K. T. Paul, Henry Whitehead, the Joint Committee on Union, and the NCC. His participation at 'Edinburgh 1910,' and his outspoken advocacy of unity at the Lambeth Conferences of 1920 and 1930[45] and the international conferences on Faith and Order in Lausanne (1927) and Edin-

44. Brief mainly because the subject has been dealt with extensively elsewhere, notably in Bengt Sundkler's *Church of South India, op. cit.* The archives at Selly Oak College, Birmingham, also contain a sizable collection of primary materials relating to the unity negotiations, including copies of Joint Committee Reports and the journal *Church Union News and Views (CUNV)*, I, 1 (July 1930), to XV, 3 (March 1945). See boxes labeled 'Pamphlets (Old) 275' and 'Pamphlets on South India Church Union Scheme,' the collection of papers labeled 'Church of South India–Negotiations for and Inauguration of the Union,' and the collection donated by Lesslie Newbigin. See also Ruth Rouse, 'Voluntary Movements and the Changing Ecumenical Climate,' and K. S. Latourette, 'Ecumenical Bearings of the Missionary Movement and the International Missionary Council,' in *A History of the Ecumenical Movement, 1517-1948* (London, 1954), pp. 309-402; G. S. Eddy, *Religion and Politics in India*, 6: 125, Eddy Papers, YDS. Surprisingly, Azariah's name does not appear in the index to Michael Hollis, *The Significance of South India* (London, 1966).

45. *Proceedings at the Sixth Lambeth Conference, Third Day, 7 July 1920*, 105: 191-95; *12th Day, 31 July 1920*, 108: 176-77; *Proceedings of the Seventh Lambeth Conference, Third Day, Wed. 9 July 1930*, 146: 232-41, *Mon. Aug. 4, 1930*, 148: 203-4; all in Lambeth Conference Papers, LP. For interesting commentary on unity debates at the Lambeth Conferences, see H. H. Henson, *Retrospect of an Unimportant Life, II, 1920-1939* (London, 1943). Also, vols. 28-29, Papers of Archbishop Temple, LP, and Alan M. G. Stephenson, *Anglicanism and the Lambeth Conferences* (London, 1978), pp. 139-41.

burgh (1937)[46] — all were essential contributions towards building an international consensus in favor of ecumenical cooperation in the early part of this century. The papers of Edwin Palmer, Bishop of Bombay and another central figure in the unity negotiations, reveal Azariah's thorough acquaintance, as a leader, organizer, and publicist, with every aspect of the unity negotiations during the last twenty-five years of his life.[47]

Azariah began his active involvement in this interdenominational struggle by convincing Henry Whitehead of the importance of organic union for India as early as 1910.[48] The Bishop of Dornakal participated in all of the major interdenominational meetings with an ecumenical thrust during the period between 1910 and 1918 (such as the Edinburgh Continuation meetings of 1910-13 and the meetings related to the Evangelistic Forward Movement during 1910-18), and was the primary organizer and leader of the now famous meeting at Tranquebar in 1919 which initiated the specific negotiations between episcopal and non-episcopal churches that succeeded in 1947.[49] Azariah then served as a leading member of the Joint Committee on Union from its inauguration in 1920 to his death in 1945.

Azariah took a strong position from the start on the need to retain an historic episcopate in the united church (by far the most divisive issue at stake) and argued against division along caste, racial, or linguistic lines.[50] In this respect, Azariah was in full agreement with the Catholic tradition in the Anglican church; as his conviction regarding this issue strengthened over the years, he came into regular confrontation with his non-Anglican colleagues, especially the Congregationalists.[51] But unlike

46. VSA: 'The Necessity of Christian Unity for the Missionary Enterprise of the Church,' in *Faith and Order: Proceedings of the World Conference, Lausanne, August 3-21, 1927*, ed. H. N. Bate (London: SCM, 1927), pp. 491-95, and discussions on pp. 102-3, 418-23; Address delivered on 3 Aug. 1937, *The Second World Conference on Faith and Order, Edinburgh, Aug. 3-18, 1937*, ed. Leonard Hodgson (London: SCM, 1938), pp. 49-55 and pp. 69, 167, 173, 197, 205.

47. For example, see 2969: 297, 2978: 13, 89-90, 97-104, 111-15, 148, 150-52, 171-72, 233-38, 274-85, 312, 341, 344-53, 357-59, 366-72, Papers of E. J. Palmer, LP.

48. G. S. Eddy, *Religion and Politics in India*, 6: 125, Eddy Papers, YDS.

49 Sundkler, *op. cit.*, pp. 61-130. This meeting was an Indian initiative with Sherwood Eddy as the only western delegate (as at the foundation of the NMS). See VSA, 'What Happened at Tranquebar,' *CUNV*, I, 4 (Jan. 1931), pp. 144-45.

50. See, e.g., Azariah's debate with Bernard Lucas in 1919 in Sundkler, *op. cit.*, pp. 108-11; VSA, 'Church Union in South India,' *HF*, XXXIX, 9 (Sept. 1919), p. 333.

51. Sundkler, *op. cit.*, p. 185.

his Anglo-Catholic colleagues, Azariah took a broad position regarding the possibility of intercommunion, a contentious issue by the early 1930s. Azariah stood alone with the Bishop of Tinnevelly, F. J. Western, in defying Anglican Catholic opinion to partake in the elements at Methodist and SIUC communion services during the Joint Committee meeting of February 1932 in Madras.[52] This constituted one of the more important turning points in the negotiations, creating a new sense of goodwill among participants that was translated later into an agreement on full unification.

The unity movement was one of the primary means by which Azariah became a world-renowned churchman. The Indian efforts were watched with great interest by Anglicans and nonconformists around the world who recognized their historical importance. At both the Lambeth Conferences of 1920 and 1930 and the Faith and Order Conferences of 1927 and 1937, Azariah publicized and promoted the South Indian scheme of union, and he fearlessly upbraided western churches for not taking denominational divisions seriously enough.

The bishop's dedication to the cause of unity was prompted by several interrelated factors. First and foremost was his commitment to evangelism and his recognition that denominationalism weakened the effectiveness of missionaries in India. Jesus Christ's prayer for unity in the Gospel of John — 'that all of them may be one, . . . so that the world may believe that you have sent me'[53]— made it clear to him that unity was essential for successful missions. Azariah's experience as an evangelist bore out the truth of this biblical passage. Interdenominational disputes were not a rare occurrence in his diocese and 'sheep stealing' by other Christian denominations was a vexing problem. His missionary work at the grassroots level in Dornakal provided him with both his rationale for and his undisputed authority in the ecumenical dialogue.

Secondly, Azariah's quest for a united church of India expressed his concern for the development of an authentically indigenous church. Azariah argued that a unified church would be a more genuine expression of a native Indian Christianity than one divided into ecclesiastical compartments formed by western controversies dating back to the Reformation. Denominationalism was an alien export from Europe that offended Indian Christian sensibilities very much like English cloth exported from Lancashire offended Indian nationalist sensibili-

---

52. *Ibid.,* pp. 240-41.
53. John 17:21.

ties.[54] Indian Christians had not participated historically in the sectarian conflicts from which denominational divisions emerged, Azariah argued, nor had they shared in the 'social discriminations, political partisanships, or racial characteristics' which perpetuated sectarian cleavages in the West. To Indian Christians, western denominational boundaries were 'totally meaningless' and destructive of their unity as a community.[55]

Worst of all to Azariah, denominationalism inhibited Indian Christians from overcoming their own prejudices of 'race, language, caste and social status.'[56] Initially meaningless sectarian divisions inherited from the West were being reinterpreted, Azariah warned, to reinforce India's indigenous sociological divisions. Denominationalism permitted Indian converts of different castes to preserve and even strengthen their social separations by joining churches of different denominations. Thus, Azariah claimed, 'separate castes merge into separate denominations and once more continue their unholy warfare of generations.'[57]

Azariah viewed the problem of denominationalism in much the same way as his contemporary, H. Richard Niebuhr, who identified various sociological determinants of ecclesiastical sectarianism as 'the accommodation of Christianity to the caste-system of human society.' To Niebuhr, 'the evil of denominationalism' lay in 'the failure of the churches to transcend the social conditions which fashion them into caste organizations.'[58] Both men regarded church divisiveness as a moral failure falling short of the ideal of Christian brotherhood as presented in the Bible.

54. Interestingly, the American Protestant proponent of the theology of the 'social gospel,' Walter Rauschenbusch, also described denominational divisions as 'nearly all an historical heritage, imported from Europe.' 'The Social Principles of Jesus,' in *The World Treasury of Modern Religious Thought*, ed. Jaroslav Pelikan (Boston, 1990), p. 591. It is likely that Azariah's thinking in this area was stimulated by American attitudes towards European Christianity articulated by another proponent of the social gospel, his close friend Sherwood Eddy.

55. VSA, Address delivered on 3 Aug. 1937, *The Second World Conference on Faith and Order, Edinburgh, August 3-18, 1937, op. cit.,* p. 52.

56. *Ibid.*

57. VSA, 'The Necessity of Christian Unity for the Missionary Enterprise of the Church,' in *op. cit.* (1927), p. 494.

58. H. Richard Niebuhr, *The Social Sources of Denominationalism* (New York, 1929), pp. 6, 21. I have been unable to establish whether Azariah was familiar with Niebuhr's works. Like Azariah, Niebuhr relied on the historical research of A. Harnack in his analysis. It is conceivable that the influence of Azariah and the South Indian unity movement provoked Niebuhr to utilize the terminology of caste in condemning denominationalism.

Both believed that the ecumenical movement was rediscovering what they regarded as the church's true vocation of transcending the divisions of the 'world' (class, race, nation) to create an international fellowship of love. This idealistic mandate provided the foundation for the World Council of Churches, whose inauguration in Amsterdam in 1948 represented a worldwide extension of the ecumenical vision to which Azariah and his colleagues had given local expression in India.

The South Indian ecumenical movement never drew its inspiration, however, from the type of secular political vision that became associated in the postwar period with the World Council of Churches; its inspiration came, rather, from the more traditional missionary objective of converting India to Christianity. The many westerners and Indians who joined Azariah in the quest for Indian ecclesiastical unity were, for the most part, ardent evangelists who recognized that denominationalism was a barrier to the effective propagation of the gospel. Men such as J. J. Banninga, J. H. Maclean, V. Santiago, J. S. M. Hooper, H. A. Popley, and Rajaiah D. Paul joined Azariah and other Anglican bishops in believing that 'the realm of the spirit' (later to become the preserve mainly of evangelicals) was 'integrally related to a new vision of the Church as one body' (later to become the realm primarily of ecumenicals).[59] After the Second World War, these two tendencies bifurcated into the acrimonious 'ecumenical-evangelical standoff' that reached its climax during the 1960s and continues today.[60] Conservative evangelicals rarely see ecumenism as a necessary part of evangelism; and liberal ecumenists tend to regard traditional evangelism as a divisive rather than a unifying force. From the perspective of the late twentieth century it is therefore difficult to imagine that, in Azariah's day, ecumenism was regarded as the very key to South Indian evangelism.

Azariah's greatest contribution to the unity debates may well have been his promotion of an Indian Christian identity that was both national and transnational in character.[61] The bishop often described church unification as part of a larger program of church indigenization: 'We must have one Church. We want a Church of India, a Church which can be our spiritual home, a Church where the Indian religious genius can find natural expression,' he argued in 1927. However, he also stressed that the Indian church was 'a living branch of the Holy, Catholic and Apostolic Church,' whose emerging ecumenical character would provide 'a visible symbol of

59. Lesslie Newbigin, *Unfinished Agenda: An Autobiography* (London, 1985), p. 176.
60. W. R. Hutchison, *Errand to the World, op. cit.*, pp. 102-18, 176-83.
61. B. Sundkler, *op. cit.*, p. 110.

unity in that divided land (India).'[62] Because Azariah always tempered nationalism with universalism, he regarded reunification less as an act of national self-assertion than as an 'act of atonement and reparation . . . of penitence and sorrow . . . for the sad condition of divisions in which we find ourselves.'[63]

The bishop paid a heavy price toward the end of his life for defending a universal ecumenical vision against the growing nationalist demand for freedom from the West. Indian Christian liberals of the 'Christo Samaj' attacked the Joint Committee negotiations for being too western in their composition and approach.[64] 'The religious ethic of India was not compatible with one centralized structure,' the Indian layman, P. Chenchiah, claimed in 1938. 'Hinduism is a federation of different Hindu temples and charitable institutions.'[65] But, to Azariah, a centralized episcopal system was essential in India to block caste divisions and to maintain Christian sacramental worship and community life.

Azariah opposed many efforts of this more radical group to liberate the Indian church from its western 'captivity.' As the bishop's youngest son recalled to this author: 'Church of England Christianity has in it an ingredient of Socrates, Plato and Aristotle and, if this element is removed and in its place Ramayana, Sankaracharya and Yoga introduced, the end product will be a very different type of Christianity; and Father was totally opposed to it.'[66] The bishop's concern for building a united Indian church upon the historical foundations of the Judeo-Graeco-Roman tradition as introduced to India by western parent churches (and by the ancient Thomas Christians) frustrated more impatient advocates of thorough indigenization. But Azariah's solution was not to turn his back on traditions inherited from the West, but to improve and build upon them.

By the opening of the 1938 International Missionary Council conference at Tambaram, the now elderly Azariah felt isolated among a new generation of Indian clergy and laity whose criticisms of western missions ap-

---

62. VSA, 'The Necessity of Christian Unity for the Missionary Enterprise of the Church,' in *op. cit.* (1927), p. 495.

63. VSA, *South India Union: An Examination of the Scheme from the Anglican Point of View* (Madras: CLS, 1936), p. 35.

64. B. Sundkler, *op. cit.,* p. 185.

65. Quoted in I. David, 'The Development of the Concept of Indigenization,' in *op. cit.,* p. 67.

66. Interview, 23 March 1986, Madras. On the problem generally, see R. H. S. Boyd, *India and the Latin Captivity of the Church, op. cit.*

peared to Azariah as essentially unjust and narrow-minded.[67] Although the bishop promoted structural and cultural indigenization in his diocese, he remained faithful to a vast majority of the traditions associated with Christianity's western (and, to a lesser extent, Eastern Orthodox) incarnations, and was distressed that many younger Indian Christians felt more resentment than gratitude towards the work of western missionaries.

At Tambaram, Azariah also defended the unpopular minority position articulated by Hendrik Kraemer which asserted the uniqueness and superiority of the Christian revelation against a growing spirit of religious relativism.[68] M. K. Gandhi's focus on Jesus Christ as a 'supreme model of passive resistance and *satyagraha*,' and on the Sermon on the Mount 'as one of the highest moral standards of conduct,' had greatly enhanced India's appreciation of Jesus 'as a great Prophet, a *Nabi*, as a World-Teacher, a *jagatguru*,' Azariah had written in 1932. But, he continued, Gandhi had failed to communicate to India that Christianity also 'stands for proclaiming a salvation from sin by faith' and joining a community fellowship 'which is the source of the Christian life.'[69]

Azariah faced a new generation at Tambaram content to preach Gandhi's ethical Christ of the Sermon on the Mount and to engage in Christian charitable projects but increasingly doubtful about preaching the supernatural Christ of the cross (i.e., atonement for sin), the resurrection, and pentecost. A desacralized church for social reform rather than evangelism was the goal and symbol of this new attitude. But doubts about Christianity's claim to be the only 'true' religion would, Azariah argued, eventually undermine the success of any missionary enterprise. Gandhi and many liberal Christians who expected missionaries to engage in charitable service without seeking conversions did not understand the importance of 'the spirit of the religion of Jesus Christ' in mission work, the bishop wrote shortly before the conference:

> To ask us to engage in all these activities without demanding obedience to Christ, is to ask railways to run without engines, and electric installations to be effected without the power-house.'[70]

---

67. I am indebted to Azariah's son Ambrose for his vivid description of his father's frustration as he faced his younger and more radical colleagues during the conference discussions. Interview, 23 March 1986, Madras.

68. Hendrik Kraemer, *The Christian Message in a Non-Christian World* (London, 1938), was the volume he prepared on this subject especially for the conference.

69. VSA, 'The Missionaries' Message,' *NCCR*, LII, 1 (Jan. 1932), pp. 14, 17.

70. VSA, 'The Christian Contribution to India,' *op. cit.* (1938), p. 807.

Azariah's struggle to unite different denominations was ultimately successful, although he did not live to see the institutional fruits of his labor. As he worked to heal divisions within Christendom, the ground shifted under his feet so that what began as a dynamic effort to free the Indian church from western denominationalism was regarded, by the end of his life, as a conservative move to preserve the church's western character. Azariah's successful solution to the rifts in post-Reformation Christendom had been overtaken by the power of a more xenophobic nationalism.

CHAPTER 8

Overcoming Caste and Culture in India

Azariah's second major challenge was to overcome the constant friction between local Andhra culture and the transformative agenda of Christianity. The differences between the Christian and non-Christian cultures in his diocese widened over time and were at least as critical to Azariah as the internal rifts within Christendom. The mass movements to Christianity demanded radical adjustments to Andhra village life, particularly in outcaste and low-caste sections. Azariah encouraged the reinterpretation of Christianity within the Telugu context, but could not always predict the outcome. There were many surprises: some good and some bad. Azariah's church was never totally successful in realizing desired change. However, Azariah did successfully resolve many of the cultural disputes in his diocese through a pragmatic balancing of change and continuity, of innovation and accommodation. His solutions were neither purely western nor purely indigenous, but a creative adaptation of grassroots cultural expressions to universalized Christian values.

Azariah's central challenge as a church builder in rural Andhra was to distinguish between those local cultural elements that were compatible with Christian social ethics and those that were not. As Niebuhr reminds us, this task has always been one of the most difficult duties of the church.[1] Azariah drew upon indigenous traditions of architecture, liturgy, music, and drama in an attempt to forge an authentically Indian expression of Christianity. At the same time, he believed that many values and practices of Indian and Telugu culture — particularly those connected

1. H. Richard Niebuhr, *The Social Sources of Denominationalism, op. cit.*, p. 273.

with untouchability — were incompatible with the new faith; and he aimed to establish, not just a new body of worshippers, but a new type of 'community' animated by radically different social principles.

Azariah wanted this new society to resist the pressure experienced by other 'introduced' religions in India (Islam, Zoroastrianism, and Judaism) to adopt the prevailing social order by participating in India's established system of *jati* (Telugu: *kulam*) relations. If the beliefs and policies behind his Christianization of the Dornakal Diocese had complex social results that did not altogether fulfil his dream, the bishop's dual advocacy of change and continuity in cultural standards and customs provided guidelines for the new community to define a double identity as both 'Indian' and 'Christian.' This is a useful starting point for exploring Christianity's impact on local culture in Andhra, where, during this brief period in the twentieth century, Anglicanism made a dramatic mark.

Christianity's relation to culture has been complex from its foundation. Jesus Christ both participated in Jewish culture and challenged the ways of Pharisees and Sadducees, thereby leaving his followers no simple normative pattern for relating to their own cultures. Christians throughout history have defined their relations to culture in diverse ways, some welcoming close association with their societies (embracing the 'world'), others rejecting it by retreating into religious communities, and still others finding an intermediate path.[2]

The relationship between 'Christ and culture' was a central problem of Bishop Azariah's life. Its solution required the daily disassociation of the essentials of the Christian faith (so-called 'substantive' Christianity) from the western cultural accretions imported to India by missionaries

---

2. H. Richard Niebuhr identified two radical and three moderate types of solutions that have been devised historically to the problem of 'Christ and culture.' Tertullian, Tolstoy, and the monastic tradition fundamentally opposed Christianity to culture; ancient Gnosticism, Abelard, and the modern Ritschl maintained the opposite position that Christianity and culture were in essential agreement. These two radical options were largely rejected by the 'church of the center' in favor of three intermediate answers: (1) the synthetic option in which Christ was the fulfillment of a perverted but perfectible culture, (2) the dualist option in which only transhistorical salvation could overcome the fundamental polarity between Christ and culture, and (3) the conversionist option in which Christ transformed culture via conversion. Concrete historical examples rarely fit neatly into such a typology, as Niebuhr admitted, but they provide a useful organizing principle for the discussion of a complex issue. H. Richard Niebuhr, *Christ and Culture* (New York, 1951), pp. 39-44.

('adjective' Christianity),[3] and the evaluation of every aspect of Indian culture in the light of fundamental Christian principles. Azariah did not write a systematic theoretical treatise on the subject of separating acceptable from unacceptable Indian traditions, but defined his position in practice during three decades of managing diocesan affairs.

The records of Azariah's episcopal career and the various references to Christianity's relation to culture in his writings suggest that he rejected both extremist positions: that Christ and culture are fundamentally in opposition or in agreement. He favored instead an intermediate position whereby Christianity was both the 'fulfillment' and 'transformer' of culture.

Azariah saw a close, almost indistinguishable link between culture and religion and, especially, between Indian culture and the Hindu religion.[4] He did not believe, like Tillich, that religion and culture were inseparable,[5] but he did consider religion to be the most important factor in the character of his own culture and the key to any meaningful reform:

Purposeless, partial, and powerless are all enterprises to redeem and reconstruct society that are not vitally related to God. The social and economic evils of society have at bottom moral and spiritual causes. Moral

3. Substantive Christianity refers to the essentials of the faith (as defined by the Apostles' Creed) which ought never to change, while adjective Christianity refers to those elements which may change. This distinction as drawn by K. M. Banerjee would exclude the sacraments from the substantive category, an exclusion which Azariah would certainly have protested. I. David, *op. cit.,* p. 65.

4. Although much of Azariah's diocese fell within the boundaries of the Muslim-ruled state of Hyderabad, necessitating regular contact with Muslim officials, the number of Muslim converts to Christianity was negligible and most of the bishop's day-to-day work in evangelism, worship, and administration brought him in touch with the so-called 'untouchables' and caste 'Sudras' who partook in the complex set of popular beliefs and rituals loosely known as 'Hinduism.' The vast majority of Azariah's statements on the subject of 'Christ and culture' refer only to Hinduism; his writings pay little attention to Islam and offer no detailed analysis of the rival monotheistic faith. It is worth noting, however, that Azariah incorporated Saracenic architectural elements into the design of the Dornakal Cathedral in a deliberate attempt to reflect all aspects of Indian culture, broadly conceived. As early as 1906 he wrote to his wife about impressive churches in Ahmednagar and Peshawar which utilized Muslim architectural forms such as the dome. VSA to Anbu, 16 Sept. 1906, Azariah Collection, Madras.

5. 'Religion is the substance of culture, culture is the form of religion.' Tillich, quoted in Kaj Baago, 'The Discovery of India's Past and Its Effect on the Christian Church in India,' in *History and Contemporary India,* ed. J. C. B. Webster (London, 1971), p. 26.

regeneration to be permanent must be based on religion. God is the source and power of all moral regeneration.[6]

Azariah therefore regarded evangelism as the single most important instrument of cultural change. He stressed the importance of Christian social service, particularly in response to the otherworldly, Indian 'ascetic temperament,' where 'the highest religious ideal has been absorption in the Infinite rigorously leaving the present world with its moral, social and political problems to their fate.'[7] But Azariah never wavered in his bedrock belief that the church's primary vocation was to share the gospel and that the type of charity advocated by the 'social gospel' movement, which influenced churches and student organizations like the YMCA during the interwar period, would never succeed in India in the absence of more fundamental religious conversion.

The Struggle against Caste

Hinduism was responsible for most of what Azariah perceived to be the negative aspects of Indian culture, and the Christian gospel would provide the only truly effective corrective.

> It is by the proclamation of this truth that the early Church turned the world upside down. It was this that rebuilt society in the corrupt pagan Roman world. It is this that will to-day redeem Indian society and emancipate it from the thralldom of centuries.[8]

Azariah accordingly insisted that all beliefs, rituals, practices, and cultural manifestations of Hinduism that the church judged to be evil should be renounced at baptism. Chief among these 'evils' was the caste system, with its dehumanizing conceptualization and rationalization of 'pollution' and 'untouchability' — relegating up to one-fifth of society to perpetual thraldom. Azariah believed the caste system to be so integral to the Hindu religion that, without caste, Hinduism would lose its core identity. In an essay published in response to an article by the Brahmo Samajist and critic of Christian missions, Manilal C. Parekh, Azariah wrote:

6. VSA, 'The Place of the YMCA in the Christian Movement in India,' *YMIB&C*, XLV, 6 (June 1933), p. 271.
7. *Ibid.*, p. 269.
8. *Ibid.*, p. 271.

Hinduism has never set forth a body of doctrines which every follower of that religion should more or less accept; it presents a scheme of life. A Hindu may believe in anything and everything, or nothing; he will still be a Hindu if only he does not transgress the social restrictions of that particular caste in which he was born, to which he belongs through life, and in which he must die. In this limited sense, caste is Hinduism and Hinduism is caste. In other words, Hinduism represents a scheme of life; it is a bundle of practices and observances that have caste as their centre and circumference.

Azariah contrasted Hindu society's caste-centeredness with Christianity's Christ-centeredness:

But what is Christianity? It is often said that Christianity is Christ. That is true; but it is also a way of life. 'The Way' was the name given to it in the days of the apostles. Christianity is not a doctrine about God; it is not hero-worship of Jesus, it is a scheme of life in a society; it is an organism, a family, a fellowship, a brotherhood — whose centre, radius and circumference is Christ. In fellowship with all others who are attached to the Lord, bound together by outward rules and rites and throbbing with one inward pulse and purpose, men and women of all ages, races, tongues, colours and nationalities have accepted this scheme of life, and separated from all others are more and more experiencing in this fellowship the impetus and power issuing from the Spirit who is its indweller and life-giver.[9]

As ways of life, Christian and Hindu norms were therefore radically opposed to each other: 'The Hindu way of life stands for caste and exclusiveness; the Christian way of life for catholicity and inclusiveness.' In contrast to Parekh, who believed, with Keshub Chunder Sen, that in the 'New Dispensation of the Spirit' it was possible to remain loyal to both the Christian and Hindu religions, Azariah stressed the radical discontinuity between the two religious systems and the necessity of choosing between allegiance to caste and the fellowship of Christ.[10]

The bishop's response to Parekh has been criticized more recently by the late Indian theologian, M. M. Thomas, for stressing the historical manifestation of life in the Church as the essence of faith at the expense of the more eschatological, or transcendent, aspects of Christianity. Thomas

9. VSA, 'India and Christ,' *IRM*, XVII (1928), pp. 155-56.
10. See M. M. Thomas, *The Acknowledged Christ of the Indian Renaissance* (London, 1969), p. 80.

suggested that, by absolutizing Christian religion and Christian society, Azariah overlooked the degree to which Christ may transcend His own manifestation as 'Christian religion and society' and create 'spiritual ferment' within Hindu society and religion, as for example, in the internal efforts of Hindus to reform the caste system. For, Thomas asked, 'when Hinduism itself has rejected that scheme as inadequate and is engaged in a struggle to express a new idea of society more in tune with the Christian scheme, can this be considered in some sense a movement of Hinduism to Christ?'[11]

Although Azariah sounded like many nineteenth-century British missionaries when discussing Hindu religion, Thomas may have an inadequate appreciation of Azariah's recognition of the value of modern Hindu reform movements. In the bishop's book *The Church and Evangelism,* Azariah described Hindu social service organizations, the Harijan uplift movement, the demand for temple entry for all, and the attempts to reform social evils as 'signs of the moving of the Spirit of God' and as 'providential preparations for the Gospel of our Lord Jesus Christ.' He also portrayed 'centuries of Hinduism . . . with sacraments, with ideas of incarnation, with its insistence upon the invariable results of sin and its emphasis on the need of deliverance . . . as preparing the way of the Lord.' Azariah assigned a more positive value than most nationalists would to foreign imperial power when Christian conversion was the result. He believed in the efficacy of an extra-ecclesiastical 'Providence' functioning as a *praeparatio evangelica* both in the Roman Empire during the time of Christ and in the British Empire during his own lifetime. And Azariah never ruled out the possibility that God worked through Hinduism itself to achieve His own eschatological purposes.[12]

Throughout his tenure in Dornakal, however, the bishop argued for the complete repudiation of caste loyalties in order to achieve a successful 'new brotherhood' that would be inclusive rather than exclusive. The Christian community should not be considered just another static communal group, but something dynamic and different that included 'all races, all tongues and all castes. . . . Our status is not to be a caste among the many Hindu castes.'[13] 'The moment a person is baptized, he is no longer a Mala, a Madiga or a Sudra, but all are one in Christ Jesus,' Azariah

---

11. *Ibid.*

12. VSA, *The Church and Evangelism, op. cit.* (1936), pp. 32-37.

13. VSA, 'Christians and the New Government: The Bishop of Dornakal's Call for Support,' *MDM,* XXXIII, 2 (Feb. 1938), pp. 60-62.

wrote,[14] echoing the vast majority of missionaries who, from the mid-nineteenth century, had formed a consensus of opposition to the caste system.[15]

The struggle against caste feeling was therefore one of the central struggles of his ministry in Dornakal, and a constant theme in diocesan records. Azariah frequently enjoined his diocese to pray against 'the spirit of faction' caused by 'caste . . . quarrels about land . . . pride.'[16] A 1934 evangelism campaign report described how caste loyalties hindered the integration of outcastes and non-Brahmin low-castes within the same congregations and churches:

> The stronghold of caste is being very badly shaken by the assault of the Christian message of salvation for all, yet it is a stronghold still. In a village of Japanapalle pastorate the caste people asked whether they could not have a separate church of their own instead of joining with the outcaste Christian church.
>
> In Rottamakuruvu the caste people fear their caste landlord who threatens to drive them out if they become Christians. In Kommagudem the caste people asked the preaching Band: 'Have you not seen that our idols and shrines are fallen down? We have left off worshipping them; we worship now the only true God the Creator of all, but because of caste we cannot become Christians.'[17]

In addition to preventing a new brotherhood from emerging between caste groups, the caste system prescribed a complex set of ritual rights and responsibilities which defined and regulated relationships between village subgroups. The Christian 'way' threatened to undermine this complex system in several crucial areas.

Azariah's diocese strictly enforced a prohibition against Sunday work, despite the provocation it represented to higher-caste employers and the persecution it brought to some converts.[18] It also required aban-

---

14. *DDM,* XIII, 1 (Jan. 1936), pp. 10-11.

15. D. B. Forrester, *Caste and Christianity, op. cit.*

16. For example, *DDM,* V, 5 (May 1928), p. 2.

17. 'Report on the United Evangelistic Campaign, 1934,' *DDM,* XII, 3 (March 1935), p. 17.

18. See, e.g., 'Diary of the Bishop's Tour,' *MDM,* I, 7 (July 1906), p. 319; *DDM,* VIII, 7 (July 1931), p. 4. The cessation of Sunday work was required in most mass movement areas. See S. Manickam, *The Social Setting of Christian Conversion in South India* (Wiesbaden, 1977), p. 105; J. Clough, *Social Christianity in the Orient, op. cit.*, pp. 159-84.

doning caste appellations for new Christian names (called 'civilized names') taken either from the Bible (Rachel, Job, and Abraham) or from Telugu and Sanskrit words for important virtues (*Dina* for humility).[19] Problems sometimes arose when new converts hastily adopted unfamiliar names, as Bishop Elliot reported from a village during a 1935 Dornakal Diocese confirmation tour:

> One specially quiet nice-looking girl-candidate had, I found for some extraordinary reason been christened Jezebel. We took the opportunity of making a change, and she chose the name Mary.[20]

The church also required male converts to shave the *juttu* (the tonsure, or tuft of hair, that signified their Hindu identity), and women to remove the caste mark (traditionally removed at the death of a husband).[21]

Like most nineteenth-century Protestant missions and many Hindu reform movements, Azariah's church condemned and forbade idol worship, although it had particular difficulty enforcing this ban. The destruction of the village shrine followed by the erection of a church (in which hymns ridiculing idol worship might be sung) usually provided the most dramatically visible sign of conversion in the untouchable hamlets.[22]

Converts were expected to abandon the performance of most of the duties previously required of them in Hindu sacrifices, rituals, and festivals; as a result they were often threatened with physical harm or loss of income. One Màdiga convert recorded the loss of customary gifts and income (*mamool*, or 'custom') earned previously from *zamindars* (or landholders) for performance of certain sacrifices. Another convert named Yesuratnam narrowly missed a beating and loss of wages when he refused to perform the traditional boundary sacrifice in which the blood of a sacrificed chicken was poured on boiled rice and sprinkled on the land's boundaries to invoke the blessing of a local goddess on the crop.[23] One Hindu *pujari* (or priest, de-

19. *DDM*, IX, 9 (Sept. 1932), p. 16; X, 5 (May 1933), pp. 7, 10; XII, 8 (Aug. 1935), pp. 8-9; interview with Rev. Daniel, 31 March 1986, Dornakal. This was also the practice in the neighboring diocese of Medak. P. Y. Luke and J. B. Carman, *Village Christians and Hindu Culture* (London, 1968), pp. 190-92.

20. *DDM*, XII, 9 (Sept. 1935), p. 9.

21. *DDM*, XIII, 4 (April 1936), p. 1; IX, 8 (Aug. 1932), p. 12.

22. *DDM*, IX, 5 (May 1932), p. 13; S. Estborn, *The Church among the Tamils and Telugus, op. cit.,* p. 40; interview with Pedamuthyam Joseph, 4 April 1986; Thirumapalayem, A. P. See also *Andhra Christian Lyrics, op. cit.,* p. 300.

23. *DDM*, VII, 9 (Sept. 1930), pp. 8-9; V, 4 (April 1928), pp. 3-4.

scribed as a devout 'worshipper of Ganganamma') gave up his regular sacrifices after his conversion; another *asadi*, who used to tell the story of Peddamma (the village goddess) in a drunken state for the amusement of caste onlookers at Hindu festivals, also gave up this practice.[24]

The rejection of traditional authority represented not just the repudiation of old idols by new converts, but also a challenge to the social order by long suppressed lower classes. The higher castes were quick to disparage efforts by members of the depressed classes to assume 'new airs.'[25] Sometimes the persecution became so intense that converts migrated to new Christian 'Villages of Refuge' such as Vedanayagapuram.

Many villagers who placed themselves on the church rolls as 'enquirers' (i.e., they were still non-baptized) were not willing or able to abide by many of the church's rules regarding former Hindu practices. In 1928, some 2,000 villagers in the Kistna (Krishna) district were struck off the registers for having 'fallen back,' another 300 were expelled for not having attended church in fifteen months, and 2,000 others were discharged for 'indifference.'[26] Excommunications (the required discipline for communicant members) were pronounced regularly for apostasy — both on individuals and on groups. In the 1929 case of a village that converted its chapel into a Hindu temple, all but one of its Christian families were excommunicated.[27]

Azariah warned that the church's permanence and strength depended on expressing outwardly 'by repentance and new life' the inner experience of faith in Jesus Christ, which permitted no conciliation with 'pagan rites.' 'Compromise with evil, leniency in regard to discipline, indifference in the matter of worship and instruction — these will always spell serious loss to Church life,' he wrote in 1934.[28] Azariah presented Anglican Christianity to Andhra's depressed classes as a dramatic alternative to their former religious practices and was often frustrated by the tendency of converts to treat the new faith and its practices as complements to the old.

24. *DDM*, VI, 5 (May 1929), p. 3; XII, 3 (March 1935), p. 16.
25. S. Manickam, *The Social Setting of Christian Conversion, op. cit.*, pp. 105, 249.
26. *DDM*, V, 5 (May 1928), pp. 1, 5.
27. *DDM*, VI, 8 (Aug. 1929), p. 12; *Church Censures: Diocese of Dornakal*, vol. 1: 1914-32, DDA. This volume of *Church Censures* and a similar one for 1933-45 contain handwritten lists of the church's disciplinary actions during the period under investigation. I discovered them in an old trunk in the Dornakal Cathedral Compound and believe they constitute a unique and hitherto neglected type of source material.
28. *DDM*, XI, 10 (Oct. 1934), p. 3.

However, the church also sought to forge some links with existing Hindu village culture, drawing distinctions between 'harmless' duties performed by the depressed classes for *ryots* at village festivals (cleaning up houses, preparing grain, etc.), 'debatable' duties (leading up animals for slaughter as offerings to Hindu gods), and those 'definitely forbidden to Christians' (sprinkling the blood of the sacrifice, i.e., taking part in Hindu *puja*).[29] Christians also sought creative and theologically acceptable ways to insert their new religion into traditional rituals, such as using prayers to Jesus as a substitute for previous sacrificial incantations during the traditional boundary sacrifice.[30]

But in Dornakal, as elsewhere, many Hindu ceremonies and customs were never fully given up.[31] One evening in 1938, an entire body of Christian village elders near Nandyal participated in a *devara* (a buffalo sacrifice).[32] Continued deference to Hindu custom was reflected in the common practice of avoiding weddings on the inauspicious days of Tuesday or Saturday and having baptisms in the second month after birth — practices which persist to this day.[33] An animated discussion with Indian Christian teachers' wives in 1938 about 'superstitions' remaining in the church caused one missionary to exclaim: 'there are so many interesting lapses to record.'[34] Many Hindu practices were clearly still considered to be both useful and legitimate by many converts and viewed less as 'lapses' from Christianity than as integrated parts of an emergent Indian Christian culture within Hindu society.[35]

The type of information available in diocesan and missionary ar-

29. *DDM*, XV, 8 (Aug. 1938), p. 10.

30. *DDM*, V, 4 (April 1928), pp. 3-4.

31. S. Estborn, *The Church among the Tamils and Telugus, op. cit.*, p. 40. Estborn shows that sometimes certain members of *kulams* did not join the mass movements in order to enable their caste to continue fulfilling its Hindu duties.

32. *DDM*, XV, 8 (Aug. 1938), p. 10. Although the elders agreed afterwards that they had 'sinned,' they protested that the *ryots* were drunk, had 'bullock whips in their hands,' and would have killed them if they had refused their traditional participation in the *devara*.

33. Interview with Bishop Solomon, 1 April 1986, Dhyana Ashram.

34. *DDM*, XV, 8 (Aug. 1938), p. 9.

35. This approach was (and is) common to many other Indian Christian communities. See especially S. B. Kaufmann, 'A Christian Caste in Hindu Society,' *op. cit.*, pp. 203-34, and 'Popular Christianity, Caste and Hindu Society in South India,' *op. cit.* Evidence supporting a similar conclusion may also be found throughout. P. Y. Luke and J. B. Carman, *Village Christians and Hindu Culture, op. cit.*; P. Wiebe, 'Protestant Missions in India: A Sociological Review,' *Journal of Asian and African Studies*, V (1970b), pp. 297-98.

chives does not permit a complete description of the sociological implications of conversion to Christianity. Most primary written materials are devoid of the sort of subtle ethnographic distinctions found in modern scholarly studies.[36] Whether Mala converts belonged to the 'land-holding,' right-handed, Saiva section *(Reddi-Bhumalu)* or to the 'service-giving,' left-handed, Vaishna sections *(Murikinai* or *Pokanati)* was clearly less important to the church than the numbers of Malas converting. Neither diocesan journals nor missionary accounts provide much sense of whether certain subgroups of Malas or Madigas tended to be more receptive to conversion, whether conversion was linked to particular social changes (such as the breaking of rules related to group endogamy), or even the precise *jati* identity of most converts. Nor do the *Church Censures,* which recorded all infractions of diocesan rules, contain much detail about the nature of the 'heathen practices' and the 'Hindu rites' for which its members were so frequently excommunicated. However, both scattered evidence in primary records and interviews with elderly church leaders in Dornakal suggest that, although some progress was made, the church did not succeed in eradicating many of the caste practices it condemned.[37] In this sense, the Christianization of Azariah's diocese always remained incomplete.

The bishop's most frequently articulated social goals were to lessen the age-old animosities between Malas and Madigas and to soften the negative feelings of 'Sudras' towards 'untouchables.'[38] His sermons, writ-

36. Such as T. R. Singh, *The Madiga: A Study in Social Structure and Change, op. cit.;* Sydney Nicholson, 'Social Organization of the Malas — An Outcaste Indian People,' *op. cit.,* pp. 91-103. Henry Whitehead's ethnographic writings provide relatively detailed observations of depressed class practices. See, e.g., his description of Mala priests *(Pambalas)* in *MDM,* I, 7 (July 1906), p. 320; *Village Gods of South India, op. cit.* (1916), and 'A Lecture on Some Religious Customs of the Hindus in South India . . . Delivered in the Regimental Theatre at Wellington,' *MDM,* I, 5 (May 1906), pp. 207-17.

37. P. Y. Luke and J. B. Carman, *Village Christians and Hindu Culture, op. cit.* This was also the conclusion drawn by M. V. Rajagopal in *Andhra Pradesh District Gazetteers: Khamman* (Hyderabad, 1977), p. 40.

38. The term 'Sudra' — like the term 'untouchable' — will strike any informed reader today as both outdated and highly problematical. Sudra was a Brahmin designation for all those who, to them, were not to be deemed 'twice born.' As such, it was much resented by caste non-Brahmins, some of whom had been the rulers of their own villages for centuries. Just as Dalits have rejected the term 'untouchable,' so Kammas and Reddis have rejected the term 'Sudra.' But this does not change the fact that these were the terms used historically by Azariah himself and by his peers. I therefore use these awkward terms in this text in order to maintain consistency with the historical sources, but not to otherwise validate their usefulness.

ings, and informal teachings were uncompromising in their denunciation of caste as a system of social organization. He used Telugu Christian lyrics to popularize his call on Christians to 'destroy caste feelings.'[39] Converts of different caste backgrounds were required to attend the same chapels, to drink from the same communion cup, to send children to the same schools (where they could receive training in occupations reserved traditionally for their own, or for rival castes), and to eat together at public celebrations such as marriages, harvest festivals, and other community *jatras*.

Although Azariah recognized that the struggle to abandon notions of ritual purity and impurity which delineated and reinforced caste boundaries was difficult for all, he believed it was especially so for those commonly labeled 'Sudras' and/or 'Tribals.' A Yerukala (Erukala) convert named Premamma refused for four years after her conversion to join former Malas and Madigas at Christian wedding feasts, insisting that she cook and eat her food separately. She eventually abandoned the belief that interdining would result in ritual pollution. Azariah reported that during the remaining seventeen years before her death in 1932, she betrayed no caste spirit and provided a powerful witness 'to the transforming power of Christ.'[40]

Diocesan literature contains substantial evidence that conversion to Christianity was accompanied by the abandonment of many attitudes and practices regulated by the caste system — particularly those related to the customary subordination of untouchables by the higher castes.[41] The unusual conversions of non-Brahmins (mostly Kammas) to Christianity throughout Telugu country during this period were accompanied by discernible 'softenings' of prejudice towards outcastes. By December 1931, there were approximately 26,000 Christians of so-called 'Sudra' origin in Andhra, over 10,000 of whom had been received into the church during the previous five years. Azariah attributed these conversions and concurrent changes in attitude towards untouchability primarily to improvements in the lives of outcastes resulting from Christianity. A survey of caste accessions to Telugu churches conducted by American Methodist Bishop J. Waskom Pickett noted that (1) 'Sudra' conversions were most

39. Interview with Rev. M. Daniel, 8 April 1986, Dornakal.
40. *DDM*, X, 1 (Jan. 1933), pp. 9-11.
41. For specific examples of improved relations between Christian converts of different caste origins, see *DDM*: VII, 1 (April 1930), p. 1; VIII, 10 (Oct. 1931), p. 9; IX, 4 (April 1932), pp. 2-3; IX, 6 (June 1932), pp. 3-4; IX, 8 (Aug. 1932), pp. 13-14; X, 4 (April 1933), pp. 1-2; XII, 3 (March 1935), pp. 12-19; XII, 12 (Dec. 1935), pp. 4-5; XIII, 4 (April 1936), p. 1.

numerous in areas where mass movements among outcastes were most successful (both numerically and in terms of changed lifestyle), and (2) wherever 'Sudras' had converted to Christianity relations improved between caste and outcaste.[42]

Notwithstanding these changes, Azariah found varied and numerous obstacles to eradication of caste. The church's goal was, after all, tantamount to changing an entire way of life. Caste provided, in the words of one commentator, 'a framework for all social activity, quite literally from conception to the afterlife, at the local level of the village community.'[43] The tenacity of caste loyalties displayed itself most forcefully in the struggle between Malas and Madigas. Each tried desperately to avoid being the lowest ranking group. That the Christian community had not fully abandoned this animosity was illustrated by a riot which erupted when an assistant pastor of Madiga origin attempted to preside at a wedding in a predominantly Mala congregation. One woman was injured, and the entire congregation temporarily defected to the Roman Catholic Church.[44] Another pastor remembered how the Malas of his village introduced IMS missionaries to their own Mala friends and relatives but 'would not allow' them to visit the Madigas who converted to Christianity until only much later.[45] Temporary closures of schools, defections to other denominations, and a reluctance to welcome converts of different castes into the church hindered an otherwise energetic missionary program and attested to the continuing persuasiveness of notions of ritual pollution and caste rank within the new Christian society. 'We deplore the many exhibitions of caste spirit within the Church,'

---

42. *DDM,* IX, 6 (June 1932), pp. 1-4. The study was conducted under the auspices of the NCC and included the Anglican Church, the United Lutheran Church, The American Baptist Telugu Mission, the Canadian Baptist Mission, and the London Missionary Society, but excluded the Wesleyan Methodist Church of Medak. Its results were published, with a foreword by Azariah, as: J. W. Pickett, *Christ's Way to India's Heart op. cit.* (1937).

43. Barrington Moore, Jr., *Social Origins of Dictatorship and Democracy: Lord and Peasant in the Making of the Modern World* (Boston, 1966), p. 315.

44. The congregation defected when the case was referred to the Deanery Chairman (a Brahmin Christian), who defended the Madiga pastor. The unhappy Malas returned to the Anglican church when they discovered that the Roman Catholics would require re-baptism. They eventually accepted the ministrations of the Madiga pastor, but only with great reluctance. Interview with Carol Graham, 19 Dec. 1984, Oxford. On the persistence of Mala-Madiga rivalry in the Telugu Baptist church, see A. T. Fishman, *For This Purpose* (Madras, 1958), pp. 76-77; and his *Culture Change and the Underprivileged* (Madras, 1941).

45. Interview with Rev. M. Daniel, 31 March 1986, Dornakal.

lamented Azariah in 1935.[46] But the pages of his diocesan magazine bore repeated testimony to the survival of such caste prejudices.[47] As in virtually all other areas of India, the church was apparently unable to produce a sense of total community strong enough to replace caste.[48]

Of particular concern to Azariah as leader of the ultimately successful ecumenical effort to unite South India's churches was the way in which Christian denominationalism permitted and even exacerbated caste divisions. As he observed in 1932:

> In many places, the Baptist Church has all the Madigas of a village; the Church of India (Anglican) has all the Malas of the village. In the Kurnool District in many a small village we may see two chapels, two village schools and two teachers — each serving one, and only one, of the two great out-caste communities in the area. At one of our Pastorate centres, the Baptist chapel (entirely consisting of Madiga converts) stands at a distance of twenty yards from our chapel! . . . These divisions pander to the age-long caste spirit of the people. Malas and Madigas hate to sit side by side, never eat in each other's houses, yea, never drink from the same well. Denominationalism then comes and panders to this inter-caste hatred. If one section joins one Church, the other joins another, and caste is thus perpetuated within the Church. The resulting local Church has thus no chance of becoming really Christian or truly Catholic, but for ever remains sectarian, racial and caste-ridden.[49]

Far from eradicating caste, the divided Christian church provided new alliances around which rival *kulams* might organize themselves and reinforce their sense of distinctiveness from other groups. Denominationalism thus undermined the anti-caste policy of Andhra's churches and further complicated the already elusive goal of making conversion to Christianity the occasion for overcoming caste distinctions.[50]

46. *DDM,* XII, 12 (Dec. 1935), p. 3.

47. See *DDM:* V, 1 (Jan. 1928), p. 12; V, 5 (May 1928), pp. 2, 5-6; IX, 12 (Dec. 1932), p. 3; X, 12 (Dec. 1933), p. 7; XI, 1 (Jan. 1934), pp. 11-12; XII, 12 (Dec. 1935), p. 3; XIII, 1 (Jan. 1936), pp. 10-11; XIII, 10 (Oct. 1936), p. 8.

48. S. Estborn, *The Church among the Tamils and Telugus, op. cit.,* p. 27.

49. *DDM,* IX, 8 (Aug. 1932), pp. 4-5. On this subject, see also VSA, 'Caste and Denomination,' *HF,* XLI, 7 (July 1921), pp. 246-53. On fate of western denominationalism in South India, see Lionel Caplan, 'Class and Christianity in South India,' *op. cit.,* pp. 645-71.

50. Archival evidence and interviews in Dornakal confirm that caste rivalries persisted in the diocese after Azariah's death. See, e.g., 'Petition from Christians of

Although Azariah always rejected the exclusivity of caste (its treatment of the 'other'), he valued some aspects of caste as an integrative system which helped to preserve the community life of its members. Azariah remained adamant to his death that converts of all castes should 'show in practice that all are brethren in Christ,'[51] but his opposition to caste was tempered by his recognition that caste also served some more positive social functions. In particular, Azariah saw caste structures as natural and effective instruments for publicizing the gospel and vehicles for encouraging conversion. His experience with the mass movements in Andhra convinced him that group conversions along caste lines were much less socially disruptive than individual accessions.

Azariah agreed fully with (and influenced) Pickett's conclusion that 'mass' movements were more 'natural' for Indians trained from birth to act and behave in groups than for people from western countries with their more individualistic ways. Group movements protected converts from social dislocation, preserved the social frameworks in which converts could exercise a stabilizing influence over one another, and minimized the danger of westernization by permitting the survival of Indian social patterns and customs so that the life of the group, in its external aspects, remained 'natural, real and therefore genuinely indigenous.'[52] Having entered the church in groups ranging from families to entire village *kulams,* they could remain in their homes and continue to pursue their former occupations in the company of non-Christians. Persecution from employers angry at the new Christians' refusal to work on Sundays could be endured collectively without isolation in mission compounds (though some persecuted Christians did move to 'model' Christian villages such as Vedanayagapuram, where they leased land from the church). The church and its missionaries also continued to use caste channels of communication to spread the Christian message and news of the conversion movements.[53]

In perhaps his most distinctive break with the commonly accepted

---

Raghavapuram,' Aug. 1947, 5: 2/2, Dornakal, MACIPBC. That this was not a problem confined to Dornakal Anglicans, see: Paul D. Wiebe, *Christians in Andhra Pradesh* (Madras, 1988), pp. 123-28; P. Y. Luke and J. B. Carman, *Village Christians and Hindu Culture, op. cit.*

51. *DDM,* XII, 12 (Dec. 1935), p. 3.

52. VSA, *India and the Christian Movement, op. cit.* (1935), pp. 76-77.

53. G. A. Oddie, 'Christian Conversion among Non-Brahmans in Andhra Pradesh, with Special Reference to the Anglican Missionaries and the Dornakal Diocese, c. 1900-1936,' in *op. cit.,* p. 83.

anti-caste policies of western Protestant missionary colleagues, Azariah allowed some church leaders in Dornakal to make substantial, if short-term, concessions to the caste sensibilities of non-Brahmin converts. The author of a diocesan report on a special mission to the 'Sudras' urged Mala and Madiga converts to be patient towards caste converts who felt they had made an enormous 'sacrifice' by joining former untouchables. Compelling caste converts immediately to eat with former outcastes would put unnecessary stumbling blocks in the way of the 'Sudras' progress,' and would constitute 'not only foolishness but a great sin.' Better to allow 'Sudras' to make decisions regarding such 'social matters' according to their own consciences, which would be persuaded over the long run to abandon caste prejudices by exposure to Christian teaching and practice.[54] Undesirable elements of caste rank and privilege were thus to be tolerated reluctantly and temporarily in order to establish the church's roots in local Telugu culture, though caste affinities would have to be abandoned eventually. 'While the gathering in of peoples along communal lines may be justifiable in the early stages of missionary work,' wrote Azariah in 1934, 'to be content with such a state of affairs for ever may positively prove a great hindrance to the progress of the Gospel.'[55]

Azariah desired nothing less than to replace caste by a whole new framework of life from conception to afterlife. But membership in the new Christian community in Dornakal would entail many social rights and responsibilities similar to those formerly imposed by caste. Thus caste provided some positive elements to build upon. Ideally, the Christian community, like the former *kulam,* would be an endogamous group, not marrying outsiders. Azariah condemned 'mixed marriages' between Christians and non-Christians, although he contended that Christians ought not to be 'yoked with unbelievers'[56] on biblical grounds rather than on the basis of the indigenous practice of marrying within the *kulam.* He prescribed excommunication, like outcasting, as the proper punishment for the offense.[57] Such disciplinary actions were executed in a manner similar to that of the former *kulam.* Bodies of church elders were constituted as informal village *panchayats* in every village and entrusted with limited disciplinary powers.

In most cases, the same people who served as village elders (*pedda-*

---

54. *DDM,* IX, 8 (Aug. 1932), pp. 13-14.
55. *DDM,* XI, 1 (Jan. 1934), p. 12.
56. 1 Cor. 7:39; 2 Cor. 6:14-16.
57. VSA, 'Mixed Marriages,' *NCCR,* LXI, 11 (Nov. 1941), pp. 528-34.

garus) before conversion continued to serve as church elders after baptism.[58] 'The congregation elders are for the most part none other than the old community elders, for in the mass movement as a rule the whole community has come over to Christianity together,' wrote one observer in 1933.[59] Like their non-Christian counterparts, the informal *panchayats* of Christian elders settled quarrels, inquired into misdemeanors, and had the power to inflict small fines. The church elders were associated with the local lay Christian teacher and area pastor much as were non-Christian elders and village headmen. Both the Christian pastor and the village headman officiated as priests at weddings and arbitrated difficult matters affecting the village by calling formal *panchayats* composed of the village elders (and, occasionally, elders from other villages). The Christian *panchayat*'s findings in matters of discipline were reported to the Bishop's Local Council (of clergy and laymen), and, if necessary, to the bishop who held the final power of excommunication or restoration of church privileges. Non-Christian *panchayats* could impose more serious sanctions (heavy fines and outcasting) and usually functioned as the final court of appeal in caste affairs, unlike their Christian counterparts who deferred to the bishop's decision on heavier penalties. Some non-Christian castes had regional *panchayats* ruling over specific territories, while others had caste gurus judging on caste affairs in a manner somewhat comparable to that of Christian bishops.

Excommunication from the church was not all that different from outcasting from the *kulam*. Azariah forbade Christians to 'keep on friendly terms with the excommunicated' and insisted that they 'hold no intercourse with such and not even . . . eat with them.'[60] He based his policy prohibiting interdining and social intercourse with Christian outcastes on 'apostolic command' rather than on Indian social traditions, and he consistently resisted the idea that the Christian community was to become just another caste like all previously introduced religions in India. Yet Azariah saw the advantage of preserving certain traditional or 'natural' social structures and modes of behavior that could be helpful in establishing an independent Indian Christian community and need not be incompatible with its ideals. The church's disciplinary system closely resembled the system it replaced, even if the standards for judging crimes

---

58. Although with one major exception, as Azariah made an effort to include women elders on the *panchayats*.

59. 'Lay Work in Dornakal Diocese,' *DDM*, X, 4 (April 1933), p. 8.

60. *DDM*, V, 5 (May 1928), p. 2.

and misdemeanors changed. The most direct and serious threat to the power of traditional village elders in Andhra during this period came from the intrusive external authority of the police and the law courts rather than the church. Many Christians and non-Christians alike were turning to formal litigation as a final court of appeal — and often revenge. One of Azariah's primary goals in establishing a strong system of Christian village *panchayats* was to provide a humane local mechanism for solving disputes without recourse to outside courts.[61]

The Reform and Integration of Local Customs

Azariah also believed that some dimensions of Hindu culture and institutions ought to be incorporated into indigenous expressions of Indian Christianity, particularly in order to attract more caste people to a faith they were initially inclined to dismiss as an 'outcastes' religion.' Incorporating certain spiritually neutral, culturally familiar elements from Hindu ritual and custom into Christian life and worship thus became another of Azariah's central preoccupations in Dornakal.

Azariah drew from Hindu and, occasionally, Muslim traditions in devising indigenous new forms of liturgy, music, drama, architecture, festivals, and Christian expression in his diocese. He devised a new Christian marriage service that adapted Hindu symbols (rather than circling a fire, the bride and groom walked around a cross), and advocated use of the Christian *tali* (a small gold cross, anchor, or heart fastened by a string round the neck of a married woman) as a substitute for the western wedding ring.[62] This service was intended especially to satisfy caste converts who objected to the brevity of the Christian marriage service. As one missionary recalled, 'A Brahmin wedding goes on for five days. What is twenty minutes in a church?' Bishop Azariah's new wedding service accommodated these traditional sensibilities 'by having

61. *DDM*, X, 4 (April 1933), pp. 8-9; 14 July 1915, *PIMS*, IMSA.
62. Azariah did not introduce the idea of a Christian *tali,* but he abandoned the practice of placing it on a plate which was passed around to receive the blessings of the elderly. Rather, he suggested that the *tali* be put around the bride's neck and that the groom touch it while saying his vows. Thamil Selvan, 'Research on Bishop Azariah and his Theology' (B.D. thesis, Tamil Theological Seminary, Madurai, 1985). Azariah designed a *tali* for his family decorated with a cross, anchor and heart representing faith, hope, and charity. Interview with Grace Aaron, 24-26 Sept. 1985, Ottawa, Canada.

plenty of singing and processions round the church (which) made the service last for two hours.'[63]

Hoping to provide a substitute for the Hindu festival of Divawli, Azariah instituted a Festival of Lights in which families lit oil lamps in church and then distributed the light throughout the village, symbolizing that Christ was the light of their homes, of their hearts, and of their families.[64] Although the bishop required the cutting of the *juttu*, he permitted use of a vermilion cross on the forehead as a substitute for traditional caste markings.[65]

Azariah's most visible contribution to indigenization was his Dornakal Cathedral, which mixed architectural elements and symbolism from Hindu, Muslim, and Christian traditions into a wholly unique synthesis. The Cathedral Church of the Epiphany, which took twenty-five years to build, combined the domes of Muslim mosques with the pillars of South Indian Hindu temples, and was suffused with Christian symbology. Thus, twelve pillars bearing up the church nave stood for the twelve apostles; each was decorated with an apostle's symbolic shield and by carvings of the lotus flower, representing India, of the datura flower, representing death, and of the shoot from the banana tree which brings new life. All of these decorations were placed under the cross, which symbolized their ultimate reconciliation in Christ. This cathedral, entirely hand-carved and hand-built by local people, was the bishop's most dramatic statement of Christianity's potential as the 'fulfillment' — of good but incomplete Indian faiths and of beautiful but imperfect Indian cultures.[66]

Azariah balanced his condemnation of caste and other undesirable Hindu practices with a willingness to integrate other elements of Indian culture into Christian life so that the church might serve a dual role as an agent of both cultural change and cultural continuity. Indo-Anglican Christianity had little direct cultural impact beyond the untouchables and low-castes in Andhra (except in the important area of education, where many students came from the upper non-Brahmin and Brahmin castes). But within the lower strata of society from which Azariah's con-

---

63. Elva Jackson, *Indian Saga*, op. cit., p. 226. See also in *DDM:* IX, 6 (June 1932), p. 2; XII, 10 (Oct. 1935), p. 8.

64. In this idea, Azariah borrowed from Easter (and probably also Epiphany) traditions of the Greek Orthodox Church. T. Selvan, *op. cit.*

65. *Ibid.*

66. For examples of relatively positive assessments of Hinduism in Azariah's writings, see VSA, *India and the Christian Movement, op. cit.* (1935), pp. 55-58; *The Church and Evangelism, op. cit.* (1936), pp. 36-37.

verts came, the church played an increasingly important role as the bearer, not only of the Christian religion, but also of what Azariah called 'civilization.' The bishop claimed that Christianity possessed 'power to bring cleanliness, power to civilize, power to drive away degrading habits, power to raise the economic status, to instill righteousness, and to make the illiterate villager an effective witness.' Azariah's gospel message contained not only the 'power of God unto salvation' but also 'a power of God unto rural up-lift, unto economic freedom and unto social advance.' In short, it contained the 'secret of national regeneration.'[67]

By 1935, the Dornakal diocese, with 250 ordained Indian clergy and more than 2,000 village teachers,[68] was sponsoring an extensive network of schools and medical dispensaries, cooperative societies and banks, printing presses, agricultural settlements, and industrial projects, in addition to leading the worship and providing pastoral services for over 218,879 Anglicans.[69] The church initiated a wide range of activities aimed at improving living conditions for its converts. Azariah frequently referred to the 'four Demons — Dirt, Disease, Debt, and Drink' — which plagued the rural villages of his diocese. He urged clergymen and missionaries to look for opportunities to introduce cleanliness and sanitation, to start cottage industries for the augmentation of daily wages, to 'wage war incessantly against drink,' and to promote literacy. 'Educate, educate and educate every child and adult that you can get hold of.'[70]

In sermons, literature, and activities, Azariah's church condemned and apparently succeeded in reducing a wide range of practices it considered to be un-Christian. Smoking tobacco was discouraged.[71] Lying, quarreling, cheating, and taking bribes were condemned and reduced,[72] and crimes like theft, cattle poisoning, and murder were constantly denounced.[73] The church also

67. *DDM,* XIII, 4 (April 1936), pp. 3-4. See also VSA, 'The Church in Rural India,' *op. cit.* (1928), pp. 1-12. ('Where Christianity goes, education, civilization and habits of cleanliness in body, dress and food, in speech and conduct, are the concomitant results.' *Ibid.,* p. 3.)

68. Elva Jackson, *Indian Saga, op. cit.,* p. 7.

69. These and the following figures are taken from *Directory of Christian Missions and Churches in India, Burma and Ceylon, 1940-41, op. cit.*

70. 'The Bishop's Letter,' *DDM,* XI, 12 (Dec. 1934), p. 4.

71. *DDM:* V, 11 (Nov. 1928), p. 4; VI, 9 (Sept. 1929), p. 3.

72. *DDM,* XIII, 4 (April 1936), pp. 1-4; K. Luke, *Ḍārṇakal Tiraṇalvēli Iṇḍiyan Miṣaṇarī Sanghamu, op. cit.,* p. 101; J. W. Pickett, *Christ's Way to India's Heart, op. cit.,* pp. 42-43.

73. *DDM:* V, 4 (April 1928), p. 3; VIII, 10 (Oct. 1931), p. 15; IX, 5 (May 1932), pp. 13-14; X, 1 (Jan. 1933), pp. 9-11; XIII, 3 (March 1936), pp. 2-3; XIII, 4 (April 1936), pp. 1-4;

encouraged thrift,[74] resisted costly weddings and dowries,[75] established programs of direct assistance as well as cooperative credit societies to free converts from debt,[76] and arbitrated land disputes.[77]

In an effort to help new congregations become self-supporting, the diocese adapted in 1912 the indigenous system of *inam* or endowment lands in which a small piece of arable tax-free church land (3-4 acres) was purchased and provided with a house, a plow, and a pair of bullocks. Christian teachers were allowed to cultivate this land on the condition that they lead village worship and conduct evening classes for children and adults.[78] Furthermore, the church bought land to establish special Christian 'Villages of Refuge': the aforementioned Vedanayagapuram for persecuted converts,[79] and Kiritipuram for famine relief victims who converted to Christianity.[80]

K. Luke, *Ḍārnakal Tiranalvēli Inḍiyan Miṣanari Sanghamu, op. cit.,* pp. 97-101; Pickett, *Christ's Way to India's Heart, op. cit.,* p. 42; 'The Bishop's Diary,' *MDM,* XVI, 3 (March 1921), pp. 51-59; David Packiamuthu, *Valikāṭṭi, op. cit.,* Act II, Scene I; Thamil Selvan, 'Research on Bishop Azariah and His Theology,' *op. cit.,* p. 32; C. Graham, *Azariah of Dornakal, op. cit.,* p. 58. Cattle poisoning was considered a more serious crime by Indian Hindus who venerated the cow than it was by westerners. It was a crime to both, nevertheless.

74. Converts claim they often gave up 'spending lots of money' after baptism. Interview with Padamuthyam Joseph, 4 April 1986, Thirumapalayem, A. P.

75. Azariah was opposed to expensive marriages (his own cost 40 rupees) and to the dowry system (he took no dowry from his son's wives, nor did he ask his wife to provide one). Interview with Grace Aaron, 24-26 Sept. 1985, Ottawa, Canada.

76. *DDM,* XI, 3 (March 1934), p. 18; VSA, 'Sermon Preached by the Bishop of Dornakal on Sunday, November 28, 1920 at St. George's Cathedral, Madras, on behalf of the CMS Centenary Celebrations,' *MDM,* XVI, 1 (Jan. 1921), pp. 13-22; Knud Heiberg, *V. S. Azariah: Biskop af Dornakal, op. cit.,* pp. 94-95; J. Z. Hodge, *Bishop Azariah of Dornakal, op. cit.,* pp. 32-33. The IMS liberated one of its first converts, Kodama Gundula Luka, from debt slavery for Rs 7: D. Packiamuthu, *Valikāṭṭi, op. cit.,* Act I, Scene 3. Mrs. Whitehead initiated one of the diocese's early efforts to establish cooperative societies by founding the Khammamett Workers Society. *MDM,* XI, 1 (Jan. 1916), p. 8. On cooperatives, see also 14 July 1915, *PIMS,* IMSA.

77. One case led indirectly to conversion. A Christian priest helped a 'rich Sudra' to win a land dispute, but then the priest refused to accept three acres of land worth Rs 900 offered to him by the grateful victor. 'This aroused the Sudra's interest and he eventually became a Christian': *DDM,* IX, 8 (Aug. 1932), p. 12.

78. *MTDM,* VII, 5 (May 1912), p. 139.

79. The land for Vedanayagapuram was purchased, with the help of Bishop Whitehead, to provide for a group of Banjara converts who were barred from burying their dead in their own village. The settlers built their own homes, worked the land, and paid a rent/tax to the church. Interview with Rev. M. Daniel, 29 March 1986, Dornakal.

80. This practice of creating villages of refuge, based on Old Testament patterns, had been revived during the Tinnevelly mass movements, so it was one with

Medical and health assistance was an integral part of the church's work. Vaccinations were distributed with gospel tracts, inoculations with magic lantern talks about Jesus. As Azariah wrote: 'God's servants cannot be messengers of God and of His salvation without also being ministers of health and good-living.' The church sponsored an annual 'medical evangelistic tour' which it viewed as part of its broader commission to further 'health propaganda and preventative work.'[81] Its workers provided for the sick a combination of Christian prayer and western medicines such as quinine, eye drops, and dysentery remedies. Interestingly, Christians often accepted western remedies but continued to go to village medicine men for native cures for ailments such as jaundice or when it was believed that *diams* (possessing evil spirits) were responsible. Christians in Dornakal today apparently continue to visit a Hindu woman for treatments.[82]

In addition to making medical care available at several hospitals and dispensaries,[83] an IMS missionary, Dr. J. S. William, traveled frequently throughout the diocese giving talks on disease (leprosy, yaws, and cholera were particularly prevalent) and sanitation while dispensing medicines and vaccinations.[84] He established a Rural Medical Relief Association which sent trained workers into the villages with medicines, and hosted an annual Health Week for all diocesan workers.[85] During a cholera epidemic in 1928, the church distributed chlorogen (a water sterilizer) and assisted officials in disinfecting water reservoirs and wells. While the epidemic strengthened the faith in some villages, it caused others to renounce the faith by joining non-Christians in making vows to 'Maramma, the cholera goddess.' Azariah observed: 'An epidemic of this kind is a searching test to many a religious profession. . . . it confirms one village in the faith, and drives back another to Hinduism. It tests the teachers: one runs away and another suffers with his people.'[86]

---

which Azariah was personally familiar. In Andhra, Kiritipuram was settled by Mala workers who constructed the Dornakal Cathedral. Construction jobs and rice from Burma were provided as relief during the *thella jonnala karuvu,* or 'white corn famine' of 1920. Interview with Rev. M. Daniel, 8 April 1986, Dornakal.

81. For example, *DDM,* IX, 7 (July 1932), pp. 10-11.

82. Interview with Rev. M. Daniel, 31 March 1986, Dornakal.

83. The 1932 annual report for the Bishop Whitehead Hospital recorded 11,686 outpatients and 131 inpatients. *DDM,* IX, 7 (July 1932), pp. 10-11.

84. *DDM:* V, 1 (Jan. 1928), pp. 8-9; V, 12 (Dec. 1928), pp. 1-2; VI, 5 (May 1929), p. 1; VI, 7 (July 1929), p. 16.

85. *DDM,* VIII, 1 (Jan. 1931), pp. 12-15.

86. *DDM,* V, 9 (Sept. 1928), pp. 2-3. Rev. Daniel, of Dornakal, described how Hindu Malas and Madigas of his native village worshipped the same gods, but

The diocese integrated health education into its training for village teachers and for clergymen. Azariah argued that 'village sanitation, personal hygiene, conduct during epidemics and the like are as essential for village service as 'Principles of Education' and 'Child Psychology.'[87] Village *dais* (midwives) were trained and equipped with boxes of necessary equipment, and the use of bore-hole latrines was advocated.[88] Christian villages developed the tradition of having an annual 'house whitewash,' and Azariah exhorted converts to commend Christianity to Andhra by, among other traits, a 'clean and well cared for body, home and village.'[89] Although the persistent problem of impure water was not solved, diocesan records suggest a marked improvement of sanitation in Christian villages.[90] Before conversion in one village

> the Zamindars [landholders] . . . would consider it pollution to walk through the village: they stood on the road and called for the men. Now they do not hesitate to walk through the street; they even go into the court-yard and knock at the door of the teacher. [Azariah] asked for the reason for this change. Cleanliness was the answer.[91]

In the area of marriage and sexual morals, the church faced the difficult task of trying to impose its standards upon a great variety of local practices. Bishop Azariah addressed the complex subject of adapting the Christian law of marriage as defined by the 'Table of Kindred and Affinity' included in the *Book of Common Prayer* to Indian conditions and to sometimes divergent civil and ecclesiastical regulations. The handbook on marriage he published for Anglican clergy and religious workers in

---

each had a different *Muthyalamma gudi* (shrine) at which they sacrificed animals. If Muthyalamma got angry, he said, she would send cholera and other serious diseases. The Malas offered goats and sheep as sacrifices; the Madigas offered chickens. When the Sudras sacrificed a buffalo, they would give all but the leg to the Madigas to eat. (The Malas would not eat the buffalo.) "People were afraid of Muthyalamma, but not the Christian God." Interview with Rev. Daniel, 8 April, 1986, Dornakal.

87. *DDM*, V, 9 (Sept. 1928), p. 4, also pp. 1-3. See also *DDM*, VIII, 1 (Jan. 1931), pp. 12-15; IX, 7 (July 1932), pp. 10-11.

88. 'Thirty Years' Report of the Dornakal Mission,' *DDM*, XI, 12 (Dec. 1934), pp. 7-8.

89. *DDM*, V, 2 (Feb. 1928), p. 6.

90. *DDM*, VIII, 10 (Oct. 1931), p. 13. Some wells were provided by a 'Well Fund' established for villages otherwise reliant on surface water. See *DDM*, V, 4 (April 1928), pp. 1-2.

91. *DDM*, XIII, 4 (April 1936), p. 2.

India[92] traced the origins of Christian laws of marriage to universally applicable natural laws ('the need to secure the preservation of the human race'), to Jewish laws, and, finally, to christological and apostolic injunctions. He argued that peoples in India had 'trespassed' against these laws with child marriage, which violated both the natural law of mutual consent and the Christian tradition of free consent between marriage partners. He saw divorce and remarriage as violations not only of a natural law demanding lifelong partnership but also of declarations by Christ and the apostles concerning the permanence of marriage. Several widely practiced unions in India (a man marrying a sister's daughter or a deceased wife's sister) also violated the unions declared permissible under Anglican guidelines.[93]

Azariah stressed that the Anglican church in India forbade marriages of Christians with non-Christians even though such 'mixed' marriages were deemed legal under the Indian Christian Marriage Act of 1872 (which made the children of such marriages legitimate and qualified them for property inheritance). This was one of several areas in which the church decreed excommunication as the penalty for a marriage that was technically legal. As Azariah wrote in 1941:

> Christian standards and ideals stand firm and unaltered, whatever the State legislation may say. Mixed marriages are wrong according to Christian ideals, and it is the duty of the Churches by ecclesiastical action to give clear guidance to their ministers and to uphold the Christian standards by Church discipline.[94]

Regarding child marriage, the church adhered to standards set by the 1872 Act, which required parental consent in cases where either party was under 21 years, and the Child Marriage Restraint Act of 1929 (the Sardha Act), which prohibited marriages of men under 18 years and of women under 14 years in British India.[95] Azariah also called for the aboli-

---

92. VSA, *Holy Matrimony: Being Chapters on the Christian Law of Marriage* (Madras, 1941; revised and enlarged in 1942). Published also in Tamil, Telugu, Hindi, Urdu, and Marathi.

93. An 'Archbishop's Commission on Kindred and Affinity as Impediments to Marriage' recommended in the 1940s greater lenience regarding marriage to a deceased wife's sister, but still prohibited marriage to a sister's daughter. *Ibid.*, pp. 84-85.

94. VSA, 'Mixed Marriages,' *op. cit.* (1941), p. 533.

95. VSA, *Holy Matrimony, op. cit.*, p. 46; *DDM*, VI, 10 (Oct. 1929), pp. 4-5.

tion of the dowry system and its 'bargain marriages' in order to foster harmonious Christian family life.[96]

Azariah and fellow church leaders in Andhra had more difficulty changing marriage practices than any others. When the IMS missionaries conducted their first Christian marriage ceremony in the Manukota pastorate in 1917, they ran up against three local customs that were particularly deeply rooted. By insisting on the English tradition of reading the banns of marriage on three consecutive Sundays before the wedding, they went directly against the village custom of having the ceremony as soon as possible after the completion of marriage negotiations (and in accordance with an auspicious date set by a Brahmin priest usually less than a week in advance).[97] By requiring marriages to be held in the village place of prayer, they took the ceremony out of the family home. By insisting that marriages be held during the day, they defied the custom of night marriages. These last changes proved so hard to accomplish that Azariah sometimes sent Christian teachers with musical instruments to homes where a wedding was imminent, with instructions to provide evening 'entertainment' and thereby insure that no ceremony could be held until the following morning.

Elsewhere in Andhra, Telugu Baptists found that, whereas idols were often destroyed eagerly, child marriage could be regulated only with strict discipline.[98] A study of Christianity in formerly Methodist areas of Andhra also recognized that, despite all legislation, child marriages still persisted among Christians and that mixed marriages were more common than unmixed ones. Indeed, Christians were more inclined to marry non-Christians of their own *jati* than Christians of different *jatis*, demonstrating the relative importance of traditional caste allegiances in comparison with introduced religious affiliations.[99]

Although articles in Azariah's *Dornakal Diocesan Magazine* claimed that the church had successfully introduced Christian marriage rites and celebrations free of alcohol consumption in a community free of 'early marriage,'[100] church disciplinary records reveal many violations. The

96. VSA, *Holy Matrimony, op. cit.,* pp. 63-65.

97. *TMI-IMS,* XIV, 5 (May 1917), p. 45; P. Y. Luke and J. B. Carman, *Village Christians and Hindu Culture, op. cit.,* pp. 195-96.

98. A. T. Fishman, *For This Purpose, op. cit.,* p. 83.

99. P. Y. Luke and J. B. Carman, *Village Christians and Hindu Culture, op. cit.,* pp. 5-6, 192-98.

100. For example, *DDM,* VI, 9 (Sept. 1929), p. 2. It is interesting to note that the first girl to attend the IMS Boarding School, established in 1906, had taken refuge with the missionaries from child marriage: *DDM,* XI, 12 (Dec. 1934), p. 6. Also, a Cen-

Church Censures for the years 1914 to 1945 contain more excommunications for improprieties connected with marriage and sexual relations than for any other type of sin. Among the volumes' 6,347 entries (giving name, offense, and punishment), the most frequently mentioned transgressions were 'heathen marriages,' 'arranging, contracting, conducting or abetting heathen marriages,' and 'adultery.' Other offenses mentioned were 'marrying wife's sister,' 'living in sin with a heathen,' 'living in sin with a married non-Christian woman,' 'living with a man without any legal marriage,' and 'fornication.'

It is difficult to derive anything but general conclusions from diocesan disciplinary records because the exact nature of each offense was usually not specified. For instance, it is unclear if the frequently used term 'irregular marriage' meant child marriage, mixed marriage, or something else entirely. In 1920, a couple was excommunicated for 'giving their junior daughter in heathen and irregular marriage in Kurnool/ Nandyal.' However, such detail was rare for these records, the usefulness of which thus lies in their testimony to the general fact that the church encountered much more resistance to its regulations, particularly in the area of marriage and sexual morals, than is indicated by published records.[101]

Azariah was perfectly frank when addressing his clergy about the average number of excommunications that occurred each year (about 200) and the general nature of the offenses (of 972 excommunications during a four-year period, 425 were for 'non-Christian practices', 281 were for 'living in adultery,' and 255 were for 'apostasy').[102] By 'non-Christian practices' the bishop explained that he meant 'non-Christian connections' associated with sexual immorality:

> A large proportion of these cases arise out of bad social customs. Parents very often arrange the marriages; free consent is not obtained of the young people; ignorance and incompatibility soon drive them apart, resulting in one or both of them seeking other connections after their own hearts.[103]

---

sus Commissioner whom Azariah described as 'an impartial student of racial progress' praised the church in 1921 for abolishing child marriage and permitting widow remarriage: *DDM*, V, 10 (Oct. 1928), p. 3.

101. *Church Censures: Diocese of Dornakal*, vol. 1: 1914-32; vol. 2: 1933-45, DDA.

102. VSA, *A Charge Delivered at Bezwada on Wednesday, October 29th, 1941, op. cit.*, p. 5.

103. *Ibid.*, p. 20.

Azariah reported in 1941 that this seemingly large total number of excommunications for 'immorality' (i.e., 281 for adultery and 425 for non-Christian connections) represented a great improvement over previous years.

> These figures are about half of what they were ten years ago, which shows that the younger generation on the whole are setting before themselves higher standards of Christian family life.[104]

Continued child marriage among Christians in Azariah's diocese is also suggested by examination of surviving marriage registers. The register for the IMS Telugu mission reveals a large number of marriages involving partners of age 14 and 15 — just over the legal limit of 14 for girls. One entry in 1924 involved a wife of 11 years, another in 1925 a wife of 10 and a husband of 14.[105] Individuals still living in Dornakal confirm the continuance of this practice. One elderly Christian woman and sweet seller in Dornakal described how she became a Christian at the age of 5 (changing her name from Venkamma to Nama Ruth) and was married at the age of 10 to a Hindu (who subsequently became a Christian and changed his name from Narsaiah to Jeremiah).[106] Another pastor who worked under Azariah confirmed that Christians and non-Christians continued to intermarry despite church prohibitions, prompting the bishop to compromise by allowing such marriages if non-Christians were first baptized.[107] It is evident that both child marriages and mixed marriages were reduced but were by no means eradicated in the diocese.

Other areas of reform were accepted more readily by Dornakal's converts, chiefly because they satisfied the moral scruples of western missionaries without offending higher-caste Indian notions of defilement via certain forms of ingestion. Azariah scored one of his biggest successes by opposing alcohol consumption in the villages. On this issue, Indo-Anglican bishops were influenced by western temperance movements.[108] They joined critics of the government's liquor laws and condemned the exploi-

104. *Ibid.,* p. 20.

105. Marriage Register, *Indian Missionary Society of Tinnevelly: Telugu Mission,* DDA.

106. Interview with Nama Ruth, 9 April 1986, Kiritapuram.

107. Interview with Rev. Daniel, 31 March 1986, Dornakal.

108. By the late nineteenth century, there were already several Anglican temperance societies at work in India: the Church of England Temperance Society, the Army White Cross, and the Church of England Purity Society. *Report of the Episcopal Conference, 1897* (handwritten), BHA, Calcutta.

tation of indigenous demand for liquor to increase revenues via taxes *(abkari)*, a practice inherited from pre-Raj times. The problem of liquor consumption in India was not an indigenous problem, according to an article published in the *Madras Diocesan Magazine* in 1918, but was created by British self-interest.[109] The Indo-Anglican leadership adopted a moral position of opposition to alcohol consumption and supported (although not unanimously) new prohibition decrees instituted by Congress ministries in provincial legislatures in 1937.[110]

Through the Dornakal Diocese's enthusiastic support for prohibition[111] and its establishment of a popular temperance society, the *Andhra Christo Purushula Samajam* (ACPS), the church achieved notable successes in lowering the rate of alcohol consumption among its adherents in Andhra.[112] Founded in 1914, the ACPS boasted 1,142 branches by 1941, with a total of 10,486 adult members and 1,673 junior members.[113] Upon admission, ACPS members promised to abstain from drink and to witness to the power of Jesus Christ through both their improved moral lives and their conversations with friends and family. Each member received a cross and a prayer card which recorded their date of admission.[114]

109. 'Prohibition Issue in India,' *MDM*, XIII, 11 (Nov. 1918), pp. 263-64.

110. Herbert Anderson, *Prohibition Progresses in India* (London: Indian Conciliation Group, 1938).

111. *Proceedings of the Eighth Session of the Dornakal Diocesan Council held at Bezwada on 6-7 Jan. 1938*, 5: 2/2, Dornakal, MACIPBC. This session applauded the Prohibition Act of 1937 and pledged to continue to aid the now-supportive government in the cause of temperance. The Anglican church was much more in harmony with Indian public opinion on this issue than with some branches of the British and Indian governments. See 'Prohibition Issue in India,' *op. cit.*, pp. 263-64.

112. For evidence of reduced alcohol consumption, see *DDM*, V, 4 (April 1928), p. 4; V, 11 (Nov. 1928), p. 4; VI, 5 (May 1929), p. 1; VI, 6 (June 1929), p. 14; VI, 9 (Sept. 1929), p. 3; VII, 5 (May 1930), pp. 6-7; VII, 9 (Sept. 1930), p. 8; IX, 5 (May 1932), p. 13; X, 10 (Oct. 1933), p. 9; XIII, 4 (April 1936), pp. 2-3. Also J. W. Pickett, *Christ's Way to India's Heart, op. cit.*, p. 42; 'The Bishop's Diary,' *MDM*, XVI, 3 (March 1921), pp. 51-59; Rajaiah D. Paul, 'V. S. Dornakal,' in *Birth Centenary of Bishop Azariah, 1974, op. cit.*, p. 59; K. Luke, *Ḍārnakal Tiranalvēli Indiyan Miṣanari Sanghamu, op. cit.*, p. 101. There is relatively little published evidence that drinking remained a severe problem in Christian congregations, but for some indication of intemperance in the church, see *DDM*, V, 5 (May 1928), p. 2; XII, 4 (April 1935), p. 4. Also 'The Bishop's Diary,' *MTDM*, IX, 2 (Feb. 1914), p. 26.

113. 1,293 of its adult members and 400 of its junior members were on 'probation' in 1941. 'ACPS Report,' *Proceedings of the Twentieth Meeting of the Standing Committee of the Diocesan Council, 29 Oct. 1941, Bezwada*, 5: 2/2, Dornakal, MACIPBC; *MTDM*, IX, 6 (June 1914), p. 167; G. B. Redman, 'Telugu Church Temperance Society,' *MDM*, XI, 4 (April 1916), pp. 121-2. See also *TMI-IMS*, XXVII, 6-7 (June-July 1928), pp. 49-52.

114. Interviews with Alfred Bunyan, 29 and 30 March 1986, Dornakal.

The ACPS became the diocese's most important social improvement agency, sponsoring about sixty-three conferences per year in which the virtues of temperance were presented alongside the claims of the gospel. Its members engaged in activities such as street and house cleaning, visiting sick people, tutoring in reading and writing, discouraging the use of indecent language, and assisting the village teacher by promoting regular attendance at morning prayers and participation in evangelistic activities such as the 'week of witness.'

Where drinking remained a problem among Christians, it was treated at first as a relatively minor offense punishable by suspension from holy communion.[115] However, with the introduction of prohibition in 1938, drinking and illicit distilling became causes for excommunication. In an exhortation that demonstrated Azariah's own support for the stronger regulations against alcohol, the bishop urged his diocese to pay careful attention to the newly rigorous standards of both church and state:

> The time when drinking among Church workers was treated as a minor fault and given a slight punishment has passed. . . . Our Christian congregations must be made to pledge themselves not to allow any toddy at marriage feasts, funerals or festivals. Any village that does these things must be severely dealt with.[116]

By 1941, Azariah reported that 'about half the Pastorates say that there is still some drinking among the older people, and that too on festival and marriage occasions,' but added that much progress had been made:

> There are many Pastorates in which public drinking has entirely gone out of fashion. 'The second generation [of Christians] has entirely given up drink' says one Deanery Chairman.[117]

Azariah's campaign against alcohol consumption satisfied the moral position against drunkenness and involved him in the tradition of nineteenth- and twentieth-century western prohibition crusades. But it would not have been so successful in India without existing Hindu abhorrence for the 'doubly-defiling' substance of alcohol. The drinking of

---

115. *Church Censures: Diocese of Dornakal*, I (1914-32), II (1933-45), DDA.
116. *DDM*, XV, 7 (July 1938), p. 11.
117. VSA, *A Charge Delivered at Bezwada on Wednesday, October 29th, 1941, op. cit.*, p. 20.

strong liquor was considered especially polluting to higher *jatis,* not so much because it was defiling in itself, but because it was distilled by *jatis* of lower rank and had thus been touched by polluting people. The abandonment of distillation and of drinking alcohol was a well-recognized means of *jati* mobility throughout Indian society, non-Christian as well as Christian.[118] The progress made by converts in this area can therefore also be understood as part of an effort to elevate ritual rank in the Hindu social order as much as, or perhaps more than, being simply an effort to conform to broader Christian standards as articulated by church leaders.

Perhaps no area more clearly illustrates the degree to which Christian conversion movements provided the depressed classes with the opportunity for social mobility than the area of carrion and meat ingestion. Here, many of Dornakal's converts voluntarily adopted certain eating prohibitions not advocated by the church but regarded as highly desirable within India's broad criteria of ritual purity and impurity. Although the eating of meat — any meat — was one of the main factors associated with pollution and untouchability, there was in practice a hierarchy of meat pollution, with chicken, fish, and mutton ranking as relatively less polluting, and bats, cats, rats, dogs, crows, and snakes ranking as relatively more polluting.[119] Beef and pork were considered by the higher castes to be particularly defiling because the former came from the most sacred of all animals, the cow, and the latter came from swine which ate excrement. Indeed, one of the myths commonly used to explain the low position of Malas and Madigas in the caste hierarchy involved the killing and eating of a divine cow belonging to Parvati and Siva.[120] Dornakal diocesan records contain numerous examples of converts forsaking carrion, beef and pork in an obvious bid to improve their social rank, as defined more by India's ritual criteria than by western or 'Christian' standards.

Both western missionaries and caste neighbors disapproved of carrion-eating but for different reasons. The depressed class practice of eating carrion *(tsachina mamsamu)* was condemned by missionaries on the grounds that the meat of animals which had died of disease, old age, or starvation was dangerously unsanitary. In contrast, the higher castes disapproved of eating *tsachina mamsamu* because, as in the case of the Madigas, this almost always meant eating relatively cheap but ritually defiling beef (cattle or buf-

---

118. David G. Mandelbaum, *Society in India* (Berkeley, 1970), pp. 201, 217, 479-81, 569.
119. R. E. Frykenberg to author, 20 Oct. 1990.
120. P. Wiebe, *Christians in Andhra Pradesh, op. cit.,* pp. 53-54.

falo).[121] Caste people felt that pollution was contracted, not through the ingestion of dead animals per se (some people of higher castes ate the carrion of other animals), but through the ingestion of cow's meat. Unlike prohibitions regarding Sunday work, participation in Hindu rituals, and child marriage, which interfered with village traditions and provoked resistance from higher-caste Hindus, the prohibition against eating *tsachina mamsamu* was welcomed by dominant Hindu groups and was accepted eagerly, at least by those Christian converts with adequate dietary alternatives.[122] A pastor reported in 1931 that, 'The Madiga Christians of L— who used to eat dead flesh have now entirely left off eating it. This is a marvellous thing.'[123] Baptist Christians of Ongole became known for sitting apart when carrion was boiling in the pot.[124]

The movement against eating carrion was part of the seemingly spontaneous wider movement among Dornakal's depressed classes to abandon eating beef, pork, and presumably other defiling but unmentionable meats. Diocesan records reported that many Christian congregations (and particularly Madigas and Yerukulas) decided to abstain from eating beef and pork voluntarily, without pressure from the church, in order to remove any hindrance to caste people who wanted to become Christian. In 1928, the church reported that Christians in a Pastorate headquarters had given up pork, 'so that the use of it may not be an offence to others,' and that Christians in another area had 'three years ago bound themselves to give up drink, beef, pork and tobacco; and are keeping faithful.'[125] In 1930, church representatives from an area in which Telagas and other Sudras were pressing for baptism reported:

> For the last two or three years we have been making a vehement campaign against beef-eating since it is a hindrance in the way of caste people coming in. They deem it as abominable and the eaters thereof wicked and sinful. As a result of this campaign six families in this congregation have given it up, and the drink habit as well.[126]

121. A. T. Fishman, *For This Purpose, op. cit.,* p. 80. Other types of highly polluting meats (bats, etc.) were not specified in the literature, only beef and pork.

122. A. T. Fishman, *Culture Change and the Underprivileged, op. cit.,* pp. 5, 13-15; *For This Purpose, op. cit.,* pp. 14-15, 80.

123. *DDM,* VIII, 10 (Oct. 1931), p. 15. It was standard practice in such journals to omit village names.

124. Emma Rauschenbusch-Clough, *While Sewing Sandals: Or Tales of a Telugu Pariah Tribe* (London, 1899).

125. *DDM,* V, 11 (Nov. 1928), p. 4.

126. *DDM,* VII, 9 (Sept. 1930), pp. 8-9.

These decisions were often made by whole villages (sometimes including numerous non-Christians) and enforced by village elders as a matter of policy. So, for example, a Deanery Chairman reported in 1930 that a big hamlet of 800 Madigas, about 350 of whom were Christians, had decided to give up drink and beef-eating four months before. All had been faithful to their pledge except a few transgressors who were summoned by the village elders (all but one of whom were Christian), who 'implored them not to be unfaithful to the solemn oath they had taken.' There were apparently immediate economic benefits to this action. The Christians estimated that they had already saved 200 rupees previously spent on drink as well as the expense of killing four to five cows per week for meat. Though they had to continue as shoemakers using the ritually defiling skins of the dead cattle for tanning, the Chairman reported that they now 'bury the flesh so that no one may eat it. Almost all of them were eating the flesh of dead cattle before.' The Madigas' pledge quickly gained the attention of the higher castes. 'The Hindus are wondering at the sudden and remarkable change which has come over them. The surrounding villages also are trying to follow suit.'[127]

Azariah sympathized to some extent with neighboring Baptist missionaries who continued to eat beef in order to demonstrate their freedom from Hindu reverence for the cow.[128] The bishop was not a vegetarian and ate meats according to his personal tastes. (As it happened, inevitably poor-quality beef was not a favorite.) But unlike the Baptists who regarded beef-eating as something of a test for converts, Azariah encouraged the anti-beef (pork, etc.) campaigns in his diocese. He attested to the longterm benefits of an anti-beef campaign in 1936 when he visited a village whose Christians had been baptized eleven years before. Their voluntary commitment to giving up 'drink, beef, theft and lies' had so improved their 'cleanliness' in the eyes of village *zamindars* that spatial distance requirements had been abandoned, Azariah reported.[129] Abstention from defiling meats was one of several means by which Christians attempted with some apparent success to raise their status in the eyes of higher castes. Azariah welcomed efforts of this sort, which, he believed, would demonstrate to higher castes the ability of Christianity 'to drive away degrading habits'[130] and lead to increased numbers of caste conversions.

127. *DDM*, VII, 5 (May 1930), pp. 6-7.
128. A. T. Fishman, *For This Purpose, op. cit.,* p. 80.
129. *DDM*, XIII, 4 (April 1936), p. 2.
130. *Ibid.,* p. 2.

Dornakal's non-Brahmin conversion movements attracted international interest, both during Azariah's lifetime and in later years, as examples of rural, agrarian movements which began among client agricultural laborers and moved upwards to patron tenants and landlords.[131] Pickett's 1937 study, which demonstrated that 'Sudra' conversions always occurred in areas where there had previously been conversions among even lower classes,[132] provided powerful evidence for the theory, greatly favored by mass movement advocates, that India would be won for Christ through a process of 'upward' filtration from the lowest to the highest ranks of society.

A more recent scholarly investigation has shed some doubt on Pickett's argument, contending that many *jatis* commonly classified by Christian observers as 'Sudras' were actually either non-'Sudras,' 'in a state of limbo detached from Hindu society,' or the lowest of 'Sudra' subcastes composed of highly unstable, often nomadic, elements.[133] This important qualification applied particularly to Yerukalas and Waddars — the two largest so-called 'Sudra' groups to convert to Christianity — which were, in fact, Adivasi (aboriginal) tribal groups.

Azariah was certainly aware of these complications. The *Dornakal Diocesan Magazine* noted in 1935 that caste movements were working their way up from the lower subsections of the 'Sudra' ranks to the higher, and that conversions among higher groups such as the Kapus had occurred earlier and more frequently in northern Andhra where Kapus were poorly represented than in southern areas where they were strong, wealthy, and independent.[134] The bishop was familiar with differences between subcastes, describing Yerukalas, Yenadis, and Waddars as 'border-line Sudras,' and Kammas, Kappus, and Telagas as 'upper-class Sudras.' He knew there were many reasons for conversion.[135] But, in summarizing the results of extensive interviews, Azariah finally claimed that the primary reason for

131. Sometimes the reverse occurred as well. The movements affected trading and artisan groups (merchants, goldsmiths, blacksmiths, potters, etc.) to a lesser degree. G. A. Oddie, 'Christian Conversion among Non-Brahmans in Andhra Pradesh, with Special Reference to the Anglican Missionaries and the Dornakal Diocese, c. 1900-1936,' in *op. cit.,* pp. 80-81.

132. J. W. Pickett, *Christ's Way to India's Heart, op. cit.,* pp. 40-45; VSA, 'The Bishop's Letter,' *DDM*, IX, 6 (June 1932), pp. 1-4.

133. J. Manor, 'Testing the Barrier between Caste and Outcaste,' *op. cit.,* pp. 30-31.

134. A. Rumpus, 'Report on the United Evangelistic Campaign 1934,' *op. cit.,* p. 18.

135. *DDM*, XII, 11 (Nov. 1935), p. 4.

'Sudra' conversions was the 'social, economical and educational transformation' that conversion to Christianity had caused among the depressed classes. He recounted the response of one landlord: "'Twenty years ago we called these depressed class people by their names and in a contemptuous manner; now we cannot address them except with terms of respect."'[136] And in addition to conversions made by the positive impression of changed lives among depressed class converts, other 'Sudra' conversions resulted from the 'sub-group opportunism' and the desire to preserve both economic and social superiority over depressed class converts that have been well documented for some areas of nearby Guntur.[137]

Both Azariah and Pickett saw a causal link between depressed class and 'Sudra' conversions wherever the introduction of Christianity had led to observable change in the lives of outcastes. Frequently, Christian converts of depressed class background were compared favorably to non-Christian untouchables by caste people. Pickett's study made no mention of the anti-meat campaign and spoke only generally about the importance of temperance and improving sanitary conditions in Christian villages as a means of demonstrating the 'radical' change brought about by conversion.[138] Like most missionary accounts of the mass movements, Pickett's tended to interpret the significant changes occurring during the process of Christianization in physical, western terms by focusing on scientific effects (sanitation reduces disease, etc.) and on moral issues familiar to western Christians (drunkenness, adultery, etc.). Such changes were easily interpreted as improvements. However, western observers tended to overlook changes associated with Indian notions of ritual pollution like eating beef or pork. Because there was nothing immoral or unhealthy in western Christian terms about consuming these meats and because the very concept of ritual defilement via ingestion seemed so foreign, changes here were largely overlooked in contemporary accounts of the mass movements destined for English-speaking audiences. As a result, the important sociological reality — that the Christian movement was part of a broader bid for *jati* mobility — was underemphasized and has remained underappreciated. The commonly held assumption by western missionaries that the mass movements represented a revolt against the caste system itself was to some degree a wish-projection made possible by the fact that

---

136. *DDM,* XII, 12 (Dec. 1935), p. 4.

137. J. Manor, *op. cit.,* pp. 34-35.

138. VSA, 'Foreword,' in J. W. Pickett, *Christ's Way to India's Heart, op. cit.,* p. i. See also pp. 40-41, 48-50, 100-102, 103-5.

westerners often interpreted the changes taking place in the villages in western rather than Indian terms.

In the context of such cultural misperceptions, Azariah's own observations regarding the anti-beef campaign seem particularly enlightened. In 1929, he visited a village in which outcaste Christians had given up beefeating, they claimed, in order to remove an alleged obstacle to caste conversions to Christianity. This had apparently helped to take away some of the stigma associated with the local Christian congregation, as Azariah recounted: 'A Komati [village banker or merchant] recently remarked of Christians of a certain village that he had no objection to their coming to his shop or his touching them since now they had altogether given up beef.' The bishop added:

> I was very much amused at this anti-beef campaign by our Christians. That it should have started from them entirely and that, too, solely for the sake of removing the prejudice of the caste people against the Christian faith are most encouraging facts. If the whole of India took a similar attitude on such questions there will be no communal conflicts. The Christian spirit is certainly the best solution for all communal troubles.[139]

Far from condemning the anti-beef resolutions as symptomatic of the continuing hold of caste prejudice or of heathen cow veneration among Christians, the bishop welcomed these movements as good-humored expressions of a new, gospel-motivated desire to reconcile communal differences. The fact that converts had spontaneously opted to give up eating beef without a mandate, or even encouragement, from the church was not viewed as insubordination but rather as an encouraging sign that outcaste Christians desired to improve their reputation among higher-caste groups, which Azariah believed would ultimately help the Christian (not to mention the outcaste) cause. The issue of eating beef had been discussed already at the 1910 Edinburgh Conference, where it was concluded that 'to refrain from eating beef would remove a serious obstacle to the acceptance of the Christian faith by Hindus.'[140] But abstaining from beef had not become a policy in Dornakal, nor even a practice followed by Azariah and most other Indian church leaders. Consistent with Azariah's generally optimistic attitude about the gospel's power to transform negative aspects of Indian culture, he viewed the campaign as

139. *DDM*, VI, 5 (May 1929), pp. 2-3.
140. Quoted in A. T. Fishman, *For This Purpose*, op. cit., p. 80.

an expression of Christian power to heal communal differences rather than as the self-serving attempt by one *jati* to improve its ritual status by adopting a higher-caste practice.

That the latter motivation may often have been the more compelling is suggested by the fact that the anti-beef campaign was not confined to Christian groups, although Christians often took the lead in initiating broad resolutions on the subject. In the mainly non-Christian Madiga hamlet cited above whose 800 inhabitants had agreed to stop drinking and eating beef, the minority Christians held all but one of the positions on the village *panchayat* responsible for the initiatives. Since Indian national independence, a sizable part of the non-Christian Madiga community has also attempted to stop eating carrion and dealing with dead cattle.[141] The rise in economic position and political power which Madigas have experienced in urban areas to which they have been migrating has been accompanied by an attempt to claim better status in the eyes of higher-caste groups. But the abstention from beef-eating and from handling cattle has been the Madigas' only concession to values derived from the Sanskritic tradition. Madiga elites attempting to raise their *jati*'s status have not engaged, except sporadically, in the process of Sanskritization, have avoided incorporating Brahmin priests into their socioreligious life, and have worshipped local territorial and caste deities rather than 'the all-India gods of classical Hinduism.'[142] Their models for emulation have been derived only occasionally and partially from the Sanskritic tradition and more often from a variety of cultural heritages which include local, regional, modern-western, and secular national traditions. For example, modern Madiga interfamily relationships have been modeled increasingly on patterns established by upper-caste Andhra agriculturalists rather than by Brahmins.[143] Refraining from beef-eating appears to have been the only Brahminical practice widely adopted.

Christianization in the Dornakal Diocese with its variety of socioeconomic and cultural repercussions is, thus, perhaps best understood as one of many facets of change which occurred in the wider context of *jati* upward mobilization. Unlike some western missionaries, Azariah accepted his converts' accommodation to certain values defined by India's broad ritual criteria whereby different meats were accorded different degrees of ritual pollution. This was a realistic recognition that, although

141. T. R. Singh, *The Madiga: A Study in Social Structure and Change, op. cit.*, p. 76.
142. *Ibid.*
143. *Ibid.*, pp. 73-74.

his formerly outcaste converts resented their ostracism from Hindu society, they were still inclined to assimilate some of that culture's values in order to gain greater respect. Insofar as those indigenous values did not offend his Christian values, Azariah chose to focus instead on their potential for improving the lives of both his converts and of Indian society as a whole.

The church hoped to bring about dramatic changes in the values and practices of the depressed classes while also adapting and invigorating certain positive elements of their culture. By requesting baptism, the mass movement converts apparently welcomed many of these changes. There is little doubt that conversion to Christianity in Dornakal and in other mass movement areas entailed, in addition to spiritual experiences, the quest for a better life both economically and socially and for greater individual and group dignity.[144] The question of which motivations took priority was one of the more vexing issues Azariah had to face during his episcopal career.

The debate over the significance of Indian mass movements during and since Azariah's lifetime focused on the question of motives for conversion. Some claimed the movements were spiritual awakenings ('move-

144. Whether these goals were met in reality remains a complex subject whose results vary according to locality and time. For useful assessments see 'Mass Movement Appeal,' *MDM*, XIII, 6 (June 1918), pp. 131-34; S. Manickam, *The Social Setting of Christian Conversion in South India, op. cit.,* pp. 101-3, 108-11, 257-58; J. C. B. Webster, *The Christian Community and Change in Nineteenth Century North India* (Delhi, 1976), pp. 61-72; *A History of the Dalit Christians in India, op. cit.*

The Indian Christian community became known rather more for its educational than for its economic attainments. Literacy gave converts the opportunity to enter new professions (in railways, postal systems, government, missions). Although this mobility contributed to a significant long-term rise in social status, persecution was often the only short-term result of mass movement conversions. S. Manickam, *op. cit.,* pp. 108-11; Paul D. Wiebe, *Christians in Andhra Pradesh, op. cit.,* pp. 128-31. Pickett claimed that church-sponsored activity led to general economic improvement for the untouchables. For example, education and the breakdown of occupational restrictions led to increased earnings, improved medical care prevented loss of working days, and reduced drinking meant less wasteful expenditure and greater productivity. But he also pointed out that conversion worsened the economic condition in some respects. Educated converts often migrated to towns and cities so that villages did not benefit from their education, converts adopted new standards of expenditure in clothes, 'false ideas of dignity' which prevented them from doing ordinary work, the boycott of certain occupations, 'and the occasional development of a spirit of dependence upon the Mission.' See 'Mass Movements and Economic Reconstruction,' *DDM,* XI, 3 (March 1934), pp. 16-19.

ments of the Holy Spirit bringing about a revival of New Testament Christianity').[145] Others described them as nothing more than 'superficial' actions prompted by economic, social, or other material motives ('conversions for convenience').[146] Many Christians joined non-Christian critics in suspecting untouchables of converting in order to find relief from their poverty, to attain higher social position, or to obey family or *jati* leaders, rather than as the result of any religious experience. Azariah and Whitehead observed that 'the motives that lead people to become Christians in mass movements are strangely mixed.'[147] Because of such suspicions, many missionaries were reluctant to baptize mass movement converts, especially after depressed class conversions became the focus of the serious moral and political dispute between Christians and Hindus in the 1930s — as we shall see in the following chapter.

Concerns about the legitimacy of group conversions from depressed classes prompted the NCC (under Bishop Azariah's presidency) to commission Pickett to conduct a nationwide sociological study of the mass movements. This was published in 1933.[148] On the basis of 3,947 interviews with Christians from representative mass movement areas, Pickett and his research team concluded in 1933 that 8.1 percent had converted for secular reasons (education, better social standing, agricultural and medical aid, marriage prospects, relief of oppression by landowners), 34.8 percent for spiritual reasons, and 22.4 percent for social reasons (i.e., because family and friends had converted). The remaining 34.7 percent said they were Christians for natal reasons (i.e., because they were raised in Christian families). Despite the limitations of such classifications, the results demonstrated the complexity of motives behind conversions and were 'effective in destroying tendencies to label simplistically and derogatorily the converts in mass movement areas.'[149]

145. For example, J. Edwin Orr sees a link between revivals occurring in America and Ireland in 1858-59 and the growth of the church in Andhra. J. Edwin Orr, *Evangelical Awakenings in Southern Asia* (Minneapolis, 1975), pp. 56-72, 118-54, and *The Outpouring of the Spirit in Revival and Awakening and Its Issue in Church Growth* (Pasadena, CA, 1984).

146. For example, M. K. Gandhi, *Christian Missions: Their Place in India,* ed. Bharatan Kumarappa (Ahmedabad, 2nd ed., 1957), pp. 61-66.

147. VSA and Henry Whitehead, *Christ in the Indian Villages* (London, 1930), quoted in J. W. Pickett, *Christian Mass Movements in India* (Lucknow, 1933), pp. 154-55.

148. J. W. Pickett, *Christian Mass Movements in India* (Lucknow, 1933).

149. According to Paul D. Wiebe, *Christians in Andhra Pradesh, op. cit.,* pp. 16-17. Pickett was chosen to lead the study because he was particularly critical of collective conversions of this nature. His findings convinced him otherwise. Interview with Cyril B. Firth, 24 Sept. 1986, Romsey, Hants.

Pickett's study concluded that 'the motives that lead Indian people to Christ in mass movements are the motives that lead people anywhere to him.' Although other Christians might describe their motives differently, Pickett believed that 'the experiences behind them would be very much the same,' even when following the decision of group leaders.[150] The study's other major conclusion was that the mass movements 'constitute for many Indian people the most natural way of approach to Christ' because 'the more individualistic way preferred in Western countries is not favored by people trained from early childhood to group action.'[151] Pickett's study was the most detailed and comprehensive analysis of mass movements during this period and provided the NCC with sufficient evidence of conversion's positive effects to justify launching a nationwide evangelistic crusade in the 1930s, to be examined below.

The controversy over the motives for conversion hinged upon a distinction between the two categories of the 'spiritual' and the 'material' which Azariah did not believe were particularly relevant to either the Bible or the South Indian village. Mass movement critics, including many educated Indian Christians from urban areas, claimed that the only worthy motives for conversion were spiritual ones. In contrast, Azariah emphasized that worldly aspirations had not disqualified the disciples of Christ nor the prodigal son from spiritual fellowship.[152] Furthermore, mass conversions and baptisms had occurred throughout Christian history, beginning at pentecost.[153] By analogy, Azariah contended that 'mixed motives' on the part of the oppressed untouchables were legitimate and not necessarily devious or a mask for self-advancement. Just as the Christian God (in the incarnate person of Jesus) had not ignored the material needs of his followers, so also should Christian missionaries seriously consider the material aspirations of the depressed classes. Azariah believed that post-baptism religious instruction and long-term exposure to Christian love and fellowship would eventually

150. J. W. Pickett, *Christian Mass Movements in India*, pp. 160-61.

151. *Ibid.*, p. 319.

152. 'Our Lord did not hesitate to enroll as His disciples men who had political ambitions and who probably followed Him hoping through Him to secure freedom from Roman domination. In the parable of the Prodigal Son, our Lord was not afraid to say that the son was driven to the father's home by circumstances that brought him to the verge of starvation,' Azariah wrote. 'The Bishop's Letter,' *DDM*, XIII, 6 (June 1936), p. 4.

153. VSA, 'Living Forces behind Mass Movements,' *IRM*, XXVIII (Oct. 1929), p. 509.

enable converts to appreciate the deeper, more specifically 'spiritual' dimensions of their baptism. Even if new Christians expressed their reasons for conversion in material terms (the desire for education or suitable marriage partners), the bishop discerned that spiritual forces were at work 'beneath the surface' providing 'dynamite' for the mass movements so that, after several years of active membership in the church, converts manifested 'higher motives, nobler thoughts and fresh achievements in character.'[154]

To Azariah, a strict separation between the spiritual and material realms was neither biblically normative nor consistent with the particularities of the Indian village situation. Critics who accused untouchable converts of undue interest in material gain at the expense of spiritual motivations (that is, of being merely 'rice Christians') appear to have been using a conceptual distinction that was foreign and seemed irrelevant to the converts themselves. Anthropological work suggests that a sharp delineation between the 'purely spiritual' (the desire for union with God and salvation of the soul) and the 'purely material' (the desire for food, education, medical care, etc.) is not particularly meaningful in the context of Telugu villages where folk religious practices have direct significance for the problems of everyday 'material' life and where the cognitive differentiation so natural to secularized western culture between the 'sacred' realm of faith, miracles, and otherworldly problems and the 'scientific' realm of empirical reality does not exist to such a great extent.[155] One study of Christianity in rural Andhra noted:

> In the context of village religion . . . concern for material welfare is not the opposite of 'turning to religion' but one of its main foundations. The ceremonies which punctuate the life of the village indicate an important feature of village religion: the sense of a sacred aspect in every activity or event.[156]

Of course, village Christians, immersed as they were in the diverse practices of India's 'little' traditional belief systems, were often also aware

154. *Ibid.,* pp. 509-10.

155. Paul G. Hiebert, 'Folk Religion in Andhra Pradesh and Some Missiological Implications,' in *The Gospel among Our Hindu Neighbours,* ed. Vinay Samuel and Chris Sugden (Bangalore, 1983), pp. 87-109; 'The Flaw of the Excluded Middle,' *Missiology,* X, 1 (Jan. 1982), pp. 35-47; *Konduru: Structure and Integration in a South Indian Village* (Minneapolis, 1971).

156. P. Y. Luke and J. B. Carman, *Village Christians and Hindu Culture, op. cit.,* pp. 42-43.

of the more reflective 'great' tradition of classical Hinduism.[157] But the villagers' dominant everyday worldview was populated mainly by spiritual beings, magical forces, and astrological and other signs; and their social life was so permeated by and patterned around religiously significant ceremonies as to make the distinction between the two transcendent ideals of 'spiritual' and 'material' almost meaningless. Such concepts were more indigenous to what Max Weber would have called a 'rationalized' society in which, as Clifford Geertz has described it:

> the sense of sacredness was gathered up like so many scattered rays of light brought to focus in a lens from the countless tree spirits and garden spells through which it was vaguely diffused, and was concentrated in a nucleated . . . concept of the divine.[158]

Mass movement critics imported the basically alien analytical dichotomy of 'spiritual' versus 'material' to explain and condemn actions of village converts for whom such categories had little meaning. Azariah, the bearer of a supposedly alien religion, seems to have understood more clearly than his critics the central role of religious beliefs and practices in ordering and explaining the everyday material life of the Indian village. The sometimes desperate need for a good monsoon and harvest, for protection from an epidemic, and for blessings in work and family life — these were spiritual as much as material issues in the less secularized rural context. As Azariah wrote to his diocese in 1935:

> Connecting the every-day events of life with religion is inborn in the Indian. The Christian religion ought also to stand for the sanctification of all human life. A religion of the Holy Incarnation cannot be anything else.[159]

---

157. On the contrast and interaction between the 'little' traditional belief systems of village India and the 'great' traditional Christian, Muslim, and Hindu understandings as manifest in Andhra Pradesh, see Paul D. Wiebe, *Christians in Andhra Pradesh, op. cit.*, pp. 70-74, 87-89. Luke and Carman show that, because Sanskritization was not carried out thoroughly in these villages, many of the all-India festivals connected with Sanskritic deities are not much understood or appreciated and, instead, are occasions for 'much *tamasha*' with little religious significance.

158. Quoted in Charles Ryerson, *Regionalism and Religion, op. cit.*, p. 4. On Weber's contrast between 'societies where the "magical" or "enchanted" does not transcend everyday life (and the) "rationalized" society where transcendent concepts stand above or apart from common place existence,' see *ibid.*, pp. 3-4.

159. *DDM*, XII, 10 (Oct. 1935), p. 8.

It was perhaps somewhat condescending of mass movement critics to assume that outcaste converts were either too unspiritual and ignorant to have religious motivations for baptism or too devious to admit that their true motivations were material. Untouchable converts in Dornakal fully expected that their gods would be involved in 'worldly' matters such as healing illnesses and in guaranteeing success in marriages, house-building, crop cultivation, and the like. 'Spiritual' revivals might be sparked by rainfall after a special day of fasting and prayer for rain.[160] Their relatively undifferentiated understanding of the spiritual and material realms made it reasonable to expect religion to entail some degree of practical benefit. Telugu village culture had been as yet only indirectly affected by those forces of secularization which had led nineteenth-century Europe to distance God from the details of human existence.[161] Rather, it was a culture in which material reality was permeated with sacred significance and in which clear divisions were not delineated between the spiritual and material realms. Not for the first time in the history of cultural contact and religious change have largely inappropriate questions led to unsatisfactory answers which tell us more about the motives of the debaters than the motives of those converted.

More recently, the debate over motives for depressed class conversions has refocused upon the somewhat different question of whether Indian Christian converts regarded their baptism as a means of protest against and escape from the hierarchical values of the Indian caste system (as the missionaries, many Indian Christians, and some scholars have claimed), or whether they were merely trying to improve their positions within the traditional Indian social order. Recent studies of Indian Christian communities suggest that converts often continued to adhere to Hindu standards of social rank and precedence and that conversion move-

160. As was the case in 1931, when a village pastor described a 'revival' that took place in two congregations following the observance of a special day of fasting and prayer for rain. The group included 120 Madiga men enrolled as Christian 'hearers' (i.e., preparing for baptism) and some Hindus and Muslims because 'all the efforts of Hindus and Mohammedans for rain had hitherto proved fruitless.' As it happened, the day of Christian prayer was followed immediately by rainfall, and this event led to the subsequent religious 'revival.' *DDM*, VIII, 10 (Oct. 1931), p. 4. *DDM* contains many stories of village religious movements in which the boundary between the spiritual and the material is not at all clear.

161. Owen Chadwick, *The Secularization of the European Mind in the Nineteenth Century* (Cambridge, 1975). Only in the 1940s did Azariah begin to warn his clergy about the dangers of secularization and materialism. See VSA, *A Charge Delivered at Bezwada on Wednesday, October 29th 1941, op. cit.,* p. 7.

ments in India cannot be properly understood in isolation from these values.[162] This was certainly true in Dornakal, where conversion served, among other functions, as a means by which depressed groups tried to improve their social and economic status, to gain new self-respect, and to win the respect of higher castes.[163] Optimistic western missionaries of this period tended to regard mass movements as means by which outcastes and low castes were rejecting not only their particular position in the caste hierarchy but also the entire hierarchical value system upon which it was based. Missionaries tended to assume that, by converting to Christianity, former untouchables and 'Sudras' were adopting not only the Christian

162. S. B. Kaufmann, 'Popular Christianity, Caste and Hindu Society in South India, 1800-1915,' in *op. cit.,* pp. 15-26, 382-490; and 'A Christian Caste in Hindu Society: Religious Leadership and Social Conflict among the Paravas of Southern Tamilnadu,' in *op. cit.,* pp. 203-34. Kaufmann's argument that Christian conversion is best understood as a sectarian movement operating according to Hindu concepts of rank and social advancement (similar to bhakti movements such as *Virasaivas*) challenges the notion that Christian converts were seeking liberation from those values. For representative Christian missionary views, see S. C. Neill, *Out of Bondage* (London, 1930), pp. 48-50, 127; W. Paton, *Christianity in the Eastern Conflicts* (Westminster, 1937), p. 93; J. W. Pickett, 'The Untouchables,' in *Moving Millions* (Boston, 1938), pp. 42-74; *Bombay Representative Christian Council: Report on the Survey of Evangelistic Opportunities in Maharashtra, 1938-39* (Mysore City, 1940), p. 10. For other modern scholarly assessments of this question, see the works by R. E. Frykenberg, R. Hardgrave, G. A. Oddie, J. Manor, and D. Washbrook cited by Kaufmann, and Mark Juergensmeyer, *Religion as Social Vision: The Movement against Untouchability in 20th-Century Punjab* (Berkeley, 1982), pp. 181-92; R. Frykenberg, 'On the Study of Conversion Movements: A Review Article and a Theoretical Note,' in *op. cit.,* pp. 121-38; D. Forrester, 'The Depressed Classes and Conversion to Christianity, 1860-1960,' in *op. cit.,* pp. 35-66; J. W. Gladstone, *Protestant Christianity and People's Movements in Kerala, 1850-1936, op. cit.,* pp. 9-10, 76-81, 151-60, 201-4, 421-28; Walter Fernandes, *Caste and Conversion Movements in India* (Delhi, 1981), and 'Caste, Religion and Social Change in India: Christianity and Conversion Movements,' in *Scheduled Castes and the Struggle against Inequality,* ed. Jose Kananaikil (Delhi, 1983), pp. 115-41; S. Manickam, *The Social Setting of Christian Conversion in South India, op. cit.,* pp. 101-12, 245-49; L. L. and S. H. Rudolph, *The Modernity of Tradition: Political Development in India* (Chicago, 1967), pp. 136-37; and Dick Kooiman, *Conversion and Social Equality in India* (New Delhi: South Asia Publications, n.d.), pp. 168-208. Although this literature has not been subjected to systematic analysis, as Frykenberg notes in his 'Review Article and Theoretical Note,' it suggests generally that conversion provided a means of challenging caste disabilities and of bidding for elevation within Indian society, rather than of eradicating caste per se.

163. *DDM,* XIII, 6 (June 1936), p. 6. See also Pickett, *Christ's Way to India's Heart, op. cit.,* pp. 42-43; A. T. Fishman, *Culture Change and the Underprivileged, op. cit.,* p. 26 (Fishman notes that the prestige of association with missionaries was not unimportant); Mark Juergensmeyer, *Religion as Social Vision, op. cit.,* p. 187.

faith but also the more egalitarian values of modern western 'democratic' cultures.[164] In fact, conversion to Christianity seems to have provided in many cases an effective instrument for improving the status of depressed class groups within the caste hierarchy. The missionaries' surprise, frustration, and bewilderment at not being able to eradicate the 'remnants' of caste and other social practices from the church are at least partly accounted for by this misperception. Evidence in the Dornakal Diocese suggests that, while the mass movements were sometimes a means of protest against the prevailing caste system, they were more often a means by which subordinate groups tried to elevate their rank within the social hierarchy by accommodation to the values of dominant groups.

Most of the changes in living habits advocated by the Dornakal church (and at least partly achieved in the villages) were universally considered 'improvements' according to both Indian/Hindu and western/ Judeo-Christian values. Converts to Christianity were expected to give up a range of habits which were regarded by everyone (although often for different reasons) as contributing to their state of 'degradation.' Christianity did change outcaste culture to some degree — but not so much in the radical way that Azariah and western missionaries originally envisioned as in a manner consistent with the elevation of caste status in Andhra society. Azariah's unique contribution was to allow his church the short-term freedom to order its affairs according to principles important to local culture rather than principles important to the external cultures of the missionaries, in the expectation that the gospel would work deeper transformations on local culture over the long term.

164. This sort of perspective is reflected indirectly in Forrester's conclusion that the depressed classes were attracted to the Protestant emphasis on equality, among other factors. D. Forrester, 'The Depressed Classes and Conversion to Christianity, 1860-1960,' in *Religion in South Asia, op. cit.,* pp. 35-66. This difference between the perceptions of missionaries and converts has been noted in other contexts. See Mark Juergensmeyer, *Religion as Social Vision, op. cit.,* p. 184, where he claims that, for the missionaries, 'Christianity in the Punjab was something that rose above caste, hardly an instrument of caste identity and mobility.' On p. 192 he writes, 'Even in the cheeriest piety of church fellowship there were tensions between the global perspective of the missionaries and the parochial concerns of village Christians, and in the end the illusion of Christendom as a new society remained mostly that, an illusion.'

PART IV

THE RIFT

As a rising influence in India, particularly among hitherto neglected outcastes, Azariah necessarily came into conflict with the new political movement that was convulsing India and threatening to override preexisting local traditions: Indian nationalism. Azariah supported many of the most sacred goals of nationalism; but his growing successes seemed to threaten this emerging secular movement. By the 1930s, he was drawn unwittingly into a serious conflict with the unchallenged giant of modern Indian nationalism, Mohandas K. Gandhi.

Gandhi's lifetime almost exactly coincided with that of Azariah, and there were many striking parallels in their development. But there were also deep differences between the two Indian leaders, which came into focus in a dramatic and still controversial meeting just a decade before the final liberation of India.

CHAPTER 9

The Conflict with Gandhi
and Political Nationalism

The remarkable story of Azariah has been almost entirely excluded from the historical literature on modern India partly because his entire life was lived in the shadow of the far more famous figure of Gandhi. Gandhi has been seen not only as the tactician and embodiment of successful Indian nationalism but also as the modern exemplar of India's mysterious and ancient spiritual values.

The public image of Gandhi, and much of the scholarship about him, has tended to be idealized and hagiographic rather than critical.[1] Otherwise some mainstream attention would surely have been devoted to Gandhi's hostile relationship with Azariah, whom the Editor of *The Collected Works of Mahatma Gandhi* has described as Gandhi's 'Enemy Number One.'[2] Those who think of Gandhi as a saintly figure working to improve the lot of the Indian masses seem not to have either questioned or explored why Gandhi should have been so hostile to someone who was do-

---

1. Few historical figures have been subject to such intensive study. Already by the mid-1970s, over 400 biographies of Gandhi were available; and several definitive and balanced biographies have appeared since that time, including Judith M. Brown, *Gandhi: Prisoner of Hope* (New Haven, 1989); Antony Copley, *Gandhi: Against the Tide* (Oxford, 1987); and Susanne H. and Lloyd I. Rudolph, *Gandhi: The Traditional Roots of Charisma* (Chicago, 1983). For much less common and sometimes shrill criticism of Gandhi, see Michael Edwardes, *The Myth of the Mahatma: Gandhi, the British and the Raj* (London, 1986); and Richard Grenier, *The Gandhi Nobody Knows* (Nashville, 1983).

2. Interview with Professor K. Swaminathan, 20 March 1986, Madras.

ing precisely that at the local level within his own country. And it seems odd that the well-subsidized editors of Gandhi's massive collected works seem never to have found — or at least included — any serious documentation of Gandhi's interaction with his 'Enemy Number One.'

One can place Azariah in the broad historical context of modern India by comparing and contrasting his life with the remarkably parallel yet strikingly divergent life of Gandhi. Gandhi was born five years before Azariah, and was killed by an assassin's gun three years after Azariah was killed by a fever contracted in a remote diocesan village. At the time of his death, Gandhi dressed as an Indian peasant while living in a businessman's Delhi mansion; Azariah dressed as an Anglican bishop — complete with resplendent robes — while living in his rural village. Both men were preoccupied with the problems of poverty and untouchability; and both men had devised entirely different strategies for alleviating its hardships.

Gandhi was born into a Hindu home in the princely state of Porbandar, where his family belonged to a subcaste of shopkeepers and moneylenders known as Banyas, and his father was raised as a Vaishnavi — a member of the Hindu sect that worships Vishnu or his incarnation, Krishna. Although Gandhi came from a higher caste than Azariah, both Gandhi and Azariah began their educations in schools where they learned to read and write by drawing letters in the dirt with sticks. Both boys were shy, and few predicted their eventual importance. Gandhi began his career inauspiciously as a tongue-tied lawyer; Azariah began by failing to complete his college degree in mathematics.

Gandhi, the apostle of Indian nationalism, was actually educated in London, while Azariah, the supposed adjunct of western imperialism, was educated in India. Gandhi spent the first twenty-one years of his adult career in South Africa during the time that Azariah was traveling the length and breadth of India as a missionary advocate. When Gandhi returned to India from South Africa in 1915, he felt in many ways a foreigner in his own land. By the time the Mahatma began his famous train tour of India designed to reacquaint him with the ways of his own people, the younger Azariah had already spent almost twenty years riding trains, bullock carts, and bicycles throughout the subcontinent meeting with ordinary people and promoting his evangelistic message.

Gandhi began his extended years outside South Asia as a careful imitator of western dress and manners, and he ended them by rejecting western civilization and calling for Indian home rule. While hammering out legal and political challenges to racist politics in South Africa, he was inspired by western writers such as Tolstoy and Ruskin to reject western civilization as godless in his 1909 publication *Hind Swaraj* (Indian Home Rule). Living abroad for an extended period of time probably intensified Gandhi's need to construct a newly viable Indian identity, both personally and politically.

Azariah avoided these extremes of imitative westernization and xenophobic nationalism, at least in part because he stayed in India. He agreed in some ways with Gandhi's *Hind Swaraj* when it criticized westernized Indian professional doctors and lawyers for betraying India's innate spiritual values: Azariah, too, enjoined professional classes in India to pursue a more spiritual mission. But because Azariah believed that Christianity contained the answers to India's deepest needs and that the Christian missionary to India was therefore the truest kind of Indian patriot, he sought ways to express and validate his Indian Christianity by combining the best of both western and Indian civilizations. Azariah shared much of Gandhi's frustration and resentment toward patronizing westerners and their institutions, but he never either fully adopted or decisively rejected western cultural norms or political legitimacy.

Azariah's first personal contact with Gandhi was orchestrated, not surprisingly, by Henry Whitehead and his wife Isabel. Like his more famous Anglican colleague C. F. Andrews, Whitehead was one of Britain's earliest supporters of Gandhi's efforts in South Africa. The Bishop of Madras served as the President of the South African League, a South Indian organization which supported the cause of Indians in Natal and the Transvaal. In 1914, Whitehead delivered a speech on the injustice being done to Indians in South Africa. He advocated breaking the law to resist tyranny, and described the South African problem as 'doubly hateful' because the rulers called themselves Christian. Finally, he elevated Gandhi to Christ-like stature by concluding: 'I frankly confess, though it deeply grieves me to say it, that I see in Mr. Gandhi, the patient sufferer for the cause of Righteousness and Mercy, a truer representative of the Crucified Saviour, than the men who have thrown him into prison and yet call themselves by the name of Christ.'[3]

The Whiteheads and Azariah met Gandhi for the first time in February 1916 when the Whiteheads hosted him for a week's visit in their Madras home.[4] Gandhi arrived on February 13 by slow train, 3rd class, and immediately struck Whitehead as 'a delightful person, very simple in his

---

3. *MTDM*, IX, 1 (Jan. 1914), pp. 9-11. See also *MTDM*, X, 1 (Jan. 1915), pp. 35-36.
4. Whitehead, *Indian Problems, op. cit.*, pp. 225-50.

life and very warm-hearted and affectionate and most responsive to the appeals of poverty and suffering.'[5]

The next day Gandhi addressed a missionary conference in Madras on the subject of *Swadeshi*, the program of economic self-reliance based on production from 'one's own country.' Mrs. Whitehead, ever eager to introduce Azariah to the 'real' India, took Azariah to hear the speech delivered to an audience of nearly all the missionaries of Madras. 'He represents in rather an extreme form the modern reaction against western influences and western civilization in India, and naturally he is opposed on principle to all proselytizing on the part of the missionary,' Henry Whitehead reported after this speech.[6]

On February 15, the Whiteheads hosted a garden party at their house to introduce Mr. Gandhi to a large number of Indians (including Azariah) and a few Europeans. That the Whiteheads should have been the conduit between Gandhi and new Indian constituencies in Madras suggests once again the importance of liberal westerners in promoting Indian nationalism on the subcontinent. We have no record of Azariah's conversation with Gandhi. In the evening after dinner, Bishop Whitehead and Gandhi had a long talk about *swadeshi*, and Whitehead expressed for the first time serious concerns about Gandhi's message:

> Where I feel that [*swadeshi*] is defective is that it is opposed to the whole Christian ideal of the brotherhood of nations, and would either lead to absolute stagnation of life and thought and reduce India to the level of the South Sea Islands or would produce a race of self-sufficing and self-satisfied Pharisees, keeping entirely aloof from the rest of the world, and living their own lives and thinking their own thoughts. Mr. Gandhi said that his ideal was that a nation should supply all its needs and not interfere with other nations or be interfered with by them. That is better than the German ideal of domination, but it is certainly inferior to the Christian ideal of mutual service.[7]

Whitehead and Gandhi then turned to the more difficult question of evangelism, undoubtedly with the example of Azariah's Dornakal in mind:

> Mr. Gandhi's ideal was that the Hindus should retain their own religion but reform its abuses. What he did not realize was that the main reform

5. *MDM*, XI, 9 (Sept. 1916), p. 232.
6. *Ibid.*, p. 233.
7. *Ibid.*, p. 234. It is entirely possible that Azariah was present for this conversation.

needed is in the fundamental conceptions of God and man and the relation between them.

This was, of course, the crux of the difficulty between Gandhi and
Azariah: that Azariah favored conversion from, rather than reform of,
Hinduism. Whitehead admired Gandhi as a great hero because of 'his
wonderful self-sacrifice and endurance in championing the cause of his
fellow countrymen during their struggle for justice' in South Africa, but
he now began to question Gandhi's broader views on religion and Indian
politics.

The next day Gandhi spoke at the annual meeting of the Social Service League, a British charitable organization chaired by Mrs. Whitehead.
When two thousand students showed up, the meeting was moved to an
outside courtyard. Gandhi spoke, apparently in a rambling fashion, about
the 'appalling dirt and filth' in the Hindu temples at Benares, 'the grasp-
ing covetousness of the Brahman priests,' his experiences traveling third
class on Indian railways, and 'educated Indians who dress as Europeans
and despise their fellow passengers.' Bishop Whitehead was disappointed
with the speech, noting that 'His suggestions were not very helpful, as the
programme he put before them was the reform of the Hindu temples, the
reform of education and the reform of the habits and customs of third
class passengers on railway trains!'[8]

Years later, Whitehead recalled that Gandhi was 'a delightful and
most interesting guest and obviously a man of transparent honesty and
sincerity,' but abstract in thinking, indifferent to concrete realities, and inconsistent. Worst of all, Gandhi preached a 'perverted patriotism' and was
blind to the false consciousness created in India by indigenous religion
and philosophy. 'He could not see that the true enemy of the soul of India
was not western civilization, but Indian tradition, and that the great need
of India was a new religion and a truer philosophy,' Whitehead wrote in
1924.[9]

Azariah and Gandhi did not clash directly over these issues until the
1930s. But the fundamental religious and philosophical disagreements
that lay at the heart of their debates emerged much earlier. Gandhi's position that all religions were equally valid was directly opposite to Azariah's
position that Christianity was the only true religion. Gandhi had long believed that all religions were merely 'different roads converging to the

8. *Ibid.*, p. 235. Gandhi was much more critical of Hindu priests and temples
than Azariah.
9. Henry Whitehead, *Indian Problems, op. cit.,* pp. 240-49.

same point,'[10] and that conversion from the religion of one's birth to another was an offense against the dharmic order.[11] Azariah's evangelism, despite its obvious benefit to untouchables, offended Gandhi by its focus on conversion and baptism. Gandhi disapproved of Christian missions that went beyond social work — education, medicine, and the like — into the realm of religious confession and commitment. Azariah's emphasis on the importance of membership in the visible church set him on a collision course with the Mahatma from their earliest years.

Azariah and the Christians in his diocese were also increasingly isolated by the growing Indian nationalist consensus that Indian Christians, especially those who opposed aspects of the Independence movement, were not really patriotic. In a 1929 letter to Gandhi, the Indian Christian Community of Nandyal in Andhra — probably with Azariah's help — defended themselves from accusations of being 'unpatriotic and anti-national in outlook.' They objected that these charges were 'utterly unfounded,' defended western missionaries, and described their own church as 'an object lesson on self-government.'[12] They advocated the more moderate political goal of Dominion status for India within the empire, and cautioned 'against extreme and militant nationalism which seeks to destroy the most fundamental of all truths, viz., the Brotherhood of Man and the Fatherhood of God.'[13]

Later, after the great rift between Gandhi and Azariah, the bishop expressed the heart of his grievance against Hindu nationalists who criticized the attitudes of Indian Christians toward their countrymen:

> He has forgotten — the critic — the great service to India that Christians
> are rendering, through bringing Christ and His faith to bear upon the

10. M. K. Gandhi, 'Why I Did Not Become a Christian,' in *The Message of Jesus Christ*, ed. Anand T. Hingorani (Bombay, 1971), p. 24.

11. See, e.g., some of Gandhi's statements from the *Harijan* (citations given from both M. K. Gandhi, *Christian Missions: Their Place in India*, ed. Bharatan Kumarappa [2nd ed., Ahmedabad, 1957, hereafter *CM*], and *CWMG*, and differences noted where applicable): 'About "Conversion,"' 28 Sept. 1935, *CM*, pp. 46-50, *CWMG*, LXI, pp. 454-58; 'A Christian Letter,' 30 Jan. 1937, *CM*, pp. 70-73, *CWMG*, LXIV, pp. 325-27; 'Conversion without Conviction,' 29 March 1942, *CM*, p. 85 (not in *CWMG*). It is interesting that Gandhi did approve of reconversion for converts to the former faith of their birth. See 'What Is Neutrality,' 30 Dec. 1939, *CM*, pp. 86-88, *CWMG*, LXXI, pp. 52-53.

12. 'An Address of Welcome Presented to Mahatma Mohandas Karamchand Gandhiji by the Indian Christian Community of Nandyal,' *DDM*, VI, 6 (June 1929), p. 13.

13. *Ibid.*, p. 13.

social problems of India. My love to my countrymen and my nationalism — they think — ought to be measured by my attitude to Congress or to political problems. No, I say my love to my country may be exercised through my ex-political work. If I labour to remove illiteracy, dirt, social enslavement and superstition of the neglected and the unprivileged or underprivileged — am I to be reckoned a foreigner with foreign sympathies with no love for my country? Should I be denounced as unpatriotic, simply because I am not dressed in a particular way or do not eat in a particular style or am not a member of a political party?

Azariah concluded by calling for a 'nationalism that will not be narrow, and will not lead to nationalistic egoism.'[14] But even in the 1920s, before his conflict with Gandhi, Azariah realized that a confrontation might be inevitable between Indian Christians — whose affiliations with the religion of empire were drawing intensified criticism — and India's nationalists.

The events that precipitated confrontation in the 1930s were set in motion by the British themselves as they gradually introduced parliamentary institutions and elective government to India. The British and Indian governments used communally based categories as the basis for organizing political reform in the late nineteenth and early twentieth centuries. Some limited and indirect elections and representation for different groups had been introduced in the last quarter of the nineteenth century; but the British introduced their first major constitutional innovation in 1909 when, under the Morley-Minto reforms, they instituted elections for an expanded number of seats on the Provincial and Central Legislative Councils. At this stage, separate electorates were introduced to protect the interests of various classes and interests, especially the Muslims who insisted on separate seats for Muslim constituencies and the right to vote in general constituencies (in all provinces except Bengal, where they were in the majority). Muslims and their British allies claimed that communal electorates — which guaranteed each definable community a predetermined level of political representation — were necessary to safeguard oppressed or underprivileged groups. Indian nationalists argued, in response, that the Raj was using communal electorates to bolster its own political position in India through a policy of 'divide and rule.'

Separate electorates were given to Indian Christians in 1919 as part of the next major phase of constitutional reform: the Montagu-Chelmsford

14. 'Extracts from Letters of Bishop Azariah, with an Introduction by the Bishop of Madras' (Madras, 1945), p. 29.

reforms. Separate electorates were also granted (or re-granted) to Muslims, Sikhs, Anglo-Indians, Europeans, Mahrattas in Bombay, and Non-Brahmins and Depressed Classes in Madras. However, limitations on the franchise kept the bulk of Azariah's converts from voting until greater rights were extended through the Government of India Act of 1935. Before this, on 4 August 1932, as a result of the deliberations in London of the Second Round Table Conference, the Government issued a Communal Award which granted separate electorates to almost every possible group, including Christians and Depressed Classes. The expanded numbers of Indians on the electoral rolls were now also increasingly divided according to their religious, caste, and economic status.[15]

These complex communally based political categories for electoral and employment procedures threatened to open up many barely submerged religious and caste fissures in national politics. Both Gandhi and Azariah opposed the separate electorates, but for different reasons: Gandhi did not want the depressed classes to be separated from his conceptualization of modern Hinduism; Azariah did not want Indian Christians to be separated from Indian society more generally. Ultimately, both men were forced to accept a compromise through the intervention of yet another untouchable leader, B. R. Ambedkar, who sought to defend and maximize separate representation for the depressed classes against Gandhi's efforts to keep them in the Hindu fold.

In this new political landscape, Indian Christians were distinguished from all other groups, including non-Christian depressed classes. Conversion instantly became a highly charged political as well as spiritual act. The mass movements now threatened to take substantial numbers, not just out of a new and increasingly organized modern Hinduism, but also off the Hindu electoral registers. Furthermore, depressed class converts to Christianity would lose all special privileges inherent to their former depressed class status; and caste converts would be grouped with former outcaste converts. Problems quickly emerged after the Congress Party gained control of the Legislature in the elections of 1937, problems that became more commonplace, complex, and troublesome after Independence. By 1939, Azariah described the emergence in his diocese of widespread communal discrimination in the matter of school fees and admissions which 'is rightly resented by all':

15. J. C. B. Webster, *A History of Dalit Christians in India* (San Francisco, 1992), pp. 73-119; J. Devasikamani, 'Separate Electorates Vs. Joint Electorates,' *Guardian*, XVIII, 9 (29 Feb. 1940), pp. 133-34.

Six boys seek admission to a Board School — all of the same economic status, with parents living on daily wages, and all of Harijan origin. Three have to pay fees because they are Christians, and three pay nothing because they are non-Christians! If this is not unfair communal and religious discrimination, what is? . . . We do not wish to call our Christians Harijans for the sake of concessions. We assert however that it is iniquitous to levy on the basis of the communal, and not on the economic status of the parents. Is it right for the son of an Hon. Minister to have full fee concession because he is a Harijan Hindu, and for the son of his peon, who until recently was a Harijan, to have to pay full fees, because the father has now become a Christian? This is surely religious partiality and communal favouritism, and [is] as bad as untouchability. Educational facilities given by Government should be certainly reckoned on an impartial basis, applicable alike to all, irrespective of caste or religion. The Hon. the Educational Minister argued that after three generations, converts ought to have been so absorbed into the Christian community, that any stigma of having belonged to the 'Harijans' should have disappeared by then. True: but the removal of the stigma does not make the convert prosperous. *Is it right for the Government to penalise conversion in this way?* Fee concessions must be given on the strength of poverty certificates and not on communal affinities. Here is an injustice unworthy of any government — much more of a Government professing to be national. The Brahman and the Harijan, the Christian and the Hindu, ought to be all treated impartially by a national Government.[16]

The effects of political reforms — some intended, others unexpected — changed the role of Christian missions in India and forced leaders such as Azariah into several contentious public policy debates. Previously, most Indian nationalists had cared little about Christian mission to the untouchables; it was, if anything, merely honorable charity work. Now that Indian Christians were placed in a separate electoral category, conversion from Hinduism (or other faiths) to Christianity (or other faiths) posed a more pressing political threat to the national movement, to Gandhi's leadership of the 'Harijans,' and therefore also to Gandhi's broad moral and political agenda.

Azariah and Gandhi united in battle against the British government's communally based political reforms of the 1930's, but before long Gandhi attacked Azariah with criticisms and innuendo, and even-

16. VSA, 'Fee Concessions for Harijans,' *Guardian,* XVII, 36-37 (14 and 21 Sept. 1939), p. 567. Italics mine.

tually he undermined the effectiveness of Azariah's missionary work in his diocese. An ill-conceived reconciliation effort by yet another group of unrealistic westerners exacerbated Azariah's problems and caused him publicly to defend Gandhi against his Christian missionary colleagues. This retreat marked a significant defeat for Azariah and for the Christian missionary enterprise, since it prevented them from engaging Gandhi in a clear public debate over issues of religious freedom that still plague India today.

Azariah and Gandhi Unite in Opposition to the Communal Award

Azariah and Gandhi both opposed British plans to divide the growing Indian electorate along communal lines. In the early 1930s, Gandhi had reached the high point of his career in India. His leadership of the civil disobedience campaign in 1930, with its brilliant attacks on the government's salt monopoly and the boycott of foreign cloth, had propelled him to the peak of his all-India political influence by early 1931. But his position rapidly eroded shortly thereafter at least partly because of his failure to win the allegiance on the subnational level of communalist Muslims and communalist Hindus.[17]

Gandhi failed to break the deadlock over minority demands for separate electorates at the Second Round Table Conference in London in September 1931. This prepared the way for the Labour government of Prime Minister Ramsay MacDonald to grant the separate communal electorate to the depressed classes in August 1932 for an experimental period of twenty years. Disagreements over the 'Communal Award' helped to eclipse the faltering civil disobedience movement and, by 1934, led Gandhi to withdraw from active party leadership in order to refocus his attentions on social and religious reform.[18] By contrast, the Communal Award brought Azariah increasingly, albeit reluctantly, into the political arena to address the problems and heightened communal tensions brought on by these changes.

17. Judith M. Brown, *Gandhi and Civil Disobedience: The Mahatma in Indian Politics, 1928-34* (Cambridge, 1977), pp. 382-89; *Gandhi: Prisoner of Hope* (New Haven and London, 1989), pp. 242-43, 247-77.

18. B. D. Graham, The Congress and Hindu Nationalism' (paper presented at the international conference '100 Years of the Indian National Congress,' Oxford, Nov. 1985), pp. 1-7.

41.-5
46
47
53, 57, 63, 66
68, 71, 73, 76, 79, 82, 3, 85.-90

95, 97, 100, 102, 104, 105, 106, 7, 9, 115
121, 123, 125, 129, 131, 134, 137, 159, 13
(147-8), 151, 2, 156, 160-1, 165-, 126, 8
187, 188, 190+, 194+, 198, 201, 203, -218-9

Part III
124, 235, 236+ -243, 84, 287,
245-247, 248, 261

296-7, 300, 316, 317, 326, 335, 338, 342-3
350-1, 356, 357, 359, 366.

By separating the electorate along caste and religious lines in a time when the franchise was expanding to include new voters and new electorates, the government threatened to undermine the Congress Party's already tenuous claim to represent the Indian nation rather than merely caste Hindus. Gandhi objected publicly to separate electorates on the religious grounds that they would divide Hinduism without solving untouchability, but privately he was more concerned about their political ramifications. As Gandhi's biographer, Judith Brown, has written:

> . . . the political implications of separate electorates were very important to him. Compounding separate electorates for Muslims, a similar concession to untouchables would shatter the united polity for which he had worked so long, and would cast Congress in the role of sectarian religious party rather than representative of an Indian nation. But he did not want to publicize this dimension of the problem for he felt it would only exacerbate communal conflict.[19]

A political crisis seemed imminent but was averted by the drastic measure of Gandhi's 'fast unto death' against separate electorates for untouchables that began on 20 September 1932.[20] Capitulation to Gandhi's suicide threat resulted in the Poona Pact negotiated with the Mahar leader, B. R. Ambedkar. By this agreement, separate electorates for depressed classes were abandoned and replaced by a system in which untouchables and caste Hindus were to vote jointly to elect untouchable candidates (who would be selected in primary elections among untouchables) to a total of 148 reserved seats in the provincial legislatures (twice as many seats as had been granted under the Communal Award).[21] Depressed class representatives would now serve in Legislative Councils as members of the 'Hindu community' — a newly conceived single entity or monolithic bloc which had expanded from the urban gentry of Calcutta, Madras, and Bombay to include more and more non-Muslim peoples, lower and lower castes, and more rural backgrounds.

Gandhi's fast helped to ensure the inclusion of the depressed classes within the powerful Hindu electorate, while other religious communities

19. Judith M. Brown, *Gandhi: Prisoner of Hope, op. cit.*, p. 265.

20. Although Gandhi justified his fast in religious terms, he was fully aware of its political implications. J. M. Brown, *Gandhi: Prisoner of Hope, op. cit.*, p. 265.

21. Ravinder Kumar, 'Gandhi, Ambedkar and the Poona Pact, 1932,' *JSAS*, VIII, 1-2, pp. 87-101. Eleanor Zelliot, 'Gandhi and Ambedkar — A Study in Leadership,' in *The Untouchables in Contemporary India*, ed. J. Michael Mahar (Tucson, AZ, 1972), pp. 69-95. Horace G. Alexander, *Untouchability and the Poona Agreement* (London, 1932).

such as Muslims, Sikhs, and Indian Christians were left within their own separate electoral categories. This 'co-opting by definition' of untouchables into the Hindu fold was greatly resented by many untouchable leaders.[22] There was now growing competition for depressed class political allegiance, and this raised the potential danger that Christian evangelism and its mass conversions of untouchables might be used as political instruments. Gandhi stepped up attacks on Christian missions, implying that their work was secretly political because it was stealing Harijans from the Hindu fold. This propelled Bishop Azariah into a heated debate with the Mahatma over the extent and legitimacy of mass conversions among depressed classes.

The Indian Christian community, especially its Protestant branch, was widely opposed to the 1932 Communal Award.[23] Bishop Azariah had earlier testified before the Simon Commission that communal electorates did not serve the interests of either Christianity or Christians; he advocated merging Indian Christians into the general electorate (with reservation of seats for the community only if absolutely necessary).[24] In addition to allying the interests of Indian Christians with those of the nation as a whole, inclusion of Indian Christians in general constituencies would help to prevent discrimination against Indian Christians on religious grounds. As it was, conversion to Christianity disqualified the still-poor and underprivileged mass movement converts from Depressed Class benefits. In his testimony, Azariah criticized the Education and Labour Departments of the Madras government for denying scholarship aid to untouchables who converted to Christianity, arguing that 'religion should not become a disqualification. It is the social and economic condition that ought to determine it.'[25]

Although the bishop apparently condemned Gandhi's 1932 fast,[26] he played a major role along with Gandhi in the opposition to the 1932 Award, moving away from his previously apolitical stance to join in battle with more active Indian Christian nationalists such as S. K. Datta, an In-

---

22. R. E. Frykenberg, 'Caste, Morality and Western Religion under the Raj: A Review Article,' draft copy from author.

23. See particularly 'The Communal Award' and 'Indian Christians and the Communal Award,' *Guardian*, X, 29 (25 Aug. 1932), pp. 342-43 and 349-50 respectively; and 'The Position of Indian Christians,' *Guardian*, X, 34 (29 Sept. 1932), p. 401.

24. 'Madras and Provincial Autonomy,' *Times*, March 1928, in Clippings Album, Azariah Collection, Madras.

25. Quoted in J. C. B. Webster, *op. cit.*, pp. 86-87.

26. D. Packiamuthu, *Valikāṭṭi*, *op. cit.*, Act III, Scene 3.

dian Christian representative at the second Round Table Conference in London.[27] Azariah's first public move was a forceful statement to the English press which argued against separate electorates — seeing them as a divisive force within both the Indian Christian community and the nation as a whole.[28] Separate electorates, he protested, would encourage Indian Christians to become a separate communal body with self-centered, inward-focused political ambitions. Such an outcome would undermine his objective of identifying Indian Christians with the aspirations of a prospectively independent and politically unified, though culturally pluralistic, Indian nation. 'We have permitted ourselves not to be placed on the side of the whole country or the nation, but on the side of a religious sect, a community which seeks self-protection for the sake of its own loaves and fishes,' he wrote.[29] Factional caste allegiances which, in keeping with Christian teaching, were submerged by the experience of common life and worship would inevitably resurface during election battles, Azariah argued. Candidates would appeal to fragmentary caste and denominational loyalties in order to win votes.

> I am not imagining the impossible; all this has happened before. Peace in many congregations has been wrecked in the past because of Legislative Council elections. Congregations that had lived in peace and unity under one pastor worshipping in one Church, though originally of different caste origins, have been by the elections torn to pieces along caste lines to the great harm of all religion and piety — harm that takes years to mend.[30]

The greater national interest would be damaged if communal identities were stressed to the detriment of more important qualities of merit and

27. Datta replaced the recently deceased K. T. Paul, representative of the All-India Conference of Indian Christians at the first Round Table Conference. J. C. B. Webster, 'Christians and the Depressed Classes Movement in the 1930's: The Crucial Decade' (paper presented to the 'Seminar on Aspects of the Economy, Society and Politics in Modern India, 1900-1950,' New Delhi, 15-18 Dec. 1980), p. 7 (hereafter, *Seminar Paper*; this paper was published in *Economy, Society and Politics in Modern India*, ed. D. N. Panigrahi [New Delhi, 1985], pp. 313-44); C. S. Milford, *Church and Crisis in India* (London, 1945), pp. 22-26; *History of Christianity in India: Source Materials*, ed. M. K. Kuriakose (Madras, 1982), pp. 351-56.

28. VSA, 'The Communal Award,' *Guardian*, X, 31 (8 Sept. 1932), p. 368. Reprinted in *DDM*, IX, 10 (Oct. 1932), pp. 10-13.

29. *Ibid.*

30. *Ibid.*

ability in the determination of political processes and outcomes. However, the most ominous implication of the new policy for the bishop was its potentially negative impact upon the church's efforts to destroy sectarian boundaries and create an inclusive, cross-cultural 'gospel' community through its evangelistic program.

> The religion of Christ . . . refuses to be confined to any one race, class or caste. It seeks to embrace all. It is most true to itself when it refuses to be restricted by human fear or prejudice; if it ever becomes petrified and static, it is dead! The inclusion of Christians in 'a communal award' is a direct blow to the nature of the Church of Christ.[31]

Under the first electoral system proposed (before the Poona Pact), members of the depressed classes would lose their unique double voting privileges (along with other government benefits) at baptism.

> The Government in recent years has been showing special favours to the Non-Christian Depressed Classes — favours which are denied to their brethren who have become Christians. The Award itself affords an illustration of this partiality. The Depressed Class voter (who has not changed his religion) has two votes — one in a special constituency and the other in the general electorate. His Christian brother however must be content with one vote and he must vote for the Christian candidate only. . . . The Award puts serious strain on his loyalty to the Christian religion.[32]

The Poona Pact eliminated the double voting privilege, but it did not include Christians in the general electorate, and in most elections caste converts had to vote for Christian candidates of untouchable background. Although caste and outcaste converts shared the same religion, Azariah argued, they did not share the same social and political interests. The problems of caste converts 'are those of the farmer and the capitalist, not those of labour!'[33]

31. *Ibid.*
32. *Ibid.*
33. *Ibid.* In this article, Azariah estimated that about 25,000 caste members had converted to Christianity in the previous decade. Henry Whitehead had earlier likened the mass movements of untouchables to the English labour movement, both of which he described as uprisings 'of the underprivileged in the determination to claim the place due to them as human beings.' See William Paton, *Christianity in the Eastern Conflicts, op. cit.*, p. 77.

Immediately following the termination of Gandhi's 'epic fast,' the Mahatma asked Azariah — through a deputation from the Christa Seva Sangha, a Christian ashram in Poona — to lead a nationwide, interdenominational effort to revoke the separate electorates for Indian Christians. In response, on October 6, Azariah published a second plea to Christians for united action against the Communal Award and in favor of joint electorates.[34] Next, he called together a meeting of the All-India Christian Conference at Poona in late October, which produced an agreed-upon policy of cooperative efforts among leaders of Hindu, Muslim, Christian, and other communities to establish a joint electorate for all.[35] Azariah's vocal opposition failed to stop separate electorates, which remained in effect until after Independence,[36] but he continued his unavailing protests throughout the remaining years of his life. In a 1938 address to the clergy in Dornakal Diocese, Azariah charged:

> The civic interests of the Indian Christians are not different from those of other communities. We are as much people of India as any others. We ought to have had the privilege of voting in the General Electorate, and all the members so elected ought to be the guardians of our interests as well as those of any others; we are one with our non-Christian brethren. . . . It is therefore the duty of all Indian Christians

34. As a temporary measure, he accepted proposals for reserved seats in a general electorate but concluded: 'At the very least under the present system, Indian Christians should have the liberty to vote in the general electorate by choice.' 'Indian Christians and the Communal Award,' *Guardian*, X, 35 (6 Oct. 1932), p. 415.

35. J. C. Winslow, 'The Christa Seva Sanghva,' *DDM*, X, 3 (March 1933), pp. 8-9. Azariah did not attend the Poona Conference, but rather chose to fulfil prior episcopal duties in the diocese; specifically a confirmation tour which, he explained, could not be canceled without considerable inconvenience to scores of villages. His absence was interpreted by the *Madras Mail* and the *Times of India* as a 'defection' from his position against the Communal Award. This charge, which Azariah refuted immediately, appears to have been part of a campaign by supporters of separate electorates to belittle the importance of the Poona Conference, which, it was believed, had been 'packed' with advocates of joint electorates. In fact, those favoring separate electorates were well represented at the conference by groups from Poona and Ahmednagar. See VSA, 'The Bishop of Dornakal and the Poona Conference,' *Guardian*, X, 40 (10 Nov. 1932), p. 475. Also 'Poona Christian Conference,' *Guardian*, X, 39 (3 Nov. 1932), p. 463; 'Bishops and Politics,' *Guardian*, X, 40 (10 Nov. 1932), p. 474.

36. Separate communal electorates were abolished in accordance with Articles 325 and 326 of the Constitution of India. Abraham V. Thomas, *Christians in Secular India* (Rutherford, NJ, 1974), p. 73.

not to rest until this great disability is removed at the next favourable opportunity.[37]

The bishop was never an enthusiastic advocate of the later 'Quit India' phase of the independence movement. He wrote: 'With trembling conviction, Indian Christians see that they must be on the side of India's freedom,' but he opposed 'civil disobedience . . . non-cooperation and . . . rebellion' as means for achieving *swaraj*.[38] However, Azariah's popular reputation as a nationalist was greatly reinforced by this earlier conflict over the electoral system. A broader, non-Christian audience discovered him as a forceful figure seeking to break down the barriers between the Indian Christian community and the nation at large.[39]

The Breakdown of Consensus

Azariah's and Gandhi's alliance in opposition to the Communal Award was shattered by the destabilizing consequences of the Award itself, which became progressively more apparent by the mid-1930s. The provisions of the Award were incorporated in the Government of India Act of 1935, which greatly increased Indian self-government on the provincial level, expanded some reforms at the Center, and extended the franchise to 30,000,000 Indian voters. The age of political democratization in India, which had begun in earnest with the Government of India Act of 1919, was now fully underway. The elections of 1937 gave Congress control over nine provincial governments in India, although this era of regional self-determination ended prematurely with the outbreak of war in 1939.

The new electoral arrangements made conversion, or more often the

37. VSA, 'Our Duty as Citizens,' *DDM*, XV, 2 (Feb. 1938), p. 6; see also VSA, 'Christians and the New Government: Bishop of Dornakal's Call for Support,' *op. cit.* (1938), pp. 86-87 (and in *MDM*, XXXIII, 3 [Feb. 1938], pp. 60-62). For other examples of his later statements on the subject, see VSA, *India and the Christian Movement, op. cit.* (1935), pp. 106-7; 'The Bishop's New Year Letter,' *DDM*, XIII, 1 (Jan. 1936), pp. 8-11; 'Bishop of Dornakal on Communal Representation,' *Guardian*, XIV, 16 (16 April 1936), p. 249; and 'The Bishop's Letter,' *DDM*, XIV, 5 (May 1937), pp. 3-4.

38. 'Bishop of Dornakal on the Indian Situation,' *Guardian*, XX, 37 (17 Sept. 1942), p. 436. Also 'The Indian Christian and Politics,' *Guardian*, XX, 40 (8 Oct., 1942), p. 478, for a clarification of his views regarding Christians' responsibility towards the state, in response to a critique by R. M. Chetsingh in the previous issue.

39. 'The Late Bishop of Dornakal,' *Guardian*, XXIII, 1 (4 Jan. 1945), pp. 2, 8.

threat of conversion, a powerful political tool for depressed class leaders to gain concessions from dominant caste groups. Threats of conversion made in western India by B. R. Ambedkar (first in 1935)[40] and in Travancore by leaders of the Izhava community (especially in 1936)[41] gained widespread attention during this period. Azariah, as a committed and well-known evangelist and senior native churchman, encouraged each of these movements and thereby placed himself in a position of direct opposition to Gandhi and the Hindu nationalists with whom he had formerly been allied.

In a much publicized declaration at the Yeola Conference of October 1935, Ambedkar announced that he would lead a mass movement of his depressed class followers out of Hinduism into a religion committed to social equality. This threat was perceived by most Christian leaders, including Azariah, as a political maneuver designed to gain social, economic, and political advantage for his movement rather than as an authentic religious statement.[42] Azariah wrote:

> religion is not a matter that can be adopted or changed by fifty million people at the behest of a leader, however influential he may be. Nor would there be any spiritual gain to the followers from a religion so adopted. The end of religion is not social uplift, but knowledge of God and union with God. It is of course certain that a true religion will bring social uplift, because it will unite men to God who is Father of us all.[43]

The response of the church, including even those within it most favorable to mass movement work, to Ambedkar's declaration was therefore cautious, with Christians playing a relatively minor role in the subsequent inter-faith competition for depressed class allegiance.[44]

40. Dhananjay Keer, *Dr. Ambedkar: Life and Mission* (3rd ed., Bombay, 1971), pp. 242-79.

41. J. W. Gladstone, *Protestant Christianity and People's Movements in Kerala 1850-1936, op. cit.,* pp. 356-74.

42. 'The Question of the Depressed Classes,' *Guardian,* XIV, 23 (4 June 1936), p. 354.

43. 'The Bishop's Letter,' *DDM,* XII, 12 (Dec. 1935), p. 3. Also, 'The Bishop of Dornakal on Dr. Ambedkar's Declaration,' *Guardian,* XIII, 50 (12 Dec. 1935), pp. 791, 793.

44. Mass movement advocate J. W. Pickett expressed skepticism about Ambedkar's making religion an 'element of barter,' and urged a hesitant Azariah to approach Ambedkar personally about the decision. See J. W. Pickett, *The Movement among the Depressed Classes in India* (New York, 12 June 1936). See also J. C. B. Webster, *Seminar Paper,* pp. 13-15.

Azariah's assessment of Ambedkar's motive for seeking a new faith was also informed, however, by a broad understanding of Christian history in which tribes and even entire nations had been converted *en masse* at the behest of political leaders acting with 'impure' motives.[45] Azariah was therefore not willing to discount the importance of Ambedkar's action, nor the possibility that his seemingly political defection from modern India's newly invented brand of monolithic Hinduism, like other spiritually ambiguous events in history, might play a positive, even providential role in the Christianization of India.

In a series of articles published in the *National Christian Council Review* in 1935, the bishop noted that the Christian faith was able to expand during its first three centuries in part because of the 'political preparation' effected by the conquests of Alexander the Great and the Roman Empire. He argued that similar political circumstances in twentieth-century India ('the occupation of India by a Christian nation . . . the spread of English education, the establishment of mission colleges, the conversion of the long despised outcastes, and the social uplift that has resulted from it') might be part of a providential plan of God to bring his countrymen into the Christian church, despite the many problems posed by mass conversions for an often ill-prepared church.[46]

45. Even before the conversion of Constantine in the year 312, conversion 'from above' had made Edessa the first state with Christianity as its official religion by the end of the second century, followed by Armenia near the end of the third century. See K. S. Latourette, *A History of the Expansion of Christianity: The First Five Centuries* (London, 1947), pp. 101-6, 223-24. Azariah used the example of Armenia to illustrate dangers inherent to mass movements in 'The Bishop's Letter,' *DDM,* XI, 10 (Oct. 1934), pp. 1-3. On Constantine's conversion, see A. H. M. Jones, *Constantine and the Conversion of Europe* (Middlesex, 1962). Jones concludes that the Emperor's dominant motive was the achievement of worldly power and that his conversion was not a 'spiritual experience' insofar as Constantine 'knew and cared nothing for the metaphysical and ethical teaching of Christianity when he became a devotee of the Christian God' (p. 105).

46. VSA, 'The Expansion of Christianity in India,' *NCCR,* LV, 2-7 (Feb.-July 1935). Published under the title *The Church and Evangelism, op. cit.* (1936). See pp. 35-37. The principal problem involved provision to largely uneducated converts of adequate instruction for baptism and, eventually, for confirmation. According to guidelines set by the NCC in 1937, catechetical preparation for baptism in mass movement areas was supposed to include instruction on the life of Christ, the cardinal doctrines of Christianity, Christian ethics, and the sacraments of baptism and the Lord's Supper. Converts were also instructed to make certain changes in lifestyle before baptism (to reject caste, idolatry, and non-Christian marriages), to observe faithfully the Lord's Day, and to profess their acceptance of Christ as Savior and Lord. See 'The Bishop's Letter,' *DDM,* XIV, 4 (April 1937), pp. 1-4. To achieve and maintain such high standards re-

To those who criticized mass movements for bringing in more people than the church could handle, Azariah responded, 'At Pentecost they baptized three thousand people in one day.'[47] He agreed with Bishop Pickett, author of the 1933 mass movement study, that group conversions were the most 'natural' way for India,[48] and campaigned vigorously in the West for assistance with the mass movement work.[49] In 1937, Azariah estimated that the rate of church growth would double in the Dornakal diocese if more workers and financial support could be made available for the instruction of catechumens.[50]

Azariah recognized the sociopolitical dimensions of Ambedkar's efforts for the depressed classes and of reformist Hindu campaigns against untouchability, but saw them as reflections of God's activity on behalf of the oppressed:

> Has the momentous declaration of the Harijans of Western India no meaning for us — that all the so-called 'depressed class people' should abandon Hinduism and seek a religion in which they will have equality of status and a chance for self-development? The social service organizations, the Harijan uplift movement, the demand for Temple entry to all, the attempts to reform social evils — may not all these be so many signs of the moving of the Spirit of God?[51]

Azariah was not trying to steer the church away from evangelism and into politics by distinguishing between 'materially' motivated conversion and conversion by spiritual conviction. Rather, he argued that in the 1930s, political and social forces external to the church had unwittingly created a unique opportunity for new mass conversions. In a 1937 letter to John Mott, Azariah identified three factors contributing to this new evan-

---

quired the availability of trained teachers and ordained clergy who were willing to work in restrictive village circumstances over long periods of time. In Dornakal Diocese, Azariah attempted to limit the expansion of the church to the availability of teaching and oversight capabilities ('The Bishop's Letter,' *DDM*, XI, 10 (Oct. 1934), p. 1), and the standard of achievement for converts in his diocese was reported to be high relative to other mass movement areas, especially in the United Provinces. See J. W. Pickett, *Christian Mass Movements in India, op. cit.,* pp. 338-41, 348-50.

47. 'The Bishop's Letter,' *DDM*, XIII, 6 (June 1936), p. 4. (Cf. Acts 2:41).

48. VSA, *India and the Christian Movement, op. cit.* (1935), p. 76.

49. His appeals for men and money are well documented in Clippings Album, Azariah Collection, Madras.

50. VSA, 'India: A Present Urgent Opportunity,' *op. cit.* (1937), pp. 541-45.

51. VSA, *The Church and Evangelism, op. cit.,* pp. 36-37.

gelistic opportunity: (i) political ambitions generated by the 1935 Government of India Act, (ii) the universal spirit of nationalism producing new social unrest aimed at changing existing authorities and traditions, and (iii) striking examples of Christian under-class uplift. These factors combined to produce 'Public anti-Hindu declarations of recent years by whole classes of people' — in particular, the Mahars (led by Ambedkar) and Izhavas. Azariah believed that the new situation created a favorable evangelistic opportunity 'unsought, unprompted and uncreated by us' which Christian missionaries should nevertheless utilize.[52]

Primarily through his presidency of the NCC, Azariah became the leading spokesman for the Indian Christian establishment in its development of an appropriate strategy of outreach to depressed classes in search of a new religion. In January 1936, the bishop issued a 'Call to the Church' on behalf of the NCC, urging Christians to redouble their missionary efforts in light of the 'widespread and deep unrest among the depressed classes . . . [which] . . . constitutes a Call of God to the Christian Church which it cannot ignore.'[53]

Azariah also published a statement in response to Ambedkar describing the benefits Christianity had obtained for untouchables.[54] In his *Open Letter to Our Countrymen Who Are Classified as Belonging to the Depressed Classes,* Azariah affirmed that the new religion had 'lifted us socially . . . raised our womanhood . . . removed the customs and habits that have been the causes of our past degradation,' such as drink, and given converts new self-respect.[55] Fortified by such an understanding of Christianity's beneficent social influence, Christians should 'testify boldly to what Christ has done to us and seek to win those that are now on the look out for a new religion.'[56]

Azariah privately circulated an additional encyclical to heads of

52. VSA to Mott, 2 Feb. 1937, 1: 4/61, Mott Papers, YDS.

53. 'A Call to the Church,' *DDM,* XIII, 2 (Feb. 1936), pp. 2-4.

54. Hodge to Paton, 1 Nov. 1935, and Hodge to Paton, 11 Sept. 1936, Box 396, NCCC, IMC/CBMS, SOAS.

55. VSA, *An Open Letter to Our Countrymen Who Are Classified as Belonging to the Depressed Classes* (Dornakal, n.d.), in English and Telugu. English copy in Box: Pamphlets (Old) 275, SOCA. Published also by the Foreign Missions Conference of North America, New York, 1936, with 'A Note of Explanation' by A. L. Warnshuis; copy in I: 4/61, Mott Papers, YDS. See also *YMI, B&C,* XLVIII, 9 (Oct. 1936), pp. 253-54, and 'What Christ Has Done for Untouchables,' *MRW,* LX (March 1937), pp. 131-32.

56. VSA, 'Duty of Indian Christian Electors,' *Guardian,* XIV, 3 (16 Jan. 1936), p. 44.

churches and missions urging vigorous witness-bearing to the untouchables but stressing the new and heavy pedagogical responsibilities that mass conversions would place on the churches.[57] This letter expressed again the widespread view that, although the motives for conversion of the depressed classes were 'mixed,' they were nonetheless *bona fide* 'salvation' movements in view of the oppressive nature of the caste system.

> He who used the Egyptian bondage, the Babylonian captivity, and (in the parable) the physical hunger of the prodigal — may in these latter days use the tyranny of the Indian caste system to make the fifty millions rise up and go to the Father in whose service there is perfect freedom.[58]

Depressed class protest in the 1930s was frequently likened to earlier movements of untouchables to Christianity and to other religions in Indian history: Islam, Sikhism, and the Arya Samaj variety of Hindu reform. With the exception of certain elements from among the educated urban Indian Christian elite,[59] Azariah was joined by most of the Christian establishment in contending that evangelism to depressed class leaders and their followers was as legitimate a project in the 1930s as it had been in previous, less politically charged times. The results of Pickett's study quelled remaining doubts within the NCC.

An evangelistic campaign was independently planned and initiated by the NCC before Ambedkar made his 1935 declaration.[60] In April 1935, the Council's Executive Committee launched a five-year 'Forward Move-

---

57. VSA, *Statement to All Heads of Church and Missions* (for private circulation only) (Dornakal, May 1936); draft and printed copies in Box 395, NCCC, IMC/CBMS, SOAS.

58. *Ibid.*

59. Some from both high-caste and untouchable backgrounds resented the scandalous embarrassment of being identified with the *en masse* entry into the church of illiterate, ill-mannered, unconverted, and uncatechized outcastes. J. W. Pickett, *Christian Mass Movements in India, op. cit.,* pp. 315-18.

60. K. Baago, *A History of the National Christian Council of India, 1914-1964, op. cit.,* pp. 50-60. The new zeal for evangelism which characterized the work of the NCC throughout the 1930s was, according to Baago, due to the following factors: (i) the influence of theological trends in Europe and America, especially in relation to Karl Barth and Reinhold Niebuhr, (ii) the example of evangelistic movements in Japan and China, and (iii) the leadership of Azariah and NCC Secretary J. Z. Hodge, 'who were both on fire for the evangelistic work of the Church.' See also C. B. G. Chambers, 'A Five Year Programme of Evangelism, 1936-1940,' *DDM*, XIII, 8 (Aug. 1936), pp. 7-12; and 'The Bishop's Letter,' *DDM*, X, 2 (Feb. 1933), pp. 1-6.

ment in Evangelism' program.[61] As chairman of both the governing Executive Committee and an advisory planning committee established in the previous year, Azariah played a leading role in crafting this project. Its central features — an annual 'week of witness' and an emphasis upon ongoing local, church-based missions in preference to 'spectacular' traveling crusades — echoed Azariah's previous strategies for the Dornakal diocese.[62]

To combat rising suspicion that there were political motives for Christian evangelism, the NCC argued that it had launched the movement without any intention of increasing the Christian community's political or communal rights. 'It is unfortunate that such a religious classification for political purposes is imposed upon us under existing circumstances. We are not for such privileges and we wish our fellow-Christians would never advance their claims upon religious census figures.'[63] The NCC Council argued that its mission to and for the depressed classes was inspired only by pan-communal and pan-Indian patriotism.[64]

Ultimately, Azariah had more confidence in the effectiveness of long-term, ecclesiastically based missionary endeavors than in the superficial promise that untouchables might be brought *en masse* into the church by the persuasive power of any political leader.[65] This view was reinforced with ironic consequences in 1936 after a personal interview with Ambedkar which deeply embarrassed and disturbed Azariah, and plunged him back into renewed efforts at ecumenism and reform within the church. Ambedkar criticized the church for denominational disunity which impeded the political objectives of the untouchables *en bloc*, as well

61. 'Forward Movement in Evangelism,' *Guardian*, XIII, 29 (July 18, 1935), pp. 455, 458; also in *DDM*, XII, 7 (July 1935), pp. 9-13.

62. The object of the evangelistic movement was 'to call the churches of Christ to this primary duty of the Church to witness for Christ.' *Ibid.*, p. 458.

63. *Ibid.*, p. 458.

64. 'When India is rising to a new national life, how can Christians remain quiet, who know fully well that Christ is indispensable in this time of renaissance and all the problems of this great continent can find solution only in and through Jesus Christ.' *Ibid.*, p. 458.

65. As was apparent in his writings on the centrality of the church's role in Christian mission. See especially 'The Place of the Church in Evangelism,' in *op. cit.* (1939), pp. 32-47. Azariah's assertion of this theme at the Tambaram conference of 1938 marked a pivotal moment in the history of Christian mission, when 'it was firmly and decisively affirmed that mission is the responsibility of the whole Church,' rather than merely of the missionary societies. See Bishop Lesslie Newbigin, 'A Sermon Preached at the Thanksgiving Service for the Fiftieth Anniversary of the Tambaram Conference of the International Missionary Council — 1938' (Jan. 1988), manuscript copy from the author.

as for the persistence within it of caste prejudice. Azariah recalled later that Ambedkar asked him the question: 'If we become Christians can we all be united in one Church wherever we live? And will we be entirely free from all Caste prejudice?' To which Azariah responded: 'I have never felt so ashamed in my life because I couldn't say YES to either question — I could only come away in disgrace.'[66] Azariah often recalled Ambedkar's criticism of Christianity when seeking support in his later years for the unification of churches in South India

Ambedkar's declaration created much anticipation that there would be mass depressed class conversions, but it did not significantly influence those communities in South India already inclining towards Christianity, such as the Malas, Madigas, or Izhavas. The church in the Dornakal diocese continued to grow at a steady pace, but without dramatic increase in 1936 and 1937.[67] Despite two depressed class gatherings in his bishopric affirming Ambedkar's declaration, Azariah noted that 'the Diocese cannot be said to have come under the spell of Dr. Ambedkar.'[68]

66. C. Graham, *Azariah of Dornakal, op. cit.,* p. 101. Azariah personally related his recollections of the meeting to Graham. As she recalled in 1985: 'Having waited to see what Dr. Ambedkar would do next, when nothing happened Azariah wrote and asked Ambedkar for an interview, which was immediately granted' (Graham to author, 16 March 1985, Farnham). The interview was also described to this author by Azariah's daughter, Grace Aaron (interview, 24-26 Sept. 1985, Ottawa, Ontario, Canada); and by Azariah's son, Ambrose Azariah (interview, 23 March 1986, Madras).

Ambedkar's subsequent long delay in deciding which new religion to adopt (he eventually converted to Buddhism) provoked Azariah to write privately in 1938 that Ambedkar '. . . has not moved one inch since I saw him in 1936; if at all, he has moved in the direction of politics.' Azariah favored dropping the issue of conversion with Ambedkar and criticized Pickett and American evangelist E. Stanley Jones for continuing their efforts and making 'fools of themselves.' Hodge to Paton, 11 March, 1938, Box 396, NCCC, IMC/CBMS, SOAS.

67. Diocesan statistics revealed the following growth:

	1934	1935	1936	1937
Total Christian community	191,342	200,656	211,075	215,486
Number of baptisms	11,685	11,017	11,401	10,038
Number of catechumens	38,955	42,051	42,453	42,961

See 'The Standing Committee,' *DDM,* XIII, 10 (Oct. 1936), pp. 5; 'The Bishop's Letter,' *DDM,* XV, 3 (March 1938), p. 1.

68. 'The Standing Committee,' *DDM,* XIII, 10 (Oct. 1936), pp. 4-5. Archdeacon Emmet in the Nandyal area of the Dornakal diocese also reported that Dr. Ambedkar's pronouncement 'has scarcely affected this area.' However, the lack of non-Christian

The Izhavas of Travancore, who had hitherto perplexed missionaries by refusing to join the Nadars (their equivalent caste in Tamil country) in their mass movement to Christianity, had been considering conversion ever since the death in 1928 of their charismatic leader and social reformer, Narayana Guru. But their 1936 resolutions to convert *en masse* to Christianity apparently bore no trace of Ambedkar's direct influence. Several decades of growing communal consciousness under the influence of the Narayana Guru movement (which sought religious and social uplift through education) seems to have heightened the Izhavas' recognition of their own relative deprivation within the Hindu fold and to have independently created favorable conditions for new conversions.[69]

Azariah assisted in leading the missionary response to Izhava unrest by visiting Travancore in February 1936 for four Izhava meetings (attended by 500 to 800 people each), during which the community's leaders denied that their actions were related to Ambedkar's Mahar movement in western India.[70] As Azariah traveled, he urged churchmen, missionaries, and Izhava leaders to evangelize more aggressively. The *Dornakal Diocesan Magazine* noted in April that the Mar Thoma Church and the Church of India, Burma, and Ceylon in Travancore had arranged to send two hundred workers to evangelize the Izhavas. The June issue carried a special prayer for the conversion of the Izhava community, along with a vigorous defense by Azariah of Christian mission to depressed class groups in response to critics both inside and outside the church.[71]

Azariah thus refused to slow down, let alone stop, his energetic mission to the depressed classes. This brought him into direct conflict with

---

Adi-Andhra leaders may have contributed to this outcome. He also observed a general apathy on the part of Sikhs, Muslims, and 'Sudra masters in the villages' toward the challenge posed by the depressed classes. *DDM*, XIV, 8 (Aug. 1937), p. 17.

69. VSA, 'The Bishop's Letter,' *DDM*, XIII, 11 (Nov. 1936), pp. 1-4; J. W. Gladstone, *Protestant Christianity and People's Movements in Kerala*, in *op. cit.*, pp. 356-74; D. B. Forrester, 'The Depressed Classes and Conversion to Christianity,' in *op. cit.*, pp. 54-56; and *Caste and Christianity: Attitudes and Policies on Caste of Anglo-Saxon Protestant Missions in India* (London, 1980), pp. 85-86.

70. VSA, 'The Bishop's Letter,' *DDM*, XIII, 11 (Nov. 1936), pp. 1-4; J. W. Gladstone, *op. cit.*, pp. 367-68. Azariah's report contradicts Eleanor Mae Zelliot's claim that the Izhavas were among those few depressed class groups which supported Ambedkar's move. E. M. Zelliot, 'Dr. Ambedkar and the Mahar Movement' (University of Pennsylvania, 1969), p. 209; cited in J. C. B. Webster, *Seminar Paper*, p. 13.

71. *DDM*, XIII, 4 (April 1936), pp. 16-17; 'The Bishop's Letter,' *DDM*, XIII, 6 (June 1936), pp. 1-5.

Gandhi, who by now was deeply hostile to Azariah's evangelism. Gandhi refused Azariah's repeated invitations to visit Dornakal to observe Christian work among the untouchables firsthand,[72] and became Azariah's most powerful and vehement critic.

The Mahatma's popular and carefully cultivated political image as champion of the depressed classes had been greatly enhanced by his 'epic fast' of 1932, his 1933-34 tour on behalf of the Harijan Sevak Sangh (Order for the Service of Harijans), and his widely read columns in the *Harijan* that began to appear on 11 February 1933. His claim to be the sole spokesman for the 'suppressed' classes in India was not seriously challenged during the period from 1932 to 1935. His concentration on temple entry bills in both the Madras legislature and the Central Legislative Assembly and on the activity of the Harijan Sevak Sangh gained for his politicized anti-untouchability movement the support of numerous Christian periodicals, such as the *Guardian,* the *National Christian Council Review,* and the *Indian Witness* (a Methodist weekly in Lucknow reflecting missionary opinion). Azariah himself credited Gandhi in 1939 for having 'revolutionized the attitude of India's thinking men and women towards untouchability.'[73]

Gandhi's activities were followed attentively by other depressed class leaders, such as Ambedkar, who jealously wondered if Gandhi's movement was simply an effective power play for mobilizing mass rural support and moral credibility.[74] Despite his differences of opinion with Christian missionaries over the legitimacy of conversion and baptism, Gandhi used relatively little anti-missionary rhetoric during the early 1930s and tended to blame depressed class conversions on the oppressive practices of Hindus.[75]

This situation of relative peace disintegrated in the mid-1930s as the implications of the constitutional reforms became apparent, and Christian leaders found themselves forced to defend missionary motives in a newly politicized context where they faced fresh challenges over the nature of religious loyalty.[76] In 1936 and 1937, Gandhi's criticisms of Chris-

---

72. K. Heiberg, *V. S. Azariah: Biskop af Dornakal, op. cit.,* p. 98.

73. VSA, 'Mahatma Gandhi's Seventieth Birthday: Bishop of Dornakal's Tribute,' *Guardian,* XVII, 36 and 37 (14 and 21 Sept. 1939), p. 577.

74. As Azariah phrased it, 'Opinions may differ as to the method Mr. Gandhi has followed in attacking the evil (untouchability): All may not agree — even of the classes benefited — in the results achieved.' *Ibid.*

75. J. C. B. Webster, *Seminar Paper,* pp. 7-12.

76. *Ibid.,* pp. 13-15. Also 'The Bishop's Letter,' *DDM,* XII, 11 (Nov. 1935), p. 3.

tian missionary activity increased in both frequency and bitterness. (He rarely mentioned the activities of Muslims or Sikhs.[77]) His specific charges focused on the allegedly unfair methods and exaggerated claims of Christian missionaries. These widely publicized indictments frequently drew on the reports of A. V. Thakkar, an opponent of Christian conversion who was both Secretary of the Harijan Sevak Sangh and a member of the Servants of India Society.[78]

Several of the charges published in the *Harijan* were directed specifically against Azariah and the evangelistic work within his diocese. Gandhi accused Azariah of falsely exaggerating the number of people in his diocese coming forward for baptism. Quoting from a CMS pamphlet which claimed that 'In the CMS area of the Dornakal Diocese there are no less than three hundred villages appealing for teachers; they represent forty thousand people definitely asking for baptism. The Bishop reckons that probably about a million people in his diocese are moving Christward'; Gandhi responded, 'Though I have traveled in the Telugu area often enough I have never heard of forty thousand Harijans asking for baptism or any figure near it.'[79] Gandhi also challenged the validity of similar claims made by both Bishop Pickett in Bombay and the CMS concerning the nature and scale of untouchable and low-caste movements in the Telugu area and in Travancore.[80] But Gandhi saw the Indian Azariah as a particularly vulnerable target and accused him of dishonorably offering

77. J. C. B. Webster, *Seminar Paper, op. cit.*, p. 16. See also *The Collected Works of Mahatma Gandhi* (hereafter *CWMG*), LXIV, pp. x-xi, and LXV, pp. ix-x, where Gandhi's opposition to conversion is described in the context of Christianity only.

78. See, e.g., a few accusations from the *Harijan* in 1937: 'The Cow and the Harijan,' 13 March, *CM*, pp. 58-60, *CWMG*, LXIV, pp. 440-41; 'An Unfortunate Document,' 3 April, *CM*, pp. 75-83, *CWMG*, LXV, pp. 47-48 (*CM* version more complete); 'Our Partial Sight,' 17 April, *CM*, pp. 74-45, *CWMG*, LXV, p. 96; 'Conversion for Convenience' and 'The Social Bait,' 12 June, *CM*, pp. 61, 67-68, *CWMG*, LXV, pp. 295-96 (latter article only); 'How They Convert,' 19 June, *CM*, pp. 63-66, *CWMG*, LXV, pp. 316-18 (*CM* version more complete); 'Four Questions,' 25 Sept., *CM*, pp. 84-85, *CWMG*, LXVI, pp. 163-64.

Thakkar's reports and Gandhi's comments were described and criticized in the *Guardian* (Madras). See 'Reports about Conversion,' and 'How They Convert,' XV, 25 (June 24, 1937), pp. 386, 394-95.

79. 'Church Missionary Society,' 26 Dec. 1936, *CM*, pp. 55-58, and *CWMG*, LXIV, pp. 176-78.

80. 'Church Missionary Society,' *op. cit.*; 'What is a Miracle,' 19 Dec. 1936, *CM*, pp. 53-55, *CWMG*, LXIV, pp. 149-51; 'Shameful If True,' 5 June 1937, *CM*, pp. 61-62, *CWMG*, LXV, pp. 277-78; 'The Kottayam Interview,' 13 March 1937, *CM*, pp. 156-59, or 'Interview to Bishop Moore, Bishop Abraham, and Others,' *CWMG*, LXIV, pp. 285-86.

'baits' to the depressed classes in his *Open Letter* responding to Ambedkar's declaration.[81]

Azariah did not publicly answer Gandhi's published accusations against him, but Gandhi's more general criticisms of Christian missions had already caused widespread irritation in Dornakal. In November 1935, Azariah reported that at a recent meeting of Dornakal diocesan organizations, 'Mr. Gandhi's public pronouncement on the work of Missions, in which he wished that the Christian movement would confine itself to activities for the amelioration of the physical and social conditions of the people without disturbing their religious faiths, was still fresh in our minds.' In response, the meeting passed unanimously the following resolution:

> The representatives of all parts of the Diocese of Dornakal in meeting assembled desire to place on record their conviction that one important function of the Christian Church and every member thereof is to bear witness before all men, by life and word, to the Gospel of the revelation of God in Jesus Christ. We do this in accordance with the command of our Lord and with a view to sharing our highest happiness with our fellow men.[82]

The bishop interpreted invective by Indian national leaders against Christian missions in general as the sad outcome of the communal franchise which had politicized the whole issue of conversion. In the *Dornakal Diocesan Magazine* of May 1937, he wrote:

> The worst and the most serious evil the present system engenders is the jealousy and disfavour with which conversions to Christianity are looked upon by political leaders. And who can blame them? However strongly Christian workers may disavow such a base and unworthy motive, conversions to Christianity give room to national leaders to say that so many conversions means so many off the Hindu voters' list, and that any forward movement in Evangelism with the resulting conversions is therefore a direct move to transfer so many thousands of voters from the Hindu group to the Indian Christian group.[83]

Azariah avoided the temptation to blame Gandhi personally for the increasing attacks on conversion, placing the onus instead on the political

---

81. 'Letter to Amrit Kaur,' 17 March 1937, *CWMG*, LXV, p. 4; 'With an Indian Missionary,' *CM*, p. 162, or 'Discussion with a Missionary,' *CWMG*, LXV, p. 81.
82. 'The Bishop's Letter,' *DDM*, XII, 11 (Nov. 1935), p. 3.
83. 'The Bishop's Letter,' *DDM*, XIV, 5 (May 1937), p. 4.

system put into operation by the British as they extended the franchise and representation to increasing numbers of Indians.

A Failed Attempt at Reconciliation

The conflict between Gandhi and Christian missionary forces over depressed class conversions threatened to worsen the already growing atmosphere of intercommunal distrust in the newly open political arena. Tragically, this hostility grew when a group consisting primarily of British Quakers sympathetic to the Indian national movement attempted to intervene in the mass movement dispute of 1936 and 1937. The India Conciliation Group had been founded by associates of Gandhi's friend, C. F. Andrews, during the second Round Table Conference to represent the interests of Indian nationalists in England. Troubled by Gandhi's deteriorating relations with Christian missionary forces, several Conciliation Group leaders mounted a well-intentioned but ultimately counter-productive effort to reconcile Gandhi with the man whom they regarded as his principal Indian Christian adversary, the Bishop of Dornakal.

The most important, though least public participant in this mediatory effort was Agatha Harrison (1885-1954), personal assistant to C. F. Andrews and Secretary of the India Conciliation Group (ICG) from its establishment in 1931.[84] Harrison had accepted an informal commission from Gandhi that year to 'work for mutual understanding between Britain and India' and subsequently visited India six times on behalf of the ICG with the financial assistance of Gandhi's supporter, the Marwari industrialist G. D. Birla. Her main function was to facilitate relations between Indian nationalist leaders and influential Britons by arranging informal meetings and consultations. She attempted to work 'behind the scenes' as an unofficial diplomat free from association with the official political networks of either the Congress Party or the British Raj. She established intimate contacts within both the British government and the

84. A highly personal biography has been provided by Agatha's sister, Irene Harrison: *Agatha Harrison: An Impression by Her Sister* (London, 1956). Useful work on Agatha Harrison (hereafter AH) has also been done by Hugh Tinker, *The Ordeal of Love: C. F. Andrews and India* (Delhi, 1979), and by Barbara N. Ramusack, 'Catalysts or Helpers? British Feminists, Indian Women's Rights and Indian Independence,' in *The Extended Family: Women and Political Participation in India and Pakistan* (Delhi, 1981), pp. 109-50. Among her papers at Friends House, London, see also 'Agatha Mary Harrison,' War and India folder, 50B ICG, FH.

Indian national movement, trying to interpret one side to the other in the somewhat naive belief that better communication would solve the divisive problems at issue.[85] Her private papers provide a unique 'third party' account of a number of critical events occurring during the final years of the independence movement, including the most complete account available of the hitherto neglected Gandhi-Azariah controversy.

From November 1936 to February 1937, Harrison undertook her third trip to India in order to calm the growing crisis over depressed class conversions. Having discussed the mass movements in London with leading missionaries and ecumenists — John Mott, Basil Matthews, William Paton, A. L. Warnshuis, Merle Davies, and Godfrey Phillips — Harrison was convinced by the validity of their claims, but also knew of Gandhi's objections through personal correspondence and her reading of the *Harijan*. The urgency of the situation became apparent immediately on board ship to Ceylon, where Harrison discovered that most passengers were not only aware of the depressed class situation, but also enthusiastic supporters of Christian evangelism.[86] As her first act of 'mediation' with those on board who had 'come primed with the usual mission literature,' Harrison arranged a lecture by Dr. Batra, a Hindu government official from Bengal's Department of Public Health, who criticized missionary activity.

Once in India and before joining Gandhi at Wardha, Harrison set out to investigate for herself the truth of missionary claims about the mass movements.[87] In order to see 'the best of Christian work,' she scheduled a 24-hour visit to Dornakal diocese on 22 November.[88] After a tour of villages with Azariah's daughter Mercy, Harrison concluded that 'this work is real and deserving of support.' She was impressed that recent converts exhibited a good understanding of Christian doctrine, but remained

85. 45: 2/5, ICG, FH. She discussed Indian controversies with Lord Irwin, Lord Lothian, and Eleanor Rathbone, and was consulted by Sir Stafford Cripps before his departure for India in 1942. Harrison also served as messenger between Gandhi and Subhas Chandra Bose during the 1938 crisis over Congress leadership. She was instrumental in negotiations over political crises in princely states as well, helping to expedite a settlement during Gandhi's Rajkot fast-to-death by establishing contact with Mr. Gibson, Resident of the States of Western India. See AH, 'Record of My Visits to India 1929-49,' 45: 2/5, ICG, FH. B. N. Ramusack, *op. cit.,* pp. 134-36.

86. AH to Mr. Heath, 16 Oct. 1936, 45: 2/2, ICG, FH.

87. She failed to investigate the work of the Harijan Sevak Sangh as originally intended. AH to C. F. Andrews, 22 July 1936, 50A: CFA folder, ICG, FH. See also AH to Mahatmaji (Gandhi), 1 July 1936 and 19 Aug. 1936, 45: 2/2, ICG, FH.

88. AH to 'dears,' 22 Nov. 1936, en route to Wardha, 50c: unmarked folder, ICG, FH.

doubtful that the mass movements were as large as Bishop Azariah and western missionary societies claimed.[89]

At first, Harrison served essentially as an apologist for the missionaries against Hindu critics. In an interview with Gandhi's ally, C. Rajagopalachari, in Madras in early November, she 'tried to convey to him the honesty of purpose behind the (Christian) "forward move."' In response, he asked Harrison to speak about the mass movements to a meeting of about thirty orthodox Brahmins and high-caste Hindus at the home of Venkatarama Sastri on 13 or 14 November (it is not clear from her letters which day the meeting was held). The meeting's purpose, she wrote, was 'to stir them to a realization of what is going on.'

> I pointed out . . . that for nearly 100 years the plight of these people [outcastes] had been on our hearts. It would be true to say that the ordinary man and woman might not know much about India, but that they did know about the Untouchables, for in chapels and churches all over the country you would find people who regularly contributed money for the support of this work. From time to time missionaries returned and went round speaking of what the Christian forces were doing. . . . Then I took some time in telling . . . that when reports and urgent pleas for help had come, the mission board leaders had held 'steady' refusing to be stampeded into taking action. But that as these pleas continued to come from the Indian Christian church, attention must be paid and help given.[90]

Afterwards, she faced 'a perfect barrage of questions.' Some implied that missionaries had political motives in seeking untouchable allegiance before an election. Others wondered why Christians sought to divide a community that was already in a dire plight. Two or three emphasized the need to reform Hinduism, saying 'that when oppression ended, conversion would end.' In Madras, Harrison also met with mass movement critic A. V. Thakkar, who presented information about Christian conversions

89. *Ibid.* Harrison questioned Mercy on numerical estimates attributed to Bishop Azariah in a pamphlet whose title Harrison leaves unnamed. It is likely that this is the same pamphlet criticized by Gandhi a month later in the *Harijan* ('Church Missionary Society,' *Harijan*, 26 Dec. 1936, in *CM*, pp. 55-58 and *CWMG*, LXIV, pp. 176-78). The pamphlet, prepared by Prebendary W. W. Cash, was published by the CMS to raise an emergency fund of 25,000 pounds sterling to support missionary work in mass movement areas. In it, Bishop Azariah estimated that about one million people in his diocese were 'moving Christward.'

90. AH to Mr. Wilson, 11 Nov. 1936, Madras, 45: 2/2, ICG, FH.

that, she claimed, was 'widely divergent from that reaching the Mission Boards.'[91]

Harrison concluded that the conflict between missionaries and Hindu reformers in the religious field was serious enough to aggravate the conflict between Britain and India in the political field.[92] She also worried that, as Hindu concern about untouchable conversion clashed with Christian enthusiasm about the mass movements, it threatened 'to add to the Hindu-Muslim tension . . . a Hindu-Christian tension.'[93]

Her solution lay in trying to lessen the tension through improved communication and informal talks. She hoped that a gathering of mission leaders from throughout India and the world for three meetings of the NCC during December in Nagpur would help bridge the gap between Hindus and Christians.[94] The Bishop of Dornakal was to preside over an Executive Committee meeting of the NCC on 1-2 December, followed by a conference on the mass movements initiated by John Mott and a Biennial Meeting of the NCC from 29 December 1936 to 1 January 1937.[95]

Before the conferences, C. F. Andrews arranged an extended interview over two days between John Mott and Gandhi at nearby Wardha in which the two leaders disagreed over the legitimacy of depressed class conversions.[96] As Mott had recalled after an earlier meeting with Gandhi in 1930:

> No one thing disappointed me more with Gandhi during the three hours' talk I had with him than his evasion and gross ignorance of these untouchables. From his answers it would appear that the Christian

91. *Ibid.* Harrison does not specify the extent or nature of the divergence. See, however, 'How They Convert,' *Harijan*, 19 June 1937, in *CM*, pp. 63-66 and *CWMG*, LXV, pp. 316-18; and the Christian critique: 'How They Convert,' *Guardian*, XV, 25 (24 June 1937), pp. 386, 394-95.

92. G. L., 'A Visit to India,' 50C: unmarked folder, ICG, FH.

93. AH to Lord Brabourne, 5 Feb. 1937, Bombay, 45: 2/2, ICG, FH.

94. AH to Wilson, 11 Nov. 1936, 45: 2/2, ICG, FH.

95. III: 118/1953, Mott Papers, YDS.

96. *Ibid.* For Mahadev Desai's selective account of the discussions, see 'Dr. Mott's Visit,' *Harijan*, 19 and 26 Dec. 1936, in *CM*, pp. 169-82, and 'Discussion with John R. Mott' (dated 13/14 Nov. 1936), in *CWMG*, LXIV, pp. 33-41. Mott claimed that Desai's record of the interview in the *Harijan* was 'meagre.' There is some inconsistency over the question of the date of the meeting. Whereas Mott contended the visit took place on 13-14 November, Desai recorded it as early December. Mott seems to have been correct since Harrison referred to the meeting as already having transpired in a letter to Carl Heath, 21 Nov. 1936, Madras, 45: 2/2, ICG, FH.

movement had nothing whatever to do with the Mass Movement and if it did have a little share, then it was a distasteful part.[97]

By 1936, Gandhi had clearly learned more about these untouchables. 'Evasion and gross ignorance' were no longer the problem. But the Mahatma remained unwilling to admit a role for Christian conversion in their uplift. Christianity was still, to Gandhi, 'a distasteful part' of Harijan uplift, despite its evident (and, hence, hotly contested) successes.

Harrison arrived in Wardha on 24 November to join Andrews in his efforts to reconcile Gandhi and the missionary establishment. In her own discussions with the Mahatma at Sevagram Ashram, she was intimidated by his anger over the mass movements.

> Our talks centre round the present situation and this impasse over conversion. About the latter he is saying some portentous things. If only the missionaries would take heed. But this week there is this Mott conference only a few miles away in which they are going to discuss future steps. The thing that ought to be done is to question whether the step (sic) should be taken at all.[98]

Christian leaders in Nagpur were not receptive to Harrison's first mediatory efforts. Mott denied her permission to attend the Mass Movement Conference,[99] and appears to have ignored her subsequent request that Gandhi be invited to Nagpur 'for serious discussion of the impasse.'[100] After attending the Congress Conference in Faizpur on 27-29 December, Harrison returned to Nagpur to attend the Biennial Meeting of the NCC, where she was met by ICG Chairman Carl Heath and his wife. Coming from a meeting of Congressites to a meeting of Christians was, Harrison wrote, 'like coming into another world.'[101]

Debates over the legitimacy of mass movement evangelism dominated the Christians' Nagpur meetings, with critics counseling delay, inac-

97. 'Mass Movement Survey, India, Memoranda, Notes, etc. 1930, 1932, "CMS" Summary of Notes taken at Conference with Dr. John R. Mott, High Leigh, April 24, 1930,' Box 406, NCCC, IMC/CBMS, SOAS.

98. AH to Family, 26 Nov. 1936, Wardha, 50C: unmarked folder, ICG, FH.

99. He said that no visitors were allowed. Alice Van Doren to AH, 16 Nov. 1936, Nagpur, 45: 2/2, ICG, FH. Original records of the proceedings do not survive; see K. Baago, *A History of the National Christian Council of India, op. cit.,* pp. 57-58. However, the printed report is available in I: 4/61, Mott Papers, YDS.

100. AH to Carl Heath, 16 Nov. 1936, New Delhi, 45: 2/1, ICG, FH.

101. 'Extracts from Letters Received from Agatha Harrison,' 45: 2/2, ICG, FH.

tion, or outright opposition to the missionary program favored by Azariah and others.[102] The ICG delegates joined a dissenting faction of city-dwelling Indian Christians who had been influenced by Gandhi to question the validity of mission to the depressed classes during a period of internal Hindu reform. Azariah wrote to John Mott soon after the December meetings: 'My first concern is in regard to the attitude of certain Indian Christian leaders of urban areas whose attitude to Mass Movements and Evangelism is indifferent or critical and antagonistic.'[103]

His debates with these Indian Christian critics appear to have shaken Azariah's confidence rather severely. Pickett reported three months later:

> ... neither Bishop Azariah nor Hodge [the NCC Secretary] has showed to their best advantage in recent months. Their leadership at the last session of the NCC was halting and uncertain. My judgment is that ... [those] ... who represent the detached, non-typical Indian Christian attitude of hostility to the depressed classes and of a deference to Gandhi and the Hindu Communalists had frightened them rather severely.[104]

Harrison was annoyed by the critical attitude of most missionaries and Indian Christians toward Hindu reforms, and she cited Azariah's claim that the Travancore temple openings were mainly a 'political move' as an example of this 'unhelpful' attitude.[105] Relations between Christians and Hindus, she found, were now marked by 'suspicion and lack of faith on both sides.'[106]

Despite her broad sympathy for Gandhi, Harrison was persuaded during the Nagpur meeting that Gandhi's criticisms of Azariah, Pickett, and the CMS in the *Harijan* had still been misguided. On the last day of the conference, she told Pickett that Gandhi had been mistaken in his charges and that the Mahatma owed both Pickett and Azariah an apol-

102. 'The Bishop's Letter,' *DDM*, XIV, 2 (Feb. 1937), pp. 1-4. It is interesting to note that Azariah's fellow advocates of a relatively conservative theology supporting mass movement work, P. O. Philip and K. T. Paul, were also involved in the NMS and shared Azariah's commitments to nationalism and indigenization. D. B. Forrester, *Caste and Christianity, op. cit.*, pp. 185-87.

103. VSA to Mott, 2 Feb. 1937, I: 4/61, Mott Papers, YDS.

104. Pickett to Diffendorfer, 17 March 1937, Bombay, 1185-4-3:03, Pickett Papers, GCAH, UMC.

105. 'Extracts from Letters Received from Agatha Harrison,' 45: 2/2, ICG, FH.

106. *Ibid.*

ogy.[107] Showing Pickett a handwritten statement from Gandhi (stating that if he was convinced of the incorrectness of his charge he would offer an apology), Harrison proposed that Azariah and Pickett meet with Gandhi the following week.[108]

On 31 December, Harrison and Heath had a 'deeply interesting and illuminating private talk' with Azariah and obtained his promise to meet Gandhi.[109] Gandhi reciprocated at Wardha the following day, provoking Heath to write optimistically:

> If these two men [Azariah and Gandhi] can meet, and deal frankly and honestly with each other, I think what threatens to become a widening division may get into its proper setting.[110]

The meeting was set for mid-February, with Bishop Pickett to be included along with Gandhi and Azariah as a participant.[111] Harrison shared Heath's high hopes about this meeting, and wrote home:

> The Bishop of Dornakal etc. are to meet (Gandhi) in the middle of February. If one has done nothing else on this trip — this is perhaps worth coming for.[112]

No transcript of the subsequently controversial Gandhi-Azariah-Pickett meeting appears to have survived. The only written record of the interview was kept by Gandhi's secretary, Mahadev Desai, 'for his own files,'[113] and the participants agreed that neither these notes nor any record of the conversation would be published.[114] Because Desai's transcript seems to have disappeared from the records,[115] secondary tes-

107. Pickett to Warnshuis, 18 Jan. 1937, Bombay, 1185-4-3:03, Pickett Papers, GCAH, UMC.

108. Pickett to Diffendorfer, 2 Jan. 1937, Bombay, 1185-4-3:03, Pickett Papers, GCAH, UMC.

109. Carl Heath to Alexander Wilson, 1 Jan. 1937, Nagpur, 44: 1 (box f), ICG, FH. Also see 'Extracts from Letters Received from Agatha Harrison,' 45: 2/2, ICG, FH; and AH to Myrene, 31 Dec. 1936, Nagpur, 50C: unmarked folder, ICG, FH.

110. Heath to Wilson, 1 Jan. 1937, Nagpur, 44: 1 (box f), ICG, FH.

111. AH to Carl Heath 1 Feb. 1937, Bombay, 45: 2/2, ICG, FH.

112. AH to Family, 21 Jan. 1937, Delhi, 50C: unmarked folder, ICG, FH.

113. Hodge to Paton, 8 Aug. 1938, Box 396, NCCC, IMC/CBMS, SOAS.

114. VSA, 'Gandhiji's Alleged Threat to Christian Work: Bishop of Dornakal Repudiates Dr. McGavran's Version,' *Guardian*, XVI, 31 (4 Aug. 1938), p. 482.

115. This conclusion is based upon an extensive search in India undertaken with the valuable assistance of Dr. Rajmohan Gandhi (Editor of the *Indian Express*

timonies of the participants and others who talked with them provide the best available information about the meeting. Such accounts are often contradictory about the contents of the discussion and even about the date of the meeting, which was probably held on 12 February 1937.[116]

The three men met in the bungalow of NCC Secretary J. Z. Hodge, at Nagpur, along with four silent observers — Hodge, Desai, Pickett's wife, and Miss M. Reid.[117] Despite the agreement regarding confidentiality, rumors circulated afterwards about the outcome of the meeting, and in the following year it became the focus of a heated debate over the prospects of religious freedom for Christians under *swaraj*.

The controversy was sparked by a three-part article entitled 'The Battle for Brotherhood in India Today,' which appeared in the London-based Christian quarterly *World Dominion*. Written by an American missionary to India from the United Christian Missionary Society, Donald A. McGavran (1897-1990), the article described depressed class conversion movements as the focal point of a great battle led by Gandhi for

---

[Madras], and grandson of Mahatma Gandhi) and Professor K. Swaminathan (Editor of *The Collected Works of Mahatma Gandhi*). Neither Dr. Gandhi nor Professor Swaminathan knew about the meeting with Azariah, but both helped this author in the search for evidence. (Interviews: Dr. Gandhi, 26 Feb. 1986, Madras; and Prof. Swaminathan, 20 March 1986, Madras.) Letters supporting the conclusion that the transcript has been lost or otherwise removed from the records were received from the following: (1) R. Subrahmaniam, Secretary: the Pyarelal Foundation for Gandhian Studies and Research, Delhi, 5 April 1986 and 30 Sept. 1986 (no transcript reported in the Diaries of Mahadev Desai); (2) Mrs. Nirmala Subramaniam, *Collected Works of Mahatma Gandhi*, Delhi, 7 May 1986 (no records of meeting in her collection or at the Gandhi Museum and Library); (3) Dr. Hari Dev Sharma, Deputy Director, Nehru Memorial Museum, Delhi, 7 and 18 April 1986 (no records in this collection); (4) Mr. Narayan Desai, son of Mahadev Desai, Institute for Total Revolution, Vedchhi, 17 May and 12 June 1986 (no notes of the interview in the family's collection of his father's papers).

116. Bishop Pickett claimed in March 1937 that it took place on 12 February, although it seems to have been scheduled originally for a later date. See Pickett to Diffendorfer: 17 March 1937, Bombay, 1185-4-3:03, Pickett Papers, GCAH, UMC. It was scheduled first for 17 February. See Pickett to Warnshuis, 18 Jan. 1937, Bombay, 1185-4-3:03, Pickett Papers, GCAH, UMC. Also, AH to Heath, 1 Feb. 1937, Bombay, 45: 2/2, ICG, FH. In 1938, Azariah placed the meeting more vaguely in 'March 1937.' See VSA, 'Gandhiji's Alleged Threat to Christian Work: Bishop of Dornakal Repudiates Dr. McGavran's Version,' *op. cit.* (1938), p. 482. It seems probable that Pickett's more precisely specified date, recollected closer to the meeting time, is the accurate one.

117. Hodge to Paton, 8 Aug. 1938, Box 396, NCCC, IMC/CBMS, SOAS.

the preservation of caste and the maintenance of Hinduism.[118] The series concluded with the following account of the Gandhi-Azariah-Pickett meeting:

'We shall not allow conversions to continue,' Mr. Gandhi explained in conclusion of a three hour conference. The Christian leaders pointed out to Mr. Gandhi the unquestioned improvement which had come to the oppressed classes people who became Christians, and tried in every way to induce him to say that he was in favour of any amelioration of their lot. But his position remained adamant, namely that it was better for the oppressed classes to suffer in Hinduism than to be relieved in Christianity. Of course he would not say this. He simply refused to admit that the oppressed classes who have become Christians are at all improved. At the conclusion of the Conference, Mr. Gandhi said to Bishop Azariah, 'You Christians must stop preaching to and making disciples amongst the Depressed Classes. If you do not, we shall make you. We shall appeal to the educated Indian Christians: we shall appeal to your home constituency; and if those fail we shall prohibit by law any change of religion, and will back up the law by the force of the State.'[119]

This account fueled existing Indian Christian fears that Gandhi would restrict the religious liberty of both Indian Christians and Christian missions in an independent India.[120] Particular concern was expressed about Gandhi's threat to use state force to prevent proselytiz-

118. D. A. McGavran, 'The Battle for Brotherhood in India Today,' *World Dominion*, XVI, 1 (Jan. 1938), pp. 32-36; 2 (April 1938), pp. 131-35; 3 (July 1938), pp. 255-61. For biographical and bibliographical information on McGavran, see *God, Man and Church Growth (A Festschrift in Honor of Donald Anderson McGavran)*, ed. A. R. Tippett (Grand Rapids, 1973); and his autobiographical article, 'My Pilgrimage in Mission,' *International Bulletin of Missionary Research*, X, 2 (April, 1986), pp. 53-58. It is ironic to note, in light of his earlier polemic against caste, how McGavran's later theories of church growth admit a remarkable (although, in theory, only short-term) tolerance for caste. In an interview with the author (30 Jan. 1987, Pasadena, CA), McGavran said that he now believes that Christian brotherhood is rarely achieved instantly, and that caste practices should be allowed to persist temporarily among new converts in the interests of numerical expansion of the church. For a critique of McGavran's missiology with special reference to his experience with mass movements in India, see Philip Lewis, 'Caste, Mission and Church Growth,' *Themelios*, X, 2 (Jan. 1985), pp. 24-30.

119. D. A. McGavran, 'The Battle for Brotherhood in India Today,' *World Dominion*, XVI, 3 (July 1938), p. 261.

120. 'Gandhiji on Religion,' *Guardian*, XVI, 28 (14 July 1938), p. 435.

ation.[121] Although Gandhi had previously condoned the use of legislation to end proselytizing,[122] Christian missionaries had never before felt so seriously threatened with the possibility of coercive civil or police action.

Hindu-Christian relations seemed to be headed for another crisis when both Gandhi and Azariah denied the truth of McGavran's account. Gandhi pressed for an apology to be printed in the relevant papers (*World Dominion, Guardian,* and *Harijan*),[123] and Azariah responded vehemently in the *Guardian:*

> Every statement — without exception — attributed to Gandhiji by Dr. MacGavran (sic) is *wholly and absolutely untrue.* Whether Gandhiji made any such statement or statements, anywhere else or to anybody else, at any other time, I do not know. But simply, he *did not say or suggest, directly or indirectly, anything* like what is attributed to him in this article. The whole, as far as our interview . . . is concerned, is a cruel fabrication. And that is the only interview I have had with him in twenty years![124]

Shortly afterwards, McGavran published an apology stating that his account had been based on a composite picture emerging 'from a dozen different sources' and that it was 'erroneous'.[125]

121. For example, in the *Guardian:* 'Stray references have been made to the Gandhi-Dornakal interview, in speeches and papers. The foregoing report is a more coherent account than what we have seen on other occasions. Mahatma Gandhi's views on conversion to Christianity are well known. They have been debated, disputed or supported in public for many years. In none of them did Gandhiji betray intentions of securing State action of the kind indicated above. That he could have held this secret in his mind seems incredible. . . . Dr. MacGavran has evidently had access to information that has been denied to the public. . . . But the public will not rest content until some one directly engaged in the interview publishes a full, authentic report of what transpired. The statements published point to serious developments in the future that are of far reaching consequence to many interests.' 'Gandhiji's Alleged Threat to Christian Missions,' *Guardian,* XVI, 30 (July 1938), p. 465.

122. For instance, in a conversation with a missionary in 1935 Gandhi said: 'If I had power and could legislate I should certainly stop all proselytizing.' See Mahadev Desai, 'Interesting Questions,' *Harijan,* 11 May 1935, in *CM,* p. 106. See also S. J. Imam-Ud-Din, *Gandhi and Christianity* (Lahore, 1946), pp. 42-44.

123. Hodge to Paton, 16 Sept. 1938, Box 396, NCCC, IMC/CBMS, SOAS.

124. 'Gandhiji's Alleged Threat to Christian Work: Bishop of Dornakal Repudiates Dr. MacGavran's Version,' *op. cit.* (1938), p. 482. For Henry Whitehead's impressions of Gandhi, see 'Bishop's Diary,' *MDM,* XI, 9 (Sept. 1916), pp. 232-35; and *Indian Problems in Religion, Education, Politics, op. cit.,* p. 245. See also Knud Heiberg, *V. S. Azariah: Biskop af Dornakal, op. cit.,* p. 97.

125. 'The explanation of the publication is that I heard the story from a dozen

Despite his published disavowal, McGavran continued to believe to the end of his life that he correctly represented Gandhi's opinions.[126] His interpretation of the Gandhi-Azariah-Pickett meeting was consequently invoked by former Baptist missionary Vern Middleton to support a theory that Azariah lied in order to defend Gandhi,[127] and that Gandhi was the inspirational force behind later anti-missionary statements, such as those of the 1956 Niyogi Commission which concluded that Christian evangelism was harmful to Indian national unity.[128]

McGavran's disingenuous apology of 1938 seems to have been motivated by the desire to protect his true informer, Bishop Pickett.[129] In a 1938 letter to Azariah, McGavran claimed that he had been unaware of the agreement against publicizing the interview and had assembled his account from 'a dozen' secondhand reports, thereby presenting a con-

different sources, did not hear that it was confidential, and thus incorporated the incident in my article in all good faith.' See 'Dr. D. A. McGavran's Explanation,' *Guardian,* XVI, 38 (22 Sept. 1938), p. 594. See also *World Dominion,* XVI, 4 (Oct. 1938), p. 392.

126. McGavran to the author, 17 Oct. 1986, Pasadena, California.

127. Vern Middleton, 'Caste Issues in the Minds of McGavran and Gandhi,' *Missiology: An International Review,* XIII, 2 (April 1985), pp. 159-73. I am grateful to the Rev. Vinay Samuel of Bangalore for drawing my attention to this article. Regarding Azariah's defense of Gandhi in the *Guardian,* Middleton contends that it 'was written under considerable duress and reflects the heat behind the issue. . . . In it the Bishop [Azariah] strives to save face with Gandhi by virtually calling McGavran a liar. A portion of the letter is quoted here to demonstrate that even Bishops can brush truth aside for that which is politically expedient. I dare make such an accusation here because history has proven the accuracy of McGavran's statements.'

128. M. B. Niyogi, *Madhya Pradesh Enquiry Report* (Madhya Pradesh Government Publications, 1956), pp. 49-51; cited in P. D. Devanandan, *The Gospel and Renascent Hinduism* (London, 1959), p. 23.

129. In a letter to the author, McGavran admitted that Pickett was his informer but explained that he (McGavran) concealed this fact at the time of the incident. After receiving 'two or three indignant letters' from Azariah demanding to know the source of his 'false information,' McGavran said he accepted blame for the incident in order to protect Pickett from being drawn into 'a very embarrassing position.' McGavran to the author, 17 Oct. 1986, Pasadena, California.

This statement is consistent with the information given by McGavran in an oral interview with Vern Middleton, author of the above article in *Missiology* on 27 Oct. 1983. See Middleton, *op. cit.,* p. 161.

Indeed, in 1938 Pickett admitted privately to Hodge his role in the affair, saying that McGavran may have '. . . laid hold of something he [Pickett] had said at the Landour Conference of a year ago.' Hodge to Paton, 8 Aug. 1938, Box 396, NCCC, IMC/CBMS, SOAS.

struction derived from hearsay as Gandhi's direct quotation.[130] In the unpublished first draft of his apology to *World Dominion,* McGavran admitted that he was guilty of an inappropriate use of quotations, but not of misrepresenting Gandhi's beliefs.[131] This explanation infuriated Gandhi, Azariah, and the Editor of *World Dominion,* who insisted that he retract the second part of his excuse.[132] McGavran bowed to the pressure but denied in later years that he had either misquoted or misunderstood Gandhi.[133]

130. 'Having heard general talk on the subject I wrote an account of the interview as I understood it. As I had adopted for that article the direct discourse style, I put quotation marks on the statement, and did not give consideration to the fact that readers would regard them as meaning that I was using Mr. Gandhi's exact words.'

'As to "who my informant was" I really can't say. I have heard the story from a dozen different people, Indians and missionaries. It is quite a common story. I have also heard substantially the same thing from Hindu sources. Not, to be sure, ascribing the statement to Mr. Gandhi in conversation with you, but laying down this course of procedure as one which India now having achieved Hindu raj would be certain to follow.'

'As I always try to be accurate, this slip causes me very great regret.' McGavran to Azariah, 6 August 1938, Box 396, NCCC, IMC/CBMS, SOAS.

131. 'It must be said that this story, current quite widely and heard by the author from a dozen different sources must hence forth be accepted as mythical in view of Bishop Azariah's categorical statement. On the other hand there is no question but that some such position is widely held amongst influential Hindu leaders. . . . In conclusion, therefore, while we point out that while Mr. Gandhi did not make the statement to Bishop Azariah, the fundamental truth underlying the statement remains unchanged, namely that in the Battle for Brotherhood Christianity is facing in India a religion whose existence depends upon a denial of brotherhood, and the prevention by as many means as it has at hand of the spread of a religion of brotherhood.' McGavran to the Editor of *World Dominion,* 29 July 1938, Box 396, NCCC, IMC/CBMS, SOAS.

132. As Paton observed: 'McGavran has not grasped the essential distinction between two things: (i) his own opinions as to whether Hindus think certain things about Christian conversion and the prohibition of it and whether Mr. Gandhi more or less agrees with them, and (ii) the question whether or not certain things were said by Mr. Gandhi on a specific and stated occasion. To withdraw what he said under No. ii and then excuse it by No i is the kind of thing which makes people see red.' Paton to Hodge, 5 Sept. 1938, Box 396, NCCC, IMC/CBMS, SOAS. See also Hodge to Paton, 16 Sept. 1938, Box 396, NCCC, IMC/CBMS, SOAS.

133. 'Since Waskom Pickett was a good friend of mine, I formed the conclusion that Gandhi had indeed said this (i.e., what was attributed to him in the *World Dominion* article), but did not want the matter publicized. I did not consult Waskom Pickett. I was sure that I had quoted him exactly. . . . My present conclusion is that Gandhi unquestionably said this but that publicizing his remark was something that he did not approve of. Pickett had made a mistake in mentioning it at all, and I had made a mis-

McGavran was further isolated when two silent observers at the meeting, Hodge and Desai, also denied the truth of McGavran's account.[134] There was a conspicuous silence from the meeting's third participant, J. W. Pickett,[135] but Pickett's private correspondence suggests that McGavran's article reflected the Methodist bishop's views with some accuracy. One month after the disputed meeting, Pickett wrote:

> In the interview with Gandhi which Bishop Azariah, Hodge and I had on the 12th February, he intimated that if we continue seeking conversions from the Depressed Classes, he will draw away from the Church many educated Indian Christians who share his aversion to the conversion of Untouchables.

Furthermore, Pickett claimed:

> Affairs in India are moving to a place where, and to a time when there will be a showdown. Gandhi is increasingly antagonistic to Christian Missions. He has begun to threaten legislation to discourage, if not prohibit, conversion, in so far as it involves a change of professed creedal loyalty, which he identifies with the community label. Gandhi grows positively furious as he talks of the conversion of the Depressed Classes. He practically demands that we renounce any desire to lead members of the Depressed Classes to the Christian Faith.[136]

Bishop Pickett's assessment of Gandhi's hostile intentions towards missionaries was influenced greatly by Ambedkar, with whom Pickett had regular contact during this period. In the same letter, Pickett wrote:

> I discussed this matter last week with Dr. Ambedkar and he feels sure that the Hindus under the leadership of Gandhi are likely to make a sus-

---

take in including it in my article. It was private information.' McGavran to the author, 17 Oct. 1986, Pasadena, California.

134. Hodge wrote: 'I entirely endorse what Dornakal has written. The words that McGavran attributes to Gandhi were quite contrary to the whole tenor of his conversation.' See Hodge to Paton, 8 Aug. 1938, Box 396, NCCC, IMC/CBMS, SOAS. Mahadev Desai called on McGavran to make an apology as well. See Hodge to Paton, 16 Sept. 1938, Box 396, NCCC, IMC/CBMS, SOAS.

135. Even the files containing Bishop Pickett's correspondence with the Home Board of Missions of the Methodist Episcopal Church for 1938 (GCAH, UMC) are void of any reference to the controversy with Gandhi.

136. J. W. Pickett to R. E. Diffendorfer, 17 March 1937, 1185-4-3:03, Pickett Papers, GCAH, UMC.

tained effort to legislate for the control of conversion. But he believes that the combined efforts of the Depressed Classes, the Christians and the Moslems, can prevent anything of that sort happening.[137]

That leaders of the depressed classes and other religious groups shared Pickett's misgivings regarding Gandhi's perceived Hindu bias lends some credence to McGavran's thesis concerning Gandhi's real intentions. Anti-missionary legislation after Independence suggests that there was strong public support in India for Gandhi's alleged views, although it hardly proves the accuracy of McGavran's account.[138] The weight of available evidence concerning the disputed interview (the first-hand accounts of Azariah, Gandhi, Desai, and Hodge against McGavran's version of Pickett's testimony) indicates that McGavran misrepresented the conversation itself. There is some plausibility in his general characterizations because of Gandhi's evident anger over untouchable conversions. But, if McGavran's inflammatory account had been true, Gandhi and Desai would probably have wanted to suppress it, and it would not have been in the Christians' interest to conceal Gandhi's threats once they were already well publicized. Azariah and Hodge would have had little motivation to lie about Gandhi's threatening posture toward evangelism.

Middleton accused Azariah of disputing the accuracy of McGavran's article in order 'to save face with Gandhi.' In so doing, Azariah allegedly

137. *Ibid.* For Ambedkar's fully developed critique of Gandhi, see B. R. Ambedkar, *What Congress and Gandhi Have Done to the Untouchables* (Bombay, 1945, 2nd ed. 1946).

138. One must therefore question the reasoning behind Middleton's assertion that 'history has proven the accuracy of McGavran's statements.' The opinions of the Niyogi Commission cannot be proof or disproof of who said what in a meeting almost two decades earlier. It is not unreasonable to suggest that Middleton has fallen into precisely the same trap that snared McGavran in 1938, namely, the failure to distinguish between the particulars of the 1937 meeting and the well-known fact of Gandhi's opposition to Christian evangelism. Middleton attempts to exonerate McGavran with the use of interesting but unrelated evidence. That Gandhi was quoted in *Harijan* as saying 'If I had power and could legislate I should certainly stop all proselytizing' is irrelevant. Azariah's defense of Gandhi says nothing about Gandhi's general beliefs with respect to proselytizing. ('Whether Gandhiji made any such statement or statements, anywhere else or to anybody else, at any other time, I do not know,' Azariah wrote.) It merely defends Gandhi from McGavran's portrayal of what was said during the 1937 meeting. More significantly, it was most likely meant to defend Christians from what would have been a justified charge by Hindu nationalists and others of distorting facts for purposes of propaganda.

brushed truth aside 'for that which is politically expedient.'[139] Azariah had reason to be embarrassed that McGavran (or, more aptly, Pickett) had broken the privacy agreement, and probably desired to disassociate himself from this blunder. But it is difficult to imagine what political expediencies would have tempted the bishop to lie when any revelation of Gandhi's intention to stop proselytization by law would have given welcome ammunition to Gandhi's critics. It is possible that Azariah was scared to play a visible role in fueling Gandhi's opposition; but it seems unlikely that the bishop (not to mention Hodge and the silent observers) stood to gain either personally or on behalf of the church by protecting Gandhi.

Azariah's long activity in support of the mass conversion movements had placed him on a collision course with Gandhi well before the 1937 meeting. The bishop's evangelism could hardly have been construed as anything but an effective, if unintended, rival to Gandhi's 'Children of God' bid to secure the allegiance of the untouchables within the political fold of his charismatically Hindu form of messianic nationalism. Given Azariah's hitherto fearless and unpopular promotion of depressed class conversions to Christianity, it seems unlikely that Azariah would have been intimidated into minimizing Gandhi's opposition to evangelism in 1938. It was in Azariah's interest to preserve evangelization as a lawful activity for Christians in an independent India, and it would have been odd for Azariah to risk his integrity to save Gandhi from criticism for being opposed to the continuance of precisely that liberty. But Gandhi was a formidable opponent, and it is possible that by 1938 Azariah was simply unwilling to take on a major public battle with him.

Frequently throughout his life Azariah took independent political positions in opposition to Gandhi and the Congress Party. Although he was ultimately in favor of Indian independence and repeatedly warned Indian Christians against 'the delusion that nationalism is a contaminating influence that they should dread,'[140] he opposed civil disobedience, non-cooperation, and 'rebellion' as means to achieve political autonomy.[141] In a speech entitled 'Nationalism and Indian Christianity,' delivered to the

139. Middleton, *op. cit.*, p. 161. Apparently, Middleton was unaware that Hodge also contested McGavran's interpretation, and no explanation was given for why the NCC Secretary might have brushed truth aside as well.

140. 'Bishops and Politics,' *Guardian*, XIV, 2 (9 Jan. 1936), p. 17.

141. VSA: 'Bishop of Dornakal on the Indian Situation,' *op. cit.* (1942), pp. 436-37; 'The Indian Christian and Politics,' *op. cit.* (1942), p. 478.

Bezwada Town Congress Committee on 2 January 1936, Azariah praised the Congress Party for its national service but explained that many Indian Christians found objectionable in principle the Congress policy of civil disobedience and its use of *khadi* as a condition of membership.[142] Azariah was clearly unafraid to disagree with Congress and its leadership over fundamental principles and practical policies. But charging Mahatma Gandhi directly with a specific threat against Christian missionary activity would have been a more challenging task.

It is possible, as McGavran ultimately believed, that neither Pickett nor Azariah was lying, but merely interpreting Gandhi's words differently.[143] It is also possible that these different interpretations sprang, in part, from differences between Indian and western perceptions, sensibilities, and loyalties. McGavran believed there was a fundamental cultural or racial element to the conflict: 'Azariah and Gandhi were pulling together, were two nationals, and Pickett was a foreigner and I was a foreigner.'[144]

The problem of correctly interpreting Gandhi's words has plagued, not just westerners, but also Gandhi's closest disciples. As the Editor of *The Collected Works of Mahatma Gandhi* explained to author Ved Mehta:

> People knew very early that Gandhi was a great man, and everything he said or did was recorded and preserved. Sometimes each person near him would record his conversations with visitors. Gandhiji would then go over their records, choose the one he liked best, correct it, and send it off for publication in one of his weeklies. . . . One of his little jokes was 'You know how the gospels of Matthew, Mark, Luke, and John differ. I want only one gospel of my life.'[145]

It is particularly ironic in light of Gandhi's New Testament analogy that interpretive disputes seemed to occur with special frequency over Gandhi's statements concerning Christian conversion. While touring Travancore to see the temple openings in January 1937, Gandhi met with Christian leaders in Kottayam to discuss misunderstandings over his ac-

142. 'What the Congress Stands For' and 'Bishops and Politics,' *Guardian*, XIV, 2 (9 Jan. 1936), p. 17; 'Concerning Untouchables,' *Guardian*, XIV, 2 (9 Jan. 1936), p. 19; VSA, 'Nationalism and Indian Christianity,' *DDM*, XIII, 2 (Feb. 1936), p. 14.

143. 'Whatever Gandhi said was subject to two interpretations. Pickett made one. Azariah made another and both of them were probably according to the best of their ability. . . . Neither of them were deliberately lying.' Interview with the author, 30 January 1987, Pasadena, California.

144. Interview with the author, 2 February 1987, Pasadena, California.

145. Ved Mehta, *Mahatma Gandhi and His Apostles* (New York, 1976), p. 36.

cusations in the *Harijan* against Bishops Azariah, Pickett, and the CMS. Afterwards, Gandhi and Desai protested that an account of the Kottayam interview in the *Madras Mail* was inaccurate and that a corrected version should be published instead.[146] The American evangelist E. Stanley Jones also recalled an occasion when Gandhi claimed that a more favorable statement on the permissibility of conversion made in a private meeting at Wardha had been misrepresented by his Christian interlocutors (all of whom in turn defended the truth of their own accounts).[147]

Similar possibilities for interpretive error existed for those privy to the conversation between Gandhi, Azariah and Pickett on the sensitive topic of conversion. What is clear, in the end, is that the meeting proposed by the idealistic ICG to relieve communal tensions resulted in significantly worsening them and in driving a wedge between Azariah and Pickett, one of his closest associates in the mass movement work.

McGavran's imprudent article was not the only reason that the Gandhi-Azariah-Pickett meeting did not resolve the deteriorating communal situation. Harrison and Heath had never developed a good relationship with the missionary establishment. Although the ICG delegates described themselves as mediators and peacemakers, Azariah and most missionaries perceived them as troublesome advocates of Gandhi's anti-missionary positions. Pickett described Harrison as Gandhi's 'personal representative,' and Azariah claimed that, among different forces trying to influence the outcome of the NCC Biennial Meeting, there were 'Miss Agatha Harrison, Karl Heath and Mrs. Heath wanting us to take our directions from Mr. Gandhi.'[148]

Harrison's relations with the NCC in India had been troubled since the early 1920s when she refused to undertake industrial work for the

146. 'The Kottayam Interview,' *Harijan*, 13 March 1937, in *CM*, pp. 156-59. See also 'Interview to Bishop Moore, Bishop Abraham, and others' (dated 19 Jan. 1937, Kottayam), *CWMG*, LXIV, pp. 285-86.

147. E. Stanley Jones, *Gandhi: Portrayal of a Friend* (Nashville, 1948), pp. 66-67. The three Christian witnesses (E. Stanley Jones, Rev. S. Aldis, and Principal David Moses of Hislop College, Nagpur) claimed that Gandhi had 'unhesitatingly approved of conversion' given certain specific conditions: (i) the convert was inwardly convinced that Christ is the one to whom he should give his allegiance, (ii) he would not be denationalized, and (iii) the Christian community as a separate political entity would fade out. A retraction published six months later by Gandhi's secretary claimed that the interview had been incorrectly reported and that Gandhi did not approve of conversion.

148. Pickett to Diffendorfer, 2 Jan. 1937, 1185-4-3:03, Pickett Papers, GCAH, UMC. VSA to Paton, 25 Jan. 1937, Box 395, NCCC, IMC/CBMS, SOAS.

NCC due to disagreements over Christian doctrine. Her uncomfortable relationship with the Anglican church was broken finally in 1940 when she joined the Society of Friends.[149] During the controversies with Gandhi in the mid-1930s, she was keenly aware of her disagreements with many missionaries over basic theological questions, particularly concerning the authority of Christian revelation. Although not a theologian, Harrison had an obvious distaste for the missionary enterprise and was more inclined towards a universalist approach which implied equality and pluralism of religions; she had a correspondingly dim view of conversion. As she wrote home to her family from India:

> I have a feeling Dr. Mott feels I am an unnecessary 'maker of trouble' on this conversion business. Perhaps not. But his 'This is a movement of God' [i.e., the mass movements to Christianity] — and mine that we should try and appreciate other "Movements of God" — rather describes the situation.[150]

Her suspicions about missionary attitudes towards her were confirmed in London in 1937 when she had 'a rather wretched contretemps' by telephone with William Paton, Secretary of the International Missionary Council, who strongly criticized the positions she had taken in India on missionary affairs.[151]

Harrison's experience highlighted some of the basic divisions among different kinds of Christians over an appropriate response to Gandhi and depressed class unrest. It also illustrated the insincerity of Harrison's (and Gandhi's) claims of tolerance for all "Movements of God." Under the guise of neutral mediation in a heated controversy, Harrison and the ICG really wished to criticize the Christian missionary enterprise in India. Azariah and much of the missionary and Indian church establishment realized that their disagreements with Gandhi sprang from more than just misunderstanding, and necessitated more than just objective mediation. William Paton wrote to Hodge before the McGavran controversy erupted:

> I am very glad indeed that the [Gandhi-Azariah] meeting was held, not that I ever believed that Gandhi would change, or that there could be

149. B. N. Ramusack, *op. cit.*, p. 131.

150. AH to Family, 50C: unmarked folder, ICG, FH.

151. 'He did not feel that my intervention into the missionary field had been helpful to say the least. In fact he "was in revolt over the line I had taken." He had read my letters and said they were "abusive" and "contemptuous."' AH to C. F. Andrews, undated (probably May 1937), 50A: CFA folder, ICG, FH.

anything but a real gulf between his position and that of the Christian evangelist. It is however worth trying to remove needless obstacles and misunderstandings.[152]

Azariah agreed, and wrote to Harrison on 17 January 1937 that his differences with Gandhi were not ultimately based on a lack of understanding but on fundamental differences in matters of faith and principle.

> We (i.e. many missionaries, Indian Christians, and myself) are convinced that Christianity has always stood for conversion, and for changing people from one society to another. 'If any man is in Christ he is a new creature'; and a new creature can only thrive in a new environment. Christian life thus cannot be really lived except within the Church. This inevitably means breaking with the old fellowship and joining a new fellowship. . . . Mr. Gandhi does not favour this.[153]

Gandhi's attack on Christian missions was supported, Azariah noted, by Rajagopalachari, who 'intensely dislikes' mass movements. After the report of the 1931 Census was published, Rajagopalachari called upon Hindus 'to wake up and give up their social inequalities, in order that the depressed classes may not be driven away from Hinduism'. Azariah continued:

> Mr. Gandhi and Mr. Rajagopalachari . . . vehemently attack Missions and Missionaries for re-doubling their efforts at such a time as this. It is realized that the possibility of conversion of large numbers to Christianity is even greater today than ever before. They therefore attack foreign money, the foreign missionary; and not only these but also all indigenous propaganda work, as they have never done before.

Azariah went on to suggest an appropriate Christian response to Hindu critics which probably resembled his own response to Gandhi in their meeting less than one month later:

> What, I ask, is our duty at this time — as followers of Christ and as Indian nationalists. First and foremost it is our duty to be loyal to Christ, and therefore we must proclaim Him to all our people as the Way, the Truth and the Life. If while doing this our national leaders oppose us and misjudge us — we must bear it all — even as the early Apostles did.

152. Paton to Hodge, 3 March 1937, Box 396, NCCC, IMC/CBMS, SOAS.
153. VSA to Harrison, 17 Jan. 1937, Box 395, NCCC, IMC/CBMS, SOAS.

Christ and his message always arouse opposition. He came not to send peace (in this sense) but a sword. Conflicts are inevitable when His followers are loyal to Him. On the other hand, if unworthy methods are used in this work by any particular Mission or Church or in any particular area, it is our duty to discover these and rectify blunders. But the remedy for a mistaken method of work is not to stop the work!

My conclusion is therefore this. Mr. Gandhi and Mr. Rajagopalachari . . . must first abandon their attitude of antagonism to change of religion as such. Each religion stands for certain truths. When a man genuinely seeks after truth, he will come to a point where Truth must win his obedience. This obedience must mean abandoning one religious system and uniting with another. If a man fears this result, he will either effect a compromise with the Truth as he sees it, or yield to an unreality, professing to see in his old religion the new truth he has found in the new religion.

It is our love of country and countrymen that makes us redouble our efforts at this juncture and call for help from Christians all over the world. If Mr. Gandhi's objective is the uplift of the village, the removal of social disabilities, the raising of the poor, the unprivileged and the hitherto uncared for — and not merely the propping up of Hinduism — let him show his greatness and genuineness by sympathy with us in our effort. Hating conversion, and hating the Christian propaganda are not becoming of a true lover of India's poor.[154]

In addition to rejecting Gandhi's portrayal of Christian evangelism as an anti-nationalistic activity, Azariah was troubled by Gandhi's hostile and heterodox approach to Christian revelation. Gandhi's opposition to conversion represented a threat to both the religious duty and freedom of professing Christians, the bishop argued. Followers of Jesus Christ were required to accept, not only the Sermon on the Mount of which Gandhi approved, but all of Christ's teaching, including His specific commission to 'Go into all the world and preach the good news to all creation.'[155]

To Azariah, a partial acceptance of Jesus' teaching constituted a rejection of the normative biblical proclamation of the missionary enterprise as a *sine qua non* of faith and practice. Gandhi had no scruples about taking a selective approach to religious scriptures of all faiths — or about suggesting that he might have a more legitimate interpretation of any par-

154. *Ibid.*
155. Mark, 16:15-16.

ticular faith than the practitioners of the faith themselves.[156] Writing in the *Harijan* in 1936, he asserted: 'I rebel against orthodox Christianity as I am convinced that it has distorted the message of Jesus.'[157]

It is ironic that these two men, both profoundly religious and committed to the cause of helping India's untouchables, should have been drawn into such a conflict. In a seventieth birthday tribute, Azariah praised Gandhi for having called India back to religious ideals in an age of growing materialism and for having assisted the outcastes by changing the attitudes of caste Hindus.[158] Ultimately, however, despite certain shared affinities between the two, underlying philosophical, religious, and political disagreements kept them apart. Azariah chose to bear Gandhi's attacks, opposition, misjudgments, and antagonism 'as the early Apostles did' — remaining silent while going on with his work.

The Continuing Tension

The Gandhi-Azariah-Pickett meeting, the subsequent controversy, and further statements from Gandhi on conversion exacerbated the suspicion of many Indian Christians (and other religious minorities) that modern organized or what Professor Romila Thapar has called 'syndicated' Hinduism was becoming too closely associated with nationalism. As the *Guardian* (Madras) argued by early 1940:

> the Christian community and its leaders . . . now know that the fundamental rights of religious freedom and action cannot be safely left in the hands of Gandhiji or his communal followers . . . that this nationalism is really disguised communalism, anxious for preserving the Hindu majority and supremacy in India. . . . This is how [Gandhiji's] attitude and utterances are being interpreted by minorities in India who cannot be

156. So, e.g., Gandhi wrote in *Young India,* 8 Dec. 1927: 'If, then, I had to face only the Sermon on the Mount and my own interpretation of it, I should not hesitate to say: "Oh yes, I am a Christian."' See 'The Message of Jesus,' in M. K. Gandhi, *The Message of Jesus Christ, op. cit.,* p. 44. On the subject of Gandhi's selective reinterpretation of Sanskritic tradition, see Judith M. Brown, 'Mahatmas as Reformers: Some Problems of Religious Authority in the Indian Nationalist Movement,' *South Asia Research*, VI, 1 (May 1986), pp. 15-26.

157. *Harijan,* 30 May 1936, quoted in M. K. Gandhi, *The Message of Jesus Christ, op. cit.,* p. 89; see also pp. 43-44.

158. 'Mahatma Gandhi's Seventieth Birthday: Bishop of Dornakal's Tribute,' *op. cit.* (1939), p. 577.

blamed on the ground of lack of nationalism in face [*sic*] of the unfolding apocalypse of his communalism.[159]

Azariah himself never directly accused Gandhi of masking Hindu communalism under the cloak of nationalism. But he did criticize Indian nationalists more generally for trying to marginalize Indian Christians from national life by virtue of their religion. Azariah responded to the charge that Indian Christians were somehow inherently unpatriotic in his 1936 speech to the Bezwada Town Congress Committee. After speaking of the ways Christianity had succeeded in helping the depressed classes, Azariah asked:

> If we have attempted such tasks and succeeded in bringing new hope and life to a few millions of people, surely we ought not to be reckoned as alien and disloyal, simply because we have used a method based on religion — a religion different from the religion of the majority of the people of India. If the fifty million Harijans can be raised up to a new life of self-respect, of enlightenment and of godliness, what does it matter to us as Indian nationalists, whether that result is achieved by one religion or another? Religious interest is allowed so to dominate all thinking men that genuine patriotic national service is in danger of being discounted and even opposed, unless it is done in the name of the old religion of the country.[160]

Later, in January 1938, Azariah exhorted Christians in the Dornakal diocese 'heartily to cooperate . . . in all measures meant for the welfare of the nation, and particularly of the underprivileged' initiated by the Congress government elected in the Madras province under provisions of the new constitution of the Government of India Act of 1935. But he also called upon Congress leaders to respect the religious liberties of Christians in the interest of national unity.[161] While welcoming Congress gov-

159. 'Gandhiji and Religious Freedom,' *Guardian*, XVIII, 11 (14 March 1940), p. 163. See also the *Guardian*, XVIII, 10 (7 March 1940), pp. 146-47.

160. 'Concerning "Untouchables,"' *Guardian*, XVI, 2 (9 Jan. 1936), p. 19. See also a similar statement several months later in which Azariah countered objections to mass conversion movements from 'nationalist patriots' who 'erroneously think that for any group to give up Hinduism is to abandon Indian nationality,' asserting instead that missionaries bore the message of Jesus Christ out of a public-spirited love for India. 'The Bishop's Letter,' *DDM*, XIII, 6 (June 1936), p. 4.

161. VSA: 'Our Duty as Citizens,' *op. cit.* (1938), pp. 5-10; 'Christians and the New Government: Bishop of Dornakal's Call for Support,' *op. cit.* (1938), pp. 86-87.

ernment programs against drinking, rural indebtedness, and illiteracy, he noted that such reforms had been in the forefront of missionary policy for many years. 'Now that the Government itself is earnestly pushing these national services,' Azariah said, 'we (Christians) ought to throw ourselves into these tasks with more zest so that our ministry may reach not only Christians but others also.' Support of such Congress initiatives was an expression of the Indian Christian's civic commitment:

> Many of us . . . are true nationalists, in the sense that we truly love our motherland and our fellow-citizens, and we have longed to see our country placed on a path of progressive evolution towards freedom, enlightenment and united nationhood. Any programme, therefore, that may be adopted by the party in power with these ends in view ought to have our hearty cooperation.[162]

Azariah urged Dornakal's clergymen to take the lead in training an 'intelligent electorate' capable of placing the national interest above narrow self-interest of family, denomination, and caste. 'You must lead your people to elect not men of their family and clan, but men of undoubted ability, absolute rectitude and genuine public spirit,' he instructed his clergy.

> Unscrupulous agents may even canvass votes by offers of bribes of various kinds. At the inception of this greatly enlarged franchise, and in the unintelligent condition of the majority of electors, this perhaps is inevitable. Christian candidates and voters, however, must be above these unworthy manifestations of the electoral system.[163]

Just a year later, Azariah reported that 'in many out of the way places [of his Dornakal diocese] . . . well-to-do Congress members had paid the four-anna [party] membership fee for Christians and enrolled them as members — often without their knowledge and consent. 3,500 were said to have been made members in one area in this way and three whole villages in another.'[164] This news amused more than irritated him; but he was very serious in his calls to Christians and non-Christians alike to be honest, broadminded, and noncommunal in their politics. Indeed, Indian Christians would withdraw support for the currently elected Congress Legislature in

---

162. VSA, 'Our Duty as Citizens,' *op. cit.* (1938), p. 7.
163. *Ibid.*, p. 6.
164. VSA, 'Fee Concessions for Harijans,' *Guardian, op. cit.*, p. 567.

Madras, Azariah warned, if the Congress Party proved to be corrupt or identified too closely with the narrow interests of Hinduism.

The bishop criticized the author of 'certain articles in the *Harijan*' for identifying nationalism too closely with Hinduism:

> If the Congress party allows itself to be suspected of such a narrow conception of nationalism, the party will inevitably bring upon itself the antagonism of the followers of all faiths except those of the ancient religion of India. A government or a party has no right to call itself national if it allies itself to one particular religion out of the many professed, followed and loved by its subjects. Speaking for ourselves, our loyalty to our Master comes first, our loyalty to our motherland second. We are first Christians, then Indians. We cannot, yea we dare not, acquiesce in any act of a Government that interferes with our innermost and sacred convictions.[165]

Invoking the memory of Queen Victoria's 1858 proclamation on religious toleration — 'rightly referred to as the Magna Charta of the Indian peoples' — Azariah argued against preferential treatment of any one religion or its followers by civil authorities. The decoupling of confessional from political allegiances would be a prerequisite for gaining the cooperation of all Indian communities in the nationalist enterprise. He challenged Gandhi's many insinuations that, by converting from Hinduism, Indian Christians had betrayed their native heritage and forfeited their legitimacy as nationalists:

> We as citizens of India claim the right to live as Christians, to worship as Christians, to serve the nation as Christians, to commend our religion to others by all peaceful means, and to apply to the solution of India's problems those methods we as Christians have found most effective. We concede the same right to the followers of other religions too. We cannot admit the illogical claim made in some quarters that all religions are of equal regenerating value, and therefore the religion of a man's forefathers is the best for him for all times! Loyalty to Truth as I know it is my duty, even though thereby I might be compelled to be disloyal to my grandmother.[166]

Azariah rejected Gandhi's view that all religions are merely different paths to the same truth. The bishop believed that Gandhi was really legiti-

165. *Ibid.,* p. 8.
166. *Ibid.,* p. 9.

mizing his own newly aggressive and hegemonic relativism under the cloak of religious tolerance. A man whose power and influence was tied to such an orthodoxy could ultimately admit no place for Christian missionaries or conversion. Although Gandhi may not have threatened to legislate against conversion in his face-to-face meeting with Azariah, he challenged Azariah's general right as an Indian to be an evangelist during the interview and in his many criticisms of Christian missionary activity.

Azariah's concern over the threatened predominance of an intolerant Hindu nationalism in the independence movement resembled the misgivings of Jinnah and the Muslim League in the period after the 1937 elections. Indian Christians, like their Muslim co-nationalists during this period, increasingly suspected Gandhi and Congress of promoting intolerant Hindu communalism. A 1940 defense of minority electoral preferences in the *Guardian* accused Congress of furthering a Hindu communalist agenda by undermining the political claims of minority communities. 'The Congress is out to destroy all ['minority'] communal organizations,' the author charged, and 'does not represent India as it claims to do.' Rather, it is 'a body communal in spirit,' which 'calls upon all communities to wind up their communal organizations and merge themselves into it as the panacea for the cure of all the ills the minorities are ailing from.'[167]

Azariah publicly opposed this author's conclusion that Congress could not be trusted to represent Indian Christians, and he noted with pride that some Congressites elected to the Madras Legislature were in fact Indian Christians. He continued to hope that, by stressing common national interests over selfish communal interests, Hindus and Christians could work to make joint electorates a future possibility. In this respect, Azariah continued to support Gandhi's broad nationalist mandate. Advocates of separate electorates argued that Indian Christian leaders like Azariah had 'not taken realities of life into account,' or considered the 'full implications and dangerous consequences'[168] of merging Indian Christians into a general electorate. But Azariah never abandoned his visionary public campaign for a politics that transcended the zero-sum game of competition between minorities seeking to gain advantages at the expense of other groups.

Azariah's writings and speeches in the years before his death reveal, however, increasing distrust of the intentions of Gandhi and Congress in

167. J. Devasikamani, 'Separate Electorates Vs. Joint Electorates with Reservation of Seats,' *Guardian*, XVIII, 10 (7 March 1940), p. 149.
168. *Ibid.*

their bid for *swaraj*. While endorsing the general cause of India's freedom, Azariah asked in 1942 whether or not Christians (85 percent of whom, he estimated, came from the 'slavery and degradation' of the depressed classes) might be deprived of liberty and fundamental material and religious rights by dominant caste Hindus in an independent India:

> Would India's freedom mean a return to the old caste tyranny? From recent experiences [the Indian Christian] is not at all sure it will not. The educated Christian in an academic sort of way desires complete freedom: but would the rural Christian be free when India's freedom comes, to practise his religion, to propagate it to his countrymen and to lift up his head as one made in Christ and raised above the ignominy and disgrace that are attached even to-day to the word *Harijan?* These are [the Indian Christian's] vague fears. Congress leaders have never given the slightest consideration to clearing these doubts.[169]

Earlier in the 1930s, Azariah had belittled the suggestion that Christians would face increased dangers in an independent India, especially when British Tories used such counsels of fear to argue against Indian constitutional reform.[170] But towards the end of the decade, Azariah became concerned that the Indian church might suffer serious persecution in the future.

In a powerful sermon during the height of his controversy with Gandhi, the bishop summoned up the image of persecution of the late first-century church under the Emperor Domitian, who made universal recognition of the claims of the imperial cult a test of loyalty to the empire. In this atmosphere of antagonism between church and state, the early Christians had been accused of criminal disloyalty against the state, which was punishable by death. Azariah likened the plight of some churches in the twentieth century to that of late first-century churches in Asia Minor, though he recognized that the Indian church was threatened not so much by outright barbarism as by 'subtle oppression and intolerant interference.'

> I do not suggest that such a crisis has come in India, and probably it may never come because of the Indian genius for toleration, accommodation and sufferance.

Nevertheless, Azariah suggested that, sooner or later in India:

169. VSA, 'Bishop of Dornakal on the Indian Situation,' *op. cit.* (1942), p. 436.
170. 'The Bishop of Dornakal on Sir H. Page Croft's Scare,' *Guardian*, XII, 28 (12 July 1934), p. 436. Also 'The Bishop's Letter,' *DDM*, XI, 7 (July 1934), pp. 2-4.

Nationalism is apt to be identified with loyalty to the ancient religion of the land; and this identification might easily look with suspicion and disfavour on any religion which is not supposed to belong to the soil, and which, in addition, is pledged to propagate itself among all outside it.[171]

Persecution of Christians in an independent India was not unlikely, Azariah claimed in 1942, given the history of India herself. The Indian Christian has 'not forgotten the past,' Azariah wrote:

His forbears had sufferings from the religious intolerance of their countrymen. He still remembers that when life and light from Christ came to his forefathers, and they decided to obey the light, their own caste kith and kin, their landlords and their masters placed every obstacle imaginable on their path. They were often deprived of their homes, their property, yet sometimes their own lives had been threatened.[172]

At the last meeting of the National Christian Council over which he presided in early 1944, Bishop Azariah forcefully expressed his conviction that Christians must have the right to preach and baptize in an independent India — not in order to gain political advantage (he once again condemned communal representation), but because the church 'can do no other in the light of the command of its Founder to preach the Gospel to every creature.' The NCC statement issued under his leadership further asserted:

It is the duty of Church bodies to urge on Governments the acceptance of the rule of religious liberty; and the duty of Governments to admit no legislation which curtails rather than promotes such liberty. In particular, we would urge that in no circumstances should any penalties be inflicted on those who honestly and sincerely desire to change their religion.[173]

Azariah never withdrew his broad support for the cause of Indian independence, but his growing concern over what he perceived as the threatening

171. 'Sermon Preached by the Bishop at the Consecration of the Bishop in Travancore in St. George's Cathedral, Madras, on October 18th,' *DDM*, XV, 12 (Dec. 1938), p. 7.

172. VSA, 'Bishop of Dornakal on the Indian Situation,' *op. cit.* (1942), p. 436.

173. Azariah headed the NCC Commission on Church and State in Post-war India that issued this statement. *Proceedings of the Ninth Meeting of the National Christian Council*, Nagpur, 1944, p. 48, UTCA.

posture of Hindu nationalism, particularly vis-à-vis Christian missions to the untouchables, continued to strain his already tense relations with Gandhi, the Congress Party, and the independence movement as a whole. Azariah was among the leading Indian Christians who sought to identify his community's interests with those of an independent nation able to decide its own future without foreign interference. But his work among depressed class groups in Andhra also convinced him that many Indians preferred British rule to the prospect of a Congress-led independent government. At the 1942 Episcopal Synod, Azariah reported that the depressed classes felt they owed everything to the British and were afraid of Congress gaining control.[174] His exposure to and fundamental sympathy for such subnational concerns, combined with his interest in safeguarding the future of Christian missionary work in independent India, prevented him from joining with unqualified enthusiasm in the movement for attaining national autonomy.

By the end of his life, Azariah felt 'hand-tied, and lip-tied' by conflicting political loyalties and 'hardly able to give expression to his real convictions.'[175] Many Indian Christians were unpopular with Indian nationalists for not joining Congress. They were also unpopular with minority leaders — Depressed Class, Muslim, and even some Indian Christian — for not throwing themselves into the political struggle for community privileges through the operation of separate electorates. But Azariah and his followers believed, on the one hand, that freedom for India would not bring full freedom for Indian Christians and, on the other, that electoral and legislative battles for communal political advantage would exacerbate old conflicts and undermine the greater national good.

Like Azariah, most Indian Christians opposed the Congress decision to withdraw cooperation from Britain's war effort in August 1942 — but again with a sense of inner tension. The Indian Christian 'is torn between two loyalties,' Azariah wrote. 'He forbears taking sides. He can only pray that the British may understand his longings for his motherland and that his countrymen may understand his loyalty to his religion.'[176] The travails of Indian Christianity in the late Raj are embodied in this image of an aging Azariah 'hand-tied, and lip-tied' by conflicting loyalties in an increasingly hostile political environment in which he felt ever more unpopular and marginalized.

174. 'Episcopal Synod, 1942,' 1: 2, Episcopal Synod, MACIPBC.
175. VSA, 'Bishop of Dornakal on the Indian Situation,' *op. cit.* (1942), p. 436. His description of the Indian Christian situation reflects accurately his own situation.
176. *Ibid.*

The Bishop's Return to Diocesan Life

Politics and his conflict with Gandhi ultimately occupied only a small portion of Azariah's life and attention. Most of his time and energy were devoted to the grassroots project of church building. In his last years, Azariah turned his thoughts and efforts increasingly back to the affairs of his diocese. He spent the last days of his life traveling on dusty roads by bullock cart to visit the villages of the remote Parkal area of his diocese. An American visitor has left a detailed description of Azariah's final days in 1944 and of the village work he most loved.

Azariah began his visit to Parkal by confirming forty men and women in a mud and thatch village chapel:

> They were ragged and not yet very advanced in ways of cleanliness and order, but with persistence the Bishop finally had them seated in orderly rows on the mat-covered mud floor, and the lists of candidates by villages before him. Then came the period of 'examination,' an informal hour when the Bishop in his white cassock sat with them, friendly and fatherly, testing their knowledge of lyrics which told of the life and work of Christ, their understanding of baptism and the promises made, of the Lord's Prayer, the Creed, and asking questions about the witness of their own lives as Christians among their Hindu neighbors.
>
> Except for the [two] teachers none among them were literate, and everything of necessity depended on very simple verbal instruction together with the living witness of the pastor and teachers in their midst. As he sat listening to their lyrics, teaching, asking questions, noting their answers, his face alight with interest and often amusement, he was observing not only the village groups but individuals.[177]

After the examination,

> he talked to them especially about the Holy Spirit, about the work of the Spirit in the lives of Peter and the frightened disciples, about His promises and power to strengthen them in their own lives in the midst of difficult surroundings and temptations. Then he showed them with the help of a young teacher exactly how to kneel for the Confirmation.[178]

177. Eleanor Mason, 'The Bishop of Dornakal's Last Visitation,' typescript, Graham collection.

178. *Ibid.*

The next day Azariah returned to the small chapel to celebrate Holy Communion:

> During the very informal sermon, the Bishop frequently put questions to the people who were alert, interested and responsive. It was the 4th Sunday in Advent, the day before Christmas, and his theme was: Christ has come. He is coming again. He is with us *now,* ever present with us. Therefore *live as in His presence:* be clean, honest, faithful in prayer and worship.[179]

That afternoon Azariah traveled two hours on rough roads in his old cart to visit a small village congregation where he interviewed and encouraged people, listened to their lyrics, and directed a Hindu man who wanted to join the church with his two wives, 'that the wives, being each the wife of one man, might be brought for instruction and baptism, that the husband could not be baptized while both wives were still living but that he was welcome to come to church and join in the daily prayers.' The bishop returned late by moonlight. It was Christmas eve.[180]

On Christmas day, Azariah preached his last sermon in the small Parkal chapel. He spoke on the subject of joy to the village congregation:

> The reasons for this joy? Christ came, and with Him *forgiveness of sins.* Christ came, and *He helps us to be brave* in times of trouble, poverty, sickness. He reminded them of the time when a serious cholera epidemic had broken out in their own village. The Mohammedan moulvi who had recently won away about 100 of the Christians from their faith ran away and left them, but the Christian missionary had stayed and cared for the people helping many back to health, even when he himself was stricken. As a result of his faithfulness the deserters had all come back to the Church. This was how Christ gave courage. Another Christian couple he cited had lost their two sons, grown young men, of typhoid, but with their uncomplaining courage and faith were an inspiration to all. This was how Christ helped people to be brave. Thirdly, we have joy because of the promise of future life, *of life eternal, with Him.*[181]

Christmas celebrations followed for village children and a special St. Stephen's Day service for mission workers, to whom he spoke about the martyr's example of praying for persecutors rather than calling for revenge.

179. *Ibid.* Italics in original.
180. *Ibid.*
181. *Ibid.* Italics in original.

The following days brought more village visitations, including one 'from which he returned disheartened':

> The teacher there was not very experienced and was unable to sing and teach lyrics and [Azariah] had found the Christians very backward. But he had a tale of adventure as he returned when his bullocks had run wild and he had had to jump from the cart. The bulls had dashed into a cornfield and much to his amazement the irate owner, with no sympathy for the plight of the travellers, had demanded indignantly, 'Why have you driven your bulls into my corn?'[182]

Azariah spent many hours during these days translating the Liturgy of the Mar Thoma Syrian Church (from Malayali, presumably to Telugu), reading a book by William Palmer Ladd on prayer, examining church registers, and instructing church workers. He also studied statistics about Christians in India from the latest census reports as well as statistics about Parkal itself collected by the Nizam's administrators on a card hung from the verandah of his traveler's bungalow.

> These included among many other interesting facts about population, schools, mosques, temples — (the number of Christian churches was 0, as the little chapel could not be so classified) — such items as the number of plows and cattle, and the acreage sown with the various grains. This keen interest in the practical and economic background of his people was also shown when his teachers reported many hours wasted in waiting to buy rice which had been removed from the villages to the taluk headquarters. 'You should report it,' he said to them emphatically, and told them how a worker in another area had firmly stood for justice to the poor and had courageously persisted until he had the full cooperation of the officials of the district.[183]

Azariah's chief concern was not the distant world of national politics, but the pressing needs — both material and spiritual — of his depressed class village congregations and of their non-Christian neighbors.

Villagers still remember him as a powerful — sometimes truly formidable — advocate on their behalf against the many persecutions, both large and small, of local landlords and government officers. During the Nizam's era, villagers of Beerole remember being forced to pay high taxes and to give their chickens and eggs to state officials and local leaders. Azariah changed

182. *Ibid.*
183. *Ibid.*

all that. 'The landlords were all afraid of Bishop Azariah,' one woman explained. 'Even the *dorai zamindars* [big landholders] used to fear Azariah, his pastors and evangelists.'[184] Furthermore, villagers continue to express gratitude that Christianity has replaced their former worship of Muthyalamma, who, they recall, was unable to save a villager's uncle from death after being bitten by a scorpion while performing customary *pujas.*[185]

These practical matters of village life and faith continued to grip Azariah to the very end.

> One of the most vivid pictures that remains from these [Parkal] days is from a walk at sunset. A young herdsman was returning across the fields of stubble from his day's toil. 'What did you do about your food today?' the Bishop called out. 'I had a little with me,' the lad replied. 'Are you a Christian?' 'No.' 'Aren't there any Christians in your village?' 'No.' All the missionary in the Bishop sprang into action. He strode across the fields to the lad, erect and vigorous, walking-stick gripped firmly. *'No Christians there?'* The boy stood his ground with fear. 'No,' he said simply. 'No one has told us.' *'No one has told us!'* The Bishop returned meditatively. 'How shall they believe in Him of whom they have not heard? — and how shall they hear without a preacher? — and how shall they preach except they be sent?'

The bishop also worried about Christians in the cities — indeed, he was waiting in Parkal for news of a hoped-for reconciliation between members of urban congregations engaged in lawsuits against one another. But his real passion lay in evangelizing rural populations and transforming village culture.

Azariah died of a 'fever' — probably related to malaria — that his companions believed he contracted in Parkal during an evening trip by bullock cart and foot to 'a tiny village lying entirely surrounded by paddy fields.' His last hours were described in a rare letter by his wife Anbu to their old friend John Mott:

> On Dec. 27th, while we were staying in Parkal Traveller's Bungalow he had a sleepless night but on the next day we left for Dornakal and he said he had a fever when we reached Kazipet Station. His temperature was 102 degrees when we arrived in Dornakal in the evening. The next day the temperature was 103 degrees. Doctor thought it was only ma-

184. Interview with Mrs. S. David, 4 April 1986, Beerole.
185. Interview with Mrs. Perem Kantamma, 4 April 1986, Beerole.

laria. On the 29th the congregation people wanted to see him and pay their respects, as it was the anniversary of his consecration day. He asked them to come on the first of January. He had difficulty breathing for the last two days. . . . He was carrying on his correspondence by dictating letters to his chaplain and our daughter Mercy. We thought he was getting better but he had become extremely weak.

. . . Dr. Little saw him and told him that what he wanted was only rest. He told us that if he could get sleep for 10 hours, undisturbed he could pull through. He gave him pills and medicines for sleep, but it was all in vain. He had his morning devotions on the morning of Jan. 1st. He tried to read *Madras Mail*. He made jokes with Dr. William at 12:30. He asked me to give him some orange juice which I gave him and we left him to sleep. At 1:30 he called for the servant and Mercy went in and saw her father in a sitting posture and he said as if he saw some light and when she took some milk to him, she saw him lying down on his bed; he entered into his eternal rest.

He was ill for three days only and his dreams were all about the Diocese, about the Retreat for the Missionaries, about Bishop Hollis — Bishop of Madras whom he expected to conduct the Retreat, about Parkal Christians, and about the European Soldiers who are not attending Sunday services.

. . . It is very difficult for us not to think of him even for a second. His body is placed inside the Cathedral Compound, behind the Cathedral. He wanted to do some literary work after his retirement. I never thought that he would leave me suddenly and unexpectedly. But God our Heavenly Father knows best. We are being sustained by the prayers of our dear friends all over the world and by the comfort of the Holy Ghost.[186]

Azariah died on New Year's Day, 1945, at the age of seventy. He had served for thirty-two years as Bishop of Dornakal. He was buried in a western-style coffin, the first most villagers had seen.[187] The news of his death traveled quickly across India and the world. Mourners sent messages of sympathy to his family and associates, and countless papers published obituaries describing his achievements.[188]

186. Anbu Azariah to John Mott, 19 Feb. 1945, I: 4/61, Mott Papers, YDS.

187. The coffin replaced the customary burial cloths used to wrap the body by Madigas. Interview with Pedamuthyam Joseph, 4 April 1986, Dornakal. Azariah's wife Anbu died five years later, on 11 Oct. 1950, and was laid to rest beside her husband.

188. Good collections of obituaries may be found in the Graham collection and scattered throughout most major archival collections containing Azariah papers. See, e.g., the memorials of Azariah in *NCCR*, LXV, 2 (Feb. 1945); 'A Great Christian,' *Over-*

Services in his memory were held throughout the Dornakal Diocese, in other Indian diocesan centers, and in London at the parish church of the Houses of Parliament. A pastor told his congregation in Masulipatam that Azariah deserved to rank as one of the 'Saints of Christendom.' A diocesan school administrator told his staff and students that 'The milk of human kindness flowed from him like a fountain,' and that 'his spotless life must be a source of inspiration to the Church for generations to come.' The Archbishop of York told assembled notables in London that Azariah left 'two lasting memorials — a cathedral built in Indian style, and a greater memorial still in the lives of the thousands whom he converted to Christ.'[189]

It was left to Azariah's colleague from Tinnevelly, Bishop Stephen Neill, to read closing prayers for his friend in London:

> We commend into thy hands of mercy, most merciful Father, the soul of our dear brother, Vedanayakam Samuel Azariah, whom it has pleased thee to call home to thyself. . . .
>
> O Almighty Father, who hast joined us together in one brotherhood in Christ with our fellow-Christians in India, Uphold we pray thee, the Bishops and Pastors of thy Church in India, and all congregations committed to their charge. Grant that in sorrow and perplexity they may hold fast the tradition of witness and sacrifice bequeathed to them by this thy servant. Take from them all doubt and distrust. Lift their thoughts up to thee in heaven; and make them to know that all things are made possible to them through thy Son, our Redeemer. Amen.[190]

Shortly thereafter, Neill summarized his views and those of other mourners, that 'Vedanayagam Samuel Azariah at the time of his death was far and away the most outstanding of Indian Christians, and one of the most eminent Church leaders in the world. . . . now he has gone, and those to whom his loss seems literally irreparable are an innumerable company.'[191]

---

seas News 39 (March 1945); 'A Pioneer Indian Bishop,' *Church Times* (12 Jan. 1945) and 'A Shepherd of Souls,' *Church Times* (4 May 1945), p. 253; Carol Graham, 'The Bishop of Dornakal,' *The East and West Review,* XI, 2 (April, 1945), pp. 35-38; *Tinnevelly Diocesan Magazine,* 309 (March 1945), p. 29 (in Tamil).

189. 'Memorials and Tributes to the Bishop,' *DDM* (March and April 1945), pp. 2-6.

190. 'A Service of Thanksgiving in Memory of Vedanayakam Samuel Azariah, Bishop of Dornakal, 1912-1945,' 7 Feb. 1945, St. Margaret's Church, Westminster, Graham Collection.

191. 'Bishop Azariah of Dornakal,' *The Student Movement,* XLVII, 4 (March 1945), p. 84.

Conclusion

Azariah made his greatest impact at the local level as a church builder in Andhra and at the international level in preparing the ground for the unprecedented ecumenical achievement of church unification in South India. In an age characterized above all by political nationalism, Azariah was neither particularly political nor nationalistic. Local evangelism rather than Indian nationalism was his primary concern, and this earned him the enmity of the powerful Mahatma Gandhi.

Azariah's life was filled with ironies: he promoted an indigenous Indian missionary society partly to please a foreign friend, the American Sherwood Eddy. His appointment as the first Indian Anglican bishop was supposed to start a trend in the church, but it was in fact an aberration resisted by many Indians and western missionaries, not imitated until decades later, and misunderstood by foreign friends and admirers. Promoted widely as a symbol of a new age of Indian Christian leaders, Azariah's bishopric was more a creation of elite western liberals — like Copleston and the Whiteheads — than of any popular groundswell in either India or England. The bishop confessed secretly in letters to his wife how hard it was to maintain an authentic identity in the face of well-meaning but intrusive pressures from his 'nationalistic' western Christian friends.

This struggle continued throughout most of his life. His diocese of Dornakal became, like Azariah himself, a symbol of indigenous Christianity in India and a showpiece for the Anglican church globally. But few western patrons ever understood the complex and unpredictable sub-national pressures Azariah faced in the field. The Andhra 'awakening' created much antipathy towards Tamil missionaries in Dornakal. Intercaste

353

rivalries between Malas and Madigas combined with interregional competition to make the appointment of British bishops and missionaries a surprisingly attractive alternative to many Telugu Christians. When the liberal-minded bishops of the Episcopal Synod were bombarded with petitions in 1945 asking for an English successor to the famous 'First Indian Bishop,' it cannot have been an encouraging portent for the future of the Indian church in an independent nation.

Azariah was influenced by, and felt broad sympathy for, the growing aspirations of his countrymen for freedom and self-determination. He constructed his Indian cathedral in Dornakal utilizing architectural elements from indigenous temples and mosques to symbolize his desire to identify Indian Christianity with Indian society more generally. He opposed communal representation, arguing that the political aspirations of Indian Christians were the same as those of the Indian nation. Because of these efforts and others, Azariah is commonly described as one of the pre-eminent Indian Christian nationalists of his generation.[1] But his most fervently 'nationalist' statements concerned ecclesiastical autonomy rather than political independence. With the exception of his outspoken opposition to the Communal Award, Azariah generally kept his distance from nationalist politics, often taking independent positions against the increasingly popular Indian National Congress.

Some British missionaries tried to block Azariah's attempts to transfer ecclesiastical responsibilities (particularly financial ones) from western missionary societies to an independent Indian diocesan structure. An international group of high church Anglicans, notably led by the Anglican poet T. S. Eliot, opposed his efforts to free the Indian church from western denominationalism. But contrary to the commonly expressed view,[2] his campaigns for the devolution of missionary control over the Indian church and for the unification of Protestant churches in South India were inspired more by the imperatives of mission (and the irritating unwillingness of western missionaries to live up to their own ideals) than by the Indian national movement. The names of Henry Venn, John Thomas,

---

1. He is usually cited along with K. T. Paul and S. K. Datta as one of the few Indian Christian leaders who sought to identify the interests of the Indian Christian community with that of the nation at large. See, e.g., 'The Late Bishop of Dornakal,' *Guardian*, XXIII, 1 (4 Jan. 1945), pp. 2, 8; A. V. Thomas, *Christians in Secular India, op. cit.*, p. 102; D. B. Forrester, *Caste and Christianity, op. cit.*, p. 185; G. Hewitt, *The Problems of Success, op. cit.*, p. 44.

2. For example, G. Thomas, *Christian Indians and Indian Nationalism, 1885-1950, op. cit.*, pp. 173-74.

Roland Allen, Henry Whitehead, and Foss Westcott appear far more often in Azariah's writings than the names of non-Christian Indian nationalists.

The desire for increased Indian Christian ecclesiastical self-expression reflected primarily the growing self-assurance of a maturing indigenous church with a strong evangelistic vision.[3] Azariah borrowed the popular vocabulary of secular political nationalism, demanding 'transfer of responsibilities, responsible self-government, opportunities for self-expression' for the church,[4] and he shared his countrymen's 'strong convictions and painful heart-yearnings for a free India.'[5] But the bishop remained largely aloof from the details of politics, as did most of the organizations in which he held important positions. The National Missionary Council and the National Christian Council rarely expressed more than evasive and unenthusiastic support for the independence movement.[6] Azariah's apparent silence after the Amritsar massacre of 1919,[7] his quiet opposition to non-cooperation, civil disobedience, and other Gandhian-inspired phases of 'rebellion' against government authorities, and his condemnation of the Congress Party's withdrawal of support for Britain during the Second World War, all placed him more often than not in a pro-British position. Apart from his stand against the government's communally based electoral reforms and its 'immoral' collection of state lottery and alcohol revenues,[8] Azariah seldom opposed British policy in India. His 1942 statement that 'with trembling conviction Indian Christians see that they must be on the side of India's

3. For a refreshing example of a missions- and church-centered explanation for indigenization, see V. E. Devadutt, 'What Is an Indigenous Theology? (with special reference to India),' *Ecumenical Review*, II, 1 (Autumn 1949), pp. 40-51. ('I have heard it said again and again that the urge for "indigenisation" is inspired by nationalist feeling. On the contrary,' p. 43.) See also I. David, 'The Development of the Concept of Indigenisation,' *op. cit.*, p. 43.

4. See the *Proceedings of the National Missionary Council* for the Reports of the Committee on the Indian Church, of which Azariah was the Convener from 1916: *Proceedings of the Fourth Meeting of the National Missionary Council, Coonoor 9-13 Nov. 1917*, pp. 15-22 (quote from p. 19); *Proceedings of the Fifth Meeting of the National Missionary Council, Benares, 14-19 Nov. 1918*, pp. 13-19; *Proceedings of the Sixth Meeting of the National Missionary Council, Lahore, 13-18 Nov. 1919*, pp. 15-23.

5. 'Bishop of Dornakal on the Indian Situation,' *Guardian*, XX, 37 (17 Sept. 1942), p. 436.

6. G. Thomas, *Christian Indians and Indian Nationalism, 1885-1950, op. cit.*, pp. 165-67, 198-99; K. Baago, *A History of the National Christian Council of India, 1914-1964, op. cit.*

7. Compare Henry Whitehead's condemnation of the British role at Amritsar in *Indian Problems, op. cit.*, pp. 302-18.

8. K. Heiberg, *V. S. Azariah: Biskop af Dornakal, op. cit.*, p. 94; Thamil Selvan, 'Research on Bishop Azariah and His Theology,' *op. cit.*, p. 55.

freedom' has been criticized for expressing more trembling than conviction.[9]

To criticize Azariah for his lack of involvement in nationalist politics is to miss both the nature of his contribution to society and the importance of subnational developments. Unlike Gandhi, Azariah was not a politician and did not believe that politics and religion were virtually inseparable. He was a missionary and church builder deeply involved in agrarian conversion movements, uplifting depressed classes and promoting inter-church cooperation. His refusal in 1932 to cancel his diocesan confirmation tour in order to speak against the Communal Award at the Poona All-India Christian Conference illustrated his attitude towards politics:

> It is the duty of Church representatives like myself to be interested in the great principles underlying political or civil problems as they affect religion. When these principles are recognized, it is only right that politicians should work out the details; and we ought to be content to leave such decisions to them.[10]

Nonetheless, Azariah's mobilization of opposition to the Communal Award may have contributed to its eventual abolition after independence.[11] But the bishop did not otherwise involve himself in matters of specific policy or legislation. His main channels of influence were ecclesiastical rather than political, extending from his church center in Dornakal worldwide to other Anglican dioceses, to other denominations and to extraecclesiastical organizations. His leadership of the National Christian Council, the Joint Committee on Union, the Bible Society, the Forward Movement for Evangelism, church and missionary society conferences and study schools, his attendance at the major international Christian conferences of his day, and his authorship of articles, books, and pamphlets — all are testimony to his prodigious activity and enormous influence among Christians in India and abroad.

Azariah was a man of the church who fundamentally trusted the British, with whom he shared religious bonds. Just as he desired a free and independent Indian church to remain part of the historic and catholic An-

---

9. VSA, 'Bishop of Dornakal on the Indian Situation,' *Guardian, op. cit.* (1942), pp. 436-37.

10. VSA, 'Bishops and Politics' and 'The Bishop of Dornakal and the Poona Conference,' *op. cit.* (1932), p. 475.

11. G. Thomas, *op. cit.,* pp. 205-18.

glican communion, he also desired India to remain in close association with Britain, whose role in Indian history he viewed as essentially providential and positive. Azariah regarded even the rise of Indian nationalism as part of God's preparation of India for Christianity.[12]

As a Christian in a predominantly Hindu India, as a Tamil missionary in Telugu territory, and as a Nadar amidst Malas, Madigas, and Telugu non-Brahmins, Azariah was a perpetual foreigner in his own country. He understood the concerns of so many sub-national forces opposing national unity that it is surprising he had any nationalist sympathy at all. His close association with Andhra's depressed classes, who generally preferred British to 'Hindu or Brahmin rule,' made the bishop wary of Congressite plans for independence, particularly after his controversy with Gandhi. Azariah's political and religious affinities with the British were acceptable to most Indian Christians in Dornakal but not to non-Christian nationalists and to many liberal western colleagues. Pressure to conform to the Indian cultural stereotypes often advocated by westerners placed him in an equally awkward position with Dornakal's rural converts.

Azariah's personal and theological consistency enabled him to cope with all these competing pressures with amazing serenity. He never wavered in his commitments to evangelizing and educating Andhra's 'untouchables,' building his church, and advancing the ecumenical movement. Neither did he appear disturbed by his lonely eminence as the first and only Indian in the Episcopal Synod.

Azariah was exposed to a particularly wide variety of what anthropologists describe as 'cultural systems,' each interacting with the others to influence actions and decisions.[13] Cultural systems of caste (Nadars, Malas, Madigas, and others), language and region (Tamil and Telugu), nation (Indian, British, American), and religion (Christianity, Hinduism, and Islam with all their local, national, and international variations), all affected Azariah's life and were, in turn, affected by him.

Certain common experiences, ideas, and understandings united Azariah, Eddy, and Whitehead within a common transnational Christian cultural system, to which they brought ideas conditioned by their shared

---

12. A. M. Mundadan, *Indian Christians Search for Identity, op. cit.*, p. 191.

13. On the concept of cultural systems (defined as 'products of human interaction within whatever size demographic framework there is communication maintained over any significant length of time and by whatever means of communication'), see Jack R. Rollwagen, 'Reconsidering Basic Assumptions: A Call for a Reassessment of the General Concept of Culture in Anthropology,' *Urban Anthropology*, XV, 1-2 (1986), pp. 97-133; definition on p. 105.

participation in (and sometimes resistance to) the cultural system of Indian nationalism. Whitehead and Eddy may be aptly described as 'Indian nationalists' by virtue of their experiences and sympathies, despite their British and American origins. Azariah's appointments to the YMCA Secretariat and the Anglican episcopate both represented efforts by the Anglo-American leaders of international Christian cultural systems (student ecumenism and Anglicanism respectively) to propitiate the increasingly vocal demands of Indian nationalism. Azariah's execution of his duties in each office influenced, in turn, the nature of those international systems, making them less western and more Asian in character.

However, Azariah made an unpredictably unique and distinctive mark in the midst of these many overlapping and sometimes competing cultural systems. Even the most analytically powerful systems theory cannot fully explain the individuality of a figure like Azariah. In this respect, his biography provides an illuminating example of what R. G. Collingwood has described as 'the freedom of man as an historical agent.'[14] No single theory or model is capable of fully explaining why Azariah chose the vocation of missionary and church leader in rural Andhra and rejected the popular tendency of the interwar years to convert religious faith into secular utopianism or, at least, to substitute a 'social gospel' for the evangelical gospel message. And he resisted this trend despite the intimidating pressure of his towering contemporary, Mahatma Gandhi.

Azariah's career provides a stark contrast to that of Sherwood Eddy, whose early missionary zeal was transformed by the 1920s and 1930s into support for socialist and communist experiments.[15] After they had traveled together at the turn of the century to promote the straightforward claims of evangelical Christianity, Eddy's and Azariah's paths diverged

14. 'The discovery that the men whose actions [the historian] studies are . . . free is a discovery which every historian makes as soon as he arrives at a scientific mastery of his own subject.' R. G. Collingwood, *The Idea of History* (London, 1966), p. 318.

15. As Stalin executed his genocidal forced collectivization of the Russian peasants, Sherwood Eddy hosted annual tours of Russia for American radicals and left-wing liberals to observe, firsthand, the socialist reconstruction. Eddy published his book, *Russia Today: What Can We Learn From It?*, in 1932 shortly after cooperating with Reinhold Niebuhr in the establishment of the Fellowship of Socialist Christians. R. W. Fox, *Reinhold Niebuhr, op. cit.,* p. 123; P. Johnson, *op. cit.,* p. 260. By 1949, however, Eddy warned Indian students of 'the tyranny of Soviet Russia's police state and slave labor camps, of the Soviet's imperialistic advance and conquests through its use of every means, fair or foul, moral or immoral, in every country in the world; and the repudiation of all absolute moral standards by its dogmatic atheism.' *Religion and Politics in India* (typewritten letter from Dornakal, 1949), p. 2, II: 6/125, Eddy Papers, YDS.

when Azariah decided, against Eddy's will,[16] to leave the YMCA for Dornakal in 1909. The American's later absorption in secular social service work greatly differed from Azariah's continuing missionary work. Azariah remained throughout his life a man of faith who was largely immune to the influence of popular ideologies.

Azariah's and Eddy's gradual separation after more than a decade of united missionary effort symbolized the growing rift in the worldwide church by the 1920s between liberal proponents of the 'social gospel' and more conservative evangelicals. This rift developed after the Second World War into the so-called 'ecumenical-evangelical standoff.' The irony in this bitter intrachurch dispute is that the ecumenical movement found its roots in the evangelical mission field where denominational divisions were discovered to be a crippling obstacle. Azariah became deeply involved in the beginnings of the ecumenical movement largely because he was a committed evangelical missionary. His work as an evangelist to Telugu outcastes in his vast rural diocese motivated him to become a leader in the negotiations which led to the creation of the Church of South India shortly after his death.

His missionary work at the grassroots level was the central source of his strength and authority as a world-renowned leader of this ecumenical dialogue which produced the first formal union of episcopal and non-episcopal Christian churches of the modern era. His diocesan experience revealed the divisive effects of denominationalism on India's village congregations, where converts of different castes perpetuated their social separations by joining churches of different denominations. It was this crippling practical effect of denominationalism that impelled Azariah to engage for over three decades in the arduous work of church unification.

Azariah's inner tranquillity during a turbulent era may be attributed to the consistency of his goals. Despite being thrust almost unwittingly into a position of unprecedented international prominence, his central interests always remained local village evangelism and social uplift of the depressed classes. Stephen Neill has contended that Azariah's greatest strengths were revealed in the most ordinary circumstances:

16. He changed his mind upon witnessing Azariah's subsequent work. During a visit to the Dornakal Diocese in 1949, Eddy wrote:

When Azariah died on January 1, 1945 after thirty-two years of labour, he left in his diocese a Christian community of 230,000. They have been uplifted above carrion-eating, devil worship, robbery and drunkenness, just as St. Paul's converts 'turned from idols to serve the living God.' . . . On the whole, this Dornakal diocese is the finest piece of mission work, the most deeply spiritual and the most fruitful, that I have seen in any land. (G. S. Eddy, *Religion and Politics in India, op. cit.,* p. 3)

Azariah was at his best with groups of very simple village enquirers, with Confirmation candidates from among the depressed classes, or surrounded by village clergy and teachers, whom he had himself chosen and trained, and whom he loved to build up in their faith and knowledge by the forthright Biblical exposition of which he was a supreme master. He was invariably courteous and considerate; everyone who had to do with him knew that he would get absolutely fair treatment.[17]

His many acts of kindness, both small and large, for otherwise despised and neglected people are well remembered in the villages today and perhaps remain his greatest legacy to India. Notwithstanding his sometimes authoritarian administrative style, *Thandrigaru* is still remembered fondly as one who sacrificed his life for a 'foreign' people, as the leader who rose every morning before sunrise to read his Bible and to pray, and as the bishop who never forgot the villages despite his international acclaim.

The people Azariah most deeply influenced are precisely those whose views are least expressed in written history. The ordinary people of South India, who were closest to the man himself, lived at a subsistence level and rarely had the skills or the opportunity to write down their views. An echo has survived, however, in the largely unrecorded tradition of Telugu *bhajan* (praise) songs, which still today preserve his memory in rural Andhra.

Azariah developed a corpus of Telugu lyrics for use in the evangelization and instruction of his largely illiterate Dornakal convert populations. He taught the basics of the faith and enlivened worship services with the beauty of songs set to the indigenous and rhythmic melodies of Karnatica music. Singing in Telugu was a central part, not only of every church service, but also of his interviews with village congregants, who would often answer his questions with sung lyrics. Sometimes these songs were accompanied by liturgical dancing and drama as well. Women often sang Christian lyrics while doing their fieldwork, and, Carol Graham remembers, 'it was not unusual to find Hindu women word perfect in a long lyric about the life of Christ.'[18] Indeed, through this tradition of Telugu Christian music, Christian converts found new ways to influence their Hindu culture:

Dornakal had an orchestra of Indian instruments and the remotest village congregation had knuckle drums and cymbals. Parties of singers visited the big Hindu festivals and could hold large audiences for hours together with an indigenous form of oratorio in which a soloist nar-

17. 'Bishop Azariah of Dornakal,' *The Student Movement, op. cit.,* p. 84.
18. Carol Graham, *Between Two Worlds, op. cit.,* p. 24.

360

rated a biblical saga interspersed with lyrics sung in chorus as a running commentary.[19]

Azariah taught villagers songs about Christ's birth, the Crucifixion, the Prodigal Son, the Ten Virgins, and the Sermon on the Mount, many of which are still remembered in Dornakal today. He used lyrics to instruct converts about Christian responsibilities: one called on Christians to 'spread the gospel in this country of Hindu Desham once ruled by a king called Bharatha'; another described how women should also participate in evangelistic campaigns.[20] He also taught simple devotional songs as aids to worship:

> Oh my Savior come down to bless us,
> Maharaja, Sovereign King, you are the father of this area,
> Son of Mary, Glorious King,
> We gather here to thank you and to praise you.
> So you shower your grace and your spirit on us.
> Send your spirit on the people of Dornakal,
> Because you are a loving God.[21]

Or songs designed to reinforce the most basic tenets of the faith:

> Jesus Christ is the Supreme God
> And he is the Savior of All.
> Jesus' blessings will be on the earth forever.
> This is a true fact.[22]

Some lyrics were composed specifically to accompany dances, such as one previously mentioned song which likens God to sweet jaggery sugar (*cheruku belam*):

> Wherever there is jaggery, there are ants;
> Wherever people preach the Gospel, many people will also gather;
> Victory! Alleluia![23]

---

19. *Ibid.*, pp. 24-25.
20. Sung to the author in Telugu by Rev. Daniel, Dornakal, April 1986. 'Friends who love to serve their country. Friends who love to serve their God. Come Forward!'
21. Sung to the author in Telugu by Eluka Nakshitrama, Madiripuram, April 1986.
22. Sung to the author in Telugu by Mrs. Rachael, Mahabubabad, April 1986.
23. Sung to the author in Telugu by Mr. Kumari Joseph Samuel, Madiripuram, April 1986. This translation conveys the meaning of the song but not the

Praise songs about Azariah himself soon developed and became a tradition, alongside the diocese's growing corpus of devotional hymns and narrative songs about biblical stories. Some of these *bhajans* about Azariah seem to have been composed spontaneously by village congregations, while others were composed by a popular Telugu Christian lyricist, Subbaya, whose liturgical dramas were used throughout the diocese. Many of these Telugu lyrics about Azariah are still remembered and sung by the older people in the villages today, reflecting the affection felt for the bishop by the people he served:

> Whether it was a large town or a poor village;
> Whether in the monsoon or hot sun;
> You still tour and set up lots of camps to tell people about God.

> Oh Bishop-oo, oh Bishop-oo,
> Sri bishop-oo, Dornakal-oo,
> Head of the Diocese,
> Sri bishop-oo
> Dornakal.

> You bless those Christians in Dornakal Diocese
> who are without food or clothing,
> those who are like orphans.

> Oh Bishop-oo, oh Bishop-oo,
> Sri bishop-oo, Dornakal-oo,
> Head of the Diocese,
> Sri bishop-oo
> Dornakal.[24]

---

rhythm achieved by its repetition. For example, the second verse translates more literally as:

> For Jesus Christ, like the gathering of ants; Victory! Alleluia!
> Like ants gathering; Victory! Alleluia!
> People from surrounding areas; Victory! Alleluia!
> Gathered around Jesus Christ; Victory! Alleluia!
> There are countless benefits; Victory! Alleluia!
> These people are profited; Victory! Alleluia!

24. Sung to the author in Telugu by Mr. Kumari Joseph Samuel, Madiripuram, April 1986.

The prolific Subbaya wrote one song specially to welcome the bishop home from a world tour:

> The Bishop who has good qualities has come back safely.
> So we are thanking God!
>
> He came from England by ship,
> By God's Grace only, he came safely.
> He came like a brave man with firm ideas
> And a humble heart.
>
> The bishop who has good qualities has come back safely.
> So we are thanking God!
>
> Bishop Azariah was a beautiful and beloved
> Disciple of God in India.
> So we gather here to thank Azariah.
> Please accept our thanks and greetings.
>
> The bishop who has good qualities has come back safely.
> So we are thanking God!
>
> Since you have come to Dornakal
> You have become our protector and sole support,
> Today, you have come back like a brave warrior
> And a guru to do mighty things.
>
> The bishop who has good qualities has come back safely:
> So we are thanking God![25]

A similar lyric welcoming him home from a trip abroad hailed the 'talented, good character' of Azariah, and concluded: 'We gather here to praise thee, oh Lord, for our first Indian bishop in Asiatic lands.' Other 'welcome songs' were shorter and less formal than Subbaya's, but equally appreciative of his hard work on behalf of the villages:

> Bishop, respected bishop, we welcome you;
> The bishop does not worry about sun, heat, rain, hardships.
> You have traveled through all sorts of weather![26]

25. Sung to the author in Telugu by Eluka Nakshitrama, Madiripuram, April 1986.

26. Sung to the author in Telugu by Mr. Kumari Joseph Samuel, Madiripuram, April 1986.

Another lyric describes Azariah's contribution to the life of the depressed classes in Dornakal:

> The ship called 'Church Mission' is on the move;
>   Jesus Christ is the Captain
>   and the leaders of the church are the crew.
>
> As its rightful owner, our father Azariah
>   brought the mission here to the people;
>   Nobody else could have done this, only he.
>
> Because of the church mission, this area
>   has flourished like a beautiful garden,
>   and like Midian.
>
> This ship has come from the Madras Presidency
>   to the Telugu area,
>   And all are singing: 'Brother!' 'Jesus!' 'Hosanna!'[27]

Yet another song praises Azariah for building the Dornakal cathedral and reflects the local pride in that accomplishment:

> This is the best cathedral,
> It brings fame to Dornakal,
> It is shining beautifully like gold.
>
> There is a bell in the high dome,
>   at the entrance gate,
> It is ringing 'tang-tang,'
>   'come-come!'
>
> This is the best cathedral,
> It brings fame to Dornakal,
> It is shining beautifully like gold.
>
> The floor is made of marble,
> This marble is very costly.
> The clerestory windows are properly arranged,
> The nails are colored black, red, white and green.
>
> This is the best cathedral

27. *Ibid.*

Who built it?
Sri Azariah,
Our most respected bishop.[28]

Finally, a song asks for blessings on Azariah:

Oh God, bless us, bless us now.
Oh Savior of poor people, please bless us now.

Oh Glorious Son of Mary,
bless our bishop [*Thandrigaru*] and us too.
Oh heavenly King;
bless our respected bishop. [*Maharaja raja shri*]

Oh heavenly God, feeder of poor people.
Send your Holy Spirit
on your servant who is living in Dornakal.[29]

The testimony of villagers today, shared orally in songs and stories, speaks eloquently of Azariah's enduring contribution to the life of his co-religionists and countrymen. Some resentments remain, particularly among the more educated who felt their aspirations thwarted by Azariah's focus on village uplift. But these are balanced by the powerful testimonies of people like Nama Ruth, the Dornakal sweet seller, whose eyes filled with tears when asked by this author to share her memories of Bishop Azariah: 'Bishop Azariah brought everything to Dornakal: education, money, the gospel. He was very strict, but on the other hand he was very kind towards poor people.' Or people like Gaddikoppula Isaiah, an eighty-five-year-old Telugu evangelist who walked slowly, leaning on a walking stick, across a long distance of sun-parched terrain to contribute his memories of Bishop Azariah to this study: 'Even though he became a bishop, he still loved villages and traveled in a bullock cart. He loved me and encouraged me in my work.'[30]

The subsequent history of the Dornakal church has not been a story of unmitigated success. The nationalist campaign against evangelism was highly effective: conversions slowed and church growth tapered off after Independence. The modern state of Andhra Pradesh, which encompasses

28. *Ibid.*
29. *Ibid.*, 5 April 1986.
30. Interviews with Nama Ruth, 8 April 1986, Dornakal; and with Gaddikoppula Isaiah, 5 April, 1986, Madiripuram.

the areas of Azariah's former diocese, has witnessed some Christian revival, but the role of the Church of South India has not always been a constructive one. Infighting between rival groups — often over the election of bishops — has combined with alleged corruption and periodic lawsuits to produce a rather depressing sequel to the Azariah story. Some of the groundwork laid in the first half of the century has been seriously eroded: educated Christians have left the villages, property has been contested, bitterness remains in the wake.

These problems would have saddened Azariah, but most of them would not have surprised him. Already in the 1940s Azariah began to counsel his diocese on the particular problems and temptations of 'second generation Christians' and of the church in the postwar era: spiritual complacency, material temptation, factionalism.[31] He warned that the 'problems are under the surface and may emerge in awkward forms any day.' In discussing 'the problem of helping the Church to be the Church ... so that it may function in the power of the Risen Lord in a post-war India,' Azariah saw the church 'maligned and crucified . . . passing once again through its Gethsemane and its Calvary with its Lord.' But he ended on a note of hope:

> It will have its Easter too. The Church should realize this and prepare for the resurrection day. We must even now bear witness to the unchanging power of the Cross of Christ — power to melt hard hearts, power to inaugurate the new era, power to overcome the evil and selfish ambitions of men everywhere, and power to draw all men unto Himself.[32]

Azariah's contribution has been obscured by the more dramatic political events engulfing his motherland during his career. His legacy and the witness of his church have both been practically obliterated by the rush of events leading to Independence and by widespread hostility of Hindu and secular nationalists to Christian evangelism. But not even the long shadow of the Mahatma has completely eclipsed the bright memories that still survive in the grassroots, among ordinary Indians for whom Azariah provided a powerful and unforgettable example of Christian servanthood in troubled times.

31. VSA, 'The Care of the Christians of the Second Generation,' *NCCR*, LXII, 1 (Jan. 1942), pp. 19-25; 'Post-War Problems of Churches and Missions in India,' *NCCR*, LXIII, 8 (Aug. 1943), pp. 263-70.
32. VSA, 'Post-War Problems of Churches and Missions in India,' *op. cit.*, pp. 269-270.

Bibliography

A. Primary Materials

I. Manuscripts

Asbury College, Wilmore, Kentucky:
J. W. Pickett Papers: unprocessed collection.

Azariah Collection, in possession of Mr. Ambrose Azariah, Madras:
Clippings Album.
Original Letters of V. S. Azariah to Anbu Azariah, 1899-1930.
Family photo album

Bishop's House Archives, Calcutta (BHA):
Minutes of the Episcopal Synods Held at Calcutta from 1910 to 1936.
Minutes of the Episcopal Synods of the Province of India and Ceylon, 1863-1908 (copy also in MDA).
Proceedings of Meetings of the Provincial Assembly of the Church of the Province of India, Burma and Ceylon, 1920, 1922; of the Provincial Council of the Church of India, Burma and Ceylon, 1922, 1926; and *of the General Council of the Church of India, Burma and Ceylon, 1928, 1930.*
Proceedings of the General Council, 1930-1966.
Reports of the Episcopal Conferences 1888-97.

Bodleian Library, Oxford:
Negotiating Committee for Church Union in North India, films 1179 (44-63).
Sankey Papers, fols. 538-40.

Cambridge University Library Manuscripts Collection, Cambridge:
Cambridge Papers (Rare Book Collection), HM51 (1895-1925).
Visitors Book, "Add 6370."

Centre of South Asian Studies, University of Cambridge (CSAS):
Anglican Missions in India: Answers to Questionnaires on Missions and Missionaries in India during the British Period.
Ferrar Papers.
Irene Mott Bose Papers: two boxes.
John R. Mott Papers; file 1: Excerpts from letters to daughter Irene Mott Bose.
Taped interviews with Missionaries: Bishop F. R. Willis, 21 June 1976, MT32; Bishop W. Q. Lash, 11 June 1974, MT24; The Revd. E. and Mrs. Gallagher, 22 June 1976; Dr. Ruth Hardy, 23 June 1983.
Wadsworth Papers: Sir Sidney Wadsworth, *Lo the Poor Indian.*

Church Missionary Society Archives, University of Birmingham (CMSA):
Series G2 I2/0: 1910-14, 1922-27; G2 I9/0: 1924-31.
Series G2 I2/L16: 1911-17; G2 I2/L12, no. 106; G2 I2/L17: 1917-24; G2 I9/L1: 1924-31; G2 I9/L2: 1931-34.
Series G2 I2/P5: 1904-13; G2 I2/P6: 1910-24.

Dornakal Diocesan Archives and Cathedral Compound, Dornakal, A.P. (DDA):
Baptismal Records: *Medithapalli, 1922-36;* unmarked register 1914-47; *Register of Baptisms: Adults, August 1906-22.*
Church Censures: Diocese of Dornakal, I: 1914-32; II: 1933-45.
Clergy Leave Books.
Confirmations by the Bishop of Dornakal, 1913-44.
Inscriptions in the Cathedral Compound.
Marriage Register: *Indian Missionary Society of Tinnevelly, Telugu Mission.*
Purchase Deeds of the Old Compound, Dornakal.
Register: The Cathedral Church of the Epiphany, Dornakal.

Friends House, London (FH):
Agatha Harrison Papers, India Conciliation Group (ICG): Boxes 42-50D.

General Commission on Archives and History, The United Methodist Church, Drew University, Madison, New Jersey (GCAH, UMC):
Conferences: Bombay 383-89, 730, 735; India 315-23, 353-61, 699-705, 860; South India 366, 375, 726-29.
India Committee: 1109-3-2: 04-06.
J. W. Pickett Papers: 1185-4-3: 03-07.

J. W. Pickett: 446-47, 751, 870; Eugene Smith: 433, 748-49; H. Lester Smith: 486.

Graham Collection, in author's temporary possession:
Dornakal, September 14-23, 1948: Extracts from a diary of the Dornakal 'invasion.'
Manuscripts by Carol Graham, including: *The Consecration of Dornakal Cathedral, History of the Mothers' Union in the Dornakal Diocese, Worship in the Dornakal Diocese, Worship in the Indian Church, Christianity and the New India, The Inauguration of the Church of South India, Address to the Mothers' Union Overseas Meeting, December 5th 1944, A Dornakal Occasion, Family Gold* (in English and Telugu), *Bible Studies and Questions for Group Discussion on the Christian Home, Light in Our House* (in English, Tamil, and Telugu; this work was translated into six other Indian vernaculars by 1942), *Christian Home Festival* (in English and Tamil).
'Press Cuttings' envelope.

Harvard Divinity School, Rare Books and Manuscripts Room:
Edward C. Carter, *Among Indian Young Men,* Cambridge, Massachusetts, March 1904.

Houghton Library, Harvard University:
The American Board of Commissioners for Foreign Missions: ABC: 16.1.1 v. 32-37, 16.1.01-03, 50.

India Office Library and Records, London (IOL):
Curzon Papers, MSS Eur F. 112/21.
Datta Papers, Letter Books, Mss Eur. F. 178, 4-5.
Home Miscellaneous Series 864 (1), Diaries of Sir F. A. Hirtzel, 1905-10/1911, Photo Eur 24, reel 740, vol. 1-2.
India Ecclesiastical Proceedings, Government of India, Proceedings of the Department of Education (GOI, PODOE), 1905, 1910, 1911, 1912.
India Ecclesiastical Proceedings, Government of India, Proceedings of the Home Department (GOI, HDP), 1905, 1908, 1909, 1910, 1911.
Judicial and Public Department (J&P), 1904, 677, 1164; 1905, 3860; 1912, 1163, 2341.
Judicial and Public Department Register and Indexes (J&PDR), 1912, Z/L/PJ/6-33.
Madras Ecclesiastical Proceedings, Ecclesiastical Department, Government of Madras (ED, GOM); 1908, P/7984; 1912, P/9029.
Morley Papers, MSS Eur DS73/67.

Indian Missionary Society of Tirunelveli Archives, Palayamkottai (IMSA):

Minute Book 1922-1950: Proceedings of the Indian Missionary Society (PIMS) (in Tamil).

Minute Book, 1903-1922, Minutes of the Executive Committee: Proceedings of the Indian Missionary Society (PIMS) (in Tamil).

Suvisesha Pirabalya Varthamani (The Missionary Intelligencer) (TMI-IMS) (in Tamil).

The 11th Annual Report of the IMS of Tinnevelly, 1913-14 (in Tamil).

The 15th Annual Report of the IMS of Tinnevelly, 1917-18 (in Tamil).

The 28th Annual Report of the IMS of Tinnevelly, 1930-1931, Palamcottah, 1931 (in Tamil).

Joint Archives of the International Missionary Council and Conference of British Missionary Societies, School of Oriental and African Studies, London (IMC/CBMS, SOAS):

National Christian Council Correspondence (NCCC), Boxes 395, 396, 406, 408, 410, 414, 441.

Lambeth Palace Library, London (LP):

Address to the World Conference on Faith and Order, 1937: ms. **2636**: 52-55.

Lambeth Conference Papers: ms. **105**: 191-95; **107**: 173; **108**: 176-77; **109**: 208-9; **134**: 384-87; **146**: 232-41; **147**: 84, 95, 372; **148**: 138, 203-4, 323, 437-38.

Papers of Archbishop Davidson: vol. **178**: 356-96.

Papers of Archbishop Lang: vol. **143**: 381-413, 151, 305-8; **171**: 314-87.

Papers of Archbishop Temple: vols. **27-29**, **36**, **59**.

Papers of E. J. Palmer, Bishop of Bombay: ms. **2966**: 172-77, 181, 211, 221-23, 224, 231, 238, 264, 265-66; **2969**: 188, 227-29, 297; **2975**: 84; **2978**: 13, 89-90, 97-104, 111-15, 148, 150-52, 171-72, 233-38, 274-85, 312, 341, 344-53, 357-59, 366-72; **2986**: 53.

Recollections of 1945 — Given by the Missionary and Ecumenical Council of the Church Assembly, 1964: ms. **2551**: 158-223.

Report on Union in South India, 1938: ms. **2977**: 253-60.

Resolutions Passed by the Synod of the Province of India and Ceylon at Sessions Held in the Palace, Calcutta on 6-11, Jan. 1908.

The Minutes of the Episcopal Synod Held at Calcutta from 1910 to 1936.

Madras Diocesan Archives, St. George's Cathedral Compound, Madras (MDA):

Charges Delivered in St. George's Cathedral at the Visitations of Frederick Gell, D.D., Bishop of Madras, 1863, 1867, 1869, 1873, 1877, 1882, 1891, 1896.

Metropolitan Archives of the Church of India, Pakistan, Burma and Ceylon, Bishop's College, Calcutta (MACIPBC):
Bishops, Series 7, Boxes 1-5 (hereafter 7: 1-5/file number).
Dornakal, 5: 1, 2.
Episcopal Synod, 1.
Foss Westcott, box unmarked.
General Council, 1.
ISPCK, 1-3.
Lambeth Conference, 1, 2.
Madras, 1: 1.
Metropolitan, 1-5.
NMS, 1.
Personal, 1, 3.
Reforms and India, 1.
Tinnevelly, 1: 3.
Unity, 1-4.
Unity CSI, 1-6, 8-11.

National Missionary Society Archives, Madras (NMSA):
In His Footsteps: Report of the NMS of India, 1936.
Original Minute Books: Proceedings of the Executive Committee, I (Dec. 1905–Dec. 1923).
Original Minute Books: Proceedings of the Executive Committee, II (Jan. 1924–Nov. 1933).
Proceedings of the National Missionary Society: Minute Book (Dec. 1905–Dec. 1923).

Neill Collection, in Possession of Rev. Charles Neill, Oxford:
Unpublished mss. by Stephen C. Neill: *Autobiography/Journal,*[1] *The Christian World.*

Pastor's House, Madiripuram:
Copy of doc. by VSA, *Madiripuram Rules,* Dornakal, 26 April 1935.
Manuelraj, I. Victor. *Lambadi Mission,* Paper presented at All-India IMS Conference held at Tiruchinapally, 18-19 February 1984; typescript from author.

Selly Oak Colleges Archive and Library, Birmingham (SOCA):
Box: 'Pamphlets (Old) 275.'
Box: 'Pamphlets on South India Church Union Scheme.'
Circular Letters from Missionaries, S. India, 1937-65.

1. Since using this manuscript, it has been edited for publication by Eleanor Jackson.

Occasional Letters of Miss D. J. Stephen (Box: Pamphlets [Old] 275).

Papers labelled 'Church of South India — Negotiations for and Inauguration of the Union.'

Papers of Michael Hollis.

Serampore College, William Carey Library, Calcutta:

Letters to Rev. L. McIntosh, File 30.

Wenger, E. S. *Missionary Biographies,* four handwritten volumes, updated until author's death in 1911.

Sundkler Collection, Uppsala, Sweden:

Notes on interview with Isabel Whitehead, September 1947.

Research notes, notes of interviews, and private correspondence for *Church of South India: The Movement towards Union, 1900-1947* (London, 1954).

United Society for the Propagation of the Gospel Archives, Rhodes House, Oxford (USPG) (*indicates consultation at USPG House, London, before transfer of collections to Oxford):

CLR Series: 35 (Dornakal), 61-63 (Madras, Tinnevelly, Dornakal).

CLS Series: 25 (Dornakal), 41-44 (Madras).

D Series: 308, 315, 324, 331, 336, 342, 363a, 369, 396, 422, 449, 470, 524 (Dornakal); 1912, III (Madras and Tinnevelly);* 1922 (India I);* 1923 (India II).*

E Series: India, Dornakal, 1923, 1938.

Ladies Association and Committee for Women's Work, CWW, 1866-1930: 2, 4, 48, 55, 277/ 1-3, 311, 313, 328.

Minute Books: Standing Committee, 1909-12: 60-63; Journals, 1931.

SPG Annual Reports: 1911-15.*

SPG Publications: *Mission Field,* 1931.

United Theological College Archives, Bangalore (UTCA):

Collection of Papers Connected with the Movement of the National Church of India (Madras).

'General Assemblies of the S.I.U.C.'

Dornakal and Madras Diocesan Magazines

'Indian National Convention of YMCA Proceedings, 1891-1905.'

Letters of K. T. Paul.

Minutes of the Executive Committee, National Christian Council, 1914-48.

Washington National Cathedral Archives, Washington, D.C.:

Scrapbook, 1937, vol. 42.

Visiting Clergy, Job 129, Box 5, fol. 3. (129: 5/3)

Whitehead Collection, in Possession of Barbara Holmes, County Donegal, Ireland.
Anonymous, *Mrs. Whitehead's Work — An Appreciation.*

Yale Divinity School, Manuscripts and Archives, New Haven, CT (YDS):
Papers of George Sherwood Eddy (Eddy Papers):
Register of George Sherwood Eddy Papers, Chronology of G. S. Eddy.
Series I, Box 3, fols. 50-57, 'Corres: Report Letters from India' (hereafter I: 3/50-57).
I: 3/58, 'Corres: A Trip to Japan.'
II: 6/101-2, 6/107, 6/109, 6/113, 6/116-18, 6/124-25, 'Writings and Articles.'
II: 7/138, II: 14/14-5.
III: 18/193-94.
IV: 23/238-39.

Papers of John R. Mott (Mott Papers):
Register of John R. Mott Papers, Biographical Note.
Series I, 'General Correspondence,' Box 4, fol. 61 (hereafter I: 4/61), Mott-Azariah Correspondence.
I: 25/469-73, Mott-Eddy Correspondence.
I: 54/1002, Mott-McGavran Correspondence, 1936-40.
I: 99/1740, Mott-Whitehead Correspondence.
III: 117/1930-32, Records of World Tour, 1895-97.
III: 117/1936, World Trip 1901-2: Records.
III: 118/1950, Records of World Tour, 1928-29.
III: 118/1953, Diary of Trip to Great Britain, India, and the Near East, 1936-37.
III: 118/1954, Diary of Trip to India, 1938-39.

Archives of the Student Volunteer Movement for Foreign Missions:
'Historical Sketch of the Student Volunteer Movement for Foreign Missions,' Register of Ms. Group No. 42.

Archives of the YMCA — Student Division:
'Historical Note,' Register of Ms. Group No. 58.
Uncatalogued collection on South India.

II. Interviews

Aaron, Grace (Azariah's only surviving daughter), 24-26 September 1985, Ottawa, Ontario, Canada.
Appasamy, S. P., 27 February 1986, Madras.
Appleton, Rt. Rev. George, August 1984, Oxford.

Asirvatham, V. (of Peddamupparam), 5 April 1986, Madiripuram, A.P.

Azariah, Ambrose J. (Azariah's only surviving son), 24 February, 2 March, 23-24 March, 3 June 1986, Madras.

Azariah, M., 27 February 1986, Madras.

Azariah, Onras, 4 April 1986, Peddamupparam, A.P.

Brown, Judith M., 6 December 1985, University of Manchester.

Bunyan, Alfred, 29-30 March, 8 April 1986, Dornakal.

Carman, John, 16 September 1987, Cambridge, Massachusetts; 2-4 November 1990, Madison, Wisconsin.

Clarke, Rt. Rev. Sundar, 3 March 1986, Madras.

Coilpillai, Poomani, March 1986, Palayamkottai.

Cole, John R., 2 February 1987, Duarte, California.

Craig, Rt. Rev. Kenneth, 8 October 1986, Oxford.

Daniel, M., 29 and 31 March, 8 April 1986, Dornakal.

David, Immanuel, 2 May 1986, Bangalore.

David, Mr., 9 April 1986, Dornakal.

David, Mrs. S., 4 April 1986, Beerole, A.P.

David, Samuel D., 9 March 1986, Palayamkottai.

David, Swamiappan, June 1986, Bible Society of India, Madras.

Devadanam, Godishala, 4 April 1986, Peddamupparam, A.P.

Devadas, B., 4 April 1986, Beerole, A.P.

Devadason, John, 8 March 1986, Palayamkottai.

Devadason, R. Jeyakumar, 9 March 1986, Megnanapuram.

Devairakkam, Vedapodakam, 8 March 1986, Palayamkottai.

Dharmaraj, Rt. Rev. Jason S., 7 and 14 March 1986, Palayamkottai.

Duraisingh, C., 22 January 1986, Council for World Mission, London.

Ebinezer, Mr., 13 May 1986, Bangalore.

Eddy, G., 11 March 1986, Palayamkottai.

Firth, Cyril B., 24 September 1986, Romsey, Hants.

Gandhi, Rajmohan, 26 and 28 February 1986, *Indian Express,* Madras.

Graham, Carol, 19 December 1984, Oxford; 22-23 April 1985, Farnham; 7 and 21-23 October, 4 November 1986, Woking.

Group interview with villagers 7 April 1986, Mandula Sangam area of Dornakal, in Sakruthanda, Suriathanda, Bangalathanda, Vedanayagapuram, A.P.

Group interviews with villagers 4 April 1986, Beerole, Mahabubabad, Peddamupparam, Pindipole, Thirumapalayem, A.P.

Group interviews in Megnanapuram, 9 March 1986.

Group interview with K. Thasiah, C. Christian Devaraj, and others, 10 March 1986, Vellalanvilai (Vellalanvilai interview).

Gwynn, Peter, 6 November 1986, London.

Hollis, Rt. Rev. Michael, 7 September 1984, Manormead, Hindhead.

Isaiah, Gaddikoppula, 5 April 1986, Madiripuram, A.P.

Jayasingh, J. M., 21 March 1986, General Secretary, NMS, Madras.

Jeevaratnam, Irri, 5 April 1986, Madiripuram, A.P.

Jesalee, J., 9 March 1986, Megnanapuram.

Jeyakumar, D. Arthur, 17 March 1986, Madurai.

John, G., 4 April 1986, Thirumapalayem, A.P.

John, Gauta, 4 April 1986, Peddamupparam, A.P.

Joseph, Padamuthyam, 4 April 1986, Thirumapalayem, A.P.

Kantama, Mrs. Peram, 4 April 1986, Beerole, A.P.

Knight, A. John, 27 and 28 February 1986, Madras.

Koilpillai, Poomani, 15 March 1986, Palayamkottai.

Lawrence, Sir John, 21 June 1987, London.

Lazarus, Rev., 3 April 1986, St. Paul's Church, Chandruthanda, A.P.

Lockwood, Ruth and Michael, March 1986, Madras Christian College, Tambaram.

Manuel, Basil, 18 April 1986, Calcutta.

Manuelraj, Victor, 2-5 April 1986, Madiripuram, A.P.

Matthews, Rt. Rev. James, Washington, D.C.

McGavran, Donald, 30 January and 2 February 1987, Fuller Theological Seminary, Pasadena, California.

Muller, G., 8 March 1986, Palayamkottai.

Nagalakshmi, M. R., 9 March 1986, Megnanapuram.

Nakshitrama, Eluka, 5 April 1986, Madiripuram, A.P.

Neill, Rt. Rev. Stephen C., 10, 12 May 1984, Wycliffe Hall, Oxford.

Packiamuthu, David and Sarojini, 6 and 13 March 1986, Perumalpuram, Tirunelveli.

Pandiaraj, Vimalavathy, 9 March 1986, Megnanapuram.

Pearline, Annie A., 9 March 1986, Megnanapuram.

Punithavathy, Jesumani, 9 March 1986, Megnanapuram.

Rachel, Mrs. Kocherla, 4 April 1986, Mahabubabad, A.P.

Rajshekar, V. T., May 1986, Dalit Sahitya Akademy, Bangalore.

Rao, Edwin, 9 April 1986, Dornakal.

Rao, K. Sanjeera, 4 April 1986, Mahabubabad, A.P.

Ratnam, Jesu, 4 April 1986, Thirumapalayem, A.P.

Ratnam, Pasunori, 5 April 1986, Madiripuram, A.P.

Ruth, Nama, 9 April 1986, Kiritapuram, Dornakal.

Samuel, Kumari Joseph, 5 April 1986, Madiripuram, A.P.

Samuel, Undata (of Thirumapalayem), 5 April 1986, Madiripuram, A.P.

Sanneh, Lamin, 17 September 1987, Cambridge, Massachusetts.

Santosham, M., 28 February 1986, President, IMS, Madras.

Sathianandam, Nialan, 4 April 1986, Pindipole, A.P.

Solomon, Rt. Rev. P., 31 March 1986, Dornakal; 1-2 April 1986, Dhyana Ashram, Paloncha, A.P.

Stackpole, Alberic, 23 June 1986, St. Benet's Hall, Oxford.
Swaminathan, K., 20 March 1986, Editor, *Collected Works of Mahatma Gandhi*, Madras.
Thasiah, K., 10 March 1986, Vellalanvilai.
Thomas, Glory, March 1986, Sarah Tucker School, Palayamkottai.
Wightman, Harry, 5 June 1985, Solihull, W. Midlands.
William, Mrs. C., June 1986, Madras.

III. Letters

Aaron, Grace, 23 November 1984; 12 January 1985, 20 August 1985, 24 October 1985, 26 December 1985; 9 January 1986, 24 January 1986; 9 July 1987; 15 June 1988, Ottawa, Ontario.
Appasamy, S. P., 1 June 1985, Kodaikanal; 10 July 1985, Madras; 21 February 1986, Madras.
Austin, Joyce, 18 June 1986, Bishop's College, Calcutta.
Azariah, Ambrose J., 2 April 1985, 15 June 1985, 10 August 1985; 27 February 1986, 3 March 1986, 21 March 1986, 23 March 1986, 14 May 1986, 8 May 1986, 19 May 1986, 30 October 1986; 26 February 1988, 28 June 1988, 28 August 1988, 12 November 1988; 28 January 1989; 7 October 1989, Madras.
Azariah, Glory C., 28 December 1984; 17, 19, and 24 March 1985, Jabalpur, M.P.
Azariah, Mrs. P., 4 December 1984, Cleveland, Ohio; 9 April 1985; 28 January 1987, 10 May 1987, 3 July 1987, Columbus, Ohio (enclosure: photocopies of Azariah's sermon notes).
Bagshaw, A., 16 July 1985, Kodaikanal.
Ballhatchet, Kenneth, 15 March 1985, SOAS, London.
Barrington-Ward, Simon, 18 January and 15 March 1985, General Secretary, Church Missionary Society, London.
Benedikz, B. S., 4 November 1985, University of Birmingham.
Blair, James, 15 November 1985, Oxford Mission, Barisha, Calcutta.
Brown, Judith M., 28 November 1985; 8 November 1988, University of Manchester.
Brown, Rt. Rev. Leslie, 30 October 1984, Cambridge.
Brown, Sylvia U., 11 November and 16 December 1986; 22 September 1987, Asbury Theological Seminary, Wilmore, Kentucky.
Budgett, Robin, 1 May 1987, Norfolk, U.K.
Bywater, V., 4 November 1985, Campion Hall, Oxford.
Caplan, Lionel, 28 November 1985, London.
Chinnadorai, D. S., 29 March 1986, National Council of Y.M.C.A.s of India, New Delhi.

Chowdhury, A. K., 16 May and 2 September 1986, National Council of YMCAs of India, New Delhi (enclosures: Chowdhury, A. K., to Richard A. Stirling, 15 May 1986, National Council of YMCAs of India, New Delhi; and Chowdhury, A. K., to Harris Manickam, 15 May 1986, National Council of Y.M.C.A.s of India, New Delhi).

Christadoss, D. A., 24 March 1986, Bethel, Danishpet.

Costelloe, M. Joseph, to Fathers Michael Amaladoss, Bernard D'Souza, and Noel D'Souza, 19 June 1985, Biblioteca Curia Generalizia della Compagnia di Gesù, Rome.

David, K., 23 April 1986, Andhra Christian Theological College, Gandhi Nagar, Secunderabad.

Desai, M. V., 14 January 1987, New Delhi.

Desai, Narayan, 17 May and 12 June 1986, Institute for Total Revolution, Vedchhi, Gujarat.

Devaraj, C. Christian, 7 April 1987, Vellalanvilai.

Dharmaraj, Rt. Rev. Jason, 28 January, 25 February and 20 March 1986, and 11 April 1987, Tirunelveli; 8 December 1988, Lincoln.

Dillistone, F. W., 29 April 1988, Oxford.

Downs, Frederick S., 10 and 24 October 1984, UTC, Bangalore.

Eagleston, Clare, 14 May 1985, Balliol College, Oxford.

Faulkner, Peter, 3 October 1986, St. Andrew's Church, Didcot.

Firth, Cyril B., 25 August 1986, Romsey, Hants.

Forman, Charles W., 12 December 1984; 20 March 1985, Yale Divinity School, New Haven.

Francis, M., 30 September 1986, Catholic Church, Dornakal.

Freeborn, Jack, 26 October 1984, Salterhebble, Halifax.

Frykenberg, R. E., 20 October 1990, Madison, Wisconsin.

Garforth, Lawson, 30 September 1986, Weston-super-Mare, Avon.

Graham, Carol, 11 September, 30 October, 6 December 1984; 29 January, 6 February, 12 and 16 March, 12 and 30 April, 18 June, 26 August, 31 October, 19 November, 3 December 1985; 8 January 1986, Farnham and Woking, U.K.

Green, J. A. S., 16 October 1986, County Archivist, Berkshire Record Office.

Gwynn, Peter, 1 and 21 October 1986, Bromley, Kent.

Hall, David, 17 June 1986, Newcastle-upon-Tyne.

Hambye, E. R., 9 November 1985, Delhi.

Hanson, A. T., 21 October and 23 December 1984; 31 March and 9 May 1985; 16 April, 1986; 29 March and 11 April, 1988, Thirsk, N. Yorks.

Hardie, Mrs. C. G., 21 May 1985, Sussex.

Higgins, Kathleen, 23 and 29 September 1984, Maidstone.

Holmes, Barbara (Henry Whitehead's closest surviving relative), 19 October 1986 and 10 July 1987, County Donegal, Northern Ireland.

Hopkins, Hugh Evan, 15 January 1986, Cambridge.

Israel, G., 20 November and 22 December 1986; 23 June and 21 November 1987, Nazareth and Tiruchy.

Jackson, Eleanor M., 24 May 1985, Kodaikanal; 12 March 1985, 20 July 1985, 31 December 1985, 21 February 1986, 29 March 1986, Serampore College; 24 December 1986; 5 March and 9 May 1987, Cambridge; 21 January 1991, Birmingham.

James, N. W., 13 November 1985, The Royal Commission on Historical Manuscripts, London.

John, Geetha, 11 November 1986, Dornakal.

Kendall, D. G., 21 May 1985 and 3 October 1986, Statistical Laboratory, Oxford.

Kuriakose, M. K., 4 October 1984; 19 March 1986, UTCA, Bangalore.

Lacy, Elizabeth, 26 September 1986, Venice (daughter of Bishop Pickett).

Lawrence, Sir John, 22 and 25 May 1987, London.

Lowe, Victor (Alfred North Whitehead's biographer), 10 June 1985, Baltimore (enclosure: letter from Michael Hollis about Henry Whitehead, 25 April 1969, Suffolk).

MacGregor, Margaret S., 26 March 1986, Bishop's College, Calcutta.

Manickam, S., 6 and 17 March 1986, 10 November 1986, General Secretary of IMS, Tirunelveli.

Manor, Jim, 22 October 1984, University of Leicester.

Manuelraj, Victor, 10 March, 24 July 1986, Madiripuram, A.P.; 2 January 1987, Balimela-Orkel, Orissa.

Mason, Eleanor D., 11 October 1984, Roslindale, Massachusetts.

Matthew, R., 1 April 1986, Andhra Christian College, Guntur, A.P.

McCandlish, Pauline, 6 August 1984, Stanford-in-the-Vale, Faringdon.

McGavran, Donald, 17 October and 10 December 1986, Fuller Theological Seminary, Pasadena, California.

Moses, Jane E., 8 March 1986, Madras.

Muthuraj, J. Gnanaseelan, 11 June 1985 and 11 March 1986, Madurai.

Newell, Graham P., 31 October 1985, Oxford Mission, Hampshire.

Nicholls, C. S., 4 November 1985, Dictionary of National Biography, Oxford.

Packiamuthu, David, 25 September, 9 and 30 December 1986, Tirunelveli.

Paul, B. C., 3 April 1986, Andhra Christian Theological College, Gandhi Nagar, Secunderabad.

Paulraj, Rt. Rev. R., 17 March 1986, Tiruchirapalli.

Rajakumar, A., 5 March 1986, Church Growth Research Centre, Madras.

Ramsay, Kay, 4 June 1987, Church of Scotland Department of World Mission and Unity, Edinburgh.

Rao, Rt. Rev. T. B. D. Prakasa Rao, 5 April 1986, Vijayawada, A.P.

Samuel, Rt. Rev. D. Noah, 5 April, 4 October 1986, Dornakal.

Scovil, F. W. J., 7 May 1985, 15 May 1985, Magdalen College, Oxford.

Sharifa, B. S., 31 October 1986, Dornakal.

Sharma, Hari Dev., 7 and 18 April 1986, Nehru Memorial Museum and Library, New Delhi.

Shepherd, Bert, n.d., Stockport (enclosure: report of Manchester Cathedral Archivist).

Solomon, Rt. Rev. P., 3 November 1984, Paloncha, A.P.

Subrahmanyam, R., 5 April and 30 September 1986, Pyarelal Foundation for Gandhian Studies and Research, New Delhi.

Subramaniam, Nirmala, 7 May 1986, *Collected Works of Mahatma Gandhi,* New Delhi.

Sundkler, Bengt, 7 April 1987 and 31 January 1991, Uppsala, Sweden.

Symonds, Richard, 6 June and 29 July 1986; 29 March 1988, Oxford.

Tangayya, Joy, 6 September 1986, Madras.

Walls, Andrew F., 29 January and 1 August 1986, University of Aberdeen, Scotland.

Weaver, Alison, 10 June 1985; 27 February, 21 April, 23 September 1986; 30 May 1986, Dornakal.

Wightman, Harry, 8 and 23 May 1985, Solihull, W. Midlands.

Woodridge, J., 23 March 1985, Peterborough.

Wylie, S., 9 October 1986, Cambridge.

Zachariah, Mathai, 7 April 1986, General Secretary, NCC, Nagpur.

IV. V. S. Azariah's Publications[2]
(listed by date of publication)

1896

'What I Saw,' *YMI,* VII, 9 (Sept. 1896), pp. 98-99.

'A Visit to South Tranvancore,' *YMI,* VII, 11 (Nov. 1896), pp. 121-22.

2. Many of Azariah's earliest articles and addresses were published anonymously and are therefore not represented in this bibliography (see 'V. S. Azariah,' *NMI,* III, 10, [June 1909], pp. 79-82). Some of Azariah's works, particularly his biblical commentaries in Tamil, Telugu, and other Indian vernaculars, have proven exceedingly difficult to find. They are preserved neither in India's principal Protestant theological college libraries, nor in Dornakal or other Telugu diocesan centres. Even Azariah's principal publisher, the Christian Literature Society, possesses neither records nor surviving copies of many works which are known by this author to have existed (S. P. Appasamy to author, 10 July 1985; and interview with S. P. Appasamy, 27 February 1986, Madras). In hopes that Azariah's 'lost works' may one day be located, this bibliography includes available information about every book he is known to have published, however incomplete. All works are in English, unless otherwise noted. English transliterations of Tamil and Telugu titles are provided only for those few works whose titles were not already translated into English by Azariah or his editors and translators.

'Smaller Associations,' *Proceedings of the Fourth Indian National Convention of the Y.M.C.A.'s Held at Calcutta, 26-30 Dec. 1896,* pp. 40-44.

1897
'The Tamil District Conference,' *YMI,* VIII, 7 (Aug. 1897), p. 98.
'The Morning Watch,' *YMI,* VIII, 8 (Sept. 1897), pp. 124-26.

1898
'The Needs of India,' *YMI,* IX, 3 (March 1898), pp. 30-31.
'The Life of Faith,' *YMI,* IX, 6 (June 1898), pp. 83-84.

1899
'Oh to be Nothing,' *YMI,* X, 1 (Jan. 1899), pp. 7-8.
'Tamil Secretary's Report,' *YMI,* X, 7 (July 1899), p. 113.
'Tamil Secretary's Statement,' *Report of the Indian National Union and Proceedings of the Fifth National Convention of the Y.M.C.A., Bombay, 28 Dec. 1899–1 Jan. 1900,* pp. 9-10.

1900
'Lessons in Prayer,' *YMI,* XI, 11 and 12 (Nov. and Dec. 1900), pp. 192-93, 210-11.

1901
'The Mutual Relations of the Associations: The Duty of All to Each Other, through (a) the National Union (b) District Union,' *YMI,* XII, 2 (Feb. 1901), pp. 23-25.
'Tamil Secretary's Statement,' *Report of the Indian National Union and Proceedings of the Sixth National Convention of the YMCA., Allahabad, 26-29 Dec. 1901,* p. 11.

1902
with G. S. Eddy. Charles G. Finney, *Lectures on Revivalism,* edited and translated into Tamil, 1902.
Andrew Murray, *Humility: The Beauty of Holiness,* translated into Tamil, c. 1902; later also into Telugu (see *Extracts from Letters of Bishop Azariah,* Madras, 1945, pp. 17-18).

1904
'Missionary Work and the Spirit of the Association,' *YMI,* XV, 3 (March 1904), pp. 43-46.

1905

'The Indian Missionary Society of Tinnevelly and Fields of Work,' *HF* (new series), XVI, 1 (Jan. 1905), pp. 17-29.

'Unoccupied Fields,' *YMI,* XVI, 2 (Feb. 1905), pp. 25-27.

'Associations in Small Towns,' *YMI,* XVI, 2 (Feb. 1905), pp. 39-41.

1906

'The Unoccupied Fields of India,' *YMI,* XVII, 1 (Jan. 1906), pp. 12-16.

with E. C. Carter. 'Letter,' *YMI,* XVII, 2 (Feb. 1906), p. 17.

'The National Missionary Society of India,' *HF* (new series), XVII, 7 (July 1906), pp. 245-51. See also *MRW,* XIV, 7 (July 1906).

'The Swadeshi Spirit,' went to press by August 1906 in undesignated publication, according to letter from VSA to his wife.

1907

'Enlisting Students in the Extension of Christ's Kingdom,' *Report of the Conference of the World Student Christian Federation: Held at Tokyo, Japan, April 3-7, 1907,* New York: WSCF, pp. 124-26.

1908

Introductory Lessons on India and Missions for Mission Study Classes, Calcutta: Student Volunteer Movement of India and Ceylon, 1908, 1915; London, Madras, and Colombo: CLS, 1909, 2nd edn. (revised and enlarged), 1913. Tamil edition: Madras: CLS, 1925. Telugu and Malayalam editions.

'The Missionary Effort of the Tinnevelly Church,' *CMR,* LIX (1908), pp. 554-60.

'Triennial Report of the Indian National Council,' *YMI,* XIX, 3 (March 1908), pp. 37-40.

1909

'The Growth of Self-Extension in the Church of India,' *MRW* (new series), XXII (April 1909), p. 283.

1910

'The Problem of Co-Operation between Foreign and Native Workers,' *World Missionary Conference, 1910: The History and Records of the Conference: Together with Addresses Delivered in the Evening Meetings,* Edinburgh and London: Oliphant, Anderson and Ferrier; New York: Fleming H. Revell Co., IX, pp. 306-15. See also *MTDM,* V, 11 (Nov. 1910), pp. 422-33.

1915

The Heritage of India Series, ed. V. S. Azariah and J. N. Farquhar, London: Oxford University Press, and Calcutta: Association Press, from 1915.

1916

A Letter concerning 'The Real Issues Involved in the War,' with a Foreword by the Metropolitan, Madras, n.d. Tamil edition: Madras: SPCK. Telugu edition: Bezwada (referred to in *MDM,* XI, 8 [August 1916], p. 217).

1917

Report on the Indian Church in 1917, for the Committee of the National Missionary Council.

1918

Founding editor of the *Tamil Church Deepika,* until 1920. See *'The Tamil Church Deepika,' MDM,* XXIV, 10 (Oct. 1929), p. 341. In Tamil.

1919

Holy Baptism. Tamil editions: Madras: CLS, 1919; and Madras: ISPCK, 1942. Telugu edition: *Parisuddha Baptismana,* Madras: CLS, 1919. See also *MDM,* XIV, 12 (Dec. 1919), pp. 283-85 and *MDM,* XIV, 12 (Dec. 1919), pp. 283-85.
'Church Union in South India,' *HF,* XXXIX, 9 (Sept. 1919), pp. 333-41.
'The Transfer of Responsibility from the Mission to the Church,' *MDM,* XIV, 11 (Nov. 1919), pp. 256-66.

1920

'The Church's Ideal,' *CMR,* LXXI (1920), pp. 148-63 (sermon preached for the 121st Anniversary of the CMS on 3 May 1920 at St. Bride's Church, Fleet St., London).
'Lambeth Resolutions,' *MDM,* XV, 12 (Dec. 1920), pp. 276-86.

1921

'Sermon Preached by the Bishop of Dornakal on Sunday, November 28, 1920 at St. George's Cathedral, Madras, on behalf of the CMS Centenary Celebrations,' *MDM,* XVI, 1 (Jan. 1921), pp. 13-22.
'The Book of Common Prayer and National Churches,' *EWR,* XIX, 73 (Jan. 1921), pp. 16-26.
'Caste and Denomination,' *HF,* XLI, 7 (July 1921), pp. 246-53.

1923

'The Training of the Village Worker,' *IRM,* XII (July 1923), pp. 360-67.
'The Maoris and Their Religion,' *MDM,* XVIII, 10 (Oct. 1923), pp. 237-40.

'Self-Government for the Church of England in India,' *HF,* XLIII (I in new series), 12 (Dec. 1923), pp. 446-52. On this subject see also 'The Bishop's Letter,' *DDM,* V, 1 (March 1928), p. 5.

1925

with J. D. Asirvadam. 'Students and the Church: Student Christian Conference, Madras, Dec. 24-31, 1924,' *Guardian,* III, 7 (12 Feb. 1925), pp. 79-81.

1926

'The Christian Gospel and the Villager,' *NCCR,* XLVI, 10 (Oct. 1926), pp. 583-89.

1927

'The Necessity of Christian Unity for the Missionary Enterprise of the Church,' *Faith and Order: Proceedings of the World Conference, Lausanne, August, 3-21, 1927,* ed. H. N. Bate, London: SCM, 1927, pp. 491-95, and discussions on pp. 102-3, 418-23. See also *Guardian,* V, 37 (22 Sept. 1927), pp. 443-45.

1928

'The Bishop's Letters,' published monthly in *DDM.* Copies available from V, 1 (Jan. 1928) to XXII, 1 (Jan. 1945).

'India and Christ,' *IRM,* XVII (1928), pp. 154-59.

with E. J. Palmer. *The New Freedom of the Church in India: Two Sermons,* 1928, pp. 11-16.

'The Bishop's Charge: Being extracts from a charge delivered by the Bishop to the clergy of the diocese in S. Saul's Church Bezwada on Dec. 1st, 1927,' *DDM,* V, 2 (Feb. 1928), pp. 1-6.

'Wanted Village Wells,' *DDM,* V, 4 (April 1928), pp. 1-2.

'A Confirmation Examination,' *DDM,* V, 4 (April 1928), pp. 2-4.

'Bishop of Dornakal's Sermon,' *DDM,* V, 4 (April 1928), pp. 7-12.

'The Church in Rural India,' *DDM,* V, 10 (Oct. 1928), pp. 1-12 (taken from an article in *Yearbook of Indian Missions.*).

1929

Address: *The Jerusalem Findings as Related to India: Report of the Enlarged Meeting of the National Christian Council of India, Burma and Ceylon held in Madras, December 29, 1928–January 2, 1929,* Poona: NCC, pp. 42-43.

'The People of the Villages,' *The Christian Task in India,* ed. J. McKenzie, London: Macmillan, 1929, pp. 27-42.

Mass Movement Work in India: Findings of a Conference of the CMS Mass Movement

Commission, Bezwada, Nov. 21-28, 1928. With a Foreword by the Rt. Rev. the Bishop of Dornakal, Kottayam: CMS Press, 1929, pp. 1-5.

'The Anglican Church in India,' *The Reunion of Christendom: A Survey of the Present Position,* ed. Sir James Marchant, London: Cassell and Co., and New York: Henry Holt and Co., 1929, pp. 281-99.

'Andhra University, Third Convocation, 1929. Addresses by V. S. Azariah and the Vice-Chancellor Mr. C. R. Reddy.' Copy in Azariah Collection, Madras.

'Age for Marriage,' *DDM,* VI, 10 (Oct. 1929), pp. 4-5.

'Living Forces behind Mass Movements,' *IRM,* XXVIII (Oct. 1929), pp. 509-17. See also I: 4/61, Mott Papers, YDS.

1930

with Henry Whitehead. *Christ in the Indian Villages,* London: Students Christian Press, 1930.

'Mission of Help to the Older Churches,' *NCCR,* L, 2 (Feb. 1930), pp. 59-61.

'Prayer Book of 1928,' *DDM,* VII, 3 (March 1930), pp. 6-7.

'Lambeth and South India: Question of Unity,' *CUNV,* I, 2 (Sept. 1930), pp. 67-70.

'A Visit to Palestine,' *DDM,* VII, 11 (Nov. 1930), pp. 3-7; and VII, 12 (Dec. 1930), pp. 3-6.

1931

Studies in First Corinthians. Tamil edition: Madras: CLS, 1931 (CLS ref. no. 97). Telugu edition: Madras: ISPCK, 1931; ISPCK, 1956.

'What Happened in Tranquebar in 1919,' *CUNV,* I, 4 (Jan. 1931), pp. 144-45.

A Charge: Delivered to the Clergy of the Diocese of Dornakal at Bezwada, October 7, 1931, Madras: Diocesan Press, 1931.

1932

'Dornakal Diocese (Its Life and Opportunities),' *DDM,* IX, 1 (Jan. 1932), pp. 9-16 (extracts from an address to Diocesan Council, Oct. 1931).

'The Missionary's Message,' *NCCR,* LII, 1 (Jan. 1932), pp. 14-17.

'Bishop Azariah on Theological Education: Partial Text of Convocation Address Delivered at Serampore University on January 30, 1932,' *Guardian,* X, 13 (5 May 1932), pp. 155-56 (full text published in *Student's Chronicle*).

'The Kotagiri Missionary Conference,' *Guardian,* X, 15 (19 May 1932), pp. 178-80.

'The Communal Award,' *Guardian,* X, 31 (8 Sept. 1932), p. 368. Reprinted in *DDM,* IX, 10 (Oct. 1932), pp. 10-13.

'The Caste Movement in South India,' *IRM,* XXI, 36 (Oct. 1932), pp. 457-67.

'Indian Christians and the Communal Award,' *Guardian*, X, 35 (6 Oct. 1932), p. 415.

'The Bishop of Dornakal and the Poona Conference,' *Guardian*, X, 40 (10 Nov. 1932), p. 475.

'Peace on Earth,' *Guardian*, X, 46 (22 Dec. 1932), pp. 545-46.

1933

Tamil translation and adaption of *Selections from Bishop Andrewes' Devotions*, Bezwada: Church Book Room, 1933, 1934; 2nd edn. published by Rev. Canon S. Paul Manickam: Tirunelveli, 1976 (excerpts published in *Tamil Church Deepika*).

'The Place of the YMCA in the Christian Movement in India,' *YMIB&C*, XLV, 6 (June 1933), pp. 268-73.

'The Bishop of Dornakal's Address at the Thirtieth Anniversary of the Indian Missionary Society of Tinnevelly,' *TMI*, XXX, 7 (July 1933), pp. 78-81.

'The South India Church Union: A Plea to the Anglican Church,' *Guardian*, XI, 34 (24 August 1933), pp. 400-401. See also *CENs* (28 July 1933).

'The Church in the Mind of Christ,' *DDM*, X, 8 (Aug. 1933), pp. 12-16; and *DDM*, IX, 9 (Sept. 1933), pp. 5-10. See also *CUNV*, III, 6 (May 1933).

1934

Collections of Prayer Meditation, Beshavada: Beshavada Church Book Room, 1934.

'Evangelization and Its Challenge,' *NCCR*, LIV, 1 (Jan. 1934), pp. 8-17.

'The Bishop of Dornakal on Sir H. Page Croft's Scare,' *Guardian*, XII, 28 (12 July 1934), p. 436. Also, 'The Bishop's Letter,' *DDM*, XI, 7 (July 1934), pp. 2-4.

'Bishop of Dornakal on the New Reforms: Speech at the Medak I.C.A.,' *Guardian* XII, 33 (16 Aug. 1934), p. 521 (excerpt from speech entitled 'Christianity and Christians in the New India' delivered to Medak Indian Christian Association).

'Forward Movement in Evangelism: Programme of Work Suggested by the National Christian Council,' Mysore City: Wesley Press and Publishing House, Dec. 1934; *Guardian*, XIII, 29 (18 July 1935), pp. 455, 458; *DDM*, XII, 7 (July 1935), pp. 9-13. Also *NCCR* (Dec. 1935).

Studies in the Acts of the Apostles, IMS, 1934 (or possibly later). Telugu edition: *Studies in the Acts*, Dornakal: Mission Press (before June 1936).

1935

Studies in the Life of Christ based on the Gospel of St. Mark. Telugu edition: Compassionate God (Krupa Nadhuni Charithra), Delhi: ISPCK, 1935.

'Assistant Bishop,' *DDM*, XII, 1 (Jan. 1935), pp. 11-13.

'The Expansion of Christianity in India,' *NCCR,* LV, 2-7 (Feb.-July 1935), pp. 64-69, 116-19, 171-74, 226-30, 283-87, 330-33.

Worship in the Indian Church: Being Substance of Addresses Delivered at the Kodaikanal Missionary Conference, May 1935, Dornakal: Mission Press, n.d. and Bezwada: Church Book Room, n.d. See also *DDM,* XII, 9 (Sept. 1935), pp. 4-8; 10 (Oct. 1935), pp. 4-8.

'South India Church Union: Revised Scheme of the Joint Committee,' *CENs,* XLII, 2150 (3 May 1935), p. 7. See also 'South India Church Union,' *Guardian,* XIII, 22 (30 May 1935), p. 343.

'Lutherans and Anglicans,' *Guardian,* XIII, 32 (8 Aug. 1935), p. 506. From *DDM,* XII, 8 (Aug. 1935), pp. 6-8.

'Church Union: A Statement by the Bishop of Dornakal,' *Guardian,* XIII, 32 (8 Aug. 1935), p. 506.

'The Bishop of Dornakal Replies to the Nagercoil Meeting,' *Guardian,* XIII, 36 (5 Sept. 1935), pp. 571-72 (reprint of letter written to *Madras Mail*).

'Indian Christian Constituencies: Letter of the Bishop of Dornakal,' *Guardian,* XIII, 39 (26 Sept. 1935), p. 622.

India and the Christian Movement, Madras: CLS, 1st edition after October 1935; 2nd ed., Madras: CLS, 1936 (CLS ref. no. 263). Tamil edition: Madras: CLS, 1937 (CLS ref. no. 147). Telugu edition not available to this author.

Notes on the *Lectionary* for village congregations, after October 1935. See 'The Bishop's Letter,' *DDM,* XII, 10 (Oct. 1935), pp. 1-2; A. Elliot, *NCCR,* LXV, 2 (Feb. 1945), pp. 16-17.

'The Bishop of Dornakal on Dr. Ambedkar's Declaration,' *Guardian,* XIII, 50 (12 Dec. 1935), pp. 791-93. From *DDM,* XII, 12 (Dec. 1935), pp. 3-5.

1936

The Church and Evangelism: Being Studies on the Evangelization of India Based on Early Church History, Madras: ISPCK/CLS, 1936 (CLS ref. no. 266). Tamil edition: Madras: CLS, 1936 (CLS ref. no. 133). The substance of this book was first presented in a series of addresses delivered in Nagpur, Madras, and Dornakal in 1934 and then published as a series of articles entitled 'The Expansion of Christianity in India,' in the *NCCR* in 1935 (see entry above).

Missionary Litanies, Madras: ISPCK/CLS, 1936. See also 'The Bishop's Letter,' *DDM,* XII, 7 (July 1935), pp. 1-3; 10 (Oct. 1935), p. 2. Copy in Azariah Collection, Madras. (VSA contributed to this as a member of the Liturgical Committee of the Episcopal Synod.)

The Pastor and the Pastorate: Being a Book on Pastoralia for Use of Those in Charge of Indian Congregations, Madras: ISPCK/CLS, 1936.

South India Union: An Examination of the Scheme from the Anglican Point of View, Madras: CLS, 1936 (CLS ref. no. 265).

'Missionary Propaganda Films: Views of the Bishops of Madras and Dornakal,' *Guardian*, XIV, 1 (2 Jan. 1936), p. 12 (includes letter by Azariah to *Madras Mail*).

'Duty of Indian Christian Electors,' *Guardian*, XIV, 3 (16 Jan. 1936), p. 44. From *DDM*, XIII, 1 (Jan. 1936), pp. 8-11.

'Nationalism and Indian Christianity,' *DDM*, XIII, 2 (Feb. 1936), p. 14 (report of speech to Bezwada Town Congress Committee, 2 Jan. 1936). See also: 'What the Congress Stands For' and 'Bishops and Politics,' *Guardian*, XIV, 2 (9 Jan. 1936), p. 17; 'Concerning Untouchables,' *Guardian*, XIV, 2 (9 Jan. 1936), p. 19; and *Madras Mail*.

'Bishop of Dornakal on Communal Representation,' *Guardian*, XIV, 16 (16 April 1936), p. 249.

Statement to All Heads of Church and Missions (for private circulation only), Dornakal: Mission Press, May 1936. Copies in Box 395, NCCC, IMC/CBMS, SOAS.

'The Indian Church and the Depressed Classes,' *Guardian*, XIV, 21 (21 May 1936), p. 325.

The Church Evangelism, Telugu edition: Dornakal: Mission Press, before June 1936.

with other members of the Joint Committee on Union. 'A Union Problem,' *Guardian*, XIV, 23 (4 June 1936), p. 362.

'Church Union in South India,' *Guardian*, XIV, 31 (30 July 1936), p. 493. From *DDM*, XIII, 7 (July 1936), pp. 1-3.

An Open Letter to Our Countrymen Who Are Classified as Belonging to the Depressed Classes, Dornakal: Mission Press, n.d. Copy in Box: Pamphlets (Old) 275, SOCA. Telugu edition: Dornakal: Mission Press. n.d.

Also published as brochure for North American audiences with 'A Note of Explanation' by A. L. Warnshuis, Secretary of the International Missionary Council: New York: Foreign Missions Conference of North America, 1936. Copy in I: 4/61, Mott Papers, YDS. See also *YMIB & C*, XLVIII, 9 (Oct. 1936), pp. 253-54; and 'What Christ Has Done for Untouchables' (see below, 1937).

1937

Foreword to J. Waskom Pickett, *Christ's Way to India's Heart*, Lucknow, 1937.

Lessons on Miracles. Telugu: SPCK Committee of the Dornakal Diocesan Council, 1937.

'Mass Movements,' *Guardian*, XV, 6 (11 Feb. 1937), p. 92. From *DDM*, XIV, 2 (Feb. 1937).

'Commemoration Service Address,' *MCCM*, Centenary Number (March 1937), pp. 111-14.

'What Christ Has Done for Untouchables,' *MRW*, LX (March 1937), pp. 131-32.

'The Unity Which Christ Wills,' *CMO*, LXIV (July 1937), pp. 150-52 (concluding part of the 1937 CMS Annual Sermon preached in St. Bride's Church, Fleet St., London). Copy also in CMSA, AR(MS), 1936-37; referred to in G. Hewitt, *The Problem of Success, op. cit.*, pp. 110, 389.

Address delivered on 3 August 1937, *The Second World Conference on Faith and Order: Held at Edinburgh, August 3-18, 1937,* ed. Leonard Hodgson (London: SCM Press, 1938), pp. 49-55, and pp. 69, 167, 173, 197, 205. See also 'Bishop of Dornakal on Church Union: Address Given at the Edinburgh World Conference on Faith and Order,' *Guardian*, XV, 35 (2 Sept. 1937), pp. 548-49.

'A Call That Was Answered,' *CMO*, LXIV (Oct. 1937), pp. 223-35.

'India: A Present Urgent Opportunity,' *The Spirit of Missions*, U.S.A. (autumn 1937), pp. 541-45, Graham Collection.

The Fellowship of the Church: The East, Cincinnati, Ohio: The Woman's Auxiliary to the National Council, n.d. (part of a series of addresses presented at the Triennial Meeting of the Woman's Auxiliary to the National Council, Cincinnati, Ohio, 1937).

1938

'The Christian Church in India,' *Moving Millions,* Boston: The Central Committee on the United Study of Foreign Missions, 1938, pp. 163-95.

'The Bishop's Message (Silver Jubilee of the Diocese of Dornakal Held on 29th December 1937),' *Guardian*, XVI, 1 (6 Jan. 1938), p. 12.

'Christians and the New Government: Bishop of Dornakal's Call for Support,' *Guardian*, XVI, 6 (10 Feb. 1938), pp. 86-87 (report of Azariah's address to his Diocesan Synod, 6 Jan. at Bezwada). See also *MDM*, XXXIII, 2 (Feb. 1938), pp. 60-62; *YMI*, L, 3 (March 1938), pp. 73-74. Also published in the *Hindu*.

'Our Duty as Citizens (Being an extract from the Bishop's charge to the Clergy at his Visitation on January 6th),' *DDM*, XV, 2 (Feb. 1938), pp. 5-10.

'Our Duty as Members of the Church,' *DDM*, XV, 3 (March 1938), pp. 5-11.

'Our Duty as Members of the Church of India,' *DDM*, XV, 4 (April 1938), pp. 5-8.

Christian Graces in a Christian Home (Madras: Fenn Thompson & Co., n.d.) (a sermon preached at the marriage of his son Henry to Glory Srinivasagam on 2 June 1938).

'Self-Support: False or True,' *IRM*, XXVII, 107 (July 1938), pp. 361-71.

'Prohibition Measures in Dornakal Diocese,' *Guardian*, XVI, 30 (28 July 1938), p. 475.

'Gandhiji's Alleged Threat to Christian Work: Bishop of Dornakal Repudiates Dr. McGavran's Version,' *Guardian*, XVI, 3 (4 Aug. 1938), p. 482.

'Self-Support,' *NCCR*, LVIII, 10 (Oct. 1938), pp. 536-43.

'Sermon Preached by the Bishop at the Consecration of the Bishop in

Tranvancore in St. George's Cathedral, Madras, on October 18th,' *DDM*, XV, 12 (Dec. 1938), pp. 4-11.

'The Christian Contribution to India,' *The Indian Review*, XXXIX, 12 (Dec. 1938), pp. 804-7. Reprinted in *NCCR*, LIX, 3 (March 1939), pp. 118-23.

1939

'The Place of the Church in Evangelism,' *Evangelism: International Missionary Council Meeting at Tambaram, Madras, December 12th to 29th, 1938*, London: Oxford University Press, 1939, pp. 32-47.

'The Church and Its Mission,' *Addresses and Other Records: International Missionary Council Meeting at Tambaram, Madras, December 12th to 29th, 1938*, London: Oxford University Press, 1939, pp. 40-42.

Christian Giving: A Series of Studies in Christian Stewardship. Madras: CLS, 1939 (CLS ref. no. 297), 1940, 1941. Republished as *Christian Giving*, edited with an introduction by Stephen Neill, London: World Christian Books, no. 2, USCL, Lutterworth Press, 1954; New York: Association Press, 1955. Tamil editions: CLS Madras: 1939, 1940 (CLS ref. no. 166). Bengali edition: Calcutta: Calcutta Christian Tract and Book Society, 1958. Telugu edition not available to this author.

Perhaps Azariah's most widely read work, *Christian Giving* was apparently written originally in Tamil and then translated into English by an anonymous associate. The original English translation was revised by Stephen Neill for the 1954 World Christian Books publication (S. C. Neill to George Appleton, 5 August 1953, Neill Collection, Oxford). Azariah's son Ambrose believes that the book was written first in English and then translated into Tamil (interview, 5 March 1986, Madras).

Devotional Studies in the Book of Revelation (or *Commentary on Revelation*). Tamil edition: Madras: ISPCK, 1939. Telugu edition: Madras: ISPCK, 1939.

The Story of the Dornakal Cathedral, Madras: Diocesan Press, 1939. Published also in *DDM*, XVI, 2 and 3 (Feb. and March 1939), pp. 17-23 (statement read by V. S. Azariah, 6 Jan. 1939).

'Fee Concessions for Harijans,' *Guardian*, XVII, 36-37 (14 and 21 Sept. 1939), p. 567. From *DDM*, vol. unavailable.

'Mahatma Gandhi's Seventieth Birthday: Bishop of Dornakal's Tribute,' *Guardian*, XVII, 36 and 37 (14 and 21 Sept. 1939), p. 577 (taken from a souvenir volume prepared by S. Radhakrishnan).

with J. Z. Hodge. 'The National Christian Council and the Situation Created by the War,' *Guardian*, XVII, 43 (2 Nov. 1939), p. 664.

1940

Studies in the Book of Job. Tamil edition: *Jobunukam Vijarkkiarnam*, Madras: ISPCK and CLS, 1940 (CLS ref. no. 171). Telugu edition: Madras: ISPCK and CLS, 1941.

'Church Union in South India: Bishop of Dornakal's Account of Joint Committee's Proceedings,' *Guardian*, XVIII, 2 (11 Jan. 1940), p. 26.

'Bishop of Dornakal on Travancore Educational Notification,' *Guardian*, XVIII, 51 (19 Dec. 1940), p. 755.

1941

Holy Matrimony: Being Chapters on the Christian Law of Marriage (first published in Tamil and Telugu but pre-1941 editions not available). English editions: Madras: ISPCK, 1941 (trans. Carol Graham); revised and enlarged, 1942. Tamil edition: Madras: CLS, 1943, 1954 (CLS ref. no. 352). Translations also into Hindi, Urdu, and Marathi.

A Charge: Delivered at Bezwada on Wednesday, October 29th, 1941, Dornakal: Mission Press, 1941. For extracts see 'Second Generation of Indian Christians,' *Guardian*, XIX, 46 (20 Nov. 1941), pp. 544-45; 47 (27 Nov. 1941), pp. 556-57.

'Mixed Marriages,' *NCCR*, LXI, 11 (Nov. 1941), pp. 528-34.

1942

Confirmation. Tamil edition: Madras: ISPCK, Church Teaching Series No. 5, 1942.

Sabbath or Sunday, SPCK India, n.d. and Madras: Diocesan Press, 1942.

South India Union Scheme: Authority of Bishops, Dornakal, 1942.

'The Care of the Christians of the Second Generation,' *NCCR*, LXII, 1 (Jan. 1942), pp. 19-25.

'Church Union in South India,' *Guardian*, XX, 8 (26 Feb. 1942), pp. 89-90.

'Indian Christians and the War,' *Guardian*, XX, 22 (4 June 1942), p. 256.

'Bishop of Dornakal on the Indian Situation,' *Guardian*, XX, 37 (17 Sept. 1942), pp. 436-37. From *DDM*, volume unavailable.

'Christian Education,' *NCCR*, LXII, 10 (Oct. 1942), pp. 405-10.

'The Indian Christian and Politics,' *Guardian*, XX, 40 (8 Oct. 1942), p. 478.

1943

Devotional and Expository Studies in Second Corinthians. Tamil edition: Madras: ISPCK, 1943. Telugu edition: ISPCK.

'South India Union,' *The Student Outlook* (Feb. 1943).

'Indian Christians and the Political Situation,' *EWR* (April 1943), pp. 49-51 (reprinted from *DDM*).

'The Late Dr. C. Frimodt-Moller,' *Guardian*, XXI, 20 (20 May 1943), p. 236.

'The Bishop of Dornakal's Address at the Fortieth Anniversary of the Indian Missionary Society of Tinnevelly,' *TMI*, XL, 7 July 1943, pp. 35-39. (in Tamil).

'Post-War Problems of Churches and Missions in India,' *NCCR*, LXIII, 8 (Aug. 1943), pp. 263-70.

'The Pledge,' *CUNV,* XIV, 1 (Sept. 1943), pp. 9-13.

1944
'The Indian Christian's Dilemma Today,' *The Methodist Woman* (March 1944), p. 9 (copy in I: 4/61, Mott Papers, YDS).

1945 and posthumously
'The Bishop's Last Letter,' *DDM,* XXII, 1 (Jan. 1945), pp. 3-7.

Extracts from Letters of Bishop Azariah, with an Introduction by the Bishop of Madras, Madras: Diocesan Press, 1945.

'Bishop Azariah's Last Sermon,' *DDM,* XXIII, 2 (Feb. 1946), pp. 4-7 (based on notes taken by B. Gnanaprakasam).

'An Illustration from V. S. Azariah,' *The Ministry of the Spirit: Selected Writings of Roland Allen,* ed. David M. Paton, London: World Dominion Press, 1960, pp. 131-33.

Studies in the Life of Christ. Tamil edition: Madras: ISPCK, n.d. Telugu edition: ISPCK, 1956.

Pentecost Spirit (Pentecostal Spirit or *Holy Spirit).* Tamil editions: CLS; Tinnevelly: Diocesan Press, 1975.

Undated Published Writings
Tamil translation of the *Confessions* of St. Augustine, n.d. (Grace Aaron to author, 9 January 1987).

My Mother. Tamil edition: n.d. (Mrs. P. Azariah to author, n.d.).

Foreword to Henry Whitehead, *The Outcastes of India and the Gospel of Christ,* London, n.d.

Studies in the Book of Amos.

with G. S. Eddy; biography of Charles G. Finney (1792-1875), Tamil pamphlets on Prayer, expository studies of Paul's Letters to the Galatians and Ephesians, and a brochure entitled 'Divisions and Unity of the Body of Christ.' In Tamil.

John Mott, *The Pastor and Modern Missions,* translated into unspecified number of Indian vernaculars.

V. Henry Whitehead's Published Writings and Addresses[3]

1890
Address to 'The Annual Meeting,' *The Oxford Mission to Calcutta: Annual Report,* Oxford, October 1890, pp. 24-39.

---

3. For further bibliography on Henry Whitehead, see Professor Bengt Sundkler, *Church of South India: The Movement towards Union, 1900-1947* (London, 1954), p. 439.

1891

The Oxford Mission to Calcutta: Annual Report, London, 1891.

1896

Address to 'The Annual Meeting,' *The Oxford Mission to Calcutta: Annual Report,*
London, 1896, pp. 16-34.

1897

India: A Sketch of the Madura Mission, London, 1897.

1899

Address to 'The Annual Meeting,' *Oxford Mission to Calcutta: Annual Report,*
London, 1899, pp. 18-25.

The Bishop's First Sermon delivered at St. George's Cathedral, Madras, *MDR,*
XIII, 4 (Oct. 1899), pp. 145-49.

'Pastoral Letter' and 'Diary' published quarterly in *Madras Diocesan Record
(MDR),* 1899-1905; and monthly in *Madras Diocesan Magazine (MDM),*
1906–April 1907; *Madras and Tinnevelly Diocesan Magazine (MTDM),* May
1907-1915; *Madras Diocesan Magazine (MDM),* 1916-22. (copies in MDA
and UTCA).

1901

'Caste Suppression Society,' *MDR,* XV, 4 (Oct. 1901), pp. 180-81.

1902

'Address by Bishop Whitehead,' *Decennial Missionary Conference,* Madras, 1902;
copy in Box: 'Pamphlets (Old) 275,' SOCA, Birmingham.

*A Charge to the Clergy Delivered at His Primary Visitation in the Cathedral Church of
St. George, Madras, on Wednesday, January 15th, 1902,* Madras, 1902.

1905

'The Future of Indian Christianity,' *TE&TW* (Jan. 1905), pp. 9-22.

1906

'A Lecture on Some Religious Customs of the Hindus in South India . . . Delivered in the Regimental Theatre at Wellington,' *MDM,* I, 5 (May 1906),
pp. 207-17.

'The Future of Christianity in India,' *MDM,* I, 11 (Nov. 1906), pp. 528-32.

1907

Our Mission Policy in India, Madras, 1907.

1909

'Relations between Europeans and Indians,' *MTDM*, IV, 6 (June 1909), pp. 169-72.

1911

'The New Movement in India and the Old Gospel,' *TE&TW*, IX, 1 (Jan. 1911), pp. 1-11.

1912

Work among Indian Outcastes, London, 1912.
'Christianity in India,' *Indian Review*, XIII, 6 (June 1912), pp. 508-11.
'Sermon at Canterbury,' *MTDM*, VII, 9 (Sept. 1912), pp. 263-72.

1913

'The Mass Movement towards Christianity in the Panjab,' *IRM*, III (1913), pp. 442-53.

1914

'A Retrospect of 1913,' *YMI*, XXV, 1 (Jan. 1914), pp. 1-9.

1916

The Village Gods of South India, London and New York, 1916; 2nd ed., Calcutta, 1921; Delhi, 1976; New York, 1980.

1924

Indian Problems in Religion, Education, Politics, London and Bombay, 1924.

1930

Mass Movements in India, London, 1930.
with V. S. Azariah. *Christ in the Indian Villages,* London, 1930.
'The Church in the Telugu Villages,' *CMO*, LVII (Aug. 1930), pp. 155-57.

1932

with Sir George Anderson. *Christian Education in India,* London, 1932.

VI. Printed Primary Sources

'A Call to the Church,' *DDM*, XIII, 2 (Feb. 1936), pp. 2-4.
'An Indian Grievance,' *TE&TW*, XIX, 73 (Jan. 1921), pp. 74-75.
'Bishops and Politics,' *Guardian*, X, 40 (10 Nov. 1932), p. 474.
'Bishops and Politics,' *Guardian*, XIV, 2 (9 Jan. 1936), p. 17.
'Branches Old and New,' *NMI*, III, 6 (Feb. 1909), p. 51.

'Calls and Excuses,' *NMI*, II, 10 (June 1908), pp. 90-93.

'Christian Responsibility after the All-Religions Conference of the All-India Depressed Classes Conference, Lucknow, U.P. — May 22-24, 1936,' *Depressed Classes Awakenings*, 24 June 1936, copy in I: 54/ 1002, Mott Papers, YDS.

'Fifth Annual Report, Madras,' *YMI*, VI, 3 (March 1895), pp. 31-33.

'Forward Movement in Evangelism,' *Guardian*, XIII, 29 (18 July 1935), pp. 455, 458.

'"Forward Movement in Evangelism" — Report of a Conference on Mass Movement Work in the Andhra Area: Guntur, August 18-19, 1938,' *NCCR*, LVIII (new series), 11 (Nov. 1938), pp. 642-50.

'Gandhiji and Religious Freedom,' *Guardian*, XVIII, 10 and 11 (7 and 14 March 1940), pp. 146-47, 163, 175.

'Gandhiji on Religion,' *Guardian*, XVI, 28 (14 July 1938), p. 435.

'Gandhiji's Alleged Threat to Christian Missions,' *Guardian*, XVI, 30 (28 July 1938), p. 465.

'Indian Christians and the Communal Award,' *Guardian*, X, 29 (25 Aug. 1932), pp. 349-50.

'Korea: The Marvellous Successes of the Gospel,' *NMI*, II, 10 (June 1908), pp. 95-97.

'Letter from an Indian Pastor of Tinnevelly,' *YMI*, X, 10 (Oct. 1899), p. 162.

'Mahatma Gandhi on Christian Missions,' *YMI*, XXXVII, 9 (Sept. 1925), pp. 517-26.

'Mass Movement Appeal,' *MDM*, XIII, 6 (June 1918), pp. 131-34.

'Mass Movements and Economic Reconstruction,' *DDM*, XI, 3 (March 1934), pp. 16-19.

'National Missionary Society,' *NMI*, II, 5 (Jan. 1908), pp. 40-41.

'Notes,' *NMI*, II, 12 (Aug. 1908), p. 122.

'Poona Christian Conference,' *Guardian*, X, 39 (3 Nov. 1932), p. 463.

'Prohibition Issue in India,' *MDM*, XIII, 11 (Nov. 1918), pp. 263-64.

'Report: Eleventh Quadrennial Conference of the National YWCA of India, Burma and Ceylon, April 30–May 9, 1938,' *NCCR*, LVIII, 7 (July 1938), pp. 401-7.

'Sixth Biennial Report of the Indian National Council,' *YMI*, XIII, 1 (Jan. 1902), pp. 19-23.

'Some Thoughts on Present Discontent,' *HF*, XVIII, 5 (new series) (May 1907), pp. 167-69.

'Statistics of Telugu Christianity,' *DDM*, XI, 8 (Aug. 1934), p. 6.

'The Communal Award,' *Guardian*, X, 29 (25 Aug. 1932), pp. 342-43.

'The Fourth Tamil Camp,' *YMI*, XIX, 6 (June 1908), pp. 98-99.

'The Indian Census,' *DDM*, X, 11 (Nov. 1933), pp. 9-12.

'The Indian Christian Attitude towards Indian National Aspirations,' *NMI*, II, 9 (May 1908), pp. 84-85.

'The National Missionary Society of India,' 'The Meeting at Serampore,' 'The Constitution of the National Missionary Society of India,' *YMI*, XVII, 1 (Jan. 1906), pp. 1-10.

'The Position of Indian Christians,' *Guardian*, X, 34 (29 Sept. 1932), p. 401.

'The Pushkaram Festival at Bezwada,' *DDM*, X, 10 (Oct. 1933), pp. 10-14.

'The Question of the Depressed Classes,' *Guardian*, XIV, 23 (4 June 1936), p. 354.

'The Rt. Rev. Bishop Whitehead,' *HF*, XLII, 6 (June 1922), pp. 216-17.

'The Standing Committee,' *DDM*, XIII, 10 (Oct. 1936), pp. 4-8.

'The Tamil Church Deepika,' *MDM*, XXIV, 10 (Oct. 1929), p. 341.

'The World Missionary Conference,' *CMG*, XXXVII, 436 (April 1910), p. 64.

'The Year's Harvest — YMCA Rural Work,' *HF*, XL, 12 (Dec. 1920), p. 470.

'What Is "Dalit" and Dalitism?' *Dalit Voice*, II, 16 (1-15 June 1983), pp. 1-2, 11.

A Brief Report of the Missionary Work of the Church of South India, CSI Synod Board of Missions, 1949; in 'Church of South India Pamphlets, Misc.,' SOCA, Birmingham.

A Collection of Papers Connected with the Movement of the National Church of India (Madras), Madras, 1893.

Allen, Roland. *Missionary Methods: St. Paul's or Ours: A Study of the Church in the Four Provinces*, 1st ed. London, 1912; 2nd ed., London, 1927; 6th ed., Grand Rapids, 1962.

Allen, Roland. *Missionary Principles*, Grand Rapids, 1964.

Allen, Roland. *The Spontaneous Expansion of the Church and the Causes Which Hinder It*, Grand Rapids, 1962.

Ambedkar, B. R. *What Congress and Gandhi Have Done to the Untouchables*, Bombay, 1945; 2nd ed. 1946.

Ambedkar, B. R. (Babasahib). *Why Go for Conversion?*, Bangalore, 1984.

Anderson, Herbert. 'The Modern National Spirit, the Indian Church and Missions,' *IRM*, VI, 23 (July 1917), pp. 400-413.

Anderson, Herbert. *Prohibition Progresses in India*, India Conciliation Group, London, 1938.

Andhra Christian Lyrics (Baptist Edition), Madras, 1939.

Andhra Pradesh District Gazetteers: Khammam, Hyderabad, 1977.

Andrews, C. F. 'A New Year's Message,' *NMI*, II, 5 (Jan. 1908), p. 35.

Andrews, C. F. 'Indian Christians and the National Movement,' *YMI*, XIX, 9 (Sept. 1908), pp. 147-51.

Andrews, C. F. *Gandhi's Fast: Will Untouchability be Ended by It?* London, 1932.

Appaswami, A. S. 'The Conversion of India by Indians,' *NMI*, III, 6 (Feb. 1909), pp. 49-51.

Arden, A. H. ('By the Author of "Foreign Missions and Home Calls"') *Are Foreign Missions Doing Any Good?*, London, 1894.

Arden, A. H. ('By the Author of "Are Foreign Missions Doing Any Good?"') *Foreign Missions and Home Calls*, London, 1893.

Azariah, A. J. *A Biographical Sketch of Samuel Vedanayagam Thomas (1855-1890)*, Madras, 1970.

Azariah, Anbu, ed. *A Talk to a Christian Girl on Her Coming of Age*, Madras: CLS, 1951 (in Tamil).

Azariah, Anbu, ed. *A Talk to a Christian Girl Who Is about to Be Married*, Madras: CLS, 1951 (in Tamil).

Azariah, Anbu, ed. *A Talk to Those Who Expect to Be Mothers*, Madras: CLS, 1951.

Azariah Family Newsletters, 30 March 1964 and 3 December 1967, Madras; in Azariah Collection, Madras.

Azariah, G. S. C. 'The Diocese of Dornakal,' *CMO*, LVII (Oct. 1930), pp. 201-3.

Azariah, Henry S. 'Rural Leadership,' *NCCR*, LXII, 6 (June 1942), pp. 241-45.

Azariah, M. 'Thirty Years' Report of the Dornakal Mission of the Indian Missionary Society of Tinnevelly, 1903-1933,' *DDM*, XI, 12 (Dec. 1934), pp. 5-8.

Azariah, Mercy. *A Drama for Children to Act*, in Azariah Collection, Madras.

Azariah, Mercy. *Naomi: A Drama for Women Actors*, Madras: CLS, 1948.

Azariah, Mercy. *Onesimus: A Play for Boys*, Madras: CLS, 1948.

Banninga, J. J., et al. *The Problem of Race Relationship*, Pasumalai, n.d., brochure for private circulation only; in Letters of K. T. Paul, UTCA.

Bell, G. K. A., ed. *The Stockholm Conference 1925. The Official Report of the Universal Christian Conference on Life and Work, 19-30 August 1925*, London, 1926.

Bible Lands: Quarterly Paper of the Jerusalem and the East Mission, VII, 114-17 (Oct. 1927–July 1928); VIII, 124 (April 1930).

Bombay Representative Christian Council: Report on the Survey of Evangelistic Opportunities in Maharashtra, 1938-39, Mysore City, 1940.

Brinton, P. R. *Edwin James Palmer — 7th Bishop of Bombay, 1908-1929: A Memoir*, August 1955.

Brittain, Arthur H. B., ed., *The Secunderabad Magazine: A Record of Church Work in an Indian Parish*, III (June 1900–April 1901), Madras, 1901.

Brown, Leslie. 'Anglican Episcopacy in Africa,' in *Bishops: But What Kind?*, ed. Peter Moore, London, 1982, pp. 135-48.

Butterfield, Kenyon L. *The Christian Mission in Rural India: Report and Recommendations*, New York, 1930.

Cambridge University Reporter, L, 2297, 20 July 1920.

Carter, Edward C. 'Indian Christian Leadership and the Indian Church,' *YMI*, XXIV, 3 (March 1913), pp. 154-57.

Carter, Edward C. *Among Indian Young Men*, Cambridge, MA, March 1904; copy in Harvard Divinity School: Rare Books Division.

Chakkarai, V. 'The Indian National Congress and the Indian Christian Community,' *NMI*, IX, 1 (Jan. 1915), p. 1.

Chambers, C. B. G. 'A Five Year Programme of Evangelism, 1936-40,' *DDM*, XIII, 8 (Aug. 1936), pp. 7-12.

Chandler, J. S. 'The Awakening in Japan: Its Lessons for India,' *HF,* XIV, 12 (new series) (Dec. 1903), pp. 450-64.

Chapman, G. 'A Literary Institute at Kavali,' *DDM,* XIV, 9 (Sept. 1937), pp. 13-15.

Christian Patriot, weekly issues of *CP* from VI, 46 (14 Nov. 1895); microfilm in UTCA, Bangalore.

Church of South India, Madras, Thanksgiving Service on Birth Centenary of Bishop Azariah, 6 October 1974, St. George's Cathedral.

Church of South India: Silver Jubilee Celebrations Souvenir: 1945-1972.

Church Union News and Views: Organ of the Continuation Committee of the South India Joint Committee on Union, Madras, I, 1 (July 1930) — XV, 3 (March 1945).

Clarke, W. D. 'In Memoriam: Samuel Satthianadhan,' *MDM,* I, 5 (May 1906), pp. 245-47.

Clarke, W. D. *The Centenary of the South Indian Mission of the Church Missionary Society,* Madras, 1914.

Clough, John E. *Social Christianity in the Orient: The Story of a Man, a Mission and a Movement,* New York, 1914.

CMS Outlook: Wartime Edition, 31, January 1943, p. 1.

Constitution and Rules of the Chapter of the Cathedral Church of the Epiphany, Dornakal, Dornakal, n.d.

Constitution of the Dornakal Diocesan Council (as amended to October 1934), Dornakal, n.d.

Copleston, Reginald S. *Buddhism Primitive and Present in Magadha and in Ceylon,* London, 1st ed., 1892; 2nd ed. 1908.

Cotelingam, J. P. 'How to Promote the Missionary Spirit among Indian Christians,' *HF,* XIV, 10 (new series) (Oct. 1903), pp. 364-68.

Cotelingam, J. P. 'Swadeshi and the South India United Church,' *HF,* XIX, 9 (new series) (Sept. 1908), pp. 346-49.

CSI News, nos. 96-104 (Feb. 1985–Feb. 1989).

Datta, S. K. 'The Problems of the Bible Study Department of the Association,' *YMI,* XI, 7 (July 1900), pp. 118-19.

Day, Lal Behari. 'The Desirableness and Practicability of Organizing a National Church in Bengal: Lecture Delivered at the Bengal Christian Association, Monday, 13 December 1869,' Calcutta, 1870.

De, Brajendra Nath. 'Reminiscences of an Indian Member of the Indian Civil Service,' Memoirs published serially in *Calcutta Review,* LLXXVII (April 1953), pp. 43-56, (June 1953), pp. 233-40; CXXVIII (Aug. 1953), pp. 141-50; CXXIX (Nov. 1953), pp. 155-69, (Dec. 1953), pp. 253-67; CXXX (Jan. 1954), pp. 16-26, (Feb. 1954), pp. 141-53, (March 1954), pp. 265-80; CXXXI (April 1954), pp. 25-38, (June 1954), pp. 227-42; CXXXII (Aug. 1954), pp. 85-98, (Sept. 1954), pp. 171-85; CXXXIII (Nov. 1954), pp. 82-96, (Dec. 1954), pp. 220-34; CXXXIV (Jan. 1955), pp. 49-62, (Feb. 1955), pp. 162-78, (March 1955), pp. 279-86; CXXXV (April 1955), pp. 25-31, (May 1955), pp. 147-54, (June 1955), pp. 175-84; CXXXVI (July 1956), pp. 27-36.

Depressed Classes Awakenings: News and Views of the All-India Depressed Classes Conference, Lucknow, 24 June 1936, copy in I: 54/ 1002, Mott Papers, YDS.

Desai, Mahadev. 'Interesting Questions,' *Harijan,* 11 May 1935, in *CM,* p. 106.

Directory of Christian Missions and Churches in India, Burma and Ceylon, 1940-1941, Nagpur, 1940.

Dornakal Diocesan Magazine, V, 1 (Jan. 1928) through XV, 12 (Dec. 1938); XVI, 2-3 (Feb.-March, 1939); XVIII, 4 (April 1941); XVIII, 6 (July 1941); XXII, 1 (Jan. 1945); XXII, 5 (May 1945); XXII, 8 (Sept.-Oct. 1945); XXIII, 2 (Feb. 1946).

Eddy, G. S. 'A Month in Jaffna,' *The Student Movement,* 1899, copy in I: 3/55 (and also as *Report Letter 19,* 3/52), Eddy Papers, YDS.

Eddy, G. S. 'A National Church for India,' *HF,* XXXI, 6 (June 1911), pp. 205-24. See also reprint copy in II: 6/ 102, Eddy Papers, YDS.

Eddy, G. S. 'Seeking to Reach the Educated Hindus,' *The Missionary Review of the World,* December 1903, pp. 922-27, copy in II: 6/101, Eddy Papers, YDS.

Eddy, G. S. 'Signs of Promise in India: The Missionary Spirit in the Native Church,' *The Missionary Review of the World,* June 1904, pp. 430-33, copy in II: 6/101, Eddy Papers, YDS.

Eddy, G. S. 'The Ceylon Conference,' *YMI,* VIII, 7 (Aug. 1897), p. 99.

Eddy, G. S. 'The Japan Conference,' *YMI,* XVIII, 7 (July 1907), pp. 87-91.

Eddy, G. S. 'The Missionary Spirit,' *YMI,* XIV, 10 (Oct. 1903), pp. 169-71.

Eddy, G. S. 'The Present Situation in India,' *IRM,* V, 18 (April 1916), pp. 267-76.

Eddy, G. S. 'The Unoccupied Fields of India,' *The Missionary Review of the World,* April 1905, pp. 247-59, copy in II: 6/ 102, Eddy Papers, YDS.

Eddy, G. S. *A Month in Tinnevelly: Report Letter No. 29,* September 1902, copy in I: 3/55, Eddy Papers, YDS.

Eddy, G. S. *Eighty Adventurous Years: An Autobiography,* New York, 1955.

Eddy, G. S. *How God Became Real to Me: A Message to India's Youth,* Coimbatore, 1948.

Eddy, G. S. *India Awakening,* New York, 1911, copy in I: 3/58, Eddy Papers, YDS.

Eddy, G. S. *Pathfinders of the World Missionary Crusade,* New York, 1945.

Eddy, G. S. *Religion and Politics in India,* 1949, copy in II: 6/125, Eddy Papers, YDS.

Editorial on the Swadeshi Movement, *HF,* XVIII, 10 (new series) (Oct. 1907), pp. 361-64.

Editorial, *CMG,* XXXVII, 440 (Aug. 1910), pp. 113-17.

Editorial, *HF,* XIV, 7 (new series) (July 1903), pp. 241-42.

Eleventh Annual Report of the IMST, 1913-14; in IMSA, Palayamkottai.

Eliot, T. S. *Reunion by Destruction: Reflections on a Scheme for Church Union in South India,* London, 1943.

Emmet, Archdeacon (P. B.). 'Lay Work in the Dornakal Diocese,' *DDM,* X, 4 (April 1933), pp. 7-10.

Emmet, P. B. 'The Proposed Scheme and the Telugu Anglican Area,' *CUNV,* XI, 1 (July 1931), pp. 32-35.

Farquhar, J. N. 'A National Missionary Society for India,' *HF,* XVII, 2 (new series) (Feb. 1906), pp. 58-63.

Farquhar, J. N. *Christianity in India,* London, 1908.

Farquhar, J. N. *Modern Religious Movements in India,* London, 1929.

Ferguson, W. L. 'The Growth of the Church in the Mission Field: The Telugu Mission of the American Baptist Foreign Mission Society,' *IRM,* I (1912), pp. 688-703.

Fifteenth Annual Report of the IMS of Tinnevelly, 1917-18; in IMSA, Palayamkottai.

Findings of the National Conference held in Calcutta, December 18th to 21st, 1912: Under the Presidency of Dr. J. R. Mott, Chairman of the Continuation Committee of the Edinburgh World Missionary Conference, n.d. (copies in SOC Library and UTCA)

Forsyth, P. T. *Missions in State and Church: Sermons and Addresses,* London, 1908.

Fraser, A. G., et al. *Village Education in India: The Report of a Commission of Inquiry,* London, 1920.

Fremantle, W. H. *The World as the Subject of Redemption: Being an Attempt to Set Forth the Functions of the Church as Designed to Embrace the Whole Race of Mankind,* London, 1885.

Gairdner, William Henry Temple. *Edinburgh 1910: An Account and Interpretation of the World Missionary Conference,* 2nd ed., Edinburgh, 1910.

Gandhi, M. K., 'Swadeshi,' *HF,* XXXVI, 4 (April 1916), pp. 126-32.

Gandhi, M. K. *Capital and Labour,* ed. Anand T. Hingorani, Bombay, 1970.

Gandhi, M. K. *Christian Missions: Their Place in India,* ed. Bharatan Kumarappa, 2nd ed., Ahmedabad, 1957.

Gandhi, M. K. *God Is Truth,* ed. Anand T. Hingorani, Bombay, 1971.

Gandhi, M. K. *Modern v. Ancient Civilization,* ed. Anand T. Hingorani, Bombay, 1970.

Gandhi, M. K. *My Religion,* ed. Bharatan Kumarappa, Ahmedabad, 1955.

Gandhi, M. K. *The Collected Works of Mahatma Gandhi* (New Delhi), LXIV (3 Nov. 1936-14 March 1937), LXV (15 March 1937-31 July 1937).

Gandhi, M. K. *The Law of Love,* ed. Anand T. Hingorani, Bombay, 1970.

Gandhi, M. K. *The Message of Jesus Christ,* ed. Anand T. Hingorani, Bombay, 1971.

Gandhi, M. K. *The Village Reconstruction,* ed. Anand T. Hingorani, Bombay, 1966.

Gell, Frederick. *Charges Delivered in St. George's Cathedral, Madras, at the Visitations of Frederick Gell, Bishop of Madras,* Madras, 1863-1896. Copy in MDA.

Gledstone, F. F. *South India,* London, 1930.

Gledstone, F. F. *The Story of the Masulipatam Cyclone of 1864 and Some Early Records of the Telugu Church,* Masulipatam, n.d.

Godbey, J. E. and A. H. *Light in Darkness; or, Missions and Missionary Heroes:. An illustrated history of the Missionary work now carried on by all Protestant denominations in heathen lands, taking up principally the work in India, Burmah, Siam, China, Japan, Polynesia, Egypt, Syria, Armenia, Africa, South America, Greenland and Labrador. Being a history of these countries naturally, socially and politically, and also the missionary work that has been done in them; the religions of pagan and heathen countries and their influence, as shown in the customs and character of the people and the idols they worship. To which is added the Adventures of Missionaries among the uncivilized races of the world; the path-breakers and standard-bearers of the church militant; their apostolic zeal and faith, the perils which they endured, and the success of their labors,* St. Louis, MO, 1893.

Graham, Carol. 'The Christian Home Festival,' *NCCR,* LXIII, 11 (Nov. 1943), pp. 391-94.

Graham, Carol. 'The Consecration of the Dornakal Cathedral,' *The Mission Field,* May 1939, pp. 144-48 (Graham Collection).

Graham, Carol. 'Women in the Indian Church,' *IJT,* VII, 4 (Oct.-Dec. 1958).

Graham, Carol. *Between Two Worlds,* private publication in England, n.d.; Madras, 1980.

Graham, Carol. *By Bread Alone?* Madras, 1974.

Graham, Carol. *Christ among the Telugus,* London, 1938.

Graham, Carol. *Christ in Our Home,* Madras, 1948 (in English, Tamil, and Telugu).

Graham, Carol. *Dornakal: Every Christian a Witness,* London, 1945.

Graham, Carol. *Family Prayers for Christian Homes,* Madras, 1951 (in English and Telugu).

Graham, Carol. *God in Our Home,* Madras, 1952 (in English, Tamil, and Telugu).

Graham, Carol. *Praying Places along the Way of the Cross: A Book for Lent,* Madras, 1963.

Graham, Carol. *The Church of South India — A Short Handbook,* Brighton, 1951; 2nd ed., 1954; 3rd ed. (entitled *The Church of South India — A Further Stage in Development*), 1956; 4th ed., 1960.

Graham, Carol. *The Holy Spirit in the Home,* Madras, 1962.

Graham, Carol. *The Meaning and Practice of Prayer,* Madras, 1959 (in English, Tamil, and Telugu).

Gulliford, Henry. *Extracts from the Diary of the Rev. Henry Gulliford, Concerning the Meetings of the Joint Committee on Church Union in South India,* n.d.

Hartman, L. O. 'The Emancipator of Indian Outcastes,' *MRW*, 59, 4 (April 1936), pp. 170-71.

Havell, E. B. 'Christian Architecture in India,' *MTDM*, IX, 2 (Feb. 1914), pp. 49-51.

Hayter, O. C. G. 'Conversions of Outcastes,' *The Asiatic Review*, XXVI, 87 (July 1930), pp. 603-11.

Heinrich, J. C. *The Psychology of a Suppressed People*, London, 1937.

Henson, Herbert Hensley. *Retrospect of an Unimportant Life, vol. II, 1920-1939*, London, 1943.

Hibbert-Ware, G. *Mass Movements in India*, Croydon, 1918.

Historical Sketch of the Student Volunteer Movement for Foreign Mission, Register of Ms. Group Number 42, Archives of the Student Volunteer Movement for Foreign Missions, YDS, New Haven, CT.

Hogg, A. G. 'The Function of the Christian College,' *IRM*, January 1934; reprint Morrison & Gibbs, Ltd., London, n.d.

Hollis, Michael. 'Christian Unity in South India,' reprint from March and May 1961 issues of *World Outlook*, New York, 1961.

In His Footsteps: Report of the National Missionary Society of India, 1936, Madras: NMS Press, 1936; in NMSA, Madras.

Jackson, Elva. *Indian Saga*, Devonport, New Zealand, 1980.

'J. N. R.' 'John Gibson Paton,' *NMI*, II, 12 (Aug. 1908), pp. 116-21.

Job, G. V. et al. *Rethinking Christianity in India Today*, D. M. Devasahayam and A. N. Sudarisanam, eds. Madras, 1938.

Jones, E. Stanley. *The Christian Programme for Reconstruction*, Lucknow, 1936.

Khammamett in 1913, Madras, 1914.

Knight, Gell. *General Meditations on the Seven Words of the Cross*, Madras, 1942 (in Tamil).

Kraemer, Hendrik. 'The Missionary Implications of the End of Western Colonialism and the Collapse of Western Civilization,' in *History's Lessons for Tomorrow's Mission*, Geneva, 1960, pp. 195-206.

Kraemer, Hendrik. *Religion and the Christian Faith*, London, 1956.

Kraemer, Hendrik. *The Christian Message in a Non-Christian World*, London, 1938.

Kuriakose, M. K., ed. *History of Christianity in India: Source Materials*, Madras, 1982.

Laflamme, H. F. 'The Telugu Christian Weekly Newspaper, "Ravi",' *HF*, XIV, 8 (new series) (Aug. 1903), pp. 297-99.

Lamb, Frederick. *The Gospel and the Mala: The Story of the Hyderabad Wesleyan Mission*, Mysore, 1913.

Lamb, Frederick. *The Story of Haidarabad*, London, n.d.

Larsen, L. P. 'A Serious Missionary Problem,' *HF*, XIV, 10 (new series) (Oct. 1903), pp. 368-83.

Laubach, Frank C. *Thirty Years with the Silent Billion: Adventuring in Literacy*, London, 1961.

Lefroy, George Alfred (Bishop of Calcutta). 'Historical Statement of the Anglican Episcopate in India,' *MTDM*, X, 1 (Jan. 1915), pp. 18-22.

London Missionary Society. *Report for the Telugu Districts (Cuddapah, Kurnool, and Anantapur), 1933,* Nagercoil, Travancore, 1934.

Madras and Tinnevelly Diocesan Magazine, II, 5 - X, 12 (May 1907–Dec. 1915).

Madras Diocesan Committee for 1896, Madras, 1906.

Madras Diocesan Magazine, I, 1 – II, 4 (Jan. 1906–April 1907); XI-XXXIII (1916-38).

Madras Diocesan Record, X-XIII (1896-1899); XIV, 1 (Jan. 1900); XV, 4 (Oct. 1901); XVII-XIX (1903-1905).

Maduram, S. G. *South India Church Union Scheme: A Review,* Madras, 1930.

Manikam, Rajah B. *The Christian College and the Christian Community,* Madras, 1938.

Mason, Eleanor. *The Bishop of Dornakal's Last Visitation,* offprint sent by author.

Mayhew, Arthur. 'Mahatma Gandhi and the Christian Mission,' *The Mission Field,* LXXVI, 907 (July 1931), pp. 150-54.

McConaughy, David. 'Second Paper,' *Report of the Third Decennial Missionary Conference, Bombay, 1892-1893,* I, Bombay, 1893, pp. 185-95.

McGavran, Donald Anderson. 'An Unparalleled Situation in India,' *World Dominion,* XV, 1 (Jan. 1937), pp. 12-21.

McGavran, Donald Anderson. 'My Pilgrimage in Mission,' *International Bulletin of Missionary Research,* X, 2 (April 1986), pp. 53-58.

McGavran, Donald Anderson. 'The Battle for Brotherhood in India Today,' *World Dominion,* XVI, 1 (Jan. 1938), pp. 32-36; XVI, 2 (April 1938), pp. 131-35; XVI, 3 (July 1938), pp. 255-61; XVI, 4 (Oct. 1938), p. 392.

McGavran, Donald Anderson. *Education and the Beliefs of Popular Hinduism: A Study of the Beliefs of Secondary School Boys in the Central Provinces, India, in regard to Nineteen Major Beliefs of Popular Hinduism,* Jubbulpore, 1935.

McGavran, Donald Anderson. *How Churches Grow: The New Frontiers of Mission,* London, 1955.

McGavran, Donald Anderson. *The Bridges of God: A Study in the Strategy of Missions,* London, 1955.

McLeish, Alexander. 'An Unprecedented Opportunity in India,' *World Dominion,* XV, 3 (July 1937), pp. 229-37; XV, 4 (Oct. 1937), pp. 385-97.

McLeish, Alexander. 'Lessons of Indian "Mass Movements",' *World Dominion,* XVI, 4 (Oct. 1938), pp. 383-92.

Milford, C. S., *Church and Crisis in India,* London, 1945.

Milton, John. *Poongavana Piralayam or Paradise Lost, Books I and II,* trans. S. V. Thomas, Trichinopoly: Southern Star Press, 1887; 2nd ed., Madras: CLS, 1978.

Minutes of the Episcopal Synod held at Calcutta from 1910 to 1936, Calcutta, 1936 (copy in BHA).

Minutes of the Episcopal Synod of the Province of India and Ceylon, 1863-1908, Calcutta, 1911 (copies in BHA and MDA).

Minutes of the Executive Committee, National Christian Council, 1914-48 (copy in UTCA).

Mission of Sawyerpooram in the District of Tinnevelly and Diocese of Madras, 7th ed., London, 1845.

Mission of Sawyerpooram, Part Second, Journal of the Rev. G. U. Pope, 5th ed., London, 1846.

Mission of Sawyerpooram, Part Third, Report of the Rev. G. U. Pope, January 1845, 4th ed., London, 1847.

Moberly, Sir Walter, et al. *The Churches Survey Their Task: The Report of the Conference at Oxford, July 1937, on Church, Community and State.* London, 1937.

Modak, S. *Directory of Protestant Indian Christians,* Ahmednagar, 1900.

Moore, Peter. 'The Anglican Episcopate: Its Strengths and Limitations,' in *Bishops: But What Kind?,* ed. Peter Moore, London, 1982, pp. 127-34.

Moorhead, Max Wood, ed. *The Student Missionary Enterprise: Addresses and Discussions of the Second International Convention of the Student Volunteer Movement for Foreign Missions, Detroit, Michigan, February 28–March 4, 1894,* Chicago, n.d.; in NMSA, Madras.

Moorman, J. R. H. 'The Anglican Bishop,' in *Bishops: But What Kind?,* ed. Peter Moore, London, 1982, pp. 116-26.

Mott, John R. *Experiences and Impressions during a Tour in Asia in 1912-1913, Being Extracts from Personal Letters of John R. Mott,* Privately Published, copy in III: 117, John Mott Papers, YDS, New Haven, CT.

Mott, John R. 'Some Impressions of Missions in Asia,' *The Congregationalist and Christian World,* 1 March 1902, p. 303; 8 March 1902, pp. 344-45. Copies in III: 117/ 1936, John Mott Papers, YDS, New Haven, CT.

N.M.S. of India, 1905, Calcutta, 1905; in NMSA, Madras.

National Missionary Intelligencer (journal of the NMS), monthly issues from II, 2 (Oct. 1907) to III, 10 (June 1909); in UTCA, Bangalore.

Nehru, Jawaharlal. *The Unity of India: Collected Writings, 1937-1940,* London, 1941.

Newbigin, Lesslie. 'A Sermon Preached at the Thanksgiving Service for the Fiftieth Anniversary of the Tambaram Conference of the International Missionary Council — 1938,' January 1988, manuscript copy from author.

Palmer, Edwin James. *South India: The Meaning of the Scheme for Church Union,* London, 1944.

Paton, David, and Charles H. Long. *The Compulsion of the Spirit: A Roland Allen Reader,* Grand Rapids, 1983.

Paton, David M., ed. *The Ministry of the Spirit: Selected Writings of Roland Allen,* London, 1960.

Paton, William. 'Personal Relationships between Indians and Europeans,' *IRM,* VIII, 32 (Oct. 1919), pp. 522-30.

Paul, K. T. 'A Call to Missionary Service,' *YMI,* XXIV, 2 (Feb. 1913), pp. 101-4.

Paul, K. T. 'Among the Syrians,' *NMI,* II, 3 (Nov. 1907) and II, 4 (Dec. 1907), pp. 28-29.

Paul, K. T. 'How Missions Denationalize Indians,' *IRM,* VIII, 32 (Oct. 1919), pp. 510-21.

Paul, K. T. 'Indian Christians and the National Movement,' *YMI,* XX, 1 (Jan. 1909), pp. 3-4.

Paul, K. T. 'Should British Young Men and Young Women Be Still Called to Missionary Work in India?' *Guardian,* II, 46 (13 Nov. 1924), pp. 548-49.

Paul, K. T. 'The Good versus the Best,' *NMI,* VIII, 4 (April 1914), pp. 21-22.

Paul, K. T. 'Twelve Years of Rural Work: Some Lessons and Warnings,' *The Indian Review,* June 1926, pp. 1-6; copy in Letters of K. T. Paul, UTCA.

Paul, K. T. *The British Connection with India,* London, 1927.

Paul, K. T. *The Missionary Spirit in the Indian Church,* Madras, 1909.

Perrill, Fred M. 'Dr. Ambedkar and the Christian Message,' address delivered at the Landour Community Conference, 10 June 1936, Lucknow, n.d.; typescript in Box: Pamphlets (Old) 275, Selly Oak Colleges Library.

Phillips, Godfrey E. *The Outcastes' Hope,* London, 8th ed. 1922 (1st ed. 1912).

Pickett, J. Waskom. 'Christian Mass Movements in India,' *MRW,* LIX, 4 (April 1936), pp. 167-69.

Pickett, J. Waskom. 'Donald A. McGavran: Missionary, Scholar, Ecumenist, Evangelist,' in *God, Man, and Church Growth: A Festschrift in Honor of Donald Anderson McGavran,* ed. A. R. Tippett, Grand Rapids, 1973, pp. 5-12.

Pickett, J. Waskom. 'The Untouchables,' in *Moving Millions,* Boston, 1938, pp. 42-74.

Pickett, J. Waskom. *Christian Mass Movements in India,* Lucknow, 1933.

Pickett, J. Waskom. *Christ's Way to India's Heart, with a Foreword by the Bishop of Dornakal,* Lucknow, 1937.

Pickett, J. Waskom. *The Movement among the Depressed Classes in India,* New York, 12 June 1936.

Pickett, J. Waskom, et al. *Church Growth and Group Conversion,* Lucknow, 1956.

Pickett, J. Waskom, D. A. McGavran, and G. H. Singh. *Mass Movement Survey Report for Mid-India,* Jubbulpore, C. P., n.d. (survey conducted 1936-37).

Pollard, C. 'Christianity and the Census of 1911,' *HF,* XXXII, 9 (Sept. 1912), pp. 342-50.

Pope, G. U. *The Folly of Demon Worship,* Madras, 1866 (in Tamil).

Popley, H. A. 'The Awakening among the Middle Classes of South India,' *IRM,* VII, 27 (July 1918), pp. 289-305.

Pratt, B. 'Mission Work among the Malas in Hyderabad,' *HF,* XIII, 8 (new series) (Aug. 1902), pp. 289-303; XIII, 9 (new series) (Sept. 1902), pp. 332-39.

Proceedings of the National Christian Council, 1924, 1926, 1929, 1930, 1933, 1934-35, 1936-37, 1939-40, 1944 (UTCA).

Proceedings of the National Missionary Council, 1914-19 (UTCA).

Proceedings of the South India Missionary Conference held at Ootacamund, April 19–May 5, 1858, Madras, 1858.

Rauschenbusch-Clough, Emma. *While Sewing Sandals: Or Tales of a Telugu Pariah Tribe,* London, 1899.

Rayappan, S. Paul. 'Adventures in Singareni Mission,' *DDM,* XXIII, 2 (Feb. 1946), pp. 7-11.

Redman, G. B. 'Telugu Church Temperance Society,' *MDM,* XI, 4 (April 1916), pp. 121-22.

Report of a Conference on Mass Movement Held under the Auspices of the National Christian Council in Nagpur on December 3 and 4, 1936, copy in I: 4/ 61, John Mott Papers, YDS, New Haven, CT.

Report of the Fifth Session of the All-India Conference of Indian Christians, Nagpur, December 28-31, 1918, Nagpur, 1919.

Report of the Fourth Session of the All-India Conference of Indian Christians, Bombay, December 27-29, 1917, Bombay, 1918.

Report of the General Missionary Conference Held at Allahabad, 1872-1873, London, 1873; in UTCA, Bangalore.

Report of the Jerusalem Meeting of the International Missionary Council, March 24th–April 8th, 1928, I-VIII, London, 1928.

Report of the Third Decennial Missionary Conference, Bombay 1892-93, I, Bombay, 1893; in UTCA Bangalore.

'Report of the Wesleyan Mission, Hyderabad Field,' *HF,* XXXVIII, 12 (new series) (Dec. 1918), pp. 472-73.

Rumpus, A. 'Report on the United Evangelistic Campaign, 1934,' *DDM,* XII, 3 (March 1935), pp. 12-19.

Sathianadhan, S. 'Indian Christians and Missionaries,' *HF,* XIV, 12 (Dec. 1903), pp. 464-66.

Satthianadhan, W. T. 'The Native Church in South India,' *Report of the General Missionary Conference Held at Allahabad 1872-73,* London, 1873, pp. 251-52.

Sell, Rev. Canon. *The Glorious Company of the Apostles and Other Sermons,* Madras, 1927.

Service in Recognition of the Inauguration of the Church of South India Held under the Auspices of the Foreign Missions Conference of North America and Union Theological Seminary in the James Memorial Chapel, Sunday, September 28th, 1947, n.p., n.d..

Sharrock, J. A. 'The Caste Suppression Society,' *HF,* IX, 8 (third series) (Aug. 1898), pp. 302-5.

Sharrock, J. A. *South Indian Missions: Containing Glimpses into the Lives and Customs of the Tamil People,* London, 1910.

Shriver, George. 'Dornakal Cathedral — Symbol of Christ in the East,' 1945: unmarked ms. in I: 4/61, Mott Papers, YDS.

Simon, P. M. 'Evangelistic Work at Alampur,' *DDM*, X, 10 (Oct. 1933), pp. 9-10.

SPG Madras Diocesan Committee Brief Annual Report for 1898, Madras, 1906.

Statement by Twenty-Five British Missionaries in India, India Conciliation Group, London, 1943.

Suvisesha Pirabalya Varthamani, XIV (1917); XVI (1919); XXVII (1928); XXIX (1932); XXX (1933); XXXIV (1937); XXXVII (1940); XXXX (1943); XXXXII (1945).

Swamidas, S. V. 'A New Development in Dornakal,' *CMO,* LVII (Nov. 1930), pp. 233-34.

Tambaram Series: Following the Meeting of the International Missionary Council at Tambaram, Madras, 12-29 December 1938, vol. III, *Evangelism;* vol. VII, *Addresses and Other Records,* London, 1938.

The Cambridge Review, XLI, 1024 (28 May 1920), p. 352; XLI, 1027 (18 June 1920), p. 426.

The Cathedral Age, XII, 2-3 (Midsummer–Autumn 1937), pp. 99-100.

The Church Missionary Atlas, London, 1896.

The Collected Works of Mahatma Gandhi (New Delhi), LXI, LXIV, LXV, LXVI, LXXI.

The Dependence of CSI on Foreign Funds, n.d. (but pre-1954) or place of publication (copy in SOCA).

The Depressed Classes: A Chronological Documentation, St. Mary's College, Kurseong, Calcutta, n.d.

The First Ten Years of the National Missionary Society, 1905-1916, Salem: T.A.C. Press, n.d.; in NMSA, Madras.

The Guardian (Madras), I, 1 (5 Jan. 1923) through XXIII, 5 (1 Feb. 1945).

The Indian Situation: Manifesto by British Missionaries in India, Society of Friends, London, 1930.

The Inquirer (a supplement to *The Young Men of India*), monthly issues from I, 1 (Sept. 1899); in UTCA, Bangalore, and YMCA Headquarters, UTC, Bangalore.

The Jerusalem and the East Mission: 40th Annual Report for the Year ending March 31, 1928.

The Jerusalem Findings as Related to India: Being a Report of the Enlarged Meeting of the National Christian Council of India, Burma and Ceylon Held in Madras, December 29, 1928–January 2, 1929, Poona.

The Meeting at Serampore, Madras, 1947; in NMSA, Madras.

The Missionary Intelligencer (journal of the IMS, in Tamil), monthly issues of TMI from XIV, 1 (Jan. 1917); in IMSA, Palayamkottai.

The National Christian Council of India, Burma and Ceylon and Its Work, Nagpur, 1934.

The Oxford Mission to Calcutta, Annual Reports, 1880, 1890, 1891, 1896, 1899.

The Silver Jubilee: Diocese of Dornakal, 1912-1937, Mysore City, n.d.

The Twenty-eighth Report of the IMS of Tinnevelly, 1930-31, Palayamkottai, 1931; in IMSA, Palayamkottai.

The World Mission of Christianity: Messages and Recommendations of the Jerusalem Meeting of the International Missionary Council, March 24th–April 8th, 1928, London, 1928.

The World Mission of the Church: Findings and Recommendations of the Meeting of the International Missionary Council, Tambaram, Madras, India, December 12-29, 1938, London, 1939.

Thomas, Samuel V. *Essays by Samuel V. Thomas, M.A. (Medalist in Sanskrit, University of Madras),* n.d. or place of publication. Bound into one volume with Milton, *Poongavana Piralayam or Paradise Lost, Books I and II,* trans. S. V. Thomas, Trichinopoly: Southern Star Press, 1887; and E. Muthiah Pillai, *The Manners and Customs of Native Christians* and *Rules and Regulations of European Missionaries,* Palamcottah: Chinthamani Press, 1894. Volume in possession of Dr. David Packiamuthu, Palayamkottai.

Thompson, E. W. 'Medak — A Study of Method in Dealing with Mass Movements,' *HF,* XXXII, 8 (Aug. 1912), pp. 294-310; XXXII, 9 (Sept. 1912), pp. 331-37.

Time for Magnanimous Action in India: Reprint of Open Letter from Scottish Missionaries to Members of Parliament Representing Scottish Constituencies, Society of Friends, London, 1932.

Twenty-five Years of Service through Village Women's Classes, 1931-1956, Velacheri, Madras Diocese, n.d.

Tyndale-Biscoe, C. E. *Tyndale-Biscoe of Kashmir: An Autobiography,* London, 1951.

Village Education in India: The Report of a Commission of Inquiry, Oxford, 1920.

Waller, E. H. M. 'Lambeth and the Union of Churches,' *CMO,* LVII (Nov. 1930), pp. 221-3.

Ward, Rev. W. *A View of the History, Literature, and Religion of the Hindoos: Including a Minute Description of Their Manners and Customs, and Translations from Their Principal Works,* 5th ed., Madras, 1863.

Wesleyan Methodist Provincial Synod, South India. *Report of the Mass Movement Commission,* Mysore, 1919.

White, J. Campbell. 'The Future of the Young Men's Christian Association in India,' *HF,* XIII, 10 (new series) (Oct. 1902), pp. 378-86.

Whitehead, A. N. *Adventure of Ideas,* New York, 1933.

Whitehead, A. N. *Religion in the Making* (Lowell Lectures), Cambridge, 1927.

Wigam, M. H. 'Educated Women and the Missionary Vocation,' *NCCR,* LXVIII, 10 (Oct. 1948), pp. 408-13.

Williams, A. T. P. *Church Union in South India,* London, 1944.

Winslow, J. C. 'The Christa Seva Sanghva,' *DDM*, X, 3 (March 1933), pp. 8-9.

Young Men of India, monthly issues from V, 5 (July 1894); in UTCA, Bangalore and YMCA Headquarters, UTC, Bangalore.

Younghusband, Francis. *Religion and Empire*, Printed for Private Circulation, London, 1914. See Curzon Papers, MSS Eur, F. 112/21, IOL.

B. Secondary Materials

I. *Works about Azariah*[4]

'A Great Christian,' *Oversea News*, 39 (March 1945), p. 1.

'A Pioneer Indian Bishop,' *Church Times* (12 Jan. 1945), Mott Papers.

'A Pioneer Indian Bishop: Death of Dr. Samuel Azariah,' unidentified newspaper clipping, Graham Collection.

'A Shepherd of Souls: Bishop Azariah's Last Days,' *The Church Times* (4 May 1945), p. 253.

'Bishop Azariah Dies,' *The Living Church*, CX, 3 (21 Jan. 1945), p. 10.

'Bishop Azariah's Family and Early Life,' *DDM*, XXII, 5 (May 1945), pp. 4-8.

'Bishop of Dornakal's Early Career,' *Guardian*, XXIII, 2 (11 Jan. 1945), p. 15.

'Death of the Bishop of Dornakal,' *Guardian*, XXIII, 1 (4 Jan. 1945), pp. 7-8.

'Death of the Bishop of Dornakal: A Tribute from a Correspondent,' *Record* (12 Jan. 1945), Graham Collection.

'Dr. V. S. Azariah: Bishop of Dornakal,' unidentified newspaper clipping, Graham Collection.

'Memorials and Tributes to the Bishop,' *DDM*, XXII, 3-4 (March and April 1945), pp. 2-10.

'The Late Bishop Azariah,' *NCCR*, LXV, 2 (Feb. 1945), pp. 13-15.

'The Late Bishop of Dornakal,' *Guardian*, XXIII, 1 (4 Jan. 1945), pp. 2, 8.

'V. S. Azariah,' *NMI*, III, 10 (June 1909), pp. 79-82.

'V. S. Azariah — An Appreciation,' *YMI*, XX, 9 (Sept. 1909), pp. 144-46.

'V. S. Azariah: First Bishop of Dornakal,' *CMS Outlook* (March 1945), Mott Papers.

A Service of Thanksgiving in Memory of Vedanayakam Samuel Azariah, Bishop of Dornakal, 1912-45, Wednesday, February 7th, 1945, St. Margaret's Church, Westminster; original program, Graham Collection.

4. Works chosen for this list devote all or significant portions of their space exclusively to Azariah. The list excludes treatments of Azariah in general ecclesiastical histories such as Eyre Chatterton, *A History of the Church of England in India since the Early Days of the East India Company* (London, 1924), pp. 325-28. A significant number of the Printed Primary Sources also contain discussions of Azariah, as indicated in footnotes throughout this book.

Abraham, Gondi Theodore. 'An Estimate of the Missionary and Pastoral Ministry of Bishop Azariah from 1922 to 1945,' B.D. thesis, United Theological College, Bangalore, 1966.

Anbudian, M. R. RyJ. 'Episodes in the Early Life of Bishop Azariah and the IMS Mission to Dornakal,' *TMI-IMS*, XXXVII, 5 (May 1940), pp. 64-47, (in Tamil).

Azariah, Mercy. *Bishop Azariah of Dornakal: A Play*, Madras, 1948; Tamil edition: Nagercoil: Mission Press, 1948.

Birth Centenary Celebrations of Bishop V. S. Azariah, Dornakal, 1974.

Birth Centenary of Bishop Azariah — 1974, Madras Diocesan Press, 1974. See full reference below under *The Church of South India . . . etc.*.

Bishop Azariah Birth Centenary Souvenir, 1974, Bishop Azariah High School for Girls: Vijayawada, 1974.

Book Reviews of Carol Graham, *Azariah of Dornakal*, 'Press Cuttings' envelope, Graham Collection.

Chirgwin, Arthur Mitchell. *These I Have Known*, London: LMS, April 1964, pp. 19-21.

Christadoss, D. A. *Acariyā Attiyaṭcar*, Tirunelveli: IMS, 1974 (in Tamil).

Downes, R. D. 'The Consecration of Bishop Azariah,' *YMI*, XXIV, 2 (Feb. 1913), pp. 112-13.

Eddy, Sherwood. *Pathfinders of the World Missionary Crusade*, New York, 1945.

Elliot, A. B. 'A Servant of the Servants of God: Bishop Azariah's Episcopate,' *NCCR*, LXV, 2 (Feb. 1945), pp. 16-17.

Emmet, Percy Barnabas. *Apostle of India: Azariah — Bishop of Dornakal*, London: SCM Press, 1949.

Graham, Carol. 'Azariah of Dornakal,' *G.D.A. Letter*, 50 (May 1946), Graham Collection.

Graham, Carol. 'Bishop Azariah and the Contribution of Women to the Church,' *Mothers in Council*, LVII, 221 (Dec. 1945), pp. 133-38.

Graham, Carol. 'Memories of the Bishop of Dornakal,' *Oversea News*, 39 (March 1945), p. 1; original ms. in Graham Collection.

Graham, Carol. 'The Bishop of Dornakal,' *The East and West Review*, XI, 2 (April 1945), pp. 35-38.

Graham, Carol. 'The Bishop of Dornakal,' unidentified newspaper clipping, Graham Collection.

Graham, Carol. 'The Legacy of V. S. Azariah,' *IBMR*, IX, 1 (Jan. 1985), pp. 16-19.

Graham, Carol. *Azariah of Dornakal*, London: SCM Press, 1946; 2nd ed., Madras: ISPCK/CLS, 1972.

Heiberg, Knud. *V. S. Azariah: Biskop af Dornakal*, Copenhagen: Det Danske Missionsselskab, 1950 (in Danish).

Hodge, John Zimmerman. *Bishop Azariah of Dornakal*, Madras: CLS, 1946.

Hooper, J. S. M. 'Bishop Azariah and Church Union,' *NCCR*, LXV, 2 (Feb. 1945), pp. 19-21.

Job, G. V. *Samuel Vethanayagam Azariah*, Madras: CLS, 1954 (in Tamil).

John, Puvvada. 'Dornakal Bishop's First Visit to Khammamett,' *DDM*, XXII (March and April 1945), pp. 10-11.

Lane, W. R. 'V. S. Azariah: First Bishop of Dornakal,' *C.M.S. Outlook*, 57 (March 1945), p. 2.

Macnicol, Nicol. 'The Bishop of Dornakal,' *British Weekly* (18 Jan. 1945), Graham Collection.

Manickam, Canon S. Paul. *Life and Work of Late Bishop Vethanayagam Samuel Azariah (Brief History)*, private publication: Tirunelveli, 1974 (in Tamil). Copy in Azariah Collection.

Mason, Eleanor. *The Bishop of Dornakal's Last Visitation*, Reprint from author.

Neill, Stephen C. 'Azariah, Vedanaiakam Samuel,' in *The Concise Dictionary of the Christian World Mission*, ed. S. Neill, G. H. Anderson and J. Goodwin, Nashville: Abingdon Press, 1971, p. 47.

Neill, Stephen C. (Stephen Tinnevelly). 'Bishop Azariah of Dornakal,' *The Student Movement*, XLVII, 4 (March 1945), p. 84.

Neill, Stephen C. 'Vedanayagam Samuel Azariah, 1874-1945,' in VSA, *Christian Giving*, London: Lutterworth Press, 1954, pp. 9-26.

Obituary of V. S. Azariah, *Tinnevelly Diocesan Magazine*, 309 (March 1945), p. 29 (in Tamil).

Packiamuthu, David. 'Azariah, the Apostle of India,' in *Birth Centenary of Bishop Azariah — 1974*, Madras: Diocesan Press, 1974, pp. 81-84.

Packiamuthu, David. *Valikāṭṭi*, Tirunelveli: IMS, 1963; Madras: CLS, 1974 (in Tamil); unpublished translation into English by Sarojini Packiamuthu.

Paul, Rajaiah D. 'V. S. Dornakal,' in *Birth Centenary of Bishop Azariah — 1974*, Madras: Diocesan Press, 1974, pp. 59-60.

Premachendrudu, Nathala. *Apostle of the Indian Church — A Life of the Rt. Rev. Vedanayagam Samuel Azariah, L.L.D., Bishop of Dornakal, 1912-45*, Madras: CLS, 1946 (in Telugu).

Premsagar, B. D. 'The Life and Work of Bishop Azariah with Special Reference to His Contribution to the Indigenisation of the Church,' Diploma thesis, United Theological College, Bangalore, 1969.

Rajomony, D. D. 'A Biography of Azariah,' *TMI-IMS*, XXXXII, 1 (Jan. 1945), pp. 2-4 (in Tamil).

Rallia Ram, B. L. 'The Bishop of Dornakal: An Apostle of the Indian Church,' *NCCR*, LXV, 2 (Feb. 1945), pp. 17-19.

Sahayam, V. D. 'The Bishop of Dornakal: An Apostle of Evangelism,' *NCCR*, LXV, 2 (Feb. 1945), pp. 21-22.

Selvan, Thamil. 'Research on Bishop Azariah and his Theology' B.D. thesis, Tamil Theological Seminary, Madurai, 1985.

Shriver, George. 'Bishop Azariah,' *Living Church* (4 Feb. 1945), Mott Papers, YDS.

Soundararaj, G. 'V. S. Azariah as YMCA Secretary,' in *Birth Centenary of Bishop Azariah — 1974*, Madras: Diocesan Press, 1974, pp. 35-37.

The Church of South India, the Indian Missionary Society, Madras, and the National Missionary Society of India Jointly Celebrate the Birth Centenary of Bishop Azariah on 5th and 6th October, 1974, in Madras, Madras: Diocesan Press, 1974 (abbreviated form, *Birth Centenary of Bishop Azariah — 1974*).

Whitehead, Henry. 'Vedanayakam Samuel Azariah,' *IRM*, XXXIV, 134 (April 1945), pp. 184-86.

II. Printed Secondary Sources

'Problems of Missionary Work,' *IRM*, XI (1922), pp. 430-38.

A Father of the Mill Hill St. Joseph's Society. *History of the Telugu Christians*, Trichinopoly, 1910.

A Hundred Years in Mysore: Being a Review of the Work of the Wesleyan Mission during the Century 1821-1921, Mysore, 1922.

A Statistical Atlas of the Madras Presidency, Madras, 1895, 1924, 1936.

Abhishiktananda. *Hindu-Christian Meeting Point*, Delhi, 1976.

Abhishiktananda. *Towards the Renewal of the Indian Church*, Cochin, 1970.

Abraham, C. E. *The Founders of the National Missionary Society of India*, Madras, 1947.

Abraham, Joseph. *Fifty Years' History of the Indian Missionary Society of Tirunelveli (1903-1953)*, Palayamkottai, 1955.

Adas, Michael. *Prophets of Rebellion: Millenarian Protest Movements against the European Colonial Order*, Cambridge, 1979.

Addleshaw, G. W. O. 'The Law and Constitution of the Church Overseas,' in *The Mission of the Anglican Communion*, ed. E. R. Morgan and R. Lloyd, London, 1948, pp. 74-98.

Ady, Cecilia M. 'From the Restoration to the Present Day,' in *Apostolic Ministry: Essays on the History and the Doctrine of Episcopacy*, ed. Kenneth E. Kirk, London, 1946, pp. 433-60.

Ahlstrom, Sydney E. *A Religious History of the American People*, New Haven, 1972.

Ahlstrom, Sydney E., ed. *Theology in America: The Major Protestant Voices from Puritanism to Neo-Orthodoxy*, Indianapolis, 1967.

Alexander, Horace. *Untouchability and the Poona Agreement*, London, 1932.

Allen, W. O. B., and Edmund McClure. *Two Hundred Years: The History of the Society for Promoting Christian Knowledge, 1698-1898*, New York, 1898, reprinted 1970.

Allier, R. *La psychologie de la conversion chez les peuples non-civilisés*, Paris, 1928.

Altholz, Joseph L. *The Churches in the Nineteenth Century*, New York, 1967.

Anand, Mulk Raj. *Untouchable*, New Delhi, 1983.

Anderson, Gerald H., ed. *The Theology of the Christian Mission*, London, 1961.

Andrews, C. F. *Sadhu Sundar Singh: A Personal Memoir*, London, 1934.

Andrews, C. F. *The Renaissance in India: Its Missionary Aspect*, London, 1914.

Annett, E. A. *Conversion in India: A Study in Religious Psychology*, Madras, 1920.

Annual Missionary Surveys for British India and Ceylon, IRM, II-IV (1913-15), pp. 28-41, 30-44, 21-31; VI-VII (1917-18), pp. 25-37, 22-33; X (1921), pp. 16-27; World Survey of India, Burma, and Ceylon, XVII (1928), pp. 32-46.

Appadorai, A. *Indian Political Thinking in the Twentieth Century from Naoroji to Nehru: An Introductory Survey*, Calcutta, 1971.

Apparao, P. S. R., ed. *Historical Tables*, Hyderabad, 1981.

Appasamy, A. J. 'Episcopacy in India,' *Church Union News and Views*, I, 3 (Nov. 1930), pp. 103-11.

Appasamy, A. J. *A Bishop's Story*, Madras, 1969.

Appasamy, A. J. *My Theological Quest*, Bangalore, 1964.

Appasamy, A. J. *Sundar Singh: A Biography*, Madras, 1966.

Arasaratnam, S. 'The Christians of Ceylon and Nationalist Politics,' in *Religion in South Asia: Religious Conversion and Revival Movements in South Asia in Medieval and Modern Times*, ed. G. A. Oddie, London, 1977, pp. 163-82.

Arnold, David. *The Congress in Tamilnad*, New Delhi, 1977.

Asirvadam, J. D. *History of the Lutheran National Missionary Society, 1916-1955*, Madras, 1965.

Axling, William. *Kagawa*, London, 1937.

Ayrookuzhiel, A. M. Abraham. *The Sacred in Popular Hinduism: An Empirical Study in Chirakkal, North Malabar*, Madras, 1983.

Baago, K. *A History of the National Christian Council of India, 1914-1964*, Nagpur, 1965.

Baago, Kaj. 'The Discovery of India's Past and Its Effect on the Christian Church in India,' in *History and Contemporary India*, ed. J. C. B. Webster, London, 1971, pp. 26-45.

Baago, Kaj. 'The First Independence Movement among Indian Christians, *ICHR*, I, 1 (June 1967), pp. 65-78.

Baago, Kaj. *Pioneers of Indigenous Christianity*, Madras, 1969.

Baago, Kaj. *The Movement around Subba Rao: A Study of the Hindu-Christian Movement around K. Subba Rao in Andhra Pradesh*, Madras, 1968.

Babb, Lawrence A. 'The Satnamis — Political Involvement of a Religious Movement,' in *The Untouchables in Contemporary India*, ed. J. Michael Mahar, Tucson, AZ, 1972, pp. 143-51.

Badley, Brenton Thoburn. *The Making of a Bishop: The Life-Story of Bishop Jashwant Rao Chitambar*, Lucknow, 1942.

Baker, C. J. and D. A. Washbrook. *South India: Political Institutions and Political Change: 1880-1940,* Delhi, 1975.

Baker, Christopher John. *The Politics of South India, 1920-1937,* Cambridge, 1976.

Ballhatchet, Kenneth. 'Missionaries, Empire and Society: The Jesuit Mission in Calcutta, 1834-1846,' in *Asie du Sud. Traditions et Changements,* Colloques Internationaux du C.N.R.S., No. 582, pp. 301-9.

Ballhatchet, Kenneth and Helen. 'Asia,' in *The Oxford Illustrated History of Christianity,* ed. John McManners, Oxford, 1990, pp. 488-518.

Bandopadhyay, Arun . 'The Communal Riots in Tinnevelli in 1899: Some Reconsiderations,' in *Caste and Communal Politics in South Asia,* ed. Sekhar Bandopadhyay and Suranjan Das, Calcutta, 1993, 29-45.

Barzun, Jacques. 'From the Nineteenth Century to the Twentieth,' in *Chapters in Western Civilization,* 3rd ed., New York, 1962, pp. 441-64.

Baskaran, S. Theodore. 'Christian Folk Songs of Tamil Nadu,' *Religion and Society,* XXXIII, 2 (June 1986), pp. 83-92.

Bates, Crispin N. *Congress and the Tribals,* unpublished ms. from author.

Bayart, J., 'Protestant Denominations in India,' *The Clergy Monthly,* VI, 6 (Dec. 1942), pp. 166-76.

Bayart, J., 'The Story of Protestant Missions,' *The Clergy Monthly,* VI, 8 (Feb. 1943), pp. 225-37; VI, 10 (April 1943), pp. 296-303.

Bayly, Susan. *Christians and Competing Fundamentalisms in South Indian Society,* Paper Presented to the Fundamentalism Project, Chicago Conference, 5-7 November 1990 (see also Susan Kaufmann).

Bays, Daniel H. *Christian Revivalism in China, 1900-1937,* Paper for Conference on Modern Christian Revivalism, Wheaton, March-April 1989.

Beaglehole, J. H. 'The Indian Christians — A Study of a Minority,' *Modern Asian Studies,* I, 1 (Jan. 1967), pp. 59-80.

Bearce, George D. *British Attitudes towards India: 1784-1858,* Oxford, 1961.

Bell, G. K. A. *Documents on Christian Unity: Third Series, 1930-1948.* London, 1948.

Bell, G. K. A. *Randall Davidson: Archbishop of Canterbury,* II, London, 1935.

Bennett, George, ed. *The Concept of Empire, Burke to Attlee, 1774-1947,* 2nd ed., London, 1962.

Beyerhaus, Peter and Carl F. Hallencreutz, eds. *The Church Crossing Frontiers: Essays on the Nature of Mission in Honour of Bengt Sundkler,* Uppsala, 1969.

Béteille, André. *Caste, Class, and Power: Changing Patterns of Stratification in a Tanjore Village,* Berkeley, 1971.

Bharati, Agehananda. 'Hindu Scholars, Germany, and the Third Reich,' *Contents,* VI, 3 (Sept. 1982), pp. 44-52.

Binfield, Clyde. *George Williams and the Y.M.C.A.: A Study in Victorian Social Attitudes* (London, 1973).

Bingle, E. J. 'A Hundred Years — 1837-1937: History of the Christian College,'

The Madras Christian College Magazine, Centenary Number (March 1937), pp. 130-36.

Bingle, Richard J. 'Outline of the Discussion,' in *Asie du Sud. Traditions et Changements*, Colloques Internationaux du C.N.R.S., No. 582, pp. 287-89.

Blauw, Johannes. *The Missionary Nature of the Church: A Survey of the Biblical Theology of Mission*, London, 1962.

Bliss, Kathleen. *The Service and Status of Women in the Churches*, London, 1952.

Boer, Jan Harm. *Missionary Messengers of Liberation in a Colonial Context: A Case Study of the Sudan United Mission*, Amsterdam, 1979.

Boggs, W. E. *Record of Telugu Mission Work Carried On by the American Baptist Telugu Mission and Other Societies*, Madras, 1904.

Boyd, Robin H. S. *India and the Latin Captivity of the Church: The Cultural Context of the Gospel*, Cambridge, 1974.

Braidwood, John. *True Yoke-fellows in the Mission Field: The Life and Labours of the Rev. John Anderson and the Rev. Robert Johnston, Traced in the Rise and Development of the Madras Free Church Mission*, London, 1862.

Brian, J. B. *Christian Indians in Natal: 1860-1911*, Cape Town, 1983.

Brou, Alexandre. 'L'Inde. Encore le problème des intouchables,' *Etudes*, 227 (1936), pp. 652-59.

Brou, Alexandre. 'Les origines du clergé indigène dans l'Inde,' *Revue d'Histoire des Missions*, VII, 1 (March 1930), pp. 46-73.

Brou, Alexandre. 'Notes sur les origines du clergé indigène au pays Tamoul,' *Revue d'Histoire des Missions*, VII, 1 (March 1930), pp. 188-210.

Brown, Judith M. 'Mahatmas as Reformers: Some Problems of Religious Authority in the Indian Nationalist Movement,' *South Asia Research*, VI, 1 (May 1986), pp. 15-26.

Brown, Judith M. *Gandhi and Civil Disobedience: The Mahatma in Indian Politics. 1928-34*, Cambridge, 1977.

Brown, Judith M. *Gandhi and the I.N.C.: A Centenary Assessment*, Paper Presented at the International Conference on '100 Years of the I.N.C.,' Oxford, November 1985.

Brown, Judith M. *Gandhi: Prisoner of Hope*, New Haven and London, 1989.

Brown, Judith M. *Men and Gods in a Changing World: Some Themes in the Religious Experience of Twentieth-Century Hindus and Christians*, London, 1980.

Brown, Judith M. *Modern India: The Origins of an Asian Democracy*, Delhi, 1985.

Brown, Leslie W. 'Anglican Episcopacy in Africa,' in *Bishops: But What Kind?*, ed. Peter Moore, London, 1982, pp. 135-48.

Brown, Leslie W. *Three Worlds: One Word: Account of a Mission*, London, 1981.

Brown, Leslie W. *The Indian Christians of St. Thomas: An Account of the Ancient Syrian Church of Malabar*, Cambridge, 1956, 1982.

Bruckner, Pascal. *The Tears of the White Man: Compassion as Contempt*, New York, 1983.

Bibliography

Brumberg, Joan Jacobs. *Mission for Life: The Story of the Family of Adoniram Judson, the Dramatic Events of the First American Foreign Mission, and the Course of Evangelical Religion in the Nineteenth Century,* London, 1980.

Bryce, L. Winifred. *India at the Threshold,* New York, 1946.

Butterfield, Herbert. *Christianity and History,* London, 1957.

Butterfield, Herbert. *History and Human Relations,* London, 1951.

Butterfield, Herbert. *The Whig Interpretation of History,* Middlesex, 1973.

Butterfield, Herbert. *Writings on Christianity and History,* ed. C. T. McIntire, New York, 1979.

Butterfield, Kenyon L. *The Christian Mission in Rural India,* London, 1930.

Caldwell, R. *A Political and General History of the District of Tinnevelly in the Presidency of Madras from the Earliest Period to Its Cession to the English Government in A.D. 1801.* Madras, 1881.

Caldwell, R. *Lectures on the Tinnevelly Missions: Descriptive of the Field, the Work, and the Results; with an Introductory Lecture on the Progress of Christianity in India,* London, 1857.

Campbell, Ernest Y. *The Church in the Punjab: Some Aspects of its Life and Growth,* Lucknow, 1961.

Campbell, John McLeod. *Christian History in the Making,* London, 1946.

Caplan, Lionel. 'Class and Christianity in South India: Indigenous Responses to Western Denominationalism,' *MAS,* XIV, 4 (Oct. 1980), pp. 645-71.

Caplan, Lionel. 'The Popular Culture of Evil in Urban South India,' in *The Anthropology of Evil,* ed. D. J. Parkin, New York, 1985.

Carmichael, Amy Wilson. *Walker of Tinnevelly,* London, 1916.

Carstairs, G. M. *Death of a Witch: A Village in North India: 1950-1981,* London, 1983.

Carus, William. *Memoirs of the Life of the Rev. Charles Simeon, M.A.,* London, 1847.

Chadwick, Owen. *The Reformation,* Middlesex, 1964.

Chadwick, Owen. *The Secularization of the European Mind in the Nineteenth Century,* Cambridge, 1975.

Chadwick, Owen. *The Victorian Church, Part I,* 3rd ed., London, 1971; *Part II,* London, 1970.

Chandra, Bipan. 'Historians of Modern India and Communalism,' *Communalism and the Writing of Indian History,* 2nd ed. New Delhi, 1977, pp. 39-61.

Chatterton, Eyre. *A History of the Church of England in India Since the Early Days of the East India Company,* London, 1924.

Chatterton, Eyre. *Our Anglican Church in India, 1815-1946,* London, 1946.

Chatterton, Eyre. *Our Church's Youngest Daughter: A Sketch of the Anglican Church in India,* London, 1928.

Chaturvedi, Benarsidas, and Marjorie Sykes. *Charles Freer Andrews,* London, 1949.

Chaudhuri, Nirad C. *A Passage to England,* London, 1966.

Chaudhuri, Nirad C. *Hinduism: A Religion to Live By,* Oxford, 1979.

Chaudhuri, Nirad C. *The Autobiography of an Unknown Indian,* London, 1951.

Chaudhuri, Nirad C. *Thy Hand, Great Anarch!,* New York, 1987.

Cherian, P. 'Some Recollections of an Eventful Decade (1880-1890),' *The Madras Christian College Magazine,* Centenary Number (March 1937), pp. 170-74.

Chetti, O. Kandaswami. 'The Maker of the Christian College,' *The Madras Christian College Magazine,* Centenary Number, March 1937, pp. 137-41.

Chetty, O. Kandaswamy. *Dr. William Miller,* Madras, 1924.

Christadoss, D. A. *Life and Work of Rev. John Thomas of Megnanapuram: Apostle of South Tirunelveli,* Palayamkottai, 1977 (in Tamil).

Christadoss, D. A. *Life of the Rev. Thomas Gajetan Ragland: Apostle of North Tirunelveli,* Tirunelveli, 1975 (in Tamil).

Christensen, Torben, and William R. Hutchison. *Missionary Ideologies in the Imperialist Era: 1880-1920,* Aarhus, Denmark, 1982.

Church of South India Silver Jubilee Celebrations: 1947-1972. Dornakal Diocese Souvenir, Dornakal, 1972.

Clarke, Sundar. 'Lest We Forget,' *CSI Review* (Sept. 1984), pp. 8-10.

Clarke, Sundar. *Let the Indian Church Be Indian,* Madras, 1980.

Cnattingius, Hans. *Bishops and Societies: A Study of Anglican Colonial and Missionary Expansion, 1698-1850,* London, 1952.

Cohn, Bernard S. 'Society and Social Change under the Raj,' *South Asian Review,* IV, 1 (Oct. 1970), pp. 27-49.

Cohn, Bernard S. 'The Changing Status of a Depressed Class,' in *Village India: Studies in the Little Community,* ed. McKim Marriot, Chicago 1955, pp. 53-77.

Cohn, Bernard S. *Colonialism and Its Forms of Knowledge: The British in India,* Oxford UP: Delhi, 1997.

Collingwood, R. G. *The Idea of History,* Oxford, 1961.

Conrad, Dieter. 'Gandhi's Egalitarianism and the Indian Tradition,' in *Indology and Law: Studies in Honour of Professor J. Duncan M. Derrett,* ed. Günther-Dietz Sontheimer and Parameswara Kota Aithal, Wiesbaden, 1982, pp. 359-410.

Copley, Antony. *Gandhi: Against the Tide,* Oxford, 1987.

Coupland, R. *Indian Politics, 1936-1942: Report on the Constitutional Problem in India, Part II,* London, 1943.

Cowasjee, Saros. *So Many Freedoms: A Study of the Major Fiction of Mulk Raj Anand,* Delhi, 1977.

Cragg, A. K. *The Christian and Other Religions: The Measure of Christ,* Oxford, 1977.

Cronin, Vincent. *A Pearl to India: The Life of Roberto de Nobili,* London, 1959.

Cronin, Vincent. *The Wise Man from the West,* London, 1984.

Crowther, M. A. *Church Embattled: Religious Controversy in Mid-Victorian England,* Hamden, CT, 1970.

D'Souza, Herman. *In the Steps of St. Thomas,* Madras-Mylapore, 1983.

Dalton, Dennis. 'The Gandhian View of Caste, and Caste After Gandhi,' in *India and Ceylon: Unity and Diversity: A Symposium,* ed. Philip Mason, London, 1967, pp. 159-81.

Daniel, Desari Victor. 'Toward More Effective Communication of the Gospel in Andhra Pradesh,' M.Th. thesis, Fuller Theological Seminary, Pasadena, CA, 1976.

Daniel, Philip. 'Theology of Conversion in the Indian Context,' Doctor of Missiology thesis, Fuller Theological Seminary, Pasadena, CA, 1984.

Datta, S. K. 'Causes of the Expansion or Retrogression of Religions in India: A Study of the Census of 1911,' *International Review of Missions,* IV (1914), pp. 639-58.

David, S. Immanuel. 'God's Messengers: Reformed Church in America Missionaries in South India: 1839-1938,' Doctor of Theology thesis, Lutheran School of Theology, Chicago, 1983.

David, S. Immanuel. 'History of Christianity in India: Changing Perspectives,' *Bangalore Theological Forum,* XVII, 4 (Oct.-Dec. 1985), pp. 55-62.

David, S. Immanuel. 'The Development of the Concept of Indigenisation among Protestant Christians in India from the Time of Henry Venn,' M.Th. thesis, United Theological College, Bangalore, 1975.

De Silva, K. M. 'Christian Missions in Sri Lanka and Their Response to Nationalism, 1910-1948,' in *Senarat Paranavitana Commemoration Volume,* ed. Leelananda Prematilleke Karthigesu Indrapala and J. E. Van Lohuizen-De Leeuw, Leiden, 1978, pp. 221-33.

De Silva, K. M. 'From Elite Status to Beleaguered Minority: The Christians in Twentieth Century Sri Lanka,' in *Asie du Sud. Traditions et Changements,* Colloques Internationaux du C.N.R.S., Paris 1979, No. 582, pp. 347-52.

Deminger, Sigfrid. *Evangelist På Indiska Villkor: Stanley Jones och den indiska renässansen, 1918-1930,* Örebro, Sweden, 1985 (in Swedish).

Dettman, Paul R. *The Forgotten Man (Church of South India Layman in Historic Perspective),* revised and enlarged ed., Madras, 1968 (from unpublished ms. in Neill collection, Oxford).

Deutsch, Karl W. 'Imperialism and Neocolonialism,' *The Papers of the Peace Science Society (International),* XXIII (1974), pp. 1-25.

Deutsch, Karl W. *Nationalism and Social Communication: An Inquiry into the Foundations of Nationality,* Cambridge, Massachusetts, 1966.

Devadason, E. D. *A Study on Conversion and Its Aftermath,* Madras, 1982.

Devadason, Samuel. 'Friends Missionary Prayer Band, India: A Study of Its Origin, Growth, Achievements, and Future Strategy,' M.Th. thesis, Fuller Theological Seminary, Pasadena, CA, 1977.

Devadason, Samuel. 'Indian Missionary Societies: A Study of Their Historical Background, Today's Opportunities and Strategies,' Doctor of Missiology thesis, Fuller Theological Seminary, Pasadena, CA, 1978.

Devadutt, V. E. 'From Mission to Younger Churches,' *History's Lessons for Tomorrow's Mission,* World's Student Christian Federation, Geneva, 1960, pp. 207-16.

Devadutt, V. E. 'What Is an Indigenous Theology? (with special reference to India),' *Ecumenical Review,* II, 1 (Autumn 1949), pp. 40-51.

Devanandan, P. D. *The Gospel and Renascent Hinduism,* London, 1959.

Dhanagare, D. N. *Peasant Movements in India: 1920-1950,* Delhi, 1983.

Dharmalingam, A. M. *Dr. B. R. Ambedkar and Secularism,* Bangalore, 1985.

Diehl, Carl Gustav. *Church and Shrine: Intermingling Patterns of Culture in the Life of Some Christian Groups in South India,* Uppsala, 1965 (in Tamil.)

Donovan, Vincent J. *Christianity Rediscovered: An Epistle from the Masai,* London, 1985.

Downs, Frederick S. *Christianity in North East India: Historical Perspectives,* Delhi, 1983.

Dubois, Abbe J. A. *Hindu Manners, Customs and Ceremonies,* trans. Henry K. Beauchamp, 3rd ed., Oxford, 1906.

'E. S.' *One Hundred Years: Being the Short History of the Church Missionary Society,* London, 1898.

Eastman, Addison J., ed. *Branches of the Banyan: Observations on the Church in Southern Asia,* New York, 1963.

Ebright, Donald Fossett. 'The National Missionary Society of India, 1905-1942: An Expression of the Movement toward Indigenization within the Indian Christian Community,' Ph.D. thesis, University of Chicago, 1944.

Edwardes, Michael. *The Last Years of British India,* London, 1963.

Edwardes, Michael. *The Myth of the Mahatma: Gandhi, the British and the Raj,* London, 1986.

Edwardes, Sir Herbert and Herman Merivale. *Life of Sir Henry Lawrence,* 3rd ed., London: Smith Elder, 1873.

Eliot, T. S. *Christianity and Culture: The Idea of a Christian Society and Notes towards the Definition of Culture,* New York, 1968.

Elliot, Elisabeth. *A Chance to Die: The Life and Legacy of Amy Carmichael,* Old Tappan, NJ, 1987.

Elwin, Verrier. *The Aboriginals,* Oxford, 1943.

Embree, Ainslie Thomas. *Charles Grant and British Rule in India,* London, 1962.

Erikson, Erik H. *Gandhi's Truth: On the Origins of Militant Nonviolence,* New York, 1969.

Estborn, S. *The Church among Tamils and Telugus: Reports of Some Aspect Studies,* Lucknow, 1961.

Fernandes, Walter. 'Caste, Religion and Social Change in India: Christianity and Conversion Movements,' in *Scheduled Castes and the Struggle against Inequality: Strategies to Empower the Marginalised,* ed. Jose Kananaikil, Delhi, 1983, pp. 115-41.

Fernandes, Walter. *Caste and Conversion Movements in India: Religion and Human Rights,* Delhi, 1981.

Fey, Harold E., ed. *The Ecumenical Advance: A History of the Ecumenical Movement,* II, London, 1970.

Field, Harry H. *After Mother India,* New York, 1929.

Finnegan, Ruth H. *Oral Poetry: Its Nature, Significance and Social Context,* Cambridge, 1977.

Firth, Cyril Bruce. *An Introduction to Indian Church History,* Madras, 1961.

Fischer, Louis. *Gandhi: His Life and Message for the World,* New York, 1954.

Fishman, Alvin Texas. *Culture, Change and the Underprivileged: A Study of the Madigas in South India under Christian Guidance,* Madras, 1941.

Fishman, Alvin Texas. *For This Purpose,* Madras, 1958.

Fiske, Adele. 'Scheduled Caste Buddhist Organizations,' in *The Untouchables in Contemporary India,* ed. J. Michael Mahar, Tucson, AZ, 1972, pp. 113-42.

Fleming, Daniel John. *Devolution in Mission Administration: As Exemplified by the Legislative History of Five American Missionary Societies in India,* London, 1916.

Florovsky, Georges. *Christianity and Culture,* Belmont, MA, 1974.

Forbes, Geraldine. *The Politics of Respectability: Indian Women and the I.N.C.,* Paper Presented at the International Conference on '100 Years of the I.N.C.,' Oxford, November 1985.

Forrester, Duncan B. 'Christianity and Early Indian Nationalism,' Paper Presented at SOAS, London, 1 February 1978.

Forrester, Duncan B. 'Christianity and Early Indian Nationalism,' in *Asie Du Sud. Traditions et Changements,* Colloques Internationaux du C.N.R.S., No. 582, Paris, 1979, pp. 331-37.

Forrester, Duncan B. 'Indian Christian Attitudes to Caste in the Twentieth Century,' *ICHR,* IX, 1 (1975).

Forrester, Duncan B. 'The Depressed Classes and Conversion to Christianity, 1860-1960,' in *Religion in South Asia: Religious Conversion and Revival Movements in South Asia in Medieval and Modern Times,* ed. G. A. Oddie, New Delhi, 1977, pp. 35-66.

Forrester, Duncan B. *Caste and Christianity: Attitudes and Policies on Caste of Anglo-Saxon Protestant Missionaries in India,* London, 1980.

Fox, Henry W. *Memoir of G. T. Fox: Missionary to the Teloogoo People,* London, 1861.

Fox, Richard W. *Reinhold Niebuhr: A Biography,* New York, 1985.

France, W. F. *The Oversea Episcopate: Centenary History of the Colonial Bishoprics Fund, 1841-1941,* London, 1941.

Frykenberg, Robert Eric. 'Caste, Morality and Western Religion under the Raj: A Review Article,' draft copy from author.

Frykenberg, Robert Eric, 'Constructions of Hinduism at the Nexus of History and Religion,' *Journal of Interdisciplinary History,* XXIII: 3 (Winter 1993), 523-50.

Frykenberg, Robert Eric. 'Conversion and Crises of Conscience under Company Raj in South India,' in *Asie du Sud. Traditions et Changements; 4th European Conference on South Asian Studies Sevres, 8-13 juillet,* Marc Gaborieau and Alice Thorner, eds., Paris: Colloques Internationaux du C.N.R.S., No. 582, 1979, pp. 311-21.

Frykenberg, Robert Eric. 'Fundamentalism and Revivalism in South Asia,' in *Fundamentalism, Revivalists and Violence in South Asia,* ed. James W. Björkman, Riverdale, MD, 1988, pp. 20-39.

Frykenberg, Robert Eric. 'Modern Education in South India, 1784-1854: Its Roots and Its Role as a Vehicle of Integration under Company Raj,' *The American Historical Review,* 91, 1 (Feb. 1986), pp. 37-65.

Frykenberg, Robert Eric. 'On the Comparative Study of Fundamentalist Movements: An Approach to Conceptual Clarity and Definition,' Paper Presented at the Wilson Center, Washington, DC, 22 April 1986.

Frykenberg, Robert Eric. 'On Roads and Riots in Tinnevelly: Radical Change and Ideology in Madras Presidency during the 19th Century,' offprint from author, pp. 34-52.

Frykenberg, Robert Eric. 'On the Study of Conversion Movements: A Review Article and a Theoretical Note,' *IESHR,* XVII, 1 (1980), pp. 121-38.

Frykenberg, Robert Eric. 'State, Empire and Nation in South India: Demythologizing as a Scholar's Enterprise,' in *Region and Nation in India,* ed. P. Wallace, New Delhi, 1985, pp. 60-84.

Frykenberg, Robert Eric. 'The Concept of "Majority" as a Devilish Force in the Politics of Modern India,' *Journal of Commonwealth and Comparative Politics,* XXV, 3 (Nov. 1987), pp. 267-74.

Frykenberg, Robert Eric. 'The Emergence of Modern "Hinduism" as a Concept and as an Institution: A Reappraisal with Special Reference to South India,' in *Hinduism Reconsidered,* ed. Günther D. Sontheimer and Hermann Kulke, South Asian Studies No. XXIV, New Delhi, 1989, pp. 29-49.

Frykenberg, Robert Eric. 'The Impact of Conversion and Social Reform upon Society in South India during the Late Company Period: Questions concerning Hindu-Christian Encounters, with Special Reference to Tinnevelly,' in *Indian Society and the Beginnings of Modernization, c. 1830-1850,* ed. C. H. Philips and M. D. Wainwright, London, 1976, pp. 187-243.

Frykenberg, Robert Eric. 'The Indian National Congress as the Third "Corporate Dynasty" within the Political System of Modern India,' Paper Presented at the International Conference on '100 Years of the I.N.C.,' Oxford, November 1985.

Frykenberg, Robert Eric. 'The Myth of English as a "Colonialist" Imposition

Upon India: A Reappraisal with Special Reference to South India,' *Journal of the Royal Asiatic Society*, II, 1988, proof pp. 001-0011.

Frykenberg, Robert Eric. 'The Socio-Political Morphology of Madras: An Historical Interpretation,' *Proceedings of Seventh European Conference on Modern South Asian Studies*, London, 7-11 July 1981, K. A. Ballhatchet et al., eds., Hong Kong: Asian Research Service, 1983, Vol. III; *Changing South Asia: City and Culture.*

Frykenberg, Robert Eric. *Guntur District, 1788-1848: A History of Local Influence and Central Authority in South India*, Oxford, 1965.

Frykenberg, Robert Eric. *Historical Knowledge, Ideology and Religion: A Comparative Assessment of Major Historiographic Traditions*, Proposal for Seminar in Comparative World Historiography.

Frykenberg, Robert Eric. *The Emergence of 'Free' Religion under the Company's Raj in South India*, typescript from author, University of Wisconsin-Madison, 1984.

Fuchs, Stephen. *Rebellious Prophets: A Study of Messianic Movements in Indian Religions*, Bombay, 1965.

Geertz, Clifford. *The Interpretation of Cultures*, New York, 1973.

George, Alexandra. *Social Ferment in India*, London, 1986.

George, S. K. *Gandhi's Challenge to Christianity*, Ahmedabad, 1960.

Gibbs, M. E. *The Anglican Church in India, 1600-1970*, Delhi, 1972.

Gierth, Roland. *Christian Life and Work at the Pastorate Level and Practical Theology in South India*, Madras, 1977.

Gittings, Robert. *The Nature of Biography*, Seattle, 1978.

Gladstone, J. W. *Protestant Christianity and People's Movements in Kerala, 1850-1936*, Kannamoola, Trivandrum, 1984.

Gokhale, Jayashree B. 'Castaways of Caste,' *Natural History* (Journal of the New York Museum of Natural History) (Oct. 1986), pp. 31-37.

Goodall, Norman. *The Ecumenical Movement: What It Is and What It Does*, London, 1961.

Goodall, Norman, et al. *A Decisive Hour for the Christian Mission: The East Asia Christian Conference 1959 and the John R. Mott Memorial Lectures*, London, 1960.

Gosling, David L. 'Christian Response within Hinduism,' *Religious Studies*, X, 4 (Dec. 1974), pp. 433-39.

Gover, C. E. *Folk-songs of Southern India*, 2nd ed., Madras, 1959.

Graham, B. D. 'The Congress and Hindu Nationalism,' Paper presented at the International Conference on '100 Years of the Indian National Congress,' Oxford, November 1985.

Grant, John Webster. *God's People in India*, Madras, 1965.

Gray, Mrs. H. 'The Progress of Women,' in *Modern India and the West: A Study of the Interaction of their Civilizations*, ed. L. S. S. O'Malley, London, 1941, pp. 445-83.

Greenberger, Allen J. *The British Image of India: A Study in the Literature of Imperialism, 1880-1960,* London, 1969.

Grenier, Richard. *The Gandhi Nobody Knows,* Nashville, 1983.

Grey-Edwards, A. H. *Memoir of the Rev. John Thomas: C.M.S. Missionary at Megnanapuram, Tinnevelly, South India, 1836-1870,* London, 1904.

Grierson, Janet. *The Deaconess,* London, 1981.

Griffiths, Bede. *Christian Ashram: Essays towards a Hindu-Christian Dialogue,* London, 1966.

Grimes, Cecil John. *Towards an Indian Church: The Growth of the Church of India in Constitution and Life,* London, 1946.

Guptara, Prabhu. *Indian Spirituality,* Bramcote, Nottinghamshire, 1984.

Hansen, Bent Smidt. 'Indigenization of Worship: A Concern among South Indian Christians,' in *South Asian Religion and Society,* ed. Asko Parpola and Bent Smidt Hansen, London, 1986, pp. 236-62.

Hansen, Holger Berut. *Mission, Church and State in a Colonial Setting: Uganda, 1890-1925,* London, 1984.

Hardgrave, Robert L. 'The Breast-Cloth Controversy,' *IESHR,* V (June 1968), 171-81.

Hardgrave, Robert L. *Essays in the Political Sociology of South India,* Delhi, 1979.

Hardgrave, Robert L. *The Dravidian Movement,* Bombay, 1965.

Hardgrave, Robert L. *The Nadars of Tamilnad: The Political Culture of a Community in Change,* Berkeley, 1969.

Hardiman, David. *Peasant Nationalists of Gujarat: Kheda District 1917-1934,* Oxford, 1981.

Hardiman, David. *The Coming of the Devi: Adivasi Assertion in Western India,* Delhi, 1987.

Hargreaves, Cecil. *Asian Christian Thinking: Studies in a Metaphor and Its Message,* Delhi, 1972.

Harper, Edward B. 'Social Consequences of an "Unsuccessful" Low Caste Movement,' in *Social Mobility in the Caste System in India,* ed. James Silverberg, The Hague, 1968, pp. 35-65.

Harper, Susan B. 'The Politics of Conversion: The Azariah-Gandhi Controversy over Christian Mission to the Depressed Classes in the 1930's,' *Indo-British Review,* XV, 1 (1988), pp. 147-75.

Harrison, Irene. *Agatha Harrison: An Impression by Her Sister,* London, 1956.

Hart, Frank. *Rahator of Bombay: The Apostle to the Marathas,* London, 1936.

Hastings, Adrian. *A History of African Christianity, 1950-1975,* Cambridge, 1979.

Hayter, O. C. G. 'Conversion of Outcastes,' *The Asiatic Review,* XXVI, 87 (July 1930), pp. 603-11.

Hayward, Victor E. W. *The Church as Christian Community: Three Studies of North Indian Churches,* London, 1966.

Heimsath, Charles H. *Indian Nationalism and Hindu Social Reform,* Princeton, 1964.

Heinrich, J. C. *The Psychology of a Suppressed People,* London, 1937.

Hellmann-Rajanayagam, Dagmar. 'Arumuka Navalar: Religious Reformer or National Leader of Eelam,' *IESHR,* XXVI, 2 (1989), pp. 235-57.

Herklots, H. G. G. *Frontiers of the Church: The Making of the Anglican Communion,* London, 1961.

Hesselgrave, David J., ed. *Dynamic Religious Movements,* Grand Rapids, 1978.

Hewitt, Gordon. *The Problems of Success: A History of the Church Missionary Society, 1910-1942,* II, London, 1977.

Hibbert-Ware, G. *Christian Missions in Telugu Country,* Westminster, 1912.

Hiebert, Paul G. 'Folk Religion in Andhra Pradesh: Some Missiological Implications,' in *The Gospel among our Hindu Neighbours,* ed. Vinay Samuel and Chris Sugden, Bangalore, 1983, pp. 87-109.

Hiebert, Paul G. 'The Flaw of the Excluded Middle,' *Missiology: An International Review,* X, 1 (Jan. 1982), pp. 35-47.

Hiebert, Paul G. *Konduru: Structure and Integration in a South Indian Village,* Minneapolis, 1971.

Himmelfarb, Gertrude. *Marriage and Morals among the Victorians and Other Essays,* New York, 1987.

Himmelfarb, Gertrude. *Victorian Values and Twentieth-Century Condescension,* London, 1987.

Hiro, Dilip. *The Untouchables of India,* Minority Rights Group Report No. 26, London, 1982.

Hirschmann, Edwin. *The 'White' Mutiny: The Ilbert Bill Crisis in India and the Genesis of the Indian National Congress,* New Delhi, 1980.

History of Christianity in India with Its Prospects: A Sketch, Vepery, 1895.

Hocking, William Ernest. *Re-thinking Missions: A Laymen's Inquiry after One Hundred Years,* New York, 1932.

Hodge, J. Z. *Salute to India,* London, 1944.

Hogg, William Richey. *Ecumenical Foundations: A History of the International Missionary Council and Its Nineteenth-Century Background,* New York, 1952.

Hollis, Michael. *Paternalism and the Church,* Oxford, 1962.

Hollis, Michael. *The Significance of South India,* London, 1966.

Hooper, J. S. M. *The Bible in India,* London, 1938.

Hopkins, C. H. *John R. Mott: 1865-1955: A Biography,* Grand Rapids, 1979.

Hopkins, Hugh Evan. *Sublime Vagabond: The Life of Joseph Wolff, Missionary Extraordinary,* Worthing, 1984.

Hough, James. *History of Christianity in India,* London, IV: 1845; V: 1860.

Houghton, Frank. *Amy Carmichael of Dohnavur,* London, 1954.

Houghton, Graham. 'Caste and the Protestant Church: A Historical Perspective,' Paper Presented at the Consultation on Caste and the Church, 9-12 February 1984, Bangalore.

Houghton, Graham W. 'The Development of the Protestant Missionary

Church in Madras 1870-1920: The Impoverishment of Dependency,' Ph.D. thesis, University of California, Los Angeles, 1981.

Houpert, J. C. *Catholic Church History: India and Ceylon, AD 50-1930,* Trichi, 1932.

Houtart, François, and Geneviève Lemercinier. *Genesis and Institutionalization of Indian Catholicism,* Louvain-la-Neuve, 1981.

Houtart, François, and Geneviève Lemercinier. *Size and Structures of the Catholic Church in India,* Louvain-la-Neuve, 1982.

Hughes, Derrick. *Bishop Sahib: A Life of Reginald Heber,* Worthing, 1986.

Hutchins, Francis G. *The Illusion of Permanence: British Imperialism in India,* Princeton, 1967.

Hutchison, William R. *Errand to the World: American Protestant Thought and Foreign Missions,* Chicago, 1987.

Imam-Ud-Din, S. J. *Gandhi and Christianity,* Lahore, 1946.

India and Oxford: Fifty Years of the Oxford Mission to Calcutta, London, 1933.

Iremonger, F. A. *William Temple: Archbishop of Canterbury, His Life and Letters,* London, 1948.

Irschick, Eugene F. 'Peasant Survival Strategies and Rehearsals for Rebellion in Eighteenth-Century South India,' *Peasant Studies,* IX, 4 (Summer 1982), pp. 215-41.

Irschick, Eugene F. *Politics and Social Conflict in South India: The Non-Brahman Movement and Tamil Separatism, 1916-1929,* Bombay, 1969.

Isaacs, Harold Robert. *India's Ex-Untouchables,* New York, 1964.

Jackson, Eleanor M. *Red Tape and the Gospel: A Study of the Significance of the Ecumenical Missionary Struggle of William Paton (1886-1943),* Birmingham, U.K., 1980.

James, I. M. *The Mathematical Works of J. H. C. Whitehead,* I, Oxford, 1962.

James, William. *The Varieties of Religious Experience,* New York, 1982.

Jayakumar, K. C. 'A Closer Look at Meenakshipuram: An Instance of Conversion or Social Uprising,' Report Prepared by World Vision Consequent to a Visit to Meenakshipuram, 13-14 January 1982, and Presented at the Consultation on Caste and the Church, 9-12 February 1984, Bangalore.

Jayasingh, Joshua M. 'The History of the National Missionary Society of India: A Critical Study,' Asian Centre for Theological Studies and Mission, M.Th. thesis, Seoul, Korea, July 1983.

Johnson, Paul. *Modern Times: The World from the Twenties to the Eighties,* New York, 1983.

Jones, A. H. M. *Constantine and the Conversion of Europe,* Middlesex, 1962.

Jones, E. Stanley. *A Song of Ascents: A Spiritual Autobiography,* Nashville, 1968.

Jones, E. Stanley. *Along the Indian Road,* New York, 1939.

Jones, E. Stanley. *Christ at the Round Table,* New York, 1928; London, 1930.

Jones, E. Stanley. *Gandhi: Portrayal of a Friend,* Nashville, 1948.

Jones, E. Stanley. *Mahatma Gandhi: In Interpretation,* Lucknow, 1948, 2nd ed. 1963.

Jones, E. Stanley. *The Christ of the Indian Road,* New York and London, 1925.

Jones, E. S. *Conversion,* London, 1960.

Jordens, J. T. F. 'Reconversion to Hinduism, the Shuddhi of the Ary Samaj,' in *Religion in South Asia: Religious Conversion and Revival Movements in South Asia in Medieval and Modern Times,* ed. G. A. Oddie, New Delhi, 1977, pp. 145-61.

Jost, Christian. 'Of Caravans and Wanderlust: The Banjaras,' *The India Magazine,* II, 4 (March 1982), pp. 40-47.

Juergensmeyer, Mark. *Religion as Social Vision: The Movement against Untouchability in 20th-Century Punjab,* Berkeley, 1982.

Juergensmeyer, Mark. *Religious Nationalism Confronts the Secular State,* Oxford UP: Delhi, 1993.

Kadambavanam, Paul S. *Origins of the Diocese of Tirunelveli,* 2nd ed., Madras, 1967 (in Tamil).

Kailasapathy, K. *Tamil Heroic Poetry,* Oxford, 1968.

Kaufmann, Susan B. 'A Christian Caste in Hindu Society: Religious Leadership and Social Conflict among the Paravas of Southern Tamilnadu,' *MAS,* XV, 2 (April 1981), pp. 203-34.

Kaufmann, Susan B. 'Popular Christianity, Caste, and Hindu Society in South India 1800-1915: A Study of Travancore and Tirunelveli,' Ph.D. thesis, Cambridge University, 1980.

Keer, Dhananjay. *Dr. Ambedkar: Life and Mission,* 3rd ed., Bombay, 1971.

Keller, Rosemary Skinner. 'Creating a Sphere for Women,' *Women in New Worlds: Historical Perspectives on the Wesleyan Tradition,* Nashville, 1981, pp. 246-60.

Kiernan, Victor Gordon. *The Lords of Human Kind: European Attitudes towards the Outside World in the Imperial Age,* London, 1969.

Kirk, J. Andrew. 'Race, Class, Caste and the Bible,' *Themelios,* X, 2 (Jan. 1985), pp. 4-14.

Klostermaier, Klaus. *Hindu and Christian in Vrindaban,* London, 1969.

Knoll, Louis Fred. 'State and Religions in British India, 1814-1865,' Ph.D. thesis, Graduate Theological Union, Berkeley, California, 1971.

Koestler, Arthur. *The Lotus and the Robot,* London, 1960.

Kooiman, Dick. *Conversion and Social Equality in India: The London Missionary Society in South Travancore in the 19th Century,* New Delhi: South Asia Publications, n.d.

Kulandran, Sabapathy. *A History of the Tamil Bible,* Bangalore, 1967 (in Tamil).

Kumar, Dharma, ed., *The Cambridge Economic History of India, II: c. 1757-1970,* Delhi, 1982.

Kumar, Ravinder. 'Gandhi, Ambedkar and the Poona Pact, 1932,' *JSAS,* VIII, 1-2, pp. 87-101.

Kuriakose, M. K., ed. *History of Christianity in India: Source Materials,* Madras, 1982.

Kuruvilla, K. K. *A History of the Mar Thoma Church and Its Doctrines,* Madras, 1950.

Laird, M. A. *Missionaries and Education in Bengal, 1793-1837,* Oxford, 1972.

Latourette, Kenneth S. 'Community and Church: An Historical Survey and Interpretation,' *Church and Community* (Church, Community, and State Series, V), London, 1938.

Latourette, Kenneth S. 'Ecumenical Bearings of the Missionary Movement and the International Missionary Council,' *A History of the Ecumenical Movement, 1517-1948,* Ruth Rouse and S. N. Neill, eds., London, 1954, pp. 357-402.

Latourette, Kenneth S. *A History of the Expansion of Christianity: The First Five Centuries,* London, 1947.

Latourette, Kenneth S. *A History of the Expansion of Christianity: The Great Century, A.D. 1800–A.D. 1914, in Northern Africa and Asia,* London, 1947.

Lawrence, John, and Audrey Woodiwiss, eds. *The Journals of Honoria Lawrence: India Observed 1837-1854,* London, 1980.

Lawrence, John. *India and Britain: More Than a Marriage of Convenience* and *With the Piffers,* offprint from author, n.d.

Leonard, Hodgson. *Anglicanism and South India,* Cambridge, 1943.

Leonard, John. 'Politics and Social Change in South India: A Study of the Andhra Movement,' *Journal of Commonwealth Political Studies,* V, 1 (March 1967), pp. 60-77.

Leonard, Karen I. and John G. 'Social Reform and Women's Participation in Political Culture: Andhra and Madras,' in *The Extended Family: Women and Political Participation in India and Pakistan,* ed. G. Minault, Delhi, 1981, pp. 19-45.

Lewis, Philip. 'Caste, Mission and Church Growth,' *Themelios,* X, 2 (Jan. 1985), pp. 24-30.

Ling, Trevor. *A History of Religion East and West,* London, 1968.

Ling, Trevor. *Karl Marx and Religion in Europe and India,* London, 1980.

Lobo, V. *Nationalism and the Church in India,* Trichi, 1920.

Lockhart, J. G. *Cosmo Gordon Lang,* London, 1949.

Long, Charles H., and Anne Rowthorn. 'The Legacy of Roland Allen,' *International Bulletin of Missionary Research,* XIII, 2 (April 1989), pp. 65-70.

Longridge, George. *A History of the Oxford Mission to Calcutta,* 2nd ed., London, 1910.

Lotz, Denton. '"The Evangelization of the World in This Generation": The Resurgence of a Missionary Idea among the Conservative Evangelicals,' Ph.D. thesis, Hamburg, 1970.

Low, D. A. *Lion Rampant: Essays in the Study of British Imperialism,* London, 1973.

Lowe, Victor. *Alfred North Whitehead: The Man and His Work: Volume I: 1861-1910,* Baltimore, 1985.

Lucas, Bernard. 'The Position of the Anglican Church in India,' *HF*, XXXII, 9 (Sept. 1912), pp. 325-30.

Luke, P. Y., and John B. Carman. *Village Christians and Hindu Culture: Study of a Rural Church in Andhra Pradesh, South India*, London, 1968.

Luke, Rev. K. *Dārnakal Tiranalvēli Iṇḍiyan Miṣanarī Sanghamu: 1906-1956*, Vijayawada, 1956.

Lumb, J. R. *The Modern Pilgrimage*, London, 1937.

Lynch, Owen M. *The Politics of Untouchability: Social Mobility and Social Change in a City of India*, New York, 1969.

M. Edwin Rao, ed. *Dornakal Mission: Indian Missionary Society of Tirunelveli 75 Years' History 1906-1981, Platinum Jubilee Book*, Hyderabad, 1981 (in Telugu).

Machin, G. I. T. *Politics and the Churches in Great Britain, 1832-1868*, Oxford, 1977.

MacKinnon, Donald. *The Stripping of the Altars: The Gore Memorial Lecture and Other Pieces*, Collins: Fontana Library, U.K., 1969.

Macnicol, Nicol. 'Indian Christianity and Some Notable Indian Christians,' *IRM*, IX, 34 (April 1920), pp. 214-28.

Macnicol, Nicol. *The Making of Modern India*, Oxford, 1924.

Macnicol, R. S. 'Landmarks in College History,' *The Madras Christian College Magazine*, Centenary Number (March 1937), pp. 142-53.

Majumdar, R. C., H. C. Raychaudhuri, and Kalikinkar Datta. *An Advanced History of India*, London, 1956.

Mandelbaum, David G. *Society in India*, I-II, Berkeley, 1970.

Mangan, J. A. *The Games Ethic and Imperialism: Aspects of the Diffusion of an Ideal*, New York, 1986.

Manickam, S. *Studies in Missionary History: Reflections on a Culture-Contact*, Madras, 1988.

Manickam, Sundararaj. *The Social Setting of Christian Conversion in South India: The Impact of the Wesleyan Methodist Missionaries on the Trichy-Tanjore Diocese with Special Reference to the Harijan Communities of the Mass Movement Area, 1820-47*, Wiesbaden, 1977.

Manor, James G. 'Testing the Barrier between Caste and Outcaste: The Andhra Evangelical Lutheran Church in Guntur District,' *ICHR*, V, 1 (1971), pp. 27-41.

Manor, James G. *Political Change in an Indian State: Mysore, 1917-1955*, New Delhi, 1977.

Mansergh, Nicholas. 'Imperialism: The Years of European Ascendancy,' *Chapters in Western Civilization*, Contemporary Civilization Staff at Columbia College, eds., 3rd ed., New York, 1962, pp. 401-40.

Manuelraj, I. Victor. 'An Evaluation of the Work of the Indian Missionary Society of Tirunelveli in the Dornakal Field from 1954-1974', Bachelor of Divinity thesis, Serampore University, 1976.

Marriott, McKim, ed. *Village India: Studies in the Little Community*, Chicago, 1955.

Martin, Hugh. *Beginning at Edinburgh: A Jubilee Assessment of the World Missionary Conference, 1910*, London, 1960.

Marty, Martin E. *Pilgrims in Their Own Land: 500 Years of Religion in America*, Boston, 1984.

Mathews, Basil. *John R. Mott: World Citizen*, New York, 1934.

Mathis, Michael A. *India: A Mission Investigation*, Cincinnati, 1926.

Maury, Philippe, ed. *History's Lessons for Tomorrow's Mission: Milestones in the History of Missionary Thinking*, Switzerland, 1960.

Mayer, Adrian C. *Culture and Morality: Essays in Honour of Christoph von Fürer-Haimendorf*, Delhi, 1981.

Mayhew, A. I. 'The Christian Ethic and India,' in *Modern India and the West*, ed. L. S. S. O'Malley, London, 1941, pp. 305-37.

Mayhew, Arthur. *Christianity and the Government of India: An Examination of the Christian Forces at Work in the Administration of India and of the Mutual Relations of the British Government and Christian Missions, 1600-1920*, London, 1929.

Mayo, Katherine. *Mother India*, London, 1927.

McCully, B. T. *English Education and the Origins of Indian Nationalism*, New York, 1940.

McGlinchey, J. F. *Mission Tours: India*, Boston, 1925.

McKenzie, John, ed. *The Christian Task in India*, London, 1929.

McLane, John R. *Indian Nationalism and the Early Congress*, Princeton, 1977.

Meersman, A. 'The Catholic Church in India since the mid-19th Century,' in *Christianity in India: A History in Ecumenical Perspective*, ed. H. C. Perumalil and E. R. Hambye, Allepey, 1972, pp. 248-66.

Mehta, Ved. *Mahatma Gandhi and His Apostles*, New York, 1976.

Meyendorff, John. 'Christ as Word: Gospel and Culture,' *IRM*, LXXIV, 294 (April 1985), pp. 246-57.

Middleton, Vern. 'Caste Issues in the Minds of McGavran and Gandhi,' *Missiology: An International Review*, XIII, 2 (April 1985), pp. 159-73.

Milford, C. S. *Church and Crisis in India*, London, 1945.

Milford, C. S. *South India's New Church*, London, 1947.

Miller, D. B., ed. *Peasants and Politics: Grass Roots Reaction to Change in Asia*, London, 1979.

Milsome, John. *From Slave Boy to Bishop: The Story of Samuel Adjai Crowther*, Cambridge, 1987.

Mills, Frederick V. *Bishops by Ballot: An Eighteenth Century Ecclesiastical Revolution*, New York, 1978.

Minault, Gail. 'The Extended Family as Metaphor and the Expansion of Women's Realm,' in *The Extended Family: Women and Political Participation in India and Pakistan*, ed. G. Minault, Delhi, 1981, pp. 3-18.

Bibliography

Minogue, Kenneth. 'Societies Collapse, Faiths Linger On: Christians and Communists in Confusion,' *Encounter* (March 1990), pp. 3-16.

Minogue, Kenneth. 'The Idea of Liberty and the Dream of Liberation: Two Themes in the Western Political Tradition,' *Encounter*, LXIX, 2 (July-Aug. 1987), pp. 5-14.

Miranda, J. L. *On the Formation of a National Indian Clergy,* Trichinopoly, 1920.

Modak, S. *Directory of Protestant Indian Christians,* Ahmednagar, 1900.

Moffatt, Michael. *An Untouchable Community in South India: Structure and Consensus,* Princeton, 1979.

Mohansingh, Samuel, et al. 'India,' in *The Encyclopedia of World Methodism,* ed. Nolan B. Harmon, Nashville, 1974, I, pp. 1202-8.

Montefiore, Arthur. *Reginald Heber, Bishop of Calcutta, Scholar and Evangelist,* London, n.d.

Montgomery, H. H. *The Life and Letters of George Alfred Lefroy,* London, 1920.

Moon, Penderel. *The British Conquest and Dominion of India,* London, 1989.

Moore, Barrington, Jr. *Social Origins of Dictatorship and Democracy: Lord and Peasant in the Making of the Modern World,* Boston, 1966.

Moore, R. J. *Liberalism and Indian Politics, 1872-1922,* London, 1966.

Moorman, J. R. H. 'The Anglican Bishop', in *Bishops: But What Kind?: Reflections on Episcopacy,* ed. Peter Moore, London, 1982, pp. 116-26.

Mudaliar, Chandra Y. *The Secular State and Religious Institutions in India: A Study of the Administration of Hindu Public Religious Trusts in Madras,* Wiesbaden, 1974.

Muller, D. S. George, and V. Joseph Abraham. *The Trail of the Tirunelveli Church,* Palamcottah, 1964.

Muller, D. S. George, and R. S. Jacobs, eds. *Bicentenary of the Tirunelveli Church, 1780-1980, Commemoration Souvenir,* Palayamkottai, 1980.

Muller, D. S. George. *The Birth of a Bishopric (Being a History of the Tirunelveli Church from early beginnings to 1896),* Palayamkottai, 1980.

Mundadan, A. Mathias. *Indian Christians: Search for Identity and Struggle for Autonomy,* Bangalore, 1984.

Muzurewa, Bishop Abel Tendekai. *Rise Up and Walk: An Autobiography,* ed. Norman E. Thomas, London, 1979.

National Christian Council. *Directory of Christian Missions and Churches: 1940-1941,* Nagpur, 1940.

National Missionary Society of India, Platinum Jubilee Souvenir 1980, Tiruvalla, 1980.

Nehru, Jawaharlal. *The Discovery of India,* New York, 1959.

Nehru, Jawaharlal. *Toward Freedom: The Autobiography of Jawaharlal Nehru,* New York, 1941.

Neill, Stephen C. 'Conversion,' *Scottish Journal of Theology,* III, 4 (Dec. 1950), pp. 352-62.

Neill, Stephen C. 'The Participation of Indian Christians in Political Affairs,' in *The Church Crossing Frontiers: Essays on the Nature of Mission in Honour of Bengt Sundkler,* ed. P. Beyerhaus and C. F. Hallencreutz, Uppsala, 1969, pp. 67-82.

Neill, Stephen C. 'The Problem of Communication,' *Scottish Journal of Theology,* I, 1 (June 1948), pp. 85-96.

Neill, Stephen C. *A History of Christian Missions,* Harmondsworth, Middlesex, 1964.

Neill, Stephen C. *A History of Christianity in India, 1707-1858,* Cambridge, 1985.

Neill, Stephen C. *A History of Christianity in India, The Beginnings to A.D. 1707,* Cambridge, 1984.

Neill, Stephen C. *Anglicanism,* 4th ed., New York, 1977.

Neill, Stephen C. *Bhakti: Hindu and Christian,* Madras, 1974.

Neill, Stephen C. *Christian Partnership,* London, 1952.

Neill, Stephen C. *Colonialism and Christian Missions,* London, 1966.

Neill, Stephen C. *Creative Tension: The Duff Lectures, 1958,* London, 1959.

Neill, Stephen C. *Letters to His Clergy,* Palamcottah, 1944.

Neill, Stephen C. *Men of Unity,* London, 1960.

Neill, Stephen C. *Out of Bondage: Christ and the Indian Villager,* London, 1930.

Neill, Stephen C. *Rome and the Ecumenical Movement,* Grahamstown, 1967.

Neill, Stephen C. *The Christian Society,* London, 1952.

Neill, Stephen C. *The Church and Christian Union: The Bampton Lectures for 1964,* London, 1968.

Neill, Stephen C. *The Cross over Asia,* London, 1948.

Neill, Stephen C. *The Story of the Christian Church in India and Pakistan,* Madras, 1972.

Neill, Stephen C., ed. *Twentieth Century Christianity: A Survey of Modern Religious Trends by Leading Churchmen,* London, 1961.

Neill, Stephen C., and Tom Wright. *The Interpretation of the New Testament, 1861-1986,* 2nd ed., Oxford, 1988.

Newbigin, Lesslie. 'Bishops in a United Church,' in *Bishops: But What Kind?* ed. Peter Moore, London, 1982, pp. 149-61.

Newbigin, Lesslie. 'The Call to Mission — A Call to Unity?' in *The Church Crossing Frontiers: Essays on the Nature of Mission in Honour of Bengt Sundkler,* Uppsala, 1969, pp. 254-65.

Newbigin, Lesslie. 'The Good Shepherd': *Meditations on Christian Ministry in Today's World,* Madras, 1974.

Newbigin, Lesslie. *Christ Our Eternal Contemporary,* Madras, 1968.

Newbigin, Lesslie. *Honest Religion for Secular Man,* London, 1966.

Newbigin, Lesslie. *South India Diary,* London, 1951.

Newbigin, Lesslie. *The Household of God: Lectures on the Nature of the Church,* London, 1953.

Newbigin, Lesslie. *The Open Secret: Sketches for a Missionary Theology,* Grand Rapids, 1978.

Bibliography

Newbigin, Lesslie. *The Other Side of 1984: Questions for the Churches,* Geneva, 1984.

Newbigin, Lesslie. *The Reunion of the Church: A Defence of the South India Scheme,* London, 1960.

Newbigin, Lesslie. *Unfinished Agenda: An Autobiography,* London, 1985.

Newsome, David. *Godliness and Good Learning: Four Studies of a Victorian Ideal,* London, 1961.

Nicholson, Sydney. 'Social Organization of the Malas — An Outcaste Indian People,' *Journal of the Royal Anthropological Institute of Great Britain and Ireland,* LVI (Jan. to June 1926), pp. 91-103.

Niebuhr, H. Richard. *Christ and Culture,* New York, 1951.

Niebuhr, H. Richard. *The Social Sources of Denominationalism,* New York, 1959.

Niebuhr, Reinhold. *Moral Man and Immoral Society: A Study in Ethics and Politics,* New York, 1947.

Niyogi, M. B. *Madhya Pradesh Enquiry Report,* Madhya Pradesh Government Publications, 1956.

Noble, John. *A Memoir of the Rev. Robert Turlington Noble: Missionary to the Telugu People of India,* London, 1867.

Nock, A. D. *Conversion: The Old and the New in Religion from Alexander the Great to Augustine of Hippo,* Oxford, 1933.

O'Connor, Daniel. *The Testimony of C. F. Andrews,* Madras, 1974.

O'Hanlon, Rosalind. *Caste, Conflict and Ideology: Mahatma Jotirao Phule and Low Caste Protest in Nineteenth-Century Western India,* Cambridge, 1985.

Oddie, G. A. 'Christian Conversion among Non-Brahmans in Andhra Pradesh, with Special Reference to Anglican Missions and the Dornakal Diocese, c. 1900-1936,' in *Religion in South Asia: Religious Conversion and Revival Movements in South Asia in Medieval and Modern Times,* ed. G. A. Oddie, New Delhi, 1977, pp. 67-99.

Oddie, G. A. 'Christian Conversion in the Telugu Country, 1860-1900: A Case Study of One Protestant Movement in the Godavery-Krishna Delta,' *IESHR,* XII, 1 (Jan.-March 1975), pp. 61-79.

Oddie, G. A. 'Christianity in the Hindu Crucible: Continuity and Change in the Kaveri Delta, 1850-1900,' *ICHR,* XV, 1 (June 1981), pp. 48-72.

Oddie, G. A. 'Hook-Swinging and Popular Religion in South India during the Nineteenth Century,' *IESHR,* XXIII, 1 (Jan.-March 1986), pp. 93-106.

Oddie, G. A. 'India and Missionary Motives,' *Journal of Ecclesiastical History,* XXV, 1 (Jan. 1974), pp. 61-74.

Oddie, G. A. 'Indian Christians and the National Congress, 1885-1910,' *ICHR,* II, 1 (June 1968), pp. 45-54.

Oddie, G. A. *Social Protest in India: British Protestant Missionaries and Social Reforms 1850-1900,* Columbia, MO, 1978 and New Delhi, 1979.

Oldham, J. H. *The Churches Survey Their Task: The Report of the Conference at Oxford, July 1937, on Church, Community, and State,* London, 1937.

Oliver, Roland. *The Missionary Factor in East Africa*, London, 1952.

One Hundred Years in Mysore. Mysore, 1921.

Orr, J. Edwin. *Evangelical Awakenings in India in the Early Twentieth Century*, New Delhi, 1970.

Orr, J. Edwin. *Evangelical Awakenings in Southern Asia*, Minneapolis, 1975.

Orr, J. Edwin. *The Outpouring of the Spirit in Revival and Awakening and Its Issue in Church Growth*, Pasadena, CA, 1984.

Orwell, George. *A Collection of Essays*, New York, 1946.

Östör, Akos, Lina Furzzetti, and Steve Barnett. *Concepts of Person: Kinship, Caste, and Marriage in India*, Cambridge, MA, 1982.

Packer, J. I. *All in Each Place: Towards Reunion in England*, Appleford, Abingdon, 1965.

Packiamuthu, Sarojini. 'A Brief History of the Tamil Bible,' in *175th Anniversary of the Bible Society of India (1811-1986)*, Madras, 1986.

Page, Jesse. *Samuel Crowther: The Slave Boy of the Niger*, London, n.d. (before 1932).

Palmer, E. J. 'The Anglican Communion: India,' in *Episcopacy Ancient and Modern*, ed. Claude Jenkins and K. D. MacKenzie, London, 1930, pp. 200-24.

Panikkar, Raimundo. *The Unknown Christ of Hinduism*, 1st ed., London, 1964; rev. and enl. ed. 1981.

Parrinder, Geoffrey. *Avatar and Incarnation*, New York, 1982.

Paton, Alan. *Apartheid and the Archbishop: The Life and Times of Geoffrey Clayton, Archbishop of Cape Town*, London, 1973.

Paton, David M. *Christian Missions and the Judgment of God*, London, 1953.

Paton, David M., ed. *Reform of the Ministry: A Study in the Work of Roland Allen*, London, 1968.

Paton, William. 'The Indigenous Church,' *IRM*, XVI (1927), pp. 46-57.

Paton, William. *Christianity in the Eastern Conflicts: A Study of Christianity, Nationalism and Communism in Asia*, Westminster, 1937.

Paul, John J., and Robert E. Frykenberg. 'A Research Note on the Discovery of Writings by Savariraya Pillai, A Tamil Diarist of Mid-Nineteenth-Century Tinnevelly,' *Journal of Asian Studies*, XLIV, 3 (May 1985), pp. 521-28.

Paul, R. C. *History of the Telugu Christians*, Madras, 1929.

Paul, Rajaiah D. *Chosen Vessels: Lives of Ten Indian Christian Pastors of the Eighteenth and Nineteenth Centuries*, Madras, 1961.

Paul, Rajaiah D. *Ecumenism in Action: A Historical Survey of the Church of South India*, Madras, 1972.

Pavier, Barry. *The Telengana Movement, 1944-1951*, New Delhi, 1981.

Pelikan, Jaroslav, ed. *The World Treasury of Modern Religious Thought*, Boston, 1990.

Perumalil, H. C., and E. R. Hambye. *Christianity in India: A History in Ecumenical Perspective*, Allepey, 1972.

Pfaffenberger, Bryan. *Caste in Tamil Culture*, Syracuse, NY, 1982.

Philip, T. V. 'Krishna Mohan Banerjea and Arian Witness to Christ: Jesus Christ and True Prajapati,' *The Indian Journal of Theology*, XXIX, 2 (April-June 1980).

Philip, T. V. 'Protestant Christianity in India since 1858,' in *Christianity in India: A History in Ecumenical Perspective*, ed. H. C. Perumalil and E. R. Hambye, Allepey, 1972, pp. 267-99.

Piggin, Stuart, and John Roxborogh. *The St. Andrews Seven: The Finest Flowering of Missionary Zeal in Scottish History*, Edinburgh, 1985.

Pollock, J. C. *Shadows Fall Apart: The Story of the Zenana Bible and Medical Mission*, London, 1958.

Polo, Angelo. *Pastoral Letter on the Conversion of India*, Trichi, 1923.

Popley, H. A. *K. T. Paul: Christian Leader*, 1st ed., Calcutta, 1938; 2nd ed., Madras, 1987.

Porter, Dale H. *The Abolition of the Slave Trade in England, 1784-1807*, Hamden, CT, 1970.

Prabhakar, M. E., and Philip Mathew, eds. 'Focus on Christian Dalits,' *Samata*, Bangalore, 1986.

Pretorius, H. L. *Bitter as the Juice of an Aloe: A Profile of Conversion: Motives and Attitudinal Changes*, Pretoria, 1983.

Priestley, Eber. *The Church of South India: Adventure in Union*, London, 1970.

Raboteau, Albert J. *Slave Religion: The 'Invisible Institution' in the Antebellum South*, Oxford, 1978.

Radhakrishnan, S. *Religion and Society*, London, 1947.

Raj, Ebenezer Sunder. 'Caste and the Church,' Paper Presented at the Consultation on Caste and the Church, 9-12 February 1984, Bangalore.

Raj, Sunder. *The Confusion Called Conversion*, New Delhi, 1986.

Rajagopal, M. V. *Andhra Pradesh District Gazetteers: Khammam, Krishna, Medak, Nellore*, Hyderabad, 1977.

Rajshekar, V. T. *Ambedkar and His Conversion*, Bangalore, 1983.

Rajshekar, V. T. *Brahminism (The Curse of India)*, Bangalore, 1981.

Rajshekar, V. T. *Class–Caste Struggle: Emerging Third Force*, Bangalore, 1980.

Rajshekar, V. T. *Hinduism, Fascism and Gandhism*, Bangalore, 1985.

Rajshekar, V. T. *Hinduism vs Movement of Untouchables in India*, Bangalore, 1983.

Rajshekar, V. T. *How Marx Failed in Hindu India*, Bangalore, 1984.

Rajshekar, V. T. *How to Destroy Caste System (Strategy for Revolution)*, Bangalore, 1981.

Rajshekar, V. T. *Muslims and the Liberation of the Oppressed*, Bangalore, 1986.

Rajshekar, V. T. *The Dilemma of Class and Caste in India*, Bangalore, 1984.

Rajshekar, V. T. *The Un-Christian Side of the Indian Church (The Plight of the Untouchable Converts)*, Bangalore, 1985.

Rajshekar, V. T. *Tribal Unrest: Whom to Blame?*, Bangalore, 1980.

Rajshekar, V. T. *Who Is Ruling India?*, Bangalore, 1982.

Rajshekar, V. T. *Who Is the Mother of Hitler?*, Bangalore, 1984.

Rajshekar, V. T. *Why Godse Killed Gandhi,* Bangalore, 1983, 2nd ed. 1986.

Raju, B. Rama. *Folklore of Andhra Pradesh,* New Delhi, 1978.

Ramachandra Rao, D. S. *Dhnnavada Anantam: 1850-1949,* Calcutta, 1956.

Ramaswamy, Uma. 'Self-Identity among Scheduled Castes: A Study of Andhra,' *Economic and Political Weekly,* IX, 47 (23 Nov. 1974), pp. 1950-64.

Ramusack, Barbara N. 'Catalysts or Helpers? British Feminists, Indian Women's Rights and Indian Independence,' in *The Extended Family: Women and Political Participation in India and Pakistan,* ed. Gail Minault, Delhi, 1981, pp. 109-50.

Ransom, C. W. *The Christian Minister in India: His Vocation and Training,* London, 1946.

Rao, Edwin M. *Church of South India, The Diocese of Dornakal, IMS, The Dornakal Mission, Platinum Jubilee, January 5-7, 1982,* Hyderabad, 1982.

Rao, K. Ranga. 'Peasant Movement in Telangana,' in *Social Movements in India, I: Peasant and Backward Classes Movements,* ed. M. S. A. Rao, Columbia, MO, 1979, pp. 149-68.

Rao, M. S. A. 'Changing Moral Values in the Context of Social-Cultural Movements,' in *Culture and Morality,* ed. A. C. Mayer, Delhi, 1981, pp. 191-208.

Rao, P. Raghunadha. *History of Modern Andhra,* New Delhi, 1978; rev. ed., 1983.

Rao, R. R. Sundara. *Bhakti Theology in the Telugu Hymnal,* Madras, 1983.

Rao, Raja. *Kanthapura,* New York, 1963.

Rauschenbusch, Walter. 'The Social Principles of Jesus,' in *The World Treasury of Modern Religious Thought,* ed. Jaroslav Pelikan, Boston 1990, pp. 586-92.

Rawlinson, A. E. J. *The Church of South India: The Lichfield Cathedral Divinity Lectures 1950,* London, 1951.

Reddi, N. Subha. 'Community-Conflict among the Depressed Castes of Andhra,' *Man in India,* XXX, 4 (Oct.-Dec. 1950), pp. 1-12.

Richter, Julius. *A History of Missions in India,* trans. Sydney H. Moore, Edinburgh, 1908.

Robert, Dana L. 'The Origin of the Student Volunteer Watchword: "The Evangelization of the World in This Generation,"' *International Bulletin of Missionary Research,* X, 4 (Oct. 1986), pp. 146-49.

Roberts, P. E. *History of British India under the Company and the Crown,* 3rd ed., Delhi, 1977.

Robertson, Roland, ed. *Sociology of Religion,* Middlesex, 1969.

Robinson, Ronald, and John Gallagher. *Africa and the Victorians: The Official Mind of Imperialism,* London, 1965.

Robinson, Thomas, and Richard Clarke. *Rise and Progress of the Missions in Tinnevelly: Being the Substance of Two Addresses to the Society for the Propagation of the Gospel on Friday, March 14, 1845,* London, 1846.

Roghair, G. *The Epic of Palnadu,* Oxford, 1982.

Rollwagen, Jack R. 'Reconsidering Basic Assumptions: A Call for a Reassessment of the General Concept of Culture in Anthropology,' *Urban Anthropology*, XV, 1-2 (1986), pp. 97-133.

Rosenthal, Michael. *The Character Factory: Baden-Powell's Boy Scouts and the Imperatives of Empire*, New York, 1986.

Ross, Alan. *The Emissary: G. D. Birla, Gandhi and Independence*, London, 1986.

Rosselli, John. *Lord William Bentinck: The Making of a Liberal Imperialist, 1774-1839*, Berkeley, 1974.

Rossillon, P. 'The Apostolate among Sudras in Southern India,' *The Clergy Monthly*, IV, 4 (Oct. 1940), pp. 99-104.

Rouse, Ruth. 'Voluntary Movements and the Changing Ecumenical Climate,' in *A History of the Ecumenical Movement, 1517-1948*, ed. R. Rouse and S. C. Neill, London, 1954, pp. 309-49.

Rouse, Ruth. *The World's Student Christian Federation: A History of the First Thirty Years*, London, 1948.

Rouse, Ruth, and Stephen C. Neill, eds. *A History of the Ecumenical Movement: 1517-1948*, London, 1954.

Rowland, Benjamin. *The Art and Architecture of India*, Middlesex, 1984.

Rudolph, Lloyd I. and Susanne H. 'Confessional Politics, Secularism and Centrism in India,' in *Fundamentalism, Revivalists and Violence in South Asia*, ed. James W. Björkman, Riverdale, MD, 1988, pp. 75-87.

Rudolph, Lloyd I. and Susanne H. *The Modernity of Tradition: Political Development in India*, Chicago, 1967.

Rudolph, Susanne H. and Lloyd I. *Gandhi: The Traditional Roots of Charisma*, Chicago, 1983.

Ryerson, Charles. *Regionalism and Religion: The Tamil Renaissance and Popular Hinduism*, Madras, 1988.

Sackett, F. Colyer. *Posnett of Medak*, London, 1951.

Said, Edward W. *Orientalism*, New York, 1979.

Saldanha, J. A. *Civil-Ecclesiastical Law in India*, Trichi, 1922.

Saldanha, J. A. *Legal Position of the Catholic Church in British India*, Trichi, 1934.

Samarth, Anil. *Shivaji and the Indian National Movement*, Bombay, 1975.

Samuel, George. 'Incorporation of Seekers into the Church and the Sociological Reality of Caste in Kerala,' Paper Presented at the Consultation on Caste and the Church, 9-12 February 1984, Bangalore.

Samuel, V., and C. Sugden. *Christian Mission in the Eighties — A Third World Perspective*, Bangalore, 1982.

Samuel, Vinay, and Chris Sugden. *Sharing Jesus in the Two-Thirds World*, Bangalore, 1983.

Samuel, Vinay, and Chris Sugden, eds. *The Gospel among Our Hindu Neighbours*, Bangalore, 1983.

Sandeen, Ernest R., ed. *The Bible and Social Reform*, Philadelphia, 1982.

Sanneh, Lamin. 'Christian Mission in the Pluralist Milieu: The African Experience,' *IRM*, LXXIV, 294 (April 1985), pp. 199-211.

Sanneh, Lamin. *Translating the Message: The Missionary Impact on Culture,* Maryknoll, NY, 1989.

Sanneh, Lamin. *West African Christianity: The Religious Impact,* London, 1983.

Sarasvati, Pandita Ramabai. *The High-Caste Hindu Woman,* New York, 1901.

Saraswathi, S. *Minorities in Madras State: Group Interests in Modern Politics,* Delhi, 1974.

Sargant, N. C. *From Missions to Church in Karnataka,* Madras, 1987.

Sargant, N. C. *The Dispersion of the Tamil Church,* Delhi, 1962.

Sargent, John. *The Life and Letters of Henry Martyn,* Edinburgh, 1985.

Sastri, Nilakanta. *A History of South India: From Prehistoric Times to the Fall of Vijayanagar,* 3rd ed., London, 1966; 4th ed., Madras, 1976.

Satthianadhan, S. *W. T. Satthianadhan,* Madras, 1893.

Schmitthenner, Peter. *Telugu Resurgence, 1800: C. P. Brown and Cultural Consolidation in South India,* New Delhi: Manohar, in press.

Schweitzer, Albert. *Indian Thought and Its Development,* trans. C. E. B. Russell, London, 1936.

Scopes, Wilfred. *Indian Opportunity,* London, 1961.

Scott, Drusilla. *A. D. Lindsay: A Biography,* Oxford, 1971.

Scott, Waldron. *Karl Barth's Theology of Mission,* Exeter, 1978.

Seal, Anil. *The Emergence of Indian Nationalism: Competition and Collaboration in the Later Nineteenth Century,* Cambridge, 1971.

Sekharam, K. Balendu. *The Andhras through the Ages,* Hyderabad, 1973.

Selwyn, G. T. *Memoir of the Rt. Rev. G. T. Selwyn,* Palayamkottai, 1958.

Seunarine, J. F. *Reconversion to Hinduism through Suddhi,* Madras, 1977.

Sharpe, Eric J. *John Nicol Farquhar: A Memoir,* Calcutta, 1963.

Sharpe, Eric J. *Not to Destroy But to Fulfil: The Contribution of J. N. Farquhar to Protestant Missionary Thought in India before 1914,* Uppsala, 1965.

Shaw, Ellis O. *Rural Hinduism: Some Observations and Experiences,* ed. S. P. Appasamy, Madras, 1986.

Shedd, Clarence P. *History of the World's Alliance of Young Men's Christian Associations,* London, 1955.

Shedd, Clarence P. *Two Centuries of Student Christian Movements,* New York, 1934.

Shenk, Wilbert R. 'The Contribution of Henry Venn to Mission Thought,' *Anvil,* II, 1 (1985), pp. 25-42.

Shenk, Wilbert R. *Henry Venn — Missionary Statesman,* Maryknoll, NY, 1983.

Shirer, William L. *Gandhi: A Memoir,* London, 1981.

Sider, Ronald J., ed. *Toward a Theology of Social Change,* Exeter, 1981.

Silverberg, James. 'Colloquium and Interpretive Conclusions,' in *Social Mobility in the Caste System in India: An Interdisciplinary Symposium,* ed. J. Silverberg, The Hague, 1968, pp. 115-38.

Singh, D. V. 'Nationalism and the Search for Identity in 19th Century Protestant Christianity in India,' *ICHR,* XIV, 2 (Dec. 1980), pp. 105-16.

Singh, K. S. *Birsa Munda and His Movement, 1874-1901: A Study of a Millenarian Movement in Chotanagpur,* Calcutta, 1983.

Singh, T. R. *The Madiga: A Study in Social Structure and Change,* Lucknow, 1969.

Slade, Ruth. *King Leopold's Congo: Aspects of the Development of Race Relations in the Congo Independent State,* London, 1962.

Smith, George. *The Conversion of India: From Pantaenus to the Present Time:* A.D. *193-1893,* London, 1893.

Smith, Paul A. *Reactions and Repercussions in the Anglican Communion to the Formation of the Church of South India,* Certificate of Theology Paper, Wycliffe Hall, Oxford, 1984.

Smith, Vincent A. *The Oxford History of India: From the Earliest Times to the End of 1911,* 2nd ed., Oxford, 1923.

Somayaji, Vidwan G. J. 'Literature and Drama: Telugu,' in *Modern India and the West,* ed. L. S. S. O'Malley, London, 1941, pp. 513-22.

Spear, Percival. *India, Pakistan, and the West,* London, 1949.

Special Committee for American Church Publications. *Christianity in India: An Historical Summary Having Particular Reference to the Anglican Communion and the Church of South India,* 2nd ed., New York, 1954.

Special Issue on 'Religious Conversion,' *Religion and Society,* XIII, 4 (Dec. 1966).

Special Issue on 'Tamil Nadu Conversions to Islam,' *Religion and Society,* XXVIII, 4 (Dec. 1981).

Srinivas, M. N., and André Béteille. 'The "Untouchables" of India,' *Scientific American,* CCXIII, 6 (Dec. 1965), pp. 13-17.

Srinivasagam, R. Theodore. 'Caste and Church Planting in Pioneer Mission Fields,' Paper Presented at the Consultation on Caste and the Church, 9-12 February 1984, Bangalore.

Statistical Atlas of India, 2nd ed., Calcutta, 1895.

Stephenson, Alan M. G. *Anglicanism and the Lambeth Conferences,* London, 1978.

Stern, Fritz. 'The Maturing of the Nation-State,' in *Chapters in Western Civilization,* 3rd ed., New York, 1962, pp. 361-400.

Stern, Fritz, ed. *The Varieties of History: From Voltaire to the Present,* New York, 1973.

Stevenson, J. Sinclair. *Robert Henderson: The Story of a Missionary Greatheart in India,* London, 1922.

Stock, Eugene. *A Short Handbook of Missions,* London, 1905.

Stock, Eugene. *The Story of Church Missions,* London, 1907.

Stokes, Eric. 'Traditional Resistance Movements and Afro-Asian Nationalism: The Context of the 1857 Mutiny Rebellion in India,' *Past and Present,* 48 (Aug. 1970), pp. 100-118.

Stoll, David. *Fishers of Men or Founders of Empire: The Wycliffe Bible Translators in Latin America,* London, 1982.

Stott, John R. W., and Robert Coote. *Down to Earth: Studies in Christianity and Culture,* London, 1980.

Strickland, W., and T. W. M. Marshall. *Catholic Missions in Southern India to 1865*, London, 1865.

Studdert-Kennedy, Gerald. 'Christian Imperialists of the Raj: Left, Right and Centre,' in *Making Imperial Mentalities: Socialisation and British Imperialism*, ed. J. A. Mangan, Manchester, 1990, pp. 127-43.

Studdert-Kennedy, Gerald. 'Woodbine Willie: Religion and Politics after the Great War,' *History Today*, 36 (Dec. 1986), pp. 40-45.

Studdert-Kennedy, Gerald. *British Christians, Indian Nationalists and the Raj*, draft copy of forthcoming book by Oxford University Press, Delhi, 1991.

Sundkler, Bengt. *Church of South India: The Movement towards Union, 1900-1947*, London, 1954.

Sundkler, Bengt. *The Christian Ministry in Africa*, London, 1962.

Sundkler, Bengt. *The World of Mission*, London, 1965.

Suntharalingam, R. *Politics and Nationalist Awakening in South India, 1852-1891*, Tucson, AZ, 1974.

Symonds, Richard. *Oxford and Empire: The Last Lost Cause?*, New York, 1986.

Symonds, Richard. *The British and Their Successors: A Study in the Development of the Government Services in the New States*, Evanston, 1966.

Tagore, Rabindranath. *Nationalism*, London, 1921.

Tambimuttu, E. L. *Dravida: A History of the Tamils from Prehistoric Times to A.D. 1800*, Colombo, 1945.

Tarlo, Emma. *Clothing Matters: Dress and Identity in India* (Chicago, 1996).

Tatlow, Tissington. *The Story of the Student Christian Movement of Great Britain and Ireland*, London, 1933.

Tawney, R. H. *Religion and the Rise of Capitalism*, New York, 1940.

Taylor, A. J. P. *English History: 1914-1945*, Middlesex, 1975.

Taylor, Howard, Mrs. *Pastor Hsi (of North China): One of China's Christians*, London, 1903.

Taylor, John. *Christianity and Politics in Africa*, London, 1957.

Taylor, Richard W. *The Contribution of E. Stanley Jones*, Madras, 1973.

Temple, William. *Nature, Man and God: Being the Gifford Lectures Delivered in the University of Glasgow in the Academical Years 1932-1933 and 1933-1934*, London, 1949.

Thanugundla, Solomon. 'Structures of the Church in Andhra Pradesh (An Historico-Juridical Study),' Dissertatio Ad Lauream in Jure Canonico, Rome, 1976.

Thapar, Romila. 'Imagined Religious Communities? Ancient History and the Modern Search for a Hindu Identity,' *Modern Asian Studies*, XXIII, 2 (May 1989), pp. 209-31.

Thapar, Romila. 'Syndicated Moksha?' *Seminar*, CCCXIII (1985), 14-22.

The Catholic Directory of India, Allahabad, 1977.

The Churchman's Diary, 1984, Madras, 1984.

The Imperial Gazetteer of India, XIII; new edition, XVI, Oxford, 1908.

Bibliography

The Lambeth Conference 1930: Encyclical Letter from the Bishops with Resolutions and Reports, London, 1930.

The National Missionary Society of India, 1905, Calcutta: Baptist Mission Press, n.d.

The National Missionary Society of India: Platinum Jubilee Souvenir, Tiruvalla, 1980.

The New Delhi Report: The Third Assembly of the World Council of Churches, 1961, London, 1962.

The Story of Dornakal Cathedral, Madras, n.d.

The Students Chronicle and Serampore College Magazine, new series, XXXV (Feb. 1913).

Thechanath, Jacob. 'Indian Signs and Symbols in Christian Liturgy,' *The South India Churchman* (Dec. 1984), pp. 12-14.

Thiel-Horstmann, Monika. 'Indian Christian and Traditional Folksong Patterns,' in *Asie du Sud. Traditions et Changements,* Colloques Internationaux du C.N.R.S., No. 582, Paris, 1979, pp. 87-91.

Thomas, Abraham Vazhayil. *Christians in Secular India,* Rutherford, NJ, 1974.

Thomas, George. *Christian Indians and Indian Nationalism, 1885-1950: An Interpretation in Historical and Theological Perspectives,* Frankfurt am Main, 1979.

Thomas, M. M. *Salvation and Humanisation: Some Crucial Issues of the Theology of Mission in Contemporary India,* Madras, 1971.

Thomas, M. M. *Some Theological Dialogues,* Madras, 1977.

Thomas, M. M. *The Acknowledged Christ of the Indian Renaissance,* London, 1969.

Thomas, M. M. *The Secular Ideologies of India and the Secular Meaning of Christ,* Madras, 1976.

Thompson, Paul R. *The Voice of the Past: Oral History,* Oxford, 1978.

Thomson, David. *England in the Twentieth Century,* Middlesex, 1982.

Thurston, Edgar. *Castes and Tribes of Southern India,* Madras, 1909.

Tierney, Brian, Donald Kagan, and L. Pearce Williams, eds. *Great Issues in Western Civilization,* II, New York, 1967.

Tiliander, Bror. *Christian and Hindu Terminology: A Study in Their Mutual Relations with Special Reference to the Tamil Area,* Uppsala, 1974.

Tinker, Hugh. *South Asia: A Short History,* London, 1966.

Tinker, Hugh. *The Ordeal of Love: C. F. Andrews and India,* Delhi, 1979.

Titus, Acharya Daya Prakash. *Fulfilment of the Vedic Quest in the Lord Jesus Christ,* Lucknow, 1982.

Toynbee, Arnold. *An Historian's Approach to Religion,* 2nd ed., Oxford, 1979.

Tucker, H. W. *Under His Banner: Papers on the Missionary Work of Modern Times,* London, 1886.

Tucker, Ruth A. *From Jerusalem to Irian Jaya: A Biographical History of Christian Missions,* Grand Rapids, 1983.

Underwood, Alfred C. *Conversion: Christian and Non-Christian: A Comparative and Psychological Study,* London, 1926.

Van Dusen, Henry P. *One Great Ground of Hope: Christian Missions and Christian Unity,* London, 1961.

Vansina, Jan. *Oral Tradition as History,* Madison, WI, 1985.

Venn, Henry. *The Missionary Life and Labours of Francis Xavier: Taken from His Own Correspondence with a Sketch of the General Results of Roman Catholic Missions among the Heathen,* London, 1862.

Vidler, Alec R. *The Church in an Age of Revolution: 1789 to the Present Day,* Middlesex, 1961.

Visser't Hooft, W. A. *Memoirs,* London, 1973.

Visser't Hooft, W. A. *No Other Name: The Choice between Syncretism and Christian Universalism,* London, 1963.

von Pochhammer, Wilhelm. *India's Road to Nationhood: A Political History of the Subcontinent,* New Delhi, 1973.

von Simson, Otto. *The Gothic Cathedral: Origins of Gothic Architecture and the Medieval Concept of Order,* Princeton, 1962.

Wagner, Peter C. *Our Kind of People: The Ethical Dimensions of Church Growth in America,* Atlanta, 1979.

Walker, J. A. K. 'Review of the Work of the Canadian Baptist Telugu Mission,' in *Among the Telugus: Report of the Canadian Baptist Telugu Missions (Working in the Ganjam, Vizagapatam, Godavari and Kistna Districts) for 1909,* ed. J. R. Stillwell, Madras, 1910.

Wallis, Jim. *The Call to Conversion,* New York, 1981.

Wand, J. W. C. *Anglicanism in History and Today,* London, 1961.

Wand, J. W. C., ed. *The Anglican Communion: A Survey,* London, 1948.

Wapinski, Roman. 'On Mass Movements and Their Leaders,' in *The Book of Lech Walesa,* Middlesex, 1982, pp. 138-45.

Warburg, Margit. 'Conversion: Considerations before a Field-work in a Baha'i Village in Kerala,' *South Asian Religion and Society,* ed. A. Parpola and B. S. Hanson, U.K., 1986, pp. 223-35.

Warren, Max. *Social History and Christian Mission,* London, 1967.

Warren, Max. *The Missionary Movement from Britain in Modern History,* London, 1965.

Warren, Max, ed. *To Apply the Gospel: Selections from the Writings of Henry Venn,* Grand Rapids, 1971.

Washbrook, D. A. *The Emergence of Provincial Politics: The Madras Presidency, 1870-1920,* Cambridge, 1976.

Watson, Francis. *A Concise History of India,* London, 1979.

Weber, Hans-Ruedi. *Asia and the Ecumenical Movement, 1895-1961,* London, 1966.

Weber, Max. *On Capitalism, Bureaucracy and Religion: A Selection of Texts,* ed. and trans. Stanislav Andreski, London, 1983.

Weber, Max. *The Protestant Ethic and the Spirit of Capitalism,* 2nd ed., London, 1976.

Webster, J. B. *The African Churches among the Yoruba, 1888-1922,* Oxford, 1964.

Webster, J. C. B. 'Christianity in the Punjab,' *Missiology: An International Review,* VI, 4 (Oct. 1978), pp. 470-71.

Webster, J. C. B. 'Christians and the Depressed Classes Movement in the 1930's: The Crucial Decade,' Paper Presented to the 'Seminar on Aspects of the Economy, Society and Politics in Modern India, 1900-1950,' 15-18 December 1980, New Delhi. Published in *Economy, Society and Politics in Modern India,* ed. D. N. Panigrahi, New Delhi, 1985, pp. 313-44.

Webster, J. C. B. 'Punjabi Christians and the Indian Nationalist Movement, 1919-1947,' *ICHR,* XIV, 2 (Dec. 1980), pp. 66-89.

Webster, J. C. B. 'The History of Christianity in India: Aims and Methods,' *Bangalore Theological Forum,* X, 2 (July-Dec. 1978), pp. 110-48.

Webster, J. C. B. *A History of the Dalit Christians in India,* San Francisco, 1992.

Webster, J. C. B. *The Christian Community and Change in Nineteenth Century North India,* Delhi, 1976.

West, Charles C., and David M. Paton, eds. *The Missionary Church in East and West,* London, 1959.

Whitcombe, E. 'Irrigation and Railways,' in *The Cambridge Economic History of India,* ed. D. Kumar and T. Raychaudhuri, II, pp. 677-737.

Wiebe, Paul D. 'Protestant Missions in India, A Sociological Review,' *Journal of Asian and African Studies,* V (1970), pp. 293-301.

Wiebe, Paul D. *Christians in Andhra Pradesh: The Mennonites of Mahbubnagar,* Madras, 1988.

Williams, C. Peter. *The Ideal of the Self-Governing Church: A Study of Victorian Missionary Strategy,* Leiden, 1990.

Williams, Garfield H. 'The Missionary Significance of the Last Ten Years: India,' *IRM,* XII (1923), pp. 326-43.

Williams, John Bob. *Research Studies in the Economic and Social Environment of the Indian Church: A Study of the Economic Status and Self-Support of the Church of the Four Protestant Missions in the Andhra Area,* Guntur, 1938.

Williams, Monier. *Religious Thought and Life in India: An Account of the Religions of the Indian Peoples, Based on a Life's Study of Their Literature and on Personal Investigations in Their Own Country, Part I: Vedism, Brahmanism and Hinduism,* London, 1883.

Willis, J. J., et al. *Towards a United Church: 1913-1947,* London, 1947.

Wilson, Bryan. *Contemporary Transformations of Religion,* Oxford, 1976.

Wilson, Bryan R. *Magic and the Millennium,* St. Albans, Hertfordshire, 1975.

Wilson, Everett A. 'Revival and Revolution in Latin America,' Paper for Conference on Modern Christian Revivalism, Wheaton, March-April 1989.

Wilson, K. *The Twice Alienated: Culture of Dalit Christians,* Hyderabad, 1982.

Winter, R. D., and S. C. Hawthorne. *Perspectives on the World Christian Movement,* Pasadena, CA, 1981.

Wiser, William H. and Charlotte V. *Behind Mud Walls, 1930-1960*, Berkeley, CA, 1971.

Wolpert, Stanley. *A New History of India*, New York, 1977.

Wolpert, Stanley. *Morley and India, 1906-1910*, Berkeley, 1967.

Woodcock, George. *Gandhi*, London, 1972.

Worman, E. C. 'Early History of the YMCA,' published serially in *YMI* (Oct. 1922–Jan. 1923); bound volume in YMCA Headquarters, UTC, Bangalore.

Wright, Harrison M., ed. *The 'New Imperialism': Analysis of Late Nineteenth-Century Expansion*, Boston, 1961.

Yates, T. E. *Venn and Victorian Bishops Abroad: The Missionary Policies of Henry Venn and Their Repercussions upon the Anglican Episcopate of the Colonial Period, 1841-1872*, Uppsala, 1978.

Young, Richard Fox. *Resistant Hinduism: Sanskrit Sources on Anti-Christian Apologetics in Early Nineteenth-Century India*, Vienna, 1981.

Zachariah, Mathai. *Christian Presence in India*, Madras, 1981.

Zachariah, Mathai, ed. *Freedom of Religion in India*, Nagpur, 1979.

Zaehner, R. C. *At Sundry Times: An Essay in the Comparison of Religions*, London, 1958.

Zelliot, Eleanor. 'Gandhi and Ambedkar — A Study in Leadership,' in *The Untouchables in Contemporary India*, ed. J. Michael Mahar, Tucson, AZ, 1972, pp. 69-95.

Zimmer, Heinrich. *Myths and Symbols in India Art and Civilization*, ed. Joseph Campbell, Princeton, 1974.

Zimmer, Heinrich. *Philosophies of India*, ed. Joseph Campbell, New York, 1951.

Index

(VSA = Vedanayakam Samuel Azariah)

272-73, 338; culture of, in Indian
Christianity, 261-87, 360; and idol
worship, 15-16, 195, 251-52, 279; and
mass movements, 133-35, 184, 281,
298-99, 320; and reform movements,
32-33, 43, 51, 202, 249, 251, 309,
311; relation of, to Christianity, 176,
295, 320-21, 323, 327; and revivalism, 32, 46; and tensions with Chris-
tians, 32, 50-51, 59-61, 81-82, 195-96,
197n.57
Hirtzel, Arthur, 127-28, 132n.135
Hislop, Stephen, 29n.75
Hislop College (Nagpur), 334n.147
History of the Expansion of Christianity, The
(Latourette), 210n.106
Hodge, J. Z., 5n.5, 311n.60, 323, 325,
328n.129, 330-32, 335
Hollis, Arthur Michael, 72n.14,
117n.78, 166n.80, 175
Holy Baptism (VSA), 199
Holy Catholic Church of Japan, 99n.19
Holy Matrimony (VSA), 199
Holy Trinity Church (Vellalanvilai),
22n.47, 23
Home Missionary Society (American
Baptist), 74
Honda, Yoitsu, 99n.19
Hooker, Richard, 107n.51
Hooper, J. S. M., 240
Horsley, Cecil Douglas, 166n.79,
167n.80
Hort, F. J. A., 199
Hoskyns, E. C., 199
hostels, student, 27, 31, 32n.85, 117-18
Howell, William, 180n.12, 183-84
Hubback, George C., 167n.80
Humility: The Beauty of Holiness (Murray),
25
Hyderabad State, 95, 205n.88, 246n.3.
See also Nizam of Hyderabad

ICG. See India Conciliation Group
ICS. See Indian civil service
iddli, 151
Ilbert bill (1883), 124
Imperial Durbar (1911), 142

IMS. *See* Indian Missionary Society of
Tinnevelly
inam, 264
Independence movement, 106, 149,
241, 243. *See also* Gandhi, Mohandas
K.
India and the Christian Movement (VSA),
199
India Bishops and Courts Act (1823),
104
India Conciliation Group, 318, 323,
334-35
India Council, 126-28
Indian Bishopric Fund, 123
Indian Christian Marriage Act (1872),
267
Indian civil service, 81, 134, 160
Indian Express (Madras), 324n.115
Indianization, 140-53, 169-71
Indian Missionary Society of
Tinnevelly, 202n.80, 206, 265, 270; in
Dornakal, 79-80, 90, 93-97, 119, 122,
135, 188; funding of, 77-79, 82, 120,
206; as indigenous missionary soci-
ety, 73, 75-83, 94-96, 204-6; opposi-
tion to, 77, 79, 207n.95, 224n.4; VSA
as missionary with, 138, 195, 201
Indian National Congress, 24, 46, 80,
130, 134, 161, 354
Indian National Convention of YMCAs:
first (1891), 47, 52; second (1892),
49-50; third (1894), 34, 55
Indian National Council of YMCAs, 55
Indian National Union of YMCAs, 52
Indian Witness, 315
India Sub-Committee of the SPG (London), 132
indigenization, 3-4, 21, 68-69, 138-53,
158-59, 172, 198, 205-20; influence
of westerners on, 2, 137, 151-53
Ing-ong, Ding, 99n.18
Institute for Total Revolution,
325n.115
International Alliance of YMCAs, 47
International Missionary Council, 335;
Jerusalem, 1928, 212; Tambaram,
1938, 212, 241-42, 312n.65